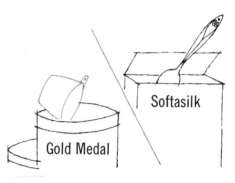

Gold Medal

Softasilk

1 Dip nested measuring cups into flour sack or canister. In using cake flour, spoon flour to overflowing into nested cups.

2 Level off with spatula or straight edged knife. (Do not tap cup or pack more flour into cup before leveling off.)

3 Pour flour into mixing bowl with other ingredients. Just stir to blend.

Dear Homemaker:

As you know, accurate measurements are necessary for good baking results. We have done a great deal of testing in our kitchens and in homes of women throughout the country to determine the best method for measuring flour.

We are happy to tell you that our new, modern "dip-level-pour" method, described on this page, gives consistently uniform measurements and beautiful bakings. Many homemakers prefer this method because of its ease and time-saving convenience. However, you may still follow the traditional sifting method, if you prefer. Use either method without altering the amounts of flour.

Betty Crocker

Betty Crocker's
NEW PICTURE
COOK BOOK

Decorations by Joseph Pearson

FIRST EDITION

Second Printing

McGRAW HILL BOOK COMPANY, Inc.

NEW YORK · TORONTO · LONDON

Reception Area Its beautiful furnishings skillfully combine the new and the old with a sectional sofa in gay paprika-colored print and a handsome old French chest decorated with Oriental figures.

THE *Betty Crocker* KITCHENS IN GOLDEN VALLEY

Homemaker Kitchen This light bright, new-as-tomorrow kitchen combines many special work areas. Here recipes for cook books are perfected.

Early American Dining Room Long remembered for its air of gracious hospitality, the dining room is charmingly furnished with pewter accessories and antiques.

Test Kitchens This bright kitchen is always busy with cooking, baking, tasting and demonstrating with each home economist at work in her own completely equipped area. In Kamera Kitchen, picture-perfect foods are readied for the photographer. New products and methods are developed in Experimental Kitchen. Products are judged for uniformity in Quality Control Kitchen.

Dear Friend,

Cooking and meal planning will bring you greater
success and deeper satisfaction with this new
cook book as your guide.
Between these covers you'll find wonderful recipes,
over 1,850 of them: time-proven recipes, exciting
new ones, recipes with step pictures for the
new cook, fancy foods for the culinary artist, recipes
from faraway lands, simple foods to tempt children,
tantalizing recipes to delight guests, quick ideas for
busy days, long-cooking recipes for quiet days,
the recipes shown in the inspiring color pictures.
Use these recipes confidently, for every one has
been tested for you, both in Betty Crocker's
Kitchens and in American homes like yours.
Woven among the recipes are hints and helps for meal
planning, use of leftovers, table service,
calorie counts and garnishes.
We are proud to be the publishers for Betty Crocker,
foremost author of cook books today. Over 5,500,000
copies of her original Picture Cook Book are being
used and enjoyed throughout the world. For practical
help in all sorts of cooking, for inspiration for
family and company meals and for the sheer pleasure
of browsing through its colorful pages, we believe
that Betty Crocker's New Picture Cook Book
is unsurpassed.

Sincerely yours,

McGRAW-HILL BOOK COMPANY

KITCHEN KNOW-HOW

HINTS FOR THE HOMEMAKER

PLAN AHEAD

Write menus for a week's meals at a time. Shop for staples once a week, fresh fruits and vegetables twice weekly.

When cooking, assemble all ingredients and utensils before beginning to prepare the dish.

If you have a freezer, make several cakes, pies, cookies, main dishes or sandwiches at a time and freeze some for future use. See freezer information *pp. 19-23.*

COMBINE JOBS

Bake cake or cookies while washing dishes or cooking dinner. Pare vegetables while meat is browning.

Plan leftovers. Cook some foods to be served more than once, such as beef roast; use again for beef sandwiches, beef hash and beef pie.

Plan and organize daily work while working with hands (peeling potatoes, sweeping floor, etc.).

REFRESH YOUR SPIRITS

Every morning before breakfast, comb hair, apply makeup and a dash of cologne. Does wonders for your morale and your family's, too!

Think pleasant thoughts while working and a chore will become a "labor of love."

Have a hobby. Garden, paint pictures, look through magazines for home planning ideas, read a good book or attend club meetings. Be interested—and you'll always be interesting!

If you have a spare moment, sit down, close your eyes and just relax.

ORGANIZE WORK

Have a weekly plan for scheduling such tasks as washing, ironing, baking, shopping, cleaning the refrigerator or washing floors. One task done each day provides a sense of accomplishment and keeps work from piling up.

Alternate sitting-down tasks and standing-up tasks. Don't be on your feet too long.

Let the family help you. Very young children can set the table; older ones help cook and wash the dishes. Include them in party plans.

BE COMFORTABLE

Wear comfortable shoes and easy-fitting clothes while working.

Stand erect. Good posture prevents fatigue.

Have sink, work table, counter tops at height that is comfortable to eliminate strain. If dishpan is too low, set it on a box.

Use a dust mop and long-handled dust pan. Use self-wringing mop to prevent stooping.

KITCHEN KNOW-HOW

HOW TO GET PERFECT RESULTS FROM RECIPES IN THIS BOOK

1. Read recipe carefully! Every word of it. And do be *sure* to see if there's anything to be purchased or done—like chopping nuts or melting chocolate before you start mixing.

2. Look at the pictures! They show the "how-to-do" you need for every step.

3. Turn on the heat! If the cookies are to be baked immediately after mixing, see that the oven is heated to correct temperature.

4. Get your ingredients together! Saves time and steps to have them all in one place.

5. Collect utensils, too! Gather together all you need . . . from the mixing bowl to the baking pan.

6. Measure exactly—just as a druggist follows a doctor's prescription! Two minutes spent measuring carefully may save you hours of grief.

7. Mix carefully as directed (cream or stir or beat or fold in). Follow every step exactly as described in the recipe and pictures.

8. Bake or cook or otherwise prepare exactly as the recipe indicates. Correct cooking or baking is necessary for complete success.

MEASURING UTENSILS

Liquid measuring cup . . . has rim above the 1-cup line. Use for measuring any liquid ingredient.

Nested measuring cups . . . ¼, ⅓, ½, 1 cup. Use to measure dry ingredients or shortenings.

Measuring spoons . . . ¼, ½ and 1 teaspoon, 1 tablespoon. Use for measuring less than ¼ cup.

HOW TO MEASURE

FLOUR *Dip-Level-Pour Method*

For GOLD MEDAL Flour, dip nested measuring cup into sack or canister.

For SOFTASILK Flour, spoon flour into measuring cup to overflowing.

Level off with spatula or straight-edged knife. Do not tap cup or pack flour. Pour flour into mixing bowl with other ingredients; just stir to blend.

Sifting Method. Sift flour onto paper before measuring. Spoon sifted flour into nested measuring cup. Level off with spatula.

SUGAR

1. Granulated sugar. Needs sifting only if lumpy. Spoon lightly into "dry" measuring cup. Level off with knife. Don't knock or tap cup.

2. Brown sugar. Pack into "dry" measuring cup until sugar holds its shape when turned out of cup. Level off. To soften brown sugar, see p. 15.

3. Confectioners' sugar. Sift or press through sieve to remove lumps. Spoon lightly into "dry" measuring cup. Level off. Don't knock or tap cup.

HOW TO MEASURE

BAKING POWDER, SODA, SALT, CORNSTARCH, CREAM OF TARTAR, SPICES, ETC.

Stir, then fill measuring spoon. Level off with straight-edged knife or spatula.

BUTTER

For approximate measure:
4 sticks (1 lb.) = 2 cups
1 stick (¼ lb.) = ½ cup
½ stick (⅛ lb.) = ¼ cup

MOLASSES OR SYRUP

Fill cup. It rounds up, so fill slowly. Scrape out with rubber scraper or flexible spatula.

SOFT BREAD CRUMBS

Pack lightly into measuring cup. Press gently until level with top.

SHORTENING

Have shortening at room temperature. Pack firmly into measuring cup. Level off with straight-edged knife.

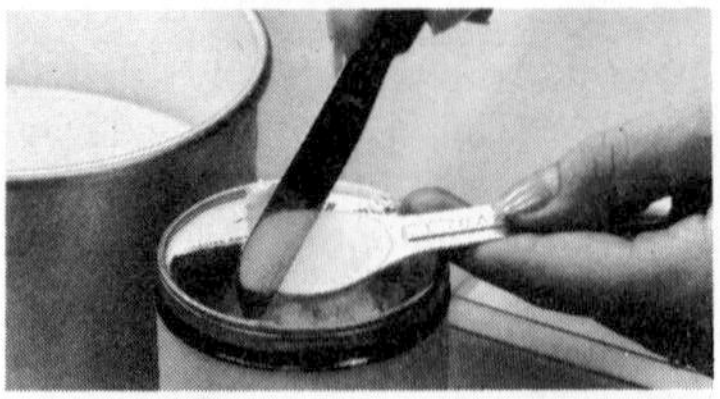

In measuring less than ¼ cup, use a tablespoon (hold fingers under bowl to prevent breaking where it joins handle).

EGGS

Whole	Egg Whites	Egg Yolks
1 medium = ¼ cup	2 = ¼ cup	3 = ¼ cup
2 medium = ⅓ to ½ cup	3 = ⅜ cup	4 = ⅓ cup
3 medium = ½ to ⅔ cup	4 = ½ cup	5 = ⅜ cup
4 medium = ⅔ to 1 cup	5 = ⅔ cup	6 = ½ cup

Size varies ... so measure whole eggs, whites and yolks in most recipes. Do not use less or more than the amount specified in recipe.

(For ways to use leftover egg whites or egg yolks, see p. 44.) Refer to index for recipes using eggs, whites and yolks.

LIQUIDS

Use "liquid" measuring cup to prevent spilling. Pour into cup on table. Have measuring line at eye level.

FINE DRY BREAD CRUMBS

Spoon lightly into measuring cup. Level off. Don't shake cup.

NUTS, COCONUT AND DRIED FRUIT

Pack shredded coconut or shelled nuts or raisins, dates, figs, etc. lightly into measuring cup level with top.

SHREDDED OR GRATED CHEESE

Pack lightly into measuring cup until level with top.

7

KITCHEN KNOW-HOW

INGREDIENT TERMS USED IN THIS BOOK

BAKING POWDER

Any of the nationally distributed brands of double-acting baking powder give good results. Do not use single-acting baking powder with recipes in this book.

CHOCOLATE

Unsweetened, semi-sweet or sweetened: use the type stated in the recipe. 1 sq. equals 1 oz.

COCONUT

Shredded coconut that is moist, either from a can or a package ... or shredded from a fresh coconut (see p. 27). Flaked coconut should be used where stated in recipe.

COFFEE

It is used in either liquid or powdered instant form. The form is indicated.

CREAM

Commercial sour . . . . .20% butterfat
Whipping . . . . .30 to 35% butterfat
Coffee . . . . .20% butterfat
Half and half . . . . .12% butterfat

FLOUR

All-purpose: Gold Medal "Kitchen-tested" Enriched Flour—recipes calling for it have been perfected for Gold Medal only.

Cake: Softasilk Cake Flour. It is specially milled from selected "soft" winter wheats to make exceptionally delicate, fine-textured cakes. Use where called for.

Rye: flour made from rye. Wheat flour is usually used with it to make bread light.

Whole wheat or graham: the fine or coarsely ground whole kernels of wheat including bran and germ.

GELATIN

Unflavored: each envelope contains 1 tbsp.; 1 tbsp. will gel 2 cups of liquid.

Flavored: gelatin with sugar, color and flavoring added. We specify the 3-oz. pkg.

HERBS

Garden fresh, dried crushed, powdered: must be fresh, full-bodied.

MILK

Fresh sweet: unless otherwise indicated.

Buttermilk and sour milk: may be used interchangeably. Pasteurized and homogenized milk must be "soured" with vinegar (see p. 26).

Evaporated: whole milk from which 60% of the water has been evaporated.

Condensed: whole milk commercially concentrated by evaporation, then sweetened.

MUSHROOMS

Fresh and canned: both are usually sautéed in butter before using (see p. 28). Follow individual recipes.

MUSTARD

Dry: ground mustard seed in powdered form.

Prepared: paste made of dry mustard blended with vinegar, sometimes specially seasoned. Use dry mustard unless recipe calls for prepared.

PEPPERS

Black: ground from whole peppercorns.

White: from peppercorns with outer bark removed.

Paprika (mildly pungent), *red* (sharper), *cayenne* (hottest of all): all ground from red pepper pods.

RAISINS

Seeded raisins are the large variety from which seeds have been removed. The sweetness released when they were slit open makes them sticky.

Seedless raisins are the small variety, both dark and light ... dried from seedless grapes. Cut or chop them to get the full sweetness and flavor.

SHORTENING

Any fresh, mild-flavored solid fat ... animal or vegetable. Butter is indicated in certain recipes for flavor.

SUGAR

Granulated, brown or confectioners' (powdered): as indicated in recipe.

VEGETABLE OIL

Any fresh, mild-flavored oil of vegetable origin.

YEAST

Active dry: in granular form. Requires no refrigeration (see expiration date on pkg.).

Compressed: in cake form (see p. 102). Refrigerate.

A DICTIONARY OF FOOD TERMS

Everyday and Special

A

à la mode. In the fashion. When referring to pie, with ice cream; referring to beef, a marinated beef, braised in marinade.

angelica. The candied leafstalk of a European herb . . . used in decorating cakes, candies, desserts, etc.

antipasto. Italian for assorted appetizers of fish, cold cuts or vegetables.

aspic. A jelly made from concentrated vegetable, meat or fish stock . . . with gelatin.

au beurre. With, or cooked in, butter.

au gratin. With a browned covering of bread crumbs, often mixed with butter or cheese.

B

baba. A French cake, made with a yeast dough, and usually flavored with rum or fruit juice.

bake. To cook by dry heat in oven.

barbecue. To roast meat on a grill or spit over hot coals . . . basting it with a highly seasoned sauce. Similar results may be obtained in the oven.

bar-le-duc. A jam originally made in Bar-le-duc, France, from currants and honey. The seeds were laboriously pushed out with a needle. Made in the United States with the seeds left in.

baste. To moisten food while it is cooking (as meat while roasting) by spooning liquid or fat over it.

batter. A mixture of flour and liquid, or in combination with other ingredients . . . thin enough to pour. Used to coat foods for frying.

beat. To mix with vigorous over-and-over motion with spoon, whip or beater (to make smooth or incorporate air).

beurre noir. Browned butter sauce.

bisque. 1. A rich cream soup (usually from fish, vegetables or game). 2. Or a frozen dessert, usually ice cream, with nuts in it.

blanch. To plunge into boiling water; then, in certain cases, into cold water. Nuts and fruits are blanched to remove skin easily.

blend. To mix thoroughly.

boil. To cook in steaming liquid in which bubbles are breaking on surface.

bombe. Frozen dessert made by lining a round or melon-shaped mold with one kind of ice cream and filling it with another.

borsch. A Russian soup made with beef broth and several vegetables including beets.

bouillabaisse. A French soup of several varieties of fish and other ingredients.

bouillon. A clear meat broth.

bouquet garni. Combination of herbs tied in cheesecloth used to season soups, stews, other foods.

braise. A method for cooking meat. See p. 302.

bread. To coat with flour, egg and crumbs.

brioche. A slightly sweetened French breakfast yeast bun.

broil. To cook directly under heating unit or over fire.

brush. To spread thinly with a brush.

C

café au lait. Coffee served with hot milk.

canapé. A tiny piece of fried or toasted bread topped with cheese, meat or sea food. See p. 59.

caramelize. To melt granulated sugar over medium heat to a golden brown syrup. See p. 141.

caviar. Prepared and salted roe (eggs) of the sturgeon and other large fish. May be black or red. Served as an appetizer.

chantilly. A dish in which whipped cream is one of the ingredients. Name derived from that of a castle north of Paris.

charlotte. A gelatin dessert containing flavored whipped cream, molded in a form lined with sponge cake strips or ladyfingers.

chill. To allow to become thoroughly cold.

chop. To cut in fine or coarse pieces with sharp knife or chopper.

chowder. Thick soup made of fish and/or vegetables, cooked in milk.

chutney. A spicy, somewhat sweet relish, made from several fruits and vegetables. Originally from India and served mainly with curry.

coat. To cover with thin film as flour, fine crumbs, icing, sugar or crushed nuts.

coddle. To simmer gently in liquid for a short time.

compote. 1. A stemmed dish. 2. A "stew" of fruits cooked slowly in syrup, during which time fruits retain their natural shape.

condiment. Pungent substance such as catsup, chutney, mustard to make food more appetizing.

consommé. A clear broth made of veal and/or chicken.

cool. Let stand at room temperature until no longer warm.

cracklings. The crisp residue of fat after the lard has been cooked out of it.

cream. To rub or work shortening and sugar against side of bowl with spoon or by beating on mixer until thoroughly blended and creamy.

A DICTIONARY OF FOOD TERMS (cont.)

creole. Well seasoned food containing tomato, green pepper and onion; the influence of early French and Spanish settlers of Louisiana.

crepe. A very thin crisp pancake. French origin.

croquette. Finely chopped meat with thick white sauce, shaped, coated with egg and crumbs and fried until crisp.

croustade. A toast case.

croutons. Small cubes of bread, fried or toasted until crisp; to serve with soups or as garnish.

cube. To cut food into solids of 6 equal sides (usually ¼ to ½″ in size).

curry. A stew cooked or flavored with curry.

cut in. To incorporate fat into a flour mixture using a pastry blender, a fork or two knives.

cutlet. A small piece of meat, cut from leg or ribs, for broiling or frying. Or mixture such as fish, shaped like a meat cutlet.

D

demitasse. The French for "half cup." A small cup for or of after-dinner coffee.

devil. To prepare with hot seasoning or sauce.

dice. To cut into very small cubes (about ¼″).

dough. A mixture of flour and liquid in combination with other ingredients, thick enough to roll, knead or drop off a spoon.

dredge. To coat thickly with flour or flour mixture.

drippings. Fat and juice from meat that collects in bottom of roasting pan.

E

éclair. Cream puff paste baked in oblong shape and filled with whipped cream or custard.

en brochette. French term for cooked on a skewer.

entrée. In formal dinners, a small "made" dish that is served as a separate course between the heavy courses. In informal meals, the chief dish of the main course . . . of meat, poultry, fish or meat substitute.

F

filet mignon. Small, tender strip of meat, usually from beef tenderloin.

fillet. Long, thin, boneless strip of lean meat or fish— usually a choice cut.

flake. To break lightly into small pieces.

fold in. To cut down through center of a batter with edge of spoon, rubber scraper or spatula, bringing up close to bowl, then turning over, cutting down through again . . . turning bowl a quarter turn at same time. Repeat until ingredients are blended.

fondant. Sugar syrup cooked to the soft ball stage (234°), cooled and kneaded to creaminess.

fondue. 1. A baked dish of eggs, cheese, milk and bread or bread crumbs. 2. A cheese dip for bread usually containing wine. Swiss origin.

frappé. Diluted sweetened fruit juice, frozen to a mushy consistency.

French fry. To cook in hot fat deep enough to float the food.

fricassee. Properly, to cook by braising. For chicken it means stewing . . . the browning process may be omitted.

frizzle. To pan-fry until the edges curl.

fromage. French word for cheese.

frost. To cover with icing.

fry. To pan-fry in a small amount of fat or shallow or deep-fry in a larger amount.

G

garnish. To decorate with portions of colorful and contrasting food.

glacé. 1. Coated with a sugar syrup cooked to the "crack" stage. 2. Frozen.

glaze. To add luster to a food by coating with a syrup or jelly—then heating or chilling.

goulash. A thick Hungarian beef or veal stew flavored with vegetables and paprika.

grate. To rub against grater to shred food.

grind. To cut or crush in a food grinder.

grits. Hulled and coarsely ground corn or other grain.

gumbo. A soup usually thickened with okra or filé. Typical Creole dish.

H

herbs. Aromatic plants used for garnish and seasonings, also used medicinally.

hollandaise. A sauce of egg yolks and butter with seasonings, served hot with vegetables and fish. Dutch origin.

hors d'oeuvres. Variety of appetizers. See p. 58.

I

ice. 1. A frozen dessert made of fruit juice, sugar and water. 2. To frost.

J

julienne. To cut food into match-like strips. See p. 373.

junket. A milk dessert coagulated by rennet; sweetened and flavored.

K

kisses. Small meringues.

knead. To work dough with a pressing motion accompanied by folding and stretching. Or to press dough with heel of hand . . . alternately folding and pushing and stretching it. See p. 103.

L

lard. 1. To insert strips of fat into or on top of uncooked meat before roasting for flavor and moisture. 2. Fat from swine.

leavening. An ingredient in baked products to make them light and porous by releasing or forming gas during baking.

leek. Onion-like bulb, but smaller, more pungent than onion.

legumes. Vegetables which bear their fruit or seeds in pods, such as peas, beans, lentils.

lyonnaise. Seasoned with onions, parsley.

M

macaroons. Small cakes made from egg whites, sugar and almond paste or powdered almonds.

macédoine. A mixture of fruits or vegetables.

maitre d'hotel. A French term meaning "head steward or cook."

Marguerites. Salty crackers covered with a mixture of boiled frosting and nuts or coconut . . . baked in the oven until browned.

marinade. An oil-acid mixture used to give flavor and sometimes to tenderize meats or vegetables.

marinate. To let food stand in oil-acid mixture (usually French dressing) for added flavor.

marzipan. A confection; a paste of almonds and sugar formed into fruit and vegetable shapes and colored. European origin.

meringue. A stiffly beaten mixture of egg whites and sugar (1) used to cover the top of a pie and usually browned in the oven, or (2) made into small cakes or cookies and baked.

mignon. 1. A French term meaning "favorite, delicate, darling." 2. A meltingly tender cut of boneless beef tenderloin.

mince. To chop or cut into very small pieces.

minestrone. Italian for thick vegetable soup.

mix. To combine ingredients, as by stirring.

mocha. Coffee-flavored or a combination of coffee and chocolate.

monosodium glutamate (MSG). A white crystalline substance made from vegetable proteins. Enhances natural flavor of foods.

mousse. 1. Light creamy dessert, sometimes frozen. 2. Dishes containing whipped egg white or cream. See p. 245.

P

pan-broil. To cook uncovered in ungreased or lightly greased hot skillet, pouring off fat as it accumulates.

pan-fry (sauté). To cook in small amount of fat in skillet.

parboil. To partially cook food in boiling water. The cooking is then completed by another method.

parch. To brown with dry heat.

pare. To cut off outside skin as from apple or potato.

parfait. 1. A frozen dessert of whipped cream, eggs cooked with syrup, and flavoring. 2. Ice cream in tall stemmed glasses.

pasteurize. To partially sterilize a liquid at a temperature (140 to 180°) which destroys bacteria (as for pasteurized milk).

paté de foie gras. Goose liver paste.

patty. A shell of puffed paste filled with a creamed mixture of chicken, fish, etc.

peel. To strip off outside covering as from orange, banana or tomato.

petits fours. Little fancy iced cakes, made by cutting sheet cakes into special shapes (squares, diamonds, etc.). Frosting is poured on and decorations added.

pilaf (pilau). Main dish of rice, seasonings and meat, fish or poultry. Far Eastern origin.

pit. To remove pits or seeds from fruit.

poach. To cook by surrounding with simmering (not boiling) water or other liquid, using care to retain shape of food.

polenta. Italian for a corn meal or farina mush to which cheese is often added.

purée. 1. To press fruit or vegetables through a fine sieve. 2. A smooth, thick mixture made by rubbing cooked foods through a sieve.

R

ragout. A highly seasoned thick meat stew.

ramekin. An individual baking dish.

ravioli. Small shapes of Italian or noodle paste spread with a meat or vegetable filling folded over and poached in meat stock.

relish. A highly flavored food used with other foods to stimulate appetite.

render. To free fat from connective tissue over low heat.

rice. To put through ricer or sieve.

rissole. A savory meat mixture enclosed in rich pastry and fried in deep fat.

roast. To cook by dry heat . . . usually in oven, sometimes in ashes or on heated stones or metals.

KITCHEN KNOW-HOW

A DICTIONARY OF FOOD TERMS (cont.)

roe. Eggs of fish. Roe herring means herring with the eggs.

roll. 1. To place on a board and spread thin with a rolling pin. 2. A small shape made from dough and baked.

rosette. A thin batter baked in a fancy shape by means of a special iron and served with creamed foods, fruit or ice cream. Sometimes called a timbale case.

roux. A cooked mixture of flour and butter used to thicken sauces or main dishes.

S

salt. To season or cure with salt.

sauté. To brown or cook in small amount of fat in skillet.

scald. To heat to temperature just below boiling point until a skin forms over the top.

scallion or shallot. A bulbless onion.

scallop. 1. To bake in a sauce. 2. A sea food.

score. To cut narrow gashes part way through outer surface of food to prevent curling.

sear. To brown surface quickly.

sherbet. A frozen dessert made of fruit juice, sugar and milk or cream.

shortening. A fat suitable for baking or frying.

shred. To tear or cut into small, but long narrow pieces.

sift. To pass through a sieve to remove lumps.

simmer. To cook in liquid just below boiling point on top of range.

skewer. 1. A long pin of wood or metal on which food is placed and held in shape while cooking. 2. To fasten meat with skewers to keep it in shape during cooking.

slice. To cut a thin, flat piece off and across large food mass, such as meat loaf or roast.

sliver. To cut or shred into long thin pieces.

soak. To immerse in liquid for a time.

soufflé. A delicate baked custard containing cheese, fruit, minced meat or vegetables ... made light by stiffly beaten egg whites.

sponge. 1. A high, light cake leavened with air and steam. 2. A batter made with yeast.

steam. To cook in the steam which arises from a pan of boiling water or other liquid.

steam-bake. To cook in the oven in a pan or baking dish set in a pan of water for steaming.

steep. To extract flavor, colors or other qualities from a substance by allowing it to stand in liquid just below the boiling point.

sterilize. To destroy microorganisms by boiling in water, by dry heat or by steam.

stew. To cook slowly in a small amount of liquid for a long time.

stir. To mix, with a spoon, by rotary motion.

stock. The liquid in which meat, poultry, fish or vegetables have been cooked.

T

tamale. A highly seasoned Mexican dish of ground meat, seasonings, cooked corn meal, beans, ripe olives and fat, rolled in oiled cornhusks, steamed or boiled.

timbale. An unsweetened custard or white sauce combined with vegetables, meat, poultry or fish and baked in individual molds.

timbale case. A small shell fried on timbale iron. See p. 96.

toast. To brown by direct heat.

torte. A rich cake, usually made from crumbs, eggs and nuts ... or a meringue in the form of a cake. See pp. 238–240.

tortilla. A thin round Mexican cake ... made of corn meal and hot water and baked on a griddle. Mexican hot mixtures are often rolled in them. See p. 276.

toss. To lightly mix ingredients without mashing them.

truss. To tie a fowl or other meat so that it will hold its shape.

tutti-frutti. Mixed fruit.

U

until set. Until a liquid has become firm ... often refers to a gelatin or custard mixture.

W

whip. To beat rapidly to produce expansion through the incorporation of air, as in egg whites and whipping cream.

Z

zwieback. A kind of toasted bread or rusk.

KITCHEN KNOW-HOW

COMMON FOOD EQUIVALENTS

(See bottom of page for nuts and dried fruits most frequently used in baking.)

	UNIT	APPROXIMATE MEASURE
Apples	1 lb.	3 medium (3 cups sliced)
Bananas	1 lb.	3 medium (2½ cups sliced)
Butter and Other Fats	1 lb.	2 cups
Cheese, Cheddar	1 lb.	4 cups grated
Cheese, Cottage	1 lb.	2 cups
Cheese, White Cream	3-oz. pkg.	6 tbsp.
	½-lb. pkg.	16 tbsp. (1 cup)
Chocolate, Unsweetened	½-lb. pkg.	8 1-oz. squares
Coconut, Shredded	1 lb.	5 cups
Coffee, Ground	1 lb.	80 tbsp.
Cream, Whipping	1 pt.	2 cups (4 cups whipped)
Flour		
All-purpose	1 lb.	4 cups (*sifted*)
Cake	1 lb.	4½ cups (*sifted*)
Whole Wheat	1 lb.	3½ cups
Rye	1 lb.	4½ to 5 cups
Lemon, Medium		
Juice	1	2 to 3 tbsp.
Rind, lightly grated	1	1½ to 3 tsp.
Marshmallows	¼ lb.	16
Orange, Medium		
Juice	1	⅓ to ½ cup
Rind, lightly grated	1	1 to 2 tbsp.
Sugar		
Granulated	1 lb.	2 cups
Brown	1 lb.	2¼ cups (firmly packed)
Confectioners'	1 lb.	3½ cups (*sifted*)

EQUIVALENT WEIGHTS AND MEASURES

Nuts and Fruits Most Commonly Used

	NUTS IN SHELL	SHELLED NUTS
ALMONDS	1 lb. = 1 to 1¾ cups nutmeats	1 lb. = 3½ cups nutmeats
PECANS	1 lb. = 2¼ cups nutmeats	1 lb. = 4 cups nutmeats
PEANUTS	1 lb. = 2¼ cups nutmeats	1 lb. = 3 cups nutmeats
WALNUTS	1 lb. = 1⅔ cups nutmeats	1 lb. = 4 cups nutmeats

1 CUP WHOLE SHELLED NUTS = (broken) = (cut-up) = (coarsely chopped) 1 cup minus 1 tbsp. = (finely chopped) ⅞ CUP

	WHOLE	PITTED	CUT-UP	FINELY CUT
DATES	1 lb. = 2¼ cups	2 cups	1¾ cups	1½ cups
PRUNES	1 lb. = 2⅓ cups	4 cups (cooked)	3 cups (cooked)	2⅞ cups (cooked)
FIGS	1 lb. = 2¾ cups	———	2⅔ cups	2½ cups
RAISINS	15-oz. pkg. = 3 cups	———	2¾ cups	2½ cups
CANDIED FRUIT	½ lb. = ———	———	1½ cups	———
CANDIED PEELS	½ lb. = ———	———	1½ cups	———

13

KITCHEN KNOW-HOW

SUBSTITUTIONS FOR EMERGENCIES

It's best to use ingredients
The recipe recommends;
But if you have to substitute,
This list solution lends.

FOR	USE
1 tbsp. cornstarch (for thickening)	2 tbsp. flour (approximately)
1 whole egg	2 egg yolks plus 1 tbsp. water (in cookies, etc.)
1 whole egg	2 egg yolks (in custards and such mixtures)
1 cup fresh whole milk	½ cup evaporated milk plus ½ cup water
1 cup fresh whole milk	1 cup reconstituted nonfat dry milk plus 2 tbsp. butter
1 cup fresh whole milk	1 cup sour milk or buttermilk plus ½ tsp. soda (decrease baking powder 2 tsp.)
1 cup sour milk or buttermilk	1 tbsp. lemon juice or vinegar plus enough fresh whole milk to make 1 cup
1 sq. unsweetened chocolate (1 oz.)	3 tbsp. cocoa plus 1 tbsp. fat
1 cup honey	1¼ cups sugar plus ¼ cup liquid
1 cup canned tomatoes	about 1⅓ cups cut-up fresh tomatoes, simmered 10 min.

If you are a
Good Mathematician
You May Safely

REDUCE RECIPES

To make half a recipe:

Use exactly *one-half the amount of each ingredient.* (See Equivalents, p. 13, and How to Measure, pp. 6–7, for help in dividing or multiplying ingredients.)

If the divided recipe calls for less than 1 egg, beat up a whole egg. Measure with a tablespoon. Divide. (Use egg that is left in scrambled eggs, sauces, etc.)

Baking pans used for half recipes of cakes, pies, etc. should measure about half the area of those for the whole recipe. Approximate baking time and oven temperature the same.

INCREASE RECIPES

To double a recipe:

Use exactly *twice the amount of each ingredient.* Add extra minute of beating for cakes.

If the increased recipe calls for uneven amounts of ingredients, it is a help to remember that

$\frac{2}{3}$ cup = ½ cup plus 2⅔ tbsp.
$\frac{5}{8}$ cup = ½ cup plus 2 tbsp.
$\frac{7}{8}$ cup = ¾ cup plus 2 tbsp.

Use twice as many pans of the same size indicated for the original recipe or a pan double in area . . . so that the batter will be the same depth in the pan and same baking time and temperature may be maintained.

STORING FOODS

BERRIES

Keep *fresh* berries wrapped in paper in refrigerator; wash and hull shortly before using. Keep leftover *hulled* berries in tightly covered glass jar in refrigerator.

BREADS

Keep cooled bread at room temperature in ventilated metal bread box. Or keep in refrigerator (here, it stales more quickly than in bread box but is less subject to mold).

CAKES

After cake is cool, store in a container with a tight cover; or invert a large bowl over cake.

Fruitcake: (see p. 162).

Cake with Cream Filling: store in refrigerator until served.

CHEESE

Tightly cover *soft* cheese; wrap *hard* cheese in waxed paper; store covered in refrigerator. Grate leftover cheese; keep in covered jar.

COCONUT AND NUTS

Keep tightly covered in refrigerator. Renew softness of coconut by heating over hot water.

COOKIES

Thin, crisp cookies: store in can with loose cover.

Soft cookies: store in airtight container.

Slices of apple or orange in jar help mellow and moisten cookies. Change fruit frequently.

CUSTARD PUDDINGS AND SAUCES

Very perishable. Cool, then cover and store immediately in refrigerator not more than 24 hr. Never eat custard mixtures that have been kept overnight without careful refrigeration.

FLOUR AND CEREALS

Keep tightly covered in cool, dry place. Do not keep whole wheat or other coarse flours or cereals near white flour. (Damp flour may be dried by sifting before a heated oven. Breakfast foods may be crisped by heating in oven.) For long keeping, store whole wheat, corn meal and rye flours in tightly covered glass jars. In hot weather, place in refrigerator.

FRUITS

Keep *unripe* fruit at room temperature to ripen. Store *ripe* fruit (except pineapple, bananas) in cool place. Place cut lemons, oranges or melons cut-side-down on plate or in covered container and store in refrigerator.

GREENS

Refrigerate *lettuce* and wash as needed to avoid "rusting." Wash and store *parsley and water cress* in tightly covered jar in refrigerator. (For other greens, see p. 368.)

MARSHMALLOWS

Keep tightly sealed in bread box or glass jar. Soften by heating in damp bag in oven.

MILK, CREAM AND EGGS

Keep milk and cream (covered) and eggs in refrigerator.

PIES

Fruit: cover with waxed paper, transparent wrap or aluminum foil. Store at room temperature. Freshen by heating a few minutes in warm oven.

Cream, custard and whipped cream: always refrigerate both before and after serving.

SHORTENINGS

Keep *lard and butter* closely covered in refrigerator. Strain drippings directly into container and store in refrigerator. Soft *hydrogenated* shortenings (such as Crisco, Spry and Swift'ning) may be kept on cupboard shelf.

SUGARS

Keep *granulated* and *confectioners'* sugar covered in dry place. Keep *brown sugar* in airtight container. Hard brown sugar may be softened by placing any of the following in container: a slice of apple or orange on waxed paper (change fruit often to insure freshness), a crisp lettuce leaf, a damp cloth, a slice of fresh bread or a piece of moistened sponge. Replace in 2 or 3 days; cover tightly again.

VEGETABLES

Potatoes, onions, beets, carrots, other root vegetables: keep in cool, dry, well ventilated place. Keep other vegetables in crisper in refrigerator. Place cut *onions* and *garlic* cut-side-down in glass jar; cover tightly. Or wrap in aluminum foil. Store in refrigerator.

KITCHEN KNOW-HOW

SELECTING KITCHEN UTENSILS

FOR MIXING

Kitchen fork and knife . . . for many uses.

Flat wire whip . . . beats more air into egg whites.

Pastry blender . . . for cutting in shortening.

Wooden spoon . . . for creaming, stirring sauces, etc.

Blending fork . . . for thorough mixing.

Rotary egg beater (sturdy) . . . for icings, etc.

Flour sifter . . . for sifting white flour.

Sieve (medium) . . . for removing lumps from confectioners' sugar when making icings.

Mixing bowls . . . a set of convenient sizes.

FOR TOP-OF-THE-RANGE COOKING

Saucepans (3) with close-fitting covers (1, 2 and 3-qt. sizes). Lipped saucepans (2).

Double boiler (1½-qt. if you have only one).

Heavy skillet or frying pans (2) with covers (one 9 to 10" diameter, one 6 to 7").

Large kettle for soups, with steamer.

Thermometers . . . for making candy and frying in deep fat.

Pancake griddle . . . waffle iron.

Coffee maker (see p. 67). Teapot.

FOR BAKING AND ROASTING

Right size pan prevents a flop, so measure it across the top.

Square pan . . . 8x8x2" or 9x9x1¾".

Round layer pans (2) . . . 8 or 9x1½" deep.

Oblong pan . . . 13x9½x2", with cover for easy storing and carrying. Glass pans, 10x6x1½" or 11½x7½x1½".

Pie pans . . . 8 or 9" diameter measured from inside rim to inside rim, 1¼" deep.

Loaf pan . . . 9x5x3" or 8½x4½x2¾".

Tube-center pan . . . 10" diameter, 4" deep.

Baking sheet (cooky sheet) without sides . . . 14x10" or 15½x12" or 17x14".

Muffin pan . . . large, medium or small cups.

Baking dish with cover. Round, oval, square or oblong; 1, 1½ or 2-qt. size.

Roasting pan with rack. Choose size suitable for family.

Individual custard cups or ramekins. They are usually set in shallow pan to bake.

Jelly roll pan . . . 15½x10½x1".

Wire racks for cooling cakes, cookies and breads.

Oven thermometer for checking oven temperature.

Meat thermometer for registering internal temperature of meat.

Special pans for special recipes such as tiny tart pans, corn stick pans, sandbakels molds.

SELECTING KITCHEN UTENSILS (cont.)

FOR FOOD PREPARATION

Apple corer . . . to remove apple cores.

Ball cutter (small) . . . for cutting out melon balls (see p. 374), potato balls, butter balls.

Bread or pastry board . . . for kneading dough and rolling out cookies, pastry, etc. Also a canvas or heavy crash *cover* for the board.

Colander (a perforated metal pan) . . . for straining foods.

Cutters of various shapes and sizes . . . for cookies, biscuits, doughnuts, etc.

Electric mixer . . . portable or standard.

Food chopper—with fine and coarse discs . . . for grinding meats, vegetables, nuts, etc.

Funnel . . . for filling jars and bottles.

Garlic press . . . for quickly mincing cloves of garlic.

Graters (a set of) . . . to grate food to different degrees—from very fine to coarse.

Hand utensils . . . often available as a set with rack for hanging on wall.

> *Fork* . . . long-handled.
>
> *Turners* . . . for pancakes, meat patties.
>
> *Ladle* . . . for soups, jams.
>
> *Potato masher* . . . for mashing foods.
>
> *Spatulas* (flexible) . . . large and small.
>
> *Spoon with slots or holes* (large) . . . for scooping foods out of a liquid.

Kitchen scissors . . . for many uses (see pp. 25-26).

Knives

> *Bread* (with saw-tooth edge) . . . for cutting breads, fruitcake, etc. neatly.
>
> *French chef* . . . for quickly mincing and cutting nuts, celery, green pepper, etc.
>
> *Grapefruit* (with a curved blade) . . . for cutting under grapefruit sections.
>
> *Long slicer* . . . for slicing roasts evenly.
>
> *Paring* (2 or 3 sharp) . . . for paring, cutting vegetables and fruits.
>
> *Straight-edge knives* (several).

Lemon squeezer . . . for extracting juice from lemons, oranges, grapefruit.

Molds—such as ring, melon or fluted-shaped . . . for puddings or salads. Fancy-shaped individual molds, custard or muffin cups.

Openers—can, jar, bottle, corkscrew.

Pastry brush—for greasing pans, brushing dough with melted butter, etc.

Rolling pin and pastry set—a canvas or heavy crash cover for the pastry board and a white stockinet cover for the pin.

Strawberry huller . . . for hulling strawberries and picking pin feathers from poultry.

Tablespoons (several)—wooden or metal.

Tongs . . . for lifting vegetables, meats and other foods out of liquid or pan.

Vegetable parer with floating blade . . . for paring potatoes and other vegetables.

Wire strainers—fine, coarse and very fine . . . for straining foods and sieving them.

FOR STORAGE

Canister set (cans for sugar, flour, etc.).

Bread box (if not part of cabinet).

Cake safe (if not part of cabinet).

Cooky jar.

Set of refrigerator dishes with covers.

FOR SINK AND CLEANING

Rubber scraper . . . for scraping dishes clean.

Dish pans . . . when sink not used for pan.

Dish drainer.

Small scrub brush . . . *bottle brush* . . . *vegetable brush.*

Pot holders . . . *dish towels* . . . *dish cloths.*

Sink strainer.

Waste basket.

Garbage can (if no incinerator or disposal).

KITCHEN KNOW-HOW *For Weight Loss or Gain, Count Your ... CALORIES*

CALORIE CHART

FOOD	CALORIE COUNT
Apple, raw, 1 medium	76
Apricots, canned, in syrup, 4 halves	97
Asparagus, 6 to 8 stalks	25
Bacon, 2 crisp slices	97
Banana, 1 medium	88
Beans, baked, canned, 1 cup	295
Beans, green or snap, 1 cup	27
Beef, steak, club, broiled 1 large piece	410
Beef, rib roast, lean, 1 medium slice	96
Beef stew with vegetables, 1 cup	252
Beets, canned, 1 cup	82
Biscuits, 1 medium	129
Bouillon or consommé, clear, 1 cup	26
Bread, white, enriched, 1 slice	64
Bread, whole wheat, 1 slice	55
Broccoli, 1 cup	44
Butter or margarine, 1 tbsp.	100
Cabbage, raw, shredded, 1 cup	24
Cake, angel or sponge, plain 2″ wedge	110
Cake, chocolate layer, iced 2″ slice	356
Cake, coffee cake, 1 small piece	100
Cake, fruit, 1 small slice, 2x2x½″	106
Cantaloupe, ½ medium	37
Carrot, 1 whole raw	21
Cauliflower, 1 cup	30
Celery, 1 large outer stalk	7
Cheese, Cheddar, 1″ cube (1 oz.)	113
Cheese, cottage, ½ cup	107
Chicken, roast, average serving (¼ lb., no bone)	227
Chicken salad, ½ cup	185
Chocolate beverages (with milk), 1 cup	239
Chocolate fudge, 1″ sq.	116
Chocolate malted milk, 1 average (13 oz.)	601
Coffee, clear, 1 cup	0
Coffee, 1 tbsp. cream and 1 lump sugar	55
Cola beverages, 1 bottle (8 oz.)	90
Cookies, assorted, 3″ diameter, each	109
Corn on the cob, 1 medium	84
Cracker, graham, 2 medium	55
Cracker, saltine, 1 double	34
Cream, whipping (35%), 1 tbsp.	49
Cream, coffee (20%), 1 tbsp.	30
Doughnut, cake or yeast, 1 average	136
Egg, boiled or poached, 1 medium	77
Frankfurters, 1 medium	124
French dressing, 1 tbsp.	59
Grapefruit, ½ medium	72
Gravy, medium consistency, ¼ cup	107
Ham, smoked, cooked, 4½x2½x½″ slice	119
Hamburger, medium patty (1/5 lb.)	331
Ice cream, plain, commercial, ½ pt.	294

Caloric values based on the U.S. Department of Agriculture Handbook No. 8. 1950.

FOOD	CALORIE COUNT
Ice cream, chocolate, ½ pt.	385
Jam or Jelly, 1 tbsp.	55
Lamb, leg, roast, 1 medium slice	103
Lamb chops, broiled, 1 medium	178
Lemonade, 1 large glass	104
Lettuce, 1 large head	50
Liver, 1 medium slice	120
Macaroni and cheese, 1 cup	464
Mayonnaise, 1 tbsp.	92
Meat loaf, 1 medium slice	100
Milk, skim, 1 glass (8 oz.)	87
Milk, whole fresh, 1 glass (8 oz.)	166
Muffin, 1 small	134
Noodles, cooked, 1 cup	107
Nuts, mixed, 8 to 12 nuts	94
Oatmeal, cooked, ½ cup	74
Olives, green or ripe, 10 small	70
Onions, 2¼″ diameter, 1 medium	45
Orange, 1 medium	68
Orange juice, frozen, after dilution 1 glass (6 oz.)	75
Pancake, 1 medium	59
Peaches, canned, in syrup, 2 halves	79
Peanut butter, 1 tbsp.	92
Pears, canned, in syrup, 2 halves	79
Peas, canned, ½ cup	84
Pie, apple or berry, 1/7 of 9″ pie	331
Pie, lemon meringue, 1/7 of 9″ pie	302
Pie, mince, 1/7 of 9″ pie	341
Pie, pumpkin, 1/7 of 9″ pie	263
Pineapple, canned, 1 slice and juice	95
Popcorn, no butter, 1 cup	54
Pork chop, 1 medium	296
Potato, baked, 1 medium	100
Potato, sweet, baked, 1 medium	190
Potato chips, 7 large or 10 medium	108
Potatoes, mashed, 1 scant cup	159
Rice, white or brown, cooked, ½ cup	100
Roll, plain, 1 medium	118
Roll, cinnamon, 1 medium	178
Salmon, canned, red, 2/3 cup	173
Sherbets, ½ cup	118
Shrimp, canned, drained, 3 oz.	108
Spaghetti with meat sauce, 1 average serving	396
Spareribs, roasted, 3 average ribs	123
Strawberries, raw, capped, 1 cup	54
Sugar, granulated or brown, 1 tbsp.	50
Tea, unsweetened, 1 cup	0
Tomatoes, fresh, 1 medium	30
Tuna fish, drained, ⅝ cup	198
Turkey, 1 slice 4x2x¼″	100
Veal cutlet, breaded, 1 medium	217
Vegetable soup, 1 cup	82
Waffle, 1 medium with 3 tbsp. syrup	687
Watermelon, 6″ slice 1½″ thick	168
White sauce, medium, ¼ cup	107

FREEZING FOODS

GENERAL RULES FOR FREEZING

1. Use quality foods.

2. Handle carefully before freezing. Follow recipe exactly. Use special directions for cooking. See chart on the following pages.

3. Use moisture-proof, vapor-proof paper, foil or waxed cartons for storing. Wrap tightly and seal well; label, date. More information below.

4. The ideal storage temperature is 0° to −10° or lower. If possible, place next to freezing surface 24 hr. before storing closer together.

5. Handle and cook properly after removing from freezer. Follow directions on chart for reheating. See chart for special information.

6. Estimate your needs. Do not freeze more food than you can use during the length of the food's storage time (chart tells storage time).

7. A rapid turnover is important. Use the oldest food in your freezer first. Make a storage chart of your freezer's contents, when the food was placed in the freezer and when it should be used.

WRAPPING FOR FREEZING

HOW TO WRAP

Use this "drugstore wrap" when packaging with freezer paper.

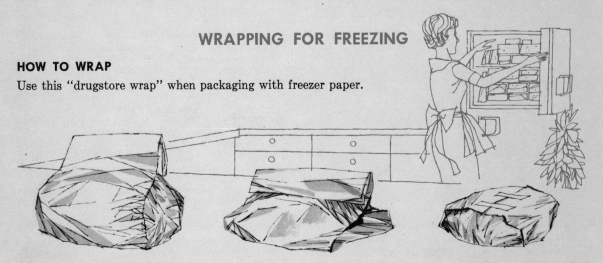

1. Place food in center of wrapping, bringing edges together evenly above food.

2. Fold edges over and over until fold is flat against food.

3. Fold inside edges and seal with freezer tape. Label plainly with contents and date.

WRAPPING MATERIALS

Good wrapping materials are resistant to moisture and vapor. For *solid foods* (meat, cake, pie, bread) use freezer-weight paper such as heavy-duty aluminum foil, cellophane, Pliofilm or other transparent film. Polyethylene bags may be used for baked goods such as bread and cookies.

Liquid-packed foods may be packaged in heavily waxed cartons, glass freezer jars, plastic or aluminum containers. Choose a size of container that holds enough for 1 meal: quarts for 4 to 6 servings; pints for 2 to 3. Use only containers with wide top openings so the food may be removed when only partially thawed. Prepared foods such as meat pies and casserole dishes may be frozen (covered and sealed with tape) in the containers in which they were baked, ready for reheating.

TO SEAL: Use freezer tape for sealing, not general utility tape. Freezer tape may also be used as a label on hard-to-mark wrapping materials.

TO LABEL: Jars, cartons and packages may be labeled with china marking pencil or soft crayon available at stationery stores. Felt pens are good for marking aluminum foil or other opaque paper. Use tie-on tags if packaging permits. Slip a square of paper into transparent wrapped package.

Food	Container or Wrap	Storage Time	
		BAKED PRODUCT	UNBAKED PRODUCT
YEAST BREADS (Plain and fancy yeast bread loaves, coffee cakes and rolls)	Polyethylene bags, Pliofilm or aluminum foil. Rolls and buns may be placed in a rigid container (coffee can or freezer box), then over-wrapped.	2 to 3 mo.	Not recommended
QUICK BREADS (Nut breads, fruit breads, biscuits, muffins, coffee cakes, waffles and pancakes)	Polyethylene bags, Pliofilm or aluminum foil. Pack biscuits and muffins as rolls (above). Stack waffles and pancakes in rigid container with waxed paper between layers.	2 to 3 mo.	Not recommended
PASTRY AND PIES Pastry shells and rounds; fruit, chiffon, pumpkin and mince pies or tarts)	Ovenproof or anodized pie pans (should not use paper pie pans) — freeze pie, then over-wrap. Place tarts in rigid box, then overwrap.	**Pastry, fruit, mince and pumpkin pies:** 4 to 6 mo. **Chiffon pies:** 2 to 3 mo.	2 to 3 mo.
COOKIES (Rolled, bar, drop and refrigerator cookies and cooky dough)	Baked: Rigid boxes, over-wrapped. Unbaked: Shape *refrigerator* cookies in roll; wrap in foil or Pliofilm. Place *drop* or *rolled* cooky dough in frozen food container.	9 to 12 mo.	9 to 12 mo.
CAKES (Butter, angel food, chiffon, double-quick, pound and fruitcakes or cupcakes)	Covered cake pans (square or oblong). Place baked round layers on cardboard rounds; overwrap. To prevent crushing, place in heavy cardboard box. Pack cupcakes as tarts (above).	**Unfrosted:** 6 mo. **Frosted:** 2 to 3 mo.	Not recommended
MAIN DISHES (Creamed dishes, chili, stews, meats with and without gravy and soups)	Freeze in ovenproof baking dishes or casseroles (ready for reheating), glass freezer jars (wide mouth-type) or alumi-num containers (with wide top).	**With sauce:** 6 mo. **Without sauce:** 3 mo.	

20

Defrosting Time		Success Tips
BAKED PRODUCT	**UNBAKED PRODUCT**	
IN OVEN (325°): Put sweet rolls, coffee cakes, etc., directly into oven for 20 min. **AT ROOM TEMPERATURE:** Thaw bread 3 hr. in wrapper.	Not recommended	For best results, bake breads before freezing. Cool thoroughly before wrapping. Bake bread to light golden brown to prevent separation of upper crust from interior of loaf.
IN OVEN (325°): Put breads directly in oven for 25 min.—biscuits, muffins, 15 to 25 min. **AT ROOM TEMPERATURE:** Thaw fruit and nut breads 1½ to 2 hr. in wrapper.	Not recommended	For best results, bake quick breads before freezing; do not overbake, as this makes reheated breads dry. Cool thoroughly; then immediately wrap and freeze.
Tarts or Pastry Rounds: Put in 325° oven 5 to 8 min. **Pies** (except chiffon): Thaw at room temp. 30 min., then heat in 325° oven 30 min. *Chiffon:* Thaw at room temp. 45 min. or in refrigerator 2 to 3 hr.	Place **tarts and pastry** directly in 475° oven 8 to 10 min. Bake **pies** at given temperature 15 to 20 min. longer than time given (lower oven shelf).	Pies baked before freezing are of best quality; if pies are frozen unbaked, the bottom crust tends to become soggy. Pastry shells or rounds freeze well, baked or unbaked. Bake or reheat pies on lower oven shelf.
AT ROOM TEMPERATURE: Thaw 10 to 15 min. Thaw on serving plate, if desired. (Do not thaw in oven.)	Thaw dough slightly at room temp.; roll, slice or drop as usual; allow few extra min. baking time for thick cookies.	Frost cookies with confectioners' sugar icing or bits of jelly just before serving to prevent sogginess. Wrap tightly to keep cookies from drying out.
AT ROOM TEMPERATURE: **Large Cake:** 2 to 3 hr. **Layers:** 1 hr. **Cupcakes:** 30 min. Thaw in wrapper or covered. (Do not thaw in oven.)	Not recommended	Baked cakes freeze best. To prevent sogginess, fill and frost just before serving. However, if frosting is desired before freezing use confectioners' sugar type.
IN OVEN (325° for thin sauces to 400° for dishes with large chunks of food): Bake 45 min. to 1 hr. **IN SAUCEPAN:** Heat with small amount fat or liquid until bubbly.		Undercook food slightly to prevent "warmed over" flavor. When reheating, stir carefully so as not to mash food. Cream sauces become smooth when stirred. Add crumb or cheese topping just before serving.

HOW TO FREEZE SANDWICHES

Both lunchbox sandwiches and fancy party sandwiches may be successfully frozen.
Also, sandwich fillings and spreads will freeze well.

To Freeze Lunchbox Sandwiches: Spread bread to the edges with softened butter (to prevent the filling from soaking into the bread). Fill and top with second slice of buttered bread. Wrap each sandwich separately in freezer paper (Pliofilm or aluminum). Label; freeze. If desired, place a number of sandwiches together in a box.

To Freeze Fancy Party Sandwiches: Spread with softened butter, then with desired filling. Decorate, if desired. Place in box in layers with waxed paper between. Wrap; label; freeze. Rolled and ribbon sandwiches may be wrapped uncut and cut after defrosting.

Length of Storage: Sandwiches may be stored up to 3 weeks. Do not refreeze.

Fillings to Freeze

Luncheon meats
Sliced roast beef
Sliced roast pork
Baked ham
Dried beef
Sliced or minced chicken or turkey

Tuna or salmon
Sliced cheese
Cheese spreads
Hard-cooked egg yolks
Peanut butter

It's Best Not to Freeze These!

Jelly, mayonnaise and salad dressing (When used as a spread, they soak into the bread, making it soggy.)

Hard-cooked egg whites
Lettuce, celery, tomatoes, carrots

To Thaw Sandwiches: Leave in original wrapping 3 to 3½ hr. for lunchbox sandwiches, 1 to 2 hr. for party sandwiches. If not used immediately, hold in refrigerator.

TIPS FOR FREEZING MAIN DISHES

Cook for shorter time than recipe directs. Cool quickly to stop cooking action. To hasten cooling, set covered pan in ice water. When cool, package immediately. Pack solidly to avoid air spaces.

Gravies and sauces packed with meats and vegetables help fill air spaces. (Note: Gravies and sauces containing large amounts of milk may appear curdled when frozen. However, they will become smooth when reheated.)

Straight-sided containers: fill pints to ½" from top; fill quarts or larger to 1" from top. Fill jars with rounded shoulders (as used in canning) only to the shoulder. Seal, label, date. Freeze. *Do not refreeze thawed food.*

Storing main dishes longer than recommended time may cause loss of flavor.

If only part of a recipe is to be frozen, take that part from the pan before completely cooked. Cool, package and freeze immediately.

Partial thawing of the frozen food *before* reheating may prevent scorching. Creamed dishes, stews, creamed soups and dishes that scorch easily may be heated in a double boiler 20 to 30 min.

Cook macaroni, spaghetti and rice to be used in frozen main dishes until *barely tender* for best texture. Freeze in baking dishes or freezer cartons. To reheat, bake in oven *at 350° 1 hr.* If too dry, add liquid when baking.

Stew should be slightly undercooked. Add vegetables when meat is nearly cooked. Meat should be tender but firm. Potatoes frozen in stew become mushy and grainy, so it is best to add them when reheating.

Meat loaf may be frozen cooked or uncooked.

Roasted meats, such as beef, pork, ham, turkey or chicken should be trimmed before freezing in order to save freezer space. Cover with gravy for prolonged storage life; freeze.

For length of storage and thawing, see pp. 20–21.

SPECIAL SUGGESTIONS

Cream Puffs: Freeze unfilled cream puffs or miniature ones (for hors d' oeuvres), since any fillings tend to make the puffs soggy. To freeze, put in layers in box with waxed paper between; overwrap box. Label, date. Cream puffs may be stored 9 to 12 months. They may be filled while frozen or may be thawed slightly in their wrap.

Meringue Shells: Wrap *unfilled* carefully for storage by putting in layers in box with waxed paper between; overwrap box. May be stored *filled* with whipped cream or ice cream (not custard or cream-type filling). To freeze, place in freezer unwrapped on level surface until filling hardens. Then place in boxes for freezing. Do not stack filled meringues.

Meringues may be stored 3 to 6 months. May be served directly from freezer or thawed slightly in wrap.

Pies: It is best not to freeze custard or meringue pies. Custards tend to separate; meringue toppings toughen, shrink, separate and stick to wrappings.

If lightweight aluminum pie pans are used, bake and reheat on baking sheet for better browning. For time and temperature, see p. 21.

Pie Fillings: Fillings such as mince, pumpkin or fruit (peach, cherry, apple, etc.) may be frozen for later use. A pint jar contains adequate filling for an 8″ pie. (Note: Use cornstarch for clear, bright fruit pie filling.)

Potatoes: Mashed potatoes and puffed potatoes in the half shell freeze well. French fried potatoes freeze best when cut very thin. For frying use a shortening or vegetable oil with a bland flavor. Candied sweet potatoes may also be frozen.

Potatoes frozen in stew become mushy and grainy upon reheating, so it is best to add them when reheating.

Cooky Pie Crusts (made from cooky crumbs or cooky-like dough): These freeze well either baked or unbaked. Baked cooky crusts may thaw at room temperature or in refrigerator; place unbaked crusts directly in oven from freezer. Other freezing information is same as cookies.

Butter Cakes Filled With Whipped Cream: Fill cake layers with plain or flavored whipped cream. Ice, if desired, with butter icing. Place in box; overwrap. Label, date. Put in freezer on level surface. Do not freeze over 3 months. To serve, place in refrigerator 3 to 4 hr. before cutting. (Note: Cakes filled with whipped cream may be refrigerated up to 2 days without becoming soggy.)

Appetizers: Tiny sandwiches may be frozen decorated, if desired. Use fillings mentioned on previous page. Pastry rounds and tiny cream puffs, however, should be frozen unfilled and filled at the last minute, since filling may make them soggy upon long standing.

Waffles, Bread, Pancakes: Reheat frozen waffles and bread slices in toaster, pancakes under broiler.

Nut Breads: Bake in small juice or soup cans; freeze right in cans. Thaw slightly and slice for round sandwiches.

Fancy Breads (Yeast or Quick): Wrap in foil to freeze. For quick thawing and warming, place directly in oven. Frost after reheating. For time and temperature, see p. 21.

For Gift Giving: Pack cookies or fruitcakes in tins ahead of time; wrap prettily; freeze.

Instant Cookies: Keep a roll of refrigerated cooky dough (pp. 192–193) in freezer; slice off and bake at an instant's notice!

GARNISHES *Garnish and serve with love.*

It may be only a ruffle of lettuce to set off a salad or a sprig of parsley to accent a platter of roast chicken. Whatever the finishing touch, be sure to make it simple and as good to eat as it is to see.

A garnish should add contrast of shape, color, crispness or flavor to the food it adorns. Notice the finishing touches suggested in many of our recipes . . . and shown in the color pictures in this book and in magazines.

GARNISHING IDEAS

For Vegetables

Just before serving, top with:
Minced parsley, chives or green onion tops
Sieved hard-cooked eggs or yolks
Quartered or sliced hard-cooked eggs
Pimiento strips
Green pepper rings or strips
Grated cheese
Thin lemon slices or wedges
Chopped toasted almonds, peanuts, cashews
Crumbled crisp bacon bits
Chili sauce, catsup or pickled red peppers

For Scrambled Eggs

Arrange small bowls of julienne ham, grated cheese, pineapple marmalade, sautéed mushrooms and chopped green pepper on a tray. Each person sprinkles one or more of the garnishes over his serving of hot creamy scrambled eggs.

For Soups

Just before serving, top with:
Toasted slivered almonds or crisp cereals . . . on creamed soups
Lemon slice . . . on black bean, jellied soup, clear tomato
Salted whipped cream or cheese popcorn . . . on tomato soup
Minced parsley or chives . . . on any cream, vegetable or jellied soup
Sprig of water cress

For Fruit Cups

Just before serving, top with:
A whole berry
A sprig of mint
A dip of fruit ice or sherbet

For Fish

Surround fish on platter with:
Lemon wedges or slices sprinkled with parsley, minced pimiento, paprika, minced green pepper
Orange slices
Grapefruit sections
Thick slices of cucumber
Tomato slices topped with thin slices of lemon and stuffed olives

For Desserts

Top plain puddings with:
Whole or sliced fresh berries or cherries
Cubes of bright colored fruit-flavored gelatin

Surround creamy or frozen desserts with:
Bright colored fresh fruits or berries

Decorate dessert plates with:
Clusters of berries or grapes
Ivy or grape leaves
A single fresh flower
Ring of berries at base of sherbet dish

For Meats

Surround meat on platter with:
Pink cinnamon apples (with pork)
Stuffed black prunes (with pork)
Slices of orange decorated with water cress or parsley (with duck)
Bunches of red, green or purple grapes (with chicken)
Molded cranberry cutouts on orange slices (with turkey and chicken)
Canned pear halves filled with green mint jelly (with lamb)
Spiced peach halves and water cress (with ham)
Sautéed mushroom caps (with steak)
French fried onion rings (with steak)
Glazed onions and buttered carrot strips (with beef)
Tiny scooped-out tomatoes filled with horse-radish (with pot roast)

For Salads

Add gaily the last minute:
Sprigs of water cress, mint or parsley
Thin strips of pimiento or green pepper
Cream cheese balls . . . may be rolled in nuts or chives
Prunes, dates, figs or cherries stuffed with seasoned cream cheese or nuts

For Sandwiches

Decorate with sprigs of water cress, sliced olives, minced parsley, green pepper or pimiento. Little bunches of sweet green grapes and grape, strawberry or mint leaves on the sandwich plates add a festive touch.

24

VEGETABLE RELISHES AND GARNISHES

CELERY CURLS

Cut stalks into short lengths. Slit both ends in narrow strips, almost to center. Ends will curl in ice water.

CARROT CURLS

Slice scraped raw carrots lengthwise paper-thin with slicer. Roll up and fasten with toothpicks. Crisp in ice water until curled.

RADISH ROSES

Cut off root end; leave bit of stem. Cut thin petals from stem to root end around radish. Place in ice water to open.

FRINGED CUCUMBER SLICES

Cut off ends. Pare, if desired. Pull sharp fork firmly down lengthwise surface. Repeat around cucumber. Slice thin. Chill.

GREEN PEPPER RINGS

Cut firm green pepper in thin slices crosswise . . . cut out all white portions and remove seeds. Crisp in ice water.

LATTICED VEGETABLES

Use lattice cutter to make attractive lattice slices and sticks from raw carrots, potatoes, turnips.

ONION CHRYSANTHEMUM

Remove outer skin from flat medium-sized sweet onion. With point of very sharp knife, cut from center into about 1/8" sections about 3/4 of the way through.

Hold onion under running hot water and spread gently. Set cut onion in red or yellow tinted water until delicately colored. Drain. Use in center of vegetable tray.

CELERY PINWHEELS

Wash celery stalks. Stuff with well seasoned cream cheese. Press 3 stalks together, overlapping as celery grows. Tie together, chill; slice 1/2" thick.

PICKLE FANS

Make four lengthwise cuts almost to end of pickle. Spread gently to form a little open fan.

CAULIFLOWERETS AND BROCCOLI BUDS

Cut away green leaves. Wash; break into bite-size flowerets. Serve chilled and crisp.

MINCED PARSLEY

Fold leaves of several stalks (washed). Hold together . . . cut fine with scissors.

HOW TO PREPARE

PREPARING NUTS

Blanched Nuts: Drop shelled nuts into boiling water. Let stand 2 to 5 min. Pour off hot water, add cold. Push off skins by pinching each nut between thumb and forefinger. Dry.

Slivered or Sliced Nuts: First blanch . . . then cut with very sharp knife or single-edged razor blade while nuts are moist and warm.

Chopped Nuts: See p. 196.

Ground Nuts: Use fine blade of food grinder for finely ground . . . coarse blade for coarsely ground. Nuts should be dry.

Toasted Nuts: Spread shelled nuts in shallow pan. Bake *at 350° 10 to 20 min.*, or until delicately browned. Watch carefully.

Salted Nuts: Stir 1 tsp. butter or oil into 1 cup nuts in pan. Toast. Drain. Sprinkle with salt.

DATES, MARSHMALLOWS

For ease in cutting, use scissors. Dip scissors in water occasionally to prevent sticking.

MELTING CHOCOLATE

Put chocolate in double boiler or small bowl. Set over hot (not boiling) water. Melt. Remove chocolate from bowl with rubber scraper.

GRATED RIND

Rub washed fruit in short strokes across small area of grater. Grate only outermost colored rind.

DISSOLVING GELATIN

Soften 1 envelope (1 tbsp.) unflavored gelatin in ½ cup cold water. Dissolve over hot water. Or follow recipe directions.

FROSTED GRAPES

Brush grapes with slightly beaten egg white. Dip in granulated sugar. Dry on a rack.

DICING CELERY, RHUBARB

Place several stalks of washed celery or rhubarb together on board. Cut through all at once.

WHIPPING CREAM

Beat chilled whipping cream (35% butterfat) in chilled deep bowl with cold rotary beater until fluffy and stiff.

SOURING MILK OR CREAM

Put 1 tbsp. vinegar or lemon juice into cup. Fill with sweet milk or cream. Let stand a few minutes.

STUFFED DATES

Fill pitted dates, prunes or figs with nuts, fondant (p. 180), cut-up marshmallows or candied ginger. Roll in sugar.

26

FRESH COCONUT

Pierce 2 holes in eyes of coconut. Drain out milk (drink or use for part of liquid in recipe).

Break shell with hammer or chisel. Remove meat from shell with knife. Pare off brown skin.

Grate or shred white meat. (Keep any not used, tightly covered, in refrigerator.)

TINT OR TOAST COCONUT

Tint coconut to desired shade by soaking in water tinted with food coloring. Drain; dry.
Toast coconut in shallow pan in mod. oven (350°) until golden brown, stirring frequently.

SHREDDING CABBAGE

For *coarsely* shredded cabbage, use a knife.
For *finely* shredded cabbage, use a grater.

GRATING CHEESE

Rub *soft cheese* lightly against a coarse grater. Use at once. Rub *dry firm cheese* against a fine grater. Can be stored, covered, in a cool place.

PINEAPPLE

Cut a thick slice from top and bottom. Remove rind by cutting down length of pineapple in long, wide strokes.

Remove eyes by cutting grooves diagonally. Then cut into ½" crosswise slices; remove core. If desired, cut slices into cubes.

Or, cut pineapple lengthwise in spears, removing core. To sweeten: mix with sugar; let stand at room temperature.

PEELING A TOMATO

Hold over flame or heat 1 min.

Or place in boiling water 1 min. Then plunge into cold water.

Slip off skin.

HOW TO PREPARE

SOFT BREAD CRUMBS

Tear day-old bread into small pieces with fingers. Or pull into crumbs with fork.

FINE DRY CRUMBS

Dry stale bread in slow oven. Put in paper bag or between waxed papers. Crush with rolling pin. Or put through food grinder.

CUBES, CROUTONS

Trim and cut bread into cubes. For *croutons*, toast tiny bread cubes in slow oven until golden. Melt butter; add cubes and toss to coat.

SANDWICH LOAF

Use a long, very sharp knife to remove crusts from loaf of sandwich bread. Leave bottom crust until last.

Cut into 4 slices. Spread with fillings. Assemble loaf; frost with cream cheese, chill. See recipe p. 120, picture p. 121.

SPIEDINI

Cut French Bread almost through in ¾" slices. Put thin slice Mozzarella cheese between slices. Tuck in a few anchovies. Pour ½ cup melted butter over loaf on baking sheet. Heat *at 350° 10 to 15 min.* Serve immediately.

FRESH MUSHROOMS

Wash mushrooms gently. (Never soak.) Trim off spots. Cut off stems. Use caps for baking, broiling. Mince stems for sauces.

Slice whole mushrooms down through stems. Sauté in butter. Use for sauce, stuffing, etc.

CANNED MUSHROOMS

To sauté: add mushrooms and liquid to melted butter in hot pan. Cook till liquid is absorbed.

POMEGRANATE SEEDS

Cut washed pomegranate in two. Remove seeds with fork. Sprinkle on salads for a festive touch.

CHOPPING OR MINCING ONION

Peel onion. Cut off end slice. Cut exposed surface into tiny squares. Cut crosswise in thin slices.

GRATING ONION

Rub onion against a coarse grater. Push off any from grater with a knife.

MEAL PLANNING

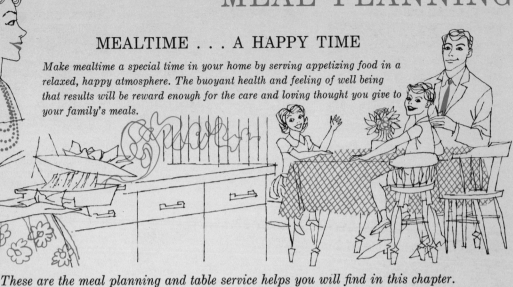

MEALTIME . . . A HAPPY TIME

Make mealtime a special time in your home by serving appetizing food in a relaxed, happy atmosphere. The buoyant health and feeling of well being that results will be reward enough for the care and loving thought you give to your family's meals.

These are the meal planning and table service helps you will find in this chapter.

ONCE-IN-A-LIFETIME PARTIES

Wedding Reception

Party Punch (*p. 72*)
Chicken Salad (*p. 381*)
Olives   Radishes   Pickles
Tiny Hot Buttered Rolls or Finger Sandwiches
Ice Cream Molds
Wedding Cake (*p. 170*)   Groom's Cake (*p. 151*)
Salted Nuts   Bon Bons
Coffee

Golden Wedding Anniversary

Tray of Beautiful Cut-up Fresh Fruits
with Cheese Straws (*p. 54*) and
Buttered Nut Bread (*p. 91*)
Double Ring Wedding Cake
(Yellow-frosted Twin Angel Cake, *p. 171*)
Ice Cream Balls
Mint Wafers   Mixed Nuts
Coffee   Tea   Punch

PLANNING MEALS FOR TWO

Make one-half or one-third of the recipes in this book (see *p. 14*). For further help, see Betty Crocker's Dinner For Two Cook Book.

PLANNING MEALS FOR MANY

Double, triple or quadruple the recipes in this book (see *p. 14*). For further help, write Betty Crocker for quantity cookery recipes.

PLANNING FOODS THAT GO TOGETHER

Something soft and something crisp
 Should always go together,
And something hot with something cold
 No matter what the weather;
Serve bland foods with tangy sauce
 And garnish them with green
If you will use these simple rules
 You'll be your family's queen!

WHEN PLANNING MEALS, SELECT FOODS FOR:

Color: An attractive plate is quite important, for it is often said that we eat with our eyes! If the meat is a drab brown, liven it up with a colorful garnish of tomato or pepper relish. Serve a colorful vegetable, such as beets or carrots or broccoli . . . along with a mound of snowy white mashed potatoes, with yellow butter melting on top and a sprinkle of paprika.

Garnishes are a good way to show artistic flare with food to liven their appeal. See suggestions for garnishing, *pp. 24–25.*

Form: Serve a variety of sizes, shapes and proportions. Meals lose interest if all foods are cut in same size pieces. If beef stew is served, add sliced tomatoes (*not* apple-carrot salad) and a piece of cake (not a fruit cup).

Variety: It is important to serve a variety of foods within a meal . . . as well as a variety within the day. If scrambled eggs are served for breakfast, avoid serving creamed eggs for supper. Complement your luncheon dish with flaky biscuits or a new kind of bread. Serve a variety of beverages during the day . . . cocoa for breakfast, milk for lunch, lemonade for snack, tea or coffee for dinner.

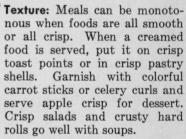

Texture: Meals can be monotonous when foods are all smooth or all crisp. When a creamed food is served, put it on crisp toast points or in crisp pastry shells. Garnish with colorful carrot sticks or celery curls and serve apple crisp for dessert. Crisp salads and crusty hard rolls go well with soups.

Temperature: Be sure to serve *hot foods hot* and *cold foods cold.* As a rule, lukewarm foods have lukewarm appeal. Try to plan meals so that foods are at the right temperature when eaten. Rolls hot from the oven are a treat . . . as well as the crisp coolness of a tossed salad.

Flavor: For appetite appeal, plan *flavor contrasts*—such as fish and lemon or turkey and cranberries — within a meal. Avoid serving more than one strong-flavored food.

Serve mild-flavored foods early in the meal, then the stronger ones—with something sweet for dessert.

Use *spices and herbs* to enhance the natural flavors in foods. Do not overspice so that food flavor is overwhelmed. See herb and spice charts, *pp. 51–52,* for flavoring suggestions.

Use *condiments*, such as catsup, mustard, Worcestershire sauce and pickle relish—but use them sparingly! A little will complement, but too much will overpower.

TYPES OF TABLE SERVICE

Family Service (English)

Most suitable for the average family.

The first course such as fruit juice or soup is on the table when the family is seated. For a change of pace, you might like to serve this first course in the living room or on the patio. When ready for the main course, the meat and vegetables are placed in front of the host and served by him on the plates placed directly in front of him or a little to the left. The hostess serves the salad, beverage and a second vegetable. Other members of the family or guests pass the plates, passing to the left. Bread, butter and jelly or relishes are placed on the table and passed by those who are nearest them.

After the family has finished the main course, the table is cleared of serving dishes and plates. Dessert may be served at the table by the hostess or it may be served from the kitchen.

The alternate method of family service is to place all the food on the table and have each person pass it in turn. It does not matter whether foods are passed to the left or the right, just so all foods are passed the same direction.

What is the correct way to serve and remove dishes?

Serve and remove all dishes at the left except beverages. Beverages are served and removed at the right. Table service should be done unobtrusively and quietly without interrupting conversations.

What should be removed before serving dessert?

Everything except the centerpiece and the water glasses or goblets. If necessary, remove crumbs with folded napkin and small plate. Dessert silver may then be put in place or served directly on dessert plates.

Salad as Appetizer: In California it is popular to serve the salad as an appetizer. It is usually served in individual wooden bowls or abalone shells in place when guests are seated.

Formal Service (Russian)

Suited to the household with a servant.

The appetizer course is served after the guests are seated, placed on the service plates, if they are used.

Food is arranged on the individual plates in the kitchen and placed before each guest. Or the meat is carved in the kitchen by the servant and the food brought in and passed by her, each guest helping himself.

Some prefer to serve the hostess first, so she may lead the way. Others serve the guest of honor first, continuing in order around the table. The hostess' plate is removed first at the end of each course.

Where does the guest of honor sit?

Whether you use formal or family service, a woman guest of honor sits at the host's right and a male guest of honor sits at the hostess' right.

What is the difference between dinner and supper?

Dinner is the main meal of the day. In America it is usually served in the evening. However, on Sundays and holidays it is generally served in the middle of the day. The evening meal, following the midday dinner, is supper. Buffet meals are always referred to as suppers when served in the evening.

When is the coffee served?

Coffee may be served with the main course as well as with the dessert course at informal dinners or luncheons. At formal dinners, serve it last, either at the table or in the living room. Small demitasse cups may be used.

Summer Beverages: In summer, iced tea or coffee or a tall fruit beverage may be in place on the table before guests are seated.

TABLE SERVICE *The table sets the mood.*

HOW TO SET AN ATTRACTIVE TABLE AT MEALTIME

For a formal table, use fine china, silver and linens. For an informal table, choose pottery or earthenware,
silverplate or stainless steel ware and place mats or inexpensive cloths.

TABLE LINENS

For formal dinners, use white, cream or pastel-colored tablecloths of damask, linen or organdy. For informal dinners, luncheons and breakfasts, use place mats of linen, cotton, straw, plastic or paper. If the china or glassware is colorless, select colored cloths. Linens should always be spotless.

Napkins: Choose napkins to harmonize with the cloth or place mats. The napkin, folded in square or rectangle, with open corner at lower right, is placed in center of each cover. If the first course is in place, put napkin to the left of the forks.

PLACING OF CHINA AND GLASSWARE

Water glass or Goblet: directly above point of knife.

Cups and Saucers: at right of spoons, with handles to right. **Bread-and-Butter Plates:** directly above forks. (They are not usual at very formal dinners.) **Salad Plates:** at left of fork or forks. **Dinner Plates:** in center of each place 1″ from edge of table. China and glassware should be sparkling.

Service Plates: always used at formal dinners, often at informal dinners and luncheons, they are usually 10″ plates, attractive in design. Place them on table in center of each place 1″ from edge of table. Leave on table during appetizer and soup courses; remove just before placing main course plates.

CENTERPIECE

The centerpiece should enhance but not obstruct the view of the diners. For formal dinners, it must be in the exact center. For an informal table, it may be placed on the unused side or end. The soft glow of candlelight lends a festive air to the evening meal. Candles should not be used for a daytime meal unless illumination is needed; then the curtains may be drawn and the candles lighted.

FLAT SILVER

Place silver 1″ from edge of table in straight line, with no more than 3 pieces on each side of plate . . . and place each piece in order of use, beginning at outside. Silver should always be shining.

PLACING OF FLAT SILVER

Knives: at right of plate with sharp edge toward plate.

Butter spreader: across top of bread-and-butter plate.

Beverage and Soup Spoons: at right of knives. Or beverage spoon on saucer; tiny after-dinner coffee spoon always on saucer. **Forks:** all but cocktail fork at left of plate, prongs up. Salad fork at left of dinner fork if salad is served as first course; to right, if served with main course. When salad accompanies main course, dinner fork may be used for both meat course and salad. Cocktail fork on appetizer plate or at extreme right.

Dessert Silver: At informal meals, dessert silver may be on table at beginning of meal. For formal service, it is brought on with the dessert.

TEAS AND RECEPTIONS ("At Homes")

One of the easiest and loveliest ways to entertain.

Arrange the table with simple elegance, tea service at one end, coffee service at the other . . . with cups, plates and spoons. (*See sketch below.*) Accompaniments for each should be nearby . . . the food placed conveniently for passing to guests who may stand or be seated. A hostess pours the tea or coffee. Guests may be invited to help themselves.

HOW TO SET THE TABLE FOR A TEA

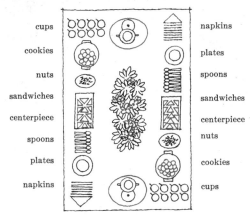

cups — napkins
cookies — plates
nuts — spoons
sandwiches — sandwiches
centerpiece — centerpiece
spoons — nuts
plates — cookies
napkins — cups

Tea or Coffee Menu
Assorted Fancy Sandwiches
Petits Fours (*p. 171*)
Fancy Cookies
Salted Nuts   Peppermints
Tea   Coffee

For a Reception: Serve a fruit punch like Party Punch (*p. 72*) from a punch bowl instead of serving tea or coffee.

BUFFET SUPPERS AND LUNCHEONS

A simple, delightful way of entertaining.

The food, with the exception of the dessert, is all placed on the table at one time. The plates, silver and napkins are so arranged as to make self-service easy. Guests love to help themselves . . . and immediately feel "at home" . . . thus an atmosphere of informal hospitality prevails. Keep hot foods hot for second servings with candle warmers and electrically heated trays.

HOW TO SET A TABLE FOR A BUFFET LUNCHEON OR SUPPER

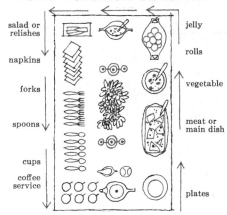

salad or relishes — jelly
napkins — rolls
forks — vegetable
spoons — meat or main dish
cups —
coffee service — plates

Buffet Luncheon Menu
Sea Food à la Newburg (*p. 269*)
in Buttercups (*p. 120*)
Buttered Peas with Mushrooms
Slices of Grapefruit and Avocado in Lettuce Cups
Tiny Hot Rolls
Coconut Cake (*p. 140*)
Coffee

For Buffet Supper: Add Baked Canadian Bacon (*p. 314*).

Table set for a smorgasbord in our Early American dining room. For menu, see p. 48.

33

FESTIVE THANKSGIVING DINNER

Menu, page 50.

MEAL PLANNING

Use the Basic Four in Planning Healthful Meals.

SERVING YOUR FAMILY A BALANCED DIET will keep them healthy, vital and alert. This means preparing for them a daily selection of all the food nutrients essential for good health.

TO SIMPLIFY MEAL PLANNING AND FOR BEST NUTRITION, the Basic Four Food Groups have been devised as a daily meal-planning guide.

GROUP I

Enriched or Whole Grain Bread, Flour, Cereals

Every day, choose FOUR servings from the following grain foods:

BREADS:
  Whole Wheat
  Dark Rye
  Enriched

CEREALS:
  Whole Wheat
  Rolled Oats
  Brown Rice

Other Cereals, if whole grain or enriched
Corn Meal, whole grain or enriched
Converted Rice
Grits, enriched
Macaroni, Noodles, Spaghetti, enriched

GROUP II

Meats, Eggs, Dry Beans

TWO OR MORE servings of meat or other protein-rich foods are needed daily.

Serve AT LEAST ONE of these every day:

Beef
Lamb
Mutton
Veal
Variety Meats
  (liver, heart,
  kidney, brains,
  tongue, etc.)

Game
Poultry (chicken, duck,
  goose, turkey)
Fish
Luncheon meats (bologna,
  wieners, etc.)

OTHER PROTEIN-RICH FOODS to include in the diet to meet daily requirements:

Eggs
Lentils
Nuts
Peanuts
Cheese (natural
  or processed)

Dried Beans or Peas
Peanut Butter
Soya flour and
  grits
Soybeans

GROUP III

Milk, Ice Cream, Cheese

DAILY MILK NEEDS:

Adults........................2 or more cups
Children.....................3 to 4 cups
Teen Agers...................1 quart or more
Pregnant Women..............1 quart or more
Nursing Mothers.............1½ quarts or more

May use one of these for 1 CUP MILK as part of daily requirement:

½ cup evaporated milk
3 tbsp. nonfat dry milk solids (dry form)
1⅓ cups cottage cheese
1½ slices Cheddar-type cheese
1¾ cups ice cream

GROUP IV

Vegetables and Fruits

Serve AT LEAST FOUR helpings daily from this group.

Choose ONE OR MORE VITAMIN C-rich foods:

Broccoli
Cabbage (raw)
Cantaloupe
Grapefruit (or juice)
Salad Greens
Lemons

Limes
Pepper (green or red)
Oranges (or juice)
Strawberries
Tangerines
Tomatoes (or juice)

Choose ONE OR MORE VITAMIN A-rich foods:

Apricots
Broccoli
Cantaloupe
Carrots
Chard, leaves
Collards
Endive, green
Escarole
Mango

Mustard Greens
Okra
Parsley
Spinach
Squash, winter, yellow
Sweet Potatoes
Turnip Greens
Other Greens, including
  Salad Greens

NOTE: Fats and sugars will also be added to the diet in cooking and during meals. Fats' and sugars' chief contribution to the diet is calories for energy.

35

MEAL PLANNING *Breakfast and lunch or supper.*

A GOOD BREAKFAST EVERY DAY FOR EVERYONE

Start everyone in your family off with fuel for the morning's activities. Breakfast can have as much variety as other meals. More breakfast menus on pp. 38, 41.

Fruit
Cereal and milk
Egg, meat or cheese
Bread and butter
Milk or other beverage

Fruit	Egg or Meat	Bread or Cereal
Orange juice	Bacon and eggs	Buttered toast
Applesauce	Poached egg on toast	Cereal
Peaches	Scrambled eggs	Pancakes
Grapefruit sections	Creamed dried beef on toast	Cereal
Pears	French toast	Cereal
Mixed fruit	Fried egg in a frame	Cereal
Orange slices	Omelet	Coffee cake

LUNCH OR SUPPER IS THE "THIRD" MEAL

Lunch or supper should be a third well planned meal, lighter than dinner but well balanced and nutritious. See p. 38 for more delicious lunch and supper menus.

Main Dish
(meat, egg or cheese)
Vegetable or fruit
Bread and butter
Dessert
Milk

Main Dish	Vegetable or Fruit	Dessert
Welsh rabbit	Vegetable salad	Fruit and cooky
Omelet	Cole slaw	Hot fudge pudding
Texas hash	Lettuce wedge with French dressing	Molded fruit gelatin
Tuna burgers	Buttered green peas	Apple crisp
Asparagus spears on toast with cheese sauce	Radishes and little green onions	Rice pudding
Summer macaroni salad	Fresh peaches	Ginger cookies
Meat sandwich	Vegetable soup	Custard and brownie

DINNER IS AN IMPORTANT TIME OF DAY

Not only a place for good nutrition, dinner is one of the happiest times the family has together. *Good* food is important for family pleasure. See pp. 39–41 for a variety of carefully planned dinner menus.

Juice or soup
Meat and potatoes
Vegetables
Salad
Bread and butter
Dessert
Milk

Meat	Potatoes	Vegetable	Salad	Dessert
Chuck roast	Mashed potatoes	Buttered carrots	Vegetable salad	Apple pie
Broiled hamburgers	Parsley potatoes	Corn-tomato casserole	Lettuce salad	Pineapple up side-down cake
Pork chops	Oven-fried potatoes	Broccoli	Apple salad	Gingerbread
Italian spaghetti		Buttered green beans	Cole slaw	Snow pudding
Liver and bacon	Scalloped potatoes	Harvard beets	Jellied carrot and pineapple	Ice cream and cake
Broiled halibut	French fried potatoes	Creamed peas	Fruit salad	Chocolate pie

BETWEEN-MEAL SNACKS ARE THE "FOURTH" MEAL

In between our main meals, we eat what we like, we eat for fun. A thoughtful mother of a growing family keeps a variety of foods on hand for snacks after-play, after-school and before-bedtime. A thoughtful hostess plans snacks for her guests after-the-concert and after-the-game (whether it's football or bridge).

Chocolate Milk
Orange Drop Cookies

Red Apple
Sour Cream Cupcakes

Ready-to-eat Cereal
with fruit and milk

Checkerboard Kuchen
Hot Coffee

Spicy Tomato Soup
Grilled Cheese Sandwiches

Little Loaves of Oatmeal Bread
Café au Lait

Washington Pie
Hot Tea

Make Your Own Sundaes
Snickerdoodles

Cold Fried Chicken
Bread and Butter
Celery Stalks

BREAKFASTS

Sliced Bananas, Top Milk
*Eggs Baked in Bacon Rings
Wheaties
*Country Breakfast Muffins
Coffee or Tea

Strawberries and Cream
*Waffles
Syrup or Hot Applesauce
Pork Links
Coffee or Tea

Steamed Prunes
Cheerios
Cinnamon Toast
*Hot Cocoa

Grapefruit Half
*Broiled Ham Slice
Oatmeal
*Double-quick Coffee Bread
Coffee or Milk

Orange Juice
*Scrambled Eggs with Ham
Trix
*Popovers
Coffee or Milk

Tomato Juice
*Delicate Fluffy Pancakes
Butter   Maple Syrup
Crisp Bacon
Coffee or Milk

LUNCHES

Consommé
*Easy Denver Sandwich
Celery Sticks
*Black Midnight Cake

*Ham Shortcakes or
Ham Sandwiches
Asparagus
*Molded Fruit Salad
Cookies

*Potato Soup
Bread Sticks
Relishes
*Quick Orange Meringue Pie

*Hot French Toasted Sandwiches
Potato Chips
Dill Pickles
Apples

*Spicy Tomato Soup
*Toasted Cheese Sandwiches
Shoestring Potatoes
*Walnut Bonnie Butter Cake
with *Browned Butter Icing

*Cream of Onion Soup
Toasted Buttered Buns
*Fresh Fruit Salad
*Jubilee Jumbles

SUPPERS

*Savory Spaghetti
Sliced Zucchini and Greens
Garlic Dressing
*Italian Bread Sticks
Spumoni Ice Cream

*Cheese Soufflé
Green Beans
Orange or Grapefruit Salad
Melba Toast
*Brownies

*Boston Baked Beans
*Cabbage Salad
Dill Pickles
*Steamed Brown Bread
*Baked Apples

*Spanish Rice
Chopped Spinach
Pear Salad
*Butter Dips Orange Marmalade
*Cream Puffs filled with
ice cream

*Poppy Seed Noodle Ring with
*Creamed Salmon
Buttered Peas
*Melon Salad
Toast Points
*Southern Peach Skillet Pie

*Yankee Doodle Macaroni
Leaf Lettuce Salad
Green Tomato Relish
Hard Rolls
*Iowa Date Pudding with
whipped cream

DINNERS

*Swiss Steak
Parsley-Buttered Potatoes
*Cabbage Salad Mustard Pickles
*Quick Buttermilk Rolls
*Peach Dumplings

*Old-fashioned Beef Stew
Lettuce,
*Thousand Island Dressing
*Corn Bread
*Blueberry Pie with
whipped ice cream

*Lamb Chops
*Creamed New Potatoes
Buttered Peas
*Pineapple-Strawberry Salad
Spring Onions and Radishes
*Jumbo Bread Sticks
*Angel Food Cake
*Clear Orange Sauce

*Pot Roast with
Homemade Chili Sauce
Noodles   Buttered Carrots
*Mexican Green Bean Salad
*Old-fashioned Biscuits
*Prune Whip

*Tomato Bouillon
*Veal Supreme   *Noodle Ring
*Chinese Celery
Bibb Lettuce,
*Garlic French Dressing
Toasted English Muffins
Fruit in Season

*New England Boiled Dinner
Corn Relish Autumn Salad Bowl
*Anadama Bread
*Baked Custard topped with
maple syrup

*Cream of Spinach Soup
*Savory Meat Pie
Lettuce,
*Green Goddess Dressing
*Double-quick Dinner Rolls
*Apple Crisp

*Bouillon
*Potato Salad
Luncheon Meats and Cheeses
Crisp Relishes
Toast Triangles
*Strawberry Meringue Torte

*Stuffed Pork Chops
Apple Rings
*Skillet Creamed Potatoes
Buttered Asparagus Spears
*Tomatoes Vinaigrette
French Bread
*Spumoni Chiffon Cake

*Delmarvelous Broiled Chicken
Shoestring Potatoes
Buttered Beets *Perfection Salad
Brown 'n Serve Rolls
Peach Halves with
*Raspberry Sauce

*Stuffed Flank Steak
Boiled Potatoes   Onion Gravy
*Golden Cabbage
*Carrot-Pineapple Mold
*Refrigerator Rolls
*Floating Island

*Oxtail Stew
Mashed Potatoes
*Philadelphia Cabbage
Celery and Carrot Sticks
*Whole Wheat Bread
*Hot Fudge Pudding

*Baked Tuna Chow Mein
Casserole
*Orange-Onion Salad
*Sesame Jumbo Bread Sticks
Vanilla Ice Cream
*Montego Bay Squares

*Crispy Browned Hash
Green Beans with Dill Weed
Tomato-Green Pepper Salad,
*Sour Cream Dressing
*Whole Wheat Bread
*Cherry Carnival

*Roast Pork with
Tart Applesauce
Buttered Cauliflower
*Orange-Grapefruit Salad
*Cloverleaf Rolls
Ice Cream with
Chocolate Marshmallow Sauce

*Fluffy Meat Loaf   Catsup
*Scalloped Potatoes
Tangy Green Beans
Lettuce Salad
*Rich Egg Bread
*Fruit Sauce
*Coconut Drop Cookies

*Liver and Bacon
*Baked Potatoes
*Easy Creamed Spinach
Dill Pickles
*Tangy Tomato Aspic
*White Bread
*Gingerbread Party Dessert

*Cream of Tomato Soup
*Veal Paprika Noodles
Baby Green Limas
*Molded Gelatin Salad
Bread Sticks
*Butterscotch Sundae Cake

MENUS *Starred recipes are in this book. See general index.*

DINNERS

*Chicken Fricassee
*Dumplings
*Glazed Carrots
*Melon Salad
French Bread
*Baked Custard

*Barbecued Spareribs
*Baked Potatoes
Buttered Whole Kernel Corn
*Cole Slaw
*Bran Pan Biscuits
*Cherry Pie

*Lamb and Carrot Meat Balls
Mashed Potatoes
Chopped Spinach
*Perfection Salad
*Hot Seeded French Bread
*Frosted Mint Delight

. . . .

*Savory Chicken Pie
*Spiced Peaches
Peas and Onions
*Jellied Fruit Medley
*Dinner Rolls
Ice Cream with
*Peppermint Candy Sauce

*Roast Veal with
Spiced Pears
*Oven-Browned Potatoes
Asparagus, *Cheese Sauce
*Ambrosia Fruit Salad
*Parkerhouse Rolls
*Boston Cream Pie

*Baked Ham with
*Orange-Currant Sauce
*Potatoes au Gratin
French-cut Green Beans
*Pacific Lime Mold
*Pumpernickel
*Coconut Custard Pie

. . . .

*Lamb Stew with Mint Jelly
Tossed Green Salad
*Cloverleaf Rolls
*Strawberry Shortcake

*Chicken Jambalaya
Tossed Salad
*Corn Bread
*Oriental Orange Snow

*Spareribs and Sauerkraut
*Potato Pancakes
*Waldorf Salad
Whole Wheat Bread
*Old-fashioned Bread Pudding

. . . .

*Pork Chops Supreme
*Baked Potatoes
Buttered Chopped Spinach
Lettuce,
*Rancho Roquefort Dressing
*Anadama Bread   Apple Jelly
*One-Egg Cake,   *Broiled Icing

*Broiled Ham Slice with
*Raisin Sauce
*Stuffed Baked Potatoes
Buttered Green Limas
*Pineapple-Cottage Cheese Salad
*Swedish Limpa
Strawberry Sundae

*Veal Birds
*Scalloped Potatoes
Corn on the Cob
Cucumber-Tomato Salad
Watermelon Pickles
*Lowell Inn Crescent Rolls
*Frozen Fruit Cocktail

. . . .

*Madrilene
*Chicken Parisian
*Choice of Melon Salad
*Iris' Biscuits
*Chocolate Pudding

*Braised Lamb Shanks
Lettuce,
*Thousand Island Dressing
*Whole Wheat Buttermilk Rolls
*Pineapple Upside-down Cake

*Chicken Casserole
New Peas
Grapefruit, *Ruby Red Dressing
*Italian Bread Sticks
*Angel Pie

. . . .

*Crispy Fried Fish
*Tartar Sauce
Creamed New Potatoes
Corn on the Cob
*Fresh Spinach Salad
*Butter Fluffs
*Lemon Chiffon Pie

*Veal Cutlets
Mashed Potatoes
*Piquant Brown Sauce
Beets with savory
*Orange-Bermuda Onion Salad
*Oatmeal Muffins
*Butterscotch Pie

*Ham Loaf Superb with
*Easy Horse-radish Sauce
*Skillet Candied Sweet Potatoes
*Cauliflower Porcupine
Tokay Grape and Apple Salad
*Herb Bread
*Orange Cake

CHEERY BREAKFASTS

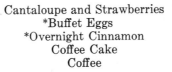

Fruit Medley
Jelly Omelet   Wheaties
*Cinnamon Coffee Cake
*Hot Cocoa

Cantaloupe and Strawberries
*Buffet Eggs
*Overnight Cinnamon
Coffee Cake
Coffee

Peach Halves and Raspberries
*Cheese Waffles
Grilled Ham Slice
*South American Chocolate

DELICIOUS LUNCHEONS

*Chicken-Rice en Casserole
Broccoli
Mixed Green Salad
*Classic French Dressing
Tiny Cinnamon Rolls
Chocolate Parfait

*Shrimp Supreme
Asparagus Tips
*Orange-Grapefruit-Avocado
Salad
Corn Meal Muffins
Currant Jelly
*Orange Chiffon Cake with
*Russian Sauce

Fruit Cup
*Cellini Pies
*Green Beans Almondine
Tossed Green Salad
*Herb Dressing
*Lowell Inn Crescent Rolls
*Baked Alaska

SUMPTUOUS COMPANY DINNERS

*Roast Beef
*Yorkshire Pudding
Brussels Sprouts with Celery
*Creamy Skillet Corn
Peach Halves with Green Grapes
*Dinner Rolls
*English Trifle

*Roast Leg of Lamb
*Oven-Browned Potatoes
*Green Beans De Luxe
*Mandarin Duet Salad
*Butter Fluffs
*Portia's Pears with
*Eggnog Sauce

Clear Consommé
*Crown Roast of Pork
Tiny Potatoes with Onions
French-cut Green Beans
*Tomato Aspic on Greens
Hard Rolls
*Caramel Custard

*Venison
*Orange-Currant Sauce
*Scalloped Potatoes Cauliflower
*Wilted Greens
*Pumpernickel
*Hot Apple Pie

*Tomato Bouillon
*Lobster Thermidor
*Baked Potato
Tossed Greens with
Cauliflowerets
*Popovers
*Aloha Chiffon Cake

*Roast Wild Duck
Lingonberries   Wild Rice
Mashed Rutabagas
*Grapefruit-Persimmon-
Avocado Salad
Poppy Seed Rolls
*Blueberry-Peach Pie

*Roast Chicken or Turkey
Cranberry Relish   *Stuffing
Mashed Potatoes   Broccoli
*24-Hour Salad
*Salt Sticks
*Autumn Pumpkin Pie with
whipped cream

*Fillet of Beef Tenderloin
Sautéed Mushroom Caps
*Oven "French Fries"
Brussels Sprouts, Hollandaise
Cantaloupe Slice with Blueberries
Hot French Bread
*Crème Brulée

*Filet de Sole Bonne Femme
Fresh Mushroom Sauce
Parsley Buttered Potatoes
*Broiled Tomatoes
Cucumbers and Onions
in Sour Cream
*Muffins
*Fruit Ambrosia

DINNERS FROM FOREIGN LANDS

From Mexico
*Black Bean Dip
with crisp crackers
*Enchiladas
Avocado Salad
*Fresh Fruit Platter

From India
*Chicken Curry
Fluffy White Rice
Bacon bits, chutney, coconut,
salted peanuts
Orange Sherbet

From Japan
*Chicken Consommé with
*Egg Rivvels
*Sukiyaki
White Rice
Mandarin Oranges
Fortune Cookies

41

American cooking is going international, thanks to the millions of servicemen and American tourists who return home praising the foods of faraway places. Let this list be your guide in preparing foods with foreign flavor.

Looking for unusual and exotic dishes to serve at your parties? This book has them—from Asparagus à la Polonaise to Zabaglione. Follow the kitchen-tested directions and you'll find out how easy entertaining with a gourmet touch can be.

Whether you call them made-overs, planned-overs or leftovers, they can be the basis for good, time-saving and economical meals. After trying a few of these suggestions, you'll soon be creating your own "second day specials."

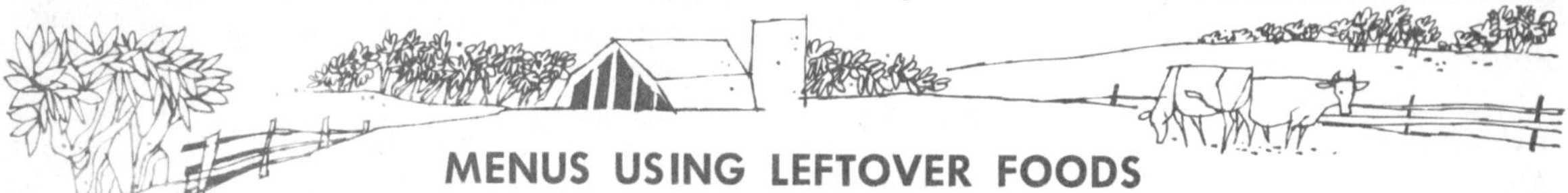

MENUS USING LEFTOVER FOODS
See general index for starred recipes.

For Breakfast	For Lunch	For Dinner

For Breakfast

*Frozen Fruit Cocktail
*Crispy Browned Hash with
Poached Eggs
*Sweet Rolls
Milk   Coffee

Chilled Strawberries
*Corn Pancakes
Maple Syrup and Butter
Crisp Bacon Strips
*Hot Cocoa

For Lunch

*Turkey and Cheese Sandwiches
*Mexican Green Bean Salad
*Snowflake Cake with
*Sunshine Sauce

*Curried Pork Slices
Buttered Carrots
*Tossed Green Salad
Bread and Butter
*Chocolate Marshmallow Cream

For Dinner

*Hot Cheese Puffs
*Fish Turbot
Asparagus Tips
*Cole Slaw
*Loaf O' Gold Cake with
Fudge Frosting

*Savory Meat Pie
Parsley Buttered Green Beans
Tomato and Lettuce Salad
Ice Cream with
*Irene's Caramel Sauce

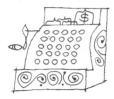

MEAL PLANNING *THRIFTY FOODS*

It's smart to be thrifty. With recipes for economical foods (like those below) at your fingertips and with careful planning, you can tempt your family with meals that are satisfying *and* easy on the budget.

Eisenhowers Enjoy Life on Gettysburg Farm

After many years of public service, former President and Mrs. Dwight D. Eisenhower are now enjoying leisurely days on their rolling farm near Gettysburg, Pa. Mr. Eisenhower (or Ike as thousands refer to him) names this menu as one of his favorites:

Broiled Sirloin Steak (*p. 301*)
Baked Potatoes   Green Beans
Green Salad with French Dressing
Apple Pie (*p. 342*) with Cheese
Coffee

United Nations Leader Chooses Dinner Favorite of Many Men

This is the favorite at-home dinner of Ralph J. Bunche, Under Secretary of the United Nations and winner of the Nobel Peace Prize. He writes: "I always ask for butter balls . . . as a youth I worked in the kitchen of a Los Angeles hotel and had to roll piles of them with the corrugated wood paddles."

Crabmeat in Tomato Halves
(or Green Turtle Soup in cold weather)
Prime Ribs of Beef (*p. 300*)
Stuffed Baked Potatoes (*p. 426*)
String Beans
Tossed Salad with French Dressing
Rolls and Butter Balls
Strawberries and Vanilla Ice Cream Scoops
Demitasse

Glamour Surrounds Simple Supper of Famous Opera Star

Helen Traubel, dear to music lovers all over America, serves a few well chosen dishes when she entertains informally.

Chicken En Casserole (*p. 268*)
Mixed Green Salad   Hard-crusted Rolls
Persian Melon
filled with
Raspberries, Cut-up Pineapple, Blueberries

Columnist Recalls Festive Breakfast on Kentucky Derby Day

Award-winning writer, Mary Margaret McBride, well remembers this bountiful breakfast served her one Derby Day in Louisville, Kentucky.

Baked Kentucky Ham
Chicken Hash   Sausages
Hot Potato Salad (*p. 377*)
Hot Biscuits (*p. 76*)   Pickled Peaches
Artichoke Hearts, Tomato and Cucumber
with Endive
Filled Cantaloupe Rings
(slice pared cantaloupe, center with fresh
pineapple, top with black cherries)

A Mexican Supper or Luncheon

From Elena Zelayeta, expert on Mexican and Spanish cookery, who is an inspiration to all who meet her or read her cook books.

Macarones Con Jocoqui (*p. 282*)
(macaroni and cheese with sour cream)
Green Salad
Guacamole (*p. 62*)   Toasted Split Buns
Fiesta Fruit Platter (*p. 218*)

Plate Dinners 'Round the Year

See color picture opposite. Food is arranged on individual plates in kitchen, then placed before each guest.

Broiled Fish Fillet (*p. 327*)
Parsleyed New Potatoes
Peas and Onions in Cream
Tomato-Cucumber Salad
Fresh Rhubarb Pie (*p. 345*)

Fried Chicken (*p. 319*)
Mashed Potatoes
Corn on the Cob   Zucchini
Pickled Peach   Celery Hearts
Strawberry Shortcake (*p. 224*)

Pan-broiled Ham Slice (*p. 311*)
Skillet Candied Sweet Potatoes (*p. 429*)
Green Beans with Cashew Sauce (*p. 430*)
Radish Roses and Raw Cauliflowerets on
Water Cress
Grape Pie (*p. 344*)

Broiled Porterhouse Steak (*p. 301*)
Stuffed Baked Potatoes (*p. 426*)
Chinese Celery   Sautéed Onion Rings
Tomatoes Vinaigrette (*p. 376*)
Apple Crisp (*p. 228*)

PLATE DINNERS 'ROUND THE YEAR

Menus and recipe references, opposite.

Circus Birthday Party Delights Caroline

Little Caroline Kennedy's birthday party is in progress and the Solarium on the third floor of the White House is alive with excitement. Centerpiece for the children's table is a circus ring with individual stuffed animals, each with a streamer leading to a child's place card. This is the party menu:

Roast Chicken
(roast extra drumsticks so there will be one each)
Mashed Potatoes with clown faces
(serve in little dishes, add carrot noses and mouths and Lima bean eyes)
Green Peas
Ice Cream Molds in clown and animal shapes
Tiered Circus Tent Birthday Cake
topped with two clowns holding placards saying:
"Happy Birthday, Caroline"

A Supper Party at Mount Vernon

For George Washington's birthday.

Old Virginia Baked Ham (p. 311)
Fried Oysters (p. 330) or
Stewed Chicken (p. 332)
Spoon Bread (p. 81)
Southern Biscuits (p. 76)
Damson Plum Preserves   Brandied Peaches
Old-time Sea Moss (same as Blanc Mange, p. 223)
Burnt Sugar Cake (p. 141)

Election Night "At Home"

In the rambling family mansion at Hyde Park one cold November night, Mrs. Franklin Delano Roosevelt welcomed neighbors to warm themselves before the crackling fire in the high-ceilinged drawing room. Then the guests stopped at the long, candlelit table in the spacious entrance hall for refreshments.

Chocolate Cake (pp. 143-146)
Coconut Cake (p. 140)
Sandwiches   Crackers and Cheese
Cider   Doughnuts (p. 83)   Coffee

Jimmy Durante's Choice

"This is what I like best for dinner," says the popular entertainer of stage and airways known as "the comedian with a heart."

Shrimp Cocktail (p. 56)
Tossed Salad with *Umbriago Dressing
Broiled Steak (p. 301)
Baked Potato with Sour Cream and Chives
Fresh Asparagus or Chopped Spinach
Fresh Fruit in Season
topped with Ice Cream or Sherbet
Tea

*Roquefort Dressing (p. 370) of olive oil, vinegar, Roquefort cheese and Worcestershire sauce, made "special" with cream, lemon and English mustard.

Island State Senator's Typical Dinner

Charming Mrs. Hiram Fong often serves this dinner to her lawmaker husband and four growing children, whether at home in Honolulu or in Washington, D. C.

Celery-Cabbage Soup
*Barbecued Chicken
Steamed Rock Fish
Green Beans
**Passion Fruit Pie
Tea   Milk

*follow directions for Pork Teriyaki (p. 310) substituting cut-up chicken for pork.
**substitute ⅔ cup passion fruit juice for ⅓ cup of the water and ⅓ cup lemon juice in Citrus Chiffon Pie (p. 356).

A Simplified Swedish Smorgasbord

Foods are listed in order as placed on the table, beginning with meat balls in the chafing dish, and moving to the right. The first group of foods—relishes and appetizers —are used as a centerpiece. See picture p. 27.

Pickled Herring   Radish Roses (p. 25)
Pickled Beets   Green and Ripe Olives
Anchovy Rolls   Celery Pinwheels (p. 25)
Swedish Meat Balls (p. 305)
Baked Ham (p. 311)   Jellied Veal
Deviled Eggs and Shrimp
Potato Salad (p. 377)   Cabbage Slaw (p. 376)
Tray of Cheeses
Fruit Gelatin Mold (p. 378) Lingonberry Sauce
Coffee for the Crowd (p. 66)

Famous Violinist Recommends Vegetable Dinner

Yehudi Menuhin, gifted concert artist, whose violin music has charmed audiences throughout the world, sent us this suggestion for a delicious and satisfying dinner without meat.

Vegetable Melange (p. 430)
*Beet Salad
**Bread Pudding (p. 227)

*Mix grated raw beets and finely grated almonds. Stir in cream and lemon juice to right consistency. Serve in individual nests of butter lettuce with olive oil and lemon dressing on only the lettuce. Note: Mr. Menuhin recommends organically grown beets and almonds and unpasteurized cream.

**Date sugar, freshly grated nutmeg, walnuts and raisins soaked in orange juice, and stone ground whole meal bread made from fresh unpasteurized cream are recommended for the Bread Pudding by Mr. Menuhin.

Alaskan Salmon Stars in Governor's Menu

From Juneau, Alaska, comes this favorite menu of William Allen Egan, governor of our faraway, yet close in spirit, forty-ninth state.

French Onion Soup (p. 406)
Broiled Salmon Steaks (p. 328)
with Lemon Butter (p. 430)
Creamed New Potatoes and New Peas
Corn Bread (p. 80)
Tossed Green Salad
Crème Brulée (p. 246) with Assorted Cookies

Former First Lady Entertains at Bridge Luncheon

Mrs. Harry S. Truman finds that her guests enjoy this simple menu when she serves it in her Independence, Missouri, home.

Chicken Salad (p. 381)
on tomato slices or in tomato cups
garnished with
water cress sprigs and olives
Hot Butter Dips (p. 77)
Frozen Lemon Pie (p. 245)
Coffee   Tea

Ranch Guests Sample Mexican Foods

Vice President Lyndon B. Johnson and his wife, Lady Bird, enjoy giving visitors to their "Lazy B Ranch" in Texas a taste of the fare of which Southwesterners are so fond.

Chili (without beans)
Pinto Beans
Hot Tamales   Enchiladas (p. 276)
Guacamole Salad
Tortillas (p. 276)
Pralines
Coffee

Dessert Masterpiece of French Chef Highlights Dinner of a Diva

Named for her and created in her honor by Louis of The Ritz in Paris, Fleur de Lily is the choice of Metropolitan Opera Star, Lily Pons, as the perfect dessert for a favorite informal dinner.

Oyster or Clam Cocktail in Season (p. 56)
*Petites Marmites
**Galantine of Chicken
Wild Rice   Petits Pois Francaise
Endive and Avocado Salad, French Dressing
Fleur de Lily (p. 248)
Demitasse

*A flavorful French soup (consommé with cooked cut-up vegetables added), served in individual casseroles or marmites. Garnish with thin slice of dry toast, sprinkle with grated Parmesan cheese, place under broiler until cheese melts.
**Jellied chicken, special French style.

Fashion Luncheon

Climaxed with a dramatic dessert from Mr. John, celebrated designer of hats that women love.

Individual Cheese Soufflés (p. 258)
with Crabmeat Sauce (p. 258)
Asparagus Vinaigrette (p. 370)
Melba Toast
French Beret Pancake Dessert (p. 248)
Coffee

A New Year's Buffet

Eggnog (*p. 70*) or Party Punch (*p. 72*)
Tray of Crackers   Bowl of Cheese Spread
Sliced Baked Ham   Sliced Roast Turkey
Buttered Thin Slices of
Rye, Whole Wheat and White Breads
Potato Salad (*p. 377*)   Cranberry Jelly
Olives   Celery   Radishes   Pickles
Tray of Fruitcake and Holiday Cookies
Coffee

St. Patrick's Day in the Evening

Let the musical background be songs of Old Erin, dreamy and gay, by Academy Award Winner Bing Crosby whose humor and versatility, both as singer and actor, have added happiness and inspiration to the lives of many.

Green-tinted Fruit Cup (*p. 56*)
or Cream of Spinach Soup (*p. 401*)
Pork Tenderloin
Stuffed Baked Potatoes (*p. 426*)
Buttered Asparagus   Cloverleaf Rolls
Molded Lime Fruit Medley (*p. 378*)
Ice Cream with Crème de Menthe
Angel Food Cake (*p. 155*) with Green Icing
Coffee

Happy Easter Dinner

Frosty Fruit Ale (*p. 57*)
Baked Ham (*p. 311*)
(basted while baking with currant jelly)
Glazed Sweet Potatoes
Buttered Asparagus
Molded Gelatin Salad (*p. 378*)
Herb Bread (*p. 105*)
Angel Pie (*p. 238*) or Fleur de Lily (*p. 248*)
Coffee

A Tea for Mother's Day

Remember a little corsage bouquet for each mother present.

Chicken Salad (*p. 381*)
in Miniature Cream Puffs (*p. 243*)
Sweetheart Cake (*p. 171*)
Red and White Mint Wafers   Salted Nuts
Coffee   Tea

July 4 Chicken Barbecue

Barbecued Chicken (*p. 322*)
Corn on the Cob   Best Tossed Salad (*p. 368*)
Hot Garlic-buttered French Bread (*p. 120*)
Strawberry or Peach Shortcake (*p. 224*) or
Fresh Fruit Pie or Ice Cream and Cake
Coffee

Halloween Refreshments

Batter Franks (*p. 314*)
Carrot Straws   Ripe Olives
Orange Sherbet
Jack-o'-Lantern Cupcakes
(orange-iced cupcakes with jack-o'-lantern faces
traced on icing with melted chocolate)

Festive Thanksgiving Dinner

See color picture p. 34.

Roast Turkey (*p. 317*)
Bread Stuffing (*p. 324*) Cranberry Sauce (*p. 332*)
Mashed Potatoes   Giblet Gravy (*p. 390*)
Creamed Onions   Mashed Squash
Carrot and Celery Curls   Ripe and Green Olives
Assorted Hot Rolls (*p. 107*)
Old-fashioned Mince Pie (*p. 348*) or
Autumn Pumpkin Pie (*p. 351*)

Christmas Eve Supper

Oyster Stew (*p. 402*)
or Cream of Tomato Soup (*p. 401*)
Celery Hearts   Salty Crackers   Radish Roses
Molded Fruit Gelatin (Red) (*p. 378*)
Stollen (*p. 110*)   Holiday Cookies
Jule Kage (*p. 116*)
Coffee

Christmas Dinner

In many homes it is traditional to serve a dinner much like the Thanksgiving dinner (above) featuring roast turkey, chicken or duck. The roast beef dinner or venison dinner (p. 41) would also make excellent Christmas dinners.

Finish the holiday meal with a flourish—with flame-wreathed English Plum Pudding (*p. 231*) or Down East Pudding (*p. 230*), White Christmas Pie (*p. 358*) or Eggnog Chiffon Pie (*p. 357*).

HOW TO USE HERBS

Use a light hand—use too little of any herb rather than too much . . . just enough to heighten natural flavors.

Start with ¼ tsp. crumbled *dried herbs* to 4 servings—to a pound of meat, poultry, fish *or* to 2 cups of sauce, vegetables, soups.

If you are using *fresh herbs*, rather than dried, use 3 to 4 times as much.

At first, use one herb in one dish at one meal. Concentrate on using one wisely. You will learn to use more later.

When several herbs are used in any one dish, one should predominate; otherwise, you will have a clash of flavors.

Add herbs at the same time as salt and pepper to meats, vegetables, sauces and soups.

In long-cooking foods, such as stews, add herbs during the last half hour of cooking time so that flavor and aroma aren't lost.

To release all flavor, powder dried herbs in the palm of your hand before measuring. If using fresh herbs, remove leaves from stems and snip with scissors into very fine pieces.

Store dried herbs in covered glass jars (preferably away from heat and steam). Air will rob them of flavor and aroma. Purchase herbs in small quantities and use within one year, if possible.

USE THESE HERBS TO ENHANCE YOUR COOKING. *Remember . . . a light hand at first!*

	Appetizers	Salads	Vegetables	Eggs, Cheeses and Meats
BASIL	Tomato Juice Sea food	Green or Fruit Salads	Tomato Dishes, Peas, Beans, Eggplant	Omelets, Rabbits, Beef, Lamb, Sausage, Pork, Spaghetti
BAY LEAF ..	Tomato Juice Bouillon	Sea food Tomato Aspic	Tomatoes, Green Beans, Rice, Carrots	Beef, Lamb, Veal, Spareribs, Kidneys, Liver, Chicken, Stews
DILL	Mayonnaise, Cream Cheese	Cole Slaw Potato Salad	Green Beans, Cabbage, Cauliflower	Cottage Cheese, Cream Cheese, Fish, Lamb Chops
MARJORAM	Bouillon	French Dressing	Peas, Carrots, Spinach	Soufflés, Baked or Creamed Fish, Roast Beef, Lamb, Veal
MINT	Iced Beverages	Fruit Salads Cabbage Salads	Carrots, Green Beans, Spinach, Peas	Cream Cheese, Lamb, Veal, Baked or Broiled Fish
OREGANO .	Vegetable Juice Cheese Spreads	Salad Dressings	Potatoes, Onions, Tomatoes, Green Beans	Omelets, Pork, Veal, Lamb, Meat Loaf, Hamburgers, Shrimp
PARSLEY ...	Garnish for Canapés, Spreads	Salad Dressings	In or over all Vegetables, Rice	Poultry, Meats, all Egg Dishes, Stews, Fish, Cheeses
ROSEMARY .	Fruit Cups Pickles	Fruit Compote	Cauliflower, Mushrooms, Cucumber, Peas, Spinach	Omelet, Deviled Eggs, Beef, Lamb, Veal, Stews, Pork
SAGE	Sharp Cheese Spreads		Eggplant, Lima Beans, Onions, Peas, Tomatoes	Cheeses: Cheddar, Cottage or Cream; Pork, Lamb
SAVORY ...	Tomato Juice Tiny Biscuits	Bean Salads Tomato Salads	Beans, Peas, Cabbage, Sauerkraut, Rice	All Egg Dishes, Fish and Shellfish, All Meats, Poultry
THYME	Sea food Liver Pâté	Tomato Aspic Pickled Beets	Tomatoes, Green Beans, Beets, Mushrooms, Onions	Cottage Cheese, Cream Cheese, Eggs, Beef, Lamb, Pork, Stews

51

HOW TO USE SPICES

Use whole spices (such as nutmeg and pepper) when possible and grind them for everyday use. You'll get more flavor that way!

Measure carefully to enhance the flavor instead of smothering it.

Season to taste—your family's taste, that is! Experiment to find out what spices your family prefers and in what amounts.

Add spices at end of cooking, if food is cooked a long time; well in advance, if food is uncooked.

Buy in small quantities so spices may be used before they become stale. They contain volatile oils which give them flavor. When oil evaporates, the flavor is lost.

Store carefully in dark, cool, dry place. Keep away from heat.

Close jars or tins tightly to protect from moisture and loss of flavor.

Refrigerate chili powder, paprika and cayenne pepper to keep them fresh longer.

USE THESE SPICES TO ADD ZEST TO YOUR COOKING *Measure, then close container tightly!*

	Appetizers and Soups	Vegetables and Fruits	Meats and Fish	Breads and Desserts
ALLSPICE . . .	Spiced Nuts, Vegetable Soup	Tomatoes, Cabbage, Apples, Peaches	Pot Roasts, Spiced Beef, Sausage	Cakes, Cookies, Fruit Pies, Plum Pudding, Mincemeat
CARAWAY .	Soft Cheese Spreads, Borsch, Goulash	Sauerkraut, Beets, Apples, Cabbage	Roast Pork, Stews, Liver, Fish Dishes	Breads (Rye), Cookies, Cakes, Pastry, Biscuits
CHILI POWDER .	Cocktail Sauces, Pea Soup, Cheeses	Corn or Cornmeal, Rice, Cauliflower	All Mexican Dishes, Pot Roast, Stew	Dust on Corn or Potato Chips
CINNAMON	Grape Juice, Spiced Punch, Milk Drinks	Squash, Sweet Potato, Apples, Peaches	Ham Glaze, Pork Roast, Pot Roast	Breads, Cake, Cookies, Candy, Rolls, Doughnuts
CLOVES	Vegetable and Fruit Juices	Tomatoes, Beans, Apples, Cranberries	Ham, Pork, Beef, Stew, Sausage	Breads, Cake (Fruitcake), Gingerbread, Cookies
CURRY POWDER .	Tomato Juice, Nuts, Pickles	Tomatoes, Carrots, Rice, Bananas, Apples	Beef, Pork, Veal, Lamb, Chicken	Biscuits, Breads
GINGER	Spiced Tea, Tomato Soup, Ginger ale	Sweet Potatoes, Pears, Apples, Figs	Steak, Pot Roast, Game, Chinese Food	Breads (Gingerbread), Cake, Cookies, Pies
*MACE AND NUTMEG .	Punches, Eggnog, Tomato Soup	Carrots, Cauliflower, Sweet Potatoes	Steak, Meat Balls, Pot Roast, Sausage	Cake (Yellow or Pound), Cookies, Breads
MUSTARD . . **(DRY)**	Cheese Spreads, Meat Soups	Almost every Vegetable, Sauces	Ham, Pork, Veal, Beef, Chicken	Biscuits, Yeast Buns
PEPPER . . . . . **(RED, BLACK)**	Cheese Spreads, All Soups	All Vegetables	All Poultry, Meat, Game, Fish	Pinwheels Made of Biscuit Dough with Meat Filling
SEEDS . . . . . . **(CELERY, SESAME, POPPY)**	Cheese Mixtures, Canapés, Cream Soups	Tomatoes, Cabbage, Corn, Peas, Turnips, Potatoes	Meat or Poultry Stuffing, Chicken, Fish, Pot Roasts	Sesame and Poppy: Sprinkle on Breads, Rolls, Cookies; Poppy: Cakes, Fillings

*Mace is the outer covering which protects the nutmeg kernel. Flavor is like nutmeg, but stronger.

APPETIZERS

Appetizers, those small portions of food or drink that whet the appetite, originated in Europe. Though the Romans munched celery or endive before their famous feasts, it was the Russians who first served hot and cold appetizers as we know them. Caviar, cold meats, vegetables vinaigrette and little filled pies were enjoyed by Russian noblemen in the 19th century.

The food-loving Scandinavians adapted and enhanced the appetizer course, producing the elaborate smorgasbord. In France, where the preparation of food is truly an art, chefs created beautiful and delicate appetizers calling them hors d'oeuvres which means "outside the work."

Hunger was the only appetizer during the frontier years here in the United States. But with increased leisure and heightened interest in entertaining, appetizers have gained popularity. Hostesses have found that having guests move about to help themselves to canapés and tidbits gets a dinner or supper party off to a friendly, informal start.

A glimpse at the following pages will reveal that our selection of appetizers comes from far and near: Rumakis from the Orient, Guacamole from Mexico, Italian Antipasto and the typically American hamburger, silver dollar size, and served in Cocktail Buns.

TO TEMPT THE APPETITE
(complete index in back of book)

TIMESAVING TIPS

Hors d'oeuvres as the first course for a sit-down dinner: have a small plate containing about 4 tangy tidbits at each place when guests are seated. A glass of a cool fruit or vegetable juice *(p. 57)* completes the course.

CALIFORNIA ONION DIP

Stir contents of 1 pkg. (1½ oz.) dehydrated onion soup mix into 2 cups commercial sour cream. Refrigerate several hours or overnight until flavors blend.

NUTS AND BOLTS

Mix 1½ cups Kix, 1 cup Cheerios, 2 cups tiny cheese crackers, 2 cups pretzel sticks and ½ lb. mixed nuts in shallow baking pan. Mix ¼ cup butter, melted, ½ tsp. Worcestershire sauce, ¼ tsp. garlic salt, ¼ tsp. celery salt; and pour over mixture. Stir and salt lightly. Bake *at 250°* (slow) for *1 hr.*, stirring every 15 min. *6 cups.*

Simple accompaniments for cocktails

Popcorn
Pretzel sticks
Ripe or green olives
Toasted seeds (sunflower,
   pumpkin or squash)

Salted nuts
A variety of crackers
   and wafers
Chips (potato, corn,
   cheese or coconut)

CHEESE STRAWS

Heat oven to 450° (hot). Make pastry as directed using 1 stick Betty Crocker Instant Mixing Pie Crust Mix—*except* add ½ cup grated sharp natural Cheddar cheese with hot water. Roll out on lightly floured board into an oblong, 13x10″, and place on baking sheet. With sharp knife cut dough into thirds lengthwise. Cut each piece of dough crosswise to make 15 strips. (Do not separate strips, they will bake apart.) Sprinkle with salt, caraway or poppy seeds and paprika. Bake *10 to 12 min.*, or until brown. Serve warm or cold. *Makes about 45 straws.*

HOLIDAY OPEN HOUSE
(see color picture pp. 60–61)

Boiled Shrimp *(p. 329)* and Vegetable Relishes *(p. 58)*
with Smoked Egg Dip *(p. 62)*
Liverwurst Pâté *(p. 62)* with crackers
Hors d' Oeuvre Tray of cheese, smoked oysters,
deviled eggs, pickles and olives
Fruit Kabobs *(p. 56)*
Canapé Tray including Dried Beef Whirls *(p. 58)*,
miniature cream puffs, Cocktail Buns *(p. 58)*
Bambinos *(p. 59)* and Tuna Pinwheels *(p. 58)*
Tomato Bouillon *(p. 57)*   Cranberry Cocktail *(p. 57)*

WHAT EVERY COOK NEEDS TO KNOW ABOUT APPETIZERS

MAKE WITH CARE

Appetizers may be the prelude to a dinner or served at an open house, reception or stand-up party. The perfect appetizers are easy to serve *and* to eat, attractive and delightful to the taste.

If your guests will be standing up or sitting about in the living room, plan a special canapé, a few simple hors d'oeuvres in a holder and crackers with a dip or bread with a spread. Serve a fruit or vegetable cocktail, either cold in tall frosty glasses or hot in mugs.

If you prefer service at the table for appetizers, choose Sea Food Cocktail (*p. 56*), an appetizer soup (*p. 400*), broiled grapefruit, or arrange several hors d'oeuvres on a plate to be eaten with a fork. Californians have popularized the custom of serving the salad planned as part of the main meal as an appetizer course (*p. 31*).

Since appetizers are a part of the whole meal, flavors should harmonize. Try not to serve any food in the main part of the meal that has been used in the appetizers.

Fortunately, many appetizers can be prepared ahead of time, thus freeing you to enjoy your guests. In fact, most spreads and dips (*p. 62*) actually improve as flavors blend in chilling. If a hot appetizer intrigues you, have it fixed, ready to heat or broil. Once hot, keep it that way on an electrified tray or in a covered chafing dish. If making canapés for a crowd, set up an assembly line with the help of a neighbor or older child for cutting bread, buttering and spreading filling.

Weight-watchers need not miss the appetizer hour. Serve Fresh Vegetable Relishes (*p. 58*) with Smoked Egg Dip (*p. 62*).

- -

SERVE WITH FLAIR

The possibilities for garnishing canapés are limited only by your imagination. Try: crispy bacon bits, minced chives, chopped nuts, slivered green or ripe olives, capers, green pepper or pimiento strips, carrot or radish slices.

Little cocktail plates are handy when serving appetizers stand-up-style. Guests may help themselves to several appetizers, then move freely about while eating them. Cocktail napkins are a must with finger foods.

NEW ADVENTURES IN APPETIZERS

Fruit Kabobs (*p. 56*)—Refreshing bits of fruit on a skewer, served with a tangy dressing.

Hot Black Bean Dip (*p. 62*)—Quickie dip for chips with south of the border flavor.

Liverwurst Pâté (*p. 62*)—Poor man's pâté de foie gras with cream cheese frosting.

Moss Ball (*p. 62*)—Blend of Bleu, Cheddar and cream cheese, named for its parsley covering.

Rumakis (*p. 58*)—Conversation-piece hors d'oeuvre to broil indoors or out.

Fruit Cup

Fresh or whole frozen fruits are ideal because they are less sweet than canned fruit. Serve whole, halved or cut in attractive sizes (not too small). Add lemon or lime juice for a refreshing tartness. To blend the flavors, prepare in advance and chill. Serve cold. Eat with spoon.

In Orange Cups: Serve any combination of fruit in hollowed-out orange halves. Garnish with water cress or mint.

Frozen Fruit Cocktail: Pour cold ginger ale over cut-up fruit and tiny sweet green grapes. Freeze to a mush. Serve in sherbet glasses.

Fruit Kabobs

See color picture pp. 60-61.

1 can (13½ oz.) pineapple chunks, drained (reserve juice)
2 bananas, cut in ½" slices
1 small avocado, cut in ½" squares
8 maraschino cherries

Dip slices of banana and avocado into pineapple juice. Alternate chunks of pineapple with slices of banana and avocado on 5 to 7" skewers. Place a cherry on the end of each skewer. Place skewer on platter of salad greens. Dip kabobs into Pineapple Fruit Salad Dressing (*p. 372*). *Makes 8.*

Fresh Strawberry Plate

Place large red strawberries (with green hulls and stems left on) in a ring around a mound of confectioners' sugar on individual plates. Dip berries into sugar and eat.

Broiled Grapefruit

Remove seeds from grapefruit halves. Cut around sections, remove center. Sprinkle lightly with sugar (brown or maple). Broil slowly until heated (15 to 20 min.).

Melon Ball Cocktail

Scoop out balls of ripe watermelon, canteloupe and honeydew melon with ball cutter or ½ tsp.-size measuring spoon (*see picture p. 374*). Fill glasses with melon balls and drip lemon or lime juice over them. Or use Aloha Sauce (*below*). Chill and serve garnished with mint sprig.

Aloha Sauce: Mix 2 tbsp. *each* strained lemon juice, orange juice and lime juice, ⅓ cup water and ⅔ cup sugar. Chill.

Oysters on the Half Shell

Medium-sized oysters are best. Wash the oysters in shells. Chill. Then open. Serve on deep halves of the shells. Arrange 5 to 7 on a plate of crushed ice. Place a tiny cup of cocktail sauce in the center and add a lemon wedge.

Sea Food Cocktail

Use fresh sea food, frozen or canned.

For each serving, use 4 to 6 cleaned, cooked shrimp or ¼ cup flaked or pieces of cooked crabmeat or lobster. Season, add minced onion, finely diced celery. Or combine sea food with pieces of pineapple, grapefruit or avocado. Serve ice cold in lettuce-lined sherbet glasses or shells . . . with Cocktail Sauce (*below*) and a garnish of lemon or seasoned mayonnaise.

Cocktail Sauce

Combine ½ cup chili sauce, ⅓ cup catsup, 2 to 4 tbsp. prepared horse-radish and 1½ tsp. Worcestershire sauce. Chill thoroughly.

NOTE: For a sharper sauce, add ¼ tsp. salt, 2 tbsp. lemon juice, dash of pepper and a few drops Tabasco.

Soup on the Rocks

Pour canned bouillon over ice cubes in tall glasses. With it, try a different cracker—Bleu cheese, perhaps, or try corn chips.

Antipasto (*Italian Appetizer Plate*)

On individual plates arrange a combination of any of the following on endive or water cress: tuna, radish slices, pickled beet cubes, pimiento-stuffed olives, hard-cooked egg slices, cheese-stuffed celery, curls of cooked ham, smoked pork slices, small green peppers. Drip olive oil over and sprinkle with salt and pepper. Serve as appetizers with bread sticks or garlic bread.

The thoughtful wife has a simple beverage (cold in summer, hot in winter) ready for her weary husband when he comes home at night. The simplest are fruit or vegetable juices served in small fruit juice glasses. See color picture pp. 60-61.

VEGETABLE COCKTAILS

Tomato Juice

Add a little salt, lemon juice, a few drops of Worcestershire sauce and onion juice to tomato juice. Serve cold or hot.

Tomato Bouillon

See color picture pp. 60-61.

Combine equal parts tomato juice and bouillon (dilute canned bouillon or use cubes with boiling water). Serve hot.

Tomato-Sauerkraut Juice

Combine 2 parts tomato juice and 1 part sauerkraut juice. Serve hot or cold.

Tomato-Clam Juice

Combine equal parts clam juice and tomato juice; season to taste with onion, salt and pepper. Serve hot.

Appetizer Soups

Recipes for jellied bouillon or consommé (good for hot weather) and other soups which can be served as appetizers are on p. 400.

Vegetable Ice Cubes

Glamour touch for vegetable drinks.

Arrange a cucumber or radish slice, carrot curl or parsley sprig in each square of ice cube tray. Add water and freeze. Serve as garnish in glasses of vegetable juices.

Muddlers

To stir seasonings into a vegetable cocktail. See color picture pp. 60-61.

Cut celery or carrot sticks 1″ longer than glass. Attach a radish slice and a pitted ripe or green olive to the end of the celery or carrot stick with a toothpick. After drinking cocktail, eat the muddler.

Gazpacho See p. 400.

FRUIT COCKTAILS

Cranberry Cocktail

See color picture pp. 60-61.

4 cups fresh or frozen cranberries
⅓ cup sugar
2 cups ginger ale
3 tbsp. lemon juice

Wash cranberries. Boil until skins pop, about 5 min., in 4 cups boiling water. Strain through 2 thicknesses of cheesecloth. There should be about 4 cups of juice. Return juice to saucepan. Stir in ⅓ cup sugar. Boil 2 min. longer. Chill thoroughly. Just before serving add ginger ale and lemon juice. *Makes about 6 cups.*

Quick Cranberry Cocktail

Chill 4 cups bottled cranberry cocktail. Before serving, add 2 cups ginger ale and 3 tbsp. lemon juice. Add sugar, if desired. *About 8 servings.*

Frosty Fruit Ale

Pour 1 qt. ginger ale into 2 refrigerator trays. Freeze to a mush, stirring 2 or 3 times during freezing. Spoon into cold sherbet glasses just before serving. Sprinkle blueberries and green seedless grapes (or raspberries and seedless grapes, frozen strawberries, etc.) over top. *10 servings.*

Minted Citrus Juice

Combine equal parts lemon juice, orange juice and water. Add a sprig of mint, crushed. Chill 2 hr. Serve cold.

Fruit Ice Cubes

A party touch for fruit cocktails.

Freeze whole strawberries or mint leaves in ice cubes. Serve in tall glasses of fruit drinks.

Fruit Soup See p. 222.

Hors d'oeuvres are dainty finger foods, colorful and varied in size and shape, often exciting, too. Serve cold ones on toothpicks in special holders. Or serve hot ones from a chafing dish. Hors d'oeuvres may be simple, such as bits of meats and cheese or more elaborate like the recipes below.

Holders for Foods on Picks

Grapefruit	Red or White Cabbage
Apple	Pineapple
Eggplant	Red Edam Cheese

Tuna Pinwheels

See color picture pp. 60-61.

1 can (6½ oz.) tuna, drained and flaked
½ cup mayonnaise
½ cup finely chopped celery
2 tbsp. chopped pickle
1 tsp. prepared mustard
20 slices square sandwich bread (crusts removed)

Combine first five ingredients and spread thinly on buttered bread. Roll like jelly roll. Cut each slice into 3 pinwheels; fasten with toothpicks. When ready to serve, brush pinwheels with melted butter, sprinkle lightly with paprika and broil until lightly toasted. *Makes about 60.*

Rumakis

Heat oven to 400° (mod. hot). Cut 6 chicken livers in half and 4 water chestnuts into slices (about 3 slices per nut). Marinate in Oriental Sauce (*below*) 4 hr. Drain; cut 6 bacon strips in half. Wrap chicken liver piece and water chestnut in bacon strip. Fasten with toothpick and roll in brown sugar. Arrange appetizers on a wire rack over a shallow roasting pan. Bake *20 min.*, or until bacon is crisp. Turn occasionally for even browning. *Makes 12.*

Oriental Sauce

¼ cup vegetable oil
¼ cup soy sauce
2 tbsp. catsup
1 tbsp. vinegar
¼ tsp. pepper
2 cloves garlic, minced

Combine all ingredients and mix well.

Dried Beef Whirls

See color picture pp. 60-61.

Spread slices of dried beef with softened cream cheese mixed with horse-radish to taste. Roll up, fasten with toothpicks, chill. Slice between picks to serve.

Some Simple Hors d'Oeuvres

Deviled Eggs (*p. 254*)	Smoked Fish
Frankfurters (1" slices)	Ripe and Green Olives
Sliced Smoked Salmon	Smoked Oysters
Lobster	Miniature Meat Balls
Pickled Herring	Vienna Sausages
Smoked Turkey	Boiled Shrimp (*p. 329*)

Fresh Vegetable Relishes

See color picture pp. 60-61.

A large bowl partly filled with crushed ice and fresh vegetable tidbits makes one of the best, easiest and most attractive of dinner appetizers. If you wish, have a flavorful dip for dunking. Keep relishes crisp in ice water.

Radishes	Cauliflowerets
Celery Hearts	Spring or Green Onions
Carrot Sticks	Broccoli Buds

Cucumber Petals: Run a sharp tined fork down the length of an unpeeled cucumber. Cut thin slices crosswise; chill in ice water.

Carrot Curls: Slice carrots lengthwise paper thin. Chill in ice water until crisp and curled.

Carrot or Turnip Strips in Olive Rings: Pull 2 or 3 very thin, 2 or 3" long, carrot or turnip strips, which have been iced, through pitted ripe olives.

Cocktail Buns

"These are just right to serve with beverages when I entertain," says Mildred Berg of our staff. See color picture pp. 60-61.

Make ½ dough for Potato Refrigerator or Easy Refrigerator Rolls (*p. 123*). Shape into tiny balls (¾ to 1"). Dip tops in Egg Yolk Glaze (*p. 115*); then dip in sesame or poppy seeds, if desired. Place 1" apart on greased baking sheet. Flatten gently. Let rise until double. Bake *at 400° (mod. hot) 8 to 10 min.*, or until golden brown. Split, butter and fill with hot Vienna sausages or hamburgers the size of silver dollars or cold sliced turkey or ham. *Makes about 7 doz.*

Canapés, designed to be eaten gracefully from the fingers, are savory little morsels of food; a base covered with a favorite topping. Often served for refreshments or with cocktails in the living room.

Instead of serving an overwhelming variety of canapés and hors d'oeuvres, concentrate on one or two that are especially picture-pretty and delicious. Offer small cocktail napkins . . . small plates, too, if you choose, when serving.

Toast Beds for Canapés

Remove crust from close-textured bread. Slice thin ($\frac{1}{8}$ to $\frac{3}{16}$"). Cut with round, star or crescent cutters. Toast *on one side only* by sautéing in a little butter in hot skillet over low heat until nicely browned. About $\frac{1}{2}$ hr. before serving, spread *untoasted side* with appetizer.

Other Popular Canapé Bases: Bite-size crispy crackers. Toasted split English muffins and tiny yeast rolls. Melba toast. Crisp, thin pastry in small shapes. Miniature cream puffs. Diminutive biscuits. Cucumber, zucchini, dill pickle slices.

Crabmeat or Shrimp Nippies

1 can (6 oz.) crabmeat or shrimp
2 tsp. mayonnaise
1 tsp. grated onion
$\frac{1}{2}$ cup grated Cheddar cheese

Flake crabmeat and toss with mayonnaise and onion. Spoon onto canapé bases (*above*). Sprinkle generously with cheese. Broil 3" from source of heat 1 to 2 min., until cheese is melted and slightly browned. Serve hot. *Makes 20 to 24 canapés.*

Shrimp Circles

Cut about 6 bread slices into 15 or 16 rounds, using $1\frac{3}{4}$" cutter. Toast, if desired. Place a thin cucumber slice on each buttered bread round, top with a dab of mayonnaise, shrimp and a few capers.

Deviled Ham Canapés

Mash deviled ham with a little horse-radish, grated onion and coarse black pepper to taste. Spread on canapé bases.

Hot Clam Canapés

A specialty of Helene Burton Kaplan, mother of four, who efficiently combines an advertising job with home-making.

Sauté finely chopped small onion and small green pepper in 3 tbsp. butter for 3 min. Add drained minced clams ($7\frac{1}{2}$ oz.), $\frac{1}{4}$ lb. grated Cheddar cheese, $\frac{1}{4}$ cup catsup, 1 tbsp. Worcestershire sauce, 1 tbsp. cooking sherry, $\frac{1}{8}$ tsp. cayenne pepper. Cook until cheese melts, stirring constantly. Serve hot over thin slice of dill pickle on buttered salty rye rounds. *8 to 10 servings.*

Hot Cheese Puffs

Beat 2 egg whites until stiff. Fold in $\frac{1}{2}$ tsp. baking powder, $\frac{1}{4}$ tsp. salt, $\frac{1}{4}$ tsp. paprika, 1 cup grated sharp Cheddar or Swiss cheese. Spread $\frac{1}{4}$" thick on toast beds. Broil until browned, about 5 min. *Makes 12.*

Bambinos

Baby pizza appe-teasers. See color picture pp. 60-61.

1 can (6 oz.) tomato paste
1 tsp. garlic salt
$\frac{1}{4}$ tsp. oregano
$\frac{1}{4}$ lb. Cheddar or Mozzarella cheese
$\frac{1}{8}$ lb. salami or pepperoni

Heat oven to 400° (mod. hot). Combine tomato paste, garlic salt and oregano. Cut cheese and salami into tiny cubes. Spoon small amounts of tomato mixture on Melba or cracker rounds. Top with cheese and meat cubes. Sprinkle with oregano. Bake *3 to 5 min.,* or until cheese melts. Serve hot. *Enough for 5 to 6 doz. canapés.*

OPEN HOUSE

Menu, page 54.

Smoked Egg Dip

Arlene Almonrode, formerly of our staff, served this unusual dip to thousands of poultry conventioneers. Delightful as a dip for Boiled Shrimp (p. 329) and Fresh Vegetable Relishes (p. 58). See color picture pp. 60-61.

12 hard-cooked eggs, finely chopped or sieved
2 tbsp. soft butter
2½ tsp. liquid smoke
1 tbsp. lemon juice
2 tsp. prepared mustard
1 tbsp. Worcestershire sauce
2 drops Tabasco
1½ tsp. salt
1 tsp. dried minced onion
¼ tsp. ground pepper
¾ cup mayonnaise or salad dressing

Combine ingredients. Blend until smooth in blender or mixer. Refrigerate at least 4 hr. Thirty min. before serving, whip to soften. *Makes 1 qt.*

Guacamole *(Gwah-ka-mo-lay)*

Beat 2 avocados, ½ medium onion, minced, 1 tbsp. vinegar, salt and pepper to taste and chopped green chili pepper to taste until smooth on medium mixer speed. Chop fine 1 very ripe peeled tomato; fold into mixture. Serve as a dip.

Hollywood Dunk

Combine ¼ cup deviled ham with 3 to 4 tbsp. horse-radish, 1 tbsp. grated onion, 2 tbsp. minced chives and 1 cup whipping cream, whipped.

Garlic-Cheese Dip

Mix 2 cups cottage cheese or 3 pkg. (3 oz. each) cream cheese, 2 cloves garlic (crushed), ½ tsp. salt, ¼ cup chopped pickles or olives and mayonnaise or milk for a good consistency. Chill.

Hot Black Bean Dip

See color picture p. 273.

Combine 1 can (10½ oz.) black bean soup, 1 can (8 oz.) tomato sauce, ½ cup shredded sharp Cheddar cheese and ¼ tsp. chili powder in small saucepan. Heat. Serve from small chafing dish. *Makes about 2 cups.*

▶ **ALL YOU HAVE TO DO**

To make decorative bowls for dips: use scooped-out tomatoes; pepper halves (seeds removed); sea shells, grapefruit, melon and avocado shells.

Liverwurst Pâté

So glamorous, yet not expensive. Developed by Jennie Lee Ragan of our staff, who has shared with us many specialties from her native state of Louisiana. See color picture pp. 60-61.

1 lb. liverwurst, mashed with fork
1 clove garlic, pressed
½ tsp. sweet basil
3 tbsp. minced onion
Cream Cheese Topping *(below)*
1 can (1½ oz.) black caviar or ¼ cup chopped
    salted peanuts or 3 tbsp. anchovy paste

Blend first four ingredients thoroughly. Shape into igloo shape on serving plate. Chill while making Cream Cheese Topping. Spread cream cheese topping over liverwurst; spread with caviar. Garnish with minced parsley. Chill overnight. Serve with crackers.

Cream Cheese Topping: Mix 1 pkg. (8 oz.) cream cheese, 1 clove garlic, pressed, ⅛ tsp. Tabasco, 1 tsp. mayonnaise.

Minced Clam-Cheese Dip

Mix 1 can (7½ oz.) minced clams, two pkg. (3 oz. each) cream cheese, 1 tbsp. lemon juice, 1 tsp. Worcestershire sauce, ½ tsp. salt, ¼ tsp. flavor enhancer (monosodium glutamate), ⅛ tsp. ground pepper and milk for a good dip consistency.

Moss Ball

From Marie Wilson of our staff.

1 pkg. (8 oz.) cream cheese
¼ to ½ lb. Bleu cheese, crumbled
¼ lb. sharp Cheddar cheese, grated
1 small onion, minced
1 tbsp. Worcestershire sauce
½ cup chopped pecans
finely chopped parsley

Place cheeses in mixer bowl and let stand at room temperature until softened. Beat on medium speed until well mixed. Add onion and Worcestershire sauce and beat well. Stir in pecans. Chill 3 to 4 hr. Roll cheese mixture into one large ball, chill and roll in parsley. Put on serving plate and chill 2 hr. or until firm. Serve the cheese ball with a variety of crackers.

Joseph Pearson

BEVERAGES

Tea and coffee, today's most popular beverages, have had romantic histories. For centuries, the serving and drinking of tea has been a ceremony in China and Japan. With the opening of trade routes to the Orient, "tay" made its debut in England in 1666.

Its popularity is illustrated by the fact that the English named their late afternoon meal, tea. The famous writer, Dr. Samuel Johnson, termed tea "a fascinating plant," and admitted that he was a "hardened and shameless tea drinker." Later the English colonists in America proved that patriotism surpassed pleasure when they staged the Boston Tea Party in protest to unfair taxation on tea.

Coffee's history may be traced from Arabia, through the Near East, to Europe and finally to the New World, where it has become a most important crop for Brazil and a most important beverage in the United States (more of its colorful history on page 66).

Another storied beverage is Wassail, the hot spicy fruit drink long enjoyed at holiday-time in England. From the Anglo-Saxon and Welsh, Wassail means literally, "be thou in health."

'Some like it hot, some like it cold' applies readily to beverages, whether coffee, tea, chocolate, or milk or fruit drinks. What could be more welcome than a tall glass of cold lemonade on a warm summer day or a steaming cup of hot chocolate on a wintry day!

BEVERAGES FOR HOSPITALITY

(complete index in back of book)

TIMESAVING TIPS

FOR QUICKEST-EVER BEVERAGES

Follow directions on each container.

Instant coffee	Instant cocoa
Instant tea	Ready-to-serve eggnog
Instant cream	Frozen fruit juice
Whole dry milk	concentrates
Non-fat dry milk	Frozen lemonade and fruit
Malted milk powders	punch concentrates

MULLED CIDER

Serve with homemade doughnuts for a perfect autumn snack.

Boil 2 qt. sweet apple cider, 1 tsp. whole cloves, 1 tsp. whole allspice, 3″ stick of cinnamon, ½ lemon, thinly sliced, and ¼ to ½ cup sugar 10 min. in covered pan. Strain; serve hot. *Makes 16 servings.*

FRUIT FRAPPÉ

Save leftover fruit juice, syrup from canned fruit (if syrup is used, add 1 tbsp. lemon juice) and fresh, canned or frozen fruit in a jar in the refrigerator. When you have 3 to 4 cups, freeze solid in refrigerator tray. To serve: break into chunks with spoon, then whip with electric mixer or blender until frozen pieces are fine. Serve with a straw. Also delicious as a dessert. To delight the children, freeze fruit frappé mixture in popsicle molds.

ORANGE FIZZ

Spoon 2 tbsp. frozen undiluted concentrated orange juice into each of 4 tall glasses. Place a scoop of vanilla ice cream in each glass. Fill with sparkling water. *4 servings.*

GLAMOUR TOUCHES FOR BEVERAGES

ICE RINGS FOR THE PUNCH BOWL: Cut thin slices of oranges and lemons in half. Arrange ½″ slices alternately in bottom of ring mold that will fit top of your punch bowl, overlapping slightly. Add just enough water to cover slices. Freeze. When frozen, fill mold ¾ full with water. Freeze. Unmold and place fruit-side-up in punch bowl.

Flower Ring: Make Fruit Ring (*above*)—*except* use flowers instead of fruit. Remove stems from *washed* flowers (carnations, roses, etc.). Place face-side-down into ring mold.

FROSTED GLASSES
See color picture p. 71.
Dip rim of each glass into water or lemon juice, then into granulated or confectioners' sugar. Put in freezer or freezing compartment a few minutes to harden sugar and to frost glasses.

UNUSUAL ICE CUBES—Coffee or Tea Cubes: Freeze regular strength coffee or tea in ice cube tray—won't dilute your iced coffee or tea.

Fruit and Vegetable Cubes: See p. 57.

Fruit Juice Cubes: Freeze lemonade or fruit juice in cubes. Serve with ginger ale.

WHAT EVERY COOK NEEDS TO KNOW ABOUT BEVERAGES

BUY WITH CARE

The fresh flavor and aroma of coffee and tea can only be obtained by using freshly ground coffee or fresh tea leaves. Buy in small quantities and keep tightly covered.

The United States consumes more coffee than any other country, and it is available here in many forms. The beans are ground for use in several types of coffee-makers, and it is important to use the correct grind for best flavor (see pp. 66–67). Instant and decaffeineated coffees, too, have become popular. Coffee substitutes, usually made of roasted ground cereals, can also be purchased.

Tea has become the favorite beverage of many (hints on making tea, p. 68). It can be bought as green tea (unfermented), which has an astringent flavor, black tea (fermented), which has a mellow flavor, or oolong (semi-fermented), which combines the qualities of both.

Keep plenty of milk on hand for Flavored Milk Drinks, Milk Shakes, Eggnogs (p. 70) and Hot Chocolate (p. 69). Nonfat dry milk, reconstituted as directed, is both convenient and economical for making milk drinks.

GARNISH AND SERVE WITH FLAIR

For beverages with a cosmopolitan touch, see suggestions from "Coffee Around the World," (p. 67) or serve "Hot Chocolate the Continental Way," (p. 69), French Chocolate (p. 69) or South American Chocolate (p. 69).

Glamorize your punch bowl with a pretty ice ring or unusual ice cubes (see opposite page).

Your guests will love to stir their Wassail Bowl (p. 72) with cinnamon sticks. Try them, too, with hot chocolate or eggnog for spicy flavor and aroma.

NEW ADVENTURES IN BEVERAGES

Caramel Milk (p. 70)—Snack in a glass.

Cold Extract of Tea (p. 68)—Make this ahead of time for the clearest iced tea you've ever served.

French Chocolate (p. 69)—Fill cups half full of chocolatey whipped cream, then pour on scalding milk from a pretty pot.

Fruit Crush (p. 72)—Easy-to-make fruit ice plus ginger ale equals refreshing summertime drink.

Hot Eggnog (p. 70)—Warming and wonderful drink of hot custardy eggnog over a fluffy meringue.

As early as 300 A.D. some sources say that coffee was discovered by Arabian shepherds who enjoyed it au naturel by chewing the bean itself. Others say monks first discovered the delightful qualities of coffee by drying the beans and boiling them . . . in 500 A.D. It came to be called "kaffia," after the shrub on which the bean grew.

It gained rapid popularity in Europe, Asia and North Africa. By the 16th century in Constantinople a wife could divorce her husband for failure to supply her with coffee. Napoleon demanded at least 7 pots a day; Bach liked it so well that he composed a special "Coffee Cantata."

SEVEN ESSENTIALS FOR A CUP OF GOOD COFFEE

See color picture p. 71.

1. Use fresh coffee. It loses its flavor when exposed to air. Buy only enough for about a week's supply. Keep tightly covered.

2. Use the correct grind for your coffee maker. "Drip" is the grind for glass vacuum makers and dripolators. "Regular" or "steel cut" is the grind for percolators or steeped (boiled) coffee.

3. Use a clean coffee maker. Wash with soap and water after each use. Stains in the coffeepot can give a musty, stale taste. Boiling water with soda in the pot removes stains. Follow directions for cleaning your type of coffee maker.

4. Start with fresh, cold water (*not hot*) from the tap. Follow directions for type of coffee maker being used (*see opposite page*).

5. Make at least ¾ capacity of pot each time. Making smaller than this quantity deprives one of the full, rich "real coffee" flavor.

6. Always measure coffee and water to keep desired strength the same.

For *weak* coffee, use . . .
    1 tbsp. to ¾ cup water
For *medium* coffee, use . . .
    2 tbsp. to ¾ cup water
For *strong* coffee, use . . .
    3 to 4 tbsp. to ¾ cup water

7. Serve coffee as soon as possible. If necessary to let it stand, remove grounds. Keep hot on asbestos pad over very low heat; or in pan of hot water. Cooled coffee loses flavor if reheated.

After-Dinner Coffee

Served in tiny, exquisite cups. It is called demitasse . . . French word for "half cup."

Make coffee about twice as strong as usual. Use about 3 to 4 tbsp. coffee to ¾ cup water. Usually served without cream or sugar.

Two Methods For Making Iced Coffee

1. Make coffee double strength; pour hot over crushed ice in tall glasses (ice melts, diluting coffee).

2. Make regular strength coffee; chill; pour over crushed ice.

Coffee For The Crowd

Old-fashioned egg coffee . . . hot and plentiful!

For 40 cups of coffee: mix 1 egg (shell and all) into 1 lb. of coffee. Add 1 cup cold water. Tie coffee in cheesecloth bag large enough to allow room for coffee to swell. Measure 7 qt. cold water into large coffeepot. Immerse coffee bag in water, bring to boil. Remove pot from heat. Leave bag in water *3 to 4 min.*, or until desired strength is reached. Remove bag and stir. Keep hot.

▶ **ALL YOU HAVE TO DO**

To keep coffee hot for later drinking: pour into thermos bottle. If you wish to store leftover coffee, place in glass jar; cover and refrigerate. Reheat slowly.

HOW TO MAKE COFFEE IN DIFFERENT TYPES OF COFFEE MAKERS

Boiled Coffee

Measure coffee (regular grind) and fresh cold water into pot. Place over heat. Stir. Bring just to boil. Stir again. Take off heat. Add dash of cold water. Strain. Serve.

Swedish Egg Coffee: Stir ½ tbsp. beaten egg or egg white into about ⅛ cup coffee before adding water.

Drip Coffee

Some drip coffeepots have no filter, only a perforated top, some have cloth and others paper filters. Scald the pot before making the coffee. Use 2 level tablespoons of coffee to a standard measuring cup of water. Put the coffee in top part of the pot and pour the briskly boiling water, 2 to 3 tbsp. at a time, over it. Heat and serve.

Dripolator

Measure coffee (drip grind) into filter section, vigorously boiling water into upper section. Cover and set over *very* low heat until water has dripped through coffee. (Do not boil!) Remove upper section, stir and serve.

Percolator

Measure fresh cold water into the pot and coffee (regular grind) into the basket. Let water boil until it has "perked" *5 to 10 min.* for desired strength.

Vacuum-Type

Measure fresh cold water into lower bowl. Fit top bowl on with filter adjusted. Put coffee (drip grind) in top. Place on heat. When water rises, lower heat. Stir once. Remove from heat after 1 min. When coffee is back in lower section, remove top, put on separate cover. Serve.

Instant Coffee

Place ½ to 1 tsp. instant coffee in serving cup, according to desired strength. Fill with briskly boiling water; stir well. For iced coffee, use 1½ tsp. coffee and ¾ cup water.

Those on special diets may prefer to drink instant decaffeinated coffee from which almost all the caffein has been removed. It is prepared in the same way as instant coffee.

COFFEE AROUND THE WORLD

Belgian: Creamy, sweetened meringue is spooned into heated cups, then topped with strong coffee.

Café Diable: Strong, black coffee is combined with cloves, cinnamon, sugar, lemon peel and cognac.

Cappuccino: Strong, dark Italian coffee combined with an equal quantity of hot milk. Poured into mugs and spiced with nutmeg or cinnamon.

Espresso: Made in special espresso coffee maker. Rich coffee flavor. Served in demitasse cups— sometimes with sugar or lemon—but never cream.

Caffé Borgia: Combine equal parts of hot espresso coffee and hot chocolate. Top with whipped cream, sprinkle of grated orange peel.

Caffé Anisette Royal: Fill large cups with espresso coffee; add ½ tsp. anisette (an anise-flavored liqueur) per cup. Top with whipped cream.

French: Coffee is served strong and black. Or it is served as Café au Lait in which equal amounts of coffee and milk are heated to scalding, then poured into the cup at the same time.

Hawaiian: Soak or cook coconut in hot milk overnight; strain and mix milk equally with strong coffee. Top with toasted coconut.

Irish: Sweetened hot coffee in warmed wine glass with Irish whiskey added. Whipped cream on top.

Turkish: Sugar and coffee are heated to a boil together three times, until very frothy. Served black in tiny cups, with a little froth in each.

Ukrainian: A rich drink is made from chocolate, sugar, coffee, milk and whipped cream.

West Indian: Milk, coffee and brown sugar blend to make a mellow drink. Stir with cinnamon stick.

TEA BEVERAGES *"Polly put the kettle on, we'll all have tea."*

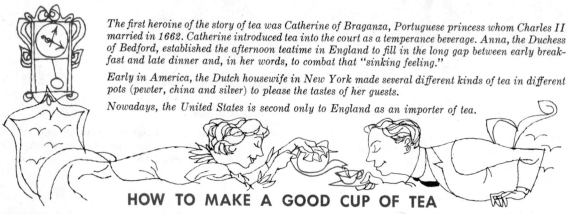

The first heroine of the story of tea was Catherine of Braganza, Portuguese princess whom Charles II married in 1662. Catherine introduced tea into the court as a temperance beverage. Anna, the Duchess of Bedford, established the afternoon teatime in England to fill in the long gap between early breakfast and late dinner and, in her words, to combat that "sinking feeling."

Early in America, the Dutch housewife in New York made several different kinds of tea in different pots (pewter, china and silver) to please the tastes of her guests.

Nowadays, the United States is second only to England as an importer of tea.

HOW TO MAKE A GOOD CUP OF TEA

Little English girls work on kettle holders in bright colored worsteds the following legend: "Unless the kettle boiling B, Filling the teapot spoils the T."

1. Use china, pottery or heat-resistant glass teapot. *Keep spotlessly clean.*

2. Preheat teapot by pouring in some scalding water just before kettle boils. Pour off water, add tea leaves to heated pot.

3. Allow 1 tsp. tea or tea bag for each cup or person plus one for the pot if you like it strong.

4. Start with fresh cold water from the tap and bring to brisk boil. Pour over the tea leaves. "Take the teapot to the kettle, never the kettle to the pot."

5. Cover the pot and let steep *3 to 5 min.* Stir and serve. Sugar, milk or lemon may be added, if desired.

HOW TO MAKE ICED TEA

See color picture p. 71.

Follow hot tea directions but use half again as much tea because melting ice dilutes to proper strength. Strain over ice in pitcher or into ice-filled glasses.

Iced Tea Tip: Tea that has steeped too long or that has been refrigerated will become cloudy. Pouring a small amount of boiling water into the tea pitcher will make it clear again.

Cold Extract of Tea

A sure method for making clear iced tea. Prepare this a day ahead of time and refrigerate.

Place in a container twice the amount of tea leaves or bags you would use for making hot tea (2 tsp. or 2 bags per glass). Add cold water and set in refrigerator for 24 hr.

For punch recipe using tea, see p. 72.

NOTES ON BUYING TEA

Buy tea in small amounts and store in airtight container, away from spices or strong-flavored vegetables, such as onions. One-fourth pound makes 35 to 45 cups of tea.

Types of Tea: Usually green teas have lighter flavor and darker teas have stronger flavor. Black tea is fermented, then dried; green tea is unfermented and oolong is semi-fermented. Scented tea is made by adding blossoms of flowers.

The name "orange pekoe" refers to the size of the tea leaf, not the kind of tea. The leaves are smaller than "pekoe" tea. "Orange pekoe" tea does not have an orange flavor.

▶ **ALL YOU HAVE TO DO**

To make tea in a hurry: use tea bags; each contains 1 tsp. tea or enough for 1 cup. Or, try the instant, soluble tea, using about 1 tsp. per cup of hot water. For iced tea, dissolve 2 tsp. instant tea in a small amount of hot water; then add cold to make 1 cup.

So history goes, Hernando Cortez was served "chocolatl" by the Emperor of the Aztecs, Montezuma, during his conquest of Mexico. Spaniards began to grow the cacao beans in their other colonial possessions and soon had built up a brisk and profitable business in the chocolate trade.

As early as 1657 wealthy Londoners were informed by a notice in the "Public Advertiser" that they could enjoy a drink of chocolate at a Public House on Bishopsgate Street. Soon chocolate houses and clubs became the fashion, and literary and political figures of the time gathered in the afternoon to gossip and drink the rare new delicacy called "jacalatte."

Hot Cocoa

Mix ¼ cup *each* sugar and cocoa. Add 1½ cups water; place over *low* heat until mixture boils, *about 4 min.* Add 6 cups milk; heat until scalded. Do not boil. Add a pinch of salt and a drop of vanilla, if desired. Just before serving, stir until smooth or beat with rotary beater. Serve hot. *6 to 8 servings.*

Hot Chocolate

See color picture p. 71.

Heat over *low* heat, 2 sq. unsweetened chocolate (2 oz.) and 1 cup water, stirring until chocolate melts and mixture is smooth. Add a pinch of salt and 3 tbsp. sugar. Boil *4 min.*, stirring. Then slowly stir in 3 cups milk. Cover and heat until scalded. Do not boil. Just before serving, beat with rotary beater until smooth and foamy. Serve hot. *6 servings.*

South American Chocolate

An unusual blend of chocolate and coffee. Good to serve with coffee cake or little cookies.

Melt over hot water ½ lb. sweet cooking chocolate (or a 6-oz. pkg. semi-sweet chocolate pieces). Add 1 cup strong hot coffee. Stir well and heat on *low* for 1 min. Scald 6 cups milk (1½ qt.); add to chocolate. Simmer until very hot. Beat with rotary beater until frothy on top. Set over hot water *10 min.* to blend flavors. Just before serving, beat again with rotary beater. *8 servings.*

Hot Chocolate Served the Continental Way

Serve small pitcher full of hot Cocoa Syrup (*at right*) along with pitcher full of scalding-hot milk. Let guests mix their own hot chocolate to desired strength.

French Chocolate

Very fancy! Scalded milk is poured over fluffy, chocolatey whipped cream for a creamy-rich drink.

¾ cup semi-sweet chocolate pieces
½ cup light corn syrup
⅓ cup water
1 tsp. vanilla
1 pt. whipping cream (2 cups)
2 qt. milk (8 cups)

Blend chocolate pieces with syrup and water over low heat until chocolate is melted. Add vanilla; pour into jar and refrigerate until cool. In large mixing bowl beat cream (medium speed) while gradually adding chocolate syrup. Continue beating until mixture mounds when dropped from spoon. Turn into serving bowl. Refrigerate. Just before serving, scald milk. Pour into heated coffee-pot or carafe. Fill serving cups half full of chocolate-whipped cream mixture. Fill with hot milk, blend. *16 to 18 servings.*

Chocolate, Maple or Fruit Ice Cream Sodas

For each soda: place 3 tbsp. Cocoa Syrup (*below*) or maple syrup or ¼ cup crushed fruit mixed with 1 tsp. sugar in tall glass. Fill glass ⅔ full with sparkling water. Add 1 scoop of ice cream; stir vigorously. Fill to top with sparkling water.

Cocoa Syrup

1½ cups sugar
dash of salt
1 cup cocoa
1 cup hot water
2 tsp. vanilla

Mix sugar, salt and cocoa. Add enough water to make a paste, then remainder of water. Bring to a boil, stirring constantly. Boil *3 min.*; add vanilla. Pour at once into jar. When cool, place in refrigerator. *Makes 2 cups.*

Eggnog

Simple, delicious egg-milk drink.

1 egg, well beaten
2 tbsp. sugar
1 cup chilled milk
*¼ tsp. vanilla

Beat egg and sugar together. Beat in milk and vanilla. Serve cold in tall glass sprinkled lightly with nutmeg. Serve immediately. *1 serving.*

*1½ tbsp. sherry flavoring and 1 tbsp. either brandy or rum flavoring may be substituted for vanilla.

Hot Eggnog

Nutritious hot drink. Warming in winter . . . wonderful for convalescents. See color picture p. 71.

4 eggs, separated
½ cup sugar
¼ tsp. salt
3 cups milk
1 tsp. vanilla or 1 tbsp. rum flavoring
3 tbsp. sugar

In large saucepan blend egg yolks, ½ cup sugar and salt. Beat in milk until thoroughly blended. Cook over medium heat, stirring constantly until heated through and bubbles form around edge. Add flavoring.

Beat egg whites until frothy. Gradually beat in 3 tbsp. sugar, a little at a time. Beat until stiff and glossy. To serve, fill cups half full with meringue. Pour hot eggnog over meringue. Sprinkle with nutmeg, if desired. *12 servings.*

Spoon-up Eggnog

Thick, rich, cold and fluffy. Eaten with a spoon, usually a holiday favorite with fruitcake.

4 eggs, separated
½ cup sugar
⅛ tsp. salt
1 to 2 tbsp. rum flavoring
2 cups whipping cream, whipped

Beat egg yolks, sugar and salt until thick and lemon-colored. Stir in flavoring. Fold egg yolk mixture into whipped cream. Beat egg whites until stiff. Fold gently into egg-cream mixture. Chill eggnog thoroughly. Serve in punch cups with spoons. Sprinkle with grated nutmeg, if desired. *12 servings.*

For thinner eggnog, fold in 1 pt. milk just before serving.

Flavored Milk Drinks

Appealing to children . . . for quick refresher or with meals.

For each serving: add one of the following syrups, fruits or flavorings to a tall glass. Fill glass with cold milk and stir thoroughly. Serve.

Banana: ½ banana, mashed.

Chocolate: 1½ to 2 tbsp. Cocoa Syrup (*p. 69*) or use canned.

Peanut Butter: 1 tbsp. peanut butter, 2 tbsp. sugar and dash of maple flavoring.

Maple: 2 tbsp. maple syrup.

Orange Blossom: ¼ to ⅓ cup orange juice, 1 tsp. sugar, about 2 drops almond flavoring.

Coffee: 1½ to 2 tsp. powdered instant coffee and 2 tbsp. sugar dissolved in 2 tbsp. water.

Berry: 2 tsp. strawberry or raspberry jam, or ice cream topping, or thawed frozen berries and 2 to 3 drops red food coloring.

Caramel: 1½ to 2 tbsp. Caramel Syrup (*below*).

Caramel Syrup

1 cup brown sugar (packed)
¾ cup hot water
1 tsp. vanilla
⅛ tsp. salt

Gradually melt sugar in heavy pan over low heat, stirring constantly, until a smooth light brown syrup forms. Remove from heat, gradually stir in water. Return to heat; simmer until smooth, stirring constantly. Cool slightly. Add vanilla and salt. *Makes 1 cup.*

Milk Shakes

Add 1 scoop vanilla ice cream to any of the Flavored Milk Drinks (*above*); stir in well.

SOME LIKE IT HOT—SOME LIKE IT COLD

Coffee
Hot Chocolate
Hot Eggnog

Party Punch with Fruit Ring
Chocolate Soda
Iced Tea
Lemonade

Lemonade

Tangy, refreshing . . . with colorful variations. See color picture p. 71.

For each serving: combine the juice of 1 lemon (about ⅓ cup) with 1 cup water and 5 tsp. sugar. Pour over ice in tall glass.

Minted Lemonade

Make Lemonade (*above*)—*except* place bruised mint leaves in bottom of glass before adding lemonade. Garnish with a sprig of mint.

Pink Lemonade

Make Lemonade (*above*)—*except* add 2 tsp. grenadine syrup and a little red food coloring.

Limeade

Make Lemonade (*above*)—*except* use juice of 1 lime in place of lemon juice. If desired, tint with green food coloring.

Orangeade

Make Lemonade (*above*)—*except* use ⅓ cup fresh orange juice plus 2 tbsp. lemon juice in place of ⅓ cup lemon juice; reduce sugar to 1 tbsp.

▶ **ALL YOU HAVE TO DO**
To make fruit drinks in a hurry: use frozen fruit juices and frozen lemonade concentrate.

Fruit Crush

Refreshing drink. From Nell Nichols, famed foods writer and epicure.

3 cups water
2 cups sugar
1 can (46 oz.) pineapple juice
1½ cups orange juice
¼ cup lemon juice
3 ripe bananas, mashed
3 qt. ginger ale or sparkling water, chilled

Mix water and sugar in saucepan; bring to boil. Remove from heat and stir in fruit juices and mashed bananas. Pour into 4 refrigerator trays and freeze until firm.

To serve, remove freezer trays and let stand at room temperature 10 to 15 min. to soften fruit mixture. Break frozen mixture into small chunks. Fill tall glasses ½ full of fruit crush, then fill to top with cold ginger ale or sparkling water. *Makes 6 qt. or about 24 servings.*

Wassail Bowl

A traditional holiday beverage in England. Serve hot, spicy cups proudly!

Heat oven to 325° (slow mod.). Stud 3 whole oranges with whole cloves (about ½" apart). Place in baking pan with a little water (just enough to cover bottom of pan). Bake *30 min.* Float the baked oranges on top of the Wassail (*below*) in punch bowl. Use cinnamon sticks for individual stirrers.

Wassail

6 cups apple cider or juice
1 cinnamon stick
¼ tsp. nutmeg
¼ cup honey
3 tbsp. lemon juice
1 tsp. lemon rind
1 can (1 lb. 4 oz.) unsweetened
   pineapple juice (2½ cups)

Heat cider and cinnamon stick in large pan. Bring to boil and simmer covered *5 min.* Add remaining ingredients and simmer uncovered *5 min.* longer. Keep hot over low heat or heat in small batches as guests arrive. *Makes 20 cups.*

Party Punch

See color picture p. 71.

4 qt. water
3 cups sugar
two cans (6 oz. each) frozen lemon juice
1 qt. apple juice
2 qt. cranberry juice
1 pt. orange juice
1 pt. strong black tea

Mix water and sugar; bring to boil. Combine with rest of ingredients. Mix well. Chill before using. *Makes 2 gal. or 40 servings.*

Raspberry Shrub

4 pkg. (10 oz. each) frozen raspberries, thawed
1 can (6 oz.) frozen lemonade concentrate
2 qt. bottles sparkling water or
   1 qt. bottle sparkling water plus
   1 qt. water

Cook raspberries *10 min.* Strain and cool. Add lemonade concentrate and sparkling water. Serve immediately with crushed ice. *12 servings.* NOTE: all ingredients except sparkling water may be mixed ahead of time.

QUICK BREADS

The stories of our delicious hot quick breads are as varied as the breads themselves. May we share with you a few excerpts from our Quick Breads notebook?

Bread serves as a plate: during the early Middle Ages meats and vegetables were served on a large piece of bread; the savory juices soaked into the bread which was eaten last.

Bannocks: Robert Burns wrote of "bannocks o' barley;" bannocks, a biscuit-like dough rolled, cut and fried on a griddle, are still enjoyed in the British Isles today.

Biscuits: Whether the menu featured fish, chicken, ham or all three, guests at a Southern plantation home before the Civil War could expect golden biscuits, just cool enough to avoid burning one's fingers, and dripping with butter.

Muffins: England's beloved Dickens had one of his characters say: "I'm glad we had muffins. It's the sort of a night for muffins."

Dumplings: Almost as famous as the seven sweets and seven sours is the Pennsylvania Dutch dish of apples and dumplings, "schnitz un knepp." Cooked, with ham as the main course or without ham as a dessert, potato dumplings crown the bubbling mixture.

Tea loaves: From England's Wiltshire county comes a currant-studded loaf called dough cake, which is surely the ancestor of our nut and fruit breads.

HOMEY HOT BREADS

(complete index in back of book)

TIMESAVING TIPS

For the best shortcut of all, use Bisquick for Drop or Rolled Biscuits, Muffins, Coffee Cake, Dumplings, Nut Breads, Pancakes, Waffles.

PUFFY RAISIN PANCAKES

Add 1 cup seedless raisins to 2-cup pancake recipe on Betty Crocker Buttermilk Pancake Mix pkg. Bake and stack with red jelly or jam between.

DOUBLE TREAT MUFFINS

Follow directions on Betty Crocker Blueberry Muffin Mix pkg.—*except* use ¾ cup water and add ½ pkg. of Orange, Date or Raisin Bran Betty Crocker Muffin Mix to the envelope of Blueberry Muffin Mix. Fold in rinsed, drained blueberries as directed. Fill greased muffin cups ½ full. Bake as directed on pkg. *Makes about 1½ doz. medium muffins.*

COFFEE WREATH

Plan a brunch around this rich, pretty, easy-to-make coffee cake.

2 cans Betty Crocker Refrigerated Biscuits
¼ cup butter, melted
¾ cup sugar
1 tbsp. cinnamon (3 tsp.)
¼ cup chopped nuts

Heat oven to 375° (quick mod.). Grease a round layer pan, 9x1½″. Separate biscuits and dip in melted butter; coat entirely with mixture of sugar and cinnamon. Place 15 biscuits around outer circle of pan overlapping to fill circle. Overlap remaining 5 biscuits around inner circle to fill pan. Pour remaining butter over top. Sprinkle with nuts. Bake *25 to 30 min.* Let stand 5 min. Turn out on rack then over again on serving plate. *10 servings.*

MEALTIME MAGIC

BREAKFAST BUFFET

(See color picture pp. 84-85.)

Fruit Juice
Waffles *(p. 94)*   Blueberry Pancakes *(p. 92)*
Bacon and Pork Sausages
Cranberry-Orange Muffins *(p. 88)*
Pineapple Nut Bread *(p. 96)*
Quick Apple Cake *(p. 78)*
Coffee

EXTRA SPECIAL COFFEE PARTY

Frosted Grapes *(p. 26)*
Danish Puff *(p. 79)*
Coffee   Tea

DESSERT FRENCH-STYLE

Crepes Suzette *(p. 248)*
Café au lait *(p. 67)*

Note: You no longer need to sift flour for recipes in this chapter. Measure Gold Medal flour by dipping nested measuring cups into flour and leveling off with spatula.

WHAT EVERY COOK NEEDS TO KNOW ABOUT QUICK BREADS

BAKE WITH CARE

Quick breads are so named because they are speedily prepared as compared to yeast breads. Let's consider this diverse family of foods according to their batters and doughs.

Biscuits (p. 76) are made from a soft dough. For flaky biscuits, cut shortening in finely so that it resembles meal. Liquid should be beaten into dry ingredients just until dough leaves sides of the bowl and rounds up into a ball. Kneading dough gently ensures a fine textured biscuit.

Muffins (p. 88) have a drop batter. They are leavened by the carbon dioxide gas which is released when the milk comes in contact with the baking powder or soda. For light, tender muffins with gently rounded tops, stir batter just enough to moisten ingredients because overmixing causes toughness and tunnels.

Corn bread, nut bread and coffee cakes are also made by the muffin method of mixing.

Popovers (p. 89) have a thin pour batter. They call for no baking powder or soda as do muffins and biscuits. The leavening is the steam created by a high proportion of milk and the high oven temperature. Popovers require just enough beating to blend ingredients; overbeating will reduce size of your popovers. If your meal plan includes lots of last minute tasks, mix all the dry ingredients for your quick bread together in the mixing bowl; have milk (and eggs, if used) ready to add.

Bake just enough biscuits or muffins for one meal as quick breads do not have the keeping qualities of other baked products which are higher in fat, sugar and eggs. If biscuits or muffins are left over, split, butter and broil them until heated through.

. . . .

SERVE WITH FLAIR

Always serve biscuits and muffins piping hot. Snuggle them in a napkin in a serving dish. Keep waffles and pancakes for second helpings between towels in warm oven until needed.

Remember quick breads at dessert time. Try Nut Waffles (p. 94) topped with ice cream. Plan a dessert party around Fritters (p. 87) or French Pancakes (p. 248).

NEW ADVENTURES IN QUICK BREADS

Cranberry-Orange Muffins (p. 88)—Polka-dotted with red cranberry halves.

Danish Puff (p. 79)—Rich 'n sweet.

Pineapple Nut Bread (p. 96)—Moist, fruity.

Potato Dumplings (p. 86)—To serve with beef.

Pumpkin Muffins (p. 89)—Spicy, raisin-filled.

Tropical Fruit Bread (p. 91)—An unusual combination of banana, apricot and bran.

75

HOW TO MAKE BISCUITS

1. Cut shortening into flour mixture.

2. Stir in milk.

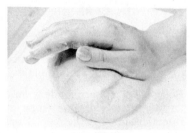
3. Round up and knead.

4. Roll dough or pat out.

5. Cut close together.

6. Place close together or apart.

Biscuits *The daily bread of earlier days in the South. See color picture page 95.*

Typical Biscuits	*Southern Biscuits*
2 cups GOLD MEDAL Flour	2 cups GOLD MEDAL Flour
3 tsp. baking powder	3 tsp. baking powder
1 tsp. salt	1 tsp. salt
¼ cup shortening	6 tbsp. shortening
¾ cup milk	⅔ cup milk

Heat oven to 450° (hot). Measure flour by dip-level-pour method or by sifting (*see p. 6*). Mix dry ingredients well in bowl. Cut in shortening with pastry blender until mixture looks like "meal." Stir in almost all the milk. If dough does not seem pliable, add enough to make a soft, puffy dough easy to roll out. (Too much milk makes dough sticky, not enough makes biscuits dry.) Round up on lightly floured cloth-covered board. Knead lightly about 6 times. Handle lightly.

Roll dough or pat out (with floured hand) to about ½″ thick (¼″ for Southern biscuits). Cut close together with floured biscuit cutter. For speed, cut in squares with knife. Fit leftover bits together. (Do not reknead.) Pat out dough, roll smooth and cut as desired. Place close together for biscuits with soft sides, an inch apart for biscuits with crusty sides, on ungreased baking sheet. Place in middle of oven. Bake *10 to 12 min.* Serve piping hot. *Makes 20 1¾″ biscuits (1″ high).*

Drop Biscuits

Make Biscuits (*above*)—*except* increase milk to 1 cup. Drop from spoon on greased pan or into greased muffin cups.

Buttermilk Biscuits

Make Biscuits (*above*)—*except*, in place of milk, use buttermilk. Use only 2 tsp. baking powder and add ¼ tsp. soda.

Bacon Biscuits

Make Biscuits (*above*)—*except* add ⅓ cup drained cooked bacon bits (about 4 strips) to flour and shortening mixture.

Herb Biscuits

Make Biscuits (*above*)—*except* add ¼ tsp. dry mustard, ½ tsp. crumbled dry sage and 1¼ tsp. caraway seeds to flour mixture.

Stir-n-Roll Biscuits

Especially rich, tender and flaky within . . . a wonderfully delicate, crispy crust on both top and bottom. Quick to make. No floury mess to clear up. So sure and easy!

Sweet Milk Biscuits

2 cups GOLD MEDAL Flour
3 tsp. baking powder
1 tsp. salt
—
⅓ cup vegetable oil
⅔ cup milk

Buttermilk Biscuits

2 cups GOLD MEDAL Flour
2 tsp. baking powder
1 tsp. salt
¼ tsp. soda
⅓ cup vegetable oil
⅔ cup buttermilk

Heat oven to 475° (very hot). Measure flour by dip-level-pour method or by sifting (*see p. 6*). Mix dry ingredients well in bowl. Pour oil and milk into measuring cup (do not stir together). Pour all at once into flour. Stir with fork until mixture cleans sides of bowl and forms a ball. To knead: turn onto waxed paper; lift paper by one corner and fold dough in half; press down firmly; pull paper back. Repeat until dough looks smooth. Pat or roll ½" thick (¼" thick for Southern biscuits) between 2 sheets of waxed paper. Cut with unfloured biscuit cutter. Place on ungreased baking sheet. Bake *10 to 12 min.*, or until golden brown. Serve piping hot with butter and jelly, honey, jam or syrup. *Makes 16 medium biscuits.*

1. Pour oil and milk into flour.

2. Knead easily . . . on waxed paper.

3. Roll out between waxed papers.

Cheese Biscuits

Golden and savory . . . with salads.

Make Biscuits (*p. 76*)—*except* add ½ cup grated sharp Cheddar cheese to flour and shortening mixture.

Iris' Biscuits

"When I was a little girl," says culinary artist Iris Davenport Mahan, Lexington, Kentucky, *"biscuits were so important a part of the meal that the homemaker made them herself, no matter how many servants the family had."*

Follow recipe for Southern Biscuits (*p. 76*) for method. But use: 2 cups GOLD MEDAL Flour, 2 tsp. baking powder, ½ tsp. soda, 2 tsp. sugar, 1 tsp. salt, ⅓ cup shortening, ⅔ cup buttermilk. Roll dough a little less than ½" thick. Cut with 1½" cutter.

Butter Dips

"These golden-crusted biscuit sticks are a wonderful addition to any meal," says Mrs. Edwin W. Fierke.

¼ cup butter
1¼ cups GOLD MEDAL Flour
2 tsp. sugar
2 tsp. baking powder
1 tsp. salt
⅔ cup milk

Heat oven to 450° (hot). Melt butter in square pan, 9x9x1¾", in oven. Remove as soon as butter melts. Measure flour by dip-level-pour method or by sifting (*see p. 6*). In bowl, stir dry ingredients together. Add milk. Stir 30 strokes with fork until dough clings together. Turn out on floured board. Knead lightly about 10 times. Roll out ½" thick into 8" square. With floured knife, cut into strips 4" wide, then cut crosswise to make 18 sticks. Dip sticks in butter; place in 2 rows in pan. Bake *15 to 20 min.* Serve hot. *Makes 18 butter dips.*

Prize Coffee Cake

With delightful changes for every occasion.

¾ cup sugar
¼ cup soft shortening
1 egg
½ cup milk

1½ cups GOLD MEDAL Flour
2 tsp. baking powder
½ tsp. salt

Heat oven to 375° (quick mod.). Grease and flour a square pan, 9x9x1¾". Mix sugar, shortening and egg thoroughly. Stir in milk. Measure flour by dip-level-pour method or by sifting (*see p. 6*). Blend dry ingredients; stir in. Spread batter in pan. Sprinkle with desired topping (*see below*). Bake 25 to 35 min., or until toothpick stuck into center comes out clean. Serve warm. *Makes 9 3" squares.*

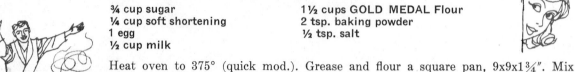

Cinnamon Coffee Cake

Tempting, spicy, delicious. Brought from Isle Royal by Esther Scarborough Chapman.

Make Prize Coffee Cake (*above*)—except sprinkle top with a mixture of ½ cup brown sugar (packed) and 1½ tsp. cinnamon.

Streusel-filled Coffee Cake

The rich cinnamony mixture both in the middle and on the top makes delightful eating.

Make Prize Coffee Cake (*above*)—except spread only half the batter in pan. Sprinkle with half the Streusel Mixture (*below*). Add the remaining batter and sprinkle remaining Streusel over top.

Streusel Mixture

Mix ½ cup brown sugar (packed), 2 tbsp. flour, 2 tsp. cinnamon, 2 tbsp. butter, melted, and ½ cup chopped nuts.

Holiday Coffee Cake

Gay and colorful with Christmas fruit.

Make Prize Coffee Cake (*above*)—except sprinkle top with mixture of ⅓ cup moist cut-up candied fruit, ½ tsp. cinnamon and 3 tbsp. sugar.

Quick Apple Cake

See color picture page 84.

Make Prize Coffee Cake (*above*)—except mix ½ cup seedless raisins into batter. Arrange apple slices in fancy design on top of batter, pressing them slightly into batter, then sprinkle top with 1 tsp. cinnamon mixed with 2 tbsp. sugar.

Blueberry Buckle

"The best of old-time Blueberry Teacakes," says Mrs. Homer Dowdy of Flint, Michigan.

Make Prize Coffee Cake (*above*)—except use 2 cups flour and carefully blend in at the last 2 cups well drained blueberries. Sprinkle top with mixture of ½ cup sugar, ⅓ cup GOLD MEDAL Flour, ½ tsp. cinnamon and ¼ cup soft butter. Bake 45 to 50 min. Delicious as dessert when served warm with cream.

Orange Coffee Cake

Refreshing orange flavor, always a favorite.

Make Prize Coffee Cake (*above*)—except use orange juice for half of the milk and add 1½ tsp. grated orange rind. Sprinkle top with mixture of ½ cup sugar, ⅓ cup GOLD MEDAL Flour, ½ tsp. cinnamon, ¼ cup soft butter and 1½ tsp. grated orange rind.

Marmalade Coffee Cake

Make Prize Coffee Cake (*above*)—except spread top with mixture of ½ cup brown sugar (packed), ½ cup GOLD MEDAL Flour, 2 tbsp. butter, 1 tbsp. cream and ½ cup orange marmalade. Topping melts down through the cake during baking.

Pineapple Coffee Cake

Make Prize Coffee Cake (*above*)—except spread top with mixture of 2 tbsp. softened butter, 2 tbsp. honey and ½ cup well drained crushed pineapple.

Danish Puff

Perfect to take along when dropping in on friends.

1 cup GOLD MEDAL Flour
½ cup butter
2 tbsp. water
½ cup butter
1 cup water
1 tsp. almond flavoring
1 cup GOLD MEDAL Flour
3 eggs

Heat oven to 350° (mod.). Measure flour by dip-level-pour method or by sifting (*see p. 6*). Measure first cup of flour into bowl. Cut in butter. Sprinkle with 2 tbsp. water; mix with fork. Round into ball; divide in half. Pat into 2 strips, 12x3". Place 3" apart on ungreased baking sheet.

Mix second amount of butter and water. Bring to boil. Remove from heat; add flavoring. Beat in flour, stirring quickly to prevent lumping. When smooth, add one egg at a time, beating well after each addition until smooth. Divide in half and spread one half evenly over each piece of pastry. Bake *about 60 min.* (Puff has a tendency to shrink while cooling, leaving a custardy portion in center.) Frost with a confectioners' sugar icing and sprinkle with chopped nuts. *8 to 12 servings.*

Sugarloaf Coffee Cake

An old-fashioned combination of raisins and spices.

2½ cups GOLD MEDAL Flour
1¼ cups sugar
3½ tsp. baking powder
1 tsp. salt
1 tsp. *each* cinnamon and nutmeg
½ tsp. *each* cloves and allspice
¾ cup shortening
1 cup raisins
1 cup milk or buttermilk
1 egg, beaten

Heat oven to 375° (quick mod.). Grease a square pan, 9x9x1¾". Measure flour by dip-level-pour method or by sifting (*see p. 6*). Mix dry ingredients well in bowl. Cut in shortening until mixture looks like meal. Set aside 1 cup for topping. To remainder, add raisins. Mix milk and egg; stir in *just until* dry ingredients are moistened. Pour into pan. Sprinkle reserved mixture over top. Bake *40 to 45 min.* Serve warm. *9 to 12 servings.*

Butterquick Coffee Cake

2 cups GOLD MEDAL Flour
1 cup sugar
3 tsp. baking powder
1 tsp. salt
⅓ cup soft butter
1 egg
1 cup milk

Heat oven to 350° (mod.). Grease a square pan, 9x9x1¾". Measure flour by dip-level-pour method or by sifting (*see p. 6*). Blend dry ingredients. Add butter, egg and milk. Beat hard 2 min. Pour into pan. Cover with Crunchy Topping (below). Bake *35 to 40 min.* Serve warm. *9 to 12 servings.*

Crunchy Topping

Mix with fork 2 tbsp. soft butter, ¼ cup brown sugar (packed), 2 tbsp. flour, 1 tsp. cinnamon and ½ cup coconut or chopped nuts.

Sugar-Nut Squares

Make Butterquick Coffee Cake (*above*)—except pour into oblong pan, 13x9½x2"; omit Crunchy Topping; sprinkle before baking with mixture of ½ cup sugar, 1 tsp. cinnamon and ¼ cup chopped nuts. Bake *about 25 min. 15 to 18 servings.*

Lemon Glazed Gems

Make Butterquick Coffee Cake (*above*)—except omit Crunchy Topping, fill greased muffin cups ⅔ full and bake *at 400° (mod. hot) 15 to 20 min.* While still warm, frost tops with Lemon Glaze (*below*). *Makes 18 medium gems.*

Lemon Glaze

Mix 1 cup *sifted* confectioners' sugar, 1 tsp. lemon juice, ½ tsp. grated lemon rind and 2 tbsp. milk.

The Indians taught the earliest colonists to parch corn and mix it with boiling water . . . and bake it in thin cakes. These were used by hunters and traders on their long journeys on foot over Indian trails; hence, the name "Journey Cake," later called "Johnny Cake." Almost as many different types of corn bread have been developed as there are different regions in our country.

HOW TO MAKE CORN BREAD

1. Beat just until smooth.

2. Pour batter into generously buttered square pan.

3. Or spoon batter into generously buttered corn stick pans.

Canary Corn Sticks

From Ohio.

1 egg
1½ cups buttermilk
½ tsp. soda
½ cup GOLD MEDAL Flour
1½ cups corn meal
1 tsp. sugar
3 tsp. baking powder
1 tsp. salt
¼ cup soft shortening
  (bacon fat is good)

Corn Cake

From Kentucky.

1 egg
1 cup plus 2 tbsp. milk
—
¼ cup GOLD MEDAL Flour
1¼ cups corn meal
2 tbsp. sugar
3 tsp. baking powder
1 tsp. salt
3 tbsp. soft shortening
  (bacon fat is good)

Corn Bread

From Arkansas.

2 eggs
2 cups buttermilk
1 tsp. soda
—
2 cups corn meal
—
—
1 tsp. salt
—

Heat oven to 450° (hot). Generously butter 12 muffin cups or corn stick pans or a square pan, 9x9x1¾". Heat in oven while mixing batter. Beat egg(s). Measure flour by dip-level-pour method or by sifting (*see p. 6*). Beat in rest of ingredients with rotary beater *just until* smooth. Pour or spoon batter into hot pans until *almost* full. Bake *10 to 15 min. for corn sticks or muffins; 20 to 25 min. for corn bread;* or just until set. Serve piping hot with butter. Cut corn bread (baked in square pan) into squares. *Makes about 12 muffins, corn sticks or pieces.*

Bacon Corn Bread

Make Corn Bread (*above*)—*except* add ⅓ cup crisply cooked bacon bits at the last, or lay short slices of partially cooked bacon on top of batter in pan (allow one piece to each serving). Bake.

Plantation Shortcake

Serve Chicken à la King (*p. 266*) over Corn Bread (*above*).

Hoe Cake and Corn Pone were the first simple forms of corn bread in the South . . . simply corn meal mixed with water, salted and baked. Hoe Cake was baked on a plank (or the cotton hoe) on hot embers. Pones were the "appones" of the Indians, shaped with the hands into small cakes, baked before the fire. Spoon Bread was evolved when an old-time Virginia cook put a dish of corn meal mush into the oven in the home of President James Monroe near Charlottesville.

Hush Puppies

When Florida hunters sat around their camp fish-fries, their dogs would whine for the good smelling food. The men tossed leftover corn patties to them calling, "Hush, puppies." Satisfied, the dogs hushed.

1½ cups corn meal
1½ cups water
⅓ cup milk
1 tbsp. vegetable oil
2 tsp. grated onion
2 eggs, beaten
1 cup GOLD MEDAL Flour
3 tsp. baking powder
2 tsp. salt
1 tsp. sugar, if desired

Cook corn meal and water, stirring until stiff and begins to roll into ball, about 6 min. Remove from heat; add milk, oil and onion. Stir until smooth. Gradually stir into beaten eggs in 2-qt. bowl. Measure flour by dip-level-pour method or by sifting (*see p. 6*). Blend dry ingredients. Add to corn meal batter; blend thoroughly. Heat fat (1″ deep) to 375°. Drop batter by teaspoonfuls into hot fat. Fry 6 to 7 min. Drain. *Makes 24 to 30.*

Old-time Johnny Cakes

Originally made from water ground corn meal.

Beat 1 egg. Stir in 2 cups white or yellow corn meal, 1 tsp. salt, 1¼ to 1½ cups milk (to make batter thick). Drop spoonfuls of batter onto a well greased hot griddle and fry to a golden brown on each side. Stir batter occasionally to keep well mixed. Serve hot with butter. *Makes 12 Johnny cakes.*

Spoon Bread

Light and soufflé-like. Often served with chicken. Virginians love it with fried tomatoes.

1½ cups boiling water
1 cup corn meal
1 tbsp. butter
3 egg yolks
1 cup buttermilk
1 tsp. salt
1 tsp. sugar
1 tsp. baking powder
¼ tsp. soda
3 egg whites, beaten only enough to hold soft peaks

Heat oven to 375° (quick mod.). Pour boiling water over corn meal. Stir until cool to keep from lumping. Add butter and egg yolks. Stir until egg is well blended. Stir in milk. Blend in salt, sugar, baking powder and soda. Fold in beaten egg whites. Pour into greased 2-qt. baking dish. Bake *45 to 50 min.* Serve hot with butter. *6 servings.*

Quick Spoon Bread (*Batter Bread*)

Soft and moist . . . custardy . . . delicious. Traditional choice with herring roe.

1 egg
¾ cup white corn meal
½ tsp. soda
½ tsp. salt
1½ cups buttermilk

Heat oven to 400° (mod. hot). Beat egg. Stir in remaining ingredients. Pour into hot 1-qt. baking dish with 1 tbsp. butter melted in it. Bake *20 to 25 min.*, or just until set. Serve hot with butter or gravy. *6 servings.*

HOW TO MAKE DOUGHNUTS

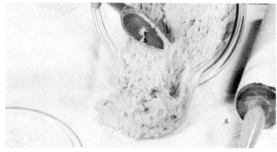

1. Turn onto floured cloth-covered board.

2. Cut with floured sharp doughnut cutter.

3. Slide into hot fat.

4. Turn and fry until brown on both sides.

Favorite Doughnuts *(Cake Doughnuts)*

The best of Old New England recipes. Subtly spiced.

4 egg yolks (or 2 whole eggs)	2 tsp. baking powder
1 cup sugar	1 tsp. soda
2 tbsp. soft shortening	½ tsp. salt
¾ cup thick buttermilk	¼ tsp. nutmeg
3½ cups GOLD MEDAL Flour	¼ tsp. cinnamon

Beat egg yolks well. Beat in sugar and shortening. Stir in milk. Measure flour by dip-level-pour method or by sifting (*see p. 6*). Blend dry ingredients; beat in until smooth. Turn part onto generously floured cloth-covered board. Turn to lightly cover with flour. Roll gently ⅓″ thick.

Place fat or oil (3 to 4″ deep) for deep fat frying in a heavy kettle or deep fat fryer. Heat to 370 to 380° (a cube of bread browns in fat in 60 seconds).

Cut dough with floured sharp doughnut cutter. Take board close to kettle to transfer. Lift with spatula; slide quickly into hot fat. Fry as many at a time as can be turned easily. Turn doughnuts as they rise to surface. Fry 2 to 3 min. total, or just until golden brown. Lift from fat with long fork. Do not prick. Drain on absorbent paper in warm place. Serve plain, sugared or glazed (*see p. 83*). *Makes 2 doz. 3″ doughnuts.*

TIPS FOR DEEP FAT FRYING

Temperature of fat should be 370 to 380° when foods are added. If fat is too hot, foods brown before they cook through. If too cool, they become grease-soaked.

Fry the "holes" for the children.

To keep fat to use again: clarify with raw potato (4 slices to 1 qt.). When fat bubbles, strain into jar or can through 2 or 3 thicknesses of cheesecloth, over wire strainer. (The potato absorbs flavors.) Keep in a cool place in light-proof, tight, covered container.

Known in England in 1536 as "imported doughty cakes," doughnuts were brought to this country by Dutch and English settlers. Originally balls or "nuts" of yeast dough, the Yankees found a quicker way. Doughnuts were as popular with soldiers of the Revolutionary War as they were with the "doughboys" of World War I and the G. I.'s of World War II.

Potato Doughnuts

Tender and light, with delicious flavor.

When mashing potatoes, set aside 1 cup before adding milk or seasonings.

3 eggs
¾ cup sugar
3 tbsp. soft shortening
2¾ cups GOLD MEDAL Flour
4 tsp. baking powder
1 tsp. salt
¼ tsp. nutmeg
1 tsp. mace
1 cup mashed potatoes (unseasoned)

Mix dough as for Favorite Doughnuts *(p. 82)*. Chill dough 2 hr. Fry as directed. *Makes 3 doz. 2½″ doughnuts.*

Sweet Milk Doughnuts

Make Favorite Doughnuts *(p. 82)—except* use sweet milk in place of buttermilk; use 4 tsp. baking powder and omit soda.

To Sugar Doughnuts: Just before serving, shake doughnuts one at a time in a paper bag with a little confectioners' sugar, granulated sugar or mixture of cinnamon and sugar.

To Glaze Doughnuts: Add ⅓ cup boiling water gradually to 1 cup confectioners' sugar. Mix thoroughly. Dip warm doughnuts into the warm glaze.

To Coat with Nuts and Sugar: Dip warm doughnuts into warm glaze *(above)*, then into mixture of ½ cup finely chopped nuts, ½ cup sugar and 1 tsp. cinnamon.

Chocolate Glaze for Doughnuts

1 sq. unsweetened chocolate (1 oz.), melted
½ tsp. vanilla
2½ cups *sifted* confectioners' sugar
about ¼ cup milk

Add melted chocolate and vanilla to confectioners' sugar. Mix thoroughly. Slowly stir in milk, mixing until smooth and of glaze consistency.

Golden Puffs

Spicy-rich little doughnut balls. Exciting and different for "coffee and doughnuts" or afternoon tea.

2 cups GOLD MEDAL Flour
¼ cup sugar
3 tsp. baking powder
1 tsp. salt
1 tsp. nutmeg or mace
¼ cup vegetable oil
¾ cup milk
1 egg

Measure flour by dip-level-pour method or by sifting *(see p. 6)*. Blend dry ingredients. Add oil, milk and egg. Mix well with fork. Drop by teaspoonfuls into hot fat (375°). Fry about 3 min., or until golden. Drain. Roll warm puffs in cinnamon-sugar mixture or glaze puffs *(see bottom left)*. *Makes 2½ doz. puffs.*

Buttermilk Nut Puffs

Make Golden Puffs *(above)—except* substitute buttermilk for milk. Reduce baking powder to 1 tsp. and add ½ tsp. soda. Roll warm puffs in granulated sugar or dip in warm glaze *(at left)* and roll in finely chopped nuts.

Raised Doughnuts See p. 124.

BUFFET BREAKFAST

HOW TO MAKE DUMPLINGS

1. Drop onto chicken or meat.

2. Remove when done.

Dumplings

Puffs as light as thistledown . . . with flavorful stews, they bring renown.
Cooking half time uncovered is the newest and best method.

1½ cups GOLD MEDAL Flour	3 tbsp. shortening
2 tsp. baking powder	¾ cup milk
¾ tsp. salt	

Measure flour by dip-level-pour method or by sifting (*see p. 6*). Blend dry ingredients. Cut in shortening. Blend in milk. Drop by spoonfuls *onto* chicken or meat in boiling meat stock (not in liquid). Cook slowly *10 min.* with kettle uncovered and *10 min.* tightly covered. To prevent soggy dumplings, use domed cover. Remove dumplings and meat to hot platter. Keep hot while making gravy. Pour part of gravy around them. Serve remainder separately. *Makes 8 to 10 dumplings.*

Parsley, Chive or Herb Dumplings

Parsley Dumplings go well with lamb stew. Try Chive or Herb Dumplings with beef or veal stew.

Make Dumplings (*above*)—*except* add 3 tbsp. minced parsley or chives or ¼ to ½ tsp. dried herbs (such as sage, celery seed or thyme) to blended dry ingredients.

Cheese Dumplings

Make Dumplings (*above*)—*except* add ¼ cup grated sharp cheese to blended dry ingredients.

Egg Dumplings

Especially delicious with chicken stew.

1 cup GOLD MEDAL Flour
1½ tsp. baking powder
½ tsp. salt
2 tbsp. vegetable oil
1 egg
¼ cup plus 2 tbsp. milk
2 tbsp. minced parsley

Measure flour by dip-level-pour method or by sifting (*see p. 6*). Mix dry ingredients in bowl. Blend in remaining ingredients. Cook as for Dumplings (*above*).

Potato Dumplings

Germans call them Kartoffelklosse. A favorite with sauerbraten and other beef dishes.

6 medium potatoes
2 slices white bread
1 egg
¼ cup plus 2 tbsp. GOLD MEDAL Flour

Pare and boil potatoes until tender. Put through ricer while hot. Let cool. Meanwhile, cut bread into small cubes and toast in 2 tbsp. butter, melted in skillet, until golden brown. When potatoes are cool, blend in egg, flour and salt to taste. Form potato mixture into 8 to 10 balls, placing three cubes of toasted bread in center of each ball. Gently place the balls in boiling salted water and simmer *10 to 15 min.*, or until light and fluffy. *Makes 8 to 10 dumplings.*

Fritters are fruits or vegetables dipped in batter and fried until golden brown outside and tender inside. The name also applies to chopped or grated foods folded into a thick batter and fried in balls. Fritter batters are also used as the coating for French fried meats and sea foods.

FRITTERS AND BATTER-DIPPED FRENCH FRIED FOODS

<table>
<tr><td>

Thick Fritter Batter

1 cup GOLD MEDAL Flour
1 tsp. baking powder
1 tsp. salt
2 eggs
½ cup milk
1 tsp. melted fat or vegetable oil

</td><td>

Thin Fritter Batter

1 cup GOLD MEDAL Flour
1 tsp. baking powder
½ tsp. salt
1 egg
1 cup milk
¼ cup vegetable oil

</td></tr>
</table>

Measure flour by dip-level-pour method or by sifting (*see p. 6*). Blend dry ingredients in bowl. Mix eggs, milk and oil. Add to dry ingredients. Beat with rotary beater until smooth. Prepare food to be fried (suggested foods below). Thaw frozen foods completely before frying. Parboil foods where indicated. Heat fat or vegetable oil to 375°, using either a frying kettle or skillet. Kettle should not be more than ⅓ full of oil or fat; oil in skillet should be 1″ deep—just deep enough to float food.

Dry food thoroughly. Coat with flour. Using tongs or fork, dip food into batter, letting excess drop off. Either Thick or Thin Fritter Batter will work well for most foods. Use Thin Batter when you want to retain shape of food, such as shrimp, fruit slices or onion rings. Fold chopped or grated foods into Thick Batter. Fry until golden. Frying time depends on food. Foods dipped in Thick Batter will take about 1 min. longer. Drain on absorbent paper. Serve meat and sea food fritters as appetizer or main dish; fruit and vegetable fritters as meat accompaniment; fruit fritters as dessert with confectioners' sugar or a sauce.

SUGGESTED FOODS

<table>
<tr><td>

Sea Food

Shrimp, deveined
Scallops
Oysters
Fillets

</td><td>

Meat

Chicken (parboil if chicken is
    larger than 2½ lb.)
Cutlets
Luncheon meat, cubed

</td></tr>
<tr><td>

Fruits

Pineapple slices
Bananas, quartered
Apples, sliced

</td><td>

Vegetables

Onion rings (*p. 425*)
Cauliflowerets
Corn

</td></tr>
</table>

Dip food in batter. Fry until golden.

Corn Fritters

Make Thick Fritter Batter—*except* add 1 cup grated cooked corn or drained canned corn to batter. Drop by spoonfuls into hot fat. Serve hot with syrup. *12 to 15 fritters.*

Apple or Pineapple Fritters

Make Thick Fritter Batter—*except* add 1 apple, chopped, *or* 1 cup drained, crushed pineapple to batter. Drop by spoonfuls into hot fat; fry. Roll in confectioners' sugar. *12 to 15 fritters.*

French Fruit Fritters (*Creole Beignets*)

Sprinkle cut-up fresh fruits (figs, pears, orange, pineapple or apple slices) with sugar and grated lemon rind. Let stand 2 to 3 hr. Drain and dip into Fluffy Fritter Batter (*below*). Fry in deep fat at 375°. Drain and serve hot with confectioners' sugar or a sweet syrup or sauce.

Fluffy Fritter Batter: Beat together 2 egg yolks, ⅔ cup milk, 1 cup GOLD MEDAL Flour, ½ tsp. salt, 1 tbsp. butter, melted, and 2 tbsp. lemon juice with rotary beater. Fold in 2 egg whites, stiffly beaten.

HOW TO MAKE MUFFINS

1. Beat egg slightly. Stir in milk and oil.

2. Mix dry ingredients and stir in lightly.

3. Fill well greased muffin cups ⅔ full.

4. Baked muffins will have gently rounded tops.

Muffins *The name means "little muffs" . . . to warm the fingers.*

Popular Muffins

1 egg
1 cup milk
¼ cup vegetable oil or melted shortening
2 cups GOLD MEDAL Flour
¼ cup sugar
3 tsp. baking powder
1 tsp. salt

Sweeter Muffins

1 egg
½ cup milk
¼ cup vegetable oil or melted shortening
1½ cups GOLD MEDAL Flour
½ cup sugar
2 tsp. baking powder
½ tsp. salt

Heat oven to 400° (mod. hot). Grease bottom of muffin cups or use paper baking cups. Beat egg with fork. Stir in milk and oil. Measure flour by dip-level-pour method or by sifting (*see p. 6*). Blend dry ingredients; stir in just until flour is moistened. *Batter should be lumpy.* Do not overmix. Fill muffin cups ⅔ full. Bake *20 to 25 min.,* or until golden brown. Muffins will have gently rounded and pebbled tops. Loosen immediately with spatula. Serve warm. *Makes 12 medium muffins.*

Whole Wheat Muffins (*Graham Gems*)

Make Popular Muffins (*above*)—except use only 1 cup flour and 2 tsp. baking powder. Add 1 cup whole wheat (graham) flour to the dry ingredients in the mixing bowl.

Surprise Muffins

The secret's inside.

Make Popular Muffins (*above*)—except fill muffin cups half full of batter, drop scant teaspoonful of jelly on center of batter, add more batter to fill cup ⅔ full. Discovering the jelly inside the baked muffin is the surprise.

Cranberry-Orange Muffins

See color picture page 85.

1 cup fresh or frozen cranberries, halved
½ cup sugar
1 egg
1 cup milk
2 tbsp. melted shortening
1 tbsp. grated orange rind
2 cups GOLD MEDAL Flour
3 tsp. baking powder
2 tbsp. sugar
1 tsp. salt

Combine cranberries and the ½ cup sugar. Let stand while mixing batter and add to batter at the last. Mix and bake as for Muffins (*above*).

Blueberry Muffins

Make Sweeter Muffins (*p. 88*)—*except* at the last blend in carefully 1 cup well drained fresh blueberries. If canned berries are used, ¾ cup.

Sour Milk Muffins

Make Popular Muffins (*p. 88*)—*except* use only 2 tsp. baking powder and add ½ tsp. soda; substitute soured milk (*see p. 26*) for sweet milk.

Wheaties Muffins

An ideal hot bread for dinner.

Make Popular Muffins (*p. 88*)—*except* use only 1 cup flour and ½ cup milk. Carefully fold in 2 cups WHEATIES at the last.

Apple Muffins

A Sunday breakfast or supper treat.

Make Sweeter Muffins (*p. 88*)—*except* blend ½ tsp. cinnamon with dry ingredients. Add 1 cup grated raw tart apple (unpared) with shortening. Bake *25 to 30 min.* If desired, sprinkle top before baking with Nut-Crunch Topping (*below*).

Nut-Crunch Topping

Mix ⅓ cup brown sugar (packed), ⅓ cup broken nuts and ½ tsp. cinnamon.

Prune Muffins

Studded with the glossy dark fruit.

Make Popular Muffins (*p. 88*)—*except* add ¼ cup brown sugar and ¼ tsp. nutmeg to flour mixture; at the last, fold in ¾ cup cut-up well drained pitted cooked prunes.

Popovers

Pumpkin Muffins

A spicy, pumpkin-flavored muffin filled with raisins.

1 egg
½ cup milk
½ cup mashed cooked or canned pumpkin
¼ cup melted shortening
1½ cups GOLD MEDAL Flour
½ cup sugar
2 tsp. baking powder
½ tsp. salt
½ tsp. cinnamon
½ tsp. nutmeg
½ cup seedless raisins

Heat oven to 400° (mod. hot). Grease bottom of muffin cups or use paper baking cups. Beat egg slightly with fork. Stir in milk, pumpkin and shortening. Measure flour by dip-level-pour method or by sifting (*see p. 6*). Blend dry ingredients and stir in just until flour is moistened. *Batter should be lumpy.* Fold in raisins. Fill greased muffin cups ⅔ full. Sprinkle ¼ tsp. sugar over each muffin. Bake *18 to 20 min.* Serve hot. *Makes 12 muffins.*

Date, Fig or Raisin Muffins

Make Popular Muffins (*p. 88*)—*except* add 1 cup finely cut-up dates or figs or raisins.

High hat muffins, popped so they are crusty shells, hollow inside. Spectacular bread for a dinner party; also delicious filled with creamed sea food or meat as a main dish. See color picture page 95.

| 1 cup GOLD MEDAL Flour | 1 cup milk |
| ½ tsp. salt | 2 eggs |

Heat oven to 425° (hot). Grease well *deep* muffin cups or custard cups. Measure flour by dip-level-pour method or by sifting (*see p. 6*). Beat all ingredients with rotary beater just until smooth. Overbeating will reduce volume. Fill greased muffin cups ¾ full or custard cups ½ full. Bake *40 to 45 min.* Serve immediately. *Makes 5 to 9 popovers.* This batter is used for Yorkshire Pudding (*p. 300*).

"Light-as-Feather" Muffins

One of the specialties of Mrs. K's Toll House, Silver Spring, Maryland, famous for its wonderful food and charming atmosphere.

¼ cup sugar
¼ cup soft shortening
1 egg
1¾ cups SOFTASILK Flour
4 tsp. baking powder
½ tsp. salt
1 cup milk

Heat oven to 375° (quick mod.). Grease bottom of muffin cups or use paper baking cups. Mix sugar and shortening well. Blend in egg. Measure flour by dip-level-pour method or by sifting (*see p. 6*). Blend dry ingredients; stir in alternately with milk. Fill muffin cups ⅔ full. Bake *20 to 23 min.* Serve hot. *Makes 14 to 16 small muffins.*

Oatmeal Muffins

They're marvelous! So moist and rich.

1 cup rolled oats
1 cup buttermilk or soured milk (*see p. 26*)
⅓ cup soft shortening (part butter)
½ cup brown sugar (packed)
1 egg
1 cup GOLD MEDAL Flour
1 tsp. baking powder
½ tsp. soda
1 tsp. salt

Heat oven to 400° (mod. hot). Grease bottom of muffin cups or use paper baking cups. Soak rolled oats in milk 1 hr. Mix shortening, sugar and egg well. Measure flour by dip-level-pour method or by sifting (*see p. 6*). Blend dry ingredients; stir into shortening mixture alternately with rolled oats and milk. Fill muffin cups ⅔ full. Bake *20 to 25 min.* Serve hot. *Makes 12 medium muffins.*

Best Bran Muffins

Make Oatmeal Muffins (*above*)—*except* omit rolled oats. After blending dry ingredients, mix with 3 cups bran, stir into shortening mixture alternately with 1 cup buttermilk.

French Breakfast Puffs

Miss Esoline Beauregard of Fort Lauderdale, Florida, said, "Please try my mother's recipe."

⅓ cup soft shortening (part butter)
½ cup sugar
1 egg
1½ cups GOLD MEDAL Flour
1½ tsp. baking powder
½ tsp. salt
¼ tsp. nutmeg
½ cup milk
⅓ cup butter, melted
½ cup sugar
1 tsp. cinnamon

Heat oven to 350° (mod.). Grease bottom of muffin cups or use paper baking cups. Mix shortening, ½ cup sugar and egg thoroughly. Measure flour by dip-level-pour method or by sifting (*see p. 6*). Blend flour, baking powder, salt and nutmeg. Stir in alternately with milk. Fill muffin cups ⅔ full. Bake *20 to 25 min.* Immediately roll in the melted butter, then in mixture of ½ cup sugar and cinnamon. Serve hot. *Makes 12 medium muffins.*

Country Breakfast Muffins (*Sour Cream*)

With that "so good" flavor and tenderness.

1 egg
1 cup commercial sour cream
2 tbsp. sugar
1 tbsp. soft shortening
1⅓ cups GOLD MEDAL Flour
1 tsp. baking powder
½ tsp. soda
½ tsp. salt

Heat oven to 400° (mod. hot). Grease bottom of muffin cups or use paper baking cups. Beat egg until light. Blend in cream, sugar and shortening. Measure flour by dip-level-pour method or by sifting (*see p. 6*). Blend dry ingredients; stir in. Fill muffin cups ⅔ full. Bake *20 to 25 min.* Serve hot. *Makes 12 medium muffins.*

White Nut Bread

Makes moist, tasty sandwiches for luncheons and lunch boxes.

¾ cup sugar
2 tbsp. soft shortening
1 egg
1½ cups milk

3 cups GOLD MEDAL Flour
3½ tsp. baking powder
1 tsp. salt
¾ cup chopped nuts

Heat oven to 350° (mod.). Grease a loaf pan, 9x5x3″ or three 20-oz. cans. Mix sugar, shortening and egg thoroughly. Stir in milk. Measure flour by dip-level-pour method or by sifting (*see p. 6*). Blend dry ingredients; stir in. Blend in nuts. Pour into pan or cans. Bake *60 to 70 min.*, or until toothpick stuck into center comes out clean. (Crack in top of loaf is characteristic.) Cool thoroughly before slicing with a thin, sharp knife.

Banana Nut Bread

Make White Nut Bread (*above*)—*except* increase sugar to 1 cup. Use only ¾ cup milk and add 1 cup mashed bananas.

Prune Nut Bread

Make White Nut Bread (*above*)—*except* use only ¼ cup milk. Add ¾ cup prune juice and 1 cup well drained, chopped, pitted, cooked prunes.

Orange Nut Bread

Make White Nut Bread (*above*)—*except* use only ¾ cup milk. Add 4 tsp. grated orange rind and ¾ cup orange juice.

Apricot Nut Bread

Make Orange Nut Bread (*above*)—*except* increase sugar to 1 cup and add 1 cup finely chopped dried apricots with the nuts.

Date-and-Nut Bread

Served by Mrs. Jack Bruce of Winnetka, Illinois.

1½ cups boiling water
1½ cups cut-up dates
½ cup brown sugar (packed)
1 tbsp. soft shortening
1 egg
2¼ cups GOLD MEDAL Flour
1 tsp. soda
½ tsp. salt
1 cup broken nuts

Heat oven to 350° (mod.). Grease a loaf pan, 9x5x3″. Pour boiling water over dates; let cool. Mix sugar, shortening and egg. Stir in dates. Measure flour by dip-level-pour method or by sifting (*see p. 6*). Blend dry ingredients; stir in. Blend in nuts. Pour into pan. Bake *60 to 70 min.*

Tropical Fruit Bread

Unusual combination of banana, apricot and bran. Given to us by Esther Roth of our staff.

⅔ cup sugar
⅓ cup shortening
2 eggs
1 cup mashed ripe bananas (2 to 3)
¼ cup buttermilk
1¼ cups GOLD MEDAL Flour
1 tsp. baking powder
½ tsp. salt
½ tsp. soda
1 cup whole bran
¾ cup chopped dried apricots
½ cup coarsely chopped walnuts

Heat oven to 350° (mod.). Grease a loaf pan, 9x5x3″. Cream sugar and shortening. Mix in eggs thoroughly. Combine bananas and buttermilk. Measure flour by dip-level-pour method or by sifting (*see p. 6*). Blend dry ingredients; add alternately with banana mixture to creamed mixture. Stir in bran, apricots and walnuts. Pour into pan. Bake *about 60 min.*

Maple Nut Bread

2½ cups GOLD MEDAL Flour
1 cup sugar
3 tsp. baking powder
½ tsp. salt
1 cup milk
1 egg, well beaten
¾ tsp. maple flavoring
1 cup coarsely chopped nuts

Heat oven to 350° (mod.). Grease a loaf pan, 9x5x3″. Measure flour by dip-level-pour method or by sifting (*see p. 6*). Blend dry ingredients in bowl. Add milk, egg and flavoring. Mix until dry ingredients are moistened. Stir in nuts. Pour into pan. Bake *1 hr.*

One of the earliest forms of baking . . . once called "hearth cakes." Dutch settlers brought pancakes to America. Whether hearty buckwheat cakes or delicate crepes, pancakes should be light, tender and uniformly golden brown. Today pancake houses featuring many varieties are gaining popularity across the nation.

HOW TO MAKE PANCAKES

1. Test griddle for right temperature.

2. Pour batter onto griddle.

3. When full of bubbles, turn pancakes.

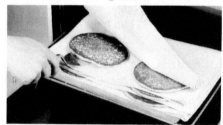

4. Keep warm until serving time.

Favorite Pancakes *The good old-fashioned kind . . . of buttermilk or sour milk.*

1 egg	1 tsp. sugar
1¼ cups buttermilk or soured milk *(see p. 26)*	1 tsp. baking powder
1¼ cups GOLD MEDAL Flour	½ tsp. soda
2 tbsp. soft shortening	½ tsp. salt

Heat griddle slowly while mixing batter. To test, sprinkle with drops of water. If bubbles "skitter around," heat is just right. (Grease griddle, if necessary.) Beat egg. Measure flour by dip-level-pour method or by sifting *(see p. 6)*. Beat in remaining ingredients until batter is smooth. Pour batter from tip of *large* spoon or from pitcher in pools a little apart (for perfectly round cakes). Turn pancakes when puffed and full of bubbles. Turn and brown other side. Keep hot by placing between folds of warm towel in warm oven. (Don't stack them!) Serve hot with butter and syrup. *Makes 16 4" pancakes.*

Sweet Milk Pancakes

Make Favorite Pancakes *(above)—except* substitute sweet milk for buttermilk, add an extra ½ tsp. baking powder and omit soda. For extra lightness, beat egg yolk, add milk, etc. Fold in stiffly beaten egg white.

▶ ALL YOU HAVE TO DO

To make pancakes thick or thin as desired: add a little more liquid to thin; make thicker by adding a little more flour.

Blueberry Pancakes

See color picture page 85.

Make Favorite Pancakes *(above)—except* add ½ cup drained fresh or frozen berries to batter, folding in carefully at the last.

Ferry Farm Sauce

As it was made by George Washington's mother.

Heat together slowly over hot water 1 cup strained honey and ½ cup maple syrup. Remove from heat and blend in 1 tsp. cinnamon.

Old-fashioned Buckwheat Cakes

They bring memories of cozy comfort at the fireside of the Henry Mausts, famous artist in Woodstock, New York.

1 pkg. active dry yeast
½ cup warm water (not hot—110 to 115°)
2 cups cold water
2 cups buckwheat flour
1 cup GOLD MEDAL Flour

1½ tsp. salt
¼ cup butter, melted
1 tbsp. molasses
1 tsp. soda dissolved in ½ cup hot water

Dissolve yeast in warm water. Add cold water. Measure Gold Medal Flour by dip-level-pour method or by sifting (*see p. 6*). Blend flours and salt; stir in. Beat vigorously until smooth. Cover; refrigerate overnight. In morning, stir in butter, molasses and soda dissolved in hot water. Let stand at room temperature 30 min. Bake as for Favorite Pancakes (*p. 92*). *Makes 36 4" pancakes.*

Wheaties Pancakes

Make Favorite Pancakes (*p. 92*)—*except* fold in ½ cup WHEATIES at the last.

Nut Pancakes

Make Favorite Pancakes (*p. 92*)—*except* add ¼ cup broken or chopped nuts to batter.

Corn Pancakes

Make Favorite Pancakes (*p. 92*)—*except* add ½ cup canned whole kernel corn, drained, to batter.

Cheese Pancakes

Make Favorite Pancakes (*p. 92*)—*except* omit sugar. Add ½ to 1½ cups grated Cheddar cheese to batter. Bake. Serve with syrup or creamed meats or vegetables.

Ham Pancakes

Make Favorite Pancakes (*p. 92*)—*except* omit sugar. Add ½ to 1½ cups ground or chopped cooked ham to batter. Bake. Serve with syrup, cranberry sauce, cheese sauce or creamed vegetables.

Banana Pancakes

Make Favorite Pancakes (*p. 92*)—*except* add 1 cup mashed ripe banana, 1 tbsp. lemon juice and 2 tbsp. sugar instead of 1 tsp. sugar. Bake. Serve with honey or currant jelly or dust with confectioners' sugar.

Delicate Fluffy Pancakes

From a wonderful cook, Mrs. Marian Bucholz of Los Angeles and Omaha.

3 egg yolks
1⅔ cups thick buttermilk
1½ cups GOLD MEDAL Flour
1 tbsp. sugar
1 tsp. baking powder
1 tsp. soda
½ tsp. salt
3 tbsp. soft butter
3 egg whites, stiffly beaten

Beat egg yolks well with rotary beater. Measure flour by dip-level-pour method or by sifting (*see p. 6*). Beat in buttermilk and mixed dry ingredients. Beat in butter. Gently fold in beaten egg whites. Bake as for Favorite Pancakes (*p. 92*). *Makes 16 4" pancakes.*

French Toast

Dip 6 slices stale bread into mixture of 2 beaten eggs, ¼ tsp. salt and ½ cup milk. Brown both sides in butter on hot griddle. Serve hot with maple syrup, jelly, honey or sprinkling of confectioners' sugar.

Oven French Toast

Heat oven to 500° (very hot). Make French Toast (*above*)—*except* place dipped slices on greased baking sheet. Bake *about 10 min.*, or until browned.

Dessert Pancakes See p. 248.

Raised Pancakes See p. 124.

The first waffle is said to have been made in 13th century England. A crusader wearing his armor accidentally sat in some freshly baked oat cakes. The cakes were flattened and bore deep imprints of the steel links. Despite this, he spread butter on the cakes and ate them. His wife, delighted with the way butter stayed in the imprints from the armor, made him put it on once a week and sit on fresh oat cakes. They were called "waffres," meaning flat honeycomb-like cakes.

Dutch colonists brought their cherished "waffre" irons to America. They were long handled and very heavy to hold over an open fire.

HOW TO MAKE WAFFLES

1. Pour batter onto center of hot waffle iron.

2. Lift off waffle carefully with fork.

Waffles *Crisp pancakes with tucks in them. See color picture page 84.*

Typical Waffles

2 eggs
2 cups buttermilk or soured milk *(see p. 26)*
1 tsp. soda
2 cups GOLD MEDAL Flour
2 tsp. baking powder
½ tsp. salt
6 tbsp. soft shortening
  (fresh bacon fat is good)

Richer Waffles

3 eggs
1½ cups buttermilk or soured milk *(see p. 26)*
1 tsp. soda
1¾ cups GOLD MEDAL Flour
2 tsp. baking powder
½ tsp. salt
½ cup soft shortening
  (fresh bacon fat is good)

Heat waffle iron while mixing batter. If no automatic heat control, test by sprinkling grids with drops of water. If water "skitters around" before evaporating, iron is just right. Beat eggs well. Measure flour by dip-level-pour method or by sifting *(see p. 6)*. Beat in remaining ingredients with rotary beater until smooth. Pour from cup or pitcher onto center of hot waffle iron. Spread to cover surface. Do not keep iron open longer than necessary. Bake until steaming stops. Lift carefully with fork. Serve hot with butter and syrup. *Makes 8 waffles.*

Sweet Milk Waffles

Make either recipe *(above)—except* omit soda and increase baking powder to 4 tsp.; substitute sweet milk for soured milk; and separate eggs. Beat egg whites until stiff and fold in last.

Nut Waffles

These are good with butter and syrup but a special treat for dessert with ice cream and chocolate sauce.

Make either recipe *(above)—except* sprinkle 2 tbsp. coarsely cut or broken toasted nuts over batter as soon as it has been poured onto iron. Bake.

Blueberry Waffles

Make Richer Waffles *(above)—except* sprinkle 2 tbsp. fresh blueberries or well drained canned blueberries over batter as soon as it has been poured onto the iron. Bake.

Cheese-and-Bacon Waffles

Make Typical Waffles *(above)—except* fold ½ cup grated Cheddar cheese into batter. Pour onto iron. Lay short strip of bacon across batter. Bake.

Raised Waffles See p. 124.

DINNER QUICK BREADS

Popovers, page 89

Biscuits, page 76

Corn Sticks, page 80

Steamed Brown Bread, page 96

Cranberry-Orange Bread

This fruity, attractive bread is a favorite of Mrs. Richard Kranz, who serves it when neighbors drop in for morning or afternoon coffee.

2 cups GOLD MEDAL Flour
1 cup sugar
1½ tsp. baking powder
½ tsp. soda
½ tsp. salt
2 tbsp. shortening
grated rind and juice of 1 orange plus
    water to make ¾ cup
1 egg, beaten
1 cup raw cranberries, cut in halves

Heat oven to 350° (mod.). Grease a loaf pan, 9x5x3″. Measure flour by dip-level-pour method or by sifting (*see p. 6*). Blend dry ingredients. Mix in shortening, orange rind, juice and egg. Fold in cranberries. Pour into pan. Bake *1 hr.* Cool thoroughly before slicing with a thin, sharp knife.

Pineapple Nut Bread

Moist new fruit loaf—with wonderful aroma and flavor of pineapple, the fruit that symbolizes hospitality. See color picture page 85.

¾ cup brown sugar (packed)
3 tbsp. soft butter
2 eggs
2 cups GOLD MEDAL Flour
2 tsp. baking powder
½ tsp. salt
¼ tsp. soda
1 can (8½ oz.) crushed pineapple
¾ cup chopped nuts
2 tbsp. granulated sugar
½ tsp. cinnamon

Heat oven to 350° (mod.). Grease a loaf pan, 9x5x3″. Cream brown sugar, butter and eggs until fluffy. Measure flour by dip-level-pour method or by sifting (*see p. 6*). Blend dry ingredients. Stir half the flour mixture into creamed mixture, add pineapple and juice, then remaining flour. Blend in nuts. Pour into pan. Mix granulated sugar and cinnamon; sprinkle over top. Bake *60 to 70 min.* or until toothpick stuck into center comes out clean. Cool before slicing with a thin, sharp knife.

Steamed Brown Bread

Serve with baked beans. See color picture page 95.

1 cup rye flour or GOLD MEDAL Flour
1 cup corn meal
1 cup whole wheat flour
2 tsp. soda
1 tsp. salt
2 cups buttermilk or soured milk (*see p. 26*)
¾ cup molasses

Measure Gold Medal Flour by dip-level-pour method or by sifting (*see p. 6*). Mix dry ingredients. Stir in milk and molasses. Beat well. Fill greased molds ⅔ full (using two 1-lb. coffee cans or one 7″ tube-center mold). Lay waxed paper over the top. Steam *3 hr.* (For method, see How to Steam and improvise steamer, *p. 230.*) Serve piping hot with butter.

Timbale Cases and Rosettes

Serve cases with creamed food, rosettes for dessert.

½ cup GOLD MEDAL Flour
1 tbsp. sugar
½ tsp. salt
½ cup water or milk
1 egg, slightly beaten
1 tbsp. vegetable oil

Measure flour by dip-level-pour method or by sifting (*see p. 6*). Blend dry ingredients. Mix remaining ingredients; stir in. Strain mixture. Heat timbale or rosette iron in hot fat (400°) 3″ deep in small saucepan. Tap off excess fat. Dip into batter until ⅔ covered. Immerse in hot fat. Fry until delicately browned. (See Tips for Deep Fat Frying, *p. 82.*) Remove, tip upside down to drain. Push off case. Stir batter each time before dipping in iron. *Makes 18.*

▶ **ALL YOU HAVE TO DO**

If rosettes don't come off iron: fry a little longer. If not crisp, fry a little slower.

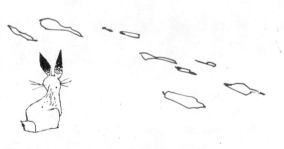

YEAST BREADS

"Back of the loaf is the snowy flour
Back of the flour, the mill,
And back of the mill is the wheat and the shower,
And the sun and the Father's will."

In these charming yet simple lines, Maltbie D. Babcock has summed up the age-old processes of milling and bread-baking from the "amber waves of grain" to the golden-crusted loaf.

Each new chapter in the history of man has brought a new chapter in the history of bread. Though the cave men baked cakes of grain in the sun, it was the ancient Egyptians who first milled flour and later lightened bread with fermentation. The Egyptians used bread as money, paying the laborers who built the pyramids three loaves of bread and two jugs of beer each day.

The arts of milling and baking soon traveled to Rome and from there to Gaul, Spain and Britain. These early European bakers used brewer's yeast or "barm," the thick scum strained from the surface of fermenting wine, to leaven bread. The class system of the medieval world made dark rye bread the staple food of the working class while the rich enjoyed fine white bread.

As time went on, each country and people developed characteristic breads which now form a rich heritage for us in America.

THE STAFF OF LIFE
(complete index in back of book)

TIMESAVING TIPS

To keep bread fresh: keep wrapped in original wrapper or wrap in polyethylene bag or in aluminum foil.

To reheat buns and rolls: place in paper bag. Sprinkle bag with water. Heat *at 400°* (mod. hot). Or heat slowly in bun warmer or heavy covered saucepan with a piece of aluminum foil in bottom. Heat *10 min.*

For yeast rolls at a moment's notice: try Brown 'n Serve rolls. For breakfast: sprinkle rolls with cinnamon-sugar or with a streusel mixture (*p. 113*) before baking.

To use leftover bread: toast and grate for crumbs or cut in cubes and dry in oven. Seal in airtight container for topping casseroles (*p. 391*) or for bread stuffing (*p. 324*). Or give the birds a treat by offering bread on a bird feeder.

To use non-fat dry milk in bread: reconstitute as directed on package, scald as recipe directs and use in recipe.

To cut cinnamon roll dough easily: pull string under roll of dough (*p. 112*), bring ends together, cross and pull until string cuts through dough. Repeat for each slice.

MEALTIME MAGIC

TEEN PIZZA PARTY

Individual Muffin Pizzas (*p. 120*)
(let teens choose toppings: pepperoni, ham, sliced mushrooms, Cheddar or Mozzarella cheese)
Carrot Sticks   Celery Sticks
Spumoni Cake (*p. 237*)
Bottled Soft Drinks

FOR THE GIRLS

Consommé
Fresh Fruit Salad
Chocolate Cinnamon Buns (*p. 122*)
Vanilla Ice Cream with
Peppermint Candy Sauce (*p. 392*)
Coffee

Note: You no longer need to sift flour for recipes in this chapter. Measure Gold Medal flour by dipping nested measuring cups into flour and leveling off with spatula.

WHAT EVERY COOK NEEDS TO KNOW ABOUT YEAST BREADS

BAKE WITH CARE

Families love the tantalizing aroma and tempting appearance of bread, rolls and coffee cakes. And you, the cook, can find such satisfaction in working with yeast doughs that the extra effort will be well worth it.

Did you know that yeast is actually a tiny plant that feeds on the sugar in the dough and causes it to rise? During rising, doughs must be kept warm (85°). If kitchen is cool, place dough on a rack over a bowl of hot water and cover completely with a towel.

To make good breads, you will need enriched all-purpose flour, fresh yeast, salt, liquid, sugar and usually fat. A special bread flour, high in protein, is available in certain areas. Recipes in this book specify active dry yeast which works best at 110 to 115° (water feels quite warm when dropped on wrist). If compressed yeast is used, crumble it into the total amount of liquid called for in the recipe. The milk or water should be 80 to 85° (feels slightly cool when dropped on the wrist).

Step-by-step directions for mixing bread and shaping the loaf are on *pp. 102–103.*

Refrigerator doughs (*p. 123*) are popular with cooks who enjoy baking fresh rolls or coffee cakes each day. Any dough except plain bread dough can be refrigerated overnight; while dough made with at least ¼ cup sugar and water will keep as long as 5 days.

Rolls, both plain and fancy, for breakfast or dinner, may be made from a basic sweet dough like Sweet Roll Dough (*p. 108*). Start with Old-fashioned Biscuits and you'll soon be turning out fancy Salt Sticks and Crescents. Sweet rolls, coffee cakes and fruited holiday breads may be made from the basic sweet dough or from their own recipes.

Newest members of the yeast bread family are the streamlined breads (*pp. 104–105*). Mixed on the electric mixer rather than being kneaded, they are moist and somewhat coarse in texture. Even a novice bread baker can turn out crusty fragrant loaves from these easy-to-follow recipes.

. . . .

SERVE WITH FLAIR

Appetite is the only garnish fresh yeast breads need—have soft butter and a favorite jelly or jam handy, of course.

Dress up sweet rolls and coffee cakes with a creamy icing and sprinkle with nuts or colored sugars.

White Bread (*p. 102*), Sour Dough French Bread (*p. 119*) or a favorite loaf from the neighborhood bakery will disappear like magic when spread with one of the savory Seasoned Butters (*p. 120*) and reheated.

NEW ADVENTURES IN YEAST BREADS

Chocolate Cinnamon Buns (*p. 122*)—True chocolate flavor in a light tender yeast roll.

Italian Bread Sticks (*p. 123*)—Impress your guests with these at your next dinner party.

Overnight Cinnamon Coffee Cake (*p. 122*)—Rich dough makes a coffee cake and 12 rolls.

Peanut Butter Bread (*p. 104*)—One of many delightful variations of our streamlined loaves.

Sour Dough French Bread (*p. 119*)—Based on old-fashioned starter dough, loaves are crusty outside, soft inside.

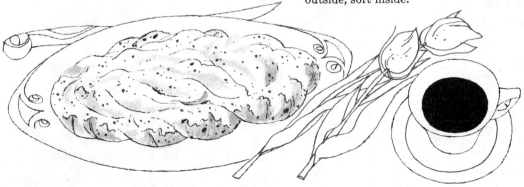

OUR DAILY BREAD

White Bread

So easy—so good! Warm mixing bowl with hot water in cold weather.

2 loaves

2 pkg. active dry yeast
½ cup warm water (not hot—110 to 115°*)
1¾ cups lukewarm milk**, water or potato water
7 to 7¼ cups GOLD MEDAL Flour
3 tbsp. sugar
1 tbsp. salt
2 tbsp. soft shortening

4 loaves

2 pkg. active dry yeast
1 cup warm water (not hot—110 to 115°*)
3½ cups lukewarm milk**, water or potato water
14 to 14½ cups GOLD MEDAL Flour
6 tbsp. sugar
2 tbsp. salt
¼ cup soft shortening

In bowl, dissolve yeast in water. Measure flour by dip-level-pour method or by sifting (*see p. 6*). Add milk, half the flour, sugar, salt and shortening to yeast. Beat until smooth and batter "sheets" off spoon. With hand, mix in enough remaining flour until dough cleans the bowl. Turn onto lightly floured board. Cover; let rest 10 to 15 min. Knead 10 min., until smooth and blistered. Place in greased bowl, bring greased side up. Cover with cloth. Let rise in warm place (85°) until double, about 1 hr.

Punch down, cover and let rise again until almost double, about 30 min. Divide into two parts. Round up and let rest 10 to 15 min. Shape into loaves (*picture directions opposite*). Place in greased loaf pans, 9x5x3", sealed-edge-down. Grease top of loaf. Cover with cloth; let rise until sides reach top of pan and center is well rounded, 50 to 60 min. Test loaf by touching gently at corner. If a slight indentation remains, loaves are ready for baking. Be careful that loaves do not rise too much.

Heat oven to 425° (hot). Place loaves in center of oven not touching each other or sides of oven. (Heat must circulate freely for even baking.) Bake *25 to 30 min.*, or until deep golden brown. To test the loaf, tap the crust. Loaf should sound hollow when done. If it doesn't, bake a few minutes longer. Immediately remove bread from pans. Place on wire cooling racks or across top edges of the bread pans. Do not place in direct draft.

*A few drops on wrist will feel quite warm. **Scalded then cooled.

WHEN MAKING BREAD AT HIGH ALTITUDES

At high altitudes, dough tends to rise more rapidly—making it coarse-grained. General principles to follow which will help give fine-textured bread at high altitudes are:

1. Allow bread to rise for a shorter time—just until doubled or until the dough reaches top of pan and center is well rounded.

2. Use less yeast, **or** allow bread to rise a third time (instead of twice) before shaping.

To make White Bread with compressed yeast: Use ½ cup lukewarm water (80 to 85°—a few drops on the wrist will feel slightly cool).

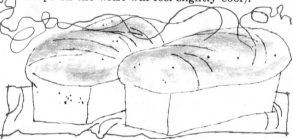

1. Flatten dough into an oblong, 12 x 8″. Press out all air with heel of hand, with back of knuckles or with fingertips.

2. Fold dough in half lengthwise. Flatten again to press out air, working from center of dough to ends. Oblong will be 12 x 8″.

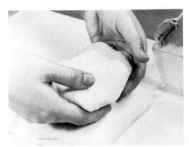

3. Bring 2 ends to center, overlap and seal well by pressing down firmly with knuckles. Press out air, keeping width same as length of pan (9″).

4. Take farthest narrow edge and roll dough toward you as tight as possible, sealing with thumbs after each roll. After last turn, seal edge carefully by pinching.

5. Roll back and forth to tighten. Seal each end by pressing with edge of hands; fold "tails" under. Smooth loaf lightly with hands.

6. Place in greased loaf pan, 9x5x3″ sealed-edge-down (pan ⅔ full). Set on rack over bowl of hot water, cover, let rise in warm place about 1 hr.

7. If slight dent remains, loaf is ready to bake.

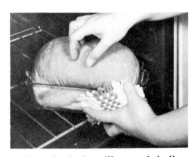

8. Tap loaf; it will sound hollow when done.

9. Cool on racks away from direct draft.

Glass, darkened metal or alumilite (dull finished aluminum) are ideal pans for baking bread. They give a good, brown crust. To darken a shiny pan, place ungreased in 425° oven for 4 to 5 hr.

For a soft, bright, tender crust, brush loaves with soft butter or other shortening after removing from pan. Cover with towel a few minutes.

For a crisp crust, do not grease loaves. Do not cover. Keep out of draft to prevent cracking.

Streamlined White Bread

Easiest bread ever . . . no kneading . . . mix dough on mixer. A crusty even-textured loaf. Extra moist so it keeps better.

1¼ cups warm water (not hot—110 to 115°)
1 pkg. active dry yeast
2 tbsp. soft shortening

2 tsp. salt
2 tbsp. sugar
3 cups GOLD MEDAL Flour

In bowl, dissolve yeast in water. Measure flour by dip-level-pour method or by sifting (*see p. 6*). Add shortening, salt, sugar and half the flour to yeast. Beat 2 min., medium speed on mixer or 300 vigorous strokes by hand. Scrape bowl frequently. Add remaining flour; blend in with spoon. Scrape batter from sides of bowl. Cover with cloth; let rise in warm place (85°) until double, about 30 min. (If kitchen is cool, place dough on a rack over a bowl of hot water and cover completely with a towel.)

Stir down batter by beating about 25 strokes. Spread batter evenly in greased loaf pan, 8½x4½x2¾" or 9x5x3". Batter will be sticky. Smooth out top of loaf by flouring hand and patting into shape.

Again let rise in warm place (85°) until batter reaches ¼" from top of 8½" pan or 1" from top of 9" pan, about 40 min.

Heat oven to 375° (quick mod.). Bake *45 to 50 min.*, or until brown. To test loaf, tap the top crust; it should sound hollow. Immediately remove from pan. Place on cooling rack or across bread pans. Brush top with melted butter or shortening. Do not place in direct draft. Cool before cutting. A saw-tooth knife is especially good for cutting. Slice with a sawing motion rather than pressing down, making slices slightly thicker than usual. *Makes 1 loaf.*

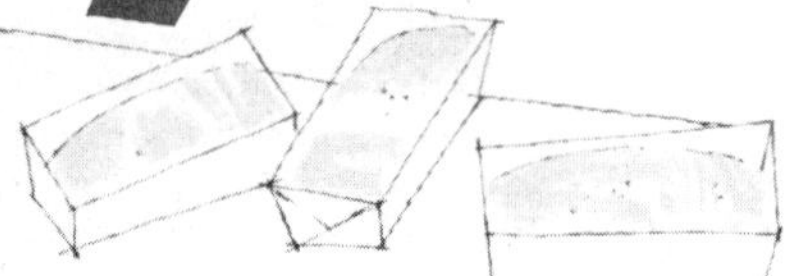

Peanut Butter Bread

A pleasing peanut butter flavor. Good fresh or toasted with jam or jelly.

1¼ cups warm water (not hot—110 to 115°)
1 pkg. active dry yeast
¼ cup chunk-style peanut butter
¼ cup finely chopped peanuts
2 tsp. salt
¼ cup brown sugar (packed)
3 cups GOLD MEDAL Flour

Mix and bake as for Streamlined White Bread (*above*). Cover loaf with brown paper during last half of baking.

Little Loaves of Streamlined Bread

Serve tiny hot-from-the-oven loaves on individual bread boards to add a special touch to a dinner party. Or serve little loaves and homemade jam as evening refreshments.

Make Streamlined White (*above*), Herb or Whole Wheat Bread (*p. 105*)—*except* divide batter into 6 greased miniature loaf pans, 4¾x2⅝x1½". Let rise until batter reaches tops of pans, about 40 min. Bake *30 to 35 min.*

Italian Christmas Bread

Baked in two 1-lb. coffee cans.

Make Streamlined White Bread (*above*)—*except* with second addition of flour add:

¼ cup raisins
¼ cup cut-up candied fruit
¼ cup chopped nuts
¾ tsp. anise
¼ tsp. vanilla

Spread batter in two greased 1-lb. coffee cans. Let rise until batter reaches ¾" from top. Bake *about 40 min.*

Swiss Christmas Bread

Make Streamlined White Bread (*above*)—*except* add ¼ tsp. nutmeg, ¼ tsp. mace, ⅛ tsp. cloves, ¼ cup raisins, ¼ cup cut-up candied cherries, 2 tbsp. chopped nuts and 2 tbsp. cut-up citron with second addition of flour. Frost while warm with a confectioners' sugar icing.

English Christmas Bread

Make Streamlined White Bread (*above*)—*except* add ¼ tsp. nutmeg, ½ tsp. allspice, ½ tsp. caraway seeds, ¼ cup currants, ¼ cup raisins and ¼ cup cut-up citron with second addition of flour.

Easy Oatmeal Bread

¾ cup boiling water
½ cup rolled oats
3 tbsp. soft shortening
¼ cup light molasses
2 tsp. salt

¼ cup warm water (not hot—110 to 115°)
1 pkg. active dry yeast
1 egg
2¾ cups GOLD MEDAL Flour

Stir together boiling water, oats, shortening, molasses and salt in large mixer bowl. Cool to lukewarm. Dissolve yeast in warm water. Measure flour by dip-level-pour method or by sifting (*see p. 6*). Add yeast, egg and half the flour to lukewarm mixture. Beat 2 min., medium speed on mixer or 300 vigorous strokes by hand. Scrape sides and bottom of bowl frequently. Add remaining flour; blend in with spoon until smooth. Spread batter evenly in greased loaf pan, 8½x4½x2¾" or 9x5x3". Smooth out top of loaf by flouring hand and patting into shape.

Let rise in warm place (85°) until batter reaches top of 8½" pan or 1" from top of 9" pan, about 1½ hr. (If kitchen is cool, place dough on a rack over a bowl of hot water and cover completely with a towel.)

Heat oven to 375° (quick mod.). Bake *50 to 55 min.* To test loaf, tap the top crust; it should sound hollow. Crust will be a dark brown. Immediately remove from pan. Place on cooling rack or across bread pans. Brush top with melted butter or shortening. Do not place in direct draft. Cool before cutting. *Makes 1 loaf.*

Rye Bread

1¼ cups warm water (not hot—110 to 115°)
1 pkg. active dry yeast
2 tbsp. soft shortening
2 tsp. salt
1 tbsp. caraway seeds, if desired
2 tbsp. brown sugar, light molasses or honey
1 cup rye flour
2½ cups GOLD MEDAL Flour

Mix and bake as for Streamlined White Bread (*p. 104*).

Whole Wheat Bread

1¼ cups warm water (not hot—110 to 115°)
1 pkg. active dry yeast
2 tbsp. soft shortening
2 tsp. salt
2 tbsp. honey, brown sugar or light molasses
1 cup whole wheat flour
2 cups GOLD MEDAL Flour

Mix and bake as for Streamlined White Bread (*p. 104*).

Herb Bread

Savory accompaniment to baked ham, roast or fried chicken.

Make Streamlined White Bread (*p. 104*)—*except* add 1 tsp. caraway seeds, ½ tsp. nutmeg, ½ tsp. crumbled or powdered sage with first addition of flour.

Anadama Bread

The name comes from a New England fisherman whose lazy wife always served him corn meal mush and molasses. One day, tired of the same corn meal mush for dinner, he mixed it with flour and yeast and baked it as bread, saying "Anna damn her." See color picture pp. 100-101.

Make Easy Oatmeal Bread (*above*)—*except* use yellow corn meal in place of rolled oats. Sprinkle dough in pan with a little corn meal and salt before baking.

Calico Bread

See color picture pp. 100-101.

Make Streamlined White Bread (*p. 104*)—*except* use only 2½ cups white flour and ½ cup *unsifted* whole wheat flour. Add 2 cups white flour in first mixing. After beating, pour half of batter into another bowl. With spoon blend in the extra ½ cup white flour. Blend whole wheat flour into second part of batter. Let rise. Spoon small amounts of light and dark batters alternately into greased loaf pan to give patchwork quilt effect. Again let rise and bake.

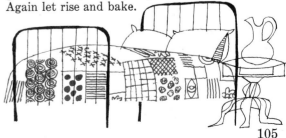

Rich Egg Bread

Yellow-rich and tender. And it makes such good toast.

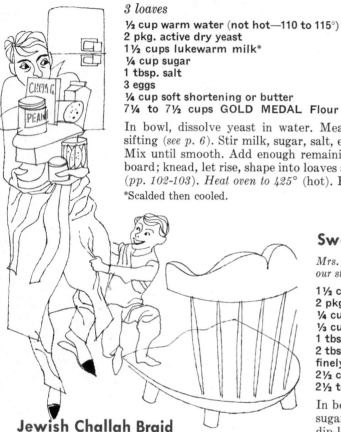

3 loaves	*1 loaf*
½ cup warm water (not hot—110 to 115°)	¼ cup warm water (not hot—110 to 115°)
2 pkg. active dry yeast	1 pkg. active dry yeast
1½ cups lukewarm milk*	½ cup lukewarm milk*
¼ cup sugar	1 tbsp. sugar
1 tbsp. salt	1 tsp. salt
3 eggs	1 egg
¼ cup soft shortening or butter	1 tbsp. soft shortening or butter
7¼ to 7½ cups GOLD MEDAL Flour	2¾ to 3 cups GOLD MEDAL Flour

In bowl, dissolve yeast in water. Measure flour by dip-level-pour method or by sifting (*see p. 6*). Stir milk, sugar, salt, eggs, shortening and half the flour into yeast. Mix until smooth. Add enough remaining flour to handle easily. Turn onto floured board; knead, let rise, shape into loaves and let rise again as directed for White Bread (*pp. 102-103*). *Heat oven to 425° (hot). Bake 25 to 30 min.*

*Scalded then cooled.

Jewish Challah Braid

Simplified version of the picturesque festival bread. Sprinkle with sesame or poppy seeds. See color picture pp. 100-101.

Make dough for 1 loaf of Rich Egg Bread (*above*). When ready to shape, divide into 3 equal parts. Roll each into a 14″ strand. Place close together on lightly greased baking sheet. Braid the strands gently and loosely. Do not stretch. Fasten ends; tuck under securely. Brush with butter. Cover with damp cloth; let rise until double, 40 to 50 min. Brush with Egg Yolk Glaze (*p. 115*). Bake at 375° (quick mod.) *25 to 30 min. Makes 1 braid.*

New England Raisin Bread

An old stand-by made for special occasions.

Make 3 loaves Rich Egg Bread (*above*)—except mix in 2 cups raisins. Before baking, brush loaves with melted butter, then sprinkle them with sugar.

Swedish Limpa (*Rye*)

Mrs. Donald F. Peterson (formerly Bernice Anderson of our staff) likes to serve Swedish Limpa on a copper tray.

1½ cups warm water (not hot—110 to 115°)
2 pkg. active dry yeast
¼ cup molasses
⅓ cup sugar
1 tbsp. salt
2 tbsp. soft shortening
finely grated rind of 1 to 2 oranges
2½ cups rye flour
2½ to 3 cups GOLD MEDAL Flour

In bowl, dissolve yeast in water. Stir in molasses, sugar, salt, shortening and rind. Measure flour by dip-level-pour method or by sifting (*see p. 6*). Mix in rye flour until smooth. Add enough remaining flour to handle easily. Turn onto floured board; knead, let rise as for White Bread (*p. 102*). Shape into 2 round, slightly flattened loaves. Place on opposite corners of greased baking sheet sprinkled with corn meal. Cover with cloth. Let rise about 1 hr. *Heat oven to 375° (quick mod.). Bake 30 to 35 min.*

Pumpernickel (*Rye*)

1½ cups warm water (not hot—110 to 115°)
3 pkg. active dry yeast
½ cup molasses
4 tsp. salt
2 tbsp. soft shortening
2 tbsp. caraway seeds
2¾ cups rye flour
3½ to 4 cups GOLD MEDAL Flour

Mix and bake as for Swedish Limpa (*above*).

Lowell Inn Crescent Rolls

These tender, rich, golden brown crescents have been made famous by Nell Palmer and her son, Arthur, of beautiful Lowell Inn, "Mount Vernon of the West," at Stillwater, Minnesota.

¾ cup warm water (not hot—110 to 115°)
2 pkg. active dry yeast
½ cup sugar
1 tsp. salt

2 eggs
½ cup soft shortening (part butter)
4 cups GOLD MEDAL Flour

In bowl, dissolve yeast in water. Measure flour by dip-level-pour method or by sifting (*see p. 6*). Stir remaining ingredients except half of flour into yeast. Add rest of flour; mix until smooth. Scrape dough from sides of bowl, cover with cloth. Let rise in warm place (85°) until double, about 1½ hr. Divide in half. Shape as Butterhorns (*p. 108*). Cover, let rise until double, 1 hr. Brush with butter. *Heat oven to 400° (mod. hot). Bake 12 to 15 min.*, or until rich golden brown. *Makes 32 rolls.*

Bran Pan Biscuits

Often made for very special luncheons in our Early American dining room.

1 cup warm water (not hot—110 to 115°)
1 pkg. active dry yeast
¼ cup brown sugar (packed)
1½ tsp. salt
½ cup whole bran or rolled oats
1 egg
3 tbsp. soft shortening
3½ to 3¾ cups GOLD MEDAL Flour

In bowl, dissolve yeast in water. Measure flour by dip-level-pour method or by sifting (*see p. 6*). Stir remaining ingredients except half of flour into yeast. Stir with spoon until smooth. Add just enough flour until easy to handle. Mix with hand. Place greased-side-up in greased bowl. Cover with cloth; let rise in warm place (85°) until double, 1½ hr. Shape into Old-fashioned Biscuits (*p. 108*). Flour or grease fingers while shaping as dough is sticky. Cover and let rise until double, 45 min. *Heat oven to 375° (quick mod.). Bake 20 to 25 min.*, *Makes 2 doz. biscuits.*

Quick Buttermilk Rolls

¼ cup warm water (not hot—110 to 115°)
1 pkg. active dry yeast
¾ cup lukewarm buttermilk
¼ tsp. soda
1 tsp. sugar
1 tsp. salt
3 tbsp. soft shortening
2½ cups GOLD MEDAL Flour

In bowl, dissolve yeast in water. Measure flour by dip-level-pour method or by sifting (*see p. 6*). Stir rest of ingredients except half of flour into yeast. Add rest of flour; mix with hand. Turn onto floured board. Knead until smooth. Shape as desired (*pp. 108–109*). Let rise until double about 1¼ hr. *Heat oven to 400° (mod. hot). Bake 15 to 20 min. Makes 1½ doz.*

Whole Wheat Buttermilk Rolls

See color picture pp. 100-101.

Make same as Quick Buttermilk Rolls (*above*)— *except* use whole wheat flour for half of white flour.

Double-Quick Dinner Rolls

Just right for the small family. Vary by sprinkling ¼ tsp. poppy or sesame seeds over each roll before second rising.

1 cup warm water (not hot—110 to 115°)
1 pkg. active dry yeast
2 tbsp. sugar
2¼ cups GOLD MEDAL Flour

1 tsp. salt
1 egg
2 tbsp. soft shortening

In bowl, dissolve yeast in water. Measure flour by dip-level-pour method or by sifting (*see p. 6*). Stir sugar, half of flour and salt into yeast. Beat with spoon until smooth. Add egg and shortening. Beat in rest of flour until smooth. Scrape sides of bowl and cover with cloth. Let rise in warm place (85°) until double, about 30 min.

Grease 12 large muffin cups. Stir down raised dough. Spoon into muffin cups filling ½ full. Again let rise in a warm place until dough reaches tops of muffin cups, 20 to 30 min. *Heat oven to 400° (mod. hot). Bake 15 to 20 min. Makes 12 rolls.*

Sweet Roll Dough

The basic magic dough to create glamorous coffee cakes, such as Swedish Tea Ring and Stollen, as well as dinner and luncheon rolls in many interesting shapes. Follow the large recipe or the small recipe according to what you plan to bake.

Large Recipe

½ cup warm water (not hot—110 to 115°)
2 pkg. active dry yeast
1½ cups lukewarm milk*
½ cup sugar
2 tsp. salt
2 eggs
½ cup soft shortening
7 to 7½ cups GOLD MEDAL Flour

Small Recipe

¼ cup warm water (not hot—110 to 115°)
1 pkg. active dry yeast
¾ cup lukewarm milk*
¼ cup sugar
1 tsp. salt
1 egg
¼ cup soft shortening
3½ to 3¾ cups GOLD MEDAL Flour

In bowl, dissolve yeast in water. Measure flour by dip-level-pour method or by sifting (*see p. 6*). Add milk, sugar, salt, egg, shortening and half of flour to yeast. Mix with spoon until smooth. Add enough remaining flour to handle easily. Turn onto lightly floured board; knead until smooth (5 min.). Round up in greased bowl, bring greased side up. Cover with cloth. Let rise in warm place (85°) until double, about 1½ hr. (If kitchen is cool, place dough on a rack over a bowl of hot water, and cover completely with a towel.) Punch down; let rise again until almost double, about 30 min. Shape, let rise and bake as directed in specific recipes.

*Scald milk then cool to lukewarm to destroy enzymes which make doughs sticky and hard to handle.

Sweet Roll Dough with Compressed Yeast

Make Sweet Roll Dough (*above*)—*except* use lukewarm water (80 to 85°—not hot, not cold when tested on wrist). Use 2 pkg. moist compressed yeast and ½ cup lukewarm water for Large Recipe, 1 pkg. moist compressed yeast and ¼ cup lukewarm water for Small Recipe.

Richer Sweet Dough

Make Sweet Roll Dough (*above*)—*except* use only ½ cup milk, 1 tsp. salt and 4½ to 5 cups flour for Large Recipe and ¼ cup milk, ½ tsp. salt and 2¼ to 2½ cups flour for Small Recipe.

▶ **ALL YOU HAVE TO DO**
To use egg yolks in these doughs: use 2 yolks plus 1 tbsp. water in place of 1 whole egg.

ROLLS OF ALL SHAPES

See color picture pp. 100-101.

Shape Sweet Roll Dough (*above*) as desired . . . just follow sketches and directions below and on p. 109. Let rise until light, 15 to 20 min. *Heat oven to 400° (mod. hot).* Bake *12 to 15 min.* in lightly greased pan, baking sheet or muffin pan. Serve piping hot.

Old-fashioned Biscuits

Form dough into balls ⅓ size desired. Place close together in a greased round pan.

Crescents (*Butterhorns*)

Roll dough about ¼″ thick into a 12″ circle. Spread with soft butter. Cut into 16 pie-shaped pieces. Beginning at rounded edge, roll up. Place on pan, point underneath.

Dinner Rolls

Roll dough into cylindrical shapes with tapered ends; place on pan.

Cloverleaf Rolls

Form bits of dough into balls about 1″ in diameter. Place 3 balls in each greased muffin cup.

Quick Four Leaf Clover Rolls

Place 2″ ball of dough in each greased muffin cup. With scissors, cut each ball of dough in half, then in quarters.

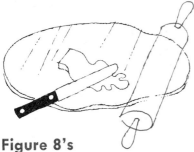

For twisted shapes *(below)*, roll dough into an oblong 12″ wide and a little less than ½″ thick. Spread with soft butter. Fold ½ of dough over the other half. Cut into strips ½″ wide and 6″ long.

Figure 8's

Hold one end of strip in one hand and twist the other end . . . stretching it slightly until the two ends when brought together on greased baking sheet will form a figure 8.

Twists

Same as Figure 8's, but give strip additional twist just before placing it on baking sheet.

Snails

Twist and hold one end of the strip down on baking sheet. Wind strip around and around. Tuck end under.

Picnic Buns

Use Small Recipe Sweet Roll Dough *(p. 108)*. Divide in 2 parts. Roll each into a 7½″ square, ½″ thick. Cut into 9 buns, each 2½″ square. Place on greased baking sheet. Let rise until double. *Heat oven to 400°* (mod. hot). Bake *12 to 15 min.,* or until brown. *Makes 1½ doz.*

Parkerhouse Rolls

Roll dough ¼″ thick. Cut with biscuit cutter. Brush with melted butter. Make crease across each with back of knife. Fold so top half slightly overlaps. Press edges together at crease. Place close together in pan.

Clothespin Crullers

Wrap strip around greased clothespin so edges barely touch. When baked, twist clothespin and pull out. May be filled with jelly or one of fruit fillings *(p. 114).*

Knots

Twist and tie each strip into a knot. Press ends down on greased baking sheet.

Toad-In-Hole *(Turk's Cap)*

Twist and tie each strip with a knot in one end of strip. Then pull the longer end through center of knot.

Butter Fluffs *(Fan Tans)*

Roll dough ⅛″ thick into oblong 9″ wide. Spread with soft butter. Cut into 6 long strips 1½″ wide. Stack 6 strips evenly, one on top of other. Cut into 1″ pieces. Place cut-side-down in greased muffin cups.

Cocktail Buns See p. 58.

Salt Sticks

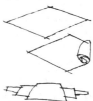

Roll dough very thin into oblong 8″ wide. Cut into 4″ squares. Starting at a corner, roll each square diagonally to opposite corner. Round the ends. Brush with egg yolk and sprinkle with coarse salt.

Stollen

Mrs. Allan B. Wilson (formerly Mary Madison of our staff) likes to bake this for friends at Christmas. See color picture opposite.

Make Small Recipe Sweet Roll Dough (*p. 108*)—*except* add with first addition of flour:

½ cup chopped blanched almonds
¼ cup *each* cut-up citron and candied cherries
1 cup raisins
1 tbsp. grated lemon rind

After dough rises, roll or pat out into an oval, about 12x8″. Spread with soft butter. Fold in two the long way. Form into a crescent. Press folded edge firmly so it won't spring open (*see below*). Place on greased baking sheet. Brush top with butter. Let rise until double, 35 to 45 min. *Heat oven to 375° (quick mod.). Bake 30 to 35 min.*, or until golden brown. Frost while warm with Quick White Icing (*below*). Decorate with blanched almond halves, pieces of citron and halves of candied cherries to simulate poinsettias. Or dust top with confectioners' sugar. *Makes 1 Stollen.*

Quick White Icing

Sift a little confectioners' sugar into bowl . . . moisten with cream or milk to spreading consistency. Add flavoring. Spread over slightly warm breads.

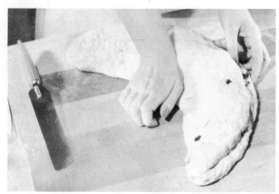

Bread-Tray Stollen

Make Stollen (*above*)—*except* divide dough into 2 parts to make 2 small Stollen. To serve, cut without separating slices, spread butter between, place on oblong bread plate.

Bohemian Braid

A fruited nut braid, elegant for the holidays. See color picture opposite.

Make Large Recipe Sweet Roll Dough (*p. 108*)—*except*, with first addition of flour, add:

2 tsp. grated lemon rind
¼ tsp. mace
1 cup raisins
1 cup chopped blanched almonds

After dough rises, divide dough into 2 portions to make 2 braids. Divide each portion into 4 equal parts. Shape 3 of the parts into 14″ strands. Place on lightly greased baking sheet. Braid loosely as shown in picture below, fastening strands at one end, then tucking under.

Divide fourth part of dough into 3 pieces and shape into 3 strands each 12″ long. Braid these 3 strands and place this small braid on top of large braid, as pictured below. Make another double braid from second portion of dough.

Cover and let rise until double, 45 to 60 min. Brush with Egg Yolk Glaze (*p. 115*), if desired. *Heat oven to 350° (mod.). Bake 30 to 40 min.*, or until golden brown. Ice while warm with Quick White Icing (*at left*), decorate with candied cherries and pecan halves. *Makes 2 large braids.*

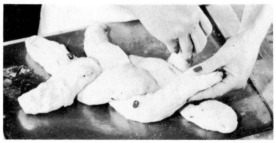

1. Braid gently and loosely. Do not stretch. Fasten ends; tuck under securely.

2. Place second braid on top. Seal braid ends by pressing firmly together and then tucking under.

TRADITIONAL HOLIDAY BREADS

Bohemian Braid, page 110

Stollen, page 110

Kulich, page 115

Jule Kage, page 116

Cinnamon Rolls

Pinwheel rolls with fragrant cinnamon-sugar butter.

Use Small Recipe Sweet Roll Dough (*p. 108*). After dough rises:

1. Roll dough into oblong, 15x9″. Spread with 2 tbsp. softened butter and sprinkle with ½ cup sugar and 2 tsp. cinnamon.

2. Roll up tightly, beginning at wide side. Seal well by pinching edges of roll together. Even up roll by stretching slightly.

3. Cut roll into 1″ slices. Place in greased 13x9″ pan or 18 greased muffin cups. Cover and let rise until double, 35 to 40 min.

4. *Heat oven to 375° (quick mod.). Bake 25 to 30 min. Frost while warm with Quick White Icing (p. 110). Makes 1½ doz. rolls.*

Butterscotch Rolls

Cinnamon rolls with butterscotch-pecan glaze.

Make Cinnamon Rolls (*above*)—*except* place cut slices in baking pan coated with mixture of:

⅓ cup butter, melted
½ cup brown sugar (packed)
1 tbsp. corn syrup
½ cup pecan halves

Bake. Immediately turn upside down on a large tray. Let pan stay over rolls a minute so that butterscotch runs down over them.

Frosted Orange Rolls

"Luscious!" says Margaret Doyle Stevning (Mrs. Oliver H.), who was in charge of our first test kitchen.

Make Cinnamon Rolls (*above*)—*except* spread dough with ½ of Creamy Orange Frosting (*below*). Let rise. Bake. Remove from pan. Spread with rest of frosting.

Creamy Orange Frosting

Mix until smooth: 3 tbsp. soft butter, 1 tbsp. grated orange rind, 2 tbsp. orange juice, 1½ cups *sifted* confectioners' sugar.

Hungarian Coffee Cake

Nut encrusted rolls—baked as a cake.

Use Small Recipe Sweet Roll Dough (*p. 108*). After dough rises, cut into pieces size of walnuts. Form into balls. Roll each ball in ½ cup melted butter. Then roll in mixture of ¾ cup sugar, 1 tsp. cinnamon, ½ cup finely chopped nuts. Place 1 layer of balls so they barely touch in well greased 9 or 10″ tube pan (if pan has removable bottom, line with aluminum foil). Sprinkle with a few raisins. Add another layer of balls, sprinkle with more raisins, pressing them in slightly. Let rise 45 min. *Heat oven to 375° (quick mod.). Bake 35 to 40 min.* Loosen from pan. Invert pan so butter-sugar mixture runs down over cake. To serve, break apart with 2 forks.

Swedish Tea Ring

Spectacular, but easy to make. People used to "oh and ah!" when Elsa Wallin Louis of our staff made it for demonstrations and cooking schools. Now she makes it for her family and friends.

Make Cinnamon Rolls (*p. 112*)—*except* sprinkle dough with ½ cup raisins in addition to sugar (granulated or brown) and cinnamon.

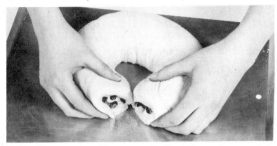

1. Roll up as for Cinnamon Rolls. Then place sealed-edge-down in ring on lightly greased baking sheet. Pinch ends together.

2. With scissors, make cuts ⅔ of the way through the ring at 1″ intervals. Turn each section on its side. Let rise until double, 35 to 40 min.

Heat oven to 375° (quick mod.). Bake *25 to 30 min.* Frost while warm with Quick White Icing (*p. 110*) and decorate with nuts and cherries. Serve warm.

Cinnamon Whirligig

See color picture pp. 100-101.

Make Small Recipe Sweet Roll Dough (*p. 108*). Let rise twice. Roll dough into an oblong, 16x8″. Sprinkle with mixture of 3 tbsp. sugar and 2 tsp. cinnamon. Roll up tightly, starting with narrow end. Seal edge. Place sealed-edge-down in well greased loaf pan, 9x5x3″. Again let rise until double, about 50 min. *Heat oven to 375°* (quick mod.). Bake *about 35 min.*, or until nicely browned.

Checkerboard Kuchen

Just the thing for get-togethers over coffee. Each one cuts the square she likes best.

Make Small Recipe Sweet Roll Dough (*p. 108*). After second rising, divide dough into 2 parts. Roll each part into a rectangle, 12x8″. Place each on separate baking sheet. Form a small edge around outside about ½″ high. Prick center with fork as for a pie shell. Let rise in warm place (85°) until double, about 40 min.

Heat oven to 350° (mod.). Carefully spread ½ cup strawberry jam, ½ cup peach jam and ½ cup finely chopped pecans mixed with 3 tbsp. honey over dough in 2″ squares, alternating colors as for a checkerboard. Sprinkle Streusel (*below*) over all. Bake *20 to 25 min.* Remove from baking sheet to cool. Cut into squares to serve.

Streusel: Mix ⅓ cup sugar, ⅓ cup GOLD MEDAL Flour, ¼ cup butter and ½ tsp. cinnamon.

Poteca (*Po-teet-za*)

A traditional bread baked by the women in the south of Yugoslavia. For them no holiday, wedding, christening or gathering is complete without Poteca.

Use Small Recipe Sweet Roll Dough (*p. 108*). After dough rises, place dough on large floured cloth and roll out almost paper-thin into an oblong, 30x20″. Spread Walnut Filling (*below*) over dough, bringing it to edges. Starting at the wide side of the oblong, lift cloth and let dough roll up like a jelly roll. Seal well by pinching edges into dough. Place in greased oblong pan, 13x9″ or on a greased baking sheet in snail shape. Let rise until almost double, 1 hr. *Heat oven to 325°* (slow mod.). Bake *40 to 45 min.*, or until brown.

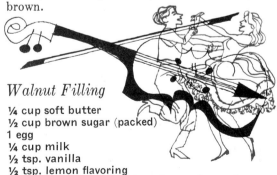

Walnut Filling

¼ cup soft butter
½ cup brown sugar (packed)
1 egg
¼ cup milk
½ tsp. vanilla
½ tsp. lemon flavoring
2 cups walnuts, finely ground (not chopped)

Mix butter, brown sugar and egg. Stir in milk, vanilla and lemon flavoring. Blend in nuts.

113

Kolache

Introduced to us by a former staff member, Mary Lapic, now Mrs. Joseph Boucher of Hopkins, Minnesota.

½ cup sugar	¾ cup warm water (not hot—110 to 115°)
½ cup soft shortening (part butter)	2 pkg. active dry yeast
1 tsp. salt	4 cups GOLD MEDAL Flour
2 eggs or 4 egg yolks plus 2 tbsp. water	

Cream sugar, shortening, salt and eggs thoroughly. Dissolve yeast in water. Measure flour by dip-level-pour method or by sifting (*see p. 6*). Add creamed mixture and 1½ cups of flour to yeast. Beat on low speed on electric mixer 10 min. Stir in remaining flour. Let rise in warm place (85°) about 1½ hr. (If kitchen is cool, place dough on a rack over a bowl of hot water and cover completely with a towel.) Stir down and turn onto a well floured board. Divide into 24 equal pieces. Shape each piece into a smooth round ball. Cover with cloth and let rest about 15 min. Shape as desired (*suggestions below*) and fill (*recipes below*). Place on greased baking sheet. Let rise about 30 min., until a depression remains when touched lightly with finger.

Heat oven to 375° (quick mod.). Bake *15 to 18 min.*, or until brown. Brush with melted butter and dust lightly with confectioners' sugar. Serve warm or cold. *Makes 24.*

1. Place 12 balls of dough on greased baking sheet about 2″ apart. Using fingers of both hands make a depression in center by pushing outward toward edge, leaving about a ½″ ridge around the outside of the circle. Fill with about 1½ tbsp. filling.

2. Form balls of dough on well floured board with fingers. Press each ball of dough into a flat 4″ square. Place 1 level tablespoonful filling in center. Bring opposite corners together. Moisten with milk, overlap about 1″ and seal well. Repeat with remaining 2 corners.

Prune-Apricot Filling

Delicious tangy filling from Alice Totushek of our staff, whose Czechoslovakian mother-in-law taught her to make Kolaches.

Simmer ½ lb. (1 cup) prunes with 4 oz. (¾ cup) dried apricots in water to cover about 30 min., or until tender. Drain; chop fruit fine and combine with ¼ tsp. allspice, ½ cup sugar, 1 tbsp. lemon juice and 1 tbsp. grated lemon rind.

Cinnamon-Apple Filling

Mix in saucepan 5 small apples, pared and cut up, ¼ cup cinnamon candies and ½ cup water. Cook until soft. Drain and press pulp through sieve.

▶ ALL YOU HAVE TO DO

To divide dough easily: cut with kitchen shears instead of knife.

114

Kulich

A delicate, sweet, fruity bread rising above tops of cans in mushroom or mosque-like shapes . . . characteristic of old Russia's holiday breads. Perfected by Bernadine Landsberg, formerly of our staff. See color picture p. 111.

Make Large Recipe Richer Sweet Roll Dough (p. 108)—*except* with first addition of flour, add ½ cup raisins, ¼ cup chopped blanched almonds and ½ tsp. vanilla. After dough rises, divide into 3 portions. Round up into 3 well rounded bun-like shapes. Place in 3 well greased 1-lb. coffee cans. Cover. Let rise until double, 30 to 40 min. or until dough is slightly above top of cans. (If kitchen is cool, place dough on a rack over a bowl of hot water and cover completely with a towel.) *Heat oven to 375° (quick mod.).* Bake *30 to 35 min.*, or until well browned. Remove from cans. Cool slightly. Using large spoon drop Confectioners' Sugar Icing (mix ½ cup *sifted* confectioners' sugar, 1½ tsp. warm water, ½ tsp. lemon juice and a bit of grated lemon rind) over tops letting it run down the sides. Decorate with tiny colored decorating candies called 100's and 1000's. *Makes 3 loaves.*

1. Place dough in cans.   2. Iced and decorated.

Hot Cross Buns *For a bountiful breakfast on Easter morning.*

1 cup warm water (not hot—110 to 115°)
1 pkg. active dry yeast
2 tbsp. sugar
2¼ cups GOLD MEDAL Flour
1 tsp. salt
1 tsp. cinnamon

¼ tsp. nutmeg
1 egg
2 tbsp. soft shortening
½ cup currants
¼ cup cut-up citron

In bowl, dissolve yeast in water. Measure flour by dip-level-pour method or by sifting (*see p. 6*). Add sugar, half of flour, salt, spices to yeast. Beat until smooth. Add egg, shortening. Beat in rest of flour, currants, citron. Scrape sides of bowl and cover with cloth. Let rise in warm place (85°) until double, 30 min. (If kitchen is cool, place dough on a rack over a bowl of hot water and cover completely with a towel.)

Grease 12 large muffin cups. Stir down raised dough. Spoon into muffin cups filling ½ full. Let rise in warm place until dough reaches tops of muffin cups, 20 to 30 min. *Heat oven to 400° (mod. hot).* Bake *15 to 20 min.*, or until brown. Make a cross on each bun with Quick White Icing (p. 110). *Makes 12 buns.*

Egg White Glaze

Mix 1 unbeaten egg white and 2 tbsp. water. Brush over breads just before baking for shiny, light finish.

Egg Yolk Glaze

Mix with fork 1 egg yolk and 2 tbsp. cold water. Brush over breads just before baking for shiny golden brown finish.

Jule Kage

A Christmas bread found on the table in Norway for a "Glad Jule." See color picture p. 111.

¼ cup warm water (not hot—110 to 115°)
1 pkg. active dry yeast
¾ cup lukewarm milk (scalded then cooled)
½ cup sugar
½ tsp. salt
½ tsp. powdered cardamom
1 egg
2 tbsp. shortening
⅓ cup cut-up citron
½ cup seedless raisins
3¼ to 3½ cups GOLD MEDAL Flour

In bowl, dissolve yeast in water. Measure flour by dip-level-pour method or by sifting (*see p. 6*). Stir in rest of ingredients except half of flour. Mix until smooth. Add rest of flour until easy to handle. Turn onto lightly floured board; knead until smooth. Round up in greased bowl; cover and let rise until double, about 1½ hr. Punch down; let rise again, about 45 min. Shape into round loaf; place in greased 9″ pie pan or on greased baking sheet. Cover, let rise 45 min., brush with Egg Yolk Glaze (*p. 115*). *Heat oven to 350° (mod.). Bake 30 to 40 min. Makes 1 loaf.*

Christmas Tree Bread

Make Small Recipe Sweet Roll Dough (*p. 108*). After dough rises, divide dough in two (one for each tree). Form each into 17 1½″ balls. Arrange on slightly greased baking sheet in a 5, 4, 3, 2, 1 pattern and with 2 balls rolled together for the trunk. Let rise until double, 20 to 30 min. *Heat oven to 350° (mod.). Bake 15 to 20 min.*, or until golden brown. Decorate with Quick White Icing (*p. 110*), candied fruits and decorating candies (including silver dragées). *Makes 2 large trees.*

Lucia Buns *(Saffron Buns)*

Since long ago, Lucia Day, December 13, has marked the opening of the Christmas season for many of Swedish descent.

In Sweden, the ceremony is very pretty. Early in the starlit morning, young girls dressed in white, wearing holly crowns set with lighted candles, wake their parents and serve them saffron buns and cups of steaming coffee.

Make Large Recipe Sweet Roll Dough (*p. 108*)— *except* dissolve ⅛ to ¼ tsp. powdered cooking saffron in 2 tbsp. boiling water. Add warm water to make ½ cup liquid for dissolving yeast.

Mix, knead and let rise as in directions for Sweet Roll Dough. To shape, divide dough into 3 parts. Roll each piece ¼″ thick on lightly floured cloth-covered board. Cut in strips, 4x½″. Cross 2 strips to make an "X" on lightly greased baking sheet. Then curl each end out and in to form a broken "8". Press 4 raisins into each bun at ends of broken 8. Brush with Egg Yolk Glaze (*p. 115*). Let rise 15 to 20 min. *Heat oven to 400° (mod. hot). Bake 10 to 12 min.*, or until golden brown. While warm, top with Quick White Icing (*p. 110*). *Makes 4 doz. buns.*

Cherry Cordial Rolls

Make Small Recipe Sweet Roll Dough (*p. 108*)— *except* add 12 maraschino cherries, chopped and drained, with first half of flour. After dough rises, roll out on lightly floured board into a rectangle, 18x9″. Mix ½ cup GOLD MEDAL Flour, ½ cup brown sugar (packed) and ¼ cup butter; spread on dough. Roll up tightly, beginning at wide side. Seal well. Cut into 18 slices. Put into greased muffin cups, cut-side-up. Cover and let rise in warm place until double, 35 to 40 min. *Heat oven to 375° (quick mod.). Bake 20 to 25 min.* Frost edges with thick confectioners' sugar icing.

Sour Cream Twists

A prize-winning recipe. It came to us from a wonderful cook in Ohio.

¼ cup warm water (not hot—110 to 115°)
1 pkg. active dry yeast
¾ cup lukewarm sour cream*
3 tbsp. sugar
⅛ tsp. soda
1 tsp. salt
1 large egg
2 tbsp. soft shortening
3 cups GOLD MEDAL Flour

In bowl, dissolve yeast in water. Measure flour by dip-level-pour method or by sifting (*see p. 6*). Stir all ingredients together. Turn dough onto floured board and fold several times to smooth. Roll into an oblong, 24x6″. Proceed as directed below. Cover, let rise in warm place (85°) 1 hr. (If kitchen is cool, place dough on a rack over a bowl of hot water and cover completely with a towel.) *Heat oven to 375°* (quick mod.). Bake *12 to 15 min.*, or until golden brown. While warm, frost with Quick White Icing (*p. 110*). *Makes 2 doz. twists.*

*To sour sweet cream: measure 1 tbsp. vinegar or strained lemon juice into measuring cup. Fill cup with sweet cream.

1. Spread with 2 tbsp. soft butter. Sprinkle half of dough with a mixture of ⅓ cup brown sugar (packed) and 1 tsp. cinnamon. Fold other half over. Cut into 24 strips 1″ wide.

2. Hold strip at both ends and twist in opposite directions. Place on greased baking sheet 2″ apart.

3. Press both ends of twist to baking sheet.

Pope Ladies

Modern adaptation of traditional New Year's bread originating in St. Albans, England. Named for mythical Popess Joan of 858 A.D.

¾ cup warm water (not hot—110 to 115°)
1 pkg. active dry yeast
2 eggs
¼ cup soft shortening
⅓ cup sugar
1 tsp. salt
2 tsp. nutmeg, if desired
3½ cups GOLD MEDAL Flour
currants

In mixer bowl, dissolve yeast in water. Measure flour by dip-level-pour method or by sifting (*see p. 6*). Add eggs, shortening, sugar, salt, nutmeg, half of flour to yeast. Beat 2 min., medium speed on mixer or 300 vigorous strokes by hand. Scrape bowl often. Add rest of flour; blend in until smooth. Cover with cloth; let rise in warm place (85°) until double, about 45 min. (If kitchen is cool, place dough on a rack over a bowl of hot water and cover completely with a towel.) Stir down by beating 25 strokes. Turn onto floured board. Cut into 12 pieces. (One for each lady.)

Body: use ½ of each piece of dough. Shape a 4″ long oval.

Head: use a little more than ½ of remaining dough. Shape a round ball. Press 2 currants in deeply for eyes; put a tiny piece of dough on for nose.

Arms: use remaining dough for arms. Make a 4″ long pencil-like roll and cut in two.

Form pope ladies about 3″ apart on greased baking sheet. Let rise in warm place (85°) until double, about 45 min. Brush lightly with 1 egg, beaten. *Heat oven to 350°* (mod.). Bake *about 15 min.*, or until nicely browned. Serve warm with butter and jam. *Makes 12 pope ladies.*

Pope Ladies (below) and
Swiss Christmas Bread (p. 104)

Double-Quick Coffee Bread

One bowl for everything. Thorough beating takes the place of kneading. No rolling or cutting of dough. These breads are fluffier, have thinner crusts and are more cake-like than kneaded breads. Delicious served warm.

Choose one of the delicious and colorful variations below; grease pan and have topping ready.

¾ cup warm water (not hot—110 to 115°)
1 pkg. active dry yeast
¼ cup sugar
1 tsp. salt

2¼ cups GOLD MEDAL Flour
1 egg
¼ cup soft shortening or butter

In bowl, dissolve yeast in water. Measure flour by dip-level-pour method or by sifting (*see p. 6*). Add sugar, salt and half the flour to yeast. Beat thoroughly 2 min. Add egg and shortening. Gradually beat in remaining flour until smooth. Drop small spoonfuls over topping in bottom of pan. Cover. Let rise in warm place (85°) until double, 50 to 60 min. (If kitchen is cool, place dough on a rack over a bowl of hot water and cover completely with a towel.) *Heat oven to 375° (quick mod.).* Bake *30 to 35 min.*, or until brown. Immediately turn out to avoid sticking. Serve warm.

1. Batter sheets off the spoon after 2 min. of mixing.

2. Drop small spoonfuls of dough over entire bottom of pan.

Cherry Butterscotch Ring

See color picture pp. 100-101.

Melt in 9″ ring mold ⅓ cup butter and ½ cup brown sugar (packed) with 1 tbsp. corn syrup. Decorate with walnut or pecan halves and candied or maraschino cherries. Cool slightly before spooning in dough.

Butterscotch Nut Buns

Melt in 10″ iron skillet ⅓ cup butter and ½ cup brown sugar (packed) with 1 tbsp. corn syrup. Add ½ cup pecans (or walnuts). Cool slightly before spooning in dough.

Browned Butter Almond Buns

Melt in 8 or 9″ square pan ⅓ cup butter. Add ½ cup slivered blanched almonds. Heat until butter foams up in pan and browns and almonds are light golden brown. (Almonds brown a little more while cooling.) Cool slightly. Mix in 2 tbsp. white corn syrup, ½ cup sugar, ½ tsp. almond extract. Spoon in dough.

Cinnamon Streusel Coffee Bread

Mix thoroughly 2 tbsp. butter, ⅓ cup granulated or brown sugar, 2 tbsp. flour, 2 tsp. cinnamon, ½ cup chopped nuts. Spoon dough into 8 or 9″ square pan. Sprinkle with streusel mixture.

Tutti Frutti Coffee Bread

Mix into finished dough ½ cup candied fruit and ¼ cup chopped nuts. Spoon into 8 or 9″ square pan. When baked, ice with a mixture of ¾ cup *sifted* confectioners' sugar and 1 to 2 tbsp. cream. Decorate top with candied fruit and nuts.

Spicy Sugar Puffs

Fill half full 16 to 20 medium-sized greased muffin cups. Let rise. Bake *15 to 20 min.* Immediately after baking, roll in ½ cup butter, melted, then in a mixture of ¾ cup sugar and 2 tsp. cinnamon. Serve hot.

Jam Puffs

Fill half full 16 to 20 medium-sized greased muffin cups. Let rise. Bake *15 to 20 min.* When baked, spread with ½ cup thick raspberry jam. Garnish with coconut or chopped nuts.

Marmalade Coffee Bread

Sprinkle ¼ cup brown sugar (packed) in 8 or 9″ square pan. Add ½ cup pineapple or orange marmalade. Spoon in dough.

Sour Dough French Bread

New version of an old favorite from our friend, Virginia Guild of San Francisco. So easy to make, moist and tender on the inside, crunchy on the outside.

First, prepare Starter Dough (*below*).

½ cup milk
1 cup water
1½ tbsp. vegetable oil
1 pkg. active dry yeast
¼ cup warm water (not hot—110 to 115°)

1½ tbsp. sugar
2½ tsp. salt
4¾ cups GOLD MEDAL Flour
2 tbsp. Starter Dough

Combine milk, water and oil; bring to boil. Cool to lukewarm (95 to 100°). Dissolve yeast in water; add with sugar and salt to cooled milk mixture. Measure flour by dip-level-pour method or by sifting (*see p. 6*). Place flour in large bowl; pour milk into well made in center of flour, add starter, blend well. *Do not knead.* Place in greased bowl; cover and let rise in warm place (85°) until double, about 1 hr. Turn onto lightly floured board. *Do not knead.* Divide in half. Roll each into an oblong, 15x10″. Roll up tightly toward you, beginning at wide side; seal edges. With hand on each end, roll to taper ends. Place on baking sheet covered with heavy foil. (Pleat foil between loaves.) With scissors, make cuts about ⅛″ deep diagonally along loaf, about 2″ apart. Let rise, uncovered, in warm place (85°) until a little more than double, about 1 hr. *Heat oven to 425° (hot). Bake 15 min. Reduce heat to 350° (mod.). Bake 15 to 20 min.* longer. Brush top and sides with 1 egg white mixed with 1 tbsp. cold water. Bake *5 min. longer.* Cool in a draft for a crisp crust. *Makes 2 loaves.*

Starter Dough

¼ cup milk
½ cup water
2 tsp. vegetable oil
1 pkg. active dry yeast
¼ cup warm water (not hot—110 to 115°)
2 tsp. sugar
1½ tsp. salt
2⅓ cups GOLD MEDAL Flour

Combine milk, water and oil; bring to boil. Cool to lukewarm (95 to 100°). Dissolve yeast in water. Add with sugar and salt to cooled milk mixture. Measure flour by dip-level-pour method or by sifting (*see p. 6*). Stir liquid into flour just enough to blend thoroughly. Cover; let stand in warm place 12 to 18 hr. to sour. *Starter for about 12 loaves.*

NOTE: Remaining starter can be stored tightly covered in refrigerator for several days. Measure amount needed, bring to room temperature before using.

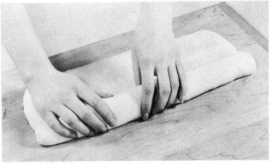

1. Roll up tightly toward you, beginning at wide side.

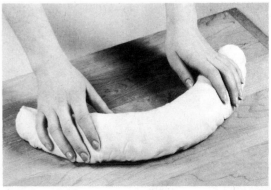

2. With hand on each end, roll gently back and forth to taper ends.

See color picture on opposite page.

Hot French Bread

Slice rye, French or Vienna bread diagonally, not quite through bottom crust. Spread with Seasoned Butters (*below*). Heat loaf *at 400°* (mod. hot) *about 15 min.*, or until piping hot and crusty. Transfer in loaf shape to basket or bread tray with a napkin to help keep bread warm.

Seasoned Butters

Cream ½ cup (¼ lb.) soft butter with:

Garlic: ½ tsp. garlic salt or a few drops garlic juice or cream butter in bowl rubbed with cut clove of garlic.

Onion: 2 tbsp. minced onion or a few drops onion juice or snipped chives.

Herb: 2 tsp. chopped parsley, ½ tsp. oregano, 2 tbsp. grated Parmesan cheese and ⅛ tsp. garlic salt.

Oregano: Generous pinch dried oregano.

Seeded: 1 tsp. poppy, caraway or sesame seeds.

Jumbo Bread Sticks

Cut unsliced loaf of bread into "sticks" (about 5x1"). Melt butter in baking pan. Roll each stick in melted butter, sprinkle with garlic salt, onion salt, celery salt, Parmesan cheese, sesame seeds or poppy seeds. Arrange in pan. Toast in oven *at 375°* (quick mod.) for *20 to 25 min.*, turning occasionally to brown evenly. Serve hot.

Hot Seeded Buttered Bread Slices

Butter slices of bread on one side. Cut each slice in half or into 6 equal strips. Place on baking sheet. Sprinkle with poppy, celery, sesame or caraway seeds. Bake in 350° oven (mod.) until crisp.

Buttercups

Brush thinly sliced bread (crusts removed) with melted butter. Press into muffin cups. Toast at 350° (mod.). Serve filled with Chicken à la King (*p. 266*).

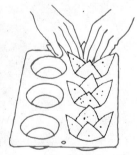

Bun Boats

Hollow out oblong rolls, brush with melted butter. Heat at 400° (mod. hot) until hot and crusty. Fill with Barbecue Hamburger Mix (*p. 292*).

Individual Muffin Pizzas

With crisp relishes or a tossed salad, they make a satisfying and "different" combination for supper, luncheon or "after ten" refreshments.

Brush halves of English Muffins with olive oil or butter. Toast under broiler. Cover each with tomato slices, catsup or tomato paste; onion rings; salami or pepperoni; and a few anchovies. Sprinkle with olive oil, salt, pepper, garlic salt and oregano. Top with a slice of Mozzarella cheese or Cheddar cheese and a mushroom cap. Return to broiler until cheese melts and bubbles. Serve hot.

Elegant Sandwich Loaf

Make ahead of time, store in refrigerator. Serve cold, garnished with lettuce, olives, radish roses and pickle fans.

Trim crust from an unsliced loaf of sandwich bread and cut the loaf into four lengthwise slices. Spread one side of each slice with ½ cup softened butter. Place one slice, buttered-side-up, on serving plate. Spread evenly with Shrimp Salad Filling. Top with second slice and spread evenly with Cheese-Pecan Filling. Top with third slice and spread evenly with Chicken-Bacon Filling. Top with remaining bread slice. Frost top and sides with mixture of two pkg. (8 oz. each) cream cheese and ½ cup cream. Decorate with sliced stuffed olives and toasted almonds. Chill in refrigerator 3 hr. or more. To serve, cut with a sharp knife into 1" slices. *12 to 14 servings.*

Shrimp Salad Filling

Mix 1 hard-cooked egg, chopped, 1⅓ cups (7-oz. can) finely chopped shrimp, ¼ cup finely chopped celery, 2 tbsp. lemon juice, ¼ tsp. salt, dash of pepper and ¼ cup mayonnaise.

Cheese-Pecan Filling

Mix 1 pkg. (3 oz.) cream cheese, softened, 1 cup (4 oz.) finely chopped toasted pecans and ¾ cup (9-oz. can) well drained crushed pineapple.

Chicken-Bacon Filling

Mix 8 slices crisp pan-broiled bacon, crumbled, 1 cup finely chopped cooked chicken, ¼ cup mayonnaise, 1 tbsp. finely chopped pimiento, ¼ tsp. salt and ⅛ tsp. pepper.

WAYS TO USE BREAD

Toasted Bun with
  Broiled Hamburger

Hot French Bread
Buttercups with
  Chicken à la King
Elegant Sandwich Loaf

Jumbo Bread Sticks
Bun Boats
Individual Muffin Pizzas

Overnight Cinnamon Coffee Cake

Rich and flavorful. Try it the next time you have week-end guests.

4 cups GOLD MEDAL Flour	¼ cup warm water (not hot—110 to 115°)
1 tsp. salt	1 pkg. active dry yeast
¼ cup sugar	3 egg yolks, beaten
1 cup soft butter (½ lb.)	1 cup milk, scalded then cooled

Measure flour by dip-level-pour method or by sifting (*see p. 6*). Stir flour, salt and sugar in large bowl. Cut in butter until mixture looks like meal. Dissolve yeast in water. Add to flour mixture with egg yolks and milk. Beat well. Chill overnight.

This amount of dough will make 2 loaves of coffee cake or about 2 doz. individual coffee cakes. Or, if desired 1 loaf and about 1 doz. smaller cakes may be made. Dough keeps well in refrigerator for at least 3 days, so half can be saved for later use.

To make loaves: Grease well a loaf pan, 9x5x3". Roll ½ recipe chilled dough into a rectangle, about 13x8". Brush with melted butter, sprinkle with mixture of ¼ cup sugar and ¾ tsp. cinnamon. Beginning at narrow end, roll up as for jelly roll. Place in pan, cover and allow to rise about 2 hr. in warm place (85°). (If kitchen is cool, place dough on a rack over a bowl of hot water and cover completely with a towel.) (Dough will not double in bulk, but will rise slightly and look light.) *Heat oven to 375° (quick mod.).* Bake *1 hr.* If loaf looks sufficiently brown after about 40 min. of baking, cover with brown paper during last of baking. Carefully remove from pan while hot and frost with Creamy Glaze (*recipe below*). Cool before cutting.

To make individual coffee cakes: Grease well about 12 medium-sized muffin cups. Roll ½ recipe chilled dough into a rectangle, about 12x10". Brush with melted butter, sprinkle with mixture of ¼ cup sugar and ¾ tsp. cinnamon. Beginning at wide side, roll as for jelly roll. With sharp knife, cut roll into 1" slices. Place in muffin cups. Cover and let rise in warm place (85°) about 1 hr. (If kitchen is cool, place dough on a rack over a bowl of hot water and cover completely with a towel.) (Rolls will rise slightly and look light.) *Heat oven to 375° (quick mod.).* Bake *20 to 25 min.*, or until golden brown. Remove from pans while hot and frost with Creamy Glaze (*recipe below*).

Creamy Glaze

Mix 1½ cups *sifted* confectioners' sugar, 2 tbsp. soft butter, 1½ tsp. vanilla and 1 or 2 tbsp. hot water to make medium thick glaze.

This recipe makes enough glaze for whole recipe of dough. If half of dough is made up at one time, half the glaze recipe will be sufficient.

Chocolate Cinnamon Buns

Cocoa lends a delicate flavor to made-with-yeast, sure-to-please buns. Created by Gladis Schmidt, an artist with yeast breads.

¾ cup warm water (not hot—110 to 115°)
1 pkg. active dry yeast
¼ cup soft shortening
1 tsp. salt
¼ cup sugar
1 egg
⅓ cup cocoa
2¼ cups GOLD MEDAL Flour
1 tbsp. soft butter
1½ tsp. cinnamon
3 tbsp. sugar
chopped pistachio nuts, almonds or pecans

In mixer bowl, dissolve yeast in water. Measure flour by dip-level-pour method or by sifting (*see p. 6*). Add shortening, salt, sugar, egg, cocoa, 1 cup of flour to yeast. Beat 2 min., medium speed on mixer or 300 vigorous strokes by hand. Scrape bowl frequently. Stir in remaining flour until smooth. Scrape batter from sides of bowl. Cover with cloth and let rise in warm place (85°) until double, about 1 hr. (If kitchen is cool, place dough on a rack over a bowl of hot water and cover completely with a towel.)

Stir down batter by beating 25 strokes. Turn out on well floured cloth-covered board (dough will be soft). Roll into a rectangle, 12x9". Spread gently with soft butter and sprinkle with mixture of cinnamon and sugar. Roll up gently beginning at wide side. Pinch edge into roll. Cut into 12 pieces Place in greased square pan, 9x9x1¾". Let rise in warm place (85°) until double, about 40 min. *Heat oven to 375° (quick mod.).* Bake *25 min.* Remove from pan; frost top immediately with Confectioners' Sugar Icing (¾ cup *sifted* confectioners' sugar moistened with cream to spreading consistency). *Makes 12.*

Potato Refrigerator Rolls

Rich and sweet.

1½ cups warm water (not hot—110 to 115°)
1 pkg. active dry yeast
⅔ cup sugar
1½ tsp. salt

⅔ cup soft shortening
2 eggs
1 cup lukewarm mashed potatoes
7 to 7½ cups GOLD MEDAL Flour

In bowl, dissolve yeast in water. Stir in sugar, salt, shortening, eggs and potatoes. Measure flour by dip-level-pour method or by sifting (*see p. 6*). Mix in flour with hand until dough is easy to handle. Turn onto lightly floured board. Knead until smooth and elastic. Place greased-side-up in greased bowl. Cover with damp cloth; place in refrigerator (*see below*). About 2 hr. before baking, shape dough into rolls, coffee cakes, etc. (*see pp. 108-109*). Cover and let rise until double, 1½ to 2 hr. *Heat oven to 400° (mod. hot). Bake 12 to 15 min. Makes 4 doz. medium rolls.*

Moravian Coffee Cake

Use half of dough for Potato Refrigerator Rolls (*above*). About 2 hr. before baking, pat dough into two well greased square pans, 9x9x1¾". Cover and let rise until double, 1½ to 2 hr. With thumb make 12 holes in top of each coffee cake. Carefully spread tops with ½ cup softened butter to avoid breaking down the raised dough. Pour ¼ cup cream into holes, sprinkle with mixture of 1 cup brown sugar (packed) and 2 tsp. cinnamon. *Heat oven to 400° (mod. hot). Bake about 25 min. 18 to 24 servings.*

Easy Refrigerator Rolls

No kneading. Fresh rolls every night.

2 cups warm water (not hot—110 to 115°)
2 pkg. active dry yeast
½ cup sugar
2 tsp. salt
¼ cup soft shortening
1 egg
6½ to 7 cups GOLD MEDAL Flour

Mix and handle dough as in Potato Refrigerator Rolls (*above*)—*except do not knead.*

TIPS ON REFRIGERATED DOUGHS

What Doughs Can I Keep in the Refrigerator?

Almost any dough except plain bread dough. Those made with at least ¼ cup sugar and milk keep about 3 days. Doughs made with water keep about 5 days. (Temperature in refrigerator should be 50° or lower.)

When Is the Dough Put in the Refrigerator?

Immediately after mixing. Or it may be allowed to rise once, punched down and then put into the refrigerator. Then it must be punched down occasionally as it rises.

Italian Bread Sticks

⅔ cup warm water (not hot—110 to 115°)
1 pkg. active dry yeast
1 tsp. salt
1 tbsp. sugar
¼ cup soft shortening
2 cups GOLD MEDAL Flour

In bowl, dissolve yeast in water. Measure flour by dip-level-pour method or by sifting (*see p. 6*). Add salt, sugar, shortening and half the flour to yeast. Beat vigorously until smooth. Mix in rest of flour. Knead on floured cloth-covered board until smooth (5 min.). Cover, let rise until double, 1 hr. (If kitchen is cool, place dough on a rack over a bowl of hot water and cover completely with a towel.) *Heat oven to 400° (mod. hot).* Divide in half. Cut each into 24 pieces. Roll each into pencil shapes, 6, 8 or 10" (depending on thickness wanted). Place on greased baking sheet 1" apart. Brush with Egg Yolk Glaze (*p. 115*). Sprinkle with sesame seeds or coarse salt. Bake *20 to 25 min. Makes 48.*

How Should I Prepare the Dough?

Grease top of dough well and cover with waxed paper or refrigerator cover; then with a damp cloth. Keep cloth damp.

Must I Bake All the Dough at Once?

No, cut off only as much as needed for number of rolls or amounts of coffee cakes. Then return remainder of dough to refrigerator.

How Long to Let Rise Before Baking?

Until doubled, 1½ to 2 hr. The time will vary with coldness of dough and size of rolls.

Raised Doughnuts

Brown and crusty . . . best served warm. New Englanders make them for breakfast and serve them with cheese.

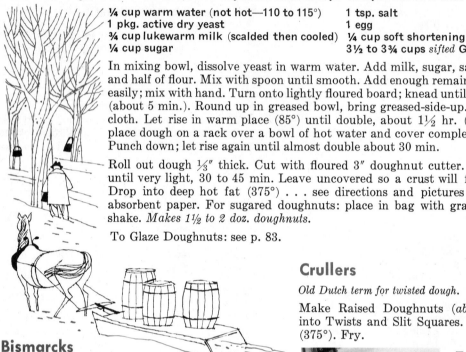

¼ cup warm water (not hot—110 to 115°)	1 tsp. salt
1 pkg. active dry yeast	1 egg
¾ cup lukewarm milk (scalded then cooled)	¼ cup soft shortening
¼ cup sugar	3½ to 3¾ cups *sifted* GOLD MEDAL Flour

In mixing bowl, dissolve yeast in warm water. Add milk, sugar, salt, egg, shortening and half of flour. Mix with spoon until smooth. Add enough remaining flour to handle easily; mix with hand. Turn onto lightly floured board; knead until smooth and elastic (about 5 min.). Round up in greased bowl, bring greased-side-up. Cover with damp cloth. Let rise in warm place (85°) until double, about 1½ hr. (If kitchen is cool, place dough on a rack over a bowl of hot water and cover completely with a towel.) Punch down; let rise again until almost double about 30 min.

Roll out dough ⅓″ thick. Cut with floured 3″ doughnut cutter. Let rise on board until very light, 30 to 45 min. Leave uncovered so a crust will form on the dough. Drop into deep hot fat (375°) . . . see directions and pictures (p. 82). Drain on absorbent paper. For sugared doughnuts: place in bag with granulated sugar and shake. *Makes 1½ to 2 doz. doughnuts.*

To Glaze Doughnuts: see p. 83.

Bismarcks

Puffy, jelly-filled, crusty, brown balls.

Make Raised Doughnuts (*above*)—*except* roll dough ½″ thick. Cut rounds with a floured 3″ cooky cutter. Fry as for Raised Doughnuts. When cool, cut a *short* slit in the side of each fried ball through the center. Thrust a teaspoonful of jelly into the center and close tightly. Roll in sugar or glaze. Serve fresh.

Raised Waffles

¼ cup warm water (not hot—110 to 115°)
1 pkg. active dry yeast
1¾ cups lukewarm milk (scalded then cooled)
2 tbsp. sugar
1 tsp. salt
3 eggs
¼ cup soft butter
2 cups *sifted* GOLD MEDAL Flour

In mixing bowl, dissolve yeast in warm water. Add milk, sugar and salt. Beat in rest of ingredients with rotary beater. Cover and let rise in warm place (85°) about 1½ hr. Stir down, cover and set in refrigerator overnight or until ready to use. Stir down again when ready to use. Pour onto hot waffle iron. Bake until brown and crisp, 3 to 4 min. *Makes about eight 7″ waffles.*

Crullers

Old Dutch term for twisted dough.

Make Raised Doughnuts (*above*)—*except* shape into Twists and Slit Squares. Drop into hot fat (375°). Fry.

Twists: Roll dough ½″ thick on lightly floured cloth-covered board. Cut in strips ½″ wide, 8″ long with kitchen shears. Shape into figure 8's sealing ends well.

Slit Squares: Roll out dough ¼″ thick. Cut in 2″ squares. Make 4 deep slits (almost through dough) in each with kitchen shears. Lift by picking up alternate strips between fingers and thumb.

Raised Pancakes

Make Raised Waffles (*at left*)—*except* pour from ¼ cup measure or tip of large spoon onto hot griddle. (Grease griddle lightly, if necessary.) Turn as soon as puffed and full of bubbles, but before bubbles break. Bake other side until golden brown.

CAKES

Cakes can be truthfully termed "food for the gods," for cakes made of flour, honey and milk were offered to the gods in both the Greek and Roman civilizations and in the Far Eastern cults.

Of course, man enjoyed cakes, too. A spicy cake much like our gingerbread is said to have been invented by a Greek on the Island of Rhodes as long ago as 2800 B.C. And the custom of serving cake at weddings dates back to Roman times with the bride and groom sharing the first slice just as they do today.

But it was not until about 1200 A.D that an ingenious nun created the forerunner of our fine-textured, delicately-flavored cakes by creaming butter with eggs and sugar for two hours. And it was she who transformed cakes from a large pudding shape to the iced layers with which we are familiar.

Cake recipes have long been jealously guarded. History reports that the countess who possessed the recipe for the currant-filled Banbury Cake was extremely popular at the court of James II.

Here in our own country, colonial cooks developed the rich Pound Cake so named because the recipe called for a pound each of sugar, butter and flour. Here too, Chiffon Cake, the first really new cake of the century, was created, combining the best qualities of both angel food and butter cakes.

CAKES FOR COMPLIMENTS

(complete index in back of book)

 TIMESAVING TIPS

Busy mothers whose children love fresh cake and cupcakes have come to rely on quick-mix cakes. Here are two favorites.

EASY BANANA CAKE

Make batter as directed on Betty Crocker Yellow Cake Mix pkg.—*except* stir ⅛ tsp. soda into mix before adding liquid. Use only ¾ cup water and add 1 cup mashed bananas (2 to 3 medium). If desired, fold ⅓ cup finely chopped nuts into batter. Bake as directed.

VELVET CRUMB CAKE

Grease and flour a square pan, 8x8x2″. Mix 1⅓ cups Bisquick, ¾ cup sugar, 3 tbsp. soft shortening, 1 egg, ¼ cup milk. Beat vigorously 1 min. Stir in ½ cup milk, 1 tsp. vanilla. Beat ½ min. Pour into pan. Bake *at 350° 35 to 40 min.* Top with Broiled Icing (*p. 176*).

 MEALTIME MAGIC

SATURDAY LUNCH AT HOME

Pea Soup
French Toasted Sandwiches (*p. 291*)
Radishes   Celery
White Nut Cake (*p. 134*) with
Glamorous Nut Topping

WINTERTIME FAVORITE

Liver and Bacon (*p. 315*)
Fried Onions   Creamed Potatoes
Tossed Salad with tomato wedges
Hot Biscuits
Red Devils Food Cake (*p. 145*)

Note: You no longer need to sift flour for recipes in this chapter. Measure Gold Medal flour by dipping nested measuring cups into flour and leveling off with spatula. Measure Softasilk flour by spooning flour into nested cups and leveling off.

WHAT EVERY COOK NEEDS TO KNOW ABOUT CAKES

BAKE WITH CARE

Baking perfect cakes is easy if you use quality ingredients, the right equipment (especially pans, *see p. 131*) and follow a tested recipe exactly. A cake recipe is a delicately balanced formula like a druggist's prescription. If you must use one ingredient in place of another (cocoa for chocolate, for example), use the substitution chart on *p. 14*.

Most cake recipes fall into two types: butter type or foam type. Cakes made with solid shortening are called butter cakes even if the shortening used is not butter or is only part butter. White, yellow, chocolate and spice cakes are butter cakes. Choose the creaming method or the double-quick method when making butter cakes (details on *p. 129*).

Creaming method is the time-honored way of making cake by creaming shortening with sugar until fluffy, then adding flour and liquid alternately. Double-quick is an electric mixer method for butter cakes.

Foam type cakes are so named because the foam of beaten egg whites provides their light, fluffy open texture. Sponge cakes, jelly rolls, angel food and chiffon cakes are foam types (step pictures for angel food cakes, *p. 154*, and chiffon cakes, *p. 156*). Remember to take out eggs and separate whites ahead of mixing as egg whites beat up best at room temperature. Bake foam cakes the full time as under-baking may cause the cake to fall out of the pan or sink.

• •

FROST AND SERVE WITH FLAIR

With your beautiful cake baked and cooled, the fun of filling and frosting it begins. Many delightful filling and frosting ideas are woven into the cake recipes in this chapter, not to mention the wide array of frostings in the Frostings chapter.

An attractive cake plate or two is a wise investment for entertaining. A cake knife or breaker and cake server are helpful in handling tender cakes. And for more and daintier pieces from your layer cakes, *see p. 145*.

NEW ADVENTURES IN CAKES

Chocolate Butter-Mallow Cake (*p. 144*)—Tender chocolate cake crowned with butterscotch filling and fluffy marshmallow frosting.

Jack Horner Cake (*p. 150*)—A spicy prune cake that is sure to be eaten quickly.

Pie 'n Cake Desserts (*p. 140*)—Cake batter baked in pie pans becomes a cherry dessert and a chocolate-topped cake.

Fruited Angel Food Cake (*p. 155*)—Candied fruit adds a holiday touch to our 12-egg white angel.

Peppermint Swirl Loaf Cake (*p. 149*)—Pink peppermint marbled through buttery pound cake.

EXQUISITE COCONUT CAKE

Silver White Cake, page 132.

HOW TO MAKE A BEAUTIFUL BUTTER CAKE . . .

Using the SIMPLIFIED CREAMING METHOD

1. Read the recipe and method carefully.

2. Heat oven to correct temperature. (If using glass pans, reduce temperature 25°.)

3. Assemble ingredients. Ingredients mix best if at room temperature. CAUTION: In hot weather, use eggs and milk directly from refrigerator. Shortening must always be at room temperature.

4. Collect utensils: standard measuring cups and spoons, bowls, beater, rubber scraper, spatula. Set up electric mixer if it is to be used. Prepare baking pan or pans of exact size called for in recipe (*see p. 131*). Bright, shiny pans are best.

Using the DOUBLE-QUICK METHOD

Follow steps for *Simplified Creaming Method*, but be sure to . . .

1. Use soft shortening (such as Crisco, Spry, Swift'ning). Butter may replace half the shortening for a better flavor.

2. Use only the size pans called for in recipe.

3. If using an electric mixer, guide the batter into the beaters with rubber scraper. If beating by hand, beat vigorously with spoon.

4. Use exact ingredients called for.

5. Have your oven checked regularly for accuracy by your local utility company.

SIMPLIFIED CREAMING METHOD—*Quick, new version of the old conventional way.*

1. First put softened shortening, sugar, whole eggs and flavoring into mixing bowl. Beat 5 min., high speed on mixer or by hand for same time until fluffy. If you are making an egg yolk cake, or one with melted chocolate, stir in yolks or chocolate after beating.

2. While mixer is creaming (or after creaming by hand), stir together flour, leavening, salt and cocoa, if cocoa cake is being made.

3. Next, mix in the dry ingredients alternately with milk. Begin and end with flour. Blend by mixer on low speed or mix by hand until smooth.

4. If you are making a white cake fold beaten egg whites in at the end. Add nuts, cherries, raisins or coconut when and as directed in recipe.

DOUBLE-QUICK METHOD—*Time-saving, one-bowl modern way.*

1. Measure flour by dip-level-pour method or by sifting (*see p. 6*). Measure dry ingredients into bowl—flour, sugar, baking powder and/or soda, salt. Blend well. If cocoa is used, stir it into flour, unless otherwise specified.

2. Measure flavoring into liquid. Add softened shortening and ⅔ of the liquid. When using all-purpose flour (GOLD MEDAL), the batter is heavier; add all liquid at once.

3. Beat on medium speed standard mixer, high speed portable mixer 2 min., scraping bowl constantly. Or beat vigorously with spoon 2 min. (150 strokes per min.).

4. Add remaining liquid, melted chocolate (if used) and unbeaten eggs, egg whites or yolks. Beat 2 min. more, scraping bowl frequently.

CAKES *From cake pan to cake plate.*

5. Divide batter evenly into prepared pans. (Batter made by Double-quick Method is thin.) Rack should be at middle of oven. Stagger layers as in picture—away from oven walls and slightly apart. This helps cake bake evenly.

6. When minimum baking time is up, test cakes made with cake flour by lightly touching middle of cake; if no imprint remains, cake is done. Test cakes made with all-purpose flour by sticking toothpick in center; if it comes out clean, cake is done.

7. Remove from oven. Let stand in pans 8 to 10 min. To remove: 1) put towel or paper towel over cake and inverted cake rack on top of towel, 2) turn over and remove cake pan, 3) put another inverted cake rack over bottom of cake and turn again.

How to Frost a Two-Layer Cake

Frost as soon as thoroughly cool. Brush away crumbs.

1. Place layer upside down. Spread with filling or frosting almost to outer edge with flexible spatula.

2. Place second layer right side up on filling. Frost sides, bringing icing up to form rim around top edge.

3. Spread frosting over top making attractive swirls. Be sure to frost to built-up edge.

How to Bake Odd-Shaped Cakes

Lamb

Bell

Christmas Tree

Star

Heart

Fill Odd-Shaped Pans

⅔ full for Creaming Method cakes (*see recipes pp. 133, 142–144, 146*).
½ full for Double-quick Method cakes (*see recipes pp. 132, 134–135, 138–141, 143, 145, 150*).

How to Measure Capacity of an Odd-Shaped Pan

Fill pan with water. Measure the water. Use ⅔ that amount of batter for Creaming Method cake; use ½ that amount for Double-quick Method cake.

How to Bake Sheet Cakes

Thinner . . . made in jelly roll pan. Used in making Petits Fours (p. 171) and cakes for weddings, buffets, etc.

Grease and flour a jelly roll pan, 15½x10½x1". Make batter for Golden Layer Cake (*p. 139*) or Silver White Cake (*p. 132*). Bake at 350° (mod.) 20 to 25 min. Make Petits Fours or frost top with desired frosting and cut into squares.

POINTERS ON PANS . . .

to give your cakes these desirable qualities.

ALL CAKES on these pages have been carefully tested using the standard-sized pans mentioned in the recipes. It is important to use the correct pan to give your cakes:

pan too big

pan too small

pan just right !

GOOD SIZE, SHAPE, CONTOUR: *Always use pan size called for in recipe.* Cakes baked in a pan of the correct size will have good shape and rounded top. Cakes baked in too large a pan will be pale, flat and shrunken. Cakes baked in too small or too shallow a pan will bulge over and lose contour. Layer pans should be at least 1½″ deep; square and oblong, 2″ deep; pound or loaf, more than 2″ deep.

FINE GRAINED TEXTURE: Baking pans with straight sides give a more velvety texture. Also, correct amount of batter in pans is an important factor (use pan size called for in recipe).

EVEN BROWNING: Shiny aluminum or tin pans distribute heat evenly and give a delicate golden brown crust to the cake. For best results when using glass baking pans, reduce the oven temperature 25° and use the same baking time called for in recipe.

use straight sided layer pans

shiny pans distribute heat

HOW TO PREPARE PANS *so that cakes are easy to remove.*

Grease generously bottom and sides of pans, using waxed paper or a narrow paintbrush to spread it evenly.

Dust the greased pans with flour until well coated on bottom and sides. Shake out excess flour.

Line loaf pans for fruitcake with aluminum foil or brown paper to keep cakes from getting too brown. (Leave "ears" for easy removal.)

HOW TO BAKE CUPCAKES *from cake recipes.*

For recipes developed just for cupcakes, see pp. 144 and 148.

Cupcakes have nicely rounded tops and hold their shape best if baked in paper cups or liners placed in muffin cups. This procedure also saves greasing and washing pan.

FILL CUPS:

⅔ full for Creaming Method cupcakes
½ full for Double-quick Method cupcakes
⅞ full for Chiffon cupcakes

TEMPERATURE: 400° (mod. hot oven).

TIME: Bake 18 to 20 min.

AMOUNT PER RECIPE: 1½ to 2 doz. cupcakes from recipe calling for 2¼ cups flour.

HIGH ALTITUDE

If you live in a high altitude (above 3,200 feet), write to Betty Crocker for adjustments on the cake recipes in this chapter. Address: Betty Crocker Kitchens, General Mills, Inc., 9200 Wayzata Boulevard, Minneapolis 26, Minnesota.

131

Silver White Cake (4 Egg Whites)

High, fluffy, showy. Delicately flavored. Reminiscent of White Mountain Cake, the rage of the Gay Nineties and the first popular "white" cake to be created. See color picture, p. 128.

2¼ cups SOFTASILK Flour	½ cup soft shortening
1½ cups sugar	1 cup milk
3½ tsp. baking powder	1 tsp. flavoring
1 tsp. salt	4 egg whites (½ to ⅔ cup), unbeaten

Heat oven to 350° (mod.). Grease and flour two layer pans, 8 or 9x1½" or an oblong pan, 13x9½x2". Measure flour by dip-level-pour method or by sifting (*see p. 6*). Blend flour, sugar, baking powder and salt. Add shortening, ⅔ cup of milk and flavoring. Beat 2 min., medium speed on mixer or 300 vigorous strokes by hand. Scrape sides and bottom of bowl constantly. Add rest of milk and egg whites. Beat 2 more min., scraping bowl frequently. Pour into pan(s). Bake *layers 30 to 35 min., oblong 35 to 40 min.* Cool. Elegant with lemon filling (*p. 177*), a fluffy icing (*p. 174*) and flaked coconut.

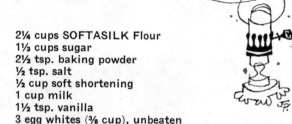

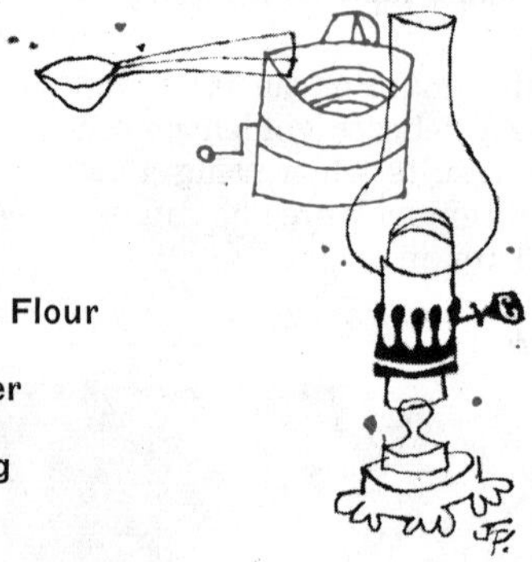

2¼ cups SOFTASILK Flour
1⅓ cups sugar
2½ tsp. baking powder
½ tsp. salt
½ cup soft shortening
1 cup milk
1½ tsp. vanilla
3 egg whites (⅜ cup), unbeaten

Mix and bake as for Silver White Cake (*above*)— *except* bake *oblong cake 35 min.*

Maraschino Cherry Cake

2¼ cups SOFTASILK Flour or 2 cups
    plus 2 tbsp. GOLD MEDAL Flour
1⅓ cups sugar
3 tsp. baking powder
1 tsp. salt
½ cup soft shortening
¼ cup maraschino cherry juice (5-oz. bottle)
16 maraschino cherries, cut in eighths
½ cup milk
4 egg whites (½ to ⅔ cup), unbeaten
½ cup chopped nuts

Heat oven to 350° (mod.). Grease and flour two layer pans, 8 or 9x1½" or an oblong pan, 13x9½x2". Measure flour by dip-level-pour method or by sifting (*see p. 6*). Stir dry ingredients together. Add shortening, cherry juice, cherries and milk. Beat 2 min., medium speed on mixer. Add egg whites. Beat 2 more min. Fold in nuts. Pour into pans. Bake *layers 30 to 35 min., oblong 35 to 40 min.*

Orange Satin Ribbon Cake

Bake Silver White Cake (*above*) in layers. Cool. Split each layer crosswise. Spread Orange Satin Filling (*below*) between layers and on top. Sprinkle ¼ cup chopped toasted almonds on top.

Orange Satin Filling

1 cup sugar
4½ tbsp. cornstarch
½ tsp. salt
1½ cups orange juice
½ cup water
4 egg yolks, beaten
¼ cup butter
3 tbsp. grated orange rind

Mix sugar, cornstarch and salt in saucepan. Gradually stir in orange juice and water. Bring to boil over low heat, stirring constantly. Remove from heat. Stir at least half of hot mixture into beaten egg yolks. Blend into remaining hot mixture. Bring to boil again; boil 1 min., stirring constantly. Remove from heat and blend in butter and orange rind. Cool.

Miracle Marble Cake

Rich chocolate and dainty white . . in intriguing marbled effect. "Guests at my home exclaim over it especially when I serve fingers of it with pink strawberry ice cream on white milk glass plates," says N. Faye Woodward of Lawrence, Kansas.

Make batter for Silver White Cake (*above*). Pour ⅔ of batter into pans. To remaining batter add 1 sq. unsweetened chocolate (1 oz.), melted, mixed with ¼ tsp. soda and 2 tbsp. warm water. Pour here and there over white batter. Cut through batter with knife several times for marbled effect. Bake. Cool. Frost with chocolate icing.

Fluffy White Cake

Old-time favorite. Luscious to eat.

½ cup soft shortening (half butter)
1½ cups sugar
2½ cups SOFTASILK Flour
2½ tsp. baking powder

1 tsp. salt
1 cup milk
1½ tsp. flavoring
4 egg whites (½ cup), stiffly beaten

Heat oven to 350° (mod.). Grease and flour two layer pans, 8 or 9x1½″ or an oblong pan, 13x9½x2″. Cream shortening and sugar until fluffy. Measure flour by dip-level-pour method or by sifting (*see p. 6*). Blend flour, baking powder and salt. Mix in alternately with milk and flavoring. Fold in egg whites. Pour into pan(s). Bake *layers 30 to 35 min., oblong 35 to 45 min.*, or until cake tests done. Cool. Finish with Egyptian Filling (*p. 177*) and a Butter Icing (*p. 172*).

Lady Baltimore Cake

A Christmas delicacy made famous long ago by cooks of the plantations of South Carolina and Maryland.

Bake Fluffy White Cake (*above*) in layers. Spread both cooled layers with Fruit-Nut Filling (*below*). Cover each with a thin layer of White Icing (*below*). Put layers together. Then cover top and sides with the remaining icing.

Lady Baltimore White Icing

1½ cups sugar
1 tsp. light corn syrup
⅔ cup water
2 egg whites (¼ cup), beaten stiff
1 tsp. vanilla

Mix sugar, corn syrup and water. Boil to 242° (or until an 8″ thread spins from spoon). Pour slowly into beaten egg whites, beating constantly. Add vanilla. Continue beating until mixture is fluffy and will hold its shape.

Lady Baltimore Fruit-Nut Filling

Take about ⅓ of icing (*above*) and mix in ⅓ cup raisins, cut fine, ⅓ cup figs, cut in strips and ½ cup chopped walnuts.

Coconut Cream Cake

Bake Fluffy White Cake (*above*) in layers. Make Cream Filling (*p. 177*). Add about ½ cup coconut to ⅓ of the filling and spread between cooled layers. Coat top and sides thinly with remaining filling. Sprinkle generously with coconut (about 1½ cups).

Pink Azalea Cake

Bake any of the Egg White Cakes in layers—*except* tint batter for one layer a delicate pink. Cool. Split layers; fill and frost with 1½ times recipe for Pink Mountain Frosting (*p. 174*) or Cherry Butter Icing (*p. 146*), alternating the pink layers with the white.

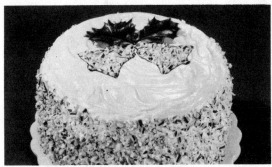

Christmas Bell Peppermint Cake

Make Fluffy White Cake (*above*)—*except* fold ⅓ cup finely crushed peppermint stick candy into batter. Fill and frost cake with White Mountain Frosting (*p. 174*). Coat sides of cake with ½ to ¾ cup crushed peppermint stick candy, reserving 3 tbsp. for decoration. Draw outline of bells atop cake freehand or use cooky cutter. Outline bell in red using toothpick dipped in food coloring. Fill bells with candy. Add holly.

Snowflake Cake

Full volumed . . . deliciously moist eating quality.

2 cups plus 2 tbsp. GOLD MEDAL Flour	½ cup soft shortening
1½ cups sugar	1 cup milk
3½ tsp. baking powder	1 tsp. flavoring
1 tsp. salt	4 egg whites (½ to ⅔ cup), unbeaten

Heat oven to 350° (mod.). Grease and flour two layer pans, 8 or 9x1½" or an oblong pan, 13x9½x2". Measure flour by dip-level-pour method or by sifting (*see p. 6*). Blend in bowl flour; sugar, baking powder and salt. Add shortening, milk and flavoring. Beat 2 min., medium speed on mixer or 300 vigorous strokes by hand. Scrape sides and bottom of bowl constantly. Add egg whites. Beat 2 more min., scraping bowl frequently. Pour into pan(s). Bake *layers 35 to 40 min., oblong 40 to 45 min.* Cool. Delicious with Pineapple Cream Filling (*p. 177*) and a white icing.

White Nut Cake

Make Snowflake Cake (*above*)—*except* fold in 1 cup chopped nuts. Finish with Glamorous Nut Topping.

Glamorous Nut Topping

Spread Butter Icing (*p. 172*)· between layers and on sides of layer cake. Stir cut-up pecans or walnuts into remaining frosting for top of the cake.

Chocolate Chip Cake

There are little surprise chunks of rich chocolate all through the white layers.

Make Snowflake Cake (*above*)—*except* fold in carefully ½ cup finely chopped sweet or semi-sweet chocolate. Bake. Finish cooled cake with a fudgy frosting or with a glossy white icing decorated with Chocolate Leaves (*at right*).

Ribbon Spice Cake

Alternate layers of white cake, lemon-flavored, and beige cake, enticingly spiced. Lemon Spice Icing.

Make Snowflake Cake (*above*)—*except* use ½ tsp. lemon flavoring. Pour half of batter into one of the prepared layer pans. To remaining batter add:

½ tsp. cinnamon
¼ tsp. nutmeg
¼ tsp. cloves
1 tbsp. molasses

Stir well and pour into the other pan. Bake. Cool. Split into 4 layers. Ice with Lemon Spice Icing (*below*) alternating spice and lemon layers.

Lemon Spice Icing

4½ cups *sifted* confectioners' sugar
4 egg yolks
½ cup soft shortening (part butter)
¼ tsp. cinnamon
⅛ tsp. *each* cloves and nutmeg
grated rind of 1 lemon
3 tbsp. lemon juice

Beat all ingredients in bowl until smooth.

▶ **ALL YOU HAVE TO DO**

To make Chocolate Leaves: wash and dry about 2 doz. leaves of varying sizes and shapes to use in decorating the cake.

Melt 2 sq. semi-sweet chocolate (2 oz.) or ½ cup semi-sweet chocolate pieces with 1 tsp. butter. Paint chocolate on backs of leaves, about ⅛" thick and just to the edges. Chill until firm. Peel off leaves; trim cake.

One-Egg Cake

Light, tender, rich and moist. Delicious any time.

2 cups SOFTASILK Flour
1¼ cups sugar
2½ tsp. baking powder
1 tsp. salt

⅓ cup soft shortening
1 cup milk
1 tsp. vanilla
1 egg (¼ cup)

Heat oven to 350° (mod.). Grease and flour two layer pans, 8x1½″ or a square pan, 9x9x1¾″. Measure flour by dip-level-pour method or by sifting (*see p. 6*). Blend flour, sugar, baking powder and salt. Add shortening, ⅔ of milk and vanilla. Beat 2 min., medium speed on mixer or 300 vigorous strokes by hand. Scrape sides and bottom of bowl constantly. Add rest of milk and egg. Beat 2 more min., scraping bowl frequently. Pour into pan(s). Bake *layers about 30 min., square 30 to 35 min.* Cool. Frost with your favorite icing.

Marble One-Egg Cake

Make One-Egg Cake (*above*)—*except* pour half of batter into another bowl and add a mixture of 1 sq. unsweetened chocolate (1 oz.), melted, ¼ tsp. soda and 2 tbsp. water. Beat ½ min. Spoon chocolate and white batters alternately into prepared pan or pans. Run knife through to give marbled effect. Frost with a chocolate icing.

Spice One-Egg Cake

Make One-Egg Cake (*above*)—*except* stir ½ tsp. cinnamon and ¼ tsp. *each* cloves, allspice, nutmeg with dry ingredients. Frost with Easy Penuche Icing (*p. 175*).

Bit o' Chocolate One-Egg Cake

Enticing bits of grated chocolate all the way through.

Make One-Egg Cake (*above*)—*except* fold 2 sq. semi-sweet chocolate (2 oz.), grated medium coarse, into the batter. Frost with Butter Icing (*p. 172*) and garnish with Chocolate Curls.

▶ **ALL YOU HAVE TO DO**

To make Chocolate Curls: barely warm a bar of chocolate (do not melt). With a razor blade or peeler, take off thin shavings from back or sides of chocolate. (They curl up.)

Butterscotch One-Egg Cake

Make One-Egg Cake (*above*)—*except* omit granulated sugar and add 1¼ cups brown sugar (packed) with the shortening. Cool and frost with Easy Penuche Icing (*p. 175*).

Toasted Walnut-Filled Cake

Make One-Egg Cake (*above*) in layers. Cool. Fill with Toasted Walnut Filling (*below*) and frost with White Mountain Frosting (*p. 174*).

Toasted Walnut Filling

½ cup brown sugar (packed)
2 tbsp. butter
1 tbsp. water
1 egg yolk, slightly beaten
¾ cup walnuts, chopped and toasted

Mix brown sugar, butter and water in saucepan. Heat until sugar is dissolved. Cook 1 min., stirring constantly. Pour at least half of the hot mixture into egg yolk. Blend into remaining hot mixture. Boil 1 min. more, stirring constantly. Cool slightly. Stir in walnuts.

Banana One-Egg Cake

Make One-Egg Cake (*above*)—*except* reduce baking powder to 1 tsp. and add 1 tsp. soda with the dry ingredients. Use ½ cup buttermilk or sour milk and 1 cup mashed ripe bananas in place of the sweet milk. Add all at once in first beating time. Finish cooled cake with sweetened whipped cream covered with banana slices.

CAKES TO CARRY

New Gold Cake

Tender . . . and rich yellow.

2 cups SOFTASILK Flour or 1¾ cups GOLD MEDAL Flour 1⅓ cups sugar 3 tsp. baking powder 1 tsp. salt	⅓ cup soft shortening 1 cup milk ½ tsp. lemon flavoring ½ tsp. vanilla 4 egg yolks (⅓ cup), unbeaten

Heat oven to 350° (mod.). Grease and flour two layer pans, 8x1½" or an oblong pan, 13x9½x2". Measure flour by dip-level-pour method or by sifting (*see p. 6*). Blend flour, sugar, baking powder and salt. Add shortening, ⅔ cup milk and flavorings. (When using GOLD MEDAL Flour, add all milk at once.) Beat 2 min., medium speed on mixer or 300 vigorous strokes by hand. Scrape sides and bottom of bowl constantly. Add rest of milk and egg yolks. Beat 2 more min., scraping bowl frequently. Pour into pan(s). Bake *layers 30 to 35 min., oblong 35 to 40 min.* Cool. Especially delicious with a fruity icing, such as Strawberry Butter Icing (*p. 172*) or Lemon or Orange Butter Icing (*p. 172*).

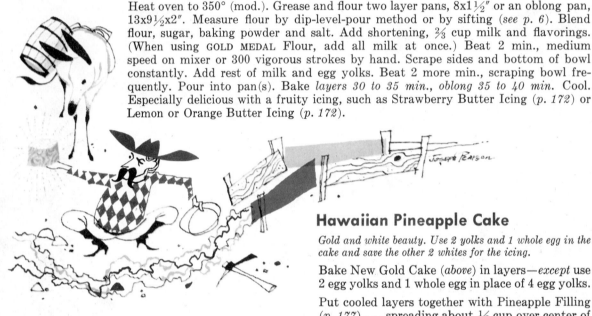

Lord Baltimore Cake

Named for George Calvert, Lord Baltimore, the English statesman who founded the state of Maryland.

Bake New Gold Cake (*above*) in layers. Spread cooled layers with Fruit-Nut Filling (*below*). Cover with thin layer of Pink Frosting (*below*). Put layers together. Cover top and sides with Pink Frosting.

Lord Baltimore Pink Frosting

Make Lady Baltimore White Icing (*p. 133*)—*except* use only ⅓ cup water and add ⅓ cup maraschino cherry juice. In place of vanilla, use ½ tsp. lemon flavoring and 1 tsp. grated orange rind.

Lord Baltimore Fruit-Nut Filling

Mix ¼ cup *each* toasted dried macaroon crumbs, toasted cut-up pecans, toasted cut-up blanched almonds and chopped maraschino cherries into ⅓ of Pink Frosting (*above*).

Hawaiian Pineapple Cake

Gold and white beauty. Use 2 yolks and 1 whole egg in the cake and save the other 2 whites for the icing.

Bake New Gold Cake (*above*) in layers—*except* use 2 egg yolks and 1 whole egg in place of 4 egg yolks.

Put cooled layers together with Pineapple Filling (*p. 177*) . . . spreading about ½ cup over center of top layer. Frost sides and a 1½" border on top with a fluffy white icing.

It is as elegant to eat as it is beautiful to look at.

138

Golden Layer Cake

Versatile with its many variations.

2¼ cups SOFTASILK Flour	½ cup soft shortening
1½ cups sugar	1 cup milk
3 tsp. baking powder	1½ tsp. flavoring
1 tsp. salt	2 eggs (⅓ to ½ cup)

Heat oven to 350° (mod.). Grease and flour two layer pans, 8 or 9x1½″ or an oblong pan, 13x9½x2″. Measure flour by dip-level-pour method or by sifting (*see p. 6*). Blend flour, sugar, baking powder and salt. Add shortening, ⅔ of milk and flavoring. Beat 2 min., medium speed on mixer or 300 vigorous strokes by hand. Scrape sides and bottom of bowl constantly. Add rest of milk and eggs. Beat 2 more min., scraping bowl frequently. Pour into prepared pan(s). Bake *layers 30 to 35 min., oblong 40 to 45 min.* Cool. Finish with filling or frosting as desired. The oblong cake is ideal finished with Broiled Icing or Choc-o-Nut Topping (*p. 176*) or with Pink Mountain Frosting (*p. 174*) sprinkled with crushed peppermint stick candy.

Maple Buttercup Cake

2¼ cups SOFTASILK Flour
1½ cups sugar
1½ tsp. baking powder
1 tsp. salt
½ tsp. soda
½ cup soft shortening (part butter)
1 cup buttermilk
1½ tsp. maple flavoring
2 eggs

Heat oven to 350° (mod.). Grease and flour two layer pans, 9x1½″ or an oblong pan, 13x9½x2″. Measure flour by dip-level-pour method or by sifting (*see p. 6*). Stir dry ingredients in bowl. Add shortening, ⅔ of the buttermilk and flavoring. Beat 2 min., medium speed on mixer or 300 vigorous strokes by hand. Scrape bowl constantly. Add rest of milk and eggs. Beat 2 more min., scraping bowl frequently. Pour into pan(s). Bake *layers 25 to 30 min., oblong 40 to 45 min.* Cool. Frost with Maple Butter Icing (*p. 172*).

Butterscotch Cake

Make Golden Layer Cake (*above*)—*except* use brown sugar in place of white and add with the shortening. Bake *oblong 35 to 40 min.* Delicious iced with a fluffy white icing or creamy Easy Penuche Icing (*p. 175*).

Daisy Cake

A marshmallow becomes a daisy in the skilled hands of Shirley Thomas of our staff, formerly of our Canadian office, Toronto.

Bake Golden Layer Cake (*above*). Cool. Fill and frost with Lemon Frosting (*p. 174*). Snip 3 marshmallows into 6 sections, cutting about ¾ of way through marshmallows. Spread sections, gently pinching to resemble petals. Arrange at one side on top of frosted cake. In center of each flower, place small yellow gumdrop. At side of each flower, make leaves with green gumdrops.

Peanut Butter Cake

Make Golden Layer Cake (*above*)—*except* use only ⅓ cup soft shortening and add ⅓ cup chunk-style peanut butter with the shortening. Bake. Cool. Finish with Peanut Butter Broiled Icing (*p. 176*) for oblong or Peanut Butter Icing (*p.172*) for layers.

New Starlight Cake

Perfect with Chocolate Cream Filling (p. 177) and Allegretti Frosting (p. 174).

2 cups plus 2 tbsp. GOLD MEDAL Flour	½ cup soft shortening
1½ cups sugar	1 cup milk
3½ tsp. baking powder	1 tsp. flavoring
1 tsp. salt	3 eggs (½ to ⅔ cup)

Heat oven to 350° (mod.). Grease and flour two layer pans, 8 or 9x1½" or an oblong pan, 13x9½x2". Measure flour by dip-level-pour method or by sifting (*see p. 6*). Blend flour, sugar, baking powder and salt. Add shortening, milk and flavoring. Beat 2 min., medium speed on mixer or 300 vigorous strokes by hand. Scrape sides and bottom of bowl constantly. Add eggs. Beat 2 more min., scraping bowl frequently. Pour into pan(s). Bake *8" layers 35 to 40 min., 9" layers 30 to 35 min., oblong 45 to 50 min.* Cool.

Butterscotch Sundae Cake

2¼ cups GOLD MEDAL Flour
3 tsp. baking powder
1 tsp. salt
1¾ cups brown sugar (packed)
½ cup soft shortening
1 cup milk
1 tsp. vanilla
2 large eggs (½ cup)

Mix and bake as for New Starlight Cake (*above*)— *except* add brown sugar with the shortening. Cool. Frost with a cooked white icing. Decorate with Butterscotch Glaze (*below*).

Butterscotch Glaze

¼ cup brown sugar (packed)
3 tbsp. butter
2 tbsp. water

Mix ingredients in saucepan. Bring to full rolling boil, stirring constantly. Then boil vigorously without stirring 1½ min. Remove from heat and immediately dribble with a teaspoon around top edge of cake. Glaze will run over sides in uneven lines. Or make a small groove around edge of cake after it has been frosted, using back of teaspoon. Dribble glaze in the groove and over the edge. This makes it look more like a Butterscotch Sundae.

Starlight Coconut Cake

Follow recipe for New Starlight Cake (*above*)— *except* add ¼ tsp. almond flavoring and 1 cup shredded coconut, finely cut, to batter. Ice with Orange Butter Icing (*p. 172*).

Kitchenette Cake

A small 1-egg cake that keeps and carries well. "This is just the right size for my sister and me," says Olga Stege of our staff.

1⅓ cups GOLD MEDAL Flour
1 cup sugar
2 tsp. baking powder
½ tsp. salt
⅓ cup soft shortening
⅔ cup milk
1 tsp. flavoring
1 egg (¼ to ⅓ cup)

Mix as for New Starlight Cake (*above*). Pour batter into greased and floured square pan, 9x9x1¾". Bake *30 to 35 min.*

Dinette Cake

Make Kitchenette Cake (*above*)—*except* use 1½ cups SOFTASILK Flour in place of GOLD MEDAL Flour.

Pie 'n Cake Desserts

Grease and flour 8 and 9" pie pans. Make batter for Kitchenette Cake (*above*) and pour into prepared pans. Bake *8" cake 25 to 30 min., 9" cake 20 to 25 min.* Immediately spread 1-lb. can prepared cherry pie filling over 9" pan. Place squares of chocolate from three ⅞-oz. milk chocolate bars over top of 8" pan and spread as they melt to form frosting. Serve cherry dessert warm in wedges; serve chocolate-topped cake later.

Burnt Sugar Cake

The real old-time, caramel-rich variety of cake that always has been first choice at church suppers. Developed by Mabel Martin of our staff.

1½ cups sugar
½ cup boiling water
2¼ cups SOFTASILK Flour
3 tsp. baking powder

1 tsp. salt
½ cup soft shortening
2 eggs (⅓ to ½ cup)
1 tsp. vanilla, if desired

Melt ½ cup sugar in heavy skillet over low heat until clear and medium brown, shaking pan gently to keep from burning. Remove from heat. Add boiling water, stirring constantly. Stir over low heat until lumps dissolve. Add water to make 1 cup. Cool.

Heat oven to 350° (mod.). Grease and flour two layer pans, 8 or 9x1½" or an oblong pan, 13x9½x2". Measure flour by dip-level-pour method or by sifting (*see p. 6*). Blend flour, 1 cup sugar, baking powder and salt. Add shortening and ⅔ cup caramel-water mixture. Beat 2 min., medium speed on mixer or 300 vigorous strokes by hand. Scrape sides and bottom of bowl constantly. Add remaining caramel-water mixture, eggs and vanilla. Beat 2 min. Pour into pan(s). Bake *8" layers 30 to 35 min., 9" layers 25 to 30 min., oblong 35 to 40 min.* Cool. Finish with Creamy Burnt Sugar Icing (below).

CARAMELIZING SUGAR

1. Melt sugar in heavy pan over low heat, shaking pan as sugar melts.

2. Heat until melted to a golden brown syrup, stirring constantly.

3. Stir in hot water (amount recipe indicates). Be careful steam does not burn hand.

Creamy Burnt Sugar Icing

½ cup sugar
¼ cup boiling water
½ cup shortening (part butter)
2½ tbsp. SOFTASILK Flour
¼ tsp. salt
3 cups *sifted* confectioners' sugar
3 tbsp. water
½ tsp. vanilla

Melt sugar in heavy skillet over low heat until clear and medium brown, shaking pan gently to keep from burning. Remove from heat. Add boiling water, stirring constantly. Stir over low heat until lumps are dissolved. Cool.

Melt shortening in saucepan. Remove from heat. Add flour and salt. Stir in caramel-water mixture, slowly. Bring to boil, stirring constantly. Boil 1 min. If mixture curdles, do not be alarmed. Remove from heat. Beat in alternately confectioners' sugar and water. Set saucepan in bowl of cold water. Beat until consistency to spread, then stir in vanilla. If too thick, add a little water.

Cinnamon Squares

A square cinnamon-nut cake that is quick and easy to make. Especially good served warm.

⅓ cup soft butter
1 cup sugar
2 eggs
1 cup GOLD MEDAL Flour
1 tsp. baking powder
1 tbsp. cinnamon
⅓ cup milk
⅔ cup broken nuts

Heat oven to 350° (mod.). Grease and flour a square pan, 8x8x2". Mix butter, sugar and eggs in mixer bowl. Beat 5 min. high speed on mixer or by hand until fluffy (5 min. total beating time). Measure flour by dip-level-pour method or by sifting (*see p. 6*). Blend flour, baking powder and cinnamon. Add alternately in three additions with milk. Start and end with dry ingredients. Beat on low speed *just* until smooth. Fold in nuts. Pour into pan. Bake *35 to 40 min.* Serve warm with a broiled icing or whipped cream.

Bonnie Butter Cake

An old-fashioned yellow cake made with butter.

⅔ cup soft butter
1¾ cups sugar
2 eggs (⅓ to ½ cup)
1½ tsp. vanilla

3 cups SOFTASILK Flour
  or 2¾ cups GOLD MEDAL Flour
2½ tsp. baking powder
1 tsp. salt
1¼ cups milk

Heat oven to 350° (mod.). Grease and flour two layer pans, 9x1½" or an oblong pan, 13x9½x2". Cream butter, sugar, eggs and vanilla until fluffy. Beat 5 min., high speed on mixer or by hand. Measure flour by dip-level-pour method or by sifting (*see p. 6*). Blend flour, baking powder and salt. Mix in alternately with milk. Use low speed on mixer. Pour into pan(s). Bake *layers 30 to 40 min., oblong 45 to 50 min.,* or until cake tests done. Cool. Delicious iced with a fluffy white icing sprinkled with coconut or Strawberry Butter Icing (*p. 172*).

Marble Bonnie Butter Cake

Make Bonnie Butter Cake (*above*)—*except* pour only ⅔ of batter into pans. Beat into remaining batter for about 30 seconds a mixture of 1 sq. unsweetened chocolate (1 oz.), melted, 2 tbsp. warm water, 1 tbsp. sugar, ¼ tsp. soda. Pour here and there over light batter. Cut through batter with knife several times for marbled effect.

Butter-Nut Filled Cake

This cake features the best filling we've tasted in years—chock-full of nuts, rich with butter. Equally good with white cake. From Margaret Wolfe, formerly of our staff.

Bake Bonnie Butter Cake (*above*) in layers. Fill with Butter-Nut Filling (*below*) and ice with White Mountain Frosting (*p. 174*).

Butter-Nut Filling

½ cup sugar
1 tbsp. flour
3 tbsp. orange juice
½ cup soft butter
¼ cup chopped dates or raisins
2 egg yolks, beaten
½ cup chopped nuts

Mix sugar, flour, orange juice, butter and dates or raisins in saucepan. Cook over low heat until mixture boils. Boil 1 min. Pour half of mixture into egg yolks, stirring constantly, then stir into filling remaining in saucepan. Bring to a boil. Add nuts. Cool before filling cake. *Makes 1¼ cups.*

Walnut Bonnie Butter Cake

Delicious nut-enriched version.

Make Bonnie Butter Cake (*above*)—*except* fold in 1 cup chopped nuts just before pouring batter into pans. Delicious finished with Browned Butter Icing (*p. 172*) or Maple Butter Icing (*p. 172*).

Pineapple Cream Cake

Bake Bonnie Butter Cake (*above*) in two layers. Cool. Split each layer crosswise in two layers. Spread Pineapple Cream Filling (*below*) between layers. Frost sides and top with 1 cup whipping cream, whipped and sweetened. Refrigerate until serving time.

Pineapple Cream Filling

1 tbsp. cornstarch
2 tbsp. sugar
1 cup milk
1 cup crushed pineapple (juice and all)
4 egg yolks, slightly beaten
1 tsp. grated lemon rind

Mix cornstarch and sugar in saucepan. Gradually stir in milk and pineapple. Bring to boil over direct heat, stirring constantly. Boil 1 min. Remove from heat. Stir at least half of hot mixture into egg yolks. Blend into rest of hot mixture. Boil 1 min. more, stirring constantly. Remove from heat and add lemon rind. Cool.

New Fudge Cake

Four squares of chocolate. Dark, delectable, fudge-like. See color picture on p. 147.

Large Cake

1¾ cups GOLD MEDAL Flour
2 cups sugar
2 tsp. baking powder
¼ tsp. soda
1 tsp. salt
¼ cup soft shortening
1½ cups milk
1 tsp. vanilla
2 eggs (⅓ to ½ cup)
4 sq. unsweetened chocolate (4 oz.), melted
1 cup chopped nuts

Small Cake

1¼ cups GOLD MEDAL Flour
1⅓ cups sugar
1¼ tsp. baking powder
¼ tsp. soda
½ tsp. salt
3 tbsp. soft shortening
1 cup milk
½ tsp. vanilla
1 egg (¼ to ⅓ cup)
3 sq. unsweetened chocolate (3 oz.), melted
⅔ cup chopped nuts

Heat oven to 350° (mod.). For Large Cake grease and flour two layer pans, 8 or 9x1½″ or an oblong pan, 13x9½x2″. For Small Cake grease and flour a square pan, 9x9x1¾″. Measure flour by dip-level-pour method or by sifting (*see p. 6*). Blend flour, sugar, baking powder, soda and salt. Add shortening, milk and vanilla. Beat 2 min., medium speed on mixer or 300 vigorous strokes by hand. Scrape sides and bottom of bowl constantly. Add eggs and chocolate. Beat 2 more min., scraping bowl frequently. Stir in nuts. Pour into pan(s). Bake *layers 35 to 40 min., oblong 40 to 45 min., square 35 to 40 min.* Cool. Ice with a fudge icing.

Chocolate Joy Cake

3 squares of chocolate. A family favorite from Mrs. Samuel C. Gale, wife of a former vice president of our company.

½ cup boiling water
3 sq. unsweetened chocolate (3 oz.), melted
½ cup soft shortening
1⅔ cups sugar
3 eggs (½ to ⅔ cup)
2¼ cups SOFTASILK Flour or 2 cups plus 2 tbsp. GOLD MEDAL Flour
2¼ tsp. baking powder
¼ tsp. soda
1 tsp. salt
1 cup buttermilk

Heat oven to 350° (mod.). Grease and flour two layer pans, 8 or 9x1½″ or an oblong pan, 13x9½x2″. Stir boiling water and chocolate until thick. Cool. Cream shortening, sugar, eggs and chocolate mixture until fluffy. Beat 5 min. high speed on mixer or by hand. Measure flour by dip-level-pour method or by sifting (*see p. 6*). Blend flour, baking powder, soda and salt. Mix in alternately with buttermilk. Use low speed on mixer. Beat just until smooth. Pour into pan(s). Bake *layers 30 to 40 min., oblong about 45 min.* Cool.

▶ **ALL YOU HAVE TO DO**

To keep chocolate cakes brown on the outside: grease and "cocoa" the pans instead of grease and "flour."

Brown Beauty Cake

2 squares of chocolate. Very rich and fudgy.

½ cup boiling water
2 sq. unsweetened chocolate (2 oz.), cut up
1 cup SOFTASILK Flour
1 cup sugar
¼ tsp. baking powder
½ tsp. soda
½ tsp. salt
¼ cup soft shortening
¼ cup buttermilk, sour milk or sweet milk
½ tsp. vanilla
1 egg

Heat oven to 350° (mod.). Grease and flour a square pan, 8x8x2″. Stir boiling water and chocolate until chocolate melts. Cool. Measure flour by dip-level-pour method or by sifting (*see p. 6*). Blend flour, sugar, baking powder, soda and salt. Stir into chocolate mixture. Add shortening. Beat 1 min., medium speed on mixer or 150 vigorous strokes by hand. Scrape sides and bottom of bowl constantly. Add milk, vanilla and egg. Beat 1 more min., scraping bowl frequently. Pour into pan. Bake *35 to 40 min.* Cool.

Chocolate Cherry Cake

Make Brown Beauty Cake (*above*) — *except* add ¼ tsp. almond flavoring and 10 maraschino cherries, chopped and drained.

Chocolate Butter-Mallow Cake

Chocolate cake with marshmallow frosting covering butterscotch filling. Given to us by Peggy Berglund Lantz.

⅓ cup soft shortening
1 cup sugar
½ cup brown sugar (packed)
2 eggs (⅓ to ½ cup)
1 tsp. vanilla
2 sq. unsweetened chocolate (2 oz.), melted

1¾ cups SOFTASILK Flour
1½ tsp. soda
¾ tsp. salt
1 cup buttermilk
¼ cup water

Heat oven to 350° (mod.). Grease and flour an oblong pan, 13x9½x2″ or two layer pans, 9x1½″. Cream shortening, sugar, eggs, vanilla and cooled chocolate until fluffy. Beat 5 min. high speed on mixer or by hand. Measure flour by dip-level-pour method or by sifting (*see p. 6*). Blend flour, soda and salt. Add alternately in three additions with buttermilk. Finally, blend in water. Pour into pan(s). Bake *oblong 35 to 40 min., layers 30 to 35 min.* Let stand 10 min., remove from pan(s). Cool. Finish with Butterscotch Filling and Marshmallow Frosting (*recipes below*).

Butterscotch Filling

1 cup brown sugar (packed)
3 tbsp. flour
1 cup milk
2 egg yolks, slightly beaten
2 tbsp. butter
1 tsp. vanilla
½ cup chopped nuts

Combine sugar and flour in saucepan. Gradually stir in milk. Cook over medium heat, stirring constantly, until mixture thickens and boils. Boil 1 min., stirring constantly. Remove from heat. Slowly stir at least half of hot mixture into egg yolks. Blend into remaining hot mixture in saucepan. Boil 1 min. more, stirring constantly. Remove from heat and blend in butter and vanilla. Cool. Spread filling over top of cake to within ½″ of edge and sprinkle with nuts.

Marshmallow Frosting

2 egg whites (¼ cup)
1½ cups sugar
¼ tsp. cream of tartar
1 tbsp. light corn syrup
⅓ cup water
¼ lb. marshmallows, quartered (about 16 whole)
½ sq. unsweetened chocolate (½ oz.), melted

Combine egg whites, sugar, cream of tartar, syrup and water in top of double boiler. Place over boiling water and beat with electric or rotary beater until mixture stands in stiff peaks. Scrape bottom and sides of pan occasionally. Remove pan from heat and add marshmallows. Continue beating until frosting is thick enough to spread. Frost top and sides of cake. Dip back of spoon in melted chocolate and swirl over top of marshmallow frosting.

Chocolate Cupcakes

Developed especially for cupcakes.

½ cup cocoa
1 cup hot water
1⅔ cups GOLD MEDAL Flour
1½ cups sugar
½ tsp. baking powder
1 tsp. soda
½ tsp. salt
½ cup soft shortening
2 eggs (⅓ to ½ cup)

Heat oven to 400° (mod. hot). Line 24 medium muffin cups with paper baking cups. Mix cocoa and water until smooth. Cool. Measure flour by dip-level-pour method or by sifting (*see p. 6*). Blend flour, sugar, baking powder, soda and salt. Add shortening and cocoa mixture. Beat 2 min., medium speed on mixer or 300 vigorous strokes by hand. Scrape sides and bottom of bowl constantly. Add eggs. Beat 2 more min., scraping bowl frequently. Pour into baking cups (½ full). Bake *15 to 20 min. Makes 24 cupcakes.*

Real Red Devils Food Cake

A rich, moist cake . . . made with cocoa. Developed by Lorraine Kilgren of our staff. See color picture, p. 147.

1 ¾ cups SOFTASILK Flour
1 ½ cups sugar
1 ¼ tsp. soda
1 tsp. salt
⅓ cup cocoa

½ cup soft shortening
1 cup milk
2 eggs (⅓ to ½ cup)
1 tsp. vanilla

Heat oven to 350° (mod.). Grease and flour two layer pans, 8 or 9x1½" or an oblong pan, 13x9½x2". Measure flour by dip-level-pour method or by sifting (*see p. 6*). Blend in bowl flour, sugar, soda, salt and cocoa. Add shortening and ⅔ cup milk. Beat 2 min., medium speed on mixer or 300 vigorous strokes by hand. Scrape sides and bottom of bowl constantly. Add rest of milk, eggs and vanilla. Beat 2 more min., scraping bowl frequently. Pour into pan(s). Bake *8" layers 35 to 40 min., 9" layers 30 to 35 min., oblong 45 to 50 min.* Cool. Finish with White Mountain or Satiny Beige Frosting (*p. 174*) or with Chocolate Butter Icing (*p. 172*).

Red Devils Food Cake

A 3-egg devils food cake made with cocoa. Long a favorite with homemakers.

1 ⅔ cups GOLD MEDAL Flour
1 ½ cups sugar
1 ¼ tsp. soda
1 tsp. salt
½ cup cocoa
½ cup soft shortening
1 cup milk
1 tsp. vanilla
3 eggs (½ to ⅔ cup)

Heat oven to 350° (mod.). Grease and flour two layer pans, 8 or 9x1½" or an oblong pan, 13x9½x2". Measure flour by dip-level-pour method or by sifting (*see p. 6*). Blend in bowl flour, sugar, soda, salt and cocoa. Add shortening, milk and vanilla. Beat 2 min., medium speed on mixer or 300 vigorous strokes by hand. Scrape sides and bottom of bowl constantly. Add eggs. Beat 2 more min., scraping bowl frequently. Pour into pan(s). Bake *8" layers about 38 min., 9" layers about 30 min., oblong about 45 min.* Cool. Frost with Brown Beauty Icing (*p. 173*).

Mardi Gras Cake

Make either of the cakes on this page in layers, but stir 1 tsp. cloves with the dry ingredients. Spread White Mountain Frosting (*p. 174*) between cooled layers and over top and sides. Decorate the icing by dipping the tip of a teaspoon into melted chocolate and making indentations in the shape of circles here and there over the entire surface.

HOW TO CUT A LAYER CAKE TO GET MORE PIECES AND DAINTIER ONES

Use a thin, sharp knife. Insert the point of knife into the cake . . . keeping the point down and handle up, slice . . . pulling the knife toward you. If frosting sticks, dip knife in hot water.

Cut around cake in a circle half way to the center. Cut pieces from outer circle. Cut pieces from inner circle. Makes 38 pieces.

OR

Cut cake in 4 quarters. Then cut each quarter into slices. The 2 pieces closest to the middle of cake may be cut in half. Makes 32 pieces.

Black Midnight Cake

Margaret Norrdin of our staff says this cake is the "best ever" . . . "especially when creamy fudge-frosted."
This cake is made with cocoa and water. See color picture, p. 147.

⅔ cup soft shortening	¼ tsp. baking powder
1⅔ cups sugar	1¼ tsp. soda
3 eggs (½ to ⅔ cup)	1 tsp. salt
2¼ cups SOFTASILK Flour	1⅓ cups water
⅔ cup cocoa	1 tsp. vanilla

Heat oven to 350° (mod.). Grease and flour two layer pans, 9x1½″ or an oblong pan, 13x9½x2″. Cream shortening, sugar and eggs until fluffy. Beat 5 min., high speed on mixer or by hand. Measure flour by dip-level-pour method or by sifting (*see p. 6*). Blend flour, cocoa, baking powder, soda and salt. Add alternately with water and vanilla. Use low speed on mixer. Pour into pan(s). Bake *layers about 35 min., oblong 40 to 45 min.* Cool. Frost with White Mountain Frosting (*p. 172*).

Cocoa Cream Cake

Make Black Midnight Cake (*above*) in layers. When cool, split each layer crosswise into two layers. For perfect cutting, use a long, thin, sharp knife.

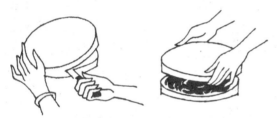

Spread sweetened whipped cream (1½ to 2 cups) between layers. Frost top and sides with Brown Beauty Icing (*p. 173*). Cake will keep in refrigerator 2 to 3 days.

They'll all take Cocoa Cream Cake.

Mocha-Frosted Chocolate Cake

Bake Black Midnight Cake (*above*) in layers. Fill and frost with Mocha Topping (*below*).

Mocha Topping

Soften 1 pkg. (8 oz.) cream cheese at room temperature. Thoroughly blend in 1 tbsp. powdered instant coffee, ½ cup brown sugar (packed), 1 tsp. vanilla and dash of salt. Fold in 1 cup whipping cream, stiffly whipped so frosting is not too soft.

Cherry-Frosted Chocolate Cake

"I like any cake . . . just so it's chocolate," says Winona Kennedy (Mrs. James G. Kennedy). "But this one is extra special. We bake it in an oblong pan to take on picnics when I'm visiting at my old home on Long Island."

Make Black Midnight Cake (*above*) or any favorite chocolate cake. Cool. Frost with Cherry Butter Icing (*below*). Decorate with drained maraschino cherry halves.

Cherry Butter Icing

⅓ cup butter
3 cups *sifted* confectioners' sugar
about ¼ cup maraschino cherry juice

Blend butter and sugar. Stir in cherry juice until smooth.

Peppermint Chocolate Cake

Make Black Midnight Cake (*above*)—*except* fold into batter ¼ tsp. peppermint flavoring. Ice with a chocolate or white icing . . . sprinkle with crushed peppermint stick candy.

CHOCOLATE CAKE AS YOU LIKE IT

New Fudge Cake, page 143
Real Red Devils Food Cake, page 145
Black Midnight Cake, opposite

Sweet Cream Cake

Easy and quick to make. Different, too!

2⅓ cups SOFTASILK Flour
 or 2¼ cups GOLD MEDAL Flour
3 tsp. baking powder
1 tsp. salt

3 eggs (½ to ⅔ cup)
1⅓ cups sugar
1⅓ cups whipping cream (30 to 35% butterfat)
1½ tsp. vanilla

Heat oven to 350° (mod.). Grease and flour two layer pans, 8 or 9x1½" or an oblong pan, 13x9½x2". Measure flour by dip-level-pour method or by sifting (*see p. 6*). Blend flour, baking powder and salt and set aside. Beat eggs until very thick in small mixer bowl (about 5 min.). Beat sugar in gradually. Transfer egg-sugar mixture into large mixing bowl. Stir in flour mixture alternately with whipping cream and vanilla. Pour into pan(s). Bake *layers 25 to 30 min., oblong about 40 min.* Cool. Finish with sweetened whipped cream or sprinkle sugar and cinnamon over top of cake 3 min. before removing from oven. Or, frost as desired.

Sweet Cream Spice Cake

Make Sweet Cream Cake (*above*)—except add 3 tsp. cinnamon, 1½ tsp. cloves and 1½ tsp. allspice to dry ingredients before stirring. Delicious with White Fudge Frosting (*p. 175*) or with peaches and cream: make double recipe Cream Filling (*p. 177*), spread on both layers, ring with drained canned peach halves, set one layer atop the other.

Whipped Cream Cake

"Iced with chocolate frosting and served with fruit gelatin, this is a favorite in our farm home," says Mrs. Lee Christopher of Jackson, Minnesota.

1½ cups whipping cream (30 to 35% butterfat)
3 eggs (½ to ⅔ cup), well beaten
1½ tsp. vanilla
2¼ cups SOFTASILK Flour
1½ cups sugar
2 tsp. baking powder
½ tsp. salt

Heat oven to 350° (mod.). Grease and flour two layer pans, 8 or 9x1½" or an oblong pan, 13x9½x2". Whip cream until stiff. Fold in eggs and vanilla. Measure flour by dip-level-pour method or by sifting (*see p. 6*). Blend flour, sugar, baking powder and salt; fold in gently with a wire whip. Pour into pan(s). Bake *layers 30 to 35 min., oblong 35 to 40 min.* Cool. Serve uniced or ice as desired.

Sour Cream Spice Cake

Mrs. George Holm of Cuba, North Dakota, says, "What is better with afternoon coffee on the farm . . . or anywhere else . . . than Sour Cream Spice Cake frosted with Easy Penuche Icing?"

1½ cups GOLD MEDAL Flour
1 tsp. baking powder
½ tsp. soda
½ tsp. salt
1¼ tsp. cinnamon
¾ tsp. cloves
¾ tsp. allspice
2 eggs (⅓ to ½ cup)
1 cup sugar
1 cup soured whipping cream (30 to 35% butterfat)
 (Put 1 tbsp. lemon juice in measuring cup, fill with cream; don't use commercial sour cream.)
1 tsp. vanilla
¼ tsp. lemon flavoring

Heat oven to 350° (mod.). Grease and flour a square pan, 9x9x1¾". Measure flour by dip-level-pour method or by sifting (*see p. 6*). Blend flour, baking powder, soda, salt and spices; set aside. Beat eggs in small mixer bowl until very thick (about 5 min.). Beat in sugar gradually. Transfer egg-sugar mixture to large mixing bowl. Stir in flour mixture alternately with cream and flavorings. Pour into pan. Bake *35 to 40 min.* Cool.

Sour Cream Cupcakes

Make batter for Sour Cream Spice Cake (*above*)—*except* omit spices and fold in ½ cup chopped nuts and ½ cup raisins. Pour into 12 medium muffin cups lined with paper baking cups (⅔ full). Bake at 400° (mod. hot) *18 to 20 min.*

Loaf o' Gold Cake

Modification of the original Pound Cake . . . in which one pound of each ingredient was used. With the modern ingredients, the cake recipe also had to be changed. Since the batter is very stiff, an electric mixer is a great help.

2¼ cups SOFTASILK Flour
or 1¾ cups GOLD MEDAL Flour
1 cup sugar
2 tsp. baking powder
1 tsp. salt

½ cup soft shortening (half butter)
1 tsp. vanilla
5 egg yolks (⅜ cup), unbeaten
¾ cup milk

Heat oven to 350° (mod.). Grease and line with paper a loaf pan, 9x5x3″. Measure flour by dip-level-pour method or by sifting (*see p. 6*). Blend dry ingredients in bowl. Add shortening, vanilla, egg yolks and ½ cup of milk. (When using GOLD MEDAL Flour, add all milk at once.) Beat 2 min., medium speed on mixer or 300 vigorous strokes by hand. Scrape sides and bottom of bowl constantly. Add rest of milk. Beat 2 more min., scraping bowl frequently. Spoon batter into pan. Bake 60 to 70 min. Cool and finish with Orange Glaze (*at right below*).

Chocolate Swirl Loaf Cake

Make Loaf o' Gold Cake (*above*)—except mix ⅓ cup batter with ½ sq. unsweetened chocolate (½ oz.), melted. Swirl chocolate batter into rest of batter with knife.

Peppermint Swirl Loaf Cake

Make Loaf o' Gold Cake (*above*)—except mix ⅓ cup batter with ¼ tsp. peppermint flavoring and 4 drops red food coloring. Swirl pink peppermint batter into rest of batter with knife.

Pecan Loaf Cake

A lovely white pound-like cake with nuts all the way through it.

2 cups SOFTASILK Flour
1¼ cups sugar
1½ tsp. baking powder
1 tsp. salt
½ cup soft shortening
½ cup milk
1 tsp. vanilla
4 egg whites (½ to ⅔ cup)
½ cup chopped pecans (toasted, if desired)

Heat oven to 350° (mod.). Grease and line with paper a loaf pan, 9x5x3″. Measure flour by dip-level-pour method or by sifting (*see p. 6*). Blend flour, sugar, baking powder and salt in bowl. Add shortening, milk and vanilla. Beat 2 min., medium speed on mixer or 300 vigorous strokes by hand. Scrape sides and bottom of bowl constantly. Add egg whites. Beat 2 more min., scraping bowl frequently. Fold in nuts. Pour into pan. *Bake 60 to 65 min.* Remove from pan and cool.

Orange Glaze

Very thin. It soaks into the warm cake, making it moist and giving it an orange flavor.

½ cup orange juice
½ tsp. grated orange rind
1 cup *sifted* confectioners' sugar

Mix ingredients. Let stand on top of oven while baking cake, stirring occasionally. When cake is baked, remove from pan and punch holes on top surface with a fork. Pour the warm glaze, a little at a time, over the top.

Lemon Loaf Cake

Make Loaf o' Gold Cake (*above*)—except fold into batter grated rind of 1 lemon (about 1 tbsp). Let cake cool 10 min. Remove from pan and punch holes on top surface with fork. Pour Orange-Lemon Glaze (*below*), a little at a time, over top.

Orange-Lemon Glaze

Blend 1¼ cups *sifted* confectioners' sugar, 2 tbsp. orange juice, 1 tsp. lemon juice, 1 tbsp. grated orange rind and 1 tsp. grated lemon rind.

149

Jack Horner Cake

A moist prune spice cake. Developed by Joy Wardner, now Mrs. Donald Bostrom of Bloomington, Indiana, when she was on our staff.

1 cup cut-up, pitted, uncooked prunes	1¼ tsp. soda
1 cup boiling water	1 tsp. *each* cinnamon, nutmeg, cloves
2 cups GOLD MEDAL Flour	½ cup vegetable oil
1½ cups sugar	3 eggs (½ to ⅔ cup)
1 tsp. salt	1 cup chopped nuts

Pour boiling water over cut-up prunes. Let stand for 2 hr. *Heat oven to 350°* (mod.). Grease and flour an oblong pan, 13x9½x2″ or two layer pans, 9x1½″. Measure flour by dip-level-pour method or by sifting (*see p. 6*). Blend dry ingredients. Add prune mixture and all other ingredients. Blend thoroughly. Beat 2 min., medium speed on mixer or 300 strokes by hand. Pour into pan(s). Bake *oblong 45 to 50 min.*, *layers 35 to 40 min.* Finish with Butter Icing (*p. 172*).

NOTE: 1 cup cut-up, pitted, unsweetened, cooked prunes may be used; substitute ⅔ cup prune juice for the 1 cup boiling water.

Prune Party Loaf

Make batter for Jack Horner Cake (*above*). Pour into greased and floured jelly roll pan, 15½x10½x1″. Bake *about 35 min.* Cool, cut in half crosswise. Cut one half into 2 rectangles, 10½x3¾″. Put together with lemon filling. Spoon lemon filling down center of top, decorate edges with whipped cream. Cut into 8 slices to serve. Frost other half of cake with confectioners' sugar icing. Sprinkle with nuts and cut into 24 bars.

Buttermilk Spice Cake

2¼ cups SOFTASILK Flour
  or 2 cups plus 2 tbsp. GOLD MEDAL Flour
1 cup sugar
1 tsp. baking powder
¾ tsp. soda
1 tsp. salt
¾ tsp. cloves
¾ tsp. cinnamon
¾ cup brown sugar (packed)
½ cup soft shortening
1 cup buttermilk
3 eggs (½ to ⅔ cup)

Heat oven to 350° (mod.). Grease and flour two layer pans, 9x1½″ or an oblong pan, 13x9½x2″. Measure flour by dip-level-pour method or by sifting (*see p. 6*). Blend dry ingredients in bowl. Add brown sugar, shortening and buttermilk. Beat 2 min., medium speed on mixer or 300 vigorous strokes by hand. Scrape sides and bottom of bowl constantly. Add eggs. Beat 2 more min., scraping bowl frequently. Pour into pan(s). Bake *layers 35 to 40 min., oblong 45 to 50 min.* Cool.

Applesauce Cake

So good with Easy Penuche Icing (p. 175).

2¾ cups SOFTASILK Flour
  or 2½ cups GOLD MEDAL Flour
2 cups sugar
¼ tsp. baking powder
1½ tsp. soda
1½ tsp. salt
¾ tsp. cinnamon
½ tsp. cloves
½ tsp. allspice
½ cup soft shortening
½ cup water
1½ cups unsweetened applesauce
2 eggs (⅓ to ½ cup)
½ cup chopped walnuts
1 cup raisins, cut up

Heat oven to 350° (mod.). Grease and flour two layer pans, 9x1½″ or an oblong pan, 13x9½x2″. Measure flour by dip-level-pour method or by sifting (*see p. 6*). Blend dry ingredients in bowl. Add shortening, water and applesauce. Beat 2 min., medium speed on mixer or 300 vigorous strokes by hand. Scrape sides and bottom of bowl constantly. Add eggs. Beat 2 more min., scraping bowl frequently. Stir in walnuts and raisins. Pour into pan(s). Bake *layers 35 to 40 min., oblong 45 to 50 min.* Cool.

▶ ALL YOU HAVE TO DO

To make 1½ cups unsweetened applesauce: wash, quarter and core 6 to 8 tart apples. Add ¼ cup water. Cover and cook to a mush, stirring occasionally. Press through a sieve or food mill.

Date-and-Nut Cake

Deliciously moist and fruity. Many like it unfrosted. But a penuche icing makes a perfect finish.

1 cup hot water
6½-oz. pkg. dates, finely cut (about 1¼ cups)
¼ cup soft shortening
1 cup sugar
1 egg

1 tsp. vanilla
1⅔ cups GOLD MEDAL Flour
  or 1¾ cups SOFTASILK Flour
1 tsp. soda
½ tsp. salt
½ cup chopped nuts

Heat oven to 350° (mod.). Grease and flour a square pan, 9x9x1¾". Pour hot water over dates. Let stand until cool.

Cream shortening, sugar, egg and vanilla together until fluffy. Beat 5 min. high speed on mixer or by hand. Measure flour by dip-level-pour method or by sifting (*see p. 6*). Blend flour, soda and salt. Mix in alternately with date-water mixture. Use low speed on mixer. Stir in nuts. Pour into pan. Bake *40 to 45 min.* Cool. Frost with Easy Penuche Icing (*p. 175*).

Raisin-Nut Cake

Rich cake with the unusual flavor that buttermilk gives. Modern version of an 18th century recipe ... when cakes with raisins or currants were favorites.

2 cups plus 2 tbsp. GOLD MEDAL Flour
1 cup sugar
1 tsp. baking powder
¾ tsp. soda
1 tsp. salt
¾ cup brown sugar (packed)
½ cup soft shortening
1 cup buttermilk
3 eggs (½ to ⅔ cup)
½ cup finely chopped nuts
½ cup finely cut-up raisins

Heat oven to 350° (mod.). Grease and flour two layer pans, 9x1½" or an oblong pan, 13x9½x2". Measure flour by dip-level-pour method or by sifting (*see p. 6*). Blend flour, sugar, baking powder, soda and salt. Add brown sugar, shortening and buttermilk. Beat 2 min., medium speed on mixer or 300 vigorous strokes by hand. Scrape sides and bottom of bowl constantly. Add eggs. Beat 2 more min., scraping bowl frequently. Fold in nuts and raisins. Pour into pan(s). Bake *layers 35 to 40 min., oblong 45 to 50 min.* Cool. Frost with White Fudge Frosting.

Dark Fruitcake

Often used as groom's cake.

Follow recipe for Golden Fruitcake (*p. 162*) except add 1 tsp. mace, ½ tsp. *each* nutmeg and allspice and ¼ tsp. cloves with dry ingredients. Instead of milk, use ½ cup fruit juice and use ½ cup *dark* jelly, beaten with fork. For fruit and nuts, use 1½ lb. seedless raisins and ½ lb. *each* currants, citron and nuts.

▶ **ALL YOU HAVE TO DO**

To cut maraschino cherries, candied cherries or dates: use kitchen scissors. Dip scissors in warm water when they begin to get sticky.

Banana-Nut Cake

Wonderfully tender. Delicate flavor of ripe bananas.

2½ cups SOFTASILK Flour
1⅔ cups sugar
1¼ tsp. baking powder
1¼ tsp. soda
1 tsp. salt
⅔ cup soft shortening
⅔ cup buttermilk
1¼ cups mashed ripe bananas (about 3)
3 eggs (½ to ⅔ cup)
⅔ cup finely chopped nuts

Heat oven to 350° (mod.). Grease and flour two layer pans, 9x1½" or an oblong pan, 13x9½x2". Measure flour by dip-level-pour method or by sifting (*see p. 6*). Blend flour, sugar, baking powder, soda and salt. Add shortening, half of buttermilk and mashed bananas. Beat 2 min., medium speed on mixer or 300 vigorous strokes by hand. Scrape sides and bottom of bowl constantly. Add eggs and rest of buttermilk. Beat 2 more min., scraping bowl frequently. Fold in nuts. Pour into pan(s). Bake *layers about 35 min., oblong 45 to 50 min.* Cool. Finish with Butter Icing (*p. 172*) or "frost" with whipped cream and decorate with sliced bananas.

USE RIPE BANANAS

Bananas should be medium yellow with brown flecks on the skins, but firm inside. Green tipped bananas aren't ripe. Never put bananas in the refrigerator.

Fluffy Sponge Cake

A lovely, high, light sponge cake—easy for the amateur.

1½ cups SOFTASILK Flour or 1½ cups GOLD MEDAL Flour	⅓ cup cold water 2 tsp. vanilla
1 tsp. baking powder	1 tsp. lemon flavoring
½ tsp. salt	1 tsp. grated lemon rind, if desired
6 egg yolks (about ½ cup)	6 egg whites (¾ cup)
1½ cups sugar	½ tsp. cream of tartar

Heat oven to 325° (slow mod.). Measure flour by dip-level-pour method or by sifting (*see p. 6*). Blend flour, baking powder and salt; set aside. Beat egg yolks in small mixer bowl until very thick and lemon-colored. Pour beaten yolks into large bowl and beat in sugar gradually. Beat dry ingredients in alternately (slowly, on low speed) with water, flavorings and rind. In large bowl, beat egg whites and cream of tartar until stiff. Gradually and gently fold egg yolk mixture into beaten whites. Pour into *ungreased* tube pan, 10x4". Bake *60 to 65 min.* Turn pan upside down with tube over neck of funnel or bottle. Cool. Remove from pan.

Egg Yolk Sponge Cake

Especially good with berries. And a wonderful way in which to use extra egg yolks.

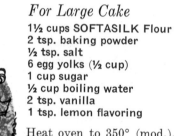

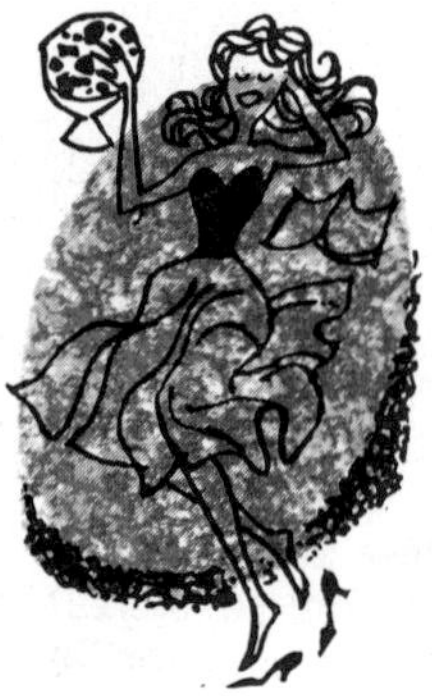

For Large Cake	*For Small Cake*
1½ cups SOFTASILK Flour	¾ cup SOFTASILK Flour
2 tsp. baking powder	1 tsp. baking powder
½ tsp. salt	¼ tsp. salt
6 egg yolks (½ cup)	3 egg yolks (¼ cup)
1 cup sugar	½ cup sugar
½ cup boiling water	¼ cup boiling water
2 tsp. vanilla	1 tsp. vanilla
1 tsp. lemon flavoring	½ tsp. lemon flavoring

Heat oven to 350° (mod.). For Large Cake grease and flour two layer pans, 8 or 9x1½" or an oblong pan, 13x9½x2". For Small Cake use one layer pan, 8 or 9x1½" or a square pan, 8x8x2" or one loaf pan, 8½x4½x2¾". Measure flour by dip-level-pour method or by sifting (*see p. 6*). Blend flour, baking powder and salt; set aside. Beat egg yolks in small mixer bowl until very thick and lemon-colored. Beat sugar in gradually. (For Large Cake, pour egg-sugar mixture into large bowl.) Blend in water and flavorings slowly, on low speed. Quickly blend in dry ingredients; pour into pan(s). Bake *oblong or loaf about 30 min., layers or square about 25 min.* Let cool upright in pans 8 to 10 min., then remove.

Hot Water Sponge Cake

Light and fluffy. Elegant with sweetened whipped cream and berries, peaches or bananas.

1¼ cups SOFTASILK Flour	¾ cup sugar
1½ tsp. baking powder	⅓ cup hot water
½ tsp. salt	1 tsp. vanilla
3 eggs (½ to ⅔ cup)	½ tsp. lemon flavoring

Heat oven to 350° (mod.). Grease and flour a square pan, 9x9x1¾". Measure flour by dip-level-pour method or by sifting (*see p. 6*). Blend flour, baking powder and salt; set aside. Beat eggs in small mixer bowl until very thick and lemon-colored. Pour beaten eggs into large mixer bowl and beat sugar in gradually. Blend in water and flavorings slowly, on low speed. Quickly blend in the dry ingredients; pour into pan. Bake *25 to 30 min.* Cool.

Jelly Roll

Lots of fun to make and serve. See "how to roll" in sketch at left below.

1 cup SOFTASILK Flour
    or 1 cup GOLD MEDAL Flour
1 tsp. baking powder
¼ tsp. salt

3 large eggs (⅔ cup)
1 cup sugar
⅓ cup water
1 tsp. vanilla

Heat oven to 375° (quick mod.). Grease a jelly roll pan, 15½x10½x1″ and line bottom with greased brown paper or with aluminum foil. Measure flour by dip-level-pour method or by sifting (*see p. 6*). Blend flour, baking powder and salt; set aside. Beat eggs in small mixer bowl until very thick and lemon-colored. Pour beaten eggs into large bowl. Gradually beat in sugar. Blend in water and vanilla, on low speed. Slowly mix in dry ingredients (low speed) just until batter is smooth. Pour into pan. Bake *12 to 15 min.* Loosen edges and immediately turn upside down on a towel sprinkled with confectioners' sugar. Remove paper. Trim off stiff edges. While hot, roll cake and towel from narrow end. Cool on wire rack. Unroll cake, remove towel. Spread with soft (not syrupy) jelly or filling. Roll again. If desired, sprinkle with confectioners' sugar. Cut in 1″ slices. *10 to 12 servings.*

Jelly Roll Jamboree

Tired of jellies and jams? Try these Fillings (p. 177).

Clear Orange   Pineapple
Clear Lemon   Chocolate Cream

To use these special fillings in a jelly roll . . . roll up a plain Jelly Roll (*above*) right after baking. Let cool. Unroll. Spread with cooled filling and reroll.

Strawberry Cream Roll

Less than an hour before serving, unroll Jelly Roll (*above*). Spread with about 1 cup Sweetened Whipped Cream (*p. 232*). Sprinkle with 2 cups sliced fresh strawberries. Reroll. Chill. Serve in thick slices.

Chocolate Roll (*Cherry Tree Log*)

"This has always been one of the best loved desserts in our home," says Mrs. William H. Lord of Foley, Minnesota. "Often we omit the icing and serve a chocolate sauce over the slices."

Make Jelly Roll (*above*)—except blend ¼ cup cocoa with the dry ingredients. Unroll, removing towel. Fill with 1 cup Sweetened Whipped Cream (*p. 232*). Roll up carefully. Frost with Thin Chocolate Icing (*p. 173*). Chill thoroughly. To serve, cut in 1″ slices. *10 to 12 servings.*

Chocolate Ribbon Cake

Make Chocolate Roll (*above*)—except do not roll cake. Cut crosswise into 4 pieces, each 10x3¾″. Stack and fill with Marshmallow Frosting (*p. 144*). Top with Thin Chocolate Icing (*p. 173*). To serve, slice or cut into squares. *12 servings.*

Lincoln's Log Cake

Bake Chocolate Roll (*above*). Run point of knife lengthwise in frosting to simulate bark. Decorate with candied or maraschino cherries and cut-up gumdrops shaped into leaves.

Guest's Name Cake

Bake Jelly Roll (*above*). Fill (*see left*), roll and ice. Write names of guests with Easy Creamy Decorating Icing (*p. 202*) across roll (name will be on each slice). Cut slices between names.

ANGEL FOOD CAKES *Light as the clouds in the heavens.*

HOW TO MAKE HIGH, LIGHT ANGEL FOOD CAKES

Separate eggs while cold and let whites warm to room temperature before beating. This gives best volume.

Be sure oven is preheated to correct temperature to assure large volume and even texture.

DO NOT GREASE angel food pan. Batter needs sides of pan to cling to for support. Also prevents cake from falling out of pan when inverted.

Beat egg whites with sugar until meringue holds stiff peaks. Use electric mixer or wire whip.

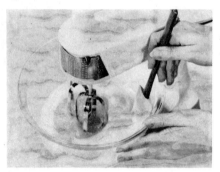

1. Stir part of sugar with flour to blend. Measure egg whites into large bowl; add cream of tartar and salt; beat until frothy. Beat in remaining sugar, *2 tbsp. at a time.* (Medium speed on mixer.)

2. Continue beating (high speed on mixer) until meringue is very firm and stiff straight peaks are formed when beater is pulled up. Fold in flavoring.

3. Sprinkle flour-sugar mixture, *3 tbsp. at a time,* over meringue. Cut and fold in gently, with spatula or wire whip, until flour-sugar mixture disappears each time.

4. Carefully push batter with rubber scraper into deep tube pan. Push and level batter gently against tube and sides to prevent large holes.

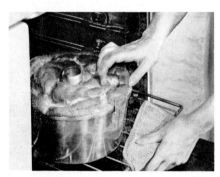

5. Bake until no imprint remains when finger lightly touches top of cake. The deep macaroon-like crust should be golden brown.

6. Immediately hang the cake, in the pan, upside down over a funnel or bottle to prevent shrinking or falling. Let hang until cool. Remove from pan, frost.

Angel Food Cake

So tender . . . light as air . . . fluffy as a cloud. But very stiff beating of the egg whites is required. Mrs. William Lilliquist (we know her as "Aunt Nannie") of Minneapolis, who loves Angel Foods above all other cakes and makes perfect ones, still prefers to beat the egg whites on a large turkey platter, using a wire whip.

Angel Food Supreme

1 cup SOFTASILK Flour
¾ cup plus 2 tbsp. sugar (granulated)
1½ cups egg whites (12)
1½ tsp. cream of tartar
¼ tsp. salt
¾ cup sugar (granulated)
1½ tsp. vanilla
½ tsp. almond flavoring

Angel Food De Luxe

1 cup SOFTASILK Flour
1½ cups sugar (*sifted* confectioners')
1½ cups egg whites (12)
1½ tsp. cream of tartar
¼ tsp. salt
1 cup sugar (granulated)
1½ tsp. vanilla
½ tsp. almond flavoring

Heat oven to 375° (quick mod.). Have ready a tube pan, 10x4", but do not grease. Measure flour by dip-level-pour method or by sifting (*see p. 6*). Stir flour and first amount of sugar together to blend. Measure egg whites, cream of tartar and salt into large mixing bowl. Beat until foamy. Gradually add second amount of sugar, 2 tbsp. at a time. Continue beating until meringue holds stiff peaks. Fold in flavorings. Sprinkle flour-sugar mixture over meringue. Fold in gently just until the flour-sugar mixture disappears. Push batter into ungreased tube pan. Gently cut through batter. Bake *30 to 35 min.* Invert on a funnel. Let hang until cold. Frost with Thin Chocolate Icing (*p. 173*) or a butter icing (*p. 172*).

Chocolate Angel Food

Make Angel Food De Luxe (*above*)—*except* substitute ¼ cup cocoa for ¼ cup of the flour (stir together to blend). Omit almond flavoring.

Fruited Angel Food

Make Angel Food De Luxe or Angel Food Supreme (*above*)—*except* save out 2 tbsp. of the flour-sugar mixture and mix with ¾ cup finely chopped candied fruit and ¼ cup finely chopped nuts, if desired. Sprinkle this mixture, ¼ cup at a time, over the batter and fold in gently. Bake.

Marble Angel Food

Make Angel Food Supreme (*above*)—*except* omit almond. Divide batter into two parts. Into one half the batter, fold 2 tbsp. sifted cocoa. Drop by spoonfuls into pan, alternating white and chocolate batter. Cut through batter several times.

See p. 234 for special angel food desserts.

Coconut Angel Food

"For birthdays, I sometimes frost it with a yellow icing, add lighted yellow candles and encircle it with a wreath of green leaves," says Mrs. Glenn M. Lewis of Knollwood, Hopkins, Minnesota, an authority on home decoration.

Make Angel Food Supreme or Angel Food De Luxe (*above*)—*except* fold in (in two additions) 1 cup shredded coconut.

Cherry Angel Food Cake

See color picture on p. 158.

Follow recipe for Angel Food De Luxe (*above*)—*except*, at the last, fold in ½ cup chopped maraschino cherries drained on paper towel.

155

HOW TO MAKE BEAUTIFUL CHIFFON CAKES

Separate eggs while cold and let whites warm to room temperature before beating. This gives best volume. Yolks may be refrigerated or at room temperature.

Be sure oven is preheated to correct temperature to assure large volume and even texture.

DO NOT GREASE chiffon cake pan. Batter needs sides of pan to cling to for support. Also prevents cake from falling out of pan when inverted.

Beat egg whites with cream of tartar until whites hold stiff peaks. Use electric mixer or wire whip.

1. Stir flour, sugar, baking powder, salt in mixing bowl. Make a well, then add in order: oil, egg yolks, water, flavoring and rind.

2. Beat with spoon until smooth. Set aside while beating egg whites.

3. Beat egg whites and cream of tartar in large bowl until they hold *very stiff* peaks. DO NOT UNDERBEAT. A rubber scraper drawn through them leaves a clean path.

4. Pour egg yolk mixture in thin stream over entire surface of egg whites, gently cutting and folding in with rubber scraper or flexible spatula.

5. Fold gently, bringing scraper across bottom of bowl, up the side and over. Turn bowl and continue until completely blended. Pour into ungreased pan.

6. Bake until surface springs back when lightly touched. Invert immediately on funnel; let hang until cold. To remove, loosen with a spatula. Turn pan over and hit edge sharply on table. Frost and trim cake, if desired.

Chiffon Cake

Light as angel food, rich as butter cake. "It's the first thing I think of when planning a party," says Dorothy Quinn (Mrs. Fred J. Quinn) of Tajunga, California. "It's so easy to make, everyone likes it and it can be served in so many glamorous ways."

Large Cake

2¼ cups SOFTASILK Flour
   or 2 cups GOLD MEDAL Flour
1½ cups sugar
3 tsp. baking powder
1 tsp. salt
½ cup vegetable oil
5 egg yolks, unbeaten (if you use
   SOFTASILK) or 7 egg yolks, unbeaten
   (if you use GOLD MEDAL)
¾ cup cold water
2 tsp. vanilla
2 tsp. grated lemon rind
1 cup egg whites (7 or 8)
½ tsp. cream of tartar

Small Cake

1 cup plus 2 tbsp. SOFTASILK Flour
   or 1 cup GOLD MEDAL Flour
¾ cup sugar
1½ tsp. baking powder
½ tsp. salt
¼ cup vegetable oil
2 egg yolks, unbeaten, if you use SOFTA-
   SILK, or 3 egg yolks, unbeaten (if you
   use GOLD MEDAL)
¼ cup plus 2 tbsp. cold water
1 tsp. vanilla
1 tsp. grated lemon rind
½ cup egg whites (4)
¼ tsp. cream of tartar

Heat oven (see temperatures below). For Large Cake use a tube pan, 10x4″ or an oblong pan, 13x9½x2″. For Small Cake use a tube pan, 9x3½″ or a loaf pan, 9x5x3″ or a square pan, 8x8x2″ or 9x9x1¾″. DO NOT GREASE PANS.

Measure flour by dip-level-pour method or by sifting (*see p. 6*). Blend flour, sugar, baking powder and salt in bowl. Make a well and add in order: oil, egg yolks, water, vanilla and rind. Beat with spoon until smooth. Measure egg whites and cream of tartar into large mixing bowl. Beat until whites form very stiff peaks. Pour egg yolk mixture gradually over beaten whites, gently folding with rubber scraper just until blended. Pour into ungreased pan. Bake. Invert on funnel. Let hang until cold.

Bake 10″ tube at 325° for 55 min., then at 350° for 10 to 15 min.
Bake 9″ tube at 325° for 50 to 55 min.
Bake oblong cake at 350° for 45 to 50 min.
Bake loaf cake at 325° for 50 to 55 min.
Bake square cake at 350° for 30 to 35 min.

Maple Pecan Chiffon

Make Large Cake (*above*)—*except* omit vanilla and lemon rind and use ¾ cup granulated sugar and ¾ cup brown sugar (packed). Use 2 tsp. maple flavoring. Gently fold in at the last 1 cup very finely chopped pecans. Frost with Maple Butter Icing. (*p. 172*).

Butterscotch Chiffon

Make Large Cake (*above*)—*except* omit sugar and lemon rind. Add 2 cups brown sugar (packed) to dry ingredients. Bake *65 to 70 min. at 325°.*

Orange Chiffon

Make Large Cake (*above*)—*except* omit vanilla and lemon rind. Add 3 tbsp. grated orange rind. Finish with Orange Butter Icing (*p. 172*).

Chocolate Chip Chiffon

Delicious chips all through.

Make Large Cake (*above*)—*except* increase sugar to 1¾ cups and omit rind. At the last, sprinkle over batter and fold in carefully with a few strokes 3 sq. unsweetened or sweet chocolate (3 oz.), shaved. Frost with Chocolate Butter Icing (*p. 172*).

Spice Chiffon

Finish with Browned Butter Icing (p. 172).

Make Large Cake (*above*)—*except* omit vanilla and lemon rind. Add to the dry ingredients 1 tsp. cinnamon, ½ tsp. *each* nutmeg, allspice and cloves. 2 tbsp. caraway seeds may be added.

Mahogany Chiffon Cake, page 159   *Cherry Angel Food Cake, page 155*

Mahogany Chiffon

See color picture on opposite page.

¾ cup boiling water
½ cup cocoa
1¾ cups SOFTASILK Flour
1¾ cups sugar
1½ tsp. soda
1 tsp. salt
½ cup vegetable oil
7 unbeaten egg yolks (medium)
2 tsp. vanilla
1 cup egg whites (7 or 8)
½ tsp. cream of tartar

Heat oven to 325° (slow mod.). Combine boiling water and cocoa, let cool. Measure flour by dip-level-pour method or by sifting (*see p. 6*). Blend flour, sugar, soda and salt in bowl. Make a well and add oil, egg yolks, vanilla and cocoa mixture. Beat until smooth. Measure egg whites and cream of tartar into large mixing bowl and beat until very stiff. Pour egg yolk mixture in thin stream over entire surface of egg whites, gently cutting and folding in with rubber spatula until completely blended. Pour into ungreased 10″ tube pan. Bake *55 min. at 325° then at 350° 10 to 15 min.* Invert. Let hang until cold. Ice with Brown Beauty Icing (p. 173).

Bit o' Walnut Chiffon

Make Small Cake (*p. 157*)—*except* omit rind. Bake in loaf pan. At the last, sprinkle over batter ... gently folding in with a few strokes ... ½ cup very finely chopped walnuts. (If black walnut flavor is desired, use black walnuts or ¼ tsp. black walnut flavoring in place of vanilla.) Frost top and sides with Browned Butter Icing (*p. 172*). Garnish with toasted walnut halves.

Holiday Fruit Chiffon

Make Large Cake (*p. 157*)—*except* add ½ tsp. cinnamon to dry ingredients. At the last, sprinkle over batter ... gently folding in with a few strokes, ¾ cup very finely cut-up candied cherries, ½ cup very finely chopped pecans, ¼ cup very finely cut-up citron.

Banana Chiffon

2¼ cups SOFTASILK Flour
1½ cups sugar
3 tsp. baking powder
1 tsp. salt
½ cup vegetable oil
5 egg yolks, unbeaten
⅓ cup cold water
1 cup mashed ripe bananas
1 tsp. vanilla
1 cup egg whites (7 or 8)
½ tsp. cream of tartar

Heat oven to 325° (slow mod.). Measure flour by dip-level-pour method or by sifting (*see p. 6*). Blend flour, sugar, baking powder and salt in bowl. Make a well and add oil, egg yolks, water, bananas and vanilla. Beat until smooth. Measure egg whites and cream or tartar into large mixing bowl and beat until very stiff. Pour egg yolk mixture in thin stream over entire surface of egg whites, gently cutting and folding in with rubber spatula until completely blended. Pour into ungreased 10″ tube pan. Bake *65 to 70 min.* Invert on funnel; let hang until cold.

Peppermint Chip Chiffon

Make Large Cake (*p. 157*)—*except* omit lemon rind and use 1 tsp. peppermint flavoring in place of the vanilla. At the last, sprinkle over batter ... gently folding in with a few strokes to give marbled effect ... ½ tsp. red food coloring. To frost, see picture on p. 156.

Cherry-Nut Chiffon

Use a 10″ tube pan. Make Large Cake (*p. 157*)—*except* omit rind, use only 1 tsp. vanilla. Use ¼ cup maraschino cherry juice and ½ cup water for the liquid. At the last, sprinkle over batter ... and fold in with a few strokes ... ½ cup *each* very finely chopped nuts and finely chopped maraschino cherries, well drained. Bake *at 325° for 65 to 70 min.*

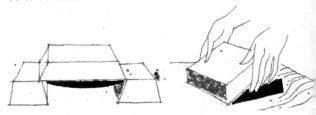

To cool a square or oblong cake .. rest edges of pan on two others.

When cold, loosen with spatula. Invert pan, hit sharply on table.

Lovelight Yellow Chiffon Cake

A whole new concept in layer cake-making, combining the fluffiness of sponge cake and the richness of butter cake. Developed by Irene Anderson, supervisor of our kitchens.

2 eggs, separated
1½ cups sugar
2¼ cups SOFTASILK Flour
3 tsp. baking powder

1 tsp. salt
⅓ cup vegetable oil
1 cup milk
1½ tsp. flavoring

Heat oven to 350° (mod.). Grease and flour two layer pans, 8 or 9x1½″ or an oblong pan, 13x9½x2″. Beat egg whites until frothy. Gradually beat in ½ cup of the sugar. Continue beating until very stiff and glossy.

Measure flour by dip-level-pour method or by sifting (*see p. 6*). Blend remaining sugar, flour, baking powder and salt in another bowl. Add oil, half of milk and flavoring. Beat 1 min., medium speed on mixer or 150 vigorous strokes by hand. Scrape sides and bottom of bowl constantly. Add remaining milk and egg yolks. Beat 1 more min., scraping bowl frequently. Fold in meringue. Pour into pan(s). Bake *layers 30 to 35 min., oblong 40 to 45 min.* Cool.

Lovelight Lemon Chiffon Cake

Make Lovelight Yellow Chiffon Cake (*above*)— *except* add 1 tsp. grated lemon rind with the vanilla. Spread Egyptian Filling (*p. 177*) between cooled layers, a white icing over top and sides.

Lovelight Chocolate Chip Chiffon Cake

Make Lovelight Yellow Chiffon Cake (*above*)— *except* fold in 2 sq. unsweetened chocolate (2 oz.), grated medium fine. Add after meringue.

Lovelight Peanut Butter Cake

2 eggs, separated
½ cup sugar
2¼ cups SOFTASILK Flour
3 tsp. baking powder
1 tsp. salt
¼ tsp. soda
1 cup brown sugar (packed)
⅓ cup chunk-style peanut butter
⅓ cup vegetable oil
1¼ cups milk

Mix and bake as for Lovelight Yellow Chiffon Cake (*above*)—*except* add brown sugar and peanut butter with oil and first addition of milk. Finish with Peanut Butter Icing (*p. 172*).

Lovelight Banana Chiffon Cake

2 eggs, separated
1⅓ cups sugar
2 cups SOFTASILK Flour
1 tsp. baking powder
1 tsp. salt
1 tsp. soda
⅓ cup vegetable oil
1 cup mashed very ripe bananas
⅔ cup buttermilk or sour milk
1 tsp. vanilla
½ cup finely chopped nuts, if desired

Heat oven to 350° (mod.). Grease and flour two layer pans, 8 or 9x1½″ or an oblong pan, 13x9½x2″. Beat egg whites until frothy. Gradually beat in ⅓ cup of the sugar. Continue beating until very stiff and glossy.

Measure flour by dip-level-pour method or by sifting (*see p. 6*). Blend remaining sugar, flour, baking powder, salt and soda in another bowl. Add oil, mashed bananas, half of buttermilk and flavoring. Beat 1 min., medium speed on mixer or 150 vigorous strokes by hand. Scrape sides and bottom of bowl constantly. Add remaining buttermilk and egg yolks. Beat 1 more min., scraping bowl frequently. Fold in meringue. Fold nuts in gently. Pour into pan(s). Bake *8″ layers 30 to 35 min., 9″ layers 25 to 30 min., oblong 40 to 45 min.*

Lovelight Chocolate Chiffon Cake

2 eggs, separated
1½ cups sugar
1¾ cups SOFTASILK Flour
¾ tsp. soda

1 tsp. salt
⅓ cup vegetable oil
1 cup buttermilk or sweet milk
2 sq. unsweetened chocolate (2 oz.), melted

Heat oven to 350° (mod.). Grease and flour two layer pans, 8 or 9x1½" or an oblong pan, 13x9½x2". Beat egg whites until frothy. Gradually beat in ½ cup of the sugar. Continue beating until very stiff and glossy.

Measure flour by dip-level-pour method or by sifting (*see p. 6*). Blend remaining sugar, flour, soda and salt in another bowl. Add oil, half of buttermilk. Beat 1 min., medium speed on mixer or 150 vigorous strokes by hand. Scrape sides and bottom of bowl constantly. Add remaining buttermilk, egg yolks and chocolate. Beat 1 more min., scraping bowl frequently. Fold in meringue. Pour into pan(s). Bake *layers 30 to 35 min., oblong 40 to 45 min.* Cool. Frost with White Mountain Frosting (*p. 174*).

Lovelight Chocolate Nut Cake

2 eggs, separated
2 cups sugar
1¾ cups GOLD MEDAL Flour
1¾ tsp. baking powder
¼ tsp. soda
1 tsp. salt
¼ cup vegetable oil
1½ cups milk
1 tsp. vanilla
4 sq. unsweetened chocolate (4 oz.), melted
1 cup finely chopped nuts

Heat oven to 350° (mod.). Grease and dust with cocoa two layer pans, 8 or 9x1½". Beat egg whites until frothy. Gradually beat in ½ cup sugar. Continue beating until very stiff and glossy.

Measure flour by dip-level-pour method or by sifting (*see p. 6*). Blend remaining sugar, flour, baking powder, soda and salt in another bowl. Add oil and 1 cup milk. Beat 1 min., medium speed on mixer or 150 vigorous strokes by hand. Scrape bowl constantly. Add remaining milk, egg yolks, vanilla and chocolate. Beat 1 more min., scraping bowl frequently. Fold in meringue. Fold in nuts. Pour into pans. Bake *35 to 40 min.*

Lovelight Spice Chiffon Cake

2 eggs, separated
½ cup granulated sugar
2¼ cups SOFTASILK Flour
1 tsp. baking powder
¾ tsp. soda
1 tsp. salt
¾ tsp. nutmeg
¾ tsp. cloves
¾ tsp. cinnamon
1 cup brown sugar (packed)
⅓ cup vegetable oil
1 cup buttermilk

Heat oven to 350° (mod.). Grease and flour two layer pans, 8 or 9x1½" or an oblong pan, 13x9½x2". Beat egg whites until frothy. Gradually beat in granulated sugar. Continue beating until very stiff and glossy.

Measure flour by dip-level-pour method or by sifting (*see p. 6*). Blend flour, baking powder, soda, salt and spices in another bowl. Add brown sugar, oil and ⅔ of buttermilk. Beat 1 min., medium speed on mixer or 150 vigorous strokes by hand. Scrape sides and bottom of bowl constantly. Add remaining buttermilk and egg yolks. Beat 1 more min., scraping bowl frequently. Fold in meringue. Pour into pans. Bake *layers 30 to 35 min., oblong 40 to 45 min.*

FRUIT CAKES *For good eating during the holidays.*

First prepare fruits: slice finely and cut up (¼ to ½″) citron, orange and lemon peel. Cut other candied fruits larger. Plump seedless raisins and currants by spreading in flat pan, covering and heating in 350° oven until they puff up.; leave whole. Heat nuts and cut them up coarsely. When measuring raisins, cut-up candied peel, candied cherries, etc., remember that: ½ lb. = 1½ cups; ¼ lb. = ¾ cup.

Golden Fruitcake

A holiday tradition in the home of Mae Chesnut, formerly of our staff.

1 cup soft shortening	½ cup light jelly
2 cups brown sugar (packed)	1 tsp. vanilla
4 large eggs (1 cup)	1 lb. white raisins
3 cups GOLD MEDAL Flour	½ lb. citron
1 tsp. baking powder	¼ lb. *each* candied cherries and pineapple
1 tsp. salt	¼ lb. *each* candied orange and lemon peel
1 tsp. cinnamon	½ lb. nuts
½ cup milk	

Heat oven to 300° (slow). Line with heavy wrapping paper and grease two loaf pans, 9x5x3″ or a tube pan, 10x4″. Cream shortening and brown sugar together until fluffy. Beat in eggs. Measure flour by dip-level-pour method or by sifting (*see p. 6*). Blend flour, baking powder, salt and cinnamon. Stir in alternately with milk, jelly and vanilla. Blend in fruits and nuts. Fill pans almost full. Bake *loaf cakes 2½ to 3 hr., tube cake 3½ to 4 hr., small cakes about 1½ hr.,* or until toothpick stuck into center comes out clean (cover with paper the last hr.). Wrap in waxed paper or aluminum foil. In old days, fruitcakes were wrapped in wine-dampened cloth to keep and mellow. Store in airtight container in *cool* place. To glaze, see below.

NOTE: For small cakes, use any small can or pudding mold.

White Fruitcake

Christmastime choice of the Old South.

1½ cups soft shortening
1½ cups sugar
2¼ cups unbeaten eggs (about 9)
3 cups GOLD MEDAL Flour
1½ tsp. baking powder
¾ tsp. salt
⅔ cup orange juice
1 lb. *each* white raisins and candied cherries
¾ lb. candied pineapple
¼ lb. candied citron
¼ lb. candied orange peel
½ lb. coconut (two 4-oz. cans or 3½ cups)
½ lb. blanched almonds
½ lb. pecans

Mix as for Golden Fruitcake (*above*). Bake in two loaf pans at 275° 2½ to 3 hr.

Fruitcake Glaze

A shiny finish for fruitcakes—not sticky.

¼ cup light corn syrup
2 tbsp. water

Combine syrup and water and bring just to a rolling boil. Remove from heat. Cool to lukewarm. Pour over cold cake before or after storing.

Old-fashioned Fruitcake

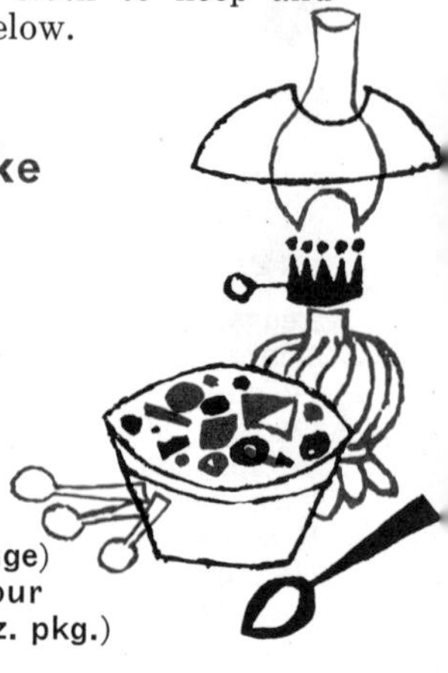

1 cup vegetable oil
1⅓ cups sugar
4 eggs
¼ cup molasses
2 cups GOLD MEDAL Flour
1 tsp. baking powder
2 tsp. salt
2 tsp. cinnamon
1 tsp. nutmeg
1 cup fruit juice (such as orange)
1 cup more GOLD MEDAL Flour
2⅔ cups seedless raisins (15-oz. pkg.)
2 cups cut-up dates (1 lb.)
2 cups mixed candied fruit (1 lb.)
1 cup nuts in large pieces

Heat oven to 275° (slow). Line with heavy wrapping paper and grease two loaf pans, 8½x4½x2¾″. Mix oil, sugar, eggs and molasses. Beat 2 min. Measure flour by dip-level-pour method or by sifting (*see p. 6*). Blend 2 cups flour, baking powder, salt and spices; stir into oil mixture alternately with fruit juice. Mix the 1 cup flour into fruits and nuts. Pour batter over fruit, mixing well. Pour into pans. Bake *2½ to 3 hr.* Let stand 15 min. before removing from pans. Cool thoroughly on racks without removing paper. Wrap in aluminum foil, store to ripen in cool place. Refrigerate after cake has been cut.

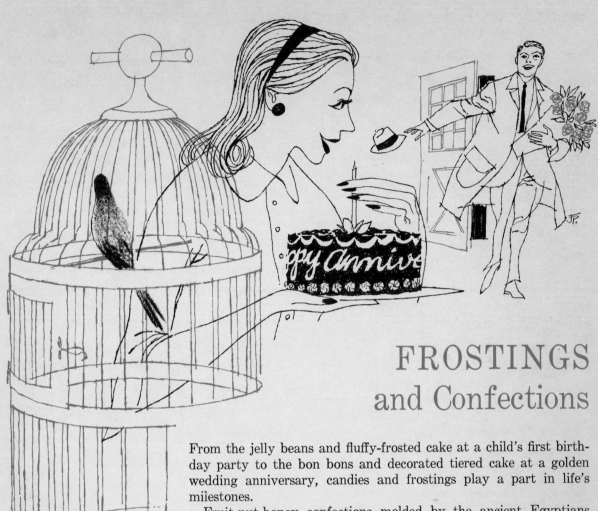

FROSTINGS
and Confections

From the jelly beans and fluffy-frosted cake at a child's first birthday party to the bon bons and decorated tiered cake at a golden wedding anniversary, candies and frostings play a part in life's milestones.

Fruit-nut-honey confections molded by the ancient Egyptians were probably the first sweets. The Romans were served candies during the entertainment following their famous feasts. But it was not until a 15th century Venetian learned to refine sugar that the art of candy-making as we know it today developed. Butterscotch toffee originated in Britain and was so named because butter was "scotched" or scorched in making it.

Of much more recent origin and definitely American is salt-water taffy. Here's the tale we were told: A candy maker located on the New Jersey shore was famous for his taffy. One day, however, something happened to his water supply; resourceful, he tried a batch of taffy with the nearby salt water. His customers loved it!

Little has been written about the origins and backgrounds of frostings. However, a famous cookery book written in 1774 gives directions for icing a great cake which called for 24 egg whites to be beaten well with a whisk for two to three hours, then spread on the cake with a thin, broad board or a bunch of feathers.

CROWNING GLORIES FOR YOUR CAKES

(complete index in back of book)

 TIMESAVING TIPS

VELVET CREAM CAKE

Bake a 9″ layer cake as directed on any flavor Betty Crocker Layer Cake Mix pkg. Cool. Split to make 4 layers. Add 2 cups desired flavor of Betty Crocker Creamy-type Frosting Mix (dry mix) to 1½ cups whipping cream (35% butterfat) and 1 tsp. vanilla for filling. Chill 1 hr., whip. Put filling between layers. Spread top with Thin Icing *(below)*; let some dribble down sides. Sprinkle top of cake with chopped nuts, if desired. Chill. *About 12 servings.*

Thin Icing: Blend rest of frosting mix (dry mix), 2 to 3 tbsp. hot water and 1 tbsp. light corn syrup. Beat until smooth. Add 1 to 2 tsp. more water, if necessary.

QUICKEST-EVER FROSTING

Easy to make with Betty Crocker Creamy-type and Fluffy-type Frosting Mixes in a full range of flavors. Just follow the easy directions on pkg.

CARAMEL APPLES

Make these a fall family tradition.

Wash 4 or 5 medium apples and dry thoroughly. Melt 1 lb. caramels with 2 tbsp. water in double boiler until smooth, stirring frequently. Stick a wooden skewer into stem end of each apple. Keeping sauce over hot water, dip apples into hot caramel sauce and turn until the apple is completely coated. Put on waxed paper and refrigerate until caramel coating is firm.

MEALTIME MAGIC

PLATTER PARTY FOR TEENS

Barbecued Hamburgers *(p. 292)*
Celery Curls and Pickle Fans *(p. 25)*
Record Cake *(p. 169)*
Milk Shakes *(p. 70)*

TO SHOWER THE BRIDE

Sea Food Salad *(p. 381)* in tomato cups
Butter Dips *(p. 77)*
Umbrella Cake *(p. 167)* or Sweetheart Cake *(p. 171)*
Coffee

WHAT EVERY COOK NEEDS TO KNOW ABOUT FROSTINGS

MAKE WITH CARE

Simplest of all icings is Butter Icing (*p. 172*). Always sift the confectioners' sugar for the smoothest icing in the shortest time.

White Mountain Frosting (*p. 174*) offers a double challenge to the cook: cooking the sugar syrup to the right consistency, and beating the syrup into the egg whites until the frosting forms glossy peaks.

Another way of making a fluffy white frosting is the double boiler method (*p. 175*), often called the seven-minute method. These fluffy frosting recipes call for corn syrup or cream of tartar which prevents sugar crystals from grouping together and making frosting grainy.

Making fudge frostings (*p. 175*) and making fudge (*p. 178*) have many techniques in common: testing to see if the syrup has cooked to the desired stage, waiting as patiently as possible while fudge cools, then beating steadily until it loses its shiny, sticky appearance and becomes soft and creamy.

Broiled icings are a wonderful quick cake topping —and most folks love warm cake. Choose one of the easy recipes (*p. 176*); be careful not to burn it.

Store your frosted cakes in a cake safe or under a large inverted bowl so that they won't dry out.

If swirls in fluffy frosting are mussed in carrying, dip a metal knife in hot water and re-swirl them.

. . . .

DECORATE WITH FLAIR

Once you've mastered the basic recipes for frostings, there's no end to the frostings you can create —with color, flavor, design and trimmings. But use color and trimmings with a light hand.

Decorating fancy cakes has become a fascinating hobby for many women. With a little practice using a small set of decorator tips and Butter Icing (*p. 172*) or Decorating Icing, you, too, can turn out pretty decorations for special occasion cakes. And someday, you will perhaps trim a tiered wedding cake for a daughter or a friend.

NEW ADVENTURES IN FROSTINGS

Birthday Bouquets (*p. 167*)—A cupcake becomes a pretty nosegay.

Bonnet Cake (*p. 168*)—Looks so real.

Chocolate-Cream Cheese Icing (*p. 173*)—Smooth cheese is shortening in this easy icing.

Designer Cake Tops (*p. 167*)—An idea to bring out the artist in you.

Glossy Web (*p. 167*)—Trace a web on butter icing with melted chocolate.

Umbrella Cake (*p. 167*)—For your next shower.

Twin Angel Cake, page 171   *Clown Cake, page 169*   *Pink Mountain Frosting, page 174*

Designer Cake Tops

Bake and frost an 8 or 9″ layer cake. Let frosting set. Make a stencil or cut-out by cutting round from waxed paper same size as cake pan. Fold in half twice. With scissors cut large patterns out of waxed paper (such as star, hat, bell, umbrella, animal, etc.). Place pattern on frosted cake. In open areas on stencil, press in one of the following: chopped coconut, shaved or grated chocolate, finely chopped nuts, crushed peppermint candy, chocolate shot, colored sugar crystals, crushed peanut brittle, toffee, etc. Remove stencil.

Washington's Birthday Cake

Frost Maraschino Cherry Cake (*p. 132*) with a white icing and trim with clusters of stemmed maraschino cherries. Use strips of green gumdrops or citron for leaves and angelica for stems.

Gift Package Cake

Bake cake in oblong pan. Place on oblong tray or plate. Ice with a chocolate or white frosting. Make white or pastel frosting ribbon tie, with bow design, on top. Use as table centerpiece with wrapped small gifts surrounding it.

Umbrella Cake

Bake a layer cake and frost with a fluffy cooked icing. Cut 3 small V's out of bottom of flat citrus candy slice to make umbrella top. Cut center out of another candy slice (same color) and use "rind" for handle. Cut a small piece off handle to make tip of umbrella. Make "umbrellas" to decorate top of cake.

Birthday Bouquets

Frost cupcakes with White Mountain Frosting (*p. 174*). Make Butter Icing (*p. 172*). Tint ½ cup pink; use petal tip for rosebud in center of each cupcake. Hold cone so wide end of tip touches cake. Make curled petal in center. Add petals to right and left, overlapping. Tint ⅓ cup light blue or yellow; use drop flower tip. Add flowers around each rosebud. Tint 3 tbsp. light green; use leaf tip. Add a few leaves. Use star tip with remaining white frosting. Complete each cupcake with a border around edge. Center each cake in a 6″ doily; add ribbon streamers for a party decoration.

SIMPLE DECORATIONS

PLAID CAKE

Frost cake with a fluffy white frosting. Dip string in food coloring; stretching it taut, press into frosting. Repeat. Use new string for each color. Make up your own plaid design.

GLOSSY WEB

Frost cake with a butter icing. Melt 1 sq. unsweetened chocolate (1 oz.). Dip knife in chocolate. Outline circles on top of cake. Draw knife out from center for web.

CRISSCROSS

Frost cake with chocolate or a favorite icing. Draw tines of fork across cake. Repeat at right angles to first markings. Place colorful candies in squares.

SCALLOPS

With teaspoon inverted, press tip into frosted cake. Repeat in rows across cake for all over design.

Butterfly Cake

Bake cake in layers. Cool. Cut each layer in half. Make double recipe White Mountain Frosting (*p. 174*). Tint a delicate yellow with 10 to 12 drops yellow food coloring. Frost cake, arranging to resemble a butterfly by placing curved sides together. Swirl icing on top of cake to resemble butterfly markings.

Easter Bunny Cake

Bake a white or yellow cake in layers. Cut one cooled layer in half to make 2 half circles. Put halves together with white frosting or whipped cream. Stand upright on cut edge. With sharp knife, cut a notch in edge to indicate the rabbit's head. Save cut-out piece for the tail. Secure with toothpick. Frost rabbit with remaining icing and cover generously with coconut. Cut ears of folded white paper; color inside pink with crayon. Use pink candies for eyes and nose. Coconut tinted green or paper grass and a few Easter eggs form an attractive nest around the bunny.

Eskimo Igloo Cake

Bake any layer cake you wish—white, yellow, chocolate, etc. Make 1½ times White Mountain Frosting (*p. 174*). Prepare a special chocolate mixture by melting together over hot water 1 sq. unsweetened chocolate (1 oz.) and ¼ tsp. shortening.

How to decorate cake: Cut each layer in half. Spread icing on one side of all halves except one. Set halves side by side on their cut edges with icing between to form a long rounded cake which makes the igloo. Frost the semi-circular top and ends with the remaining icing. To make ice blocks on igloo, mark icing into squares by dripping melted chocolate mixture from end of teaspoon.

How to cut cake: Cut crosswise in half, then cut from either flat end of cake to center. This gives flat slices of cake with icing on the top and on the sides.

Bonnet Cake

Bake your favorite layer cake in one 8″ and one 9″ layer. Use 9″ layer for brim. Frost with a butter icing. Trim other layer down to 6″ diameter. Place on 9″ layer to make crown of bonnet; frost. Use your imagination in trimming the bonnet. Tint some of frosting with food coloring to make contrasting ribbon around base of crown. To decorate, use candies, make frosting flowers with a pastry tube or gather fresh spring flowers and arrange them around crown.

Blarney Stones

Frost 3x1″ oblongs of Sponge or Chiffon Cake with Butter Icing (*p. 172*). Roll in chopped peanuts. Serve each on green shamrock paper cut-out placed on lace paper doily.

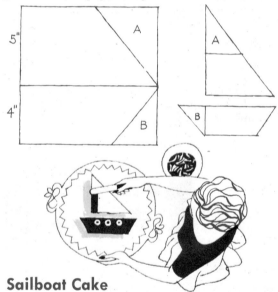

Sailboat Cake

Bake a 9″ square cake. When cool, cut cake as shown in diagram 1. Note that triangle A is slightly larger than triangle B. Arrange cake pieces on tray as shown in diagram 2. Prepare Butter Icing (*p. 172*). Put ⅓ of frosting in another bowl and thoroughly stir in 3 tbsp. cocoa. Leave remaining frosting white. Spread white frosting on sail and chocolate frosting on hull of boat. Add a line of chocolate frosting up the sail for the mast. Sprinkle flaked coconut on the sail. Add mint-flavored hard-candy circles for portholes on hull.

NOTE: For ease in frosting cut sides of cake: frost last, and add a few additional drops hot water to frosting.

Clown Cake

See color picture p. 166.

Bake two 8″ layers of cake and one cupcake. For cupcake, use ¼ cup batter in greased 3″ custard cup. Bake cupcake 15 to 20 min. Make White Mountain Frosting (*p. 174*). Save 1 cup. Tint rest of frosting light green and frost cake.

To make clown: Mark top of cake into 8 sections, heaping frosting in each section to make ruffle. Hold inverted cupcake on 3 toothpicks and frost all over with white frosting. Set in center of cake. Frost small ice cream cone or paper cup; press onto cupcake for hat.

To decorate: Blend 2½ cups *sifted* confectioners' sugar with 2 tbsp. milk. Put into star tipped decorator tube and make brim on hat. Make zig-zag design for neck ruff and border at top and base of cake. Cut gumdrops for eyes, nose, ears, mouth; add others for trim around cake.

A Day-at-the-Zoo Cake

Bake any cake you wish as long as recipe calls for a 13x9″ pan. Then make 1½ times the recipe for White Mountain Frosting (*p. 174*) or Butter Icing (*p. 172*). Tint orange or green with food coloring.

How to decorate cake: Frost cake, making icing on top about ¼″ thick. Decorate by spacing animal crackers about 1″ apart around top of cake, pressing crackers gently into icing to hold upright. Form a rectangle in center of oblong cake by setting candles into icing. Decorate sides of cake by pressing additional animal crackers flat against icing. If desired, dip animal crackers in 2 sq. unsweetened chocolate (2 oz.), melted with ½ tsp. shortening. Let dry on a wire rack.

Airplane Birthday Cake

Bake cake in an oblong pan. Turn cake out on flat platter or board to cool. Frost with Peanut Butter Icing (*p. 172*). Place a row of birthday candles along the two long sides of cake. Place several toy airplanes on top of cake.

Baseball Cupcakes

Bake cupcakes. Frost all around with Butter Icing (*p. 172*). Color part of icing brown. Draw brown stitching lines on baseballs using decorating tube. Put a birthday candle in each ball.

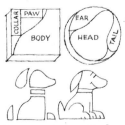

Puppy Dog Cake

Bake white, yellow or chocolate cake in an 8″ square and an 8″ round layer pan. Pour batter to the same level in both pans for uniform height. Bake, remove from pans and cool.

Cut body, paw and collar from square cake and head, tail and ear from round cake as shown in diagram above. Arrange cake pieces on a tray as shown in sketch turning ear and tail pieces over so they are in proper position. Prepare White Mountain Frosting (*p. 174*). Frost entire dog, joining all parts. Melt 2 sq. semi-sweet chocolate (2 oz.). Using small spatula, spread chocolate over frosting on ears and collar. Draw eyes and mouth with melted chocolate. Outline paws and legs (see sketch) with pieces of black licorice sticks. Give him a big, fat gumdrop nose.

Record Cake

Bake cake in layers. Make half recipe Butter Icing (*p. 172*) and spread part of it between layers. Frost top and sides with a chocolate icing, reserving ⅓ cup for decorating. Frost center with rest of Butter Icing to resemble a label. To make grooves, draw tines of fork round and round through chocolate icing. Use reserved chocolate icing to write "Happy Birthday" and make 2 or 3 notes and a dot for record hole on label. Make 2 small dancers on cake using pipe cleaners.

We used to call it the "Bride's Cake" . . . that ethereal structure of white tender cake all iced and decorated with snowy frosting. The dark fruitcake which maidens put under their pillows to dream on is traditional wedding cake. But nowadays it's the Bride's Cake that is the "Wedding Cake," and the fruitcake is the "Groom's Cake." It is sometimes given to guests in small white boxes to take home.

Make the Cake

Use recipe for Silver White Cake (*p. 132*) as basis for amount of ingredients.

Assemble ingredients for making two double recipes. Use half almond, half vanilla flavoring.

Grease generously and flour 3 round layer pans: one 12″, one 9″, one 6″ in diameter . . . at least 1½″ deep.

Each tier will consist of two identical layers (12″, 9″, 6″).

Heat oven to 350° (mod.). Mix batter for one double recipe *each time*, beating 2½ min. each mixing time. Pour a little over half of batter (4½ cups) into 12″ pan and place in center of oven, allowing plenty of space for cake to rise. Bake *30 to 40 min.* Test for doneness by inserting a toothpick in center of cake. Cool in pan.

Pour remaining batter into 9″ and 6″ pans (6″ pan requires about 1¼ cups batter). Refrigerate these layers until 12″ cake is baked. Then place 9″ layer near rear of oven and 6″ layer near front. Bake *9″ layer 30 to 35 min., 6″ layer 25 to 30 min. For second layers, repeat above process.*

Frost the Cake

While cake is still slightly warm, spread each layer with thin coating of Butter Icing (*p. 172*) (to prevent crumbs getting into final frosting and help keep moist and fresh). *Do not* put layers together.

Choose an appropriate permanent foundation such as a mirror, crystal or silver cake plate or a heavy, round cardboard covered with lace paper doilies.

Make 4 times recipe for Butter Icing (*p. 172*), using 2 tbsp. vanilla and ¾ tsp. almond flavoring. Put one 12″ layer on a mirror or cake plate. Frost top; put on other 12″ layer. Frost sides and top. Cut a 9″ cardboard circle; place on top of frosted layers. Place one 9″ layer on cardboard; frost top. Put on second 9″ layer; frost sides and top. Follow these directions for 6″ cardboard and 6″ layers.

Decorate the Cake

Make 1½ times recipe for Decorating Icing (*p. 172*). Decorate with scrolls, swags, lilies of the valley and roses as directed on opposite page. Top with miniature bride and groom, bells or flowers.

Cut and Serve the Cake

The bride cuts the first piece and shares it with the groom. Then someone else cuts pieces for the guests, cutting slices or wedges (see sketches on p. 145) starting with the second tier. The top tier is often frozen for the couple's first anniversary. Decorated sheet cakes can supplement the wedding cake.

How to Decorate a Wedding Cake (*See opposite page for baking and frosting cake.*)

1. Make scroll design for border around top and base of each layer, using flower tip.

3. Decorate top layer with lily-of-the-valley flowers and stems with writing tip. Add leaves with leaf tip.

5. Select a special decoration for top of cake, such as bride and groom, lovebirds, wedding bells or ribbon.

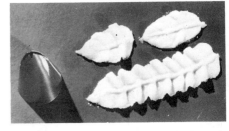

2. Make swag design around layers, using leaf tip in overlapping motion.

4. Make roses and place around cake. *To make roses:* use petal tip and flower nail. Hold cone with narrow opening of tip always up. Turning clockwise, make tiny circle for center of rose. To form first petal, make standing half circle to one side of center. Add two more petals, forming triangle. Add petals, overlapping. Remove rose from nail with kitchen shears . . . cut almost through base of rose, place on cake, cut completely through, ease rose off.

Petits Fours

Make a sheet cake (*p. 130*). When cool, cut in $1\frac{1}{2}''$ squares and cover top and sides of squares with Icing (*below*). Keep icing over lukewarm water while frosting cakes so that icing will remain thin. Frost squares upside-down so crust is on bottom. Stick fork into bottom of petits four and hold over icing pan while spooning icing on sides of square. To frost top of petits four, set square of cake on cooling rack. (Have waxed paper under rack.) Then pour icing over top with teaspoon. Decorate with nuts, colored candies, etc. (Icing which drips on waxed paper can be scraped off, reheated and reused.)

Icing

Mix 6 cups *sifted* confectioners' sugar, 5 tbsp. water, 5 tbsp. corn syrup, 1 tsp. vanilla and a few drops food coloring in top of double boiler. Heat to pouring consistency.

Twin Angel Cake

Perfect for bridal shower, small wedding reception or wedding anniversary party. See color picture p. 166.

Bake 2 angel food cakes. Cool and remove from pans. Trim slice from side of each cake. Place cakes, flat sides together, on large serving tray (18x12") or foil-covered heavy cardboard. Cover with a fluffy white frosting. Sprinkle with silver dragées. Smilax or huckleberry and sweetheart roses around the base enhance this beautiful cake.

Sweetheart Cake

Bake two 8 or 9" round cake layers or heart-shaped layers. Cool. Make Pink Mountain Frosting (*p. 174*). Reserve $\frac{1}{2}$ cup. Spread between layers and on top of cake. Tint remaining icing deep pink with food coloring. Draw heart-shaped outline on top of cake, fill it with $\frac{1}{2}$ cup frosting. Frost sides.

171

Butter Icing *For extra richness, add 1 egg yolk.*

⅓ cup soft butter
3 cups *sifted* confectioners' sugar

about 3 tbsp. cream
1½ tsp. vanilla

Blend butter and sugar together. Stir in cream and vanilla until smooth. *Makes frosting for two 8 or 9" layers or 13x9" oblong.*

Chocolate Butter Icing

Make Butter Icing (*above*)—*except* stir 3 sq. unsweetened chocolate (3 oz.), melted, into blended mixture.

Mocha Butter Icing

Make Butter Icing (*above*)—*except* omit cream and vanilla and blend in 2 tsp. powdered instant coffee dissolved in 2 tbsp. hot water. Stir in a few drops water if too thick.

Browned Butter Icing

Make Butter Icing (*above*)—*except* brown butter in saucepan over medium heat until delicate brown. Blend with sugar.

Maple Butter Icing

Make Butter Icing (*above*)—*except* omit cream and vanilla and add ½ cup maple syrup.

Decorating Icing

Tint as desired. To make roses, add more confectioners' sugar until icing is quite thick.

½ cup soft shortening (half butter, if desired)
8 cups *sifted* confectioners' sugar
¼ cup cream (20% butterfat)
2 egg whites
1 tbsp. vanilla

Blend all ingredients at low speed on mixer; beat on high speed until fluffy. *Makes 4 cups icing.* 1½ times this recipe is needed to frost the tiered wedding cake (*p. 170*).

Rich Almond Frosting

½ cup soft butter
1¾ cups *sifted* confectioners' sugar
1 unbeaten egg yolk
½ tsp. almond flavoring
4 tsp. milk

Mix butter, sugar, egg yolk, flavoring and milk thoroughly. Stir over ice water until thick enough to spread. *For top of 9" square cake, 13x9" oblong cake or especially nice on angel food cake.*

Orange (or Lemon) Butter Icing

Make Butter Icing (*above*)—*except* omit vanilla, and in place of the cream, use orange (or lemon) juice. Blend in 1½ tbsp. grated rind for extra flavor.

Pineapple Butter Icing

Make Butter Icing (*above*)—*except* omit cream and vanilla. Stir in ⅓ cup well drained crushed pineapple.

Strawberry Butter Icing

Make Butter Icing (*above*)—*except* omit cream and vanilla. Stir in 3 to 4 tbsp. crushed fresh or frozen strawberries.

Cherry Butter Icing

Make Butter Icing (*above*)—*except* omit cream and vanilla. Stir in about ¼ cup maraschino cherry juice.

Peanut Butter Icing

¼ cup chunk-style peanut butter
3 cups *sifted* confectioners' sugar
¼ to ⅓ cup milk

Stir peanut butter, sugar and milk together until creamy. *Makes frosting for two 8 or 9" layers or 13x9" oblong.*

Brown Beauty Icing *Much like a cooked fudge frosting . . . soft, dark, glossy and moist.*

1⅓ cups *sifted* confectioners' sugar
¼ cup shortening
¼ cup milk

3 sq. unsweetened chocolate (3 oz.), melted
1 tsp. vanilla
1 whole egg (or 3 egg yolks)

Blend sugar, shortening, milk, chocolate and vanilla in mixing bowl. Add egg. Beat with rotary beater *just* until frosting is smooth. Place bowl in ice water and *stir* until frosting is thick enough to spread. If frosting becomes too thick, dip bowl in hot water for a few seconds and stir to desired consistency. *Makes frosting for two 8 or 9" layers or 13x9" oblong.*

For hobnail effect, twist tip of spoon in the icing.

Glossy Chocolate Icing

3 tbsp. shortening
3 sq. unsweetened chocolate (3 oz.)
2 cups *sifted* confectioners' sugar
¼ tsp. salt
⅓ cup milk
1 tsp. vanilla

Melt shortening and chocolate together over hot water. Blend in sugar, salt, milk and vanilla. Stir until smooth. Place bowl in ice water and continue stirring until thick enough to spread. *Makes frosting for two 8 or 9" layers or 13x9" oblong.*

Thin Chocolate Icing

For Boston Cream Pie, Cream Puffs and Chocolate Roll.

1 sq. unsweetened chocolate (1 oz.)
1 tsp. butter
1 cup *sifted* confectioners' sugar
2 tbsp. boiling water

Melt chocolate and butter together over hot water. Remove from heat. Blend in sugar and water. Beat only until smooth but not stiff.

Chocolate-Cream Cheese Icing

Creamy Cocoa Icing

2⅔ cups *sifted* confectioners' sugar
⅓ cup cocoa
⅓ cup soft butter
3 to 4 tbsp. milk

Sift sugar and cocoa together. Add butter and milk. Stir until well blended. *Makes frosting for two 8 or 9" layers or 13x9" oblong.*

Cocoa-Mocha Icing

A spice cake takes this frosting treatment nicely.

Sift together 2⅔ cups *sifted* confectioners' sugar and 3 tbsp. cocoa. Add ⅓ cup *soft* butter and 1 tbsp. powdered instant coffee dissolved in 2 tbsp. water. Blend well.

Quick-As-A-Wink Chocolate Frosting

1 pkg. (6 oz.) semi-sweet chocolate pieces
2 tbsp. butter
3 tbsp. milk
1 cup *sifted* confectioners' sugar

Combine chocolate, butter and milk in saucepan. Stir over low heat until chocolate is *just* melted. Remove from heat. Stir in sugar. Beat until smooth, glossy and easy to spread. (If not glossy, stir in a few drops of hot water.) *Makes frosting for 8 or 9" square.*

Blend 1 pkg. (3 oz.) soft cream cheese and 1 tbsp. milk. Blend in well 2½ cups *sifted* confectioners' sugar. Stir in 1 to 2 sq. unsweetened chocolate (1 to 2 oz.), melted and slightly cooled, 1 tsp. vanilla and dash of salt. (Thin with more milk if necessary for desired spreading consistency.) *Makes frosting for two 8 or 9" layers or 13x9" oblong.*

FROSTINGS *Fluffy frostings to ice cakes in swirls and swirls.*

White Mountain Frosting

Soft, never grainy, spreads easily.

½ cup sugar
2 tbsp. water
¼ cup light corn syrup
2 egg whites (¼ cup)
1 tsp. vanilla

Mix sugar, water and corn syrup in saucepan. Cover saucepan, bring to rolling boil. Remove cover and cook to 242° or until syrup spins a 6 to 8″ thread. Just before syrup is ready, beat egg whites until stiff enough to hold a point. Pour hot syrup very slowly in a thin stream into the beaten egg whites. Continue beating until frosting holds peaks. Blend in vanilla. When spreading on cake, make pretty swirls with spatula. *Makes frosting for two 8 or 9″ layers or 13x9″ oblong.*

Pink Mountain Frosting

Make White Mountain Frosting (*above*)—except use 2 tbsp. maraschino cherry juice in place of water.

Lemon Frosting

Make White Mountain Frosting (*above*)—except, in place of vanilla, use 1 tbsp. lemon juice and fold in a little grated lemon rind.

Chocolate Revel Frosting

Make White Mountain Frosting (*above*). At the very last, fold in 1 sq. unsweetened chocolate (1 oz.), coarsely grated, or ½ cup semi-sweet chocolate pieces.

Allegretti Frosting

Melt over hot water 1 sq. unsweetened chocolate (1 oz.) with ¼ tsp. shortening. Using a teaspoon, drip chocolate around top edge of cake iced with a fluffy white frosting, letting chocolate run down sides in uneven lines.

Satiny Beige Frosting

Make White Mountain Frosting (*above*)—except use brown sugar in place of granulated. Use only ½ tsp. vanilla.

Peppermint Frosting

Make White Mountain Frosting (*above*)—except fold in, after beating, ½ tsp. peppermint flavoring or ⅓ cup coarsely crushed peppermint stick candy.

Boil syrup to 242°. Will spin 6 to 8″ thread.

Pour very slowly into stiffly beaten egg whites. Continue beating until frosting holds its shape.

A Candy Thermometer helps take guesswork out of making frostings and candies. To get an accurate reading, syrup must be bubbling around bulb or tip of thermometer; be careful that bulb or tip doesn't rest on metal of pan.

Marshmallow Frosting

Make White Mountain Frosting (*at left*). At the last, fold in 6 to 8 quartered soft marshmallows, stirring until blended.

Tutti-Frutti Frosting

Make White Mountain Frosting (*at left*). At the very last, fold in nuts, candied cherries, dates and raisins (all chopped).

Comfort Frosting

Divinity type.

1½ cups sugar
1 tbsp. light corn syrup
½ cup water
2 egg whites (¼ cup)
1 tsp. vanilla

Follow method for White Mountain Frosting (*at left*).

HOW TO QUICK-FROST CUPCAKES
Twirl the cupcakes in the frosting bowl.

174

Double Boiler Frosting

For two 8 or 9" layers	*For 13x9" oblong*
2 egg whites (¼ cup)	1 (2 tbsp.)
1½ cups sugar	¾ cup
¼ tsp. cream of tartar	⅛ tsp.
or 1 tbsp. light corn syrup	or 1½ tsp.
⅓ cup water	3 tbsp.
1 tsp. vanilla	½ tsp.

Mix all ingredients except vanilla in top of double boiler. Place over boiling water; beat with rotary beater until stiff peaks form. Scrape bottom and sides of pan occasionally. Fold in vanilla.

Strawberry Icing

Make Double Boiler Frosting (*above*)—*except* use frozen or fresh strawberry juice in place of water.

Lemon Butter Fluff Icing

Made with cream cheese. So delicious on angel food, sponge and chiffon cakes.

1 pkg. (3 oz.) cream cheese (room temperature)
2 tbsp. cream
½ cup soft butter (¼ lb.)
4 cups *sifted* confectioners' sugar
1 tbsp. lemon juice
2 to 3 tsp. grated lemon rind
1 tsp. vanilla

Combine all ingredients and beat until light and fluffy. *Enough for 1 large cake.*

Minute Fudge Frosting

Quick. Sure. Creamy.

2 cups sugar
¼ cup light corn syrup
½ cup milk
½ cup shortening
2 sq. unsweetened chocolate (2 oz.), cut up
¼ tsp. salt
1 tsp. vanilla

Mix all ingredients except vanilla in saucepan. Stir over low heat until chocolate and shortening melt. Bring to a full rolling boil, stirring constantly. Boil 1 min. (220°). Remove from heat and beat until lukewarm (120°). Stir in vanilla. Beat until a smooth spreading consistency. *Enough for two 8 or 9" layers or 13x9" oblong.*

Minute Penuche Frosting

Make Minute Fudge Frosting (*above*)—*except* use brown sugar in place of granulated. Omit corn syrup and chocolate.

Prize Fudge Frosting

NOTE: When fudge-type frostings become too *thick* to spread, add a little cream as needed. When too *thin*, add *sifted* confectioners' sugar.

1½ cups sugar
½ cup water
1 tbsp. light corn syrup
1 tbsp. butter
2 sq. unsweetened chocolate (2 oz.), cut up
1 tsp. vanilla

Mix all ingredients except vanilla in saucepan. Cover and cook slowly until mixture boils. Remove cover and cook without stirring until a little dropped into cold water forms a soft ball (234°). Remove from heat, let stand until cool. Add vanilla. Beat until thick enough to spread. *Enough for 9" square or 13x9" oblong.*

White Fudge Frosting

Delicious on spice and chocolate cakes.

Make Prize Fudge Frosting (*above*)—*except* omit the chocolate and use sour cream or milk in place of water. Fold in 1 cup cut-up seedless raisins, if desired.

Easy Penuche Icing

Perfect on date, spice, whole egg or chocolate cakes.

½ cup butter
1 cup brown sugar (packed)
¼ cup milk
1¾ to 2 cups *sifted* confectioners' sugar

Melt butter in saucepan. Stir in brown sugar. Boil and stir over low heat 2 min. Stir in milk. Bring to boil, stirring constantly. Cool to lukewarm (120°). Gradually stir in confectioners' sugar. Place pan in ice water and stir until thick enough to spread. *Enough for two 8 or 9" layers or 13x9" oblong.*

Easy Choco-Mint Icing

Use about 16 large chocolate-covered peppermint cream patties for frosting for 13x9" oblong cake, 12 for 9" square. The minute cake comes out of the oven, place chocolate peppermints over top. As they melt, spread quickly.

Brown Sugar Meringue

Especially delicious on a spice cake.

2 egg whites (¼ cup)
1 cup brown sugar (packed)
1 tbsp. lemon juice
½ cup nuts, cut up

Just before cake is removed from oven, beat egg whites until frothy. Gradually beat in sugar and lemon juice until stiff. Spread on hot 8 or 9″ square cake immediately. Sprinkle with nuts. Bake *at 400°* (mod. hot) *8 to 10 min.* to brown meringue.

Choc-o-Nut Topping

To be used with Brown Beauty Cake (p. 143) or your favorite 8″ square chocolate cake.

2 cups coconut, cut up
⅓ cup water
½ cup semi-sweet chocolate pieces, melted

Mix ingredients. Pour ½ of cake batter into prepared pan. Sprinkle with ½ of choc-o-nut mixture. Add remaining batter. Bake. As soon as cake is done, sprinkle with remaining choc-o-nut mixture.

Creamy White Icing

Never sugary, never grainy. S-m-o-o-t-h.

½ cup shortening (part butter)
2½ tbsp. flour
¼ tsp. salt
½ cup milk
about 3 cups *sifted* **confectioners' sugar**
½ tsp. vanilla

Melt shortening in saucepan. Remove from heat. Blend in flour and salt. Stir milk in slowly. Bring to boil, stirring constantly. Boil 1 min. Remove from heat. Stir in sugar and vanilla. Stir until thick enough to spread. (Place pan in ice water while stirring to set the icing.)

Creamy Raisin or Nut: Add about ½ cup cut-up raisins or nuts.

Creamy Orange or Lemon: Omit vanilla. In place of the milk, use orange or lemon juice. Add 1½ extra tbsp. flour. Add grated orange or lemon rind for extra flavor.

Creamy Fudge: Reduce shortening to ¼ cup. Add 2 sq. unsweetened chocolate (2 oz.), melted, after the sugar.

Creamy Browned Butter: Use all butter. Brown butter in saucepan over medium heat until a delicate brown.

Broiled Icing

Bubbles and browns under the broiler. Wonderful on Butterscotch Cake, Spice Cake and Hot Water Sponge Cake.

⅓ cup soft butter
⅔ cup brown sugar (packed)
¼ cup cream (20% butterfat)
½ cup nuts, cut up

Mix ingredients. Spread over top of warm 13x9″ cake. Place low under broiler until mixture browns. For extra goodness, add 1 cup moist shredded coconut.

Peanut Butter Broiled Icing

Delicious on Peanut Butter Cake (p. 139) or your favorite chocolate cake.

⅔ cup brown sugar (packed)
¼ cup soft butter
¼ cup cream (20% butterfat)
¼ cup peanut butter
1 cup peanuts, chopped

Mix first four ingredients. Stir in peanuts. Spread on warm 13x9″ cake, place low under broiler until mixture browns slightly.

Continental Glaze

For Applesauce Cake.

Bake Applesauce Cake (p. 150) in 9″ layers. Cool. Put layers together with half recipe of Butter Icing (p. 172). Spread a thin coating of apricot jam or clear jelly over top of cake. Make 8 apple designs around top: cut red candied pineapple slices in three thin slices for apple design and make leaf designs from thinly cut green candied pineapple slices. Use cloves for stems. Put pieces of waxed paper on plate to catch drip of glaze. Pour over top a Thin Glaze (stir over boiling water until mixture is hot, about 5 min., 2 tbsp. water, 2 cups *sifted* confectioners' sugar, 2½ tbsp. white corn syrup and 1 tsp. flavoring). Glaze has to be very thin and put on hot. It should barely coat cake so design shows through.

Cream Filling

So smooth and rich.

¼ cup sugar
1 tbsp. cornstarch
¼ tsp. salt
1 cup milk
1 egg yolk, slightly beaten
1 tbsp. butter
1 tsp. vanilla

Mix sugar, cornstarch and salt in saucepan. Gradually stir in milk. Bring to boil over medium heat, stirring constantly. Boil 1 min. Remove from heat. Stir at least half of hot mixture into egg yolk. Blend into remaining mixture. Boil 1 min. more. Remove from heat. Blend in butter and vanilla. Cool, stirring occasionally.

Almond Cream Filling

Make Cream Filling (*above*)—*except* use only ½ tsp. vanilla and add ¼ tsp. almond flavoring. Cool. Add ½ cup toasted slivered blanched almonds.

Chocolate Cream Filling

Make Cream Filling (*above*)—*except* increase sugar to ½ cup and add 1 sq. unsweetened chocolate (1 oz.), cut up, to mixed dry ingredients (¼ cup cocoa may be used in place of chocolate).

Egyptian Filling

Custard type . . . enhanced with dates and almonds.

⅔ cup cream (20% butterfat)
⅔ cup sugar
2 egg yolks
½ cup chopped dates
½ tsp. vanilla
½ cup chopped almonds, toasted

Mix first four ingredients. Cook over low heat until slightly thickened, stirring constantly (6 or 7 min.). Remove from heat; add vanilla and nuts. Cool until thick enough to spread. *Enough to fill and cover top of two 8 or 9″ layers.*

Whipped Cream Toppings and Fillings

Sweetened Whipped Cream (*p. 232*). Fruited whipped creams (*pp. 237, 238*). Cocoa Fluff Filling and Topping (*p. 238*). Caramel Fluff (*p. 234*).

Clear Lemon Filling

Wonderfully tart and delicious.

¾ cup sugar
3 tbsp. cornstarch
¼ tsp. salt
¾ cup water
1 tbsp. butter
2 tbsp. grated lemon rind
⅓ cup lemon juice

Mix sugar, cornstarch and salt in saucepan. Gradually stir in water. Bring to boil over direct heat, stirring constantly. Boil 1 min. Remove from heat. Stir in butter and rind. Gradually add lemon juice. Cool thoroughly.

Rich Lemon Filling

Use the leftover egg whites in frosting.

Make Clear Lemon Filling (*above*)—*except*, after mixture has boiled 1 min., stir half of hot mixture into 2 egg yolks, slightly beaten. Blend into remaining mixture. Boil 1 min. more. Remove from heat and add the butter, lemon rind and juice.

Clear Orange Filling

Refreshing. Full orange flavor.

1 cup sugar
¼ cup cornstarch
½ tsp. salt
1 cup orange juice (reconstituted frozen orange juice may be used)
2 tbsp. butter
2 tbsp. grated orange rind
2 tbsp. lemon juice

Follow method for Clear Lemon Filling (*above*).

Pineapple Filling

½ cup sugar
3 tbsp. cornstarch
½ tsp. salt
¾ cup pineapple juice
about 1 cup crushed pineapple, well drained
1 tbsp. butter
1 tsp. lemon juice

Follow method for Clear Lemon Filling (*above*).

HOW TO MAKE CANDY

1. *Choose a heavy cooking pan large enough* to let the sugar syrup boil freely.

2. *Prevent formation of sugar crystals.* If recipe calls for butter, use it to grease sides of pan before adding other ingredients. Stir sugar in thoroughly before placing the mixture over heat. During cooling, do not stir or agitate.

3. *Watch candy closely.* Temperature rises with great speed once it reaches 220°.

4. *Test candy carefully.* A dependable candy thermometer takes the guesswork out of testing. To get an accurate reading, be sure candy is bubbling all around bulb; and bulb is not resting against metal pan. Use cold water test if you don't have a thermometer. Drop a small amount of candy from spoon into very cold water in a cup. Be sure to remove candy from heat as you test. Use clean spoon for each test.

5. *Be patient about cooling.* Don't beat the candy before it has cooled to 110°—or when the saucepan feels lukewarm to palm of the hand.

6. *"Stir-beat."* Stir steadily, not furiously. If possible, have a second person to help beat.

7. *When it rains or humidity is high,* cook a degree or so higher than recipe states.

8. *Altitudes affect temperature.* Consult altitude table for adjustments.

CANDY TESTS

Stages	Temperature	Cold Water Tests
Soft ball	234° to 240° F.	Can be picked up, but flattens.
Firm ball	242° to 248° F.	Holds shape unless pressed.
Hard ball	250° to 268° F.	Holds shape, though pliable.
Soft crack	270° to 290° F.	Separates into hard threads, but not brittle.
Hard crack	300° to 310° F.	Separates into hard and brittle thread.

Old-fashioned Chocolate Fudge

Recalls to many their first cooking experience.

2 cups sugar
⅔ cup milk
2 sq. unsweetened chocolate (2 oz.)
   or ⅓ cup cocoa
2 tbsp. light corn syrup
¼ tsp. salt
2 tbsp. butter
1 tsp. vanilla
½ cup broken nuts

Combine sugar, milk, chocolate or cocoa, corn syrup and salt in saucepan. Stir over medium heat until chocolate melts and sugar dissolves. Cook to 234° or until a little dropped in cold water forms a soft ball. Stir occasionally. Remove from heat. Add butter. Cool to lukewarm *without stirring*. Add vanilla. Beat until thick and no longer glossy. Quickly stir in nuts. Pour into buttered 8 or 9″ square pan. When set, cut into squares. *Makes 36 (1½″) pieces.*

Mexican Fudge

Creamy candies chock-full of crunchy pecans. Shared with us by Mrs. George Lear of Fort Allen, Louisiana, a gracious hostess and winner of flower show awards.

2 cups sugar
1 cup cream (20% butterfat)
1 cup sugar
¼ cup butter
4½ cups pecan halves

Caramelize 1 cup sugar in small skillet (*see p. 141*). Combine 2 cups sugar and cream in medium saucepan. Bring to a boil. Pour caramelized sugar *very slowly* into boiling cream, stirring while pouring. Be careful steam does not burn hand. Cook over medium heat until a little dropped in cold water forms a soft ball (234°). Stir occasionally. Remove from heat. Add butter and pecans. Beat by hand until candy holds together and loses its gloss. Drop quickly by teaspoonfuls onto buttered waxed paper. *Makes 2½ to 3 doz.*

Quick Chocolate Fudge

Family Fudge (2 lb.)

1 cup semi-sweet chocolate pieces (6 oz.)
1 milk chocolate candy bar (4½ oz.), broken in pieces
⅔ cup marshmallow creme
1 tbsp. butter
1⅓ cups chopped nuts
⅔ cup undiluted evaporated milk (5⅓ oz.)
1½ cups sugar

Party or Gift Fudge (6 lb.)

3 cups (three 6-oz. pkg.) semi-sweet chocolate pieces
3 milk chocolate candy bars, broken in pieces
2 cups (1 pt.) marshmallow creme
¼ cup butter
4 cups chopped nuts
1⅔ cups (14½ oz.) undiluted evaporated milk
4½ cups sugar

Put chocolate pieces, broken candy bar, marshmallow creme, butter and chopped nuts into mixing bowl (a very large one for large recipe). Combine undiluted evaporated milk and sugar in saucepan over medium heat. Bring to boil; cook 5 min. (or 225° on candy thermometer), stirring constantly. Remove from heat and pour over other ingredients. Stir until chocolate has melted and mixture is smooth and glossy. Pour smaller recipe into ungreased 8 or 9″ square pan; larger recipe into ungreased 13x9″ oblong and 8 or 9″ square pan. Allow to cool and cut into squares.

Peanut Brittle

3 cups sugar
1 cup water
½ cup white corn syrup
¼ cup butter
1 lb. raw Spanish peanuts (round, with red skins on)
1 tsp. soda
1 tsp. vanilla

Boil sugar, water and corn syrup until it threads. Add butter and peanuts; cook slowly to 300°, stirring occasionally. Add soda and vanilla. (It will foam up.) Turn out onto two buttered baking sheets; pull out thin as it cools. When cold, break into pieces with knife handle. *Makes about 3 lb.*

Toffee Fudge

Crispy toffee squares, chocolate-coated tops. Mrs. M. E. Roy of Minneapolis makes this often for her family and friends.

1 cup pecans, chopped
¾ cup brown sugar (packed)
½ cup butter
½ cup semi-sweet chocolate pieces or 4½-oz. milk chocolate bar, broken in pieces

Sprinkle pecans on bottom of greased square pan, 9x9x1¾″. Combine sugar and butter in saucepan. Bring to boil, stirring constantly; boil 7 min. Remove from heat and spread over nuts. Sprinkle chocolate pieces over top. Cover pan so heat will melt chocolate. Spread evenly over top. Cut in squares while warm. Refrigerate to set. *Makes 36 1½″ pieces.*

Cream Caramels

Chewy. Creamy-rich.

½ cup chopped nuts
2 cups sugar
¾ cup light corn syrup
½ cup butter
2 cups cream (20% butterfat)

Sprinkle nuts in buttered 8″ square pan. Mix sugar, corn syrup, butter and half of cream in saucepan. Bring to boil over low heat, stirring constantly. Stir in rest of cream gradually. Continue stirring as mixture thickens, and cook to 250° or until a little dropped in cold water forms a hard ball. Remove from heat and pour over nuts in pan. When cold, cut into squares. *Makes about 5 doz.*

Divinity

2⅔ cups sugar
⅔ cup light corn syrup
½ cup water
2 egg whites, stiffly beaten
1 tsp. vanilla
⅔ cup broken nuts

Mix sugar, corn syrup and water in saucepan. Stir over low heat until sugar is dissolved; then cook without stirring to 260° (a little dropped into cold water forms a hard ball). Remove from heat and pour, beating constantly, in a fine stream into the beaten egg whites. Add vanilla and continue beating until mixture holds its shape and becomes slightly dull. Fold in nuts. Drop quickly from tip of buttered spoon onto waxed paper in individual peaks . . . or spread in a buttered pan and cut into 1″ squares when firm. *Makes 48 pieces.*

Popped Corn

1 cup unpopped corn makes about 5 cups popped corn.

After popping, stir in melted butter; sprinkle with salt.

Hurry-up "Popcorn"

Melt 2 to 4 tbsp. butter in heavy skillet. Add 4 cups KIX or CHEERIOS and ½ tsp. salt. Stir over medium heat 5 min.

Easy Caramel Corn

Stir ½ lb. caramels (28) and 2 tbsp. hot water over hot water until smooth. Pour over 5 cups popped corn, KIX or CHEERIOS. Mix gently until blended. Drop by spoonfuls onto waxed paper. *Makes about 3 doz.*

Wheaties Ting-a-Lings

Melt two pkg. (6 oz. each) semi-sweet chocolate pieces over hot water. Cool at room temperature. Mix in gently 4 cups WHEATIES. Drop by tablespoonfuls onto waxed paper. Place in refrigerator to set (2 hr.). *Makes 42 clusters.*

Uncooked Fondant

Ideal for party candy variations.

1 egg white
2 cups *sifted* **confectioners' sugar**
2 tsp. butter
½ tsp. vanilla

Combine ingredients in mixing bowl. Mix until creamy. Tint as desired with few drops of food coloring. Drop small spoonfuls onto waxed paper. Decorate with nuts, candied fruits or silver dragées. Let stand to become firm.

Mint Wafers

Make Uncooked Fondant (*above*)—*except* use 2½ cups confectioners' sugar. Substitute peppermint flavoring for the vanilla. Tint in shades of delicate yellow, pink and green. Knead with hands. Shape into 1" balls; place on waxed paper and flatten with tines of a fork.

Popcorn Balls

Make into interesting shapes for kiddies.

7 cups popped corn, KIX or CHEERIOS
1 cup sugar
⅓ cup water
⅓ cup light corn syrup
1 tsp. salt
¼ cup butter
1 tsp. vanilla

Put corn or cereal in large bowl. Mix sugar, water, syrup, salt and butter in saucepan. Cook to 250° or until a few drops form a hard ball when dropped into cold water. Remove from heat. Stir in vanilla. Pour in thin stream over corn or cereal, stirring constantly, to mix well. With buttered hands, shape into balls or shapes below. *Makes 12 to 15 large balls.*

Easter Bunnies

Make Popcorn Balls (*above*)—*except* form into bunny shapes. Shape slices of marshmallow for ears, half marshmallow for tail and use pipe cleaners for whiskers.

Jack-o'-Lanterns

Just the thing for "tricks or treats."

Make Popcorn Balls (*above*)—*except* add a little red and yellow food coloring for an orange-colored syrup and form into pumpkin shapes. Use small gumdrops for eyes and nose; corn candy for teeth; green gumdrop or jelly bean for stem.

Marshmallow Bars

⅓ cup butter
½ lb. marshmallows (32)
5 cups KIX or CHEERIOS

Melt butter and marshmallows over hot water. Stir occasionally. Pour syrup over cereal in large greased bowl; stir gently to coat well. Pack into greased 9" square pan. Cool. Cut into 3x1" bars. *Makes 27 bars.*

Peanut Butter-Marshmallow Bars

Make Marshmallow Bars (*above*)—*except* add ½ cup peanut butter to marshmallow mixture.

Kiddie Kones

Serve ice cream in them for special treats.

Make Marshmallow Bars (*above*)—*except* pack, with greased hands, into 12 greased custard cups, leaving centers hollow. Cool thoroughly. Remove from cups before filling with ice cream.

COOKIES

"Sugar and spice, and all things nice," the poet's description for little girls, is just as apt for cookies.

The name cooky has been traced to Holland where a tiny St. Nicholas cake called "koekje" was put in children's stockings.

The baking and serving of cookies is a generations-old custom. In twelfth century England, friends and relatives gathered for fairs and feast days and passed the day watching cockfights and bear baiting *and* munching cookies. Some of the most popular were "brandy snaps," a thin cooky rolled after baking; "fair buttons," large ginger cookies; and "Shrewsbury cake," like shortbread.

To our shores have come cookies from 'round the world. Many a mother made room among the few possessions she brought to the new homeland for a set of "sandbakkel" molds or a "springerle" rolling pin. Russian Teacakes, Petticoat Tails (French "petits gateaux tailles"), Moravian Ginger Cookies, Scotch Shortbread, Nürnberger, Finska Kakor and Canadian Honey Drops have filled our all-American cooky jar to the brim.

The cookies you bake carry your love wherever they go: wax-paper-wrapped, to school or work in a lunch box; gift-tied, to a new neighbor; holiday-boxed, to relatives and friends; carefully-packed, to a student or serviceman far away.

COOKIES—TREATS AND TREASURES

(complete index in back of book)

 TIMESAVING TIPS

Delicious cookies are easiest-ever with Betty Crocker Cooky Mixes: Brownie Mix and Date Bar Mix. And Rolled or Drop Ginger Cookies can be made with Gingerbread Mix. Try Betty Crocker Refrigerated Cookies, too ... all ready to bake.

DATE DROP COOKIES

Heat oven to 400° (mod. hot). Empty contents of Betty Crocker Date Bar Mix pkg. including date filling into mixing bowl. Add ¼ cup *hot* water and 1 egg; mix thoroughly. Drop rounded teaspoonfuls about 2″ apart on lightly greased baking sheet. Bake *8 to 10 min.* Cool on wire rack. *Makes about 2½ doz.*

GINGERSNAPS

Heat oven to 375° (quick mod.). Blend 1 pkg. Betty Crocker Gingerbread Mix with ⅓ cup shortening or vegetable oil and ½ cup milk. Beat vigorously ½ min. Drop rounded teaspoonfuls 3″ apart on ungreased baking sheet. Sprinkle with sugar. Bake *8 to 10 min. Makes about 4 doz. cookies.*

NO-BAKE PEANUT OATMEAL DROPS

Mix 1 cup sugar, ¼ cup butter, ⅓ cup evaporated milk in saucepan. Bring to rolling boil, boil 3 min., stirring frequently. Remove from heat. Stir in 1 cup peanut butter, ½ tsp. vanilla, 1 cup rolled oats and ½ cup Spanish peanuts. Drop by tablespoonfuls onto waxed paper. Let stand until set. *Makes 2½ doz.*

NOUGAT BARS

Children love these.

Melt 3 tbsp. butter and ½ lb. marshmallows over hot water, stirring occasionally. Remove from heat. Fold in 4 cups Kix or Cheerios, ¼ cup coarsely chopped nuts, ½ cup moist shredded coconut and ½ tsp. salt. Turn onto buttered square pan, 8x8x2″. With hand protected by waxed paper, pat out evenly in pan. Melt 4 sq. sweet or semi-sweet chocolate (4 oz.) and pour over top, spreading it in thin layer with spatula. Chill until set, 45 to 60 min. Cut into 2x1″ bars. *Makes 32.*

Note: You no longer need to sift flour for recipes in this chapter. Measure Gold Medal flour by dipping nested measuring cups into flour and leveling off with spatula.

WHAT EVERY COOK NEEDS TO KNOW ABOUT COOKIES

BAKE WITH CARE

Keep a well-filled cooky jar and you will be beloved by children of all ages. If you feel creative, try molded cookies like Kaleidoscope Cookies (*p. 193*) or fancy decorated cookies like Gingerbread Boys (*p. 211*). If your day will be busy, plan to bake a bar cooky (*p. 195*) or use a roll of refrigerator cookies from your refrigerator or freezer.

You will note that most of the recipes call for all-purpose flour and only a few for cake flour. Also, little or no liquid is called for as cooky doughs are usually quite stiff.

Cooky recipes in this chapter are organized according to the method of shaping with step-by-step photographs showing each type.

Drop (*pp. 186–191*)—dough is dropped from a spoon onto a lightly greased baking sheet.

Roll-and-slice (refrigerator) (*pp. 192–193*)—dough is shaped into a roll and chilled to be sliced thinly and baked.

Bar (*pp. 195–197*)—dough is baked in a square or oblong pan and cut into bars or squares after baking.

Rolled (*pp. 198–204*)—dough is rolled to desired thickness and cut with cooky cutter.

Molded (*pp. 206–209*)—dough is shaped by hand; shape is retained after baking.

Pressed (*p. 205*)—dough is soft enough to be forced through a cooky press yet stiff enough to hold its shape.

Try not to overbake cookies. Always test them for doneness as directed in the recipe. Remember that in the second between the time cookies are removed from the oven and taken from the baking sheet, they continue to bake.

Guard against using too much flour, either when making or rolling cooky dough, since excessive flour makes cookies dry. When baking drop cookies, always bake a test cooky. If dough for molded cookies seems dry, add cream, 1 tbsp. at a time.

• •

SERVE WITH FLAIR

Let cookies help build traditions in your family. Bake and decorate special cookies for holidays through the year (*suggestions on p. 211*).

If you have a freezer, keep a tin of fancy rich cookies like Spritz (*p. 205*), Shortbread (*p. 210*) or colorful Marzipan (*p. 212*) in it to brighten cooky trays.

Delight children with cut-out cookies in their favorite animal shapes. Let youngsters decorate cookies using tinted icing. For cooky place cards: bake a round molded cooky with a crease in the middle, fill crease with icing and stand decorated cut-out cooky upright.

NEW ADVENTURES IN COOKY MAKING

Coconut-Chocolate Meringue Bites (*p. 196*)—Butterscotch bottom layer, filling of chocolate and nuts, topped with a brown sugar meringue.

Fudge Meltaways (*p. 194*)—The refrigerator replaces the oven in blending flavors of this cooky-confection.

Lemon Slice Cookies (*p. 212*)—Half slices of lemon-colored cookies that look like candy.

Marzipan Cookies (*p. 212*)—Cooky copies of the attractive foreign-made candy called marzipan.

Orange-Caramel Cookies (*p. 197*)—A delicious bar cooky that is quick to mix.

PAINTED COOKIES

Paintbrush Cookies, page 198   *Painted Petite Pops, page 211*   *Marzipan Cookies, page 212*

TIPS FOR SUCCESSFUL COOKY BAKING

1. Before you start:

> Read through the recipe
> Get together the ingredients
> Collect the utensils
> Preheat the oven
> Measure the ingredients

2. Make a test cooky to see if consistency of dough is right. More flour may be added if cooky spreads more than desired.

3. Look at cookies when minimum baking time is up. Avoid overbaking—this makes cookies dry and too dark.

4. Immediately after baking, remove cookies from baking sheet to cooling rack with wide spatula. This prevents overbaking and breaking.

5. Make all cookies in batch same size. This assures even baking.

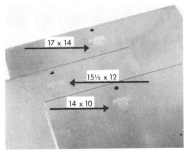

1. Use baking sheets or pans at least 2″ narrower and shorter than oven so heat circulates around it. Standard size baking sheets are 14x10″, 15½x12″ and 17x14″. SHINY, BRIGHT pans are best for light brown crusts.

2. If pan with sides is used for baking sheet, turn upside down and bake cookies on the bottom—this insures even browning. Grease cool pans as indicated with *unsalted* shortening.

3. Combine the *softened* shortening, sugar and eggs. Add also any molasses, syrup or melted chocolate in the recipe. Mix thoroughly by hand or use an electric mixer on low to medium speed.

4. Stir in the liquid (if called for) and flavoring. Mix well. Stir flour, salt and leavening (baking powder *or* · cream of tartar and soda) together and blend in; also any spices. Mix in fruit or nuts. Shape as in recipe.

5. Bake in center of oven if one rack is used. If two, divide oven in thirds with racks. Look at cookies when minimum baking time is up; *do not overbake*. Remove to wire rack.

6. Store crisp, thin cookies in container with a loose cover. Store soft cookies in container with a tight-fitting cover. Slices of orange or apple in container will mellow cookies; change fruit often.

How to Make Drop Cookies *(To mix cooky dough, see p. 185.)*

1. Drop dough by rounded or heaping teaspoonfuls, depending on size of cookies desired. With rubber spatula or another teaspoon, push dough onto baking sheet . . . being careful to peak up the dough.

2. Make filled cookies easily by dropping filling on mounds of dough on baking sheet . . . then covering filling with a little more of the dough.

Brown Sugar Drops

Soft, chewy. Wonderful brown sugar flavor.

1 cup soft shortening	3½ cups GOLD MEDAL Flour
2 cups brown sugar (packed)	1 tsp. soda
2 eggs	1 tsp. salt
½ cup soured milk *(see p. 26)*, butter-milk or water	

Mix shortening, brown sugar and eggs thoroughly. Stir in milk. Measure flour by dip-level-pour method or by sifting *(see p. 6)*. Blend flour, soda and salt; stir in. Chill at least 1 hr. *Heat oven to 400°* (mod. hot). Drop rounded teaspoonfuls of dough 2″ apart on greased baking sheet. Bake *8 to 10 min.*, or until almost no imprint remains when touched lightly with finger. *Makes about 6 doz. 2½″ cookies.*

Holiday Fruit Cookies

Elegant. Richly studded with fruits and nuts. Butterscotch-flavored. Perfect for your loveliest hospitality.

Make Brown Sugar Drops *(above)*—*except* mix into the dough 1½ cups chopped pecans, 2 cups candied cherries, cut in halves, and 2 cups cut-up dates. Place a pecan half on each cooky. Make these rich cookies smaller . . . only 2″. *Makes 8 doz. cookies.*

Easy Filled Cookies

Mrs. Edwin Korslund of Eagle Grove, Iowa, gave us this idea for making filled cookies the quickest way. See picture 2 above.

Make Brown Sugar Drops *(above)*—*except* place ½ tsp. Date Filling *(p. 204)* on each teaspoonful dough. Cover with ½ tsp. dough. Bake *10 to 12 min.*, or until lightly browned.

Jewelled Cookies

Glowing with gems of spicy gumdrops (red and green for Christmas holidays).

Make Brown Sugar Drops *(above)*—*except* mix into the dough 3 to 4 cups cut-up gumdrops.

Nut Drop Cookies

Make Brown Sugar Drops *(above)*—*except* mix into the dough 1 cup chopped nuts.

Coconut Drop Cookies

Make Brown Sugar Drops *(above)*—*except* mix into the dough 1 cup moist shredded coconut.

Rocks

Rich, buttery raisin-nut drop cooky—children will love them. Very similar to the old-fashioned hermits.

1 cup soft shortening (half butter)
1½ cups brown sugar (packed)
3 eggs
3 cups GOLD MEDAL Flour
1 tsp. soda
½ tsp. salt
2 tsp. cinnamon
1 tsp. cloves
1 cup seedless raisins
1 cup chopped nuts

Heat oven to 375° (quick mod.). Mix shortening, sugar and eggs thoroughly. Measure flour by dip-level-pour method or by sifting (*see p. 6*). Blend dry ingredients; stir in. Mix in raisins and nuts. Drop by rounded teaspoonfuls 2″ apart onto greased baking sheet. Bake *8 to 10 min. Makes about 5 doz. cookies.*

Old-fashioned Oatmeal Cookies

1 cup seedless raisins
1 cup water
¾ cup soft shortening
1½ cups sugar
2 eggs
1 tsp. vanilla
2½ cups GOLD MEDAL Flour
½ tsp. baking powder
1 tsp. soda
1 tsp. salt
1 tsp. cinnamon
½ tsp. cloves
2 cups rolled oats
½ cup chopped nuts

Simmer raisins and water in saucepan over low heat until raisins are plump, 20 to 30 min. Drain raisin liquid into measuring cup. Add water to make ½ cup. *Heat oven to 400°* (mod. hot). Cream shortening, sugar, eggs and vanilla. Stir in raisin liquid. Measure flour by dip-level-pour method or by sifting (*see p. 6*). Blend flour, baking powder, soda, salt and spices; stir in. Add rolled oats, nuts and raisins. Drop rounded teaspoonfuls 2″ apart onto ungreased baking sheet. Bake *8 to 10 min. Makes 6 to 7 doz.*

Wheaties Drop Cookies

Whole wheat flakes add extra flavor and goodness.

1 cup soft shortening
1 cup sugar
2 eggs
1 cup buttermilk
2 cups GOLD MEDAL Flour
½ tsp. soda
½ tsp. salt
1 tsp. cinnamon
½ tsp. nutmeg
½ tsp. cloves
¾ cup coarsely chopped nuts
1 cup seedless raisins
3 cups WHEATIES

Heat oven to 400° (mod. hot). Mix shortening, sugar and eggs thoroughly. Stir in buttermilk. Measure flour by dip-level-pour method or by sifting (*see p. 6*). Blend dry ingredients; stir in. Mix in nuts, raisins and Wheaties. Drop by teaspoonfuls 2″ apart onto lightly greased baking sheet. Bake *10 to 12 min. Makes 5 to 6 doz. cookies.*

Applesauce Cookies

¾ cup soft shortening
1 cup brown sugar (packed)
1 egg
½ cup applesauce
2¼ cups GOLD MEDAL Flour
½ tsp. soda
½ tsp. salt
¾ tsp. cinnamon
¼ tsp. cloves
1 cup seedless raisins
½ cup chopped nuts

Heat oven to 375° (quick mod.). Mix shortening, sugar and egg thoroughly. Stir in applesauce. Measure flour by dip-level-pour method or by sifting (*see p. 6*). Blend dry ingredients; stir in. Mix in raisins and nuts. Drop by teaspoonfuls onto greased baking sheet. Bake *10 to 12 min. Makes 4 doz. cookies.*

Jubilee Jumbles

Soft, tender, creamy-rich. Especially chosen to commemorate the seventy-fifth anniversary of the naming of GOLD MEDAL Flour. It happened in 1880 at the International Millers' Exhibition in Cincinnati, Ohio, when the flour previously known as Washburn's Superlative was awarded the medal of gold.

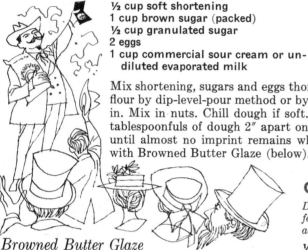

½ cup soft shortening
1 cup brown sugar (packed)
½ cup granulated sugar
2 eggs
1 cup commercial sour cream or undiluted evaporated milk

1 tsp. vanilla
2¾ cups GOLD MEDAL Flour
½ tsp. soda
1 tsp. salt
1 cup chopped nuts, if desired

Mix shortening, sugars and eggs thoroughly. Stir in sour cream and vanilla. Measure flour by dip-level-pour method or by sifting (*see p. 6*). Blend flour, soda and salt; stir in. Mix in nuts. Chill dough if soft. *Heat oven to 375° (quick mod.).* Drop rounded tablespoonfuls of dough 2″ apart onto greased baking sheet. Bake *about 10 min.*, or until almost no imprint remains when touched with finger. Spread cooled cookies with Browned Butter Glaze (below). *Makes about 4 doz. 2½″ cookies.*

Browned Butter Glaze

Melt ½ cup butter until golden brown. Blend in 2 cups *sifted* confectioners' sugar and 1 tsp. vanilla. Stir in 2 to 4 tbsp. hot water until icing spreads smoothly.

Coconut Jumbles

Make Jubilee Jumbles (*above*)—*except* mix into the dough 1 cup moist flaked coconut.

Chocolate Chip Jumbles

Make Jubilee Jumbles (*above*)—*except* mix into the dough 1 pkg. (6 oz.) chocolate pieces.

Date or Raisin Jumbles

Make Jubilee Jumbles (*above*)—*except* mix into the dough 1 cup finely cut dates or seedless raisins.

Butterscotch Jumbles

Make Jubilee Jumbles (*above*)—*except* omit granulated sugar and increase brown sugar to 1½ cups.

Chocolate Jumbles

Make Jubilee Jumbles (*above*)—*except* use only 2¼ cups flour, ½ cup cocoa, 1 tsp. soda. Frost cooled cookies with Marie's Chocolate Icing (*p. 195*).

Old-time Cinnamon Jumbles

Delicately cake-like. "So easy . . . making them is a thrill for the girls in the Home Economics classes each year," according to Miss Sarah M. Knight of Buffalo, New York.

½ cup soft shortening (part butter)
1 cup sugar
1 egg
¾ cup buttermilk
1 tsp. vanilla
2 cups GOLD MEDAL Flour
½ tsp. soda
½ tsp. salt
¼ cup sugar
1 tsp. cinnamon

Mix shortening, 1 cup sugar and egg thoroughly. Stir in buttermilk and vanilla. Measure flour by dip-level-pour method or by sifting (*see p. 6*). Blend flour, soda and salt; stir in. Chill dough. *Heat oven to 400° (mod. hot).* Drop rounded teaspoonfuls of dough 2″ apart onto lightly greased baking sheet. Sprinkle with mixture of ¼ cup sugar and cinnamon. Bake *8 to 10 min. Makes about 4 doz. 2″ cookies.*

Chocolate Chip Cookies

Also known as "Toll House" Cookies . . . originated by Kenneth and Ruth Wakefield at their charming New England Toll House on the outskirts of Whitman, Massachusetts. These cookies were first introduced to American homemakers in 1939 through our series of radio talks on "Famous Foods from Famous Eating Places."

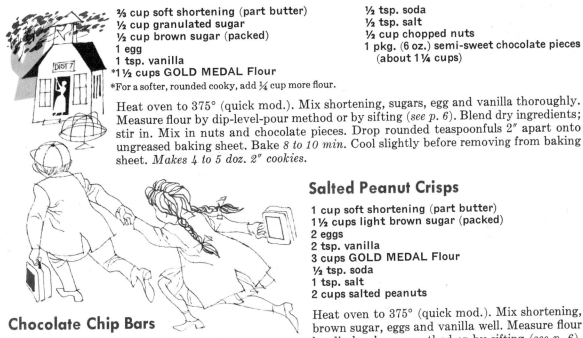

⅔ cup soft shortening (part butter)
½ cup granulated sugar
½ cup brown sugar (packed)
1 egg
1 tsp. vanilla
*1½ cups GOLD MEDAL Flour

½ tsp. soda
½ tsp. salt
½ cup chopped nuts
1 pkg. (6 oz.) semi-sweet chocolate pieces
  (about 1¼ cups)

*For a softer, rounded cooky, add ¼ cup more flour.

Heat oven to 375° (quick mod.). Mix shortening, sugars, egg and vanilla thoroughly. Measure flour by dip-level-pour method or by sifting (*see p. 6*). Blend dry ingredients; stir in. Mix in nuts and chocolate pieces. Drop rounded teaspoonfuls 2″ apart onto ungreased baking sheet. Bake *8 to 10 min.* Cool slightly before removing from baking sheet. *Makes 4 to 5 doz. 2″ cookies.*

Chocolate Chip Bars

Make dough for Chocolate Chip Cookies (*above*). Spread in greased oblong pan, 13x9½x2″. Bake *at 375° 20 to 25 min. Makes 48 bars.*

Banana Jumbos

These soft, moist cookies are like little banana cakes. Frost, if desired, with a confectioners' sugar icing.

1 cup soft shortening (part butter)
1 cup sugar
2 eggs
1 cup mashed ripe bananas (about 2)
½ cup buttermilk
1 tsp. vanilla
3 cups GOLD MEDAL Flour
1½ tsp. soda
½ tsp. salt
1 cup chopped nuts

Mix well shortening, sugar and eggs. Stir in bananas, buttermilk and vanilla. Measure flour by dip-level-pour method or by sifting (*see p. 6*). Blend flour, soda and salt; stir in. Blend in nuts. Chill 1 hr. *Heat oven to 375° (quick mod.).* Drop rounded tablespoonfuls 2″ apart onto lightly greased baking sheet. Bake *about 10 min. Makes about 3½ doz. cookies.*

Salted Peanut Crisps

1 cup soft shortening (part butter)
1½ cups light brown sugar (packed)
2 eggs
2 tsp. vanilla
3 cups GOLD MEDAL Flour
½ tsp. soda
1 tsp. salt
2 cups salted peanuts

Heat oven to 375° (quick mod.). Mix shortening, brown sugar, eggs and vanilla well. Measure flour by dip-level-pour method or by sifting (*see p. 6*). Blend flour, soda and salt; stir in. Mix in peanuts. Drop rounded teaspoonfuls 2″ apart onto lightly greased baking sheet. Flatten with greased bottom of glass dipped in sugar. Bake *8 to 10 min. Makes about 6 doz.*

Stir-n-Drop Sugar Cookies

2 eggs
⅔ cup vegetable oil
2 tsp. vanilla
1 tsp. grated lemon rind
¾ cup sugar
2 cups GOLD MEDAL Flour
2 tsp. baking powder
½ tsp. salt

Heat oven to 400° (mod. hot). Beat eggs with fork. Stir in oil, vanilla and rind. Blend in sugar until mixture thickens. Measure flour by dip-level-pour method or by sifting (*see p. 6*). Blend flour, baking powder and salt; stir in. Drop by teaspoonfuls 2″ apart onto ungreased baking sheet. Flatten with greased bottom of glass dipped in sugar. Bake *8 to 10 min.* Remove immediately. *Makes about 3 doz. 3″ cookies.*

Chocolate Drop Cookies

So chocolaty, soft and tender.

½ cup soft shortening (part butter)
1 cup sugar
1 egg
2 sq. unsweetened chocolate (2 oz.),
   melted and cooled
¾ cup buttermilk or soured milk (*see p. 26*)

1 tsp. vanilla
1¾ cups GOLD MEDAL Flour
½ tsp. soda
½ tsp. salt
1 cup chopped pecans or other nuts,
   if desired

Mix shortening, sugar, egg and chocolate thoroughly. Stir in buttermilk and vanilla. Measure flour by dip-level-pour method or by sifting (*see p. 6*). Blend flour, soda and salt; stir in. Mix in nuts. Chill at least 1 hr. *Heat oven to 400°* (mod. hot). Drop rounded teaspoonfuls of dough 2″ apart onto lightly greased baking sheet. Bake *8 to 10 min.,* or until no imprint remains when touched lightly with finger. Frost cooled cookies, if desired, with Marie's Chocolate Icing (*p. 195*). *Makes about 3½ doz. 2½″ cookies.*

Cocoa Drop Cookies

Make Chocolate Drop Cookies (*above*)—*except* omit chocolate; add ½ cup cocoa to dry ingredients.

Black Walnut Chocolate Drops

Make Chocolate Drop Cookies (*above*)—*except* use black walnuts for the nuts.

Chocolate-Cherry Drops

Make Chocolate Drop Cookies (*above*)—*except* omit nuts and mix into dough 2 cups cut-up candied or drained maraschino cherries. *Makes 4 doz. cookies.*

Orange Drop Cookies

A delightfully flavored cake-like cooky.

⅔ cup shortening
¾ cup sugar
1 egg
½ cup orange juice
2 tbsp. grated orange rind
2 cups GOLD MEDAL Flour
½ tsp. baking powder
½ tsp. soda
½ tsp. salt

Heat oven to 400° (mod. hot). Mix shortening, sugar and egg. Stir in orange juice and rind. Measure flour by dip-level-pour method or by sifting (*see p. 6*). Blend dry ingredients; stir in. Drop rounded teaspoonfuls 2″ apart on ungreased baking sheet. Bake *8 to 10 min.* Frost with Orange Butter Icing (blend 2 cups *sifted* confectioners' sugar and 2 tbsp. butter; stir in 1 tbsp. grated orange rind and about 2 tbsp. orange juice until smooth). *Makes 4 doz. 2″ cookies.*

Ginger Creams

Mildred Bennett (now Mrs. Axel Anderson), who was honored one year as national 4-H girl, brought us this recipe when she was a member of our staff.

⅓ cup soft shortening
½ cup sugar
1 small egg
½ cup molasses
½ cup water
2 cups GOLD MEDAL Flour
½ tsp. salt
½ tsp. soda
1 tsp. ginger
½ tsp. nutmeg
½ tsp. cloves
½ tsp. cinnamon

Mix shortening, sugar, egg, molasses and water thoroughly. Measure flour by dip-level-pour method or by sifting (*see p. 6*). Blend dry ingredients; stir in. Chill dough. *Heat oven to 400°* (mod. hot). Drop dough by teaspoonfuls 2″ apart onto lightly greased baking sheet. (Cookies will spread slightly during baking.) Bake *about 8 min.,* or until no imprint remains when touched lightly. While warm, frost with Easy Creamy Icing (*p. 202*). *Makes about 4 doz. 2″ cookies.*

Ginger Cream Bars

Make Ginger Creams (*above*)—*except* spread dough evenly in oblong pan, 13x9½x2″. Bake *about 30 min.* While slightly warm, frost with Easy Creamy Icing (*p. 202*). Then cut into bars.

Kisses

Moist, chewy, macaroon-like.

½ cup egg whites (4 medium)
1¼ cups sugar
¼ tsp. salt
½ tsp. vanilla
2½ cups moist shredded coconut or 2 cups finely
  chopped nuts

Heat oven to 325° (slow mod.). Beat egg whites until frothy. Gradually beat in sugar. Continue beating with rotary beater or mixer until very stiff and glossy. Stir in salt, vanilla and coconut. Drop heaping teaspoonfuls 2″ apart onto un-greased brown wrapping paper on baking sheet. Bake *about 20 min.*, or until set and delicately browned. Lift off paper, lay wet towel on hot baking sheet. Place paper of kisses on towel, let stand 1 min. Steam will loosen kisses. Slip off with spatula. *Makes about 3 doz. cookies.*

Chocolate-Coconut Kisses

Make coconut Kisses (*above*)—*except* stir into the batter 2 sq. unsweetened chocolate (2 oz.), melted and slightly cooled.

Pineapple Cookies

"These are my children's favorite cookies!" says Mrs. Frank Parauka of Grand Rapids, Michigan, who sent us the recipe.

1 cup soft shortening
1½ cups sugar
1 egg
1 can (9 oz.) crushed pineapple with juice
3½ cups GOLD MEDAL Flour
1 tsp. soda
½ tsp. salt
¼ tsp. nutmeg
½ cup chopped nuts

Mix shortening, sugar and egg well. Stir in pineapple. Measure flour by dip-level-pour method or by sifting (*see p. 6*). Blend flour, soda, salt and nutmeg; stir in. Mix in nuts. Chill 1 hr. *Heat oven to 400°* (mod. hot). Drop rounded teaspoonfuls 2″ apart onto lightly greased baking sheet. Bake *8 to 10 min.*, or until no imprint remains when touched lightly. *Makes 5 doz. cookies.*

Swedish Macaroon Teacakes

They look like tiny tarts. The rich cooky-type crust and the delicious macaroon-like filling are baked together.

1 cup soft butter
½ cup sugar
1 egg
1 tsp. vanilla
2 cups SOFTASILK Flour or GOLD MEDAL Flour

Cream butter and sugar thoroughly. Beat in egg and vanilla. Measure flour by dip-level-pour method or by sifting (*see p. 6*). Stir in flour. Drop a rounded teaspoonful of batter into each greased tiny muffin cup ... pressing batter over bottom and up around sides (¼″ thick ... center hollow). Chill. *Heat oven to 325°* (slow mod.). Fill hollows with Almond Macaroon Filling (*below*). Bake *25 to 30 min. Makes 2 doz. cookies.*

Almond Macaroon Filling

Beat 2 eggs until light and foamy. Gradually beat in ½ cup sugar until well blended. Mix in 1¼ cups blanched almonds, finely chopped, and ½ tsp. almond flavoring.

Wheaties Cherry Blinks

⅓ cup soft shortening
½ cup sugar
1 egg
1½ tbsp. milk
½ tsp. vanilla
1 cup GOLD MEDAL Flour
½ tsp. baking powder
¼ tsp. soda
¼ tsp. salt
½ cup seedless raisins or cut-up dates
½ cup nuts, chopped
1½ cups WHEATIES, crushed
candied or maraschino cherries

Heat oven to 400° (mod. hot). Mix shortening, sugar and egg. Stir in milk and vanilla. Measure flour by dip-level-pour method or by sifting (*see p. 6*). Blend dry ingredients; stir in. Mix in raisins and nuts. Drop dough from teaspoon, one at a time, into Wheaties. Roll gently until completely coated. Place 2″ apart on greased baking sheet. Top with a piece of candied or maraschino cherry. Bake *10 to 12 min. Makes about 3 doz. cookies.*

How To Make Refrigerator Cookies (*To mix cooky dough, see p. 185.*)

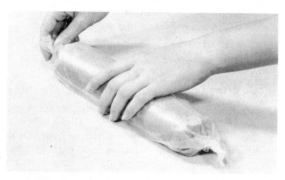

1. Press and mold dough with hands into a long roll, even and smooth, and as big around as you want your cookies to be. Wrap in waxed paper . . . twisting ends to hold the roll in shape.

2. Chill roll of dough until it is firm enough to slice easily. To speed up chilling, place in freezing compartment of refrigerator. Slice with a thin sharp knife to insure neat slices with smooth edges. Wrap and return unused dough to refrigerator so it will remain firm.

Refrigerator Cookies

Melt-in-the-mouth rich and crispy.

½ cup soft shortening (part butter)
1 cup brown sugar (packed)
1 egg
½ tsp. vanilla

1 ¾ cups GOLD MEDAL Flour
½ tsp. soda
¼ tsp. salt

Mix shortening, sugar, egg and vanilla thoroughly. Measure flour by dip-level-pour method or by sifting (*see p. 6*). Blend flour, soda and salt; stir in. Form into roll 2½″ across. Wrap in waxed paper. Chill until firm. *Heat oven to 400°* (mod. hot). With a thin sharp knife, slice ⅛″ thick. Place a little apart on ungreased baking sheet. Bake *8 to 10 min. Makes about 5 doz. cookies.*

Cooky Tarts

Make Refrigerator Cookies (*above*)—*except* spoon 1 tsp. jam on half of slices, top with rest of slices. *Seal edges.* Cut slits in top so filling shows through. Bake. *Makes 2½ doz. cookies.*

Nut Fingers

Make Refrigerator Cookies (*above*)—*except* mold level tablespoonfuls of chilled dough into rolls 3″ long. Roll in finely chopped nuts. Bake. *Makes 5½ doz. cookies.*

Nut Refrigerator Cookies

Make Refrigerator Cookies (*above*)—*except* add 1 cup finely chopped nuts. Form into 2″ rolls. Bake. *Makes 6½ doz. cookies.*

Chocolate Refrigerator Cookies

Make Refrigerator Cookies (*above*)—*except* add 1½ sq. unsweetened chocolate (1½ oz.), melted, with the shortening. Form into roll 2″ across. *Bake.* Put cooled slices together with icing. *Makes about 2½ doz. filled cookies.*

Ribbon Bar Cookies

Make Refrigerator Cookies (*above*)—*except* divide dough in halves. To one add ½ sq. unsweetened chocolate (½ oz.), melted. Form each half into 2 strips, 2″ wide and ¼″ thick. Pile strips, alternating colors. Press together. *Makes 5 doz. bar cookies.*

Chocolate Refrigerator Cookies

Butter rich . . . rolled in pecans. Developed by Jenelle Dow of Owatonna, Minnesota, formerly of our staff.

1¼ cups soft butter
1½ cups *sifted* confectioners' sugar
1 egg
3 cups SOFTASILK Flour

½ cup cocoa
¼ tsp. salt
1½ cups chopped pecans
4 oz. German sweet chocolate

Cream butter and confectioners' sugar. Blend in egg. Measure flour by dip-level-pour method or by sifting (*see p. 6*). Stir in flour, cocoa and salt. Blend well. Chill dough 1 to 2 hr. Press and mold into 2 long smooth rolls, 1½″ across. Roll in pecans. Chill overnight. *Heat oven to 400°* (mod. hot). Cut ⅛″ slices. Place on ungreased baking sheet. Bake *about 10 min.* Cool. Melt chocolate in double boiler; frost center of cookies. *Makes about 8 doz. cookies.*

Petticoat Tails

Brought from France to Scotland by Mary, Queen of Scots. The French name "Petits Gateaux Tailles" means—"little cakes cut off." But the name came to be pronounced as it sounded to the Scotch and English—"Petticoat Tails."

1 cup soft butter
1 cup *sifted* confectioners' sugar
1 tsp. flavoring (vanilla, almond,
    wintergreen or rose)
2½ cups GOLD MEDAL Flour
¼ tsp. salt

Mix butter, sugar and flavoring. Measure flour by dip-level-pour method or by sifting (*see p. 6*). Blend flour and salt; stir in. Mix with hands. Mold into a roll about 2″ across. Wrap in waxed paper and chill (several hours or overnight). *Heat oven to 400°* (mod. hot). Cut ⅛″ slices. Place a little apart on ungreased baking sheet. Bake *8 to 10 min. Makes about 6 doz. 2″ cookies.*

Date-Nut Pinwheels

Make dough for Refrigerator Cookies (*p. 192*). Divide into 2 parts. Roll each piece of dough on waxed paper into a rectangle about 11x7″. Spread rectangles with Date-Nut Filling (below). Roll up tightly beginning at wide side. Pinch edge to seal. Wrap rolls in waxed paper and chill several hours. *Heat oven to 400°* (mod. hot). Cut into ¼″ slices. Place on lightly greased baking sheet. Bake *about 10 min. Makes about 5 doz. cookies.*

Date-Nut Filling

Place in saucepan ¾ lb. moist pitted dates, cut up, ⅓ cup sugar and ⅓ cup water. Cook until slightly thickened, stirring constantly Remove from heat. Cool. Stir in ½ cup finely chopped nuts.

Kaleidoscope Cookies (*Summer Pastels*)

These multi-colored cookies remind us of the bright patterns in a kaleidoscope.

Make dough for Petticoat Tails (*at left*). If dough is dry, add 1 to 2 tbsp. cream. Divide dough into thirds. Select 3 variations (*below*) and follow directions for flavor, coloring and trim. Wrap tightly; chill until firm. *Heat oven to 375°* (quick mod.). Slice cookies ⅛″ thick. Place on ungreased baking sheet. Bake *7 to 9 min.,* or until lightly browned. *Makes 6 doz.*

Using ⅓ of the dough, add the following and mix thoroughly:

Green Cookies: Add 1 tbsp. grated lemon rind, few drops green food coloring. Roll in multi-colored sugar.

Yellow Cookies: Add 1 tbsp. grated orange rind, few drops yellow food coloring. Roll in finely chopped almonds.

Pink Cookies: Add ½ tsp. peppermint flavoring, color with few drops red food coloring. Roll in red crystal sugars.

Chocolate on Chocolate: Add 1 sq. semi-sweet chocolate (1 oz.), melted. Roll in chocolate shot.

Chocolate Drop Quickies

A quick sweet treat. No baking, just cook and drop.

2 cups sugar
½ cup butter
½ cup cocoa
½ cup milk
3 cups quick-cooking rolled oats
½ cup chopped nuts
1 tsp. vanilla

Mix sugar, butter, cocoa and milk in saucepan. Bring to boil quickly. Reduce heat to medium and boil 3 or 4 min., or until a little dropped into cold water forms a soft ball (234°). Remove from heat; stir in rolled oats, nuts and vanilla. Drop by teaspoonfuls onto waxed paper; let stand until hardened. Store in refrigerator, if desired. *Makes about 3 doz. cookies.*

Fudge Meltaways

Easy no-bake confection-like brownie melts in your mouth.

½ cup butter
1 sq. unsweetened chocolate (1 oz.)
¼ cup sugar
1 tsp. vanilla
1 egg, beaten
2 cups graham cracker crumbs
1 cup coconut
½ cup chopped nuts
¼ cup butter
1 tbsp. milk or cream
2 cups *sifted* confectioners' sugar
1 tsp. vanilla
1½ sq. unsweetened chocolate (1½ oz.), melted

Melt ½ cup butter and 1 sq. chocolate in saucepan. Blend sugar, 1 tsp. vanilla, egg, graham cracker crumbs, coconut and nuts into butter-chocolate mixture. Mix thoroughly and press into 11½x7½x1½" baking dish or square pan, 9x9x1¾". Refrigerate while making filling.

Cream ¼ cup butter, milk, confectioners' sugar and 1 tsp. vanilla. Mix and spread over crumb mixture. Chill in refrigerator. Pour 1½ sq. melted chocolate over chilled mixture and spread evenly. Store in refrigerator. Cut into squares before Meltaways are completely firm. *Makes 3 to 4 doz. squares.*

194

Toffee Squares

Rich cooky that looks and tastes like toffee candy. Especially good at holiday time.

1 cup butter
1 cup brown sugar (packed)
1 egg yolk
1 tsp. vanilla
2 cups GOLD MEDAL Flour
¼ tsp. salt
3 to 4 milk chocolate bars (⅞ oz. each)
½ cup chopped nuts

Heat oven to 350° (mod.) Cream butter, sugar, egg yolk and vanilla. Measure flour by dip-level-pour method or by sifting (*see p. 6*). Stir in flour and salt thoroughly. Spread 13x10" rectangle on greased baking sheet (leave about 1" around edge of baking sheet). Bake *20 to 25 min.* It will still be soft. Remove from oven. Immediately place separated squares of chocolate on top. Let stand until soft; spread evenly over surface. Sprinkle with nuts. Cut into small squares while warm. *Makes 6 to 7 doz. cookies.*

For a softer cake-like cooky, spread dough in an oblong pan, 13x9½x2". Bake *25 to 30 min.*

Date and Nut Squares

Chewy, rich flavored. Much like the Bishop's Bread served to circuit-riding preachers in days of Early America.

2 eggs
½ cup sugar
½ tsp. vanilla
½ cup GOLD MEDAL Flour
½ tsp. baking powder
½ tsp. salt
1 cup chopped walnuts
2 cups finely cut-up dates

Heat oven to 325° (slow mod.). Grease square pan, 8x8x2". Beat eggs until foamy. Beat in sugar and vanilla. Measure flour by dip-level-pour method or by sifting (*see p. 6*). Blend flour, baking powder and salt; stir in. Mix in walnuts and dates. Spread in greased pan. Bake *25 to 30 min.* Cut into squares. Cool; remove from pan. Dip in confectioners' sugar. *Makes 16 2" squares.*

How To Make Bar Cookies *(To mix cooky dough, see p. 185.)*

1. Spread dough in greased pan and bake as directed.

2. Cut into squares or bars when slightly cool.

3. Remove from pan with a wide spatula

Brownies

Chewy, fudge squares. A favorite of Lynn Auten of our staff who likes any food just so it's chocolate.

2 sq. unsweetened chocolate (2 oz.)
⅓ cup shortening
1 cup sugar
2 eggs

¾ cup GOLD MEDAL Flour
½ tsp. baking powder
½ tsp. salt
½ cup chopped nuts

Heat oven to 350° (mod.). Grease a square pan, 8x8x2″. Melt chocolate and shortening over hot water. Beat in sugar and eggs. Measure flour by dip-level-pour method or by sifting (*see p. 6*). Blend flour, baking powder and salt; stir in. Mix in nuts. Spread in pan. Bake *30 to 35 min.* or until slight imprint remains when touched lightly with finger. Cool slightly and cut into squares. If desired, spread with Marie's Chocolate Icing (*below*) before cutting. *Makes 16 2″ squares.*

Marie's Chocolate Icing

Melt over hot water 1 tbsp. butter and 1 sq. unsweetened chocolate (1 oz.). Blend in 1½ tbsp. warm water. Beat in about 1 cup *sifted* confectioners' sugar (until icing spreads easily).

Dainty Tea Brownies

Make Brownies (*above*)—*except* chop nuts *finely* and spread dough in *two* well greased oblong pans, 13x9½x2″. Sprinkle with ¾ cup blanched and finely sliced pistachio nuts. Bake *7 to 8 min.* Cut immediately into squares or diamonds. Remove from pan while warm.

Brownie Confections

Make Brownies (*above*). Cool. Brown ¼ cup soft butter to a delicate brown. Blend with 2 cups *sifted* confectioners' sugar. Stir in 2 tbsp. cream and 1 tsp. vanilla until smooth. Spread on Brownies.

Melt 1 sq. unsweetened chocolate (1 oz.) and 1 tbsp. butter. When cooled, spread very thin coating over butter icing. When toppings are set, cut in squares about 1″. *Makes 64 squares.*

Butterscotch Brownies

Keep deliciously soft for days in a tightly covered jar.

¼ cup butter, soft shortening or vegetable oil
1 cup light brown sugar (packed)
1 egg
¾ cup GOLD MEDAL Flour
1 tsp. baking powder
½ tsp. salt
½ tsp. vanilla
½ cup coarsely chopped walnuts

Heat oven to 350° (mod.). Melt shortening over low heat. Remove from heat. Blend in sugar. Cool. Stir in egg. Measure flour by dip-level-pour method or by sifting (*see p. 6*). Blend flour, baking powder and salt; stir in. Mix in vanilla and walnuts. Spread in well greased square pan, 8x8x2″. Bake *25 min.* DO NOT OVERBAKE. Cut into bars while warm. *Makes 18 bars 2½ x 1″.*

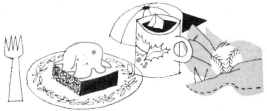

Dream Bars

Almond-coconut topping on melt-in-the-mouth crust.

½ cup soft shortening (half butter)
½ cup brown sugar (packed)
1 cup GOLD MEDAL Flour

Heat oven to 350° (mod.). Mix shortening and sugar thoroughly. Measure flour by dip-level-pour method or by sifting (*see p. 6*). Stir in flour. Flatten into bottom of ungreased oblong pan, 13x9½x2″. Bake *10 min.* Then spread with

Almond-Coconut Topping

2 eggs, well beaten
1 cup brown sugar (packed)
1 tsp. vanilla
2 tbsp. flour
1 tsp. baking powder
½ tsp. salt
1 cup moist shredded coconut
1 cup slivered almonds (or other nuts)

Mix eggs, sugar and vanilla. Mix with flour, baking powder and salt. Stir in coconut and almonds. Return to oven and bake *25 min. more.* Cool; cut in bars. *Makes about 2½ doz. 3x1″ bars.*

Chocolate Chip Dream Bars

Make Dream Bars (*above*)—except use ⅓ cup butter in bottom layer. In topping use 1 pkg. (6 oz.) semi-sweet chocolate pieces in place of coconut. Bake *15 to 20 min.* Cool; spread with Thin Chocolate Icing (*p. 173*).

HOW TO CHOP NUTS

Chop with long, straight knife. Hold point against cutting board, chop through nuts—swinging handle around in quarter circle. Chop coarsely or finely as recipe directs.

Coconut-Chocolate Meringue Bites

From Diana Williams of San Francisco, Calif., formerly of our staff, who says that they travel well.

¾ cup soft butter
½ cup brown sugar (packed)
½ cup granulated sugar
3 eggs, separated
1 tsp. vanilla
2 cups GOLD MEDAL Flour
1 tsp. baking powder
¼ tsp. soda
¼ tsp. salt
1 pkg. (6 oz.) chocolate pieces
1 cup flaked or grated coconut
¾ cup coarsely chopped nuts
1 cup brown sugar (packed)

Heat oven to 350° (mod.). Grease an oblong pan, 13x9½x2″. Blend butter, ½ cup brown sugar, granulated sugar, egg yolks and vanilla. Beat 2 min., medium speed on mixer or 300 vigorous strokes by hand, scraping bowl constantly. Measure flour by dip-level-pour method or by sifting (*see p. 6*). Blend dry ingredients; stir in. Spread dough in pan. Sprinkle with chocolate pieces, coconut and nuts. Beat egg whites until frothy; add 1 cup brown sugar gradually and beat until stiff. Spread over nuts. Bake *35 to 40 min.* Cool; cut into bars. *Makes 40 to 60 bars.*

Fancy Filbert Bars

Specialty of Mrs. George Ludcke, Jr. (formerly Jeannette Campbell of our staff).

½ cup soft shortening (half butter)
½ cup *sifted* confectioners' sugar
2 egg yolks
1 cup GOLD MEDAL Flour

Heat oven to 350° (mod.). Mix shortening, sugar and egg yolks thoroughly. Measure flour by dip-level-pour method or by sifting (*see p. 6*). Stir in flour. Flatten into bottom of ungreased oblong pan, 13x9½x2″. Bake *10 min.* Spread with ½ to ¾ cup softened currant or raspberry jelly, then with

Meringue-Filbert Topping

Beat 2 egg whites until stiff. Beat in mixture of ½ cup sugar and ¼ tsp. cinnamon gradually. Fold in 1 cup finely chopped or ground filberts (unblanched). Bake *25 min. more.* Cool; cut into bars. *Makes about 2½ doz. 3x1″ bars.*

Date Bars (*Matrimonial Cake*)

These cookies won first prize at the Minnesota State Fair.

¾ cup soft shortening (part butter)
1 cup brown sugar (packed)
1¾ cups GOLD MEDAL Flour
½ tsp. soda
1 tsp. salt
1½ cups rolled oats

Heat oven to 400° (mod. hot). Mix shortening and sugar. Measure flour by dip-level-pour method or by sifting (*see p. 6*). Blend flour, soda and salt; stir in. Mix in rolled oats. Flatten half of mixture into bottom of greased oblong pan, 13x9½x2". Spread with cooled Date Filling (*below*). Top with remaining crumb mixture, patting lightly. Bake *25 to 30 min.* While warm, cut into bars and remove from pan. *Makes about 2½ doz. 2x1½" bars.*

Date Filling

Mix 3 cups cut-up dates, ¼ cup sugar and 1½ cups water in saucepan. Cook over low heat, stirring constantly, until thickened (about 10 min.). Cool.

Christmas Mincemeat Bars

1½ cups brown sugar (packed)
2 eggs
2 tbsp. molasses
1 tbsp. soft butter
1 tsp. vanilla
2 cups GOLD MEDAL Flour
½ tsp. salt
½ tsp. soda
1 tsp. *each* cinnamon and cloves
3 tbsp. hot water
¼ cup almonds, slivered
¼ cup seedless raisins
1 pkg. (9 oz.) mincemeat, broken up with fork
1½ cups *sifted* confectioners' sugar
about 3 tbsp. hot milk
½ tsp. *each* vanilla and almond flavoring

Heat oven to 400° (mod. hot). Grease two oblong pans, 13x9½x2". Mix brown sugar, eggs, molasses, butter and vanilla. Measure flour by dip-level-pour method or by sifting (*see p. 6*). Blend flour, salt, soda and spices; stir in. Mix in hot water. Stir in almonds, raisins and mincemeat. Spread thin in greased pans. (Dough puffs and fills in any holes as it bakes.) Bake *12 to 15 min.* Spread immediately with mixture of confectioners' sugar, milk and flavorings. Cut into squares or diamonds. *Makes 6 doz. 2x1½" bars.*

Montego Bay Squares

Subtle chocolate taste hints of Jamaica and brings to mind its delightful food.

1½ cups cut-up dates
2 tbsp. sugar
¾ cup water
½ sq. unsweetened chocolate (½ oz.)
⅓ cup shortening (part butter)
½ cup brown sugar (packed)
¾ cup GOLD MEDAL Flour
¼ tsp. soda
½ tsp. salt
¾ cup rolled oats
⅓ cup finely chopped nuts

Heat oven to 400° (mod. hot). Grease a square pan, 8x8x2". Cook dates, sugar, water and chocolate over low heat, stirring constantly, until mixture thickens, about 10 min. Cool. Cream shortening and brown sugar. Measure flour by dip-level-pour method or by sifting (*see p. 6*). Blend flour, soda and salt; stir in. Mix in rolled oats and nuts. Press half of mixture over bottom of pan. Spread with date mixture; top with remaining crumbly mixture, pressing top lightly. Bake *25 to 30 min.* *Makes about 2 doz. bars.*

Orange-Caramel Cookies

Simply delicious. Borrowed from food artist, Helen Corbitt of Neiman-Marcus, Dallas, who in turn had gotten the recipe from Miss Fanny Andrews.

1½ cups brown sugar (packed)
2 eggs
1⅓ cups GOLD MEDAL Flour
⅔ cup cut-up fresh orange slices with white skin left on (1 large or 2 small oranges)
⅔ cup chopped pecans

Heat oven to 350° (mod.). Beat sugar and eggs 3 min., high speed on mixer. Measure flour by dip-level-pour method or by sifting (*see p. 6*). Stir in flour. Fold in orange pieces and pecans. Spread thin in greased jelly roll pan, 15½x10½x1". Bake *30 to 35 min.* While warm, spread with *Glaze:* mix grated rind of 1 orange, ⅔ cup *sifted* confectioners' sugar, 2 tbsp. cream. *Makes fifty 2x1½" bars.*

197

How To Make Rolled Cookies *(To mix cooky dough, see p. 185.)*

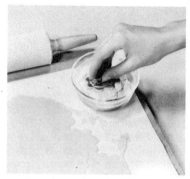

1. To prevent "sticking," slip a canvas cover over board and stockinet over rolling pin. Rub flour into the covers.

2. Roll lightly, small amount dough at a time . . . keeping the rest chilled. Roll very thin for crisp cookies.

3. Cut as many cookies from each rolling as possible. Dip cooky cutter in flour, then shake it and cut.

Mary's Sugar Cookies

The most delicious and versatile of cookies. From Mary Herman, a thoughtful friend and fine letter writer, who shared many of her special recipes with us when on our staff.

1½ cups *sifted* confectioners' sugar	½ tsp. almond flavoring
1 cup butter	2½ cups GOLD MEDAL Flour
1 egg	1 tsp. soda
1 tsp. vanilla	1 tsp. cream of tartar

Cream sugar and butter. Mix in egg and flavorings. Measure flour by dip-level-pour method or by sifting *(see p. 6)*. Blend dry ingredients; stir in. Refrigerate 2 to 3 hr. *Heat oven to 375° (quick mod.).* Divide dough in half and roll out on lightly floured pastry cloth to 3/16″ thick. Cut as shown above. Sprinkle with sugar. Place on lightly greased baking sheet. Bake *7 to 8 min.*, or until delicately golden. *Makes 5 doz. 2 to 2½″ cookies.*

Sugar Cooky Balls

Roll dough for Mary's Sugar Cookies *(above)* into small balls. Place 2″ apart on lightly greased baking sheet. Bake *about 10 min.*

Paintbrush Cookies

See color picture p. 184.

Make Mary's Sugar Cookies *(above)—except* before baking paint designs on cookies with Egg Yolk Paint *(below)*.

Egg Yolk Paint

Blend 1 egg yolk and ¼ tsp. water. Divide among several small custard cups, depending on how many different colors you wish to use. Add food coloring to each cup for desired color. Paint designs on cookies with small paintbrushes. Use a separate brush for each color.

COOKY SHORT CUT
Dough for most rolled cookies may be dropped by teaspoonfuls onto baking sheet and flattened with glass that has been greased and dipped in sugar.

Ethel's Sugar Cookies

¾ cup shortening (part butter)
1 cup sugar
2 eggs
½ tsp. lemon flavoring or 1 tsp. vanilla
2½ cups GOLD MEDAL Flour
1 tsp. baking powder
1 tsp. salt

Mix well shortening, sugar, eggs and flavoring. Measure flour by dip-level-pour method or by sifting (*see p. 6*). Blend flour, baking powder and salt; stir in. Chill at least 1 hr. *Heat oven to 400° mod. hot).* Roll ⅛″ thick on floured board. Cut with 3″ cooky cutter. Place on ungreased baking sheet. Bake *6 to 8 min. Makes about 4 doz.*

Chocolate Pinwheels

Make dough for Ethel's Sugar Cookies (*above*) using vanilla for flavoring. Divide dough into 2 parts. Into 1 part, blend 2 sq. unsweetened chocolate (2 oz.), melted and cooled. Chill. Roll white dough into an oblong, 12x9″. Roll chocolate dough same size and lay on top of white. Roll together until ³⁄₁₆″ thick. Roll up tightly beginning at wide side. Chill. Cut ⅛″ slices. Bake *at 400° (mod. hot) 8 to 10 min. Makes 7 doz.*

Butter Cookies

From Ischl, a famous Austrian resort, comes this rich cooky, contributed by Antal Dorati, internationally known conductor, to "Encore," the cookbook of favorite dishes of famous musicians, ©1958 by Random House.

1 cup soft butter
2 cups GOLD MEDAL Flour
½ cup sugar
1 cup finely chopped walnuts

Heat oven to 350° (mod.). Measure flour by dip-level-pour method or by sifting (*see p. 6*). Combine all ingredients; blend well. Roll on floured cloth-covered board to ¼″. Cut with 1½″ cooky cutter. Place on ungreased baking sheet. Bake *10 to 12 min.*, until set but not brown. Cool. Frost cookies with a bitter chocolate icing or put together with raspberry jam. *Makes 8 doz. cookies.*

Old-fashioned Sour Cream Cookies

½ cup shortening (part butter)
1 cup sugar
1 egg
1 tsp. vanilla
2⅔ cups GOLD MEDAL Flour
1 tsp. baking powder
½ tsp. soda
½ tsp. salt
¼ tsp. nutmeg
½ cup commercial sour cream

Heat oven to 425° (hot). Mix shortening, sugar, egg and vanilla. Measure flour by dip-level-pour method or by sifting (*see p. 6*). Blend dry ingredients and add to creamed mixture alternately with sour cream. Roll ¼″ thick on well floured pastry cloth. Cut with 2″ cutter, place on greased baking sheet. Sprinkle with sugar. Bake *8 to 10 min. Makes 4 to 5 doz. 2″ cookies.*

Traffic Light Cookies

A delightful frosted cooky to teach children red for "stop" and green for "go."

¾ cup shortening (half butter)
1 cup sugar
2 eggs
½ tsp. flavoring
2½ cups GOLD MEDAL Flour
1 tsp. baking powder
1 tsp. salt
¾ cup orange marmalade

Mix first four ingredients thoroughly. Measure flour by dip-level-pour method or by sifting (*see p. 6*). Blend dry ingredients; stir in. Chill 1 hr. *Heat oven to 400° (mod. hot).* Divide dough into 3 parts. Roll on well floured cloth-covered board ¼″ thick. Cut into rectangles, 3x2″ with a knife or 3″ circles with a cooky cutter. With thimble, make three indentations in cookies. Bake *6 to 8 min.* Reinforce indentations with thimble. Place 3 to 4 tbsp. marmalade in 3 separate cups. Tint one red, one green, the other is already yellow. Fill indentations with colored jelly giving the effect of a traffic light. *Makes 2½ to 3 doz.*

199

ROLLED COOKIES *Gay shapes . . . for holiday and year 'round cheer.*

Use dark-colored Gingies dough (*p. 202*) for animal shapes, toys, boy and girl figures. Use light-colored Merry Christmas Cookies dough for bells and all other shapes.

Merry Christmas Cookies

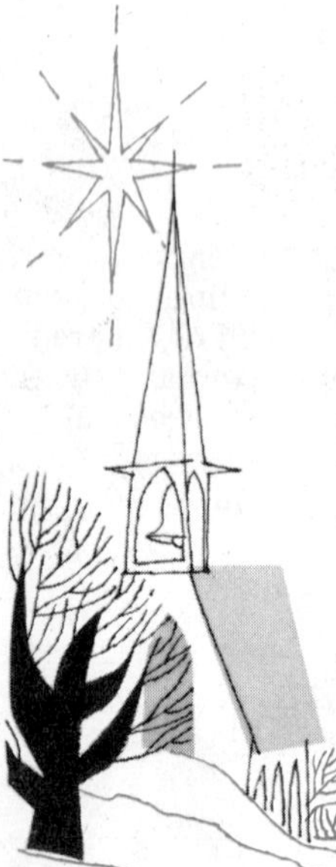

⅓ cup soft shortening
⅓ cup sugar
1 egg
⅔ cup honey
1 tsp. lemon flavoring
2¾ cups GOLD MEDAL Flour
1 tsp. soda
1 tsp. salt

Mix shortening, sugar, egg, honey and flavoring thoroughly. Measure flour by dip-level-pour method or by sifting (*see p. 6*). Blend flour, soda, salt; stir in. Chill dough. *Heat oven to 375°* (quick mod.). Roll dough ¼″ thick. Cut into desired shapes. Place 1″ apart on lightly greased baking sheet. Bake *8 to 10 min.* When cool, ice and decorate as desired. *Makes about 5 doz. 2½″ cookies.*

TO DECORATE

Use recipe for Easy Creamy Decorating Icing (*p. 202*). For decorating ideas, see below and color picture opposite. Colored or white sugar in coarse granules for decorating is available at your grocery store.

▶ **ALL YOU HAVE TO DO**

To make cookies to hang on the Christmas tree: loop a piece of green string and press ends into the dough at the underside of each cooky before baking.

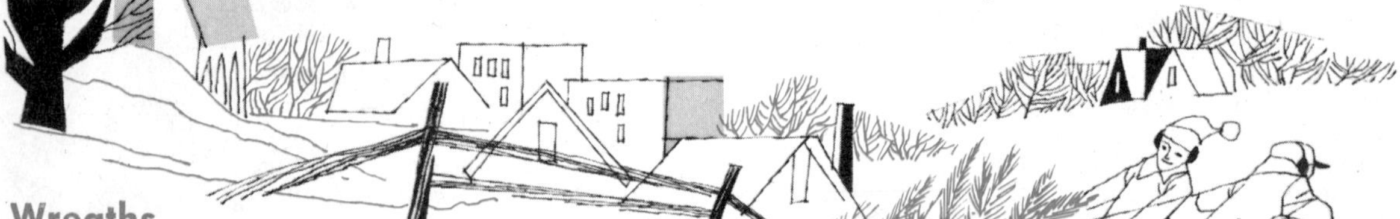

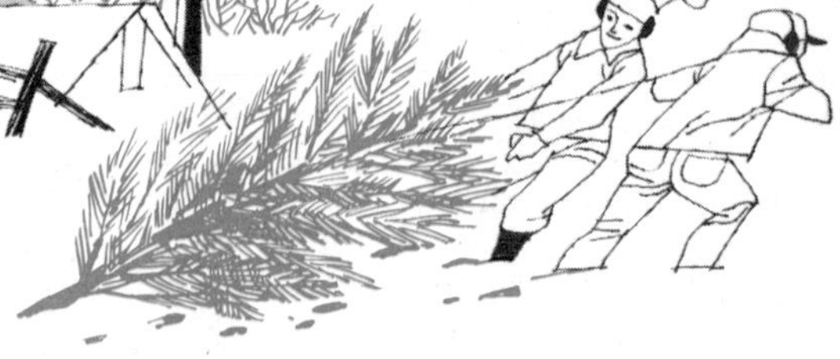

Wreaths

Cut with scalloped cutter . . . using smaller cutter for center. Cover with white icing. Sprinkle with green sugar and decorate with clusters of berries made of red icing—leaves of green icing—to give effect of holly wreaths.

Bells

Outline and make clapper with red icing. (A favorite with children.)

Stockings

Sprinkle colored sugar on toes and heels before baking. Or mark heels and toes of baked cookies with icing of some contrasting color.

Santa Claus

Outline with red icing. Fill bag with tiny colored candies. Paint boots with melted chocolate.

Angels

Frost skirt and face white; wings light blue. Trim with gold and silver dragées.

Christmas Trees

Spread with white icing . . . then sprinkle with green sugar. Decorate with silver dragées and tiny colored candies.

Toys

Outline shapes (drum, car, jack-in-the-box, etc.) with white or colored icing.

Animals

Pipe icing on animals (reindeer, elephant, horse, camel, dog, kitten, etc.) to give effect of bridles, blankets, etc.

Boys and Girls

Pipe figures with an icing to give desired effects: eyes, noses, buttons, etc.

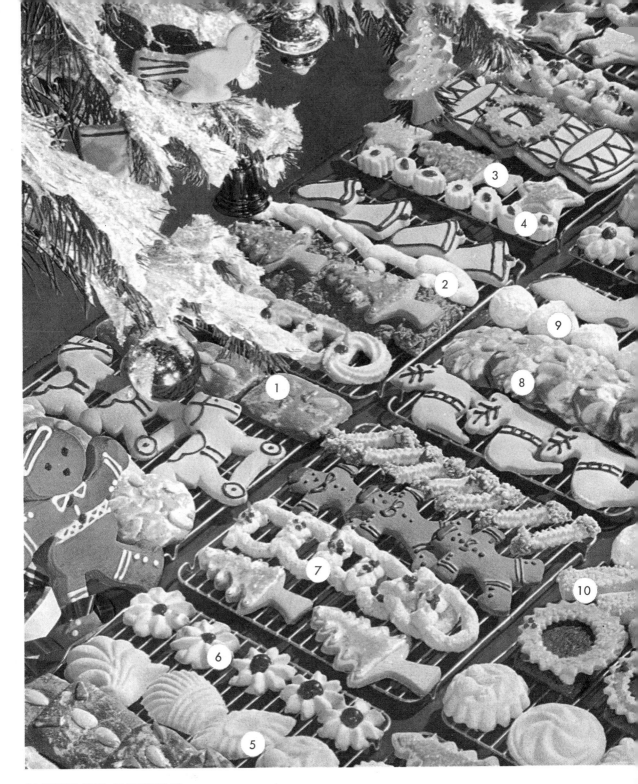

COOKIES FOR CHRISTMAS

(1) *Lebkuchen, page 203*

(2) *Spritz, page 205*

(3) *Merry Christmas Cookies, page 200*

(4) *Scotch Shortbread, page 210*

(5) *Sandbakelser, page 210*

(6) *Spritz, page 205*

(7) *Berliner Kränze, page 210*

(8) *Nürnberger, page 203*

(9) *Russian Teacakes, page 207*

(10) *Finska Kakor, page 210*

Gingies

A happy tradition at the famous Girard College, Philadelphia, Pennsylvania. The boys hoard them . . . old grads long for them. An excellent dough for Christmas cookies (p. 200).

⅓ cup soft shortening
1 cup brown sugar (packed)
1½ cups dark molasses
⅔ cup cold water
6 cups GOLD MEDAL Flour
2 tsp. soda

1 tsp. salt
1 tsp. allspice
1 tsp. ginger
1 tsp. cloves
1 tsp. cinnamon

Mix shortening, brown sugar and molasses thoroughly. Stir in water. Measure flour by dip-level-pour method or by sifting (*see p. 6*). Blend all dry ingredients; stir in. Chill. *Heat oven to 350° (mod.).* Roll ½″ thick. Cut with 2½″ round cutter. Place far apart on lightly greased baking sheet. Bake *about 15 min.,* or until no imprint remains when touched lightly. Frost cooled cookies with Easy Creamy Icing (*below*). *Makes 2⅔ doz. 2½″ cookies.*

Moravian Ginger Cookies

Crisp, spicy, paper-thin. Moravians who founded Bethlehem, Pennsylvania, on Christmas Eve, 1741, brought this cooky recipe with them.

⅓ cup molasses
3 tbsp. soft shortening
2 tbsp. brown sugar
1¼ cups GOLD MEDAL Flour
½ tsp. salt
¼ tsp. soda
¼ tsp. *each* cinnamon, ginger, cloves
dash *each* nutmeg and allspice

Mix molasses, shortening and sugar thoroughly. Measure flour by dip-level-pour method or by sifting (*see p. 6*). Blend all dry ingredients; stir in. Work with hands until well blended. Cover; chill 4 hr. *Heat oven to 375°* (quick mod.). Roll dough out paper-thin, a little at a time. Cut in desired shapes. Place on greased baking sheet. Bake *5 to 6 min.,* or until lightly browned. When cool, frost with a thin layer of Easy Creamy Icing (*at right*). *Makes about 5 doz. cookies.*

Stone Jar Molasses Cookies

Crisp and brown . . . and so delicious.

1 cup molasses
½ cup shortening
1 tsp. soda
2¼ cups GOLD MEDAL Flour
1¾ tsp. baking powder
1 tsp. salt
1½ tsp. ginger

Heat molasses to boiling point. Remove from heat. Stir in shortening and soda. Measure flour by dip-level-pour method or by sifting (*see p. 6*). Blend remaining ingredients; stir in. Chill dough. *Heat oven to 350°* (mod.). Roll thin (1/16″). Cut into desired shapes. Place on lightly greased baking sheet. Bake *5 to 7 min.* DO NOT OVERBAKE. *Makes about 6 doz. 2½″ cookies.*

Easy Creamy Icing

Blend 1 cup *sifted* confectioners' sugar, ¼ tsp. salt and ½ tsp. vanilla or other flavoring (lemon, almond or peppermint, etc.) and liquid to make easy to spread (about 1 tbsp. water or 1½ tbsp. cream). Tint, if desired, with a few drops of food coloring. Spread on cookies with spatula or pastry brush.

Easy Creamy Decorating Icing

Make Easy Creamy Icing (*above*)—*except* use less liquid . . . only enough to make icing easy to force through pastry tube—yet hold its shape (about ¾ tbsp. water or 1 tbsp. cream). Fill pastry tube and squeeze onto cookies in desired design.

▶ **ALL YOU HAVE TO DO**

To make a paper funnel for use with decorating icing: cut off a tiny corner of an envelope. An excellent substitute for a pastry tube.

Lebkuchen

The famous old-time German Christmas Honey Cakes. Adah E. M. Anderson of Hopkins, Minnesota, remembers that her grandmother, Wilhelmina Lutz Haish, said of these: "No Christmas celebration in the whole Black Forest region is ever complete without Lebkuchen."

½ cup honey
½ cup molasses
¾ cup brown sugar (packed)
1 egg
1 tbsp. lemon juice
1 tsp. grated lemon rind
2¾ cups GOLD MEDAL Flour

½ tsp. soda
1 tsp. cinnamon
1 tsp. cloves
1 tsp. allspice
1 tsp. nutmeg
⅓ cup cut-up citron
⅓ cup chopped nuts

Mix honey and molasses; bring to a boil. Stir in sugar, egg, lemon juice and rind. Measure flour by dip-level-pour method or by sifting (*see p. 6*). Blend dry ingredients; stir in. Mix in citron and nuts. Chill overnight. *Heat oven to 400°* (mod. hot). Roll small amount at a time, keeping rest chilled. Roll ¼" thick; cut into oblongs, 2½x1½". Place 1" apart on greased baking sheet. Bake *10 to 12 min.*, or until no imprint remains when touched lightly. While cookies bake, make Glazing Icing (*below*). Brush it over cookies the minute they are out of oven. Quickly remove from baking sheet. Cool; store to mellow. *Makes 6 doz. 3x2" cookies.*

Glazing Icing

Boil together 1 cup sugar and ½ cup water until first indication of a thread appears (230°). Remove from heat. Stir in ¼ cup confectioners' sugar and brush hot icing lightly over cookies. (*When icing gets sugary, reheat slightly, adding a little water until clear again.*) Icing is also good on fruitcake and other fruit bars.

Nürnberger

Round, light-colored honey cakes from the famed old City of Toys.

Make Lebkuchen (*above*)—*except*, in place of honey and molasses, use 1 cup honey and reduce spices using ¼ tsp. cloves, ½ tsp. allspice and ½ tsp. nutmeg . . . with 1 tsp. cinnamon.

Roll out the *chilled* dough ¼" thick. Cut into 2" rounds. Place on greased baking sheet. With fingers, round up cookies a bit toward center. Press in blanched almond halves around the edge like petals of a daisy. Use a round piece of citron for each center. Bake just until set. *Immediately* brush with Glazing Icing (*above*). Remove from baking sheet. Cool and store to mellow. *Makes about 6 doz. 2½" cookies.*

TO "MELLOW" COOKIES

. . . store in an airtight container for a few days. Add a cut orange or apple . . . changing it frequently to insure freshness.

Cream Wafers (*Pariserwafier*)

Mrs. G. C. Olson of Lake Minnetonka, Minnesota, brought this recipe with her from Sweden when she came to this country as a bride.

1 cup soft butter
⅓ cup whipping cream (35% butterfat)
2 cups GOLD MEDAL Flour

Measure flour by dip-level-pour method or by sifting (*see p. 6*). Mix ingredients thoroughly. Chill 1 hr. *Heat oven to 375°* (quick mod.). Roll ⅛" thick. Cut into 1½" rounds. Transfer to waxed paper heavily sprinkled with sugar . . . turning to coat both sides. Place on ungreased baking sheet. Prick in 4 places with fork. Bake *7 to 9 min.*, or until slightly puffy. Put two cooled cookies together with Creamy Butter Filling (*below*). *Makes about 5 doz. 1½" double cookies.*

Creamy Butter Filling

Blend ¼ cup soft butter, ¾ cup *sifted* confectioners' sugar, 1 egg yolk and 1 tsp. vanilla. If desired, tint pink or green with food coloring.

Filled Cooky Turnovers

Tender, creamy-white . . . with luscious fillings.

½ cup soft shortening
1 cup sugar
2 eggs
2 tbsp. cream (35% butterfat)

1 tsp. vanilla
2½ cups GOLD MEDAL Flour
¼ tsp. soda
½ tsp. salt

Mix shortening, sugar and eggs thoroughly. Stir in cream and vanilla. Measure flour by dip-level-pour method or by sifting (*see p. 6*). Blend flour, soda and salt; stir in. Chill. *Heat oven to 400°* (mod. hot). Roll ⅟₁₆″ thick. Cut 3″ rounds or squares. Place on lightly greased baking sheet. Place a rounded teaspoonful filling (*see below*) on each. Fold like a turnover, pressing edges together. Bake *8 to 10 min.*, or until delicately browned. *Makes about 6 doz. 3″ cookies.*

Date, Fig, Raisin or Prune Filling

2 cups dates, figs or raisins, finely cut up or ground, or 2 cups mashed cooked prunes (2⅔ cups uncooked)
¾ cup sugar
¾ cup water
½ cup chopped nuts, if desired

Cook fruit, sugar and water together slowly, stirring constantly, until thickened. Add nuts. Cool. *About 2⅓ cups filling.*

Pineapple Filling

1 cup sugar
¼ cup GOLD MEDAL Flour
1½ cups well drained crushed pineapple
¼ cup lemon juice
3 tbsp. butter
¼ tsp. nutmeg
¾ cup pineapple juice

Mix sugar and flour in saucepan. Stir in rest of ingredients. Cook slowly, stirring constantly, until thickened (5 to 10 min.). Cool. *About 2⅔ cups filling.*

▶ **ALL YOU HAVE TO DO**

To clean sticky fruits from your food grinder quickly and easily: run a few small pieces of dry bread through it.

Filled Cookies in Fancy Shapes

Make Filled Cooky Turnovers (*above*)—*except* cut dough with scalloped round cooky cutter or with heart, diamond or 2½″ cutter of any desired shape, cutting 2 alike for each filled cooky. (To give a decorative effect, cut the center out of the top cooky with a tiny cutter of heart, star or scalloped round shape.) Place the bottom pieces on lightly greased baking sheet. Spread desired filling (*at left*) on each . . . spreading up to edge. Cover with the top cooky. Press edges together. *Makes about 4 doz. 2½″ filled cookies.*

Spread filling almost to the edges when making filled cookies. To keep the filling in, press edges of filled cookies together with the fingers or with floured tines of a fork.

How To Make Pressed Cookies

Use a dough rich in shortening, such as that for Spritz and Peanut Butter Fingers (*below*). If very warm, chill the dough. But keep it pliable. (It crumbles if too cold.) Force dough through cooky press (or pastry tube), following manufacturer's directions, onto ungreased baking sheet.

▶ **ALL YOU HAVE TO DO**

To ensure perfect pressed cookies: have baking sheet room temperature before forcing cooky dough through press onto it. If sheet is warm, the fat in the dough will melt and the cookies will pull away from the sheet when the press is lifted.

Spritz

Crisp, fragile, buttery-tasting curlicues.

1 cup soft butter
⅔ cup sugar
3 egg yolks

1 tsp. flavoring (almond or vanilla) or
¼ cup finely chopped almonds
2½ cups GOLD MEDAL Flour

Heat oven to 400° (mod. hot). Mix butter, sugar, egg yolks and flavoring thoroughly. Measure flour by dip-level-pour method or by sifting (*see p. 6*). Work in flour. Using one-fourth at a time, force dough through cooky press onto ungreased baking sheet in desired shapes. Bake *7 to 10 min.*, or until set but not brown. *Makes about 6 doz. cookies.*

Chocolate Spritz

Make Spritz (*above*)—*except* blend into the shortening mixture 2 sq. unsweetened chocolate (2 oz.), melted.

Holiday Spritz

Colorful party cooky idea from Virginia Thuftedal, Fort Worth, Texas, formerly of our staff.

Make Spritz (*above*)—*except* omit almond or vanilla flavoring and add 1 tsp. rum flavoring. Tint dough with food coloring to light pastel shades. Glaze cooled cookies with Butter Rum Glaze (*below*).

Butter Rum Glaze

Melt ¼ cup butter in saucepan. Blend in 1 cup *sifted* confectioners' sugar and 1 tsp. rum flavoring. Stir in 1 to 2 tbsp. hot water until glaze spreads smoothly. Tint glaze to match cookies.

Peanut Butter Fingers

Peanut butter with chocolate—a winning combination.

½ cup soft shortening
½ cup peanut butter
½ cup granulated sugar
½ cup brown sugar (packed)
1 egg
1¼ cups GOLD MEDAL Flour
½ tsp. baking powder
¾ tsp. soda
¼ tsp. salt
*4 small plain chocolate bars, melted
¾ cup salted peanuts, crushed

*Melt chocolate in glass custard cup over hot water. Keep over hot water while dipping cookies.

Mix shortening, peanut butter, sugars and egg thoroughly. Measure flour by dip-level-pour method or by sifting (*see p. 6*). Blend dry ingredients; stir in. Chill 1 hr. *Heat oven to 375° (quick mod.).* Using cooky press with star shaped plate, make cookies 2½" long. Place on greased baking sheet 2" apart. Bake *8 to 10 min.* When cool, dip one end in melted chocolate and then in crushed peanuts. *Makes about 6 doz. cookies.*

How To Make Molded Cookies *(To mix cooky dough, see p. 185.)*

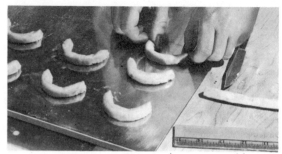

1. With hands, roll dough into balls. Flatten balls of dough with bottom of a glass dipped in flour or with a fork—crisscrossed.

2. Cut pencil-thick strips... and shape as directed... as for Berliner Kränze *(p. 210).*

Peanut Butter Cookies

Crunchy rounds. Many mothers double the recipe since they disappear so quickly.

½ cup soft shortening (half butter)
½ cup peanut butter
½ cup granulated sugar
½ cup brown sugar (packed)
1 egg

1¼ cups GOLD MEDAL Flour
½ tsp. baking powder
¾ tsp. soda
¼ tsp. salt

Mix shortening, peanut butter, sugars and egg thoroughly. Measure flour by dip-level-pour method or by sifting *(see p. 6)*. Blend all dry ingredients; stir in. Chill. *Heat oven to 375° (quick mod.).* Roll into balls size of large walnuts. Place 3" apart on lightly greased baking sheet. Flatten with fork dipped in flour ... crisscross. Bake *10 to 12 min.* Makes about *3 doz. 2½" cookies.*

Honey Peanut Butter Cookies

Make Peanut Butter Cookies *(above)*—*except* use only ¼ cup shortening and in place of brown sugar use ½ cup honey.

Peanut Butter and Jelly Cookies

Popular with children and grown-ups.

Make dough for Peanut Butter Cookies *(above)*. Chill. *Heat oven to 375° (quick mod.).* Roll dough into 1" balls. Roll in ½ cup finely chopped peanuts. Place about 3" apart on baking sheet and press thumb gently into center of each. Bake *10 to 12 min.*, or until set. Spoon small amount of preserves or jelly in thumbprint. *Makes 3½ doz. cookies.*

Date-Oatmeal Cookies

¾ cup soft shortening (half butter)
1 cup brown sugar (packed)
2 eggs
3 tbsp. milk
1 tsp. vanilla
2 cups GOLD MEDAL Flour
¾ tsp. soda
1 tsp. salt
2 cups rolled oats
1½ cups cut-up dates
¾ cup chopped nuts

Mix shortening, brown sugar, eggs, milk and vanilla thoroughly. Measure flour by dip-level-pour method or by sifting *(see p. 6)*. Blend flour, soda and salt; stir in. Mix in rolled oats, dates and nuts. Chill. *Heat oven to 375° (quick mod.).* Roll into balls size of large walnuts. Place 3" apart on lightly greased baking sheet. Flatten to ¼" thick with bottom of glass dipped in flour. Bake *10 to 12 min.* Makes about *4 doz. 2½" cookies.*

Russian Teacakes

Crunchy, sugared, nut-filled snowballs. This favorite with men came to us from Carl Burkland, a television consultant, who makes them at Christmastime.

1 cup soft butter
½ cup *sifted* confectioners' sugar
1 tsp. vanilla
2¼ cups GOLD MEDAL Flour
¼ tsp. salt
¾ cup finely chopped nuts

Mix butter, sugar and vanilla thoroughly. Measure flour by dip-level-pour method or by sifting (*see p. 6*). Blend flour and salt; stir in. Mix in nuts. Chill. *Heat oven to 400°* (mod. hot). Roll into 1" balls. Place on ungreased baking sheet. Bake *10 to 12 min.* While still warm, roll in confectioners' sugar. Cool. Roll in sugar again. *Makes about 4 doz. 1" cookies.*

Canadian Honey Drops

Mrs. W. G. Oliver of Winnipeg, Manitoba, mother of Margaret Oliver, formerly of our Canadian office in Toronto, sent us this treasured recipe.

1 cup soft shortening (part butter)
1 cup brown sugar (packed)
2 eggs
⅓ cup honey
1 tsp. vanilla
3½ cups GOLD MEDAL Flour
2 tsp. soda

Mix shortening, brown sugar and eggs thoroughly. Stir in honey and vanilla. Measure flour by dip-level-pour method or by sifting (*see p. 6*). Blend flour and soda; stir in. Chill several hours or overnight. *Heat oven to 350°* (mod.). Roll into balls size of large walnuts. Place on ungreased baking sheet. Bake *10 to 12 min.*, or until almost no imprint remains when touched lightly. When slightly cooled, put together with apricot jam. *Makes 3 doz. double cookies.*

Molasses Crinkles

Thick, chewy, with crackled, sugary tops. We begged the recipe from Mrs. Fred Fredell in St. Paul, Minnesota.

¾ cup soft shortening
1 cup brown sugar (packed)
1 egg
¼ cup molasses
2¼ cups GOLD MEDAL Flour
2 tsp. soda
¼ tsp. salt
½ tsp. cloves
1 tsp. cinnamon
1 tsp. ginger

Mix shortening, sugar, egg and molasses thoroughly. Measure flour by dip-level-pour method or by sifting (*see p. 6*). Blend all dry ingredients; stir in. Chill. *Heat oven to 375°* (quick mod.). Roll dough into balls the size of large walnuts. Dip tops in sugar. Place, sugared-side-up, 3" apart on greased baking sheet. Sprinkle each with 2 or 3 drops of water. Bake *10 to 12 min. Makes 4 doz.*

Snickerdoodles

Mrs. Ronald Anfinson (formerly Pat Roth of our staff) said, "These crunchy, crinkly-topped, spicy rounds are one of my happy childhood memories."

1 cup soft shortening (part butter)
1½ cups sugar
2 eggs
2¾ cups GOLD MEDAL Flour
2 tsp. cream of tartar
1 tsp. soda
¼ tsp. salt

Heat oven to 400° (mod. hot). Mix shortening, sugar and eggs thoroughly. Measure flour by dip-level-pour method or by sifting (*see p. 6*). Blend all dry ingredients; stir in. Roll into balls the size of small walnuts. Roll in mixture of 2 tbsp. sugar and 2 tsp. cinnamon. Place 2" apart on ungreased baking sheet. Bake *8 to 10 min.* (These cookies puff up at first, then flatten out.) *Makes about 5 doz. 2" cookies.*

BON BON COOKIES

Recipe, opposite.

Thumbprint Cookies

Nut-rich . . . the thumb dents filled with sparkling jelly. We are as delighted with this quaint addition to our cooky collection, from Ken MacKenzie, as she is when a friend presents her with antique thumbprint goblets.

½ cup soft shortening (half butter)
¼ cup brown sugar (packed)
1 egg yolk
½ tsp. vanilla

1 cup GOLD MEDAL Flour
¼ tsp. salt
1 egg white
¾ cup finely chopped nuts

Heat oven to 350° (mod.). Mix shortening, brown sugar, egg yolk and vanilla thoroughly. Measure flour by dip-level-pour method or by sifting (*see p. 6*). Blend flour and salt; stir in. Roll 1 tsp. dough into balls. Dip in slightly beaten egg white. Roll in nuts. Place 1″ apart on ungreased baking sheet; press thumb gently into centers. Bake *10 to 12 min.* Cool. Fill holes with sparkling jelly or tinted confectioners' sugar icing. *Makes about 3 doz. cookies.*

Chocolate Thumbprint Cookies

Make Thumbprint Cookies (*above*)—except substitute ½ cup granulated sugar for the brown sugar and add 1 sq. unsweetened chocolate (1 oz.), melted, with the shortening.

Lemon Snowdrops

A rich fancy cooky put together with a lemon filling.

1 cup butter
½ cup *sifted* confectioners' sugar
1 tsp. lemon flavoring
2 cups GOLD MEDAL Flour
¼ tsp. salt

Heat oven to 400° (mod. hot). Cream butter and sugar. Measure flour by dip-level-pour method or by sifting (*see p. 6*). Add flavoring, flour, salt; mix well. Measure level teaspoonfuls of dough, round into ball and flatten slightly. Place 1″ apart on ungreased baking sheet. Bake *8 to 10 min.* Cool. Put together with Lemon Butter Filling (*below*). Roll in confectioners' sugar. *Makes about 5 doz. cookies.*

Lemon Butter Filling

1 egg, slightly beaten
grated rind of 1 lemon
⅔ cup sugar
3 tbsp. lemon juice
1½ tbsp. softened butter

Blend all ingredients in top of double boiler. Cook over hot water until thick, stirring constantly. Set aside to cool.

Bon Bon Cookies

Bake them like cookies. Eat them like candies. Created by a true westerner, Mrs. Joseph J. Wallace, high in her Rocky Mountain home near Whitehall, Montana. (See color picture, opposite.)

½ cup soft butter
¾ cup *sifted* confectioners' sugar
1 tbsp. vanilla (3 tsp.)
food coloring, if desired
1½ cups GOLD MEDAL Flour
⅛ tsp. salt

Heat oven to 350° (mod.). Mix butter, sugar, vanilla and food coloring thoroughly. Measure flour by dip-level-pour method or by sifting (*see p. 6*). Blend in flour and salt. If dough is dry, add 1 to 2 tbsp. cream. Wrap level tablespoon dough around filling (a candied or well drained maraschino cherry, pitted date, nut or chocolate pieces). Place 1″ apart on ungreased baking sheet. Bake *12 to 15 min.* Cool. Dip tops of cookies in Icing (*below*). Decorate. *Makes 20 to 25 cookies.*

Chocolate Dough: Blend in 1 sq. unsweetened chocolate (1 oz.), melted.

Penuche Dough: Use ½ cup brown sugar (packed) in place of confectioners' sugar.

Icing

Mix 1 cup *sifted* confectioners' sugar, 2 tbsp. cream, 1 tsp. vanilla and food coloring, if desired.

Chocolate Icing: Add 1 sq. unsweetened chocolate (1 oz.), melted, and use ¼ cup cream.

Berliner Kränze (*Berlin Wreaths*)

Delicious and buttery, these gay little wreaths are made each holiday season in Norway.

1½ cups soft shortening (half butter)
1 cup sugar
2 tsp. grated orange rind
2 eggs
4 cups GOLD MEDAL Flour

Mix shortening, sugar, rind and eggs thoroughly. Measure flour by dip-level-pour method or by sifting (*see p. 6*). Stir in flour. Chill. *Heat oven to 400°* (mod. hot). Break off small pieces of dough; roll 6″ long and ¼″ thick. Form each piece into a circle, bringing one end over and through in a single knot. Leave ½″ end on each side. Place on ungreased baking sheet. Brush tops with meringue (made by beating 1 egg white until stiff, gradually beating in 2 tbsp. sugar). Press bits of red candied cherries on center of knot for holly berries. Add little jagged leaves cut out of green citron. Bake *10 to 12 min. Makes about 6 doz.*

NOTE: If dough seems crumbly, let it warm or work in a few drops of liquid until dough sticks together.

Scotch Shortbread

Old-time delicacy from Scotland . . . crisp, thick, buttery. Allene Moe, formerly of our staff, likes to tint the dough in assorted pastel colors before chilling it.

¾ cup soft butter
¼ cup sugar
2 cups GOLD MEDAL Flour

Mix butter and sugar thoroughly. Measure flour by dip-level-pour method or by sifting (*see p. 6*). Work in flour with hands. Chill. *Heat oven to 350°* (mod.). Roll ⅓ to ½″ thick. Cut into fancy shapes (small leaves, ovals, squares, etc.). Flute edges, if desired, as for pie crust. Place on ungreased baking sheet. Bake *20 to 25 min.* (The tops do not brown during baking, nor does shape of cookies change.) *Makes 2 doz. 1½x1″ cookies.*

Sandbakelser (*Sand Tarts*)

Fragile almond-flavored shells of Swedish origin, made in metal molds of varied designs.

*⅓ cup blanched almonds
*4 unblanched almonds
¾ cup soft butter
¾ cup sugar
1 small egg white, unbeaten
1¾ cups GOLD MEDAL Flour

*In place of the almonds, you may use 1 tsp. vanilla and 1 tsp. almond flavoring.

Put almonds through fine knife of food grinder twice. Mix in butter, sugar and egg white thoroughly. Measure flour by dip-level-pour method or by sifting (*see p. 6*). Stir in flour. Chill. *Heat oven to 350°* (mod.). Press dough into sandbakelse molds (tiny fluted forms) to form thin coating. Place on ungreased baking sheet. Bake *12 to 15 min.* Tap molds on table to loosen cookies; turn out. *Makes about 3½ doz. cookies.*

Finska Kakor (*Finnish Cakes*)

Nut-studded butter strips from Finland.

¾ cup soft butter
¼ cup sugar
1 tsp. almond flavoring
2 cups GOLD MEDAL Flour
1 egg white, slightly beaten
1 tbsp. sugar
⅓ cup finely chopped blanched almonds

Mix butter, ¼ cup sugar and flavoring thoroughly. Measure flour by dip-level-pour method or by sifting (*see p. 6*). Work in flour with hands. Chill. *Heat oven to 350°* (mod.). Roll ¼″ thick. Cut into strips 2½x¾″. Brush tops lightly with beaten egg white. Sprinkle with mixture of 1 tbsp. sugar and almonds. Carefully transfer to ungreased baking sheet. Bake *17 to 20 min. Makes about 4 doz. 2½x¾″ cookies.*

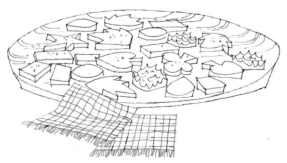

FESTIVE COOKIES

Painted Petite Pops

See color picture p. 184.

Make Mary's Sugar Cookies (*p. 198*)—except cut rolled dough into 1½" circles. Paint designs on half the cookies with Egg Yolk Paint (*p. 198*).

Bake *6 to 8 min*. To make petite pop: spread Easy Creamy Icing (*p. 202*) on plain baked cooky. Place a colored pick or 2" length of colored plastic straw across the middle, letting one end extend beyond edge of cooky. Place a painted cooky on top, pressing down slightly. *Makes 6 doz. cookies.*

Lollipop Cookies

Make Painted Petite Pops (*above*)—except cut 2½ to 3" circles and do not paint. Use flat wooden stick or colored plastic straw as handle. Decorate with faces of tinted icing.

New Year Clocks

Roll dough for Merry Christmas Cookies (*p. 200*) ¼" thick. Cut into 2½" rounds. Bake. Cool. Frost with Easy Creamy Icing (*p. 202*). Mark hours and hands pointing to five minutes of twelve with melted chocolate (using toothpick for outlining) or strands of licorice sticks.

Lincoln Logs

Cut chocolate-frosted Brownies (*p. 195*) in bars about 3x¾". Draw prongs of fork through icing down length of each to make it resemble a log. Decorate with star or with a tiny flag.

Valentine Hearts

Roll dough for Mary's Sugar Cookies (*p. 198*) ¹⁄₁₆" thick. Cut in heart shapes. Bake. Cool. Frost with pink-tinted Easy Creamy Icing (*p. 202*). Sprinkle with coconut or edge with tiny hearts.

Gingerbread Boys

Make holidays gayer than ever.

Make dough for Gingies (*p. 202*)—*except* mix in 1 more cup GOLD MEDAL Flour. Chill dough. Roll ½" thick. Cut with a gingerbread boy cutter. With a pancake turner, carefully transfer gingerbread boys to lightly greased baking sheet. Press raisins into dough for eyes, nose, mouth and shoe and cuff buttons. Use bits of candied cherries or red gumdrops for coat buttons; strips of citron for tie. Bake. Cool slightly, then carefully remove from baking sheet. With Easy Creamy Decorating Icing (*p. 202*), make outlines for collar, cuffs, belt and shoes. *Makes about 12 Gingerbread Boys.*

Shamrocks for St. Patrick's Day

Roll dough for Mary's Sugar Cookies (*p. 198*) ⅛" thick. Cut in shamrock shapes with club-shaped cutter. Bake. Cool. Frost with Easy Creamy Icing (*p. 202*) tinted pale green. Center with deeper green candy shamrock or other St. Patrick's Day symbol.

Easter Flowers

Tint dough for Mary's Sugar Cookies (*p. 198*) pastel shades of pink, green or yellow with a few drops of food coloring. Roll out ¹⁄₁₆" thick. Cut with little scalloped cutters for petal effect. Sprinkle with tinted sugar to match the dough before baking. Bits of candied orange peel or yellow gumdrops may be used for flower centers.

Halloween Cookies with Faces

Roll dough for Gingies (*p. 202*) ½" thick. Cut into 2½" rounds. Bake. Cool. Cover with orange-tinted Easy Creamy Icing (*p. 202*). Make faces with melted chocolate (using toothpick for outlining).

MORE COOKIES FOR SPECIAL OCCASIONS

Marzipan Cookies

Exciting little cookies adapted from the attractive and expensive candy called Marzipan by Willa Murphy of our staff. See color picture p. 184.

½ cup soft butter
¼ cup sugar
food coloring (see below)
⅛ tsp. almond flavoring
1¼ cups GOLD MEDAL Flour

Cream butter, sugar, food coloring of your choice and flavoring. Measure flour by dip-level-pour method or by sifting (*see p. 6*). Stir in flour; mix well. Shape as directed; for most cookies use 2 level teaspoonfuls of dough. Place on ungreased baking sheet. Chill 30 min. *Heat oven to 300°* (slow). Bake *about 30 min.* (time will vary according to size and thickness of cookies). *Makes 2 to 2½ doz. cookies.*

ORANGE DOUGH: Add 3 drops red food coloring and 2 drops yellow food coloring when creaming butter and sugar.

Oranges: Form into round ball. Insert clove in blossom end. For rough skin punch cooky with blunt end of toothpick.

Apricots: Roll dough into ball. Make crease down one side with toothpick. Stick clove in blossom end. Use red blush (see pears).

YELLOW DOUGH: Add 2 to 3 drops yellow food coloring when creaming butter and sugar.

Bananas: Roll dough into banana shape, tapering ends. Flatten top slightly to show planes on fruit and curve slightly. Paint on characteristic markings with mixture of 3 drops red, 2 drops yellow and 1 drop blue food coloring in ½ tsp. water.

Pears: Roll dough into a ball, then into cone shape. Bend top slightly. Insert stick of cinnamon for stem. For red blush, dilute ⅛ tsp. red food coloring with 1 tsp. water and paint cheeks.

RED DOUGH: Add 4 to 5 drops red food coloring when creaming butter and sugar.

Apples: Roll dough into round ball. Stick small piece of stick cinnamon in stem top and clove in blossom end. Use red blush (see pears).

Strawberries: Roll dough into a ball; form into heart shape. Cooky should be about ¾" high. For texture punch cooky with blunt end of toothpick. Roll in red crystal sugars, if desired. Place small piece of green colored toothpick or green dough into top for stem.

212

Lemon Slice Cookies

Fancy cookies that look like the well known candy and add a decorator's touch to a cooky tray or gift box. See color picture p. 71.

1 cup soft butter
1 cup *sifted* confectioners' sugar
¼ tsp. salt
¼ tsp. yellow food coloring
1 to 2 tbsp. grated lemon rind
2½ cups GOLD MEDAL Flour
yellow crystal sugars

Heat oven to 375° (quick mod.). Mix butter, sugar, salt, food coloring and lemon rind thoroughly. Measure flour by dip-level-pour method or by sifting (*see p. 6*). Add flour and blend well. Roll ¼" thick on floured cloth-covered board. Cut into 2" circles, then in half. Sprinkle with crystal sugars. Place on ungreased baking sheet. Bake *6 to 8 min.* Cool. Roll rounded edge in mixture of 1 egg white and 1 tsp. water, then in crystal sugars. Add thin line of Icing (*below*) ¼" from outside edge. *Makes 6 doz.*

Icing: Blend 1 cup *sifted* confectioners' sugar, ¼ tsp. salt and 1 tbsp. lemon juice. Fill pastry tube or paper funnel and squeeze onto cookies. If icing is too thick, add more juice or a little water.

Cherry-Coconut Bars

If desired, cut into squares and serve as dessert.

1 cup GOLD MEDAL Flour
½ cup butter
3 tbsp. confectioners' sugar
2 eggs, slightly beaten
1 cup sugar
¼ cup GOLD MEDAL Flour
½ tsp. baking powder
¼ tsp. salt
1 tsp. vanilla
¾ cup chopped nuts
½ cup coconut
½ cup quartered maraschino cherries

Heat oven to 350° (mod.). Measure flour by dip-level-pour method or by sifting (*see p. 6*). With hands, mix 1 cup flour, butter and confectioners' sugar until smooth. Spread thin with fingers in square pan, 8x8x2". Bake *about 25 min.* Stir all remaining ingredients into eggs. Spread over base. Bake *about 25 min. more.* Cool. *Makes twenty 3x1" bars.*

DESSERTS

Czars and princesses and chefs are the stars of the drama of dessert with explorers, patriots and opera stars appearing in lesser roles. Let's watch some of the action: Handsome Marco Polo, having visited Chinese sugar mills, is back home in Italy encouraging the refining of sugar, dessert's all-important ingredient.

Flames dance from a long-handled skillet as the next scene opens. Deftly, the white-hatted chef, folds the delicate crepes, pours on the bubbling sauce and presents it to the beautiful princess. Voilà! The first Crepes Suzette!

The czar, Alexander, and the chef, Louis Antoine de Câreme, appear together in another scene. Câreme has just produced a fantastic dessert from whipped cream, sugar, wine and candied fruits. The czar pronounces it delightful and names it for his first minister, Count Nestlerode.

Now the action changes to England and we see another chef being awarded a country estate for his creation of a fruit-filled steamed pudding.

More scenes from the story of desserts are presented with the recipes on the following pages. And, after mastering these fancy and famous desserts, you may be inspired to write a brand-new scene in our never-ending drama of dessert.

DESSERTS—THE GRAND FINALE

(complete index in back of book)

 TIMESAVING TIPS

COCONUT BOSTON CREAM PIE

Follow directions on Betty Crocker Boston Cream Pie Mix pkg.—*except* gently stir ⅓ cup flaked coconut into filling after mixing. Sprinkle ⅓ cup flaked coconut on top of chocolate glaze.

MILK CHOCOLATE PUDDING CAKE

Follow directions on Betty Crocker Chocolate Pudding Cake Mix pkg.—*except* use 1½ cups hot milk in place of boiling water poured over pudding mix. If desired, sprinkle with ½ cup chopped nuts. Bake *30 to 35 min.*

MINCE-GINGER UPSIDE-DOWN CAKE

Heat oven to 350° (mod.). Generously grease the bottom and corners of a square pan, 9x9x1¾". Spread 1 jar (1 lb. 12 oz.) mincemeat in pan. Prepare batter as directed on Betty Crocker Gingerbread Mix pkg. Pour evenly over mincemeat. Bake *about 50 min.,* or until top of cake is firm to touch. Run knife around edge of cake to free it from pan. Immediately invert onto serving plate. Leave pan over cake for 5 min. Remove pan and serve warm with Hard Sauce *(p. 393)* or Sweetened Whipped Cream *(p. 232). 12 to 16 servings.*

 MEALTIME MAGIC

FATHER'S DAY DINNER
Shrimp Cocktail *(p. 56)*
Filet Mignon with Mushrooms
Au Gratin Potatoes *(p. 411)*   Spinach
Greens with Italian Onion Rings
Hot Rolls
French Ribbon Cake *(p. 234)*

LUNCHEON WITH ZIP
Spicy Tomato Soup *(p. 400)*
Shrimp Curry on Rice *(p. 267)*
(toasted coconut, chutney, sieved hard-cooked egg, salted peanuts)
Butter Dips *(p. 77)*
Pears Helene *(p. 246)*

Note: You no longer need to sift flour for recipes in this chapter. Measure Gold Medal flour by dipping nested measuring cups into flour and leveling off with spatula. Measure Softasilk flour by spooning flour into nested cups and leveling off.

WHAT EVERY COOK NEEDS TO KNOW ABOUT DESSERTS

MAKE WITH CARE

Dessert is the satisfying sweet at the end of the meal. The lightest and easiest to prepare desserts are fruits (*pp. 218–219*), whether served fresh, stewed or baked.

Varied is the word for puddings. Puddings may be thickened with flour, cornstarch, rice, tapioca, bread, even corn meal (Indian Pudding, *p. 226*). Custards are an especially nutritious type of pudding made of sweetened eggs and milk, either baked (*p. 223*) without stirring or cooked with constant stirring. It's best to cook cream and tapioca puddings and custards over medium heat stirring often to prevent scorching and lumping.

Called puddings but actually cake-like in texture are Cottage Pudding (*p. 228*), cake puddings (*p. 229*) and steamed puddings (*p. 230*). Test them for doneness as you would cake.

Popular refrigerator desserts range from simple fruited gelatin through creamy mallow desserts to Bavarian cream in fancy molds. Creamy gelatin desserts require special care; cool just until the mixture mounds slightly when dropped from a spoon, then fold in whipped cream.

Refreshing frozen desserts are of two types. Those which must be beaten every so often during freezing to insure a smooth texture include ice creams, ices and sherbets (*p. 244*). Those which are frozen without stirring include parfaits and mousses (*p. 245*).

Eggs are the key ingredient for three famous desserts often shunned by the new cook as too difficult: soufflés (*p. 238*), Baked Alaska (*p. 234*) and Cream Puffs (*p. 243*). You'll be surprised how easy they are if you follow the recipes exactly.

. . . .

SERVE WITH FLAIR

Molded desserts are dramatic turned out on a large platter and surrounded with fruit or fresh lemon, ivy or grape leaves.

Serve steamed pudding flaming (*p. 230*) for a memorable climax to a holiday meal.

Cream pudding and custards take kindly to a garnish of whole berries or cherries, mandarin orange sections, toasted coconut or chopped nuts (*more suggestions on p. 24*).

NEW ADVENTURES IN DESSERTS

Aloha Chiffon Cake (*p. 237*)—Island inspired—with pineapple and coconut.

Frosted Mint Delight (*p. 220*)—Delicate fruit-mint flavor, delicate green color.

Nut Cracker Sweet (*p. 239*)—An elegant cream-filled chocolate torte.

Oriental Orange Snow (*p. 221*)—A dazzling dessert to crown a company dinner.

Steamed Pumpkin Pudding (*p. 231*)—To complete your holiday dinner.

PLAIN BUT FANCY

Fresh Fruit and Cheese

The easiest of all desserts.

A bowl heaped with colorful fruit washed, dried and chilled—a variety to choose from . . . is both decorative and tempting. Cheese and crisp unsweetened crackers are natural affinities, or crisp rich cookies are pleasant accompaniments. Serving can be very simple: just an individual dessert plate, a suitable knife for cutting fruit and spreading soft cheese. Finger bowls are correct to save linens from stubborn fruit stains but today paper napkins are often used with fruit.

Fresh Fruit Desserts in Season

Combinations always popular.

Honeydew melon with lime or lemon and garnish of mint leaves.

Cantaloupe filled with ice cream.

Peaches and raspberries, plain or with ice cream.

Strawberries, raspberries, blackberries, blueberries or sliced peaches with cream.

Sliced bananas with raspberries or sliced strawberries, topped with a mound of ice cream or with whipped cream or sour cream sprinkled with brown sugar.

Orange slices in orange juice. Orange ice added.

Fruit Ambrosia

Make it with any fruit you have on hand.

Sprinkle fruit (such as orange slices, bananas, unpared red apples, pineapple) with confectioners' sugar. Chill. Just before serving, top with plain or toasted coconut, salted peanuts or almonds or maraschino cherries.

Cheese and Fruit Partners

With bread or cracker accompaniment.

Concord grapes. Smoked, French Brie, Gouda, Edam or Swiss cheese. Salty crackers.

Red apples. Camembert, Liederkranz or New York cheese. Gingersnaps. Nuts.

Fresh pears. Bar-le-duc (currant preserves). Cream cheese. Buttered hot tiny baking powder biscuits or salty crackers.

Fresh strawberries (with hulls) around a mound of cream cheese sweetened with confectioners' sugar, a hint of rum flavoring. Dip strawberries into cheese mixture.

Tokay grapes. Mild brick or Cheddar cheese. Thin slices of buttered Pumpernickel (*p. 106*).

Melon wedges, green grapes, Bing cherries with stems. Gouda or Edam cheese (cut in wedges almost to bottom but left intact). Circles of onion and garlic-flavored cheese. Assorted crackers.

Green Gage or other plums (Italian prunes) stewed with strips of candied ginger, served chilled with Brie or other soft sharp cheese. Crackers.

Wedges of unhulled fresh pineapple, Camembert, Liederkranz or sharp New York cheese. Whole wheat crackers.

Tart plums and sugared blue grapes. Camembert, Roquefort or Bleu cheese. Thin slices of buttered caraway rye bread.

Fiesta Fruit Platter

From Elena Zelayeta of San Francisco, California, whose courageous spirit is an inspiration to us all. See color picture pp. 216–217.

On a large platter arrange clusters of Bing cherries (stems on) alternating with small bunches of green grapes around a pile of melon balls. Border with sliced peeled peaches. Lay bananas (cut in half, then split in two) over peaches like spokes in a wheel. Garnish with strawberries and mint leaves. Each person serves himself from platter, topping fruit with a swirl of cream cheese softened with milk and Raspberry Sauce (*below*) or thawed frozen raspberries.

Fresh Raspberry Sauce: Mix 1 pt. raspberries with ½ to 1 cup sugar. Let stand 2 hr. Put through sieve. *Makes 2 cups.*

Fresh Fruit Sauce

For a simple dessert or meat accompaniment.

1 qt. fresh, firm fruit (apples, peaches, pears,
    plums, cherries)
1 cup sugar
1 cup water

Wash, pare, core, cut up or leave fruit whole.
Bring sugar and water to a boil in saucepan. Add
prepared fruit. Simmer until tender and slightly
transparent. Cool. *6 to 8 servings.*

Dried Fruit Sauce

Prunes, apricots, apples, pears, peaches, figs.

Packaged Dried Fruit: Follow cooking directions
on pkg. **Bulk Dried Fruit:** Wash, soak in cold
water until plump, simmer in same water until
tender, *30 to 45 min.*, then sweeten to taste.

Old-fashioned Applesauce

*Especially good with Greenings, Wealthies, Baldwins,
Jonathans or Winesaps.*

Wash, pare, if desired, quarter and core apples.
Add water about 1/2″ deep in pan; cover and simmer *15 to 20 min.*, or until tender. Sweeten to
taste (about 1/4 cup sugar to 4 medium apples) and
again bring to boil. If desired, press through
sieve or colander. Season with cinnamon. *2 1/2 to
3 lb. (8 medium) makes 1 qt. sauce.*

Rhubarb Sauce

Wash and cut rhubarb in 1″ pieces. Use 1 cup
sugar for 4 cups rhubarb. Cook as for Old-
fashioned Applesauce *(above)—except* cook about
10 min. and omit cinnamon. *4 cups raw rhubarb
makes 4 servings sauce.*

Baked Apples

*Choose baking apples such as Rome Beauty, Jonathan,
Wealthy or Greenings.*

Heat oven to 375° (quick mod.). Wash and core
apples. Either pare upper half of apples or slit
around center. Place in baking dish; fill center of
each apple with 1 to 2 tbsp. granulated or brown
sugar, 1 tsp. butter and 1/8 tsp. cinnamon. Cover
bottom of pan with water about 1/4″ deep. Bake
about 45 min., or until tender when pierced with
fork (time varies). Baste occasionally.

Poached Fruit

Cook fruit gently in a single layer just until tender
in a thin sugar-and-water syrup of 1 1/2 cups sugar
and 3/4 cup water. Do not stir. Dip syrup over
fruit to glaze.

Apple Dumplings

First choice of husbands.

For 6 Dumplings	*For 4 Dumplings*
Pastry for 9″ Two-crust Pie *(p. 337)*	Pastry for 8″ Two-crust Pie *(p. 337)*
6 medium tart juicy apples	4
1 cup sugar	2/3 cup
2 cups water	1 1/2 cups
3 tbsp. butter	2 tbsp.
1/4 tsp. cinnamon	1/4 tsp.
1/2 cup sugar	1/3 cup
1 1/2 tsp. cinnamon	1 tsp.
1 tbsp. butter	2 tsp.

Heat oven to 425° (hot). Roll out pastry a little
less than 1/8″ thick and cut into 7″ squares. Pare
and core an apple for each dumpling. Boil next
4 ingredients together for *3 min.* Place apple on each
square of pastry. Fill cavities of apples with mixture of sugar and cinnamon. Dot each with butter.
Bring opposite points of pastry up over the apple.
Overlap, moisten and seal. Lift carefully, place a
little apart in baking dish. Pour hot syrup *around*
dumplings. Bake immediately *40 to 45 min.*, or
until crust is nicely browned and apples are
cooked through (test with fork). Serve warm with
the syrup and with cream or whipped cream.

Bring opposite points of pastry up over the apple.
Overlap, moisten and seal.

Peach Dumplings

See color picture pp. 216-217.

Make Apple Dumplings *(above)—except* use
8 pitted pared fresh peaches instead of 6 apples
and smaller squares of pastry to fit.

▶ **ALL YOU HAVE TO DO**

To pit peaches: cut a segment out of each peach. Remove the pit. Fill the hollow and replace segment.

Strawberry or Raspberry Velvet Cream

Mrs. J. H. Senseney, Webster Groves, Missouri, says, "Made-in-advance chilled desserts are my specialty in summer."

1 pkg. (3 oz.) strawberry or raspberry-flavored gelatin
1 cup whipping cream, whipped

1 pkg. (10 oz.) frozen strawberries or raspberries, thawed and drained

Dissolve gelatin as directed on pkg., using 1 cup boiling water and strawberry juice with cold water to make 1 cup. Chill until almost firm. Beat gelatin until foamy. Fold together whipped gelatin, whipped cream and drained berries. Spoon into 1-qt. mold or 6 to 8 individual molds. Chill until firm. Unmold. Garnish with fresh unhulled strawberries or other fruits. Top with whipped cream or Soft Custard (p. 223), if desired. *6 to 8 servings.*

Pineapple Velvet Cream

Make Strawberry or Raspberry Velvet Cream (*above*)—*except* use lemon-flavored gelatin and 1 cup crushed pineapple instead of frozen fruit.

Molded Fruit Gelatin

An old standby . . . a favorite for everyday meals, buffets, smorgasbords and church bazaars.

1 pkg. (3 oz.) fruit-flavored gelatin
1 to 2 cups drained cut-up fruit (fresh, frozen or canned)

Dissolve gelatin as directed on pkg., using juice from canned or frozen fruit for some of liquid, if desired. Cool until mixture begins to thicken. Then stir in fruit. Pour into 1-qt. mold or 6 individual molds. Chill until set. Unmold. Serve with cream, whipped cream or Soft Custard (p. 223). *6 servings.*

Snow Pudding

"Is there anything more refreshing?" asks Mrs. William Fulton of Minneapolis.

¾ cup sugar
1 envelope unflavored gelatin (1 tbsp.)
1¼ cups water
¼ cup lemon juice
1 tbsp. grated lemon rind
2 egg whites

Mix sugar, gelatin and water in saucepan. Cook just until boiling, stirring constantly. Blend in lemon juice and rind. Place pan in cold water and cool until mixture mounds when dropped from spoon. Beat egg whites until stiff. Slowly blend gelatin into beaten egg whites using rotary beater. When blended, stir mixture with rubber spatula until it holds its shape. Spoon into dessert dishes or mold. Chill until firm. Serve with Soft Custard (p. 223) as sauce. *6 to 8 servings.*

Frosted Mint Delight

The choice of Mrs. Dwight D. Eisenhower, whose charm made her such an asset to her husband in his busy life as military leader and later as President. See color picture pp. 216–217.

1 can (1 lb. 4½ oz.) crushed pineapple
1 envelope unflavored gelatin (1 tbsp.)
⅓ cup mint-flavored apple jelly
1 cup whipping cream
1 tsp. confectioners' sugar

Drain pineapple, reserving ½ cup juice. Blend gelatin and pineapple juice and heat just until boiling, stirring constantly. Add jelly and heat over medium heat until melted. Add pineapple and cool. Whip cream with confectioners' sugar. Fold whipped cream into jelly mixture. Put into a freezer tray and refrigerate until firm or freeze until firm, but not solid. Garnish with mint. *8 servings.*

Chocolate Marshmallow Cream

Lovely, fluffy pudding.

½ cup sugar
1 envelope unflavored gelatin (1 tbsp.)
2¼ cups milk
1 sq. unsweetened chocolate (1 oz.)
¼ lb. marshmallows (11 to 16), cut up
¼ cup ground nuts, if desired
2 egg whites, stiffly beaten
1 cup whipping cream, whipped stiff

Blend sugar, gelatin, milk and chocolate thoroughly in saucepan. Cook over medium heat, stirring constantly, just until mixture comes to a boil. Place pan in cold water; cool until mixture mounds slightly when dropped from spoon. Stir in marshmallows and nuts. Fold in egg whites and whipped cream. Chill 4 hr. Serve in sherbet glasses. *8 servings.*

Crème Vanille (*Vanilla Bavarian Cream*)

From Marjorie Child Husted who was director of our Home Service Department for twenty years. One of her many contributions, and one dear to her heart, was the editing of the first Betty Crocker Picture Cook Book.

½ cup sugar
1 envelope unflavored gelatin (1 tbsp.)
¼ tsp. salt
2¼ cups milk

4 egg yolks, slightly beaten
1 cup whipping cream, whipped stiff
1 tsp. vanilla

Blend sugar, gelatin, salt, milk and egg yolks well in saucepan. Cook over medium heat, stirring constantly, just until mixture comes to a boil. Place pan in cold water; cool until mixture mounds slightly when dropped from spoon. Fold in whipped cream and vanilla. Pour into buttered 1-qt. mold. Chill until firm (about 4 hr.). Unmold on large serving dish. Garnish with Sweetened Whipped Cream (*p. 232*) and fresh fruit, such as strawberries, raspberries or sliced peaches. *8 servings.*

Mocha Crème Vanille

Make Crème Vanille (*above*)—*except* add 3 tbsp. powdered instant coffee to mixture before cooking. Garnish with whipped cream, sprinkle with toasted slivered almonds or crushed peanut brittle.

Chocolate Crème Vanille

Make Crème Vanille (*above*)—*except* add ½ cup semi-sweet chocolate pieces to mixture before cooking. Remove from heat. Stir until chocolate pieces are entirely or partially melted.

▶ ALL YOU HAVE TO DO

To unmold gelatin desserts: dip mold in warm water (not hot) to depth of gelatin. Loosen around edge with tip of a paring knife. Place serving dish on top of mold and turn upside down. Shake, holding serving dish tightly to mold. If gelatin doesn't unmold readily, repeat.

Peppermint Cream

24 marshmallows
½ cup milk
3 drops peppermint flavoring
1 tsp. vanilla
⅛ tsp. salt
few drops green or red food coloring
1 cup whipping cream, whipped stiff

Melt marshmallows with milk over hot water. Remove from heat. Cool slightly; then stir in flavorings, salt and food coloring. Cool until mixture mounds slightly when dropped from spoon. Fold in whipped cream. Serve in sherbet glasses with frosted Brownies (*p. 195*). Or use as filling for Chocolate Cooky Crust (*p. 341*). Garnish with sprig of fresh mint.

Oriental Orange Snow

A prize-winning recipe from Mrs. Jean Dunbar, Sinks Grove, West Virginia. See color picture p. 247.

1 envelope unflavored gelatin (1 tbsp.)
½ cup sugar
½ cup milk
2 egg yolks, beaten
¼ cup fresh lemon juice
¼ cup orange juice
½ cup cottage cheese, sieved
½ cup flaked coconut
2 egg whites
1 cup whipping cream
1 can (11 oz.) Mandarin oranges, drained (reserve juice for glaze)
Orange Glaze (*below*)

Mix gelatin and sugar. Blend in milk and egg yolks. Cook over low heat until dissolved and mixture begins to bubble. Remove from heat. Add lemon juice, orange juice, cottage cheese and coconut. Chill in small mixer bowl in refrigerator until partially set, 45 min. to 1 hr.

Beat egg whites until stiff, but not dry. Whip cream until stiff. Whip chilled mixture on medium speed with electric mixer; fold in egg whites and whipped cream. Spoon into parfait or sherbet glasses, alternating with orange slices and Orange Glaze (*below*) reserving 1 orange slice and small amount of glaze for top of each. Chill until firm. *8 to 10 servings.*

Orange Glaze

Mix ⅓ cup sugar, 1 tbsp. cornstarch and ⅛ tsp. salt. Slowly blend in ½ cup Mandarin orange juice and a few drops yellow food coloring. Bring to a boil, stirring constantly; boil 1 min. Cool.

Tapioca Cream

The fluffy type.

2 egg yolks, slightly beaten
2 cups milk
2 tbsp. sugar
2 tbsp. quick-cooking tapioca
¼ tsp. salt
1 tsp. vanilla
2 egg whites
¼ cup sugar

Mix egg yolks, milk, 2 tbsp. sugar, tapioca and salt in saucepan. Cook over low heat, stirring constantly, until mixture boils. Remove from heat. Cool. Stir in vanilla. Beat egg whites until frothy. Gradually beat in the ¼ cup sugar. Continue beating until stiff and glossy. Fold into mixture in saucepan. Spoon into dessert dishes. Serve with cream or fruit juice. *6 servings.*

Chocolate Tapioca Cream

Make Tapioca Cream (*above*)—*except* fold in at the last ½ cup semi-sweet chocolate pieces.

Fruit Tapioca Cream

Try blueberries, sweet cherries, pineapple, raspberries or strawberries . . . delicious and colorful.

Make Tapioca Cream (*above*)—*except* fold in at the last 1 to 1½ cups fresh, frozen or canned fruits. Canned and frozen fruits must be thoroughly drained.

Fruit Soup *(Frukt Suppa)*

Also excellent as a meat accompaniment or as an appetizer.

2 cups mixed dried fruit (12 oz.), such as currants,
   raisins, prunes, pears, apricots, peaches, apples
3 cups water (half grape juice may be used)
½ lemon, sliced
1 tbsp. tapioca
¼ tsp. salt
½ to ⅔ cup sugar
1 stick cinnamon

Mix ingredients and cook, covered, until fruits are tender *30 to 40 min.* Serve hot or cold. *About 4 servings.*

Old-fashioned Creamy Rice Pudding

Requests come to us often for this recipe.

½ cup uncooked rice (not instant)
½ tsp. salt
¼ cup sugar
¼ tsp. cinnamon or nutmeg
2½ cups milk
½ cup seedless raisins, if desired

Combine all ingredients in top of double boiler. Cook, covered, over boiling water until rice is tender and milk is almost absorbed, *1 hr.*, stirring frequently. Serve warm with cream or a soft custard. *6 to 8 servings.*

New-fashioned Rice Pudding

1 cup uncooked instant rice
1½ cups milk
3 or 4 tbsp. sugar
½ tsp. salt
¼ tsp. cinnamon or nutmeg
¼ cup seedless raisins, if desired

Combine all ingredients in saucepan. Bring to a full rolling boil, stirring constantly. Remove from heat. Cover and let stand 12 to 15 min., stirring occasionally. Serve warm with cream. *4 servings.*

Glorified Rice

Margret Christopher Johnson of our staff says: "To me, this is the perfect dessert."

1 cup cold cooked rice
½ cup sugar
1½ cups crushed pineapple, drained
½ tsp. vanilla
1 cup whipping cream, whipped
8 marshmallows, cut up

Mix all ingredients. Chill very thoroughly before serving. *6 to 8 servings.*

222

Baked Custard

Jan Korslund of our staff suggests using brown sugar in place of granulated sugar for a dark golden delicious custard.

2 eggs (or 4 egg yolks)
⅓ cup sugar
¼ tsp. salt
2 cups milk, scalded
½ tsp. vanilla, if desired

Heat oven to 350° (mod.). Beat eggs, sugar and salt slightly to mix. Stir in scalded milk. Add vanilla. Pour into 6 custard cups or a 1½-qt. baking dish and set in pan of hot water (1" deep). Sprinkle a little nutmeg over tops. Bake *45 to 50 min.*, or just until a silver knife inserted 1" from edge comes out clean (soft center sets as it stands). Immediately remove from oven. Serve cool or chilled in same cups on dessert plates or unmold and serve. Pass grape or other fruit juice to pour over, if desired. *6 servings.*

Custard Rice Pudding

A favorite of Senator Stuart Symington of Missouri. Mrs. Symington butters the baking dish and lines it with fine bread crumbs before pouring in the rice-custard mixture, then sprinkles ½ cup chopped nuts over the pudding before baking.

Make Baked Custard (*above*)—except increase sugar to ½ cup. Add 2 cups cooked rice and ½ cup seedless raisins. Pour into 1-qt. baking dish. Sprinkle with nutmeg. Set in pan of water (1" deep). Bake *50 to 60 min.* Serve warm with cream. *6 to 8 servings.*

Baked Caramel Custard

Caramelize ½ cup sugar (*p. 141*). Pour a little into each custard cup. Move cups about so that caramel will coat sides. When caramel is hard, fill cups with custard (make recipe above—*except* add 1 more egg). When unmolded, melted caramel runs down sides forming a sauce.

Blanc Mange

French for "white food." An economical milk pudding.

Mix ⅓ cup sugar, 3 tbsp. cornstarch and ¼ tsp. salt in saucepan. Gradually stir in 2¼ cups milk. Cook over medium heat, stirring constantly, until mixture boils. Boil 1 min. Remove from heat. Blend in 1½ tsp. vanilla. Chill. Serve topped with fresh fruit, fruit juice or whipped cream. *4 to 6 servings.*

Soft Custard

Delicate pudding or sauce to dress up other desserts.

1½ cups milk
4 egg yolks (or 2 whole eggs)
¼ cup sugar
¼ tsp. salt
1 tsp. vanilla

Scald milk in top of double boiler over direct heat. Beat egg yolks in small bowl. Blend in sugar and salt. Gradually stir in scalded milk. Return to double boiler. Cook over simmering (not boiling) water, stirring constantly. When custard coats silver spoon (thin coating), remove from heat. Cool quickly. If custard should start to curdle, beat vigorously at once with rotary beater until smooth. Blend in vanilla. Serve in sherbet glasses topped with whipped cream; or use as a sauce over fruit, cake or other desserts. *6 servings.*

Fruit with Custard

Make Soft Custard (*above*) and pour over cut-up fresh fruit (bananas, orange sections, strawberries, raspberries, halved small green or seeded Tokay grapes) in individual dessert dishes or serving dish.

Floating Island

Grandma called it "float," a company dessert presented in tall glass compote. See color picture pp. 216–217.

Make Soft Custard (*above*)—except make a meringue of 2 egg whites and ¼ cup sugar. Drop this meringue as "islands" on hot custard in serving dish. Chill before serving.

Pot de Crème au Chocolat

An elegant chocolate custard cream from France. See color picture p. 247.

¼ lb. German sweet chocolate
1 tbsp. sugar
½ cup cream
2 egg yolks, slightly beaten
½ tsp. vanilla

Combine chocolate, sugar and cream in saucepan. Heat over medium heat, stirring constantly until chocolate melts and mixture is blended. Remove from heat; slowly pour into egg yolks, stirring constantly. Blend in vanilla. Pour into small individual dessert dishes or demitasse cups. Chill. Garnish with whipped cream. *4 to 6 servings.*

Strawberry Shortcake

The good old-time American dessert. First choice of Dorothy Thomale, formerly of our staff. See color picture opposite.

1 qt. fresh strawberries
2 cups GOLD MEDAL Flour
2 tbsp. sugar
3 tsp. baking powder
1 tsp. salt
⅓ cup shortening
1 cup milk

Wash berries, drain well. Then pick them over. Remove stems and hulls. Add about 1 cup sugar and let stand at room temperature an hour.

Heat oven to 450° (hot). Measure flour by dip-level-pour method or by sifting (*see p. 6*). Stir flour, sugar, baking powder, salt in bowl. Cut in shortening. Stir in milk just until blended. Spread dough in 2 greased layer pans, 8x1½″. Dot with butter. Bake *12 to 15 min.*

Place one layer on serving plate upside down; cover with sweetened berries; top with other layer, right side up; cover with more berries. Serve warm with plain or whipped cream. *6 to 8 servings.*

For a less crusty shortcake, spread all the dough in one 8″ layer pan. Bake *15 to 20 min.* Split crosswise while hot. Spread with butter, fill and top with berries.

Raspberry Shortcake

Make Strawberry Shortcake (*above*)—except use 1 qt. raspberries, sweetened.

Peach Shortcake

Mrs. Homer Westbrook and Mrs. Hugh Smith serve this during fresh peach season in their Atlanta, Georgia, home.

Make Strawberry Shortcake (*above*)—except use 1 qt. sliced fresh peaches, sweetened.

Individual Shortcakes

Make Southern Biscuits (*p. 76*)—except add 2 tbsp. sugar with the dry ingredients and pat or roll into 2½ to 3″ rounds. Bake *10 to 12 min.* Break apart while hot. Place bottom half on dessert dish, spoon over sweetened berries. Top with other half, cut-side-up, then with more berries. Serve with plain or whipped cream. *6 to 8 servings.*

Berries with Cake

Serve sweetened berries or fruit with Sponge Cake (*p. 152*) or Kitchenette Cake (*p. 140*).

Fresh Fruit Cobbler

"Cobble up" means to put together in a hurry. For the fruit, use cherries, peaches, apricots or blackberries.

⅔ to 1 cup sugar
1 tbsp. cornstarch
1 cup water
3 cups fresh fruit with any juice there might be
1 cup GOLD MEDAL Flour
1 tbsp. sugar
1½ tsp. baking powder
½ tsp. salt
3 tbsp. shortening
½ cup milk

Heat oven to 400° (mod. hot). Mix sugar, cornstarch. Gradually stir in water. Bring to boil and boil 1 min., stirring constantly. Add fruit and juice. Pour into 1½-qt. baking dish; dot with butter. Sprinkle with cinnamon. Measure flour by dip-level-pour method or by sifting (*see p. 6*). Stir flour, sugar, baking powder, salt in bowl. Cut in shortening until mixture looks like "meal." Stir in milk. Drop by spoonfuls onto hot fruit. Bake *25 to 30 min.* Serve warm with juice and cream. *6 to 8 servings.*

Canned Fruit Cobbler

Make Fresh Fruit Cobbler (*above*)—except use 2½ cups canned fruit or berries and juice in place of fresh fruit. Use only ½ cup sugar with the fruit and omit water.

Southern Peach Skillet Pie

½ recipe Southern Biscuit dough (*p. 76*)
6 fresh peaches, peeled and sliced
½ cup sugar
½ tsp. salt
¼ tsp. cinnamon
1½ tbsp. soft butter

Heat oven to 425° (hot). Make biscuit dough adding 1 tbsp. sugar. Roll or pat out dough ¼″ thick. Place in 8″ skillet, allowing some of dough to hang over edge. Top dough with peaches. Mix sugar, salt, cinnamon and butter; sprinkle over fruit. Fold hanging dough toward center, leaving a little space uncovered. Bake *25 min. 6 servings.*

OLD-FASHIONED FAVORITES

English Plum Pudding, page 231
Squares of Favorite Gingerbread, page 232

Strawberry Shortcake, page 224
White Plum Duff, page 231

Fruit Cobbler,
page 224

Indian Pudding

The Puritan women learned to make it from the Indians. In New England, it always shared the old brick oven with baked beans. Traditional dessert for a clambake.

4 cups milk
⅔ cup molasses
⅔ cup yellow corn meal
⅓ cup sugar
1 tsp. salt
¾ tsp. cinnamon
¾ tsp. nutmeg
¼ cup butter

Heat oven to 300° (slow). Heat 3 cups of milk and molasses in saucepan. Combine corn meal, sugar, salt and spices. Gradually stir corn into hot liquid. Add butter. Cook over low heat stirring frequently, until mixture thickens, about 10 min. Pour into greased 2-qt. baking dish. Pour remaining cup cold milk over pudding; do not stir. Bake *3 hr.* Serve with whipped cream or ice cream. *8 servings.*

Prune Whip

1 cup cooled cut-up prunes (cooked, drained, pitted)
3 egg whites
⅓ cup sugar
¼ tsp. salt
1 tbsp. lemon juice
¼ cup pecans, chopped

Beat prunes, egg whites, sugar and salt with rotary beater until stiff enough to hold shape, about 5 min. Fold in lemon juice and pecans, if desired. Spoon into dessert dishes. Or pour into 1½-qt. baking dish. Set in pan of hot water (1″ deep). Bake *at 350° 30 to 35 min.*, or until puffed and a thin coating has formed over the top. Serve with Sweetened Whipped Cream (*p. 232*). *6 servings.*

Vanilla Cream Pudding

½ cup sugar
2 tbsp. cornstarch
½ tsp. salt
2 cups milk
2 egg yolks, slightly beaten
2 tsp. butter
1 tsp. vanilla

Mix sugar, cornstarch and salt in saucepan. Gradually stir in milk. Cook over medium heat, stirring constantly, until mixture thickens and boils. Boil 1 min. Remove from heat. Gradually stir at least half of hot mixture into egg yolks. Then blend into hot mixture in saucepan. Boil 1 min. more, stirring constantly. Remove from heat. Blend in butter and vanilla. Pour into dessert dishes. Serve warm or cool with cream or whipped cream.

Chocolate Cream Pudding

Make Vanilla Cream Pudding (*above*)—*except* increase sugar to 1 cup and add 2 sq. unsweetened chocolate (2 oz.), cut up, with the milk or ⅓ cup cocoa with the sugar, cornstarch and salt.

Butterscotch Cream Pudding

¾ cup brown sugar (packed)
3 tbsp. cornstarch
½ tsp. salt
¾ cup water
1¼ cups milk
¼ cup butter
2 egg yolks, slightly beaten
1 tsp. vanilla

Prepare as for Vanilla Cream Pudding (*above*).

HOW TO PREPARE CREAM PUDDINGS AND CREAM OR CUSTARD FILLINGS.

1. Stir milk into mixture of sugar, cornstarch and salt.

2. Stir half of hot mixture into beaten egg yolks.

3. Blend this egg yolk mixture into remaining hot mixture.

Meringue Bread Pudding (*Queen's Pudding*)

Ed Sullivan, the famous and popular newspaper columnist and television master of ceremonies, gave us this recipe.

2 cups fine dry bread crumbs (*see p. 28*)
3 cups milk, scalded
1 whole egg plus 2 egg yolks, slightly
    beaten
⅓ cup sugar

1 tsp. vanilla
nutmeg
currant jelly
2 egg whites
¼ cup sugar

Heat oven to 350° (mod.). Place bread crumbs in ungreased 1½-qt. baking dish. Blend in milk, egg plus egg yolks, ⅓ cup sugar and vanilla. Sprinkle with nutmeg. Place baking dish in pan of hot water (1″ deep). Bake *about 1 hr.*, or until silver knife inserted 1″ from edge comes out clean. Remove from oven. Spoon thin layer of currant jelly over pudding. Beat egg whites until frothy. Gradually beat in ¼ cup sugar. Continue beating until stiff and glossy. Spread over pudding. Return to oven and bake *about 15 min.*, or until meringue is browned. Cool 20 to 30 min. before serving. *6 to 8 servings.*

Old-fashioned Bread Pudding

3 cups soft bread crumbs (*see p. 28*) (**use 4 cups for**
    firmer pudding)
2 cups milk, scalded with ¼ cup butter
½ cup sugar
2 eggs, slightly beaten
¼ tsp. salt
1 tsp. cinnamon or nutmeg
½ cup seedless raisins

Heat oven to 350° (mod.). Place bread crumbs in 1½-qt. baking dish. Blend in remaining ingredients. Place baking dish in pan of hot water (1″ deep). Bake *40 to 45 min.*, or until silver knife inserted 1″ from edge comes out clean. Serve warm, with cream. *6 to 8 servings.*

Chocolate Bread Pudding

Make Old-fashioned Bread Pudding (*above*)— *except* use ½ cup semi-sweet chocolate pieces instead of raisins. Omit the spices.

Applescotch Bread Pudding

4 cups soft bread cubes (½″) (*see p. 28*)
1 qt. sliced, pared cooking apples
¼ cup butter, melted
½ cup granulated sugar
½ cup brown sugar (packed)
½ tsp. cinnamon
¼ cup cream (20% butterfat)

Heat oven to 350° (mod.). Place half of bread cubes in greased 1½-qt. baking dish. Cover with 2 cups apples. Mix butter, sugars, cinnamon and cream. Pour half over apples. Add another layer of bread cubes and apples; top with rest of sugar mixture. Bake *1 to 1½ hr.* *8 servings.*

Danish Apple Pudding

Tart apple flavor blended with rich buttery bread crumbs and whipped cream. Ole Risom, New York art director, says this brings fond memories of his Danish homeland.

1½ cups fine zwieback crumbs or fine dry bread
    crumbs (*see p. 28*)
⅓ cup butter
2 cups applesauce (1-lb. can)
¼ tsp. salt
1 tbsp. lemon juice
½ tsp. cinnamon

Sauté crumbs in butter until evenly browned. Line greased square pan, 8x8x2″ with half of crumbs. Mix applesauce, salt, lemon juice and cinnamon. Pour half over crumbs; cover with rest of crumbs, then remaining applesauce. Top with Sweetened Whipped Cream (*½ recipe, p. 232*). Chill several hr. Serve in squares decorated with bits of red jelly, if desired. *6 to 8 servings.*

Date and Nut Torte

4 eggs
1 cup sugar
1 cup fine dry bread crumbs (*see p. 28*)
1 tsp. baking powder
2 cups finely cut pitted dates
1 cup cut-up walnuts

Heat oven to 350° (mod.). Grease a square pan, 9x9x1¾″. Beat eggs thoroughly. Gradually beat in sugar. Mix bread crumbs and baking powder; stir in. Mix in dates and walnuts. Spread in greased pan. Bake *35 min.*, or until set. Cut in oblongs, 3x2″. Serve cool with whipped cream or ice cream. *12 servings.*

227

Cottage Pudding

Fluffy, delicious, easy to make.

1¾ cups GOLD MEDAL Flour
2 tsp. baking powder
½ tsp. salt
¼ cup soft shortening

¾ cup sugar
1 egg
¾ cup milk
1 tsp. vanilla

Heat oven to 350° (mod.). Grease and flour a square pan, 9x9x1¾". Measure flour by dip-level-pour method or by sifting (*see p. 6*). Stir flour, baking powder, salt in bowl. Add remaining ingredients; beat until smooth. Pour into pan. Bake *25 to 30 min.* Serve warm cut in 3" squares with hot Vanilla, Lemon or Nutmeg Sauce (below). *9 servings.*

Vanilla, Lemon or Nutmeg Sauce

1 cup sugar
2 tbsp. cornstarch
2 cups water
¼ cup butter
2 tsp. vanilla or 2 tbsp. lemon juice with
  2 tbsp. grated lemon rind or 2 tsp. nutmeg

Mix sugar and cornstarch in saucepan. Gradually stir in water. Boil 1 min., stirring constantly. Stir in butter and flavoring. *Makes 2 cups.*

Cherry Carnival

Rich, luscious cherry favorite.

Make Cottage Pudding (*above*)—except increase sugar to 1 cup, omit vanilla. Blend in 2 cups cut-up well drained pitted sour cherries (1 lb. 4-oz. can, save juice) and ½ cup chopped nuts. Bake *30 to 40 min.* Serve hot with hot Clear Red Sauce (*below*).

Clear Red Sauce

½ cup sugar
2 tbsp. cornstarch
1 cup water
¾ cup juice from cherries or raspberries
¼ tsp. almond flavoring
few drops red food coloring, if desired

Mix sugar and cornstarch in saucepan. Gradually stir in water and juice. Boil 1 min., stirring constantly. Stir in flavoring and food coloring. *Makes 2 cups.*

Iowa Date Pudding

Virginia Van Nostrand of St. Joseph, Michigan, formerly of our staff, finds this soft, rich combination of dates and nuts a dessert to be served often.

3 eggs
1 cup sugar
¼ cup GOLD MEDAL Flour
1 tsp. baking powder
¼ tsp. salt
2½ cups chopped dates (1 lb.)
1 cup broken nuts

Heat oven to 350° (mod.). Grease a square pan, 9x9x1¾". Beat eggs until light. Beat sugar in thoroughly. Measure flour by dip-level-pour method or by sifting (*see p. 6*). Blend flour, baking powder, salt; stir in. Mix in dates and nuts. Pour into pan. Bake *30* min. Serve warm with whipped cream. *9 to 12 servings.*

Apple Crisp (*Apple Crumble*)

Mrs. Herbert A. Berg, St. Paul, Minnesota, substitutes 1 cup graham cracker crumbs for the flour and oatmeal in this recipe.

4 cups sliced, pared, cored baking apples (about 6 medium)
⅔ to ¾ cup brown sugar (packed)
½ cup GOLD MEDAL Flour
½ cup rolled oats
¾ tsp. cinnamon
¾ tsp. nutmeg
⅓ cup soft butter

Heat oven to 375° (quick mod.). Place sliced apples in greased square pan, 8x8x2" or a baking dish, 10x6x1½" or 1½-qt. baking dish. Blend remaining ingredients until mixture is crumbly. Spread over apples. Bake *30 to 35 min.*, or until apples are tender and topping is golden brown. Serve warm with cream, ice cream or Hard Sauce (*p. 393*). *6 servings.*

Lemon Cake Pudding

Delicate cake and refreshing lemon sauce in one pudding.

¼ cup GOLD MEDAL Flour
1 cup sugar
¼ tsp. salt
1 tbsp. grated lemon rind (1 lemon)

¼ cup lemon juice
2 egg yolks, well beaten
1 cup milk
2 egg whites, stiffly beaten

Heat oven to 350° (mod.). Measure flour by dip-level-pour method or by sifting (*see p. 6*). Blend flour, sugar, salt in mixing bowl. Stir in lemon rind and juice, egg yolks and milk. Fold in egg whites. Pour into 1-qt. baking dish (6½″) or 6 custard cups. Set in pan of hot water (1″ deep). Bake *50 min. 6 servings.*

Lime Cake Pudding

Make Lemon Cake Pudding (*above*)—except, in place of lemon, use lime juice and rind.

Orange Cake Pudding

Make Lemon Cake Pudding (*above*)—except, in place of lemon, use orange juice and rind.

Pineapple Cake Pudding

Make Lemon Cake Pudding (*above*)—except reduce sugar to ½ cup, use only ½ cup milk, only 1 tbsp. lemon juice. Add ¼ cup drained crushed pineapple and ¼ cup pineapple juice.

Hot Fudge Pudding

We are grateful to Mrs. Oswin Keifer of Bostwich, Nebraska, for this rich-tasting yet inexpensive dessert. See color picture pp. 216–217.

1 cup GOLD MEDAL Flour
2 tsp. baking powder
¼ tsp. salt
¾ cup sugar
2 tbsp. cocoa
½ cup milk
2 tbsp. shortening, melted
1 cup chopped nuts
1 cup brown sugar (packed)
¼ cup cocoa
1¾ cups hot water

Heat oven to 350° (mod.). Measure flour by dip-level-pour method or by sifting (*see p. 6*). Blend flour, baking powder, salt, sugar and 2 tbsp. cocoa in bowl. Stir in milk and shortening. Blend in nuts. Spread in square pan, 9x9x1¾″. Sprinkle with mixture of brown sugar and ¼ cup cocoa. Pour hot water over entire batter. Bake *45 min.* During baking, cake mixture rises to top and chocolate sauce settles to bottom. Cut into squares; invert each square onto dessert plate, spoon sauce over. Or invert entire pudding on platter. Serve warm. *9 servings.*

Lemon Cake Pie

Tender pastry, delicate cake and refreshing lemon sauce combined in this unusual dessert.

Make Pastry for 9″ One-crust Pie (*pp. 337–339*).

¼ cup GOLD MEDAL Flour
1 cup sugar
¼ tsp. salt
1 tbsp. grated lemon rind (1 lemon)
¼ cup lemon juice
2 egg yolks, well beaten
1 cup milk
2 egg whites

Heat oven to 350° (mod.). Measure flour by dip-level-pour method or by sifting (*see p. 6*). Blend dry ingredients in mixing bowl. Stir in lemon rind, lemon juice, egg yolks, milk. Beat egg whites until stiff; fold in. Pour into pastry-lined pie pan. Bake *about 50 min.*

Date Gems

Date cupcakes served hot with a simple orange sauce.

1 cup GOLD MEDAL Flour
½ tsp. baking powder
½ tsp. soda
½ tsp. salt
¼ cup soft shortening
½ cup sugar
1 egg
⅓ cup buttermilk or soured milk (*see p. 26*)
1 tbsp. grated orange rind
1 cup cut-up dates
¾ cup strained orange juice
¼ cup sugar

Heat oven to 350° (mod.). Grease 6 muffin cups. Measure flour by dip-level-pour method or by sifting (*see p. 6*). Blend first 4 ingredients in bowl. Add shortening, ½ cup sugar, egg, milk, orange rind. Beat until smooth. Blend in dates. Fill muffin cups ⅔ full. Bake *25 to 30 min.* Mix orange juice and ¼ cup sugar. Serve hot over hot gems. *6 servings.*

229

STEAMERS

1. A deep well cooker with wire frame to hold pudding mold. **2.** A deep kettle that holds water to last through the entire steaming. **3.** A steamer with holes in the bottom and a tight-fitting cover to hold in steam.

MOLDS

1. Turk's head mold with spiral fluting. **2.** Tube center mold allows steam to quickly reach center of pudding. **3.** Individual molds, custard cups or jelly glasses. **4.** Round can (coffee can, etc.) or bowl.

HOW TO STEAM

1. Pour pudding batter into generously greased molds ... filling them ½ to ⅔ full. This allows room for expansion of batter.

2. Place in steamer. Tie waxed paper loosely over mold to prevent steam which collects on cover dropping on pudding.

3. Remove from steamer after prescribed time. Remove waxed paper.

4. Loosen pudding at one side to let in air. Turn out on hot serving dish. For old-style flaming pudding: pour on heated brandy, light with a match.

5. The new way is to soak lumps of sugar in lemon or orange extract, place around pudding. Touch match to one lump and the pudding is encircled with flames.

Down East Pudding

1 cup boiling water
1 cup cut-up cranberries or raisins
2 tbsp. shortening
1 egg
½ cup sugar
½ cup molasses
1½ cups GOLD MEDAL Flour
1 tsp. *each* salt and soda

Blend first 3 ingredients; let stand few min. Beat together egg, sugar, molasses; add to cranberries. Measure flour by dip-level-pour method or by sifting (*see p. 6*). Blend flour, salt, soda; stir in. Pour into well greased 1-qt. mold (⅔ full). Steam *2 hr.* Serve with Hard Sauce (*p. 393*). *8 servings.*

Plum Duff (*Dark*)

Moist, fruity, yet delicate and light.

2 eggs, well beaten
1 cup brown sugar (packed)
½ cup shortening, melted
2 cups well drained cut-up pitted cooked prunes
1 cup GOLD MEDAL Flour
½ tsp. salt
1 tsp. soda

Blend sugar, shortening, prunes into eggs. Measure flour by dip-level-pour method or by sifting (*see p. 6*). Blend flour, salt and soda; stir in. Pour into well greased 1-qt. mold. Steam *1 hr.* Serve hot with Creamy Sauce or Hard Sauce (*p. 393*). *8 servings.*

230

An old Yorkshire tradition: "In as many homes as you eat plum pudding in the 12 days following Christmas, so many happy months will you have during the year."

Thrifty colonial homemakers evolved new variations. Modern methods and equipment have made puddings lighter, fluffier and more delicious.

To reheat steamed pudding made ahead or canned steamed pudding: wrap in foil, heat in 350° oven 15 to 20 min.

English Plum Pudding

We think it's the best of all the real English recipes for plum pudding.

1 cup GOLD MEDAL Flour
1 tsp. soda
1 tsp. salt
1 tsp. cinnamon
¼ tsp. nutmeg
¾ tsp. mace
1½ cups finely cut raisins (½ lb.)
1½ cups currants (½ lb.), plumped
¾ cup finely cut citron (¼ lb.)
¾ cup finely cut candied orange and lemon peel
½ cup chopped walnuts
1½ cups coarse soft bread crumbs
2 cups ground suet (½ lb.)
1 cup brown sugar (packed)
3 eggs, beaten
⅓ cup currant jelly
¼ cup fruit juice (old recipes called for brandy or sherry)

Measure flour by dip-level-pour method or by sifting (*see p. 6*). Blend first 6 ingredients. Mix in fruits, walnuts, crumbs. Mix remaining ingredients; blend in. Pour into well greased 2-qt. mold (or two 1-qt. molds). Steam *6 hr.* Serve hot with Hard Sauce (*p. 393*). *16 servings.*

Steamed Pumpkin Pudding

A tender, spiced, steamed pudding that will complete a traditional Thanksgiving dinner.

1¾ cups GOLD MEDAL Flour
1 tsp. baking powder
½ tsp. *each* salt, soda, cinnamon, ginger and cloves
½ cup shortening
1 cup brown sugar (packed)
2 eggs
¼ cup soured milk (*see p. 26*)
½ cup cooked or canned pumpkin

Measure flour by dip-level-pour method or by sifting (*see p. 6*). Blend flour, baking powder, salt, soda, spices. Cream shortening and sugar. Add eggs; beat well. Add flour mixture alternately with sour milk and pumpkin. Pour into greased 1½-qt. mold. Steam *1¾ hr.* Cool a few min., loosen from sides of mold, remove from mold, serve warm with Hard Sauce (*p. 393*). *About 10 servings.*

Steamed Chocolate Pudding

Many were tried, this one chosen ... the recipe was brought in by Dorothy Elliott, formerly of our staff.

1 egg
1 cup sugar
2 tbsp. soft butter
2 sq. unsweetened chocolate (2 oz.), melted
1¾ cups GOLD MEDAL Flour
1 tsp. salt
¼ tsp. cream of tartar
¼ tsp. soda
1 cup milk

Beat egg, sugar, butter, chocolate. Measure flour by dip-level-pour method or by sifting (*see p. 6*). Blend flour, salt, cream of tartar, soda; beat in alternately with milk. Steam *2 hr.* in greased 1-qt. mold. Serve with Creamy Sauce (*p. 393*). *8 servings.*

White Plum Duff

See color picture p. 225.

½ lb. prunes (1 cup cooked)
1 cup GOLD MEDAL Flour
1½ tsp. baking powder
½ tsp. salt
¼ cup soft shortening
½ cup sugar
1 egg
½ cup milk
1 tsp. vanilla

Cook prunes in 2 cups water. Drain, reserving juice. Pit prunes. Measure flour by dip-level-pour method or by sifting (*see p. 6*). Blend flour, baking powder, salt in bowl. Add shortening, sugar, egg, milk, vanilla. Beat with rotary beater or spoon until smooth. Grease generously a 1-qt. mold. Place 1 cup well drained cooked prune halves, shiny-side-down on bottom and sides of mold. Pour in batter. Cover. Steam *2 hr.* Serve hot with Prune Sauce. *6 servings.*

Prune Sauce

Mix 1½ tbsp. cornstarch, ⅓ cup sugar, 1 cup prune juice, 1 tbsp. lemon juice in saucepan. Boil 1 min., stirring constantly. Remove from heat. Blend in 1 tbsp. butter and dash of nutmeg.

Early American colonists made gingerbread much as we do today. When Lafayette returned to America in 1784, he went to Fredricksburg to visit George Washington's mother. She served him mint julep with "spiced gingerbrede." Her recipe included "West India molasses," a "wine glass of brandy," and "the juice and rind of orange" in addition to the usual ingredients.

Favorite Gingerbread

Deliciously rich, black and moist. Grandma knew it as "Fort Atkinson Gingerbread" in the popular old brown-covered GOLD MEDAL *Cook Book that was a treasure trove for brides in the 1870's.*

½ cup soft shortening	2¼ cups GOLD MEDAL Flour
2 tbsp. sugar	1 tsp. soda
1 egg	½ tsp. salt
1 cup dark molasses	1 tsp. ginger
1 cup boiling water	1 tsp. cinnamon

Heat oven to 325° (slow mod.). Grease and flour square pan, 9x9x1¾" or 9" ring mold. Mix thoroughly shortening, sugar, egg. Blend in molasses and water. Measure flour by dip-level-pour method or by sifting (*see p. 6*). Stir together dry ingredients; blend in. Beat until smooth. Pour into pan. Bake *45 to 50 min. in square pan, 45 to 50 min. in ring mold.* Serve hot cut in squares or wedges with Sweetened Whipped Cream (*below*) or applesauce. *9 servings.*

Gingerbread with Bananas and Apricot Glaze

Mix 2½ cups (1 lb. 4-oz. can) cooked apricots with juice, 1 cup sugar and ⅓ cup boiling water. Boil until thick like jam. Cool. Cover top of Favorite Gingerbread (*above*) with slices of banana. Pour apricot glaze over all.

Haddon Hall Gingerbread

Gingerbread with cream cheese and lemon sauce. "Ideal for a 'dessert and coffee' party," says Ruth Sweat, Pasadena, California, once in charge of our test kitchens.

Soften cream cheese with a little cream. Beat until fluffy. Split each serving of Favorite Gingerbread (*above*), spoon cheese between layers. Top with more cheese. Serve with Old-fashioned Lemon Sauce (*p. 393*).

Gingerbread Party Dessert

Bake Favorite Gingerbread (*above*) in square pan. Top squares of hot gingerbread with Orange Cream Cheese Topping (*below*) and canned whole or halved peeled apricots.

Orange Cream Cheese Topping

2 pkg. (3 oz. each) cream cheese
1¼ cups *sifted* confectioners' sugar
3 tbsp. orange juice
1 tsp. lemon juice

Blend all ingredients until smooth.

Washington Pie

From Civil War days when Washington, D. C., housewives could not get lard for pies. They made plain cakes, split and filled them with jelly from their cellars. Ever since, they have been called "Washington Pies."

Make Egg Yolk Sponge Cake (*p. 152*) in a layer pan or use 1 layer of Lovelight Yellow Chiffon Cake (*p. 160*). Cool. Split into 2 layers. Put together with jelly. Sprinkle confectioners' sugar on top.

Boston Cream Pie

Make Egg Yolk Sponge Cake (*p. 152*) in a layer pan or use 1 layer of Lovelight Yellow Chiffon Cake (*p. 160*). Cool. Split into 2 thin layers. Put together with cooled Cream Filling (*p. 177*). Spread Thin Chocolate Icing (*p. 173*) over top. Serve in wedges.

Sweetened Whipped Cream

1 cup chilled whipping cream (35% butterfat)
¼ cup *sifted* confectioners' sugar
flavoring, if desired

Chill deep bowl and beater. Then place all ingredients in bowl and beat together until stiff. *Makes 2 cups.*

Pineapple Upside-down Cake

Sometimes called "skillet cake." Handsome dessert to serve at table.

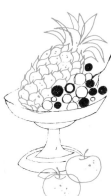

⅓ cup butter
½ cup brown sugar (packed)
1 can (1 lb. 4 oz.) sliced pineapple, drained
  (crushed may be used if well drained)
1½ cups SOFTASILK Flour
  or 1⅓ cups GOLD MEDAL Flour
1 cup sugar

2 tsp. baking powder
½ tsp. salt
⅓ cup soft shortening
⅔ cup milk
1 tsp. vanilla
½ tsp. lemon flavoring, if desired
1 egg (¼ to ⅓ cup)

Heat oven to 350° (mod.). Melt butter in heavy 10″ skillet or square pan, 9x9x1¾″. Sprinkle brown sugar evenly over butter. Arrange pineapple in attractive pattern on the butter-sugar coating. Decorate with pecan halves and cherries, if desired.

Measure flour by dip-level-pour method or by sifting (*see p. 6*). Stir flour, sugar, baking powder, salt in mixer bowl. Add shortening, milk, flavorings. Beat 2 min., medium speed on mixer or 300 vigorous strokes by hand. Scrape sides and bottom of bowl constantly. Add egg. Beat 2 more min., scraping bowl frequently. Pour batter over fruit. Bake *40 to 50 min.* Immediately turn upside down on serving plate. Leave pan over cake a few minutes. Serve warm with whipped cream.

Checkerboard Upside-down Cake

Prunes and apricots, checkerboard style.

Make Pineapple Upside-down Cake (*above*)— *except* use drained cooked apricot halves and pitted cooked prunes in place of pineapple. Arrange in checkerboard fashion in prepared pan.

Apricot Upside-down Cake

Make Pineapple Upside-down Cake (*above*)— *except* use 1 can (1 lb. 4 oz.) apricot halves, drained, instead of pineapple.

Blushing Apple Upside-down Cake

Make Pineapple Upside-down Cake (*above*)— *except* omit pineapple and arrange 2 medium cooking apples, pared and sliced, in 3 rows in pan. Spoon ½ cup whole cranberry sauce between rows. Pour batter over fruit and bake. Serve warm with whipped cream.

Baked Alaska

See color picture opposite. Mrs. George Cammack of Minneapolis says that her guests just gasp at the beauty of this mysterious dessert when she serves it on an antique silver-edged pink china cake plate.

9″ round layer Egg Yolk Sponge Cake (p. 152)
2 qt. strawberry ice cream
6 large egg whites (¾ cup)
½ tsp. cream of tartar
1 cup sugar

Pack ice cream in round bowl about 1″ smaller around than layer of cake. Place in freezing compartment of refrigerator until serving time. Shortly before serving, beat egg whites with cream of tartar until frothy. Gradually beat in sugar. Continue beating until meringue is stiff and glossy. *Heat oven to 500° (very hot).* Place cooled layer of cake on a cutting board on a baking sheet. Loosen ice cream from bowl with spatula. Invert bowl over cake. Remove bowl. Cover cake and ice cream with meringue, sealing meringue to board for a complete seal. (Ice cream will not melt in oven.) Bake *3 to 5 min.*, or until meringue is delicately browned. Slip the dessert onto a serving platter, board and all, if board is small. Serve immediately. *12 to 16 servings.*

Brick Alaska

Make Baked Alaska *(above)*—*except* use any desired cake cut 1″ larger around than a pint brick of ice cream. Use only ½ of meringue.

Chocolate Brick Alaska: Use chocolate cake, either vanilla or chocolate ice cream. Sprinkle meringue before baking with slivered almonds and shaved chocolate.

Brownie Brick Alaska: Use Brownies (p. 195), cut the right size, and peppermint ice cream.

Caramel Fluff Angel Food

Split Angel Food Cake (p. 155) into 3 layers. Spread Caramel Fluff *(below)* between layers and on top and sides. Sprinkle shaved chocolate over top. Chill 1 to 2 hr.

Caramel Fluff

Combine 2 cups whipping cream, ¾ cup brown sugar (packed) and 1 tsp. vanilla. Chill 30 min.; then whip until stiff.

Orange Almond Delight

Split a 10″ Sponge Cake (p. 152), Orange Chiffon Cake (p. 157) or Angel Food Cake (p. 155) into 2 or 3 layers. Put layers together and frost with Orange Fluff *(below)*.

Orange Fluff (Russian Sauce)

3 or 4 egg yolks (or 2 whole eggs)
½ cup sugar
⅓ to ½ cup orange juice (1 large orange)
1 tbsp. grated orange rind
1 cup whipping cream, whipped stiff
½ cup chopped toasted blanched almonds
  or fresh grated coconut

Mix egg yolks, sugar and orange juice in top of double boiler. Cook over hot water, stirring constantly, until it thickens *about 15 min.* Stir in rind. Cool. Fold in whipped cream and almonds.

French Ribbon Cake

Split a loaf of Chiffon Cake (p. 157) into 4 layers. Put layers together and frost cake with Chocolate Filling and Frosting *(below)*. Sprinkle sides of frosted cake with chopped nuts or decorate edge with blanched almond halves stuck into frosting. Chill in refrigerator several hours. *10 servings.*

Chocolate Filling and Frosting

Cream together ¾ cup soft butter and 1 cup *sifted* confectioners' sugar. Beat in 3 egg yolks, one at a time, and 3 sq. unsweetened chocolate (3 oz.), melted. Fold in 3 egg whites, beaten stiff.

Singed Angel Wings

Happy idea for a few remaining wedges of Angel Food Cake.

Brush cut sides of wedges of Angel Food Cake (p. 155) with melted butter. Lightly brown both sides under broiler (1 min. each side). Serve with Clear Orange Sauce (p. 393).

Strawberry or Raspberry Angel Food

Prepare Angel Food Cake for filling (p. 236). Prepare Strawberry or Raspberry Velvet Cream (p. 220)—except use 1½ cups whipping cream. After folding in cream and fruit, chill 10 min. (until slightly firm). Fill cake cavity and replace top of cake. Frost with remaining mixture. Chill about 4 hr., or until set. Garnish with whole fresh berries.

BAKED ALASKA

Recipe, opposite.

HOW TO FILL ANGEL FOOD CAKES

Fillings and frostings are for 10″ Angel Food Cakes (*p. 155*). It is important to have cake *completely cool*, or filling will weigh it down; make cake a day before filling, if possible. Choose desired filling and frosting from recipes below.

1. Place a 10″ Angel Food Cake upside down on plate or waxed paper. Slice entire top from cake about 1″ down. Lift off top and lay aside.

2. Cut down into the cake 1″ from outer edge, and 1″ from hole, leaving a substantial "wall" of cake about 1″ thick.

3. Remove center with a curved knife or spoon, being careful to leave a base of cake at bottom 1″ thick. Place cake on serving plate.

4. Completely fill cavity with chilled filling. Push filling well into cake hollow to avoid "holes" in cut slices.

5. Replace top of cake and press gently. Cover top and sides with the remaining chilled whipped cream.

6. Decorate appropriately and chill until well set (4 hr. or more). Cut into 12 to 16 servings.

Angel Food Delight

Choice of an epicure, Judge Leslie L. Anderson, Minneapolis, Minnesota.

Prepare Angel Food Cake as above. Fill cake cavity with Fruited Cream Filling (*below*). Replace top of cake and spread whipped cream on top and sides. Chill until set (4 hr. or more).

Fruited Cream Filling and Frosting

3 cups whipping cream
⅓ cup confectioners' sugar
¾ cup crushed pineapple, well drained
1 cup fresh strawberries, cut in halves
6 marshmallows, cut in quarters

Whip cream and confectioners' sugar until stiff. Reserve half for frosting. To remaining half of cream, fold in pineapple, strawberries and marshmallows; use to fill cake. Frost top and sides with reserved whipped cream.

Angel Food Waldorf

Tender white angel food cake filled and frosted with dark rich cocoa fluff makes a dessert of delightful contrasts. Make it ahead for easy entertaining.

Prepare Angel Food Cake as above. Fill and frost with Cocoa Fluff Filling and Topping (*below*). Chill until set (4 hr. or more).

Cocoa Fluff Filling and Topping

3 cups chilled whipping cream
1½ cups *sifted* confectioners' sugar
¾ cup cocoa
¼ tsp. salt
⅔ cup toasted slivered almonds

Mix cream, sugar, cocoa and salt in chilled bowl; beat until stiff. Fold half of almonds into half the Cocoa Fluff; use this to fill cake. Frost cake with remaining Cocoa Fluff; sprinkle sides and top of cake with rest of almonds.

236

Rainbow Dessert (*Blöte Kage*)

A dazzling dessert with fillings of rainbow colors served at exclusive hotels in Norway. The Norwegian name, Blöte Kage, means Soft Cake. It was brought to us by Mrs. Gladys Petch, formerly of Oslo, Norway, now of New York, Radio Consultant to the Norwegian Information Services.

Cut a cooled large Sponge Cake (*p. 152*) or Chiffon Cake (*p. 157*) into four 1″ layers. Whip 3 cups whipping cream and 6 tbsp. confectioners' sugar until stiff. Put cake together with Fillings (*opposite*). Cover top and sides with the remaining whipped cream (3 cups). Sprinkle with green pistachio nuts (blanched and finely chopped). Chill 3 hr. before serving. Arrange apricot halves, rounded-side-out, around base of cake. Add a few green leaves. Serve.

Pineapple Filling (*bottom*): Soften 2 tsp. unflavored gelatin in 1 tbsp. pineapple juice. Dissolve over hot water. Stir into 1 cup drained crushed pineapple. Tint with green food coloring. Chill. When partially set, fold in 1 cup of the whipped cream.

Apricot Filling (*second*): Soften 2 tsp. unflavored gelatin in 1 tbsp. pineapple juice. Dissolve over hot water. Stir into 1 cup mashed apricot pulp (sweet). Chill. When partially set, fold in 1 cup of the whipped cream.

Raspberry Filling (*third*): Soften 2 tsp. unflavored gelatin in 1 tbsp. pineapple juice. Dissolve over hot water. Stir into 1 cup thick raspberry jam. Chill. When partially set, fold in 1 cup of the whipped cream.

Aloha Chiffon Cake

After a delightful holiday in Hawaii, Beverly Steffen Brunner, formerly of our staff, developed this fancy cake dessert with island pineapple and coconut in the fillings. Served to 450 at a banquet for the Betty Crocker Homemaker of Tomorrow. See color picture p. 247.

Split a Chiffon Cake (*p. 157*) into 3 layers. Whip 3½ cups whipping cream and 1 cup *sifted* confectioners' sugar until it forms soft peaks. Put cake together with Fillings (*below*). Frost cake with remaining whipped cream, to which 2 tsp. rum flavoring has been added. Cover entire cake with 1½ cups crushed peanut brittle, about ½ lb. Chill or freeze cake before serving. If frozen, thaw 2 to 3 hr. before serving.

Pineapple Filling: To 2 cups whipped cream, add a few drops green food coloring, 1½ tsp. vanilla and 1 cup well drained crushed pineapple.

Coconut Filling: To 2 cups whipped cream, add a few drops red food coloring, 1½ tsp. vanilla and ½ cup shredded coconut, cut up.

Spumoni Chiffon Cake

Combines the colors and flavors of an Italian favorite . . . spumoni ice cream.

Bake Lovelight Chocolate Chiffon Cake (*p. 161*) in layers. Split layers to make 4 layers. Whip 3 cups whipping cream and ¾ cup *sifted* confectioners' sugar until it forms soft peaks. Divide into 4 parts. Put cake together with Fillings (*below*). Wrap aluminum foil around sides of cake and chill or freeze until serving time. If frozen, thaw 2 to 3 hr. before serving.

Green Pistachio Filling (*bottom*): To ¼ of the whipped cream, add 4 to 6 drops green food coloring, 1 tsp. vanilla and ¼ cup chopped pistachio nuts.

Pink Peppermint Filling (*second*): To ¼ of the whipped cream, add 4 to 6 drops red food coloring and ¼ cup crushed peppermint candy (about 3 sticks).

Golden Rum-flavored Filling (*third*): To ¼ of the whipped cream, add 4 to 6 drops yellow food coloring and 1 tsp. rum flavoring.

Spicy Cocoa Topping: To remaining whipped cream, add ¼ tsp. cinnamon and 3 tbsp. sifted cocoa.

NOTE: To frost cake completely with cocoa whipped cream, whip an additional cup of whipping cream with ¼ cup *sifted* confectioners' sugar and add ½ tsp. cinnamon and 3 tbsp. *sifted* cocoa. Do not cover with foil.

Meringue Torte (*Meringue Shells*)

For meringues of special shapes, draw outline on brown paper, spoon meringue inside outline. For crisp, tender meringues: beat thoroughly to stiff peaks and dry out completely by baking, then leaving in oven until cool.

3 egg whites (⅓ to ½ cup)   1 cup sugar
¼ tsp. cream of tartar

Heat oven to 275° (slow). Beat egg whites and cream of tartar until frothy. Gradually beat in sugar a little at a time. Beat until very stiff and glossy. Tint, if desired, with food coloring. Spread on heavy brown paper on baking sheet in 8 or 9″ round, heart or any desired shape. Or in 9″ round layer pan with cutter. Shape with back of spoon. Bake *60 min.* Turn off oven and leave in until cool. Fill with ice cream topped with fresh berries or cut-up fruit or chocolate or butterscotch sauce. If desired, top with Sweetened Whipped Cream (*p. 232*). *8 to 10 servings.*

▶ **ALL YOU HAVE TO DO**

To store meringue shells for later use: wrap in waxed paper and put in cupboard for several days; do not place in air-tight container.

Lemon Schaum Torte (*Angel Pie*)

The perfect finish for a hearty meal.

Make Meringue Torte (*above*)—*except* use 4 egg whites. Spread with cooled Lemon Torte Filling (*below*). Top with 1 cup whipping cream, stiffly whipped. Chill about 12 hr. before serving.

Lemon Torte Filling

Beat 4 egg yolks in small mixer bowl until thick and lemon-colored. Gradually beat in ½ cup sugar. Blend in ¼ cup lemon juice, 2 tbsp. grated lemon rind. Cook over hot water, stirring constantly, until thick, *5 to 8 min.* Cool.

Orange Soufflé

Soufflé-like dessert prepared in a double boiler. "I'm crazy about it!" says Beverly Prevey, Hopkins, Minnesota.

3 egg whites (⅓ to ½ cup)
3 tbsp. sugar
1 tsp. orange flavoring
2 tbsp. cut-up orange marmalade

Butter entire inside of top of 2-qt. double boiler including inside of cover. Beat egg whites until frothy. Gradually add sugar and flavoring. Continue beating until mixture is stiff. Fold in marmalade. Cook in covered double boiler over boiling water *1 hr.* Do not lift cover. Turn off heat, let stand until ready to serve (not more than ½ hr.). Turn out onto hot serving dish. Garnish with shaved almonds. Serve with Sunshine Sauce (*p. 394*) or Clear Orange Sauce (*p. 393*). *6 servings.*

Individual Meringue Shells

Make Meringue Torte (*above*)—except drop ⅓ cup for each shell on brown paper on baking sheet. Shape with back of spoon. *Makes 8.*

Chocolate Soufflé

¼ cup butter
¼ cup GOLD MEDAL Flour
¼ tsp. salt
¾ cup milk
2 sq. unsweetened chocolate (2 oz.), cut up
3 egg yolks
½ cup sugar
3 egg whites
¼ tsp. cream of tartar

Heat oven to 350° (mod.). Melt butter in saucepan. Blend in flour and salt; cook until smooth and bubbly. Remove from heat and stir in milk and chocolate. Bring to boil. Boil 1 min., stirring constantly. Remove from heat. Beat egg yolks until thick and lemon-colored. Gradually beat in sugar. Then blend chocolate mixture into egg yolk mixture. Beat egg whites and cream of tartar until stiff. Carefully fold in egg yolk-chocolate mixture. Pour into greased 2-qt. baking dish. Set in pan of hot water (1″ deep). Bake *about 45 min.*, or until silver knife inserted in center comes out clean. Serve immediately on warm dessert plates. Top with whipped cream and toasted sliced almonds. *6 to 8 servings.*

Torte is the old German name for a special type of rich dessert. Made light with eggs, crumbs or ground nuts that take the place of most of the flour. Often garnished with fondant in fancy shapes.

Nut Cracker Sweet

A feathery-light, nut-chocolate torte filled with rum-flavored whipped cream. Its clever name was suggested by Mrs. Joseph Yanchor, one of our recipe testers.

6 eggs, separated	2 tbsp. vegetable oil
1 cup sugar	1 tbsp. rum flavoring (½-oz. bottle)
¼ cup GOLD MEDAL Flour	1 cup finely crushed graham cracker
1¼ tsp. baking powder	crumbs (12)
1 tsp. cinnamon	1 sq. unsweetened chocolate (1 oz.),
½ tsp. cloves	grated
	1 cup finely chopped nuts

Heat oven to 350° (mod.). Line bottoms of two layer pans, 8 or 9x1½″ or an oblong pan, 13x9½x2″ with aluminum foil. In large mixing bowl, beat egg whites until frothy. Gradually fold in ½ cup sugar and continue beating until whites form firm peaks. Blend remaining sugar, flour, baking powder, cinnamon and cloves together; combine in small mixing bowl with egg yolks, oil and rum flavoring. Beat 1 min., medium speed on mixer or with hand rotary beater. Pour egg yolk mixture over beaten whites, gently folding with rubber scraper until blended. Fold in graham cracker crumbs, chocolate and nuts. Pour into prepared pans. Bake *layers 30 to 35 min., oblong 35 to 40 min.*, or until no imprint remains when touched lightly with finger. Invert immediately to cool by resting edges of pan on two other inverted pans.

When completely cooled loosen with spatula. Invert pan, hit sharply on table. Cake drops out. Split layers. Put together and top with rum-flavored whipped cream (beat 2 cups whipping cream with ½ cup *sifted* confectioners' sugar until stiff; fold in 2 tsp. rum flavoring). Garnish with grated chocolate. Refrigerate 7 to 8 hr. or overnight. Cake becomes increasingly moist and mellow with refrigeration.

Cheesecake (*Baked*)

After testing and tasting many cheesecakes, we chose this as the smoothest and fluffiest. From Mrs. Harry Goldbarg of St. Paul, who sometimes serves it with fruit sauce instead of cherry glaze. See color picture pp. 216-217. For Refrigerated Cheesecake, see p. 246.

Heat oven to 275° (slow). Butter a 9″ spring-form pan. Dust bottom and sides with a mixture of ½ cup fine zwieback or graham cracker crumbs, 1 tbsp. sugar and ¼ tsp. *each* cinnamon and nutmeg. Pour Filling (*below*) into prepared pan. Bake *70 min.* Turn off oven and leave in 1 hr. without opening oven door. Remove from oven and cool. Spread top with Cherry Glaze (*below*). Remove cheesecake from pan just before serving. *16 to 20 servings.*

Filling

5 eggs, separated
1 cup sugar
1 lb. cream cheese (room temperature)
1 cup commercial sour cream
2 tbsp. flour
1 tsp. vanilla

Beat egg yolks until thick and lemon-colored. Gradually beat in sugar. Break up cream cheese; add to egg mixture beating until smooth. Add sour cream, flour and vanilla; continue beating until smooth. Beat egg whites until stiff but not dry. Gently fold into cheese mixture.

Cherry Glaze

1 can (16 oz.) red tart pitted cherries
½ cup sugar
2 tbsp. cornstarch
few drops red food coloring, if desired.

Drain cherries, reserving liquid. Add enough water to cherry juice to make 1 cup. Combine with sugar and cornstarch in saucepan. Cook, stirring constantly, until mixture thickens. Boil 1 min. Remove from heat; stir in cherries and food coloring. When cool, spread over cooled cheesecake. Refrigerate until set.

Chocolate Vienna Torte

Easy to make . . . like a chocolate chip sponge cake.

6 egg yolks
½ cup sugar
¾ cup GOLD MEDAL Flour
1 tsp. baking powder
1 tsp. salt

6 egg whites
½ tsp. cream of tartar
½ cup sugar
¾ cup grated unsweetened chocolate
1 tsp. vanilla

Heat oven to 350° (mod.). Line with greased paper two round layer pans, 9x1½″. Beat egg yolks in small mixer bowl until thick and lemon-colored. Beat in ½ cup sugar. Measure flour by dip-level-pour method or by sifting (*see p. 6*). Blend flour, baking powder and salt; stir in. Beat egg whites with cream of tartar until frothy. Beat in gradually another ½ cup sugar. Beat until very stiff and glossy. Gently fold in chocolate and vanilla. Carefully fold in egg yolk mixture. Pour into pans. Bake *25 to 30 min.*, or until no imprint remains when touched lightly. Turn out of pans, remove paper. Cool. Put together and top with Whipped Cream Filling (*below*). *16 servings.*

Whipped Cream Filling

Soften 1 tsp. unflavored gelatin in 1 tbsp. water. Dissolve over hot water. Whip 1 cup whipping cream and ¼ cup confectioners' sugar until it begins to thicken. Gradually add dissolved gelatin. Beat until stiff. Add 1 tsp. flavoring. *Makes 2 cups.*

Caramel Almond Vienna Torte

Caramelize ¾ cup sugar (*p. 141*). Add ½ cup hot water and cook, stirring until lumps are dissolved. Two tablespoonfuls of this caramel syrup will be used in the torte, the remainder in the topping.

Make Chocolate Vienna Torte (*above*)—*except* stir 2 tbsp. of caramel mixture into egg yolk mixture. Instead of chocolate, fold ¾ cup finely chopped toasted almonds into egg white mixture. Put cooled layers together with Whipped Cream Filling (*above*) or Sweetened Whipped Cream (*p. 232*). Cover with Caramel Topping (*below*).

Caramel Topping

½ cup sugar
¼ cup butter
¼ tsp. salt
½ cup milk
caramel syrup (*above*)
¼ cup cream (20% butterfat)

Add sugar, butter, salt and milk to caramel syrup in skillet. Stir until smooth. Cook over medium heat, stirring occasionally, to soft ball stage, 234°. Add cream. Cook again to 234°. When partially cool (no stirring), pour over top of torte letting it drip down sides here and there.

Blitz Torte (*Lightning Cake*)

Beautiful . . . the meringue top encrusted with sugar and toasted almonds.

¾ cup *sifted* confectioners' sugar
½ cup soft shortening
4 egg yolks, well beaten
1 cup GOLD MEDAL Flour
1 tsp. baking powder
¼ tsp. salt
3 tbsp. milk
4 egg whites
1 cup sugar (half confectioners')
½ cup shaved blanched almonds
2 tbsp. sugar

Heat oven to 325° (slow mod.). Grease and flour two round layer pans, 8x1½″. Mix thoroughly sugar and shortening. Beat in egg yolks. Measure flour by dip-level-pour method or by sifting (*see p. 6*). Blend flour, baking powder and salt; stir in. Blend in milk. Spread batter in pans. For meringue: beat egg whites until frothy, gradually beat in sugar, beat until stiff and glossy. Spread half of meringue over batter in each pan. Sprinkle each with half of almonds and 1 tbsp. sugar. Bake *35 to 40 min.* Cool. Remove from pans. Place one layer on serving plate meringue-side-up. Spread with Rich Custard (*p. 242*). Place other layer on top meringue-side-up. If desired, pipe with Sweetened Whipped Cream (*p. 232*). *12 servings.*

Apricot Wafer Dessert

Loretta Bonde of our staff, who shared this recipe with us, prefers the flavor of dried apricots.

1½ cups crushed chocolate wafers
½ cup soft butter
1 cup *sifted* confectioners' sugar
1 egg (room temperature)
1 cup sweetened apricot pulp (from cooked dried or drained canned apricots)
1 cup whipping cream, whipped stiff

Spread half of crumbs in square pan, 8x8x2". Beat butter, confectioners' sugar and egg together until light and fluffy. Spread over crumbs in pan. Add apricot pulp. Spread whipped cream over apricots. Sprinkle with remaining crumbs. Chill 12 hr. or longer. Cut in squares to serve. *9 servings.*

Banana Wafer Dessert

From Girl Scout leader Caroline Briese of St. Paul, who makes the crust from the shortbread cookies sold by the Scouts.

Make Apricot Wafer Dessert (*above*)—*except* use vanilla wafers for the crust and in place of apricot pulp use ¼ cup maraschino cherries (cut up), 1 banana (mashed) and ½ cup chopped nuts.

Pineapple Wafer Dessert

Make Apricot Wafer Dessert (*above*)—*except* omit apricot pulp and mix 1½ cups well drained crushed pineapple with the whipped cream and spread over butter-crumb mixture.

Strawberry Meringue Torte

Luscious! The meringue is the crust.

3 egg whites
½ tsp. baking powder
1 cup sugar
10 sq. (2") soda crackers, rolled fine
½ cup cut-up pecans
1 qt. unsweetened strawberries
½ recipe Sweetened Whipped Cream (*p. 232*)

Heat oven to 300° (slow). Butter generously a 9" pie pan. Beat egg whites with baking powder until frothy. Gradually beat in sugar until whites are stiff. Fold in cracker crumbs and pecans. Spread in pie pan. Bake *30 min.* Cool. Fill with strawberries and top with whipped cream. Chill several hours. *6 to 8 servings.*

Blueberry Imperial Dessert

Bake an 8" Graham Cracker Crust (*p. 341*) in a square pan, 9x9x1¾". Spread cooled filling for 8" Vanilla Cream Pie (*p. 354*) over crust; cover with Blueberry Filling (*below*). Refrigerate several hours. Garnish with Sweetened Whipped Cream (*p. 232*).

Blueberry Filling

¼ cup sugar
2 tbsp. cornstarch
½ tsp. salt
1 can (15 oz.) blueberries, drained (reserve liquid)
1 tbsp. lemon juice
2 tbsp. butter

Mix sugar, cornstarch and salt in saucepan. Add syrup drained from blueberries; stir until smooth. Cook until thickened and clear, stirring constantly. Remove from heat and add lemon juice, butter and blueberries. Cool. *8 to 10 servings.*

Chocolate Delight

Chocolate-and-white marbled refrigerator dessert . . . bits of angel food layered with fluffy chocolate cream.

1 pkg. (6 oz.) semi-sweet chocolate pieces
4 eggs, very well beaten
1 cup whipping cream, whipped stiff
1 tsp. vanilla, if desired
¾ cup chopped nuts
½ Angel Food Cake (*p. 155*)

Melt chocolate pieces over hot water. Cool slightly. Mix with eggs. Fold in whipped cream, vanilla and nuts. Tear angel food into small pieces. Line an oblong pan, 13x9½x2" with half of cake pieces. Pour over half of the filling. Cover with remaining cake pieces and filling. Sprinkle with chopped nuts. Chill several hours. Cut in squares or oblongs. *10 to 12 servings.*

English Trifle

Sheila John, charming home economist representing our company in the British Isles, served this to us as the dessert typical of an English dinner. For picture-pretty trifle, arrange ladyfingers around sides of a glass dessert dish, see pp. 216-217.

6 ladyfingers or 9″ square sponge cake, split
⅓ cup strawberry or raspberry jam
⅓ cup orange juice
3 tbsp. sherry flavoring

6 almond macaroons, crushed
½ cup whipping cream
2 tbsp. confectioners' sugar
½ tsp. vanilla
½ cup slivered almonds, toasted

Split ladyfingers and spread with jam or split sponge cake in two and cut one layer in sections the size of ladyfingers (12 sections). Arrange in single layer in bottom of square glass baking dish, 9x9x1¾″. Mix orange juice and sherry flavoring; pour over ladyfingers or cake. Sprinkle with macaroons and cover with Rich Custard (*below*). Allow to set. Whip cream and confectioners' sugar; add vanilla and spread over custard. Decorate with toasted almonds. *9 servings.*

Rich Custard

½ cup sugar
½ tsp. salt
2 tbsp. cornstarch
2½ cups milk
4 egg yolks, beaten
2 tsp. vanilla

Mix sugar, salt and cornstarch in saucepan. Stir in milk. Cook over medium heat, stirring constantly, until mixture boils. Boil 1 min. Remove from heat. Stir a little over half this mixture into beaten egg yolks, blend into mixture in saucepan. Bring just to boil, stirring constantly. Cool and add vanilla.

▶ ALL YOU HAVE TO DO

To make dessert from leftover cake and cookies: break them up and mix lightly into Soft Custard (*p. 223*) or whipped cream. Chill.

Silhouette Pudding

Use 30 crisp, thick 3″ ginger or chocolate cookies. Whip 2 cups whipping cream with ¼ cup confectioners' sugar until stiff. Spread a spoonful on a cooky. Place another cooky on top . . . continue until there are 6 piles of 5 cookies with whipped cream between. Lay piles crosswise on serving platter (see illustration opposite). Cover the roll evenly with remaining whipped cream. Chill at least 6 hr. *8 to 10 servings.*

For **Fudge Cream Roll** (made with chocolate cookies): garnish with walnut or pecan halves. Offer a chocolate sauce.

For **Ginger Cream Roll** (made with ginger cookies): garnish with bits of candied ginger. A bit of clear apricot jam on top is delicious.

Chocolate Toffee Dessert

So rich . . . serve just a small piece.

1 cup crushed vanilla wafers (20 wafers)
⅔ cup soft butter
1⅓ cups *sifted* confectioners' sugar
2 egg yolks
two bars (4 oz. each) German sweet chocolate, melted, or 1⅓ cups semi-sweet chocolate pieces, melted
⅔ cup chopped walnuts
1 tsp. vanilla
2 egg whites, stiffly beaten

Sprinkle half of crumbs on bottom of square pan, 8x8x2″. Cream together butter and confectioners' sugar. Stir in egg yolks, chocolate, walnuts and vanilla. Fold in egg whites. Spread over crumbs in pan. Sprinkle remaining crumbs over top. Chill. Serve small squares topped with whipped cream on individual dessert plates. *9 to 12 servings.*

HOW TO MAKE CREAM PUFFS

1. Stir constantly until mixture forms a ball.

2. Drop from spoon onto baking sheet forming 8 mounds.

3. Cut off tops. Scoop out filaments, fill, replace tops.

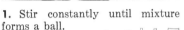

Cream Puffs *French-born delicacy . . . crisp and hollow.*

1 cup water	1 cup GOLD MEDAL Flour
½ cup butter	4 eggs

Heat oven to 400° (mod. hot). Heat water and butter to a rolling boil in saucepan. Measure flour by dip-level-pour method or by sifting (*see p. 6*). Stir in flour. Stir vigorously over low heat until mixture forms a ball (about 1 min.). Remove from heat. Beat in eggs thoroughly, 1 at a time. Beat until smooth. Drop from spoon onto ungreased baking sheet into 8 mounds 3″ apart. Bake *45 to 50 min.*, or until puffed, golden brown and dry. Allow to cool slowly, away from drafts. Cut off tops with sharp knife. Scoop out soft dough. Fill with Sweetened Whipped Cream (*p. 232*) or filling for 8″ Custard Pie (*p. 349*) or Rich Custard Filling (*p. 394*). Replace tops. Dust with confectioners' sugar. Or fill with ice cream, serve with sauce. Serve immediately or refrigerate. *Makes 8 large puffs.*

Chocolate Éclairs

Make Cream Puffs (*above*)—except put dough through pastry tube or shape with spatula into 12 fingers 4″ long and 1″ wide. Fill with filling for 8″ Custard Pie (*p. 349*). Frost with Thin Chocolate Icing (*p. 173*). *Makes 12 éclairs.*

Petits Choux *(Midget Puffs)*

A dessert of distinction. See color picture p. 247.

Make Cream Puffs (*above*)—except make 18 tiny puffs the size of a walnut. Bake *30 min.* Fill with various flavored ice creams. Serve with Quick Chocolate Sauce (*p. 392*). *6 servings.*

Cream Puff Swans

Make dough for Cream Puffs (*above*). Pipe the dough through a pastry tube into an "S" 2½ to 3″ tall; repeat to make 4 swan necks and heads. Pipe 4 comma (,) shapes for the tails. Bake *15 to 20 min.* Remove tails at 15 min., if necessary. Spoon remaining dough into 4 mounds on a baking sheet. Bake *45 to 50 min.* Cool. Cut tops from puffs and fill with 1½ cups whipping cream, whipped and sweetened. Insert a head and tail in each swan cutting a hole if necessary. Cut each top in half and insert for lifted wings. Sprinkle with confectioners' sugar. Serve immediately.

Luxury-loving Romans knew a kind of ice cream . . . snow from the high mountain passes, carried to Rome by fleet runners. There it was flavored with fruit juices. Centuries later, "Cream Ice" was so well liked by Charles I of England, that he pensioned the French chef who made it for him. Virginia cavaliers brought that idea to the new world. Later, Dolly Madison reversed the name and "Ice Cream" appeared on the White House menu.

French Vanilla Ice Cream *(For Refrigerator)*

The egg yolks make it a lovely yellow. Keep trays covered with waxed paper to help prevent crystals.

½ cup sugar
¼ tsp. salt
1 cup milk

3 egg yolks, beaten
1 tbsp. vanilla
1 cup whipping cream

Set refrigerator control for fast freezing. Blend sugar, salt, milk and egg yolks in saucepan. Cook over medium heat, stirring constantly, just until mixture comes to a boil. Cool. Add vanilla. Pour into refrigerator tray. Freeze until mixture is mushy and partly frozen, ½ to 1 hr. Whip cream until barely stiff. Empty partially frozen mixture into chilled bowl, beat until smooth. Fold in whipped cream. Pour into two refrigerator trays and freeze until firm, stirring frequently and thoroughly, during first hour of freezing. Freezing time will be 3 to 4 hr. *6 to 8 servings (1 qt.).*

French Vanilla Ice Cream

(For Crank Freezer)

Make French Vanilla Ice Cream *(above)—except,* after custard has cooled, blend in vanilla and whipping cream without whipping. Freeze according to directions on freezer.

Fruit Sherbet

¾ cup crushed fruit (pineapple, strawberries, raspberries, apricot)
2 tbsp. lemon juice
¾ cup sugar
1½ tsp. unflavored gelatin
2 tbsp. cold water
¼ cup hot milk
1 cup milk
1 egg white, beaten stiff

Mix fruit, lemon juice and sugar. Let stand until syrup forms (2 hr.). Soften gelatin in cold water, dissolve in hot milk. Add to fruit mixture. Stir in the 1 cup milk slowly. Pour into freezing tray, freeze 1 hr. Beat the partially frozen mixture in a chilled bowl with a rotary beater until creamy and frothy. Fold in beaten egg white. Return to tray. Freeze 3 to 4 hr., or until firm, stirring occasionally. *6 to 8 servings (1 qt.).*

Lemon Sherbet

Make Fruit Sherbet *(above)—except* use ¾ cup lemon juice in all, 2 tsp. grated lemon rind and 1 cup sugar.

Pineapple Ice

Refreshing dessert or meat accompaniment.

1 tsp. unflavored gelatin
¾ cup sugar
1 cup water
¼ cup lemon juice
1 cup crushed pineapple, undrained
1 egg white, stiffly beaten

Mix gelatin and sugar in saucepan. Stir in water, lemon juice and pineapple; bring to boil. Cool. Pour into refrigerator tray; freeze to a mush. Beat in chilled bowl with rotary beater until fluffy. Fold in beaten egg white. Return to tray. Freeze until firm, 2 to 3 hr., stirring occasionally. *6 to 8 servings (1 qt.).*

Raspberry or Strawberry Ice

Make Pineapple Ice *(above)—except* omit lemon juice and pineapple; add 1 pkg. (10 oz.) frozen raspberries or strawberries, undrained.

Cranberry Ice See p. 332.

Fruit Cream Sherbet

Make Fruit Sherbet *(at left)—except* use ¼ cup lemon juice, 1 tsp. gelatin, ¼ cup boiling water in place of hot milk, omit the 1 cup milk. Whip ½ cup whipping cream until stiff; fold in 1 egg yolk, beaten very light, and the egg white. Add at the last.

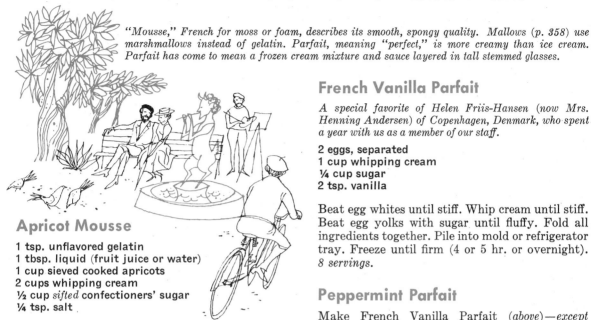

"Mousse," French for moss or foam, describes its smooth, spongy quality. Mallows (p. 358) use marshmallows instead of gelatin. Parfait, meaning "perfect," is more creamy than ice cream. Parfait has come to mean a frozen cream mixture and sauce layered in tall stemmed glasses.

Apricot Mousse

1 tsp. unflavored gelatin
1 tbsp. liquid (fruit juice or water)
1 cup sieved cooked apricots
2 cups whipping cream
½ cup *sifted* confectioners' sugar
¼ tsp. salt

Soften gelatin in liquid. Dissolve over hot water. Stir into apricots. Combine cream, confectioners' sugar and salt in chilled bowl. Whip until stiff. Fold into apricot mixture. Turn into refrigerator tray; freeze 3 to 4 hr., or until firm. *6 servings (1 qt.).*

Strawberry or Raspberry Mousse

Make Apricot Mousse *(above)—except* use slightly sweetened strawberries or raspberries, mashed, for the fruit pulp.

Easy Chocolate Mousse

From Mrs. Lewis Washburn Child of Minneapolis, who gave us several fine frozen dessert recipes.

Make Apricot Mousse *(above)—except*, in place of fruit pulp, use canned chocolate syrup.

French Vanilla Parfait

A special favorite of Helen Friis-Hansen (now Mrs. Henning Andersen) of Copenhagen, Denmark, who spent a year with us as a member of our staff.

2 eggs, separated
1 cup whipping cream
¼ cup sugar
2 tsp. vanilla

Beat egg whites until stiff. Whip cream until stiff. Beat egg yolks with sugar until fluffy. Fold all ingredients together. Pile into mold or refrigerator tray. Freeze until firm (4 or 5 hr. or overnight). *8 servings.*

Peppermint Parfait

Make French Vanilla Parfait *(above)—except* fold in 1 cup crushed (crush in cloth bag) peppermint candy (about 8 oz.).

Chocolate Parfait

Make French Vanilla Parfait *(above)—except* fold in 2 sq. (2 oz.) grated semi-sweet chocolate. Or swirl ½ cup chocolate or fudge ice cream sauce through parfait in freezer tray.

Fruit Parfait

Make French Vanilla Parfait *(above)—except* fold in 1 pkg. (10 oz.) frozen strawberries or raspberries, partially thawed and slightly mashed with fork, or ½ cup chopped maraschino cherries (about 16).

Frozen Lemon Pie

A specialty of a gracious former White House hostess, Mrs. Harry S. Truman. The Trumans' home city, Independence, Missouri, recently dedicated the beautiful library which houses 3½ million documents related to the Truman administration.

½ cup fine graham cracker crumbs
3 egg whites
½ cup sugar
3 egg yolks

1 cup whipping cream
2 to 3 tsp. grated lemon rind
¼ to ⅓ cup lemon juice

Sprinkle half of crumbs in well greased 9″ pie pan. Beat egg whites until frothy. Gradually add sugar. Beat until stiff and glossy. Beat egg yolks until thick and lemon-colored. Fold into egg white mixture. Mix cream, lemon rind and juice; beat until stiff. Fold into egg mixture. Pour into crumb-lined pie pan. Sprinkle rest of crumbs over top. Freeze to desired consistency. *6 to 8 servings.*

Refrigerated Cheesecake *(Unbaked)*

For Cheesecake (baked type), see p. 239.

2 envelopes unflavored gelatin (2 tbsp.)
¾ cup sugar
¼ tsp. salt
2 egg yolks
1 cup milk
1 tsp. grated lemon rind
1 tbsp. lemon juice
1 tsp. vanilla
3 cups cream-style cottage cheese (24 oz.)
2 egg whites
¼ cup sugar
1 cup whipping cream, whipped stiff

Mix gelatin, sugar and salt in saucepan. Beat together egg yolks and milk. Add gradually to mixture in saucepan. Bring *just* to boil over medium heat, stirring constantly. Remove from heat. Stir in lemon rind, juice and vanilla. Cool. Sieve cottage cheese into large mixing bowl. Stir in cooled gelatin mixture. Chill, stirring occasionally, until mixture mounds slightly when dropped from spoon. Beat egg whites until frothy; gradually beat in sugar. Beat until stiff. Fold into gelatin-cheese mixture. Then fold in whipped cream. Turn mixture into an 8″ spring-form pan or square pan, 8x8x2″ or 9x9x1¾″. Sprinkle with Crumb Topping *(below)*. Chill until firm, at least 4 hr. *16 servings.*

Crumb Topping

Mix ½ cup fine zwieback crumbs, 1 tbsp. sugar, ¼ tsp. cinnamon and ¼ tsp. nutmeg.

Portia's Pears

Use a whole canned pear (small) for each serving. Moisten cocoa (1 tbsp. for each pear) with some of pear juice. Fill center cavity of 1 half. Place 2 halves together, fasten with toothpick. Chill. Brush pears with pink coloring. Place in dessert dish on top of Sunshine Sauce (p. 394).

Peach Melba

Simply wonderful dessert named for Nellie Melba, beloved Australian operatic soprano. Mrs. Arthur C. Burslie, The Dalles, Oregon, can hastily prepare this tempting concoction for family and guests from the peaches raised right outside her back door. See color picture pp. 216–217.

Peel fresh peaches and poach halves in syrup (*see Poached Fruit, p. 219*). Chill. Place a peach half on a mound of ice cream in serving dish. Add sweetened mashed raspberries, chilled, or Raspberry-Currant Sauce (p. 394).

Crème Brulée *(Burned Cream)*

This elegant dish was a feature of the famous hospitality of Thomas Jefferson's Virginia home, "Monticello."

6 egg yolks
⅓ cup sugar
3 cups whipping cream
⅓ cup brown sugar (packed)
sweetened fresh strawberries, raspberries or peaches; or green gage plums or pears poached in syrup

Beat egg yolks until very thick. Gradually beat in sugar. Scald cream in top of double boiler over direct heat. Pour scalded cream gradually into egg mixture. Return to double boiler and cook over hot water, stirring frequently, until mixture thickens, *about 5 min.* Pour into heat-proof serving dish. Cool. Sprinkle top with brown sugar. Broil until sugar melts and forms glaze (about 1 min.). Chill. Spoon over the fruit in individual dessert dishes. *8 to 10 servings.*

Zabaglione

A confection-like custard from Italy.

Beat 4 egg yolks in small mixer bowl until thick and lemon-colored. Beat in ¼ cup sugar and ¼ tsp. salt thoroughly. Blend in ¼ cup sherry, Marsala or sherry flavoring. Pour into top of double boiler and cook over hot water, stirring constantly, until thickened, *5 min.* Serve hot or cold in sherbet or parfait glasses . . . or in demitasse cups. *Makes 1 cup or 4 servings.*

Pear Helene

First enjoyed at the luxurious Chateau Lake Louise in the Canadian Rockies. Sometimes served with crystallized violets.

Pare and core fresh pears. Poach halves in syrup (*see Poached Fruit, p. 219*). Chill. For each serving, arrange a pear half on a mound of vanilla ice cream in a deep dessert dish. Pass Quick Chocolate Sauce (p. 392) to pour over the ice cream and pear.

BELLE OF THE EVENING

French Pancakes *(Crepes)*

From Betty Bucholz of New York who, for years, contributed much to our Betty Crocker service on radio.

1 cup milk
2 tbsp. butter
2 eggs, beaten

½ cup GOLD MEDAL Flour
1 tsp. baking powder
½ tsp. salt

Heat milk and butter in saucepan. Measure flour by dip-level-pour method or by sifting (*see p. 6*). When slightly cooled, beat in eggs, flour, baking powder, salt. Beat until smooth. Grease a 4 or 5" skillet lightly. Heat, pour in batter to coat bottom. Tilt skillet to cover evenly. Cook 1 min. Loosen with spatula and "flip." Brown other side. To serve, follow one of recipes below. *Makes 30 3" pancakes.*

Swedish Pancakes *(Plättar)*

Make French Pancakes (*above*)—*except* bake small cakes (3"). If possible, bake on Swedish griddle (with indentations). Arrange a ring of 6 or 7 overlapping cakes on dessert plate; in center, a spoonful of lingonberries or raspberry jam, a fluff of whipped cream.

Crepes Suzette *(Pancakes in Orange Sauce)*

Original recipes call for Cointreau and brandy poured over the sauce in chafing dish after crepes are added . . . then lighted before serving.

Make French Pancakes (*above*) in advance. Cool. Keep covered so crepes will not dry out. To serve: melt ⅓ cup butter in chafing dish. Blend in 2 tbsp. sugar, ⅓ cup orange juice, a bit of grated orange rind. Turn crepes in the hot sauce, then fold them in halves or quarters. Place 3 or 4 on each dessert plate with some of the sauce spooned over.

French Beret Pancake Dessert

This delectable dessert came to us from Mr. John, of French Room hat fame, who serves pancakes with wild strawberries (fraise des bois).

2 egg whites
2 egg yolks
½ cup milk
¼ cup GOLD MEDAL Flour
2 tsp. sugar
2 tsp. butter, melted

Beat egg whites until stiff. In separate bowl, mix egg yolks and milk. Beat in flour, sugar and butter until smooth. Fold into egg whites. Heat buttered skillet. Use 2 tbsp. of batter for each pancake. Brown quickly on one side and turn to brown other side. Roll pancakes with strawberry jam. Top with thick cream. Serve 3 rolled pancakes for each serving. *4 servings.*

Fleur de Lily

Dainty, lily-shaped dessert. Created for Lily Pons, brilliant star of the Metropolitan Opera, by Louis, fabulous chef of the Ritz in Paris.

3 egg whites
½ cup sugar
⅓ cup GOLD MEDAL Flour
⅓ cup finely ground almonds
⅓ cup butter, melted and cooled
1 tsp. vanilla

Heat oven to 400° (mod. hot). Beat egg whites until frothy. Gradually beat in sugar. Beat until stiff. Measure flour by dip-level-pour method or by sifting (*see p. 6*). Fold in flour, almonds, butter, vanilla. Use 2 tbsp. batter for each lily. Drop 2" apart on greased heavy baking sheet. Bake *8 to 10 min.* Loosen with spatula; form quickly into little cones. Seal by lapping edges. Cool. Fill with Sweetened Whipped Cream (*p. 232*) into which strawberries have been folded. *Makes 10 to 12 lilies.*

Cherries Jubilee

For a glamorous touch, Mrs. Ralph Teynor, Albany, Oregon, adds ½ cup brandy just before serving. Without stirring, she lights it with a match so the flaming cherries can be spooned over each serving.

¾ cup currant jelly
1 can (1 lb.) pitted Bing cherries or 2 cups fresh
   Bing cherries, poached (*see Poached Fruit, p. 219*)
1 tbsp. grated orange rind
brandy flavoring (to taste)

Melt jelly in chafing dish over direct heat. Add cherries, rind and flavoring. Heat slowly to simmering, stirring occasionally. Serve hot over vanilla ice cream. *8 to 10 servings.*

Joseph Pearson

EGGS

Down through the ages, men have used eggs for magic, for religious purposes, for gifts and for games, but principally for food. The English of old feasted on eggs on the Saturday preceding Lent as the eating of eggs was forbidden for those 40 days. Colored Easter eggs, our childhood delight, originated in Persia as a symbol of new life. The Europeans, especially the Ukrainians, have made an art of decorating Easter eggs.

In the past some countries have prized duck eggs, in others the egg of the plover was a delicacy, though the hen's eggs are the universal favorite. Ancient Romans believed that long eggs had better flavor than round eggs; but today we know that a fresh egg, whether long or round, large or small, brown or white, is a gold mine of flavor and nutrition.

No food or ingredient is more versatile than eggs. This chapter features eggs cooked in the shell, poached, fried, scrambled, baked or transformed into an omelet or soufflé. Throughout the book you'll find eggs at work thickening custards and sauces, binding other ingredients in meat loaves and cakes, emulsifying mayonnaise (almost magically the egg keeps oil and vinegar intermixed), lightening cakes and meringues, even decorating salads.

For interesting meals at a low cost, serve eggs often.

VERSATILE EGGS

(complete index in back of book)

BREAKFAST STAND-BYS

COME FOR BRUNCH

FOR NUTRITIOUS SUPPERS

FOR GRACIOUS LUNCHEONS

FREEZER FACTS

DO NOT FREEZE dishes with large amounts of egg: custards, meringues, fluffy-type frostings, deviled eggs, etc. Egg salad sandwich filling may be frozen if finely chopped or riced.

UNCOOKED EGGS may be frozen in quantity successfully. If you desire to do so, see your local extension agent for correct freezing procedure.

STORING LEFTOVER YOLKS AND/OR WHITES

(See p. 44 for more recipe suggestions using egg whites and yolks)

EGG YOLKS: Store yolks in a tightly covered jar in refrigerator. More perishable than whites. Use 2 egg yolks for 1 whole egg in soft and baked custards, salad dressings, cream pie fillings, etc. Use 2 egg yolks plus 1 tbsp. water for 1 whole egg in yeast doughs, cookies, etc.

EGG WHITES: Store whites in a tightly covered jar in refrigerator. They keep for weeks. Use them to make angel food cakes, white butter cakes, fluffy-type icings, meringues, frozen desserts, fruit whips, glazes for breads and cookies and various cake toppings.

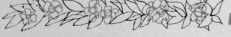

MEALTIME MAGIC

LUNCH IN THE BACKYARD

Coney Islands
Deviled Eggs (*p. 254*)
Carrot Sticks
Brownie Confections (*p. 195*)
Fresh Fruit
Milk

GRADUATION BRUNCH

Fresh Strawberry Plate (*p. 56*)
Spinach Soufflé (*p. 424*) with
Welsh Rabbit (*p. 274*)
Cherry Butterscotch Ring (*p. 118*)
Milk or Coffee

EASTER SUPPER

Eggs Florentine (*p. 254*)
Tossed Salad
Tomatoes Vinaigrette (*p. 376*)
Butter Dips (*p. 77*)
Lemon Meringue Pie (*p. 353*)
Coffee

CHRISTMAS MORN

Fruit Cup
Eggs Poached in Milk (*p. 256*)
on Hot Toast
Stollen (*p. 110*)
Jule Kage (*p. 116*)
Coffee

WHAT EVERY COOK NEEDS TO KNOW ABOUT EGGS

BUY AND COOK WITH CARE

A fresh egg has a dull shell, not shiny or bright—it makes no difference whether the shell is brown or white. A fresh egg will sink when placed in cold water. Crack open a fresh egg and you'll find a firm, upstanding yolk and a thick white. To stay fresh, eggs must be kept under refrigeration at the grocery store and be put into the refrigerator immediately at home.

Eggs for the breakfast table should be strictly fresh (top grade) of any size you prefer. For cooking (in meat loaves or custard), you may use smaller eggs. For baking (especially cakes), use large eggs (2 oz.) or their equivalent (*see p. 7*). Federal and state regulations for eggs vary. Find out what your state regulations mean. Different grades are found in all sizes of eggs. Most home-makers plan to use 2 to 5 eggs each week for each member of the family.

Always break egg into saucer before cooking or combining with other foods.

The most important thing to remember in cooking eggs is: cook eggs with low to moderate, even heat. This is true no matter how you are cooking eggs. Too high a heat toughens the protein in eggs making them leathery and curdled.

When combining hot mixtures with whole eggs or egg yolks, as in Cream Pudding (*p. 226*), always add half the hot mixture slowly to the eggs, stirring or beating constantly.

Either egg yolks or egg whites are called for in many recipes, so learn to separate them perfectly: remove from refrigerator and immediately break shell with sharp tap at its center with knife blade or on bowl edge. Press thumb tips into crack; pull shell apart, keeping yolk in one half, letting white pour out of other. Rock yolk from one half of shell to other, so rest of white pours off. If a small amount of egg yolk gets into white, it can be easily removed using a piece of egg shell as a dipper.

· ·

SERVE WITH FLAIR

For puffiest omelets, fluffiest scrambled eggs, serve eggs as soon as possible after cooking.

The mild-flavored egg combines well with so many other foods. For breakfast variety, try Eggs Baked in Bacon Rings (*p. 255*) or Scrambled Eggs with Cheese (*p. 257*).

NEW ADVENTURES IN EGG COOKERY

Buffet Eggs (*p. 257*)—Scrambled supper dish of eggs, cottage cheese and dried beef.

Deviled Eggs De Luxe (*p. 254*)—Festive appetizer.

Meat or Sea Food Soufflé (*p. 258*)—Chicken or crabmeat replaces cheese in high soufflé.

Savory Eggs (*p. 255*)—Perfectly seasoned casserole of eggs baked with cheese.

EGGS À LA GOLDENROD

Recipe, page 254.

*You like them soft to start the day,
but hard they make a garnish gay.*

1. Have eggs at room temperature to prevent "cracking" during cooking.
2. Start in cold or boiling water.
3. Cover eggs completely with water.
4. Choose large enough pan. Do not pile eggs one on top of another.
5. Time accurately, by clock or timer.
6. Cook at temperature below boiling.

How to Soft Cook Eggs

Sometimes called Coddled Eggs.

Cold Water Start: Cover eggs in saucepan with cold water. Heat until water boils. Remove from heat. Cover pan. Let stand *off heat* 2 to 4 min.

Boiling Water Start: Bring water to a boil in saucepan. With a spoon, carefully lower eggs into water to prevent cracking the shell. Reduce heat. Keep water simmering *3 to 5 min.*

How to Hard Cook Eggs

Cold Water Start: Cover eggs in saucepan with cold water. Heat until water boils. Remove from heat. Cover pan. Let stand *off heat* 23 to 25 min.

Boiling Water Start: Bring water to a boil in saucepan. With a spoon, carefully lower eggs into water to prevent cracking the shell. Reduce heat. Keep water simmering *18 to 20 min.*

To cool hard or soft-cooked eggs

Cool eggs under cold water. This makes eggs easier to handle, easier to shell and immediately stops the cooking (overcooking causes the yolks to become darkened). Cracking shells slightly before cooling makes eggs easier to peel later.

To serve soft-cooked eggs

Crack egg sharply *at large end* when egg is to be eaten from shell, set in individual egg cup. Crack egg sharply *in center* if to be turned into egg dish or cup. Season with salt, pepper and butter. "Use bone or ivory spoon," say the English.

To shell hard-cooked eggs easily: Tap to crackle. Roll between hands to loosen shells. Peel under cold water. Slice with sharp knife.

To slice hard-cooked eggs: Place shelled egg in egg slicer; pull down top. Fine wire cuts egg evenly. Use slices for garnish.

To sieve hard-cooked eggs: Press yolks and whites separately through coarse sieve. Use as garnish.

Deviled Eggs

Mounds of savory yellow egg yolks in white frames. A tasty finger food for picnics or parties.

6 hard-cooked eggs
½ tsp. salt
¼ tsp. pepper
½ tsp. dry mustard
about 3 tbsp. salad dressing or vinegar or cream
   (enough to moisten)

Cut hard-cooked eggs in halves. Slip out yolks. Mash with fork. Mix in rest of ingredients. Refill whites with egg yolk mixture, heaping it up lightly. Serve with salads or cold meat platters.

Deviled Eggs De Luxe

6 hard-cooked eggs, halved lengthwise
2 tsp. prepared mustard
1½ tsp. Worcestershire sauce
2 tsp. lemon juice
¼ tsp. salt
⅛ tsp. pepper
¼ cup mayonnaise

Save egg whites. Mash yolks and mix with rest of ingredients. Add one of the following:

1 can (6½ oz.) flaked tuna
⅛ tsp. curry powder to tuna variation
use ½ cup commercial sour cream in place of
   mayonnaise
1 can (4½ oz.) shrimp, chopped
¼ lb. crisp, cooked bacon (about 8 slices),
   crumbled
1 can (2¼ oz.) deviled ham
⅔ cup shredded sharp Cheddar cheese;
   increase mayonnaise 2 tbsp.
1 can (8 oz.) salmon, with juice (remove skin
   and small bones)

Pile into egg white halves. Garnish with parsley or sprinkle with paprika for more color.

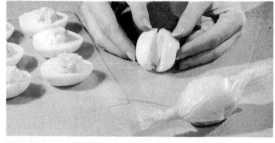

TO CARRY DEVILED EGGS TO PICNICS

Fit two halves together, wrap in waxed paper (twisting the ends).

Creamed Eggs

Offer endless possibilities for plain and fancy fare.

1 cup Medium White Sauce (p. 387)
4 hard-cooked eggs, cut into quarters

Carefully fold eggs into hot white sauce. Serve over hot buttered toast or biscuits, crisp chow mein noodles or fluffy boiled rice; or in toast Buttercups (p. 120) or patty shells. Sprinkle with paprika and garnish with sprigs of parsley or crisp bacon. *4 servings.*

Curried Eggs: Add ¼ tsp. curry powder with other seasonings when making Medium White Sauce for Creamed Eggs (above).

Eggs à la Goldenrod: Make Creamed Eggs (above), reserving 2 egg yolks. Serve on toast; press yolks through sieve or strainer to decorate tops. *See color picture p. 252.*

Creamed Tuna or Salmon and Eggs: Add 1 cup flaked tuna or salmon to Creamed Eggs (above).

Creamed Dried Beef and Eggs: Frizzle 1 cup dried beef in butter; add to Creamed Eggs (above).

Creamed Ham and Eggs: Add 1 cup diced cooked ham and ¼ cup mushrooms (browned in butter used to make White Sauce) to Creamed Eggs (above).

Eggs Florentine

Cook 1 lb. fresh or 2 pkg. (10 oz. each) frozen spinach *just* until tender; drain. Season. Chop fine. *Heat oven to 400° (mod. hot).* Spread spinach in 8″ round or square baking dish. Arrange 4 hard-cooked eggs on top. Cover with White Sauce (p. 387). Sprinkle with Crumb Topping (below). Bake *20 min. 4 servings.*

Crumb Topping: Melt 2 tbsp. butter. Add 1 clove garlic, sliced. Cook slowly about 3 min. Remove from heat; remove garlic. Mix in ½ cup dry bread or cracker crumbs and 2 tbsp. grated cheese.

How to Fry Eggs

Heat a thin layer of butter or bacon fat in heavy skillet until moderately hot. Break eggs, one at a time, into saucer; slip into skillet. Immediately reduce heat to low.

Cook *slowly*, spooning fat over eggs until whites are set and a film forms over yolks, *3 to 4 min.* Or turn eggs over quickly when whites are set and cook until done as desired. Sprinkle with salt and pepper. Serve at once on warm plate.

Poached-Fried Eggs

Lower in calories than eggs fried in fat.

Fry eggs (*see above*)—*except* use just enough fat to coat skillet. Immediately add ½ tsp. water or cream for each egg. Cover tightly. Cook to firmness desired, *5 to 6 min.*

Bacon-or-Ham and Eggs

Fry bacon or ham in skillet; remove; keep warm. Then fry eggs in some of fat in pan. Serve immediately surrounded by bacon or ham.

Eggs in a Frame

A Sunday evening treat. Easy for children to do.

Cut circle from slice of bread; then butter rest of slice generously on both sides. Place in hot buttered skillet over low heat. Drop an egg into center. Cook slowly until egg is set and underside of bread is brown. Turn. Brown on other side. Season with salt and pepper.

How to Bake or Shir Eggs

Break and slip 1 or 2 eggs into a greased individual shallow baking dish. Dot with butter. Sprinkle with salt and pepper. Add 1 tbsp. cream or milk, if desired. Bake *at 350°* (mod.) *15 to 20 min.,* or until set. Serve hot in the dish as an individual serving . . . garnish with parsley or water cress.

Eggs Baked on Corned Beef Hash

See color picture p. 259.

Spread warmed moist corned beef hash in well greased shallow baking dish. With bottom of custard cup, make deep hollows in hash. Dot each with butter and break an egg into it. Season with salt and pepper; cover with 1 tbsp. cream. Bake *at 400°* (mod. hot) *15 to 20 min.,* or until eggs are set. Serve immediately in baking dish.

Eggs Baked in Bacon Rings

Festive serving of bacon and eggs.

Bake or Shir Eggs (*above*)—*except* circle inside of each baking dish with a partially cooked bacon strip (not crisp) before adding egg.

Savory Eggs

Different and delicious lunch or supper main dish; serve with buttered spinach and a salad bowl.

1 cup grated Cheddar cheese
2 tbsp. butter
½ cup cream
1 tsp. prepared mustard
½ tsp. salt
¼ tsp. pepper
6 eggs, slightly beaten

Heat oven to 325° (slow mod.). Sprinkle cheese in square pan, 9x9x1¾". Dot with butter. Mix cream, mustard, salt and pepper; pour half over cheese. Pour eggs over top, then remaining cream mixture. Bake *25 min.* Serve at once. *6 servings.*

How to Poach Eggs

1. Fill greased skillet with hot water about 1½″ deep. Bring to boil; then reduce to simmering. Break each egg into a saucer and slip one at a time into the water. Slide egg toward side of pan to keep yolk in center. Cook below simmering *3 to 5 min.*

2. Lift eggs from water, one at a time, with slotted turner. Drain. Season with salt and pepper. Serve at once on hot buttered toast, ham-covered toast rounds, toasted split corn bread or corned beef hash slices; or in nests of cooked garden spinach.

Eggs Poached in Milk

"My mother always prepared them this way for my sisters and brothers and me when we were children. And, until we were grown up, we didn't know that eggs could be poached in any other way," says James Fish, advertising director of our company.

Poach eggs (*see above*)—*except* use milk or cream in place of water. Pour the hot milk over eggs on the hot toast.

Eggs Poached in Egg Poacher

Simple way to poach eggs with steam using special poaching pan.

Fill pan with water to 1″ and bring to boil. Add butter to little metal egg cups. Break eggs into custard cup or saucer, then turn into greased cups. Set egg cups in frame over steaming water. Cover and steam *3 to 4 min.*, or until done as desired.

Eggs à la Reine

Fit for a queen's luncheon or supper.

Place rounds of toast in baking dish. Cover with sliced mushrooms sautéed in butter . . . then with poached eggs. Pour over all hot Cheese Sauce (*p. 387*). Sprinkle with grated cheese. *Heat in 375° oven* (quick mod.) until cheese melts.

Eggs Mornay

Place poached eggs in shallow baking dish. Cover with Sauce Mornay (*p. 388*). Sprinkle with grated Parmesan cheese. Brown under broiler. Serve at once.

Eggs Benedict

The original recipe was brought to Old New Orleans by the French. See color picture p. 259.

For each serving, cover a round of split and toasted English muffin (or toast) with a thin slice of fried ham (same size). Top each with a poached egg and cover with Hollandaise Sauce (*p. 391*). Serve at once.

Eggs à la Lee

As served in Old Virginia.

For each serving, cover hot toast round with thin slice of boiled ham. Top with hot poached egg. Pour hot Mushroom Sauce (*p. 387*) over all. Serve at once.

Scrambled Eggs

Moist, tender and golden. Delicious served on toast strips covered with deviled ham, crisp bacon, creamed chicken, smoked salmon or anchovy paste.

1. Break eggs into a bowl with 1 tbsp. milk or cream for each egg, salt and pepper. Beat with fork. Heat butter or other fat (½ tbsp. for each egg) in moderately hot skillet. Pour in egg mixture and reduce heat to low. (Eggs should be scrambled slowly and gently.)

2. When mixture starts to set at bottom and sides, lift cooked portions with spatula and turn gently to cook all portions evenly. As soon as eggs are almost cooked through but are still moist and glossy, *5 to 8 min.*, quickly remove to hot platter and serve at once.

Quick Scrambled Eggs

Make Scrambled Eggs (*above*)—*except* do not mix eggs in bowl with milk. Pour eggs directly into hot fat in skillet. Add salt and pepper to taste. Stir gently to mix yolks and whites.

Creamy Scrambled Eggs

Made in double boiler without fat.

Make Scrambled Eggs (*above*)—*except* cook in top of double boiler over simmering—not boiling—water, stirring occasionally, until eggs are thick and creamy.

Scrambled Eggs with Herbs

Make Scrambled Eggs (*above*)—*except* add minced *fresh* herbs (chives, parsley, tarragon or chervil) to egg mixture.

Scrambled Eggs with Cheese

Make Scrambled Eggs (*above*)—*except*, for each egg, add 1 tbsp. grated Cheddar cheese, ¼ tsp. minced onion to egg mixture. Tomato Sauce (*p. 389*) makes a tasty complement.

Scrambled Eggs with Mushrooms

Make Scrambled Eggs (*above*)—*except* first sauté sliced fresh or canned mushrooms (1 to 2 tbsp. for each egg) in the hot fat.

Scrambled Eggs with Dried Beef or Ham

Make Scrambled Eggs (*above*)—*except* frizzle flaked pieces of dried beef or boiled ham in the hot fat before adding eggs. For something special, serve with hot Mushroom Sauce (*p. 387*).

Scrambled Eggs in Cream Puffs

Fill Cream Puffs (*p. 243*) with Scrambled Eggs (*above*). Top with Tomato Sauce (*p. 389*).

Arkansas Smoked Turkey Supreme

Top slices of hot smoked turkey with Scrambled Eggs (*above*), seasoned with chives, and Hollandaise Sauce (*p. 391*). Garnish with chopped parsley.

Buffet Eggs

Melt 3 tbsp. butter in large skillet. Add ¼ cup finely chopped green onion tops and cook until tender. Beat 9 eggs thoroughly; blend in 4 oz. (about 1⅓ cups) dried beef, cut in small strips, and 1 cup cottage cheese (cream style or dry). Add egg mixture to onion and cook like scrambled eggs. *6 servings.*

257

Cheese Soufflé

1 cup Thick White Sauce (*p. 387*)
¼ tsp. dry mustard
dash of cayenne pepper
1 cup shredded sharp cheese (¼ lb.)
3 egg yolks, well beaten
3 egg whites
¼ tsp. cream of tartar

Heat oven to 350° (mod.). Prepare thick white sauce. Add mustard, pepper and cheese to hot sauce. Remove from heat; stir gradually into egg yolks. Beat egg whites and cream of tartar until stiff. Fold in cheese mixture. Pour into ungreased 1½-qt. baking dish. For *High Hat Soufflé*, make groove 1″ from edge. Set baking dish in pan of hot water (1″ deep). Bake *50 to 60 min.*, or until puffed and golden brown. Serve immediately . . . with crisp bacon, Mushroom Sauce (*p. 387*) or Tomato-Mushroom Sauce (*p. 389*). *4 servings.*

Mushroom-Cheese Soufflé

Make Cheese Soufflé (*above*)—*except* fold 1 cup sautéed finely cut mushrooms into the Cheese Soufflé mixture at the last. Delicious with Sea Food Sauce (*below*).

Sea Food Sauce

To 1 cup Medium White Sauce (*p. 387*) carefully stir in ½ to 1 cup cooked shrimp or pieces of other sea food.

Cheese-and-Ham Soufflé

Make Cheese Soufflé (*above*)—*except* add, with the cheese, ½ cup ground cooked ham.

Meat or Sea Food Soufflé

Make Cheese Soufflé (*above*)—*except*, in place of cheese, use 1 cup finely ground cooked meat (chicken, lamb, veal) or sea food (shrimp, crabmeat, salmon seasoned with 1 tbsp. lemon juice). Serve with Mushroom Sauce (*p. 387*).

Individual Cheese Soufflés

Pour mixture into 6 custard cups. Bake *20 to 25 min.*

Dessert Soufflés See p. 238.

1. Stir cheese into sauce. **2.** Stir in beaten egg yolks.

3. Fold into beaten whites. **4.** Make groove with spoon.

Tomato Soufflé Ring

Delicate in color and flavor . . . for women's luncheons.

1 can (1 lb.) tomatoes (2 cups)
½ large onion, chopped
2 whole cloves
1 bay leaf
1 tsp. sugar
1 tsp. salt
⅛ tsp. pepper
¼ cup butter
¼ cup GOLD MEDAL Flour
3 egg yolks, well beaten
3 egg whites
¼ tsp. cream of tartar

Heat oven to 350° (mod.). Grease an 8″ ring mold or 1½-qt. baking dish. Mix tomatoes, onion, cloves, bay leaf, sugar, salt and pepper in saucepan. Simmer over low heat *15 min.* Strain and set aside 1 cup of tomato mixture. Melt butter; remove from heat and blend in flour. Stir in tomato mixture. Bring to boil, stirring constantly. Boil 1 min. Remove from heat and gradually stir in egg yolks. Beat egg whites with cream of tartar until stiff. Fold in tomato mixture carefully. Pour into prepared pan. Set in pan of hot water 1″ deep. Bake *30 to 40 min.* Soufflé is done when a silver knife stuck into the center comes out clean. To remove from mold, loosen edges slightly with a sharp knife and invert over desired serving plate. Serve immediately with creamed chicken, shrimp or mushrooms. *4 servings.*

VERSATILE EGGS

Eggs Baked on Corned Beef Hash, page 255

Jelly Omelet, page 260
Eggs Benedict, page 256

French Omelet

3 eggs   dash of salt and pepper
3 tbsp. milk or cream   1 tbsp. fat

Beat eggs until fluffy. Beat in milk or cream and seasonings. Pour into hot fat in skillet over *low* heat. Cook slowly . . . keeping heat low. As under-surface becomes set, start lifting it slightly with spatula to let uncooked portion flow underneath and cook. To add herbs, cheese or meat, sprinkle ½ tbsp. per egg over top of eggs. As soon as all of mixture seems set, fold or roll it; serve immediately. *2 servings.*

For variety add: sautéed sliced mushrooms (2 to 4 tbsp. for each egg) or 2 tbsp. sautéed cut-up fresh tomatoes for each egg.

Jelly Omelet

See color picture p. 259.

Make French Omelet (*above*)—*except* just before folding, spread with jelly.

Omelet Aux Fines Herbes

Make French Omelet (*above*)—*except* sprinkle with ½ tbsp. *each* minced *fresh* chives and parsley. Add a dash of chervil, basil, thyme, marjoram.

Puffy Omelet

A lovely main dish . . . the cook's pride.

4 eggs, separated   dash of salt and pepper
¼ cup milk or cream   2 tbsp. fat

Beat egg whites until stiff. Beat egg yolks until thick and lemon-colored; beat in milk or cream and seasonings. Fold into the beaten whites. Pour into sizzling hot butter in heavy skillet. Turn heat to low. Cook slowly until brown underneath, *about 10 min.* (Bubbles will still appear through uncooked puffy top and mixture will look moist.) Place skillet *in 350° (mod.) oven.* Bake *10 to 15 min.*, or until light brown on top and no imprint remains when touched lightly with finger. Make ½" deep crease across omelet . . . half way between handle and opposite side. Slip turner under, tip skillet to loosen omelet and fold in half without breaking. Roll omelet top-side-down onto hot platter. Garnish with hot sauce and serve at once. *2 to 3 servings.*

Favorite Omelet Sauces

Cheese Sauce (*p. 387*)
Mushroom Sauce (*p. 387 and p. 389*)
Tomato Sauce (*p. 389*)

Chicken à la King (*p. 266*)
Creamed Asparagus (*p. 411*)

Cook slowly . . . until set.

Fold or roll and serve immediately.

Bacon or Ham Omelet

Make French Omelet (*at left above*)—*except* sprinkle with 2 tbsp. crisp cooked bacon bits or flakes of cooked ham for each egg.

Fold egg yolk mixture into beaten whites.

Place in oven. Bake.

Slip turner under side and fold in half.

MAIN DISHES

Forerunner of today's increasingly popular main dishes is the "entree" or made-dish, like creamed sweetbreads or chicken patties, which preceded the roast meat course in the elegant five-course dinners of days gone by. Now expanded, the made-dish has replaced the meat course for suppers and light dinners.

Rice, a much-used main dish ingredient, is the world's number one food grain. What fun it would be to take a rice-tasting trip, sampling Creole Shrimp on rice in our southland, Fried Rice in Hawaii, Pilaf in India, Sukiyaki with rice in Japan and finish with Creamy Rice Pudding in Scandinavia.

Pasta (macaroni, spaghetti and noodles), basis of many another main dish, is as important to the Italians as opera. They have proved their ingenuity in designing pasta shapes from bowknots to lasagne *and* in creating many delicious sauces for pasta.

Vegetables, especially beans and corn, were eaten daily by pioneer families struggling for subsistence here in America and have held an honored place in our meals ever since. Baked beans, Indian pudding, hominy grits, corn breads and scrapple are among these foods of our forefathers.

We hope that you'll enjoy using these, our treasured main dish recipes, as much as we have enjoyed collecting them.

SATISFYING SUPPER DISHES

(complete index in back of book)

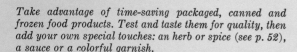 TIMESAVING TIPS

Take advantage of time-saving packaged, canned and frozen food products. Test and taste them for quality, then add your own special touches: an herb or spice (see p. 52), a sauce or a colorful garnish.

PIZZA AMERICANO

Follow steps on can of Betty Crocker Refrigerated Pizza. To complete pizza, arrange 3 skinless frankfurters (cut in quarters lengthwise) in spoke fashion, on a round pizza. Place Cheddar cheese strips across frankfurter strips. Bake.

HAM 'N CHIPS

Prepare Betty Crocker Scalloped Potatoes as directed on pkg.—except add ½ cup chopped ham and ½ cup chopped green pepper. When baked, sprinkle grated Parmesan cheese over top. *4 servings.*

HASH HATS

Heat oven to 350° (mod.). Break apart with a fork 1-lb. can corned beef hash; blend in ¼ cup finely chopped sweet pickle or pickle relish. Place four ¼" slices Bermuda onion in baking dish. Season with salt and pepper; top with butter. Mold hash in rounds on onion slices. Bake *20 min.* Serve with hot chili sauce. *4 servings.*

EASY-CREAMY SHRIMP ON RICE

Place contents of 10-oz. can frozen cream of shrimp soup in saucepan; add ½ cup milk. Heat slowly; stir often, until sauce reaches boiling point and is smooth. Add 4½-oz. can broken shrimp, drained, or whole little Italian shrimp. Heat *5 more min.* Serve over fluffy white rice tossed with chopped pimiento. *4 servings.*

MENUS FEATURING MAIN DISHES ARE ON pp. 38-40.

WHAT EVERY COOK NEEDS TO KNOW ABOUT MAIN DISHES

MAKE WITH CARE

Most main dishes are quick and easy. They can be served straight from the oven to the table, thus shortening serving time, as well as dishwashing time.

Main dishes are usually meals-in-one. They contain one or more foods high in protein, such as meat, fish, poultry, eggs, cheese or dried legumes. Vegetables and/or rice or noodles can be added and the dish is cooked with a sauce. Sometimes a pastry or biscuit topping is the finishing touch, or the dish may be topped with buttered crumbs or potato chips.

Use your imagination when seasoning main dishes. A few spices and herbs (p. 51) added can enhance the flavor—and make the dish your very own!

Hearty stews (p. 303) and skillet meals, such as Buffet Eggs (p. 257) and Chicken Almond (p. 267) are also main dish meals-in-one. Some sandwiches, such as Reuben's Sandwich (p. 292) are a meal in themselves.

When making baked casseroles, it is important to use the size baking dish called for in the recipe. Too big a dish will cause liquid to evaporate and food will be dry; liquid may bubble over if dish is too small.

Most baked casseroles may be made ahead and refrigerated. If so, let warm to room temperature before cooking, or start in a cold oven. Ovenproof glass and metal dishes, however, may be put directly into hot oven; allow 15 to 30 extra minutes to bake, depending on size.

SERVE WITH FLAIR

If your main dish is a hearty one, serve simple tossed salad, French bread or crusty rolls and light dessert. If less hearty, serve with a salad, vegetable, bread and a richer dessert.

It's fun to have several baking dishes in varying sizes, shapes and colors to suit your food—and your mood!

Garnishes are a welcome addition to main dishes. Keep a few sprigs of parsley in your refrigerator for bright green touch. Sliced raw tomatoes, carrot curls and pickles, too, are colorful garnishes.

NEW ADVENTURES IN MAIN DISHES

Avery Island Deviled Shrimp (p. 271)—With an indescribably delicious sauce.

Baked Bean and Sausage Casserole (p. 275)—Colorful and tasty . . . combining two meats, three kinds of beans . . . can be made ahead.

Cheeseburger Pie (p. 274)—Flaky crust filled with a spicy meat loaf and topped with cheese.

Lima-Corn Barbecue (p. 264)—A skillet main dish that's easy on the cook.

Mushrooms à la Boeuf (p. 265)—Will thrill guests at brunch or luncheon.

Cabbage Rolls with Sour Cream Sauce

2 cups seasoned ground meat (leftover
    meat or ground beef)
¼ cup diced onion
2 tbsp. meat drippings
½ cup diced celery
1 cup cooked rice
1 tsp. horse-radish
1 tbsp. prepared mustard
1 egg, well beaten
6 to 8 large cabbage leaves
¼ cup tomato purée
½ cup water
1 cup commercial sour cream

Heat oven to 350° (mod.). Brown meat and onion in meat drippings in a heavy skillet over low heat. Remove from heat. Mix in thoroughly celery, rice, horse-radish, mustard and egg. Cook cabbage leaves for *3 min.* in boiling salted water. Drain. Place meat mixture on cabbage leaves. Roll and fasten with toothpicks. Place close together in greased baking dish, 11½x7½". Pour tomato purée and water over cabbage rolls. Cover and bake *30 min.* Remove cabbage rolls. Pour sour cream into liquid remaining in baking dish. Serve over cabbage rolls. *6 to 8 servings.*

Stuffed Green Peppers

4 large green peppers
1 cup boiling salted water (1½ tsp. salt)
1 can (8 oz.) tomato sauce
½ lb. ground beef
1 cup coarse dry bread or cracker crumbs
1 tsp. salt
¼ tsp. pepper
1 tbsp. chopped onion

Heat oven to 350° (mod.). Cut a thin slice from the stem end of each pepper. Wash outside and inside. Remove all seeds and membrane. Cook peppers in boiling salted water *5 min.* Drain. Mix rest of ingredients. Stuff peppers lightly with meat mixture. Stand upright in small baking dish. Bake *covered 45 min.,* uncover and bake *15 min.* longer. *4 servings.*

Scalloped Ham and Potatoes

Place slices or strips of baked ham (about 1½ cups) in layers when making Easy Scalloped Potatoes (*p. 427*).

Cube Steak Stew

Serve with lettuce salad, hot corn bread and chocolate pudding for a tasty, quick lunch.

4 cube steaks, cut in 2x½" strips
3 tbsp. flour
1½ tsp. salt
¼ tsp. pepper
½ tsp. flavor enhancer (monosodium glutamate)
3 tbsp. fat
1 large onion, thinly sliced
1 clove garlic, minced, if desired
4 medium potatoes, peeled and cut in eighths
1 tsp. salt
1 can (1 lb. 4 oz.) tomatoes (2½ cups)
1 can (8 oz.) tomato sauce
1 pkg. (10 oz.) frozen peas
½ medium green pepper, seeded and
    cut into ¼" strips

Dredge meat in mixture of flour, salt, pepper and flavor enhancer. Melt fat in large heavy kettle and brown meat. Add onion, garlic, potatoes, salt, tomatoes and tomato sauce. Heat to boil, lower heat and simmer, stirring occasionally, about *30 min.,* or until meat and vegetables are almost tender. Add peas and green pepper. Heat to boil, lower heat and cook *5 min.* longer, until peas are tender, but pepper still crisp. *6 servings.*

Lima-Corn Barbecue

Vegetables and water chestnuts added to barbecued beef make a zesty skillet main dish.

1½ lb. ground beef
3 tbsp. fat
1 medium onion, chopped
1 medium green pepper, chopped
1 can (10½ oz.) tomato soup
1 can (1 lb.) baby Lima beans (drain
    and reserve juice)
1 tbsp. chili powder
1 tbsp. prepared mustard
1 tbsp. Worcestershire sauce
1½ tsp. salt
1 can (1 lb.) whole kernel corn, drained
1 can (5 oz.) water chestnuts, thinly
    sliced (if desired)

Brown meat in fat. Add onion and pepper, cook just until tender. Mix soup, juice from beans, chili powder, mustard, Worcestershire sauce and salt. Stir into meat mixture. Cover; cook over slow heat *20 min.* Add Lima beans, corn and water chestnuts. Cook *10 min.* more. *6 servings.*

Jumbo Mushrooms à la Boeuf

A gourmet entree for company breakfast. Excellent when served on toast points for luncheons.

20 to 24 large fresh mushrooms (about
   2″ in diameter)
1 lb. ground round steak
1 egg
3 tbsp. cold water
½ tsp. lemon juice
1 tsp. A-1 sauce
1 medium onion, grated
1 tsp. salt
¼ tsp. pepper
½ cup beef stock or bouillon
Mushroom Sauce (*double recipe, p. 387*)

Heat oven to 350° (mod.). Wash and drain mushrooms. Remove stems and reserve for mushroom sauce. Sprinkle mushroom caps with salt and pepper. Mix remaining ingredients except sauce. Pile ground beef mixture generously into mushroom caps. Place in shallow baking dish or jelly roll pan. Bake *20 to 30 min.*, basting about every 5 min. with beef stock or bouillon. Serve 2 to 3 mushrooms per person, with Mushroom Sauce (allow at least ¼ cup sauce per person). Garnish with crisp bacon bits. *6 to 8 servings.*

Beef Curry

A typical Chinese curry with lean beef, mushrooms, tomato and onion.

1½ tbsp. vegetable oil
1 medium Spanish onion, sliced in rings
2 to 3 tsp. curry powder
1½ lb. lean flank steak, cut in 1″ cubes
½ lb. fresh mushrooms, sliced
1 tomato, diced
1 large clove garlic, minced
2 tsp. salt
2 tsp. sugar
about 2 cups water
2 tbsp. cornstarch
2 tbsp. water
3 cups cooked rice

Heat oil in heavy skillet. Sauté onion over medium heat, just until tender. Stir in curry powder; cook 1 min. Add beef cubes and next five ingredients in order listed. Continue cooking until beef cubes are lightly browned. Add enough boiling water to barely cover beef (about 2 cups). Cover skillet and simmer gently about 1½ hr., or until beef is extremely tender. Thicken with cornstarch-water mixture. Serve with rice. *4 to 6 servings.*

Sukiyaki

A traditional dish usually prepared at the dinner table in Japan. See color picture pp. 272-273.

1 lb. round steak
½ lb. mushrooms, thinly sliced
1 bunch green onions, cut in 1½″ lengths
3 stalks celery, sliced
2 large onions, thinly sliced
1 can (8 oz.) bamboo shoots, drained
3 tbsp. water
⅓ cup soy sauce
1 chicken bouillon cube dissolved in
   ½ cup hot water
3 cups raw spinach leaves
3 cups cooked rice

Cut round steak in pieces 2x½″ and brown. Add all ingredients except spinach and rice. Simmer until vegetables are tender, about *10 min.* Add spinach; cook *5 min.* Serve on rice. *4 servings.*

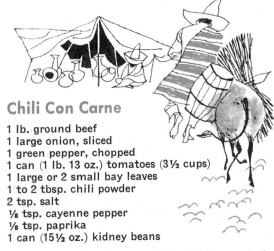

Chili Con Carne

1 lb. ground beef
1 large onion, sliced
1 green pepper, chopped
1 can (1 lb. 13 oz.) tomatoes (3½ cups)
1 large or 2 small bay leaves
1 to 2 tbsp. chili powder
2 tsp. salt
⅛ tsp. cayenne pepper
⅛ tsp. paprika
1 can (15½ oz.) kidney beans

Crumble and brown ground beef in heavy skillet (no fat added). Add onion and green pepper; cook until almost tender. Add tomatoes and seasonings. Cover. Simmer gently *2 hr.*, adding bean liquid and water a little at a time, if needed, to keep consistency of thick soup. Add kidney beans; heat through. Remove bay leaves. Serve in small bowls. *6 servings.*

Spicy Chili Con Carne

Happy addition to chili suggested by Barbara Arend, formerly of our staff, who says, "This is my husband's favorite for cool weather."

Make Chili Con Carne (*above*)—*except* add 3 whole cloves and ½ stick cinnamon with tomatoes and seasonings.

Chicken à la King

⅓ cup mushrooms (2-oz. can)
¼ cup chopped green pepper
¼ cup butter
¼ cup GOLD MEDAL Flour
½ tsp. salt
⅛ tsp. pepper
1 cup chicken broth
1 cup cream (20% butterfat)
1 cup diced cooked chicken*
¼ cup chopped pimiento

Sauté mushrooms and green pepper in butter. Blend in flour and seasonings. Cook over low heat, stirring until mixture is smooth, bubbly. Remove from heat. Slowly stir in broth and cream. Bring to boil over low heat, stirring constantly. Boil 1 min. Add chicken and pimiento. Continue cooking until meat is heated through. Serve hot in patty shells, pastry cases, biscuit rings or timbale cases; or over toast points, noodles or fluffy rice. *4 servings.*

Chicken Pie

Pastry for One-crust Pie *(pp. 337–339)*
6 tbsp. chicken fat or butter
6 tbsp. GOLD MEDAL Flour
½ tsp. salt
¼ tsp. pepper
1¾ cups chicken broth
⅔ cup cream or milk
2 cups cut-up cooked chicken*
¼ cup cut-up pimiento

Heat oven to 475° (very hot). Roll pastry and cut to fit top of 1½-qt. baking dish. Cut into 4 sections; place on baking sheet; prick. Bake *8 to 10 min. Reduce heat to 350°* (mod.). Melt fat over low heat. Blend in flour and seasonings. Cook over low heat, stirring until mixture is smooth, bubbly. Remove from heat. Stir in broth and cream. Bring to boil, stirring. Boil 1 min. Stir in chicken and pimiento. Pour into baking dish. Top with pastry. Bake *5 to 10 min. 6 servings.*

Ring Around the Chicken

Served to Dorothy Marsh of Good Housekeeping Magazine.

1½ cups GOLD MEDAL Flour
3 tsp. baking powder
¾ tsp. salt
½ to ¾ tsp. poultry seasoning
¼ cup shortening
½ cup plus 2 tbsp. milk

Heat oven to 450° (hot). Measure flour by dip-level-pour method or by sifting (*see p. 6*). Stir flour, baking powder, salt and poultry seasoning in bowl. Cut shortening in until mixture resembles meal. Mix milk in thoroughly. Spoon into an 8" ring mold. Bake *15 min.* Unmold on hot platter. Serve immediately with hot Chicken à la King (*above*) in center. *4 to 6 servings.*

*To prepare "cooked chicken" see *Stewed Chicken* (p. 322).

Chicken-Rice en Casserole

¼ cup chicken fat or butter
5 tbsp. flour
1½ tsp. salt
⅛ tsp. pepper
1 cup chicken broth
1½ cups milk
1½ cups cooked wild or white rice
  (½ cup uncooked)
2 cups cut-up cooked chicken*
¾ cup sliced mushrooms
⅓ cup chopped green pepper
2 tbsp. chopped pimiento
¼ cup slivered almonds

Heat oven to 350° (mod.). Melt fat in saucepan over low heat. Blend in flour, salt and pepper. Cook over low heat until smooth and bubbly. Remove from heat. Stir in chicken broth and milk. Bring to boil; boil 1 min., stirring constantly. Mix sauce with remaining ingredients. Pour into greased oblong baking dish, 10x6x1½". Bake *40 to 45 min. 8 servings.*

Chicken Casserole

Delicate, custardy consistency. Superb!

¼ lb. sliced fresh mushrooms or 1 can (4 oz.)
1 tbsp. butter
3 cups cut-up cooked chicken*
3 cups soft bread crumbs
1 cup milk
1 cup chicken broth
¼ cup finely chopped pimiento
2 eggs, beaten
2 tbsp. minced onion
seasonings (salt, pepper, celery salt, paprika)

Heat oven to 350° (mod.). Sauté mushrooms in butter. Mix with rest of ingredients. Pour into greased 2-qt. baking dish. Set in pan of water (1" deep). Bake *about 1½ hr.* Serve with Mushroom Sauce (*p. 387*) or Almond Velvet Sauce (*p. 388*). *6 servings.*

Chicken Curry

For a glamorous buffet . . . an East Indian dish.
See color picture p. 272.

3 tbsp. butter
¼ cup minced onion
1½ tsp. curry powder
3 tbsp. flour
¾ tsp. salt
¾ tsp. sugar
⅛ tsp. ground ginger
1 cup chicken broth (or 1 chicken bouillon cube
    dissolved in 1 cup hot water)
1 cup milk
2 cups diced cooked chicken
½ tsp. lemon juice
3 to 4 cups cooked rice (1 cup uncooked)

Melt butter over low heat in heavy saucepan. Sauté onion and curry in melted butter. Blend in flour and seasonings. Cook over low heat until mixture is smooth and bubbly. Remove from heat. Stir in chicken broth and milk. Bring to a boil, stirring constantly. Boil 1 min. Add chicken and lemon juice. Heat. *4 servings.*

Spoon Chicken Curry over the rice, then sprinkle accompaniments over the top as desired.

Curry Accompaniments

Chutney	Sieved hard-cooked eggs
Tomato wedges	Crisp bacon bits
Raisins	Sweet or sour pickles
Slivered salted almonds	Currant jelly
Chopped salted peanuts	Flaked coconut
Sautéed onion rings	India relish
Pineapple chunks	Sliced avocado

Shrimp Curry

Make Chicken Curry *(above)—except use* 2 cups cooked, cleaned shrimp in place of chicken.

Chicken Almond

As served in the Waikiki Room at Hotel Nicollet in Minneapolis, Minnesota.

2 cups diced cooked chicken
2 cups sliced celery
½ cup mushrooms, sliced
½ cup bamboo shoots, sliced very thin
½ cup sliced water chestnuts
½ cup Chinese pea pods, if available
1 tsp. salt
2 tbsp. cornstarch
1 tsp. salt
2 cups chicken broth
whole toasted almonds
4 to 5 cups cooked rice (1½ cups uncooked)

Sauté chicken in a little oil in a large skillet until lightly browned *(about 10 min.)*. Add celery, mushrooms, bamboo shoots, water chestnuts, pea pods and 1 tsp. salt. Sauté *5 min.* Mix cornstarch and 1 tsp. salt in saucepan. Stir in chicken broth gradually. Cook over medium heat, stirring constantly, until mixture thickens and boils. Boil 1 min. Add to other ingredients; stir. Cover and simmer *5 min.* more. Sprinkle with toasted almonds. Serve with hot fluffy rice and soy sauce. *6 servings.*

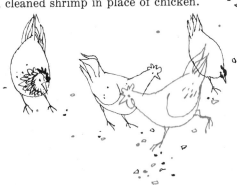

Chicken Chow Mein

¼ cup vegetable oil
1 tsp. salt
¼ tsp. pepper
2 cups sliced Chinese cabbage
3 cups thinly sliced celery
1 can (1 lb.) bean sprouts, drained
1 can (4 oz.) water chestnuts, sliced
2 tsp. sugar
2 cups chicken broth or water
2½ tbsp. cornstarch
¼ cup cold water
¼ cup soy sauce
2 cups sliced cooked chicken, cut in slivers
chow mein noodles

Heat oil, salt and pepper in deep skillet. Add cabbage, celery, bean sprouts, water chestnuts and sugar. Stir in chicken broth; cook about 10 min. Blend cornstarch, water and soy sauce. Add to vegetable mixture and stir until mixture thickens. Add chicken. Heat through. Serve over hot chow mein noodles. *4 to 6 servings.*

For *Chicken Chop Suey* serve on cooked white rice.

Chicken en Casserole

For this elegant dish, perfect for informal dinners and suppers, we are indebted to Miss Helen Traubel, illustrious star of grand opera and one of America's most beloved entertainers.

½ cup butter
1 clove garlic, quartered
4 to 5-lb. roasting chicken, disjointed
1 cup GOLD MEDAL Flour
2 tsp. salt
1 tsp. pepper
2 medium onions, thinly sliced
2 cups chopped celery
3 small carrots, chopped
½ cup fresh mushrooms, sliced
2 tbsp. minced parsley
pinch of thyme and marjoram
dash of Worcestershire sauce
6 peppercorns, coarsely cracked
1 bay leaf, crumbled

Heat oven to 350° (mod.). Put butter and garlic in large skillet over low heat. When butter bubbles, remove garlic. Dip chicken pieces in mixture of flour, salt and pepper. Brown chicken slowly in butter and transfer to a 3-qt. baking dish. Cover. Bake *1 hr.* During the last 10 min. of baking (using the same skillet), sauté onions, celery, carrots and mushrooms until slightly browned. Stir in remaining ingredients. Simmer a few minutes to blend flavors. Season to taste with salt. Remove chicken from oven. Pour vegetable mixture over chicken. Cover and return to oven for *another 30 min.* Serve hot from baking dish. *6 to 8 servings.*

Scalloped Chicken

2½ cups finely cut cooked chicken
2½ cups rich chicken gravy
1 cup fine dry bread crumbs

Heat oven to 350° (mod.). In greased 1½-qt. baking dish, place all ingredients in alternate layers until all is used. Dot with butter. Bake *20 to 30 min.* Serve hot. *6 servings.*

Chicken Jambalaya

A popular one-dish meal in the Cajun country.

3-lb. frying chicken
½ lb. ham, cubed
3 tbsp. vegetable oil
1 cup chopped green pepper (1 large)
1 cup chopped onion (1 large)
1 clove garlic, minced
2 tsp. salt
2 tsp. Worcestershire sauce
¼ tsp. thyme
¼ tsp. Tabasco
¼ tsp. black pepper
3 cups chicken broth (canned or cubes)
1½ cups uncooked rice

Cut chicken in legs, thighs, breasts, etc., leaving meat on bones. Brown chicken and ham in oil. Remove meat. Sauté pepper, onion and garlic 5 min. over low heat. Add seasonings and broth. Simmer *10 min.* Add rice and meat. Cover and cook over low heat *25 min.* Fluff rice with fork and cook *5 min.* longer. *8 servings.*

Sea Food Jambalaya: Make Chicken Jambalaya (*above*)—*except* substitute 1 pt. fresh or 1 can (12 oz.) frozen oysters, thawed, and 1 lb. peeled, cooked shrimp for chicken.

Chicken Parisian

Our adaptation of the specialty of the house of the popular French restaurant in New York, Divan Parisien.

sliced cooked chicken (about 2 chicken breasts)
2 pkg. (10 oz. each) frozen or
  2 lb. fresh broccoli, cooked
1 cup grated Parmesan cheese
1 can (4 oz.) button mushrooms
3 tbsp. butter
3 tbsp. flour
¼ tsp. salt
⅛ tsp. pepper
1½ cups milk
¼ tsp. nutmeg
⅓ cup mayonnaise
⅓ cup whipping cream, whipped
¾ tsp. Worcestershire sauce

Place slices of cooked chicken in 6 individual ramekins. On top of each slice of chicken place several pieces of broccoli. Sprinkle with half of the cheese. Top with mushrooms. Melt butter over low heat in a heavy saucepan. Blend in flour, salt and pepper. Cook over low heat, stirring until mixture is smooth and bubbly. Remove from heat. Stir in milk. Bring to boil, stirring constantly. Boil 1 min. Blend in rest of ingredients. Pour over broccoli and sprinkle with remaining cheese. Broil until brown and bubbly (*3 to 5 min.*). *4 to 6 servings.*

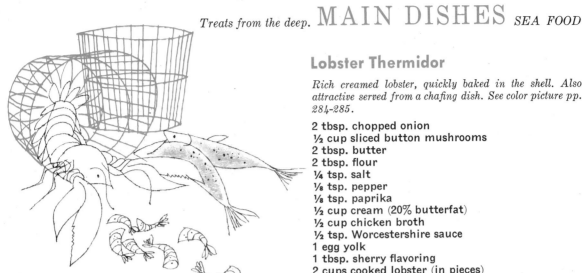

Sea Food à la Newburg

One of the dishes that helped build the fame of Delmonico's in New York. Created by Mr. Wenburg, and originally named for him—later the first three letters were reversed.

2 cups hot Medium White Sauce (*p. 387*)
2 egg yolks, beaten
1 tbsp. sherry flavoring or lemon juice
2 cups cooked sea food, in large pieces

Mix white sauce and egg yolks carefully. Just before serving, stir in flavoring and sea food. Serve hot over hot rich biscuits or toast points or in patty shells. Garnish with parsley and pimiento strips. *6 to 8 servings.*

Creole Shrimp

Prize recipe from Mrs. R. E. Smith of Redgate Plantation, Jeanerette, Louisiana.

½ cup minced onion
2 tbsp. butter
1 bay leaf, crushed
¼ cup diced celery
1 tsp. minced parsley
½ cup chopped green pepper
dash of cayenne pepper
1 tsp. salt
1 can (6 oz.) tomato paste
2½ cups water
2 cups cooked shrimp (two 7-oz. cans)

Sauté onion in butter. Blend in rest of ingredients except shrimp. Cook slowly, stirring occasionally, *about 30 min.* Stir in shrimp and heat. Serve on hot cooked rice. *6 servings.*

NOTE: When using uncooked (green) shrimp, do not precook; cook in the sauce only until pink (*10 min.*).

Sea Food Salads See pp. 381-382.

Lobster Thermidor

Rich creamed lobster, quickly baked in the shell. Also attractive served from a chafing dish. See color picture pp. 284-285.

2 tbsp. chopped onion
½ cup sliced button mushrooms
2 tbsp. butter
2 tbsp. flour
¼ tsp. salt
⅛ tsp. pepper
⅛ tsp. paprika
½ cup cream (20% butterfat)
½ cup chicken broth
½ tsp. Worcestershire sauce
1 egg yolk
1 tbsp. sherry flavoring
2 cups cooked lobster (in pieces)

Heat oven to 450° (hot). Sauté onion and mushrooms in butter. Blend in flour and seasonings. Cook over low heat until bubbly. Remove from heat and stir in cream, chicken broth and Worcestershire sauce. Bring to boil, stirring constantly. Boil 1 min. Add egg yolk, flavoring and lobster. Place mixture in shell of lobster or individual baking dishes and sprinkle with 3 tbsp. fine buttered cracker or dry bread crumbs. Bake *5 min. 6 servings.*

Cheese Pinwheels on Crabmeat

2 tbsp. chopped green pepper
2 tbsp. butter
2 tbsp. flour
⅛ tsp. pepper
1 cup chicken broth (1 cup water plus
    1 chicken bouillon cube)
1 can (6½ oz.) crabmeat, flaked
2 tbsp. sliced celery
2 tbsp. finely chopped onion
1 tsp. capers

Heat oven to 375° (quick mod.). Sauté green pepper in butter until tender. Blend in flour and pepper. Cook over low heat, stirring until mixture is smooth, bubbly. Remove from heat. Stir in chicken broth. Bring to boil, stirring constantly. Boil 1 min. Add crabmeat, celery, onion and capers. Turn into 1½-qt. baking dish; cover with Cheese Pinwheels (*below*). Sprinkle with 1 tbsp. grated Parmesan cheese. Bake *25 to 30 min.*, or until pinwheels are golden brown. *5 to 6 servings.*

Cheese Pinwheels: Make ½ recipe for Biscuits (*p. 76*). Roll dough into a 7″ square. Spread with 1 tbsp. butter, melted, and sprinkle with ½ cup grated sharp Cheddar cheese. Roll as for jelly roll. Seal edge. Slice into 10 pinwheels. Place on crabmeat mixture.

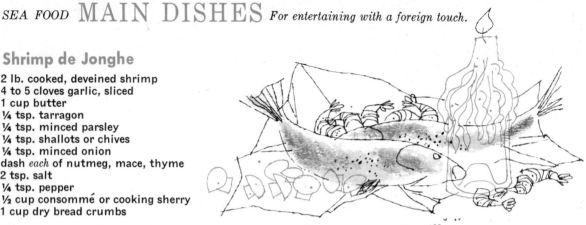

Shrimp de Jonghe

2 lb. cooked, deveined shrimp
4 to 5 cloves garlic, sliced
1 cup butter
¼ tsp. tarragon
¼ tsp. minced parsley
¼ tsp. shallots or chives
¼ tsp. minced onion
dash *each* of nutmeg, mace, thyme
2 tsp. salt
¼ tsp. pepper
½ cup consommé or cooking sherry
1 cup dry bread crumbs

Heat oven to 400° (mod. hot). Place shrimp in 8 individual baking dishes. Cook garlic in butter until butter browns; remove garlic. Add herbs, seasonings and consommé to butter. Remove ¼ cup butter mixture and toss with bread crumbs. Pour remaining butter mixture over shrimp. Top with buttered crumbs. Bake *15 min.* Before serving garnish with parsley sprigs, if desired.

NOTE: If shallots are not available, increase minced onion to ½ tsp.

Cellini Pies

A sophisticated luncheon dish.

Golden Pastry (*below*)
1 small clove garlic, minced
1 medium onion, minced
4 thin slices Swiss cheese
4 small tomatoes
12 anchovies, cut up
capers, if desired
1 cup whipping cream (35% butterfat)

Heat oven to 400° (mod. hot). Cut rounds of pastry 1½" larger than inverted 4" pie pans. Place loosely in pans; cover edges with 1½" strip of aluminum foil to prevent excessive browning. Spread over pastry a mixture of garlic and onion. Cover with cheese slices. Slice tomatoes and dip in flour. Place over cheese. Sprinkle with anchovies and capers. Pour cream over pies. Bake *25 to 30 min.* Remove foil strips 15 min. before end of baking period. *4 servings.*

Golden Pastry

Measure 1 cup GOLD MEDAL Flour by dip-level-pour method or by sifting (*see p. 6*). Blend flour, 1 tbsp. sugar, ½ tsp. salt. Cut in 6 tbsp. butter. Mix 1 egg yolk, 1½ tbsp. lemon juice, 1 tbsp. water. Blend into dry ingredients. Refrigerate. Roll on floured board.

Pompano en Papillote

Poached fish in a mushroom sauce with shrimp, baked in an envelope of aluminum foil or parchment. Worked out by Esther MacMillan, when on our staff, after she enjoyed it in New Orleans.

1 lb. pompano fillets (2 fillets) (lake trout,
   pike, halibut or red snapper may be used)
New Orleans Mushroom Sauce (*below*)
¾ cup cooked, deveined shrimp (about 12)

Cut fillets in half. Poach fillets (*p. 327*) about 3 min. Reserve ½ cup fish stock.

Heat oven to 350° (mod.). For each serving: cut a 12x8" rectangle of heavy duty aluminum foil or parchment (butter on both sides). Place 3 tbsp. mushroom sauce on half of the rectangle. Place half a fillet on sauce. Top with 3 shrimp. Cover with more sauce. Fold other half of foil over, close and seal by folding edges together. Place on baking sheet. Bake *20 min.* Serve, case and all, on dinner plates. Each person unwraps his own by cutting slits in foil or parchment and folding back. *4 servings.*

New Orleans Mushroom Sauce

4 tbsp. butter
3 tbsp. flour
¼ tsp. salt
⅛ tsp. pepper
⅛ tsp. celery salt
½ cup milk
½ cup fish stock in which 1 chicken bouillon cube
   has been dissolved
1 can (4 oz.) sliced mushrooms

Sauté mushrooms with their liquor in 1 tbsp. melted butter until liquor is absorbed. Melt remaining butter over low heat. Blend in flour and seasonings. Cook over low heat, stirring until mixture is smooth and bubbly. Remove from heat. Stir in milk. Bring to boil; boil 1 min., stirring constantly. Add fish stock and cook until thickened. Stir sautéed mushrooms into sauce.

Avery Island Deviled Shrimp

Avery Island, famous as the home of Tabasco and a fabulous bird sanctuary. The "Deviled Shrimp" is a specialty of the McIlhenny family of Avery Island. See color picture p. 284.

1 lb. deveined fresh shrimp (or thawed frozen)
1 egg, slightly beaten
¼ tsp. salt
½ cup fine bread crumbs
¼ cup butter
Deviled Shrimp Sauce (*below*)
3 cups hot cooked rice (1 cup uncooked)

Roll shrimp in mixture of egg and salt, then in bread crumbs. Brown in butter over medium heat about 10 min., until pink. Remove shrimp and keep warm while preparing Deviled Shrimp Sauce. Arrange shrimp on rice and pour sauce over all. *About 4 servings.*

Deviled Shrimp Sauce

1 medium onion, finely chopped (1 cup)
1 clove garlic, minced
2 tbsp. butter
1 can (10½ oz.) consommé
½ cup water
2 tbsp. steak sauce
1½ tsp. mustard
½ tsp. salt
¼ to ½ tsp. Tabasco
juice of 1 small lemon (1 to 2 tbsp.)

Sauté onion and garlic in butter over medium heat until tender. Add remaining ingredients except lemon juice. Bring to boil and simmer *15 min.,* or until volume is reduced to ½ (about 1 cup). Add lemon juice.

Scalloped Tuna

"A perfectly grand dish for women's luncheons!" according to a former member of our staff, Ruby Nelson (Mrs. Charles W. Turner of Delmar, New York), who first made it in our test kitchen.

2 cans (7 oz. each) tuna, in large pieces
2 cups crushed cheese crackers or potato chips
3 cups Medium White Sauce (*p. 387*)
¾ cup sliced ripe olives or sautéed mushrooms

Heat oven to 350° (mod.). Arrange ingredients in alternate layers in buttered 1½-qt. baking dish. Finish with a sprinkling of the crackers. Bake *35 min.* Serve hot. *6 servings.*

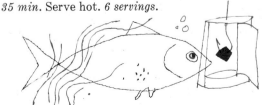

Sea Food Symphony

Flakes of white halibut, curls of pink shrimp . . . in tune with Rich Cheese Sauce.

2 lb. halibut, fresh or thawed frozen
2 lb. fresh green shrimp, cooked and deveined
  or two cans (4½ oz. each) shrimp
2 cups Rich Cheese Sauce (*p. 387*)

Poach halibut (*p. 327*). Drain fish well, flake it and place in oblong baking dish, 11½x7½x1½". Spread shrimp over halibut. Cover fish and shrimp with cheese sauce and sprinkle lightly with paprika. Place baking dish under broiler until sauce bubbles and top browns. *6 to 8 servings.*

Eggs Foo Yung

1 medium green pepper, chopped
1 medium onion, chopped
1 cup cooked deveined shrimp, chopped
1 can (5 oz.) sliced water chestnuts,
  well drained
1 cup bean sprouts, well drained
2 to 3 tbsp. soy sauce
5 eggs

Heat just enough fat or oil to cover bottom of heavy skillet. Sauté green pepper and onion until tender. Stir in shrimp, water chestnuts, bean sprouts and soy sauce. Heat mixture. Remove from heat. Beat eggs until thick, about 5 min. Blend shrimp-vegetable mixture into eggs. Heat additional oil or fat to cover bottom of skillet. Pour mixture from soup ladle or cup into skillet forming patties. When brown on one side, turn over. Patties may be kept warm until serving time between folds of towel in a warm oven. Serve with Hot Soy Sauce (*below*). *Makes about sixteen 2½" patties.*

Hot Soy Sauce: Make paste of 2 tbsp. cornstarch and ¼ cup cold water. Stir into 2 cups boiling soup stock, bouillon or consommé and 2 tbsp. soy sauce. Cook, stirring constantly, until clear and thickened.

271

WITH A FOREIGN FLAVOR

Sukiyaki from Japan, page 265
Chicken Curry from India, page 267
Enchiladas from Mexico, page 276

Welsh Rabbit *(Welsh Rarebit)*

The story goes that long ago in Wales the peasants, not allowed to hunt on the estates of noblemen, served melted cheese as a substitute for rabbit, popular prize of the hunt. It became a famous dish of Ye Olde Cheshire Inn, meeting place of England's illustrious penmen. There rare wits from Ben Jonson to Charles Dickens conversed copiously while enjoying this specialty of the house.

4 cups sliced nippy Cheddar
   cheese (1 lb.)
¾ cup cream (20% butterfat)
½ tsp. mustard

½ tsp. Worcestershire sauce
¼ tsp. salt
dash of pepper

Melt cheese over hot, not boiling, water. (Never let cheese boil.) Gradually stir in rest of ingredients. Serve at once on crisp crackers or toast with pickles. *6 servings.*

Welsh Rabbit De Luxe

Make Welsh Rabbit *(above)—except* use ginger ale in place of cream.

Welsh Rabbit with Kidney Beans

Melt in chafing dish or top of double boiler over hot water 2 cups diced Cheddar cheese (½ lb.). Stir in 2½ cups heated cooked kidney beans with liquid (1 lb. 4 oz.) and ½ cup diced green pepper. Keep hot. Serve on crisp toast or crackers.

Pink Bunny

"This is an easy Sunday supper dish for busy mothers," says Inez-Muriel McLaughlin, formerly of our staff.

Heat 1¼ cups condensed tomato soup (or seasoned cooked tomatoes). Place over hot water and stir in 2 cups shredded Cheddar cheese (½ lb.). Remove from heat and blend in 1 egg, slightly beaten, ¼ tsp. dry mustard, ¼ tsp. Worcestershire sauce. Serve hot on toast or crackers. Garnish with pickles. *4 to 6 servings.*

Brer Rabbit with Corn

Make Pink Bunny *(above)—except* add 1 cup whole kernel corn with tomato and cheese.

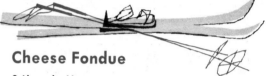

Cheese Fondue

3 tbsp. butter
3 cups bread cubes (5 slices)
1 cup shredded sharp Cheddar cheese (¼ lb.)
1 large egg, beaten
1 cup milk
½ tsp. salt
dash of pepper
⅛ tsp. mustard

Heat oven to 350° (mod.). Melt butter in skillet. Add bread cubes; stir until lightly browned. Place in greased 1-qt. baking dish in alternate layers with cheese. Mix rest of ingredients and pour over. Sprinkle with paprika. Set in pan of water (1″ deep). Bake *40 min.* Serve hot. *4 servings.*

Cheeseburger Pie

Make Pastry for 9″ One-crust Pie *(pp. 337–339).*

1 lb. ground beef
½ tsp. oregano
1 tsp. salt
¼ tsp. pepper
¼ cup chopped onion
¼ cup chopped green pepper, if desired
½ cup fine dry bread crumbs
half of 8-oz. can tomato sauce
Cheese Topping *(below)*

Heat oven to 425° (hot). Brown beef in small amount of fat. Mix in rest of ingredients except topping. Spread in pastry-lined pie pan. Spread Cheese Topping over filling. Bake *about 30 min.* Serve in wedges with sauce (equal amounts of chili sauce and remaining tomato sauce). *6 to 8 servings.*

Cheese Topping: Mix 8-oz. wedge mellow Cheddar cheese, grated, 1 egg, beaten, ¼ cup milk and ½ tsp. *each* salt, dry mustard, Worcestershire sauce.

274

Boston Baked Beans

Really "Indian" Baked Beans, originated by the Indians three centuries ago—baked in earthen pots as we bake them today. In early New England, they were traditional Saturday night fare.

2 cups navy or pea beans
½ lb. salt pork (scalded, rind scraped)
1 slice onion
3 tbsp. molasses
2 tsp. salt
⅛ tsp. pepper
¼ tsp. mustard

Soak beans overnight in cold water. Simmer in same water until tender, *1 to 2 hr.* Drain, save liquor. *Heat oven to 300° (slow).* Place beans, pork and onion in 2-qt. bean pot in layers. Combine molasses and seasonings; pour over beans. Add enough bean liquor to cover. Cover. Bake *8 hr.* Remove cover last half of baking, add a little boiling water if beans seem dry. Serve hot with hot Steamed Brown Bread (*p. 96*). *6 servings.*

Country-Baked Limas

2 cups dried Lima beans
¼ lb. bacon, cut in small pieces
1 medium onion, sliced
¼ cup light molasses
2 tbsp. chili sauce
1½ tbsp. brown sugar
2 tsp. salt
1 tsp. mustard
1 cup tomato juice

Wash beans thoroughly and soak overnight in 1 qt. cold water. Simmer in same water about *½ hr.* Drain, reserving liquor. *Heat oven to 250° (slow).* Place beans, bacon and onion in bean pot in layers. Combine remaining ingredients; pour over beans, adding enough liquor to cover beans. Cover and bake *4 to 6 hr.*, until tender. Uncover last ½ hr. to brown, if desired. *8 servings.*

Vegetarian Baked Beans

This recipe shows how tasty baked beans can be without meat.

Heat oven to 350° (mod.). Sauté ⅓ cup minced onion in 2 tbsp. butter until yellow. Stir in 1 can (1 lb.) vegetarian baked beans, 2 tbsp. dark molasses and ¼ cup catsup. Pour into 1-qt. baking dish. Bake *25 min. 4 servings.*

Baked Bean and Sausage Casserole

Our appetizing adaptation of the French "cassoulet" which includes sausage, a second meat, beans, tomato and a variety of seasonings.

1 pkg. (10 oz.) frozen Lima beans
3 cans (1 lb. each) baked beans
2 cans (1 lb. 4 oz. each) kidney beans, drained)
1 lb. Italian link sausage or pork link sausage
½ lb. smoked ham, cut in ½" cubes
1 tbsp. salt
½ tsp. pepper
½ tsp. mustard
1 can (8 oz.) tomato sauce
½ cup catsup
¼ cup brown sugar (packed)
1 medium onion, chopped

Cook Lima beans *10 min.* (see pkg.). Drain; mix with baked beans and kidney beans. Place sausage in skillet; add small amount of water. Cover and simmer *5 min.* Drain; pan fry until brown. Don't prick. Cut each sausage into 2 or 3 pieces. *Heat oven to 400° (mod. hot).* Mix sausage, ham and beans. Combine seasonings, tomato sauce, catsup, brown sugar and onion; add to beans. Pour into 3-qt. baking dish. Bake *uncovered 1 hr. 10 to 12 servings.*

Bayou Red Beans and Rice

Years ago a pot of red beans was set at the back of the stove to simmer on washday Mondays. Now many New Orleans hotels feature this at lunch.

1 lb. dried red kidney beans
1 qt. water
1 ham bone with ham*
1 large onion, chopped
¼ cup chopped celery and leaves
1 tsp. salt
½ tsp. Tabasco
3 cups hot cooked rice

Soak beans overnight in water. Pour into large heavy pan or Dutch oven. Add remaining ingredients except rice. Simmer *3 hr.* or until beans are tender. Remove ham bone, cut off meat and add to beans. Add water when necessary during cooking. Water should barely cover beans at end of cooking time. Remove 1 cup beans and mash to a paste. Add to beans and stir until liquid is thickened. Serve hot over white rice. *6 servings.*

*Plan to have 1 cup chopped ham to cook with beans.

Mexican Enchiladas

Tortillas dipped in chili-flavored tomato sauce, filled, rolled, covered with more sauce. See color picture p. 273.

Dip Tortillas (*below*) into melted fat; then dip into Enchiladas Sauce (*below*). Place large spoonful of Tortilla Filling (*below*) on each and roll up. Arrange in serving dish or baking dish. Cover with hot sauce and sprinkle with remaining filling. Serve at once or reheat before serving at 375° (quick mod.). *6 servings.*

Tortillas

1 cup GOLD MEDAL Flour
½ cup corn meal
¼ tsp. salt
1 egg
1½ cups cold water

Measure flour by dip-level-pour method or by sifting (*see p. 6*). Combine ingredients in bowl. Beat with rotary beater until smooth. Spoon 3 tbsp. batter onto a mod. hot ungreased griddle to make a very thin 6″ pancake. Turn tortillas when edges begin to look dry, not brown. Bake other side; keep warm in covered pan. *Makes 12 tortillas.*

Tortilla Filling

2 cups grated sharp Cheddar cheese
1 cup minced onion
½ tsp. salt

Mix ingredients thoroughly.

Enchiladas Sauce

2 tbsp. minced onion
2 tbsp. fat or drippings
1 tbsp. flour
1 can (1 lb. 4 oz.) tomatoes, drained
1 clove garlic, minced
2 tsp. chili powder
1 tsp. salt
¼ tsp. Tabasco

Brown onion in hot fat. Stir in flour. Then stir in rest of ingredients. Add about ½ cup tomato juice (drained from tomatoes) to make a sauce of medium thickness. Let simmer until thickened.

NOTE: Enchiladas fit perfectly in 11½x7½x1½″ baking dish or 13x9½x2″ pan. They may be kept hot in the oven for some time if covered with aluminum foil.

Italian Pizza

The variety of pizza toppings is limited only by your imagination. Why not try: browned ground beef, tuna, shrimp, bacon, sliced franks, ham or salami; ricotta or Cheddar cheese.

Dough

¼ pkg. active dry yeast (½ tsp.)
¾ cup plus 2 tbsp. warm water
  (not hot—110 to 115°)
3 to 3¼ cups GOLD MEDAL Flour

Dissolve yeast in water. Measure flour by dip-level-pour method or by sifting (*see p. 6*). Blend in flour. Knead on lightly floured surface. Place in greased bowl, turn to grease top. Cover and let rise in warm place (85°) until double (1½ to 2 hr.). *Heat oven to 425° (hot).* Divide in half. Roll into two 14x10″ rectangles or two 14″ circles. Place on pizza pan, oblong pan (shallow sides) or baking sheet. Roll edge.

Topping

3 cups tomato sauce (three 8-oz. cans)
½ tsp. oregano
½ tsp. rosemary
½ tsp. salt
¼ tsp. pepper
¼ cup vegetable oil
⅔ cup chopped mushrooms (4 oz.), sautéed
  in 1 tbsp. butter
¼ cup grated Parmesan cheese
1 lb. Italian sausage, browned and drained,
  or 2 links pepperoni
1 can (1 oz.) anchovies, if desired
2 cups grated Mozzarella cheese

Combine tomato sauce and seasonings; spread half over each pizza. Sprinkle oil over pizzas. Spread half the remaining ingredients over each pizza. Bake *25 to 30 min.* (refrigerate second pizza while first one bakes). Cut in wedges or squares and serve hot. *6 to 8 servings.*

Hamburger Stroganoff

Popular ground beef version of the famous Russian meat,
Beef Stroganoff (p. 304).

½ cup minced onion
1 clove garlic, minced
¼ cup butter
1 lb. ground beef
2 tbsp. flour
2 tsp. salt
¼ tsp. pepper
1 lb. fresh mushrooms or 1 can (8 oz.), sliced
1 can (10½ oz.) cream of chicken soup
1 cup commercial sour cream
2 tbsp. minced parsley
hot boiled noodles (5 to 6 oz. uncooked) *(p. 281)*

Sauté onion and garlic in butter over medium heat.
Add meat and brown. Add flour, salt, pepper and
mushrooms. Cook *5 min.* Add soup, simmer uncovered *10 min.* Stir in sour cream. Heat through.
Sprinkle with parsley. Serve with noodles. *4 to 6
servings.*

Connecticut Supper

*This tasty beef-potato casserole with mushroom-sour
cream gravy earned Mrs. J. W. Canfield, Newington,
Connecticut, a prize in the Larro Recipe Round-up.*

2 large onions, sliced
2 tbsp. fat
2 lb. beef chuck, cut in 1″ cubes
1 cup water
2 large potatoes, sliced ⅛″ thick
1 can (10½ oz.) cream of mushroom soup
1 cup commercial sour cream
1¼ cups milk
1 tsp. salt
¼ tsp. pepper
1 cup grated Cheddar cheese
½ cup crushed WHEATIES (1¼ cups uncrushed)

Brown onions in fat. Add meat and water. Cover.
Simmer *50 min.* Heat oven to *350°* (mod.). Pour
into baking dish, 13x9½x2″. Place potato slices
over meat. Blend soup, cream, milk, salt and
pepper. Pour evenly over top. Sprinkle with
cheese and WHEATIES. Bake *uncovered 1½ hr.,* or
until done. *6 to 8 servings.*

Fiesta Tamale Pie

Picturesque dish from Old Mexico.

1 small onion, minced
1 clove garlic, minced
1 tbsp. fat
1 lb. ground beef
¼ lb. bulk pork sausage
1 can (1 lb.) tomatoes
1 can (1 lb.) whole kernel corn, drained
1½ tsp. salt
1½ tsp. chili powder
18 pitted ripe olives
1 cup corn meal
1 cup milk
2 eggs, well beaten
1 cup grated Cheddar cheese

Heat oven to 350° (mod.). Sauté onion and garlic
in hot fat until yellow. Add meat and brown.
Pour off excess fat. Add vegetables and seasonings; bring to boil. Pour mixture into square baking dish, 9x9x1¾″. Press olives into mixture.
Combine corn meal, milk and eggs. Spoon over
filling. Sprinkle with cheese. Bake *1 hr. 6 to 8
servings.*

Philadelphia Scrapple

*Meat-filled and meat-flavored crispy fried mush from
Pennsylvania Dutch cookery.*

2 lb. lean boneless pork
2 qt. boiling salted water (2 tsp. salt)
1½ cups corn meal
2 cups cold water
¼ tsp. pepper
¼ tsp. savory and sage, mixed
salt to taste

Simmer pork in boiling salted water until meat is
very tender, *2 hr.* With fork, shred the cooked
pork into fine pieces. Bring to boil 1 qt. of the
stock. Mix corn meal and cold water. Stir into
boiling stock. Cook, stirring until thick. Add seasonings. Stir the meat into corn meal mush and
cook *5 min.* Pour into buttered loaf pan, 9x5x3″.
Chill until firm. Slice ½″ thick. Brown on each
side (for crispness, first dip slices in flour). Serve
hot . . . plain or with butter and syrup. *8 servings.*

HOW TO COOK WHITE RICE
(1 cup uncooked white rice equals 3 to 4 cups cooked)

METHOD I

A quick method for boiling rice that gives soft fluffy grains.

1 cup uncooked rice
1 tbsp. salt
8 cups water (2 qt.)

Add salt to water in large kettle; bring to rapid boil. Slowly add rice, keeping water boiling. Boil rapidly until tender, *15 to 20 min.* (Kernels feel soft when pressed between thumb and forefinger.) Occasionally lift with fork to prevent sticking; do not stir. Drain; rinse, if desired. Serve immediately.

TWO WAYS TO KEEP COOKED RICE HOT

First, run boiling water through it to separate the kernels, then . . .

1. Cover cooked rice with cloth and place over pan of hot water.

2. Place in square or oblong baking pan; cover with aluminum foil and place in slow oven. (If rice is wet, do not cover. Let dry in oven *5 to 10 min.*; fluff with fork.)

TWO WAYS TO REHEAT COOKED RICE

1. Heat over hot water, in double boiler, *about 10 min.*, or until rice is hot and fluffy.

2. Place in heavy pan with close-fitting cover. Sprinkle water over rice, using about 1 tbsp. water to 2 cups rice. Cover; heat over low heat *5 to 8 min.*, until hot and fluffy.

Rice Verte *(Fluffy Green Rice)*

Prepare cooked rice *(above)*. Toss together with any of the following greens, using 1 cup greens for 3 cups cooked rice: chopped parsley or spinach; tiny water cress sprigs, chopped; green olives, sliced; scallions, sliced and sautéed in butter until crisp.

▶ **ALL YOU HAVE TO DO**

To Make a Rice Ring: lightly press 4 cups fluffy cooked rice (1 cup uncooked) into well greased 9" ring mold. Keep hot until time to serve. Unmold on hot platter and fill center with creamed sea food or chicken and mushrooms. Serve hot. *8 servings.*

METHOD II

A method for steaming rice . . . it is cooked over low, even heat. Gives big, separate grains.

1 cup uncooked rice
1 tsp. salt
1 ½ cups cold water

Combine all ingredients in heavy saucepan with close-fitting lid. Bring to brisk boil; cover. Turn heat *very low* and continue cooking about *30 min.* (*25 min.* for long grain). Do not lift lid, as this lets steam escape. Turn off heat. Fluff rice with fork. Let stand, uncovered, 2 or 3 min.

Brown Rice

Nut-like flavor and so nutritious.

Brown rice may be cooked by either Method I or II *(above)*—except, with Method II, increase water to 1¾ to 2 cups and increase cooking time to *40 min.*

Green Rice

From Mrs. R. E. Boutell, who likes to serve this with ham or chicken.

3 cups fluffy cooked rice
   (1 cup uncooked)
1 cup chopped spinach or parsley or combination
2 eggs, well beaten
1 cup milk
1 tsp. Worcestershire sauce
1 ¼ tsp. salt
½ tbsp. grated onion or scant ¼ tsp. onion powder
¼ cup butter, melted
½ cup grated sharp cheese

Heat oven to 325° (slow mod.). Toss together rice and spinach. Add eggs, milk, Worcestershire sauce, salt and onion; stir. Pour into 10x6x1½" oblong baking dish or 2-qt. baking dish. Sprinkle with butter and cheese. Bake *30 to 40 min.* *8 servings.*

Curried Rice

Wonderful with creamed shrimp, chicken or ham.

Sauté 1 tbsp. minced onion in 2 tbsp. butter until yellow. Gently stir in 3 cups fluffy cooked rice *(above)*, ¼ tsp. salt, ¼ tsp. pepper, 1 tsp. curry powder. Serve hot with any creamed meat or sea food. *6 to 8 servings.*

278

Spanish Rice

6 slices bacon, cut up
¼ cup finely chopped onion
¼ cup chopped green pepper
3 cups cooked rice (1 cup uncooked or
    1⅓ cups precooked rice)
2 cups cooked tomatoes (1 lb.)
1½ tsp. salt
⅛ tsp. pepper

In a large skillet: Fry bacon until crisp; remove from skillet, draining off most of fat. Add onion and green pepper to bacon fat; cook over medium heat until onion is yellow. Add bacon and remaining ingredients; cook uncovered over low heat about *15 min.*, until flavors are blended and mixture is hot. *4 to 6 servings.*

In the oven: Heat oven to 400° (mod. hot). Fry bacon until crisp draining off most of fat. Remove to 1½-qt. baking dish and whisk bacon around to grease dish. Add onion and green pepper to bacon fat; cook until onion is yellow. Combine all ingredients in baking dish. Sprinkle ¼ cup grated Cheddar cheese over top. Bake *25 to 30 min.*

Frankfurter Spanish Rice

Make Spanish Rice (*above*)—*except* use ½ lb. frankfurters (cut in pieces) in place of bacon. Add 1 clove garlic, chopped, 2 tsp. Worcestershire sauce, 1 tsp. chili powder, ¼ tsp. cloves, ½ tsp. cayenne pepper with other seasonings.

Indian Pilaf

An excellent accompaniment for beef . . . adapted from a famous dish of exotic India.

1 cup long grain rice, uncooked
1 clove garlic, minced
⅓ cup butter
2½ to 3 cups beef bouillon
¼ cup raisins
2 tbsp. toasted slivered almonds

In heavy 9″ skillet, sauté rice and garlic in butter until rice turns orange. Remove from heat and add 2½ cups bouillon. Cover with tight-fitting lid or aluminum foil which fits securely around edge of skillet. Add more bouillon if needed after 30 min. of cooking. Cook *45 to 50 min.*, or until liquid is absorbed and rice is tender. Remove from heat, uncover, sprinkle with raisins and almonds. Serve immediately. *4 servings.*

Texas Hash

One of the popular supper dishes served by Georgia Kelley of Marine-on-the-St. Croix. The recipe was given to her sister by a Texas friend, now a leading hostess of Washington, D. C.

3 large onions, sliced
1 large green pepper, minced
3 tbsp. fat
1 lb. ground beef
2 cups cooked tomatoes (1 lb.)
½ cup uncooked rice
1 tsp. chili powder
2 tsp. salt
⅛ tsp. pepper

Heat oven to 350° (mod.). Sauté onion and green pepper in fat until onions are yellow. Add meat and fry until mixture falls apart. Stir in rest of ingredients. Pour into greased 2-qt. baking dish. Cover and bake *1 hr.*, removing cover last 15 min. Serve hot. *6 servings.*

Oriental Veal Casserole

Even better when made ahead and reheated. From Shirley Burr of our Marketing Research Department.

1 lb. cubed veal
3 tbsp. flour
2 tbsp. fat
1½ cups sliced celery
2 small onions, chopped
1 can (10½ oz.) cream of chicken soup
1 can (10½ oz.) cream of mushroom soup
1 soup can water
2 to 3 tbsp. soy sauce
½ cup uncooked rice

Heat oven to 325° (slow mod.). Roll meat in flour; brown in hot fat over medium heat; stir in rest of ingredients. Pour into 2-qt. baking dish. Bake covered *1½ hr.* 6 servings.

Oriental Pork Casserole

Make Oriental Veal Casserole (*above*)—*except* use 1 lb. cubed pork in place of veal.

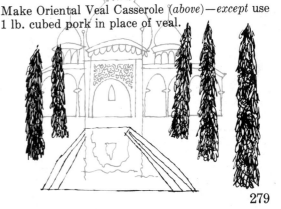

279

Wild rice is the seed of a shallow water grass. It is harvested in the marshes of Minnesota by Indians. Seated in canoes, they pull the grass heads downward over the edges of the crafts and beat out the seeds with short sticks or paddles.

This food is highly prized for its subtle flavor and excellent nutritive qualities. It is a perfect complement for game . . . and always a tempting gourmet treat.

HOW TO COOK WILD RICE

(1 cup uncooked wild rice equals 3 cups cooked)

DIRECT HEAT METHOD

1 cup wild rice
2½ cups water
1 tsp. salt

Wash wild rice by placing in wire strainer and running cold water through it; lift with fingers to clean thoroughly. Combine all ingredients in heavy saucepan. Heat to boil. Cover and simmer over low heat *40 to 50 min.*, until rice is tender. Remove cover, fluff rice with fork. Cook *5 min.* longer. *3 to 4 servings.*

NOTE: After first 30 min. of cooking, check rice to see that it is not sticking to pan. If necessary, an additional ¼ cup water may be added.

BOILING WATER METHOD

Cover 1 cup wild rice with 4 cups boiling water. Let stand covered *20 min.* Drain and repeat 3 times, using fresh boiling water each time and adding 1 tbsp. salt the last time. Add generous amount of butter and season with salt and pepper. Keep warm in oven or in double boiler, covering if held longer than 5 min.

Chicken and Wild Rice

Fried chicken on a bed of wild rice, topped with a raisin-orange sauce. This recipe won first prize for Mrs. Orville White of Medaryville, Indiana, in our Larro Recipe Round-up Contest.

2 cups wild rice, washed and drained
4 cups chicken broth
½ cup seedless raisins
½ cup orange juice
6 chicken breasts
¼ cup butter
3 tbsp. flour
½ tsp. paprika
1 tsp. salt
dash of pepper
1½ cups cream (20% butterfat)
½ cup milk

Simmer rice and broth in covered saucepan until liquid is absorbed and rice is done, *30 to 45 min.* Mix raisins and orange juice in small pan; bring to boil. Reduce heat and simmer *5 min.* Shake chicken in Seasoned Flour (*p. 302*); brown in butter in heavy skillet. Cover and lower heat. Cook ½ hr. Remove chicken and all fat except 3 tbsp. Blend in flour and seasonings. Cook over low heat, stirring until mixture is smooth and bubbly. Remove from heat. Stir in cream and milk. Bring to boil, stirring constantly. Boil *1 min.* Add raisin-orange mixture to sauce. *Heat oven to 350° (mod.).* Put cooked rice in bottom of baking dish, 13x9½x2". Cover with sauce reserving some for top of chicken breasts. Top with chicken and remaining sauce. Bake *20 min. 6 servings.*

Wild Rice with Mushrooms and Almonds

¼ cup butter
1 cup wild rice
½ cup blanched, slivered almonds
2 tbsp. chopped green onion or chives
2 cans (7 oz. each) mushroom pieces and stems, drained
3 cups chicken broth

Put all ingredients except broth in heavy frying pan and cook over medium high heat *about 20 min.*, until almonds are slightly brown. Stir often. *Heat oven to 325°* (slow mod.). When almonds are brown, add chicken broth to rest of ingredients, stir; then pour mixture into 1½-qt. deep baking dish. Cover tightly and bake about 1½ hr. 6 to 8 servings.

There are many romantic stories about the origin of macaroni. Some say that Marco Polo discovered it in the 13th century on one of his exploring expeditions to China. Others say that it was the Germans who first imported macaroni to Europe from China . . . and taught the Italians the art of making it. At any rate, it had become so popular in Italy by the 13th century that Emperor Frederick II coined the name "macaroni" from "marcus," meaning "divine dish." Its introduction into the United States has been traced back to the 16th century, the time of the exploits of Spanish explorers. But it really became an important food in our country with the influx of Italians following the Civil War. The finest macaroni products are made from durum semolina.

How to Cook Macaroni, Spaghetti and Noodles

They may be used interchangeably in soups, in place of potatoes and in main dishes.

1. Coil spaghetti into kettle.　　**2.** Test tenderness with fork.　　**3.** Drain in colander.

Add 1 tbsp. salt to 3 qt. rapidly boiling water in deep kettle. Drop 1 pkg. (7 or 8 oz.) macaroni, spaghetti or noodles into water gradually so water keeps boiling. If spaghetti strands are left whole, place one end in water. As they soften, gradually coil them around in kettle until submerged. If you wish, break spaghetti into 1½ to 2½" lengths. Cook, uncovered, at fast boil, stirring occasionally with long fork to prevent sticking. Cook just until tender* (*7 to 10 min.* or see time on pkg.). Test by cutting with fork against kettle. Drain quickly in colander or sieve. Toss with 3 tbsp. butter or sauce to prevent strands sticking together. *4 to 6 servings.*

*Thicker walled products require a longer time (15 to 18 min. or see pkg. directions).

EASY COOKING METHOD FOR MACARONI, SPAGHETTI AND NOODLES

For 1 pkg. (7 or 8 oz.) macaroni or spaghetti, or 1 pkg. (5 or 6 oz.) noodles, drop into 6 cups rapidly boiling salted water (4 tsp. salt). Bring back to rapid boil. Cook, stirring constantly, 3 min.* Cover with tight-fitting lid, remove from heat and let stand 10 min. Drain. If used in hot dishes, rinse with hot water and use immediately. If used for salad, rinse with running cold water.

*For thicker walled products, such as lasagne or kluski noodles, etc., use conventional cooking method. Follow manufacturer's directions.

A HELPFUL GUIDE

1 cup uncooked macaroni
　　(4 oz.) = 2 cups cooked
1 cup uncooked spaghetti
　　(4 oz.) = 2 cups cooked
1 cup uncooked noodles
　　(2½ oz.) = 1¼ cups cooked

SHOULD MACARONI FOODS BE RINSED?

Many American cooks rinse macaroni foods in hot water when used for a hot dish, and in cold water for a cold dish, such as a salad. But some Italian-American cooks are convinced that macaroni, spaghetti and noodles should never be rinsed if they are to be used at once—in either hot or cold dishes.

If you want to hold cooked macaroni for later use, rinse it thoroughly in cold water until all stickiness disappears. Drain well and refrigerate. Before use, freshen under running hot or cold water or by heating in butter.

Nutritionists believe rinsing causes loss of vitamins.

▶ **ALL YOU HAVE TO DO**

To keep cooked spaghetti, macaroni or noodles from sticking together: toss with butter or a few tablespoons of sauce as soon as it is drained. Then second servings will be as attractive as the first.

281

Old-fashioned Macaroni and Cheese

The simplest kind of dish.

hot boiled macaroni (7 or 8 oz.
  uncooked) (*p. 281*)
2 cups cut-up sharp Cheddar cheese
  (½" cubes) (½ lb.)
1 tsp. salt

¼ tsp. pepper
2 cups milk
paprika

Heat oven to 350° (mod.). Place cooked macaroni, cheese, salt and pepper in alternate layers in buttered oblong baking dish, 11½x7½x1½", ending with a layer of cheese on top. Pour milk over all. Sprinkle with paprika. Bake *35 to 45 min.*, or until golden brown on top. Serve hot from baking dish garnished, if desired, with parsley sprigs, pimiento strips or pepper rings. *6 to 8 servings.*

Creamy Macaroni and Cheese

Make Old-fashioned Macaroni and Cheese (*above*) —*except* use 2 cups Medium White Sauce (*p. 387*) in place of milk and seasonings.

Macaroni and Cheese with Sweet or Sour Cream

Called Macarones Con Jocoqui in the Southwest and Mexico.

Make Old-fashioned Macaroni and Cheese (*above*) —*except* use 2½ cups sweet or sour cream in place of milk.

Macaroni-Tomato Casserole

Make Old-fashioned Macaroni and Cheese (*above*) —*except* use 2½ cups well seasoned cooked tomatoes in place of milk. Bake *45 min.*, or until liquid is absorbed.

Ring of Plenty

A custardy one-dish meal from Mrs. Frank J. Ebsen of Wisconsin Rapids, Wisconsin.

hot boiled macaroni (7 or 8 oz. uncooked) (*p. 281*)
2 cups hot milk
¼ cup butter
2 cups shredded Cheddar cheese (½ lb.)
2 cups soft bread crumbs
2 eggs, well beaten
2 tbsp. *each* minced parsley, minced
  onion and chopped pimiento
2 tsp. salt
¼ tsp. pepper

Heat oven to 350° (mod.). Combine all ingredients. Pour into well greased 10" ring mold or 3-qt. baking dish. Set in pan of water (1" deep). Bake *30 to 35 min. for ring, 45 min. to 1 hr. for baking dish*, or until set. Unmold ring on hot platter; fill center with creamed sea food, chicken or vegetables. *8 servings.*

Macaroni à la Creme

6 cups water
4 tsp. salt
1 pkg. (7 or 8 oz.) uncooked macaroni
2 medium onions, finely chopped
1 cup finely diced celery
2 cups Medium White Sauce (*p. 387*)
1¼ cups cut-up sharp cheese (½" cubes) (⅓ lb.)
½ cup undiluted canned tomato soup
5 wieners, sliced pennywise or 2 slices
  partially cooked bacon, diced

Heat oven to 350° (mod.). Bring water to rapid boil. Add salt, macaroni, onions and celery. Bring back to rapid boil. Cook, stirring constantly, 3 min. Cover with tight-fitting lid, remove from heat and let stand 10 min. Rinse with hot water; drain. Prepare white sauce while macaroni is cooking. Combine macaroni mixture, white sauce, cheese and soup. Pour into square baking dish, 9x9x1¾". Arrange wieners or diced bacon over top. Bake *uncovered 20 min. 6 servings.*

Macaroni Loaf

Ruth Kerker Smith, who developed many fine recipes when on our staff, serves this for company luncheons.

Make Ring of Plenty (*at left*)—*except* bake in greased loaf pan, 9x5x3" *45 min. to 1 hr.*, or until set. Serve hot with Tomato Sauce (*p. 389*) or Mushroom Sauce (*p. 387*).

Yankee Doodle Macaroni

About the time of our Revolutionary War, there was a group of young dandies in London who were called "Macaronis." They adopted the title because it signified elegance. So when Yankee Doodle called his feather "Macaroni," he was assuring himself that it was elegant.

2 cups minced onion
2 cloves garlic, minced
¾ cup sliced mushrooms, if desired
3 tbsp. fat
1 lb. ground beef

1 can (1 lb. 13 oz.) cooked tomatoes
  (3½ cups)
1 tbsp. minced parsley
1 tbsp. salt
⅛ tsp. pepper
hot boiled macaroni (8 oz. uncooked)
  (p. 281)

Sauté onion, garlic and mushrooms in hot fat until onions are yellow. Add ground beef and cook until brown. Add tomatoes, parsley, salt and pepper; cook slowly, about *45 min.* Pour over macaroni on hot platter. Sprinkle with grated sharp Cheddar or Parmesan cheese. Serve immediately. *6 to 8 servings.*

Macaroni Sauté

Bake in oven or cook on top of range.

2 cups uncooked elbow macaroni (7 or 8 oz.)
½ cup chopped onion
½ cup chopped green pepper
1 clove garlic, crushed, if desired
½ cup fat or vegetable oil
1 can (1 lb. 4 oz.) tomato juice (2½ cups)
1 tsp. salt
¼ tsp. pepper
2 tbsp. Worcestershire sauce, if desired

Heat oven to 350° (mod.). Sauté macaroni, onion, green pepper and garlic in fat over low heat. Stir occasionally until macaroni turns slightly yellow. Heat tomato juice to boil. Add rest of ingredients. Stir into macaroni mixture. Pour into 1½-qt. baking dish. Cover. Bake *30 to 40 min.* Serve with fish or meat. *6 servings.*

To cook Macaroni Sauté on top of range: increase tomato juice to 3 cups; do not preheat. Bring just to boil over high heat. Cover. Immediately reduce to lowest heat. Cook *20 min.* without stirring.

Monday Macaroni

Sunday leftovers in a delicious dish for Monday's dinner.

2 onions, minced
2 tbsp. butter
1 tbsp. olive oil
1 cup finely chopped cooked meat
1 can (6 oz.) tomato purée or soup
2 tsp. minced parsley
bit of bay leaf
1 cup cooked vegetables
1 cup meat stock
hot boiled macaroni (8 oz. uncooked) (p. 281)

Sauté onions in butter and olive oil. Add meat and cook *5 min.* Add tomato purée, parsley and bay leaf; simmer *15 min.* Add vegetables and meat stock. Heat through. Pour over macaroni on hot platter. Sprinkle with grated sharp Cheddar or Parmesan cheese. Serve immediately. *6 to 8 servings.*

Lumberjack Macaroni

Mr. James Ford Bell, founder of General Mills, world traveler and epicure, made this dish for us himself in our test kitchen.

hot boiled macaroni (8 oz. uncooked) (p. 281)
2 cups grated Cheddar cheese (½ lb.)
3 to 5 tbsp. Worcestershire sauce
¼ cup chili sauce
salt and pepper to taste
¾ cup piping hot melted butter

Spread macaroni out on hot large platter. Sprinkle with cheese, Worcestershire sauce, chili sauce, salt and pepper. Pour hot melted butter over all. Mix with 2 forks until sauce is creamy. Serve at once on hot plates. *6 servings.*

BUFFET SUPPER DISHES

Avery Island Deviled Shrimp,
   page 271

Lobster Thermidor, page 269

Savory Spaghetti, page 287

Poppy Seed Noodles with Veal
   Paprika, page 288

Any one of these makes a sumptuous
supper with tossed salad, bread sticks
and fresh fruit compote.

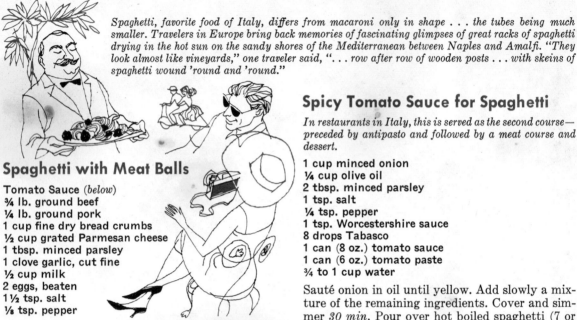

Spaghetti, favorite food of Italy, differs from macaroni only in shape . . . the tubes being much smaller. Travelers in Europe bring back memories of fascinating glimpses of great racks of spaghetti drying in the hot sun on the sandy shores of the Mediterranean between Naples and Amalfi. "They look almost like vineyards," one traveler said, ". . . row after row of wooden posts . . . with skeins of spaghetti wound 'round and 'round."

Spaghetti with Meat Balls

Tomato Sauce *(below)*
¾ lb. ground beef
¼ lb. ground pork
1 cup fine dry bread crumbs
½ cup grated Parmesan cheese
1 tbsp. minced parsley
1 clove garlic, cut fine
½ cup milk
2 eggs, beaten
1½ tsp. salt
⅛ tsp. pepper

Mix ingredients for meat balls lightly and shape into 1″ balls. Brown meat balls on all sides in hot fat. Pour off fat as it collects. Add to sauce 20 min. before sauce is done. Place hot boiled spaghetti (7 or 8 oz. uncooked) (p. 281) on warm platter. Top with sauce, surround with meat balls. Serve with grated Parmesan cheese. *4 to 6 servings.*

Tomato Sauce

½ cup chopped onion
1 clove garlic, minced
3 tbsp. olive oil
2 cans (1 lb. 4 oz. each) tomatoes, rubbed
   through sieve
1 can (8 oz.) tomato sauce
1 can (6 oz.) tomato paste
1 cup water
1 tsp. basil
2 tbsp. minced parsley
2 tsp. salt
¼ tsp. pepper

Sauté onion and garlic in oil. Add rest of ingredients. Simmer over low heat *1 hr.*

Spaghetti Valhalla

Sprinkle 2 cups grated sharp cheese over hot boiled spaghetti (7 or 8 oz. uncooked) (p. 281) in oblong baking dish, 11½x7½x1½″. On top, place alternately 1 lb. little pork sausages (parboiled *10 min.*, then browned) and 12 tomato slices. Season with salt and pepper. Pour ½ cup water over all. Bake *at 350° (mod.) 35 min. 6 servings.*

Spicy Tomato Sauce for Spaghetti

In restaurants in Italy, this is served as the second course— preceded by antipasto and followed by a meat course and dessert.

1 cup minced onion
¼ cup olive oil
2 tbsp. minced parsley
1 tsp. salt
¼ tsp. pepper
1 tsp. Worcestershire sauce
8 drops Tabasco
1 can (8 oz.) tomato sauce
1 can (6 oz.) tomato paste
¾ to 1 cup water

Sauté onion in oil until yellow. Add slowly a mixture of the remaining ingredients. Cover and simmer *30 min.* Pour over hot boiled spaghetti (7 or 8 oz. uncooked) (p. 281) on hot platter. Sprinkle with grated Parmesan or Romano cheese. Serve immediately. *6 servings.*

Clam or Oyster Spaghetti

Popular Friday and Lenten dish in New York City.

1 can (10 oz.) minced clams or 1¼ cups leftover
   steamed clams with broth or 1 can (8 oz.)
   oysters, minced
2 cloves garlic, minced
¼ cup butter
2 tbsp. minced parsley
hot boiled spaghetti (7 or 8 oz. uncooked) (p. 281)
minced parsley for garnish

Drain juice from sea food saving it for sauce. Sauté garlic in butter over low heat. Stir in juice, minced sea food and 2 tbsp. parsley. Bring to boil; simmer *3 to 5 min.* Pour over hot spaghetti and mix gently. Sprinkle with minced parsley. Serve with grated Parmesan cheese. *4 servings.*

Turkey and Ham Tetrazzini

7 oz. spaghetti, broken in 2" pieces and
   boiled (p. 281)
¼ cup butter
¼ cup flour
1 tsp. salt
¼ tsp. white pepper
¼ tsp. nutmeg
2 cups chicken or turkey broth or 1 can
   (14½ oz.) chicken broth
1 cup milk
3 tbsp. sherry flavoring
2 cups cooked turkey, cut in small pieces
½ cup cooked cubed ham
¼ cup chopped green pepper sautéed or
   4-oz. can pimiento, cut up
1 cup ripe olives, cut in large pieces or
   ½ lb. mushrooms, sliced and sautéed
   in butter 5 min.
1 egg yolk
½ cup grated Parmesan cheese or ½ cup
   slivered toasted almonds

Heat oven to 350° (mod.). Melt butter over low
heat in heavy saucepan. Blend in flour and seasonings. Cook over low heat, stirring until mixture
is smooth and bubbly. Remove from heat. Stir in
broth and milk. Bring to boil; boil 1 min., stirring
constantly. Blend in sherry flavoring. Add sauce
to cooked spaghetti. Add turkey, ham, green
pepper, olives and egg yolk to spaghetti. Pour
into 2-qt. baking dish. Sprinkle with cheese or
almonds. Bake *uncovered 25 to 30 min.* Let stand
for 10 min. before serving. *6 to 8 servings.*

Holiday Spaghetti

4 slices bacon
1 cup minced onion
¾ cup minced green pepper
1 cup sliced mushrooms
3 tbsp. hot drippings
1 lb. ground beef
2 tsp. salt
1 tsp. sugar
3½ cups cooked tomatoes, cut up
hot drained Boiled Spaghetti (8 oz.
   uncooked) (p. 281)

Heat oven to 350° (mod.). Fry bacon. Sauté onion,
green pepper, mushrooms in hot drippings until
onions are yellow. Add ground beef and cook until
browned. Add rest of ingredients and heat. Pour
into well greased 2-qt. baking dish. Sprinkle with
grated sharp cheese. Bake *30 min.* Serve hot garnished with crisp bacon and parsley. *8 servings.*

Spaghetti Pie

hot drained Boiled Spaghetti (7 oz. uncooked)
   (p. 281)
1 cup cottage cheese
2 eggs, slightly beaten
1½ tsp. salt
⅛ tsp. pepper
1 cup grated sharp Cheddar cheese
1 egg, beaten
2 tbsp. grated Parmesan cheese

Heat oven to 350° (mod.). Mix spaghetti, cottage
cheese, 2 eggs, salt, pepper and Cheddar cheese.
Place in buttered 9" pie pan. Top with mixture
of 1 egg and Parmesan cheese. Bake *45 to 50 min.*,
or until silver knife inserted in center comes out
clean. Serve warm garnished with parsley. May
be served in pie-shaped wedges with Mushroom
Sauce (p. 387) or Tomato Sauce (p. 389). *4 to 6
servings.*

Savory Spaghetti *Delicious, moist spaghetti dish that is really simple to do. See color picture pp. 284-285.*

½ lb. ground beef
¼ lb. ground pork
1 small onion, chopped
1 small green pepper, sliced
½ cup sliced ripe olives
1 can (2 oz.) mushrooms, drained
1 can (8 oz.) tomato sauce (1 cup)

2½ cups tomatoes (1 lb. 4 oz.)
2 cups water
2 tsp. salt
¼ tsp. pepper
1 tsp. Worcestershire sauce
6 drops Tabasco
4 oz. long spaghetti or noodles

Brown meat in large skillet over medium heat. Add onion, green pepper and cook
5 min. Add olives, mushrooms, tomato sauce and mix lightly. Stir mixture of tomatoes,
water, salt, pepper, Worcestershire sauce, Tabasco into meat mixture. Add *uncooked*
spaghetti and bring to boil. Cover tightly, reduce heat to low and simmer about
40 min., stirring occasionally. Uncover and simmer *15 min.* longer. *About 6 servings.*

287

Noodles are made of a dough similar to macaroni dough enriched with eggs or egg yolks. They are usually in the form of long, flat ribbons, but sometimes letters of the alphabet. Homemade egg noodles and packaged noodles may be used interchangeably in all recipes.

Homemade Egg Noodles

3 egg yolks
1 whole egg
3 tbsp. cold water
1 tsp. salt
2 cups GOLD MEDAL Flour

Beat yolks and egg well. Beat in water and salt. Measure flour by dip-level-pour method or by sifting (*see p. 6*). Stir in flour with spoon. (Dough is stiff—knead in last of flour.) Divide into 3 parts. Roll each piece *as thin as possible* (paper thin) on lightly floured cloth-covered board. Place between 2 towels until dough is partially dry (like chamois skin). Roll up as for jelly roll. With a thin sharp knife cut into strips of desired widths (⅛" for fine noodles, up to ½" for broad noodles). Shake strips and allow to dry before using or storing in covered glass jar. Cook in generous amount of boiling salted water (*p. 281*). Older, drier noodles take longer to cook until tender. *Makes 6 cups or 10 oz.*

Short Ribs and Noodles

3 lb. beef short ribs
2 tbsp. fat
2 tsp. salt
¼ tsp. pepper
½ tsp. paprika
½ cup chopped onion
1½ cups water
½ cup tomato juice
noodles (5 oz. uncooked)

Brown short ribs in fat. Add remaining ingredients except noodles. Cover tightly and simmer 2½ to 3 hr., or until short ribs are done. Add noodles and cook *15 min.* longer, or until noodles are tender. *4 to 5 servings.*

Pot Roast and Noodles with Browned Crumbs

From early German settlers of Pennsylvania.

About 15 min. before Pot Roast (*p. 302*) is ready to serve, cook 5 to 6 oz. noodles (*p. 281*). Heat ¼ cup butter in heavy skillet. Add 1 cup fine dry bread crumbs and cook over low heat, stirring frequently, until lightly browned. Add hot drained cooked noodles gently mixing the two. Serve piping hot with Pot Roast and gravy. *8 to 10 servings.*

Noodle Ring with Chicken à la King

"My sons loved this for Sunday supper," says Mrs. Charles Poor, Bozeman, Montana.

3 eggs, lightly beaten
1 tsp. salt
⅛ tsp. pepper
¾ cup milk
1 tbsp. butter, melted
hot boiled noodles (10 to 12 oz. uncooked) (*p. 281*)
Chicken à la King (*p. 266*)

Heat oven to 350° (mod.). Mix all ingredients except Chicken à la King. Place in well buttered 10" ring mold. Set in pan of water (1" deep). Bake *45 min.*, or until silver knife plunged into center comes out clean. Unmold; fill center with hot Chicken à la King. Serve immediately. *6 to 8 servings.*

Poppy Seed Noodles with Veal Paprika

Often served as the main dish of "a supper to remember" by Ruth M. Skinner of Chicago. See color picture p. 285.

1 tsp. butter
½ cup blanched almonds, slivered (if desired)
3 tbsp. butter
hot boiled noodles (5 to 6 oz. uncooked) (*p. 281*)
2 tsp. poppy seeds
Veal Paprika (*p. 308*)

Melt 1 tsp. butter in heavy skillet. Add almonds and stir over low heat until lightly browned. Add 3 tbsp. butter, noodles and poppy seeds and stir gently until heated through. Center platter with Veal Paprika arranging Poppy Seed Noodles around edge. *6 to 8 servings.*

Noodles Romanoff

Tangy, perfectly seasoned casserole of noodles, sour cream and cheese—gourmet fare.

hot boiled noodles (5 to 6 oz. uncooked) (*p. 281*)
1 cup cottage cheese
1 cup commercial sour cream
¼ cup finely chopped onion
1 clove garlic, minced very fine
1 to 2 tsp. Worcestershire sauce
dash of Tabasco
½ tsp. salt
½ cup grated sharp cheese

Heat oven to 350° (mod.). Mix all ingredients except cheese lightly and place in greased square baking dish, 8x8x2". Sprinkle with cheese. Bake *40 min.* *4 to 6 servings.*

Chili-Chicken Casserole

From Genevieve Callahan and Lou Richardson, who say that its zippy seasonings are typical of San Francisco fare, and its ease of preparation typical of the California way of life.

½ cup chopped onion
2 tbsp. butter
3 cans (10½ oz. each) condensed cream of
    mushroom soup
1 can (4 oz.) pimientos, chopped
2 tbsp. (2 oz.) finely chopped pickled hot green chili
    peppers (remove stems and seeds)*
hot boiled noodles (16 oz. uncooked) (p. 281)
3 to 4 cups diced cooked or canned
    chicken or turkey
pepper and seasoning salt
2 to 3 cups grated sharp Cheddar
    cheese (½ to ¾ lb.)

Heat oven to 350° (mod.). Sauté onion in butter until yellow. Stir in soup, pimiento and chili pepper. In buttered 4-qt. baking dish (or two 2-qt. baking dishes) layer half of ingredients in this order: noodles, chicken (sprinkle lightly with salt and pepper), soup mixture and cheese. Repeat layers, one more of each. Bake *45 min. 12 servings.*

*Amount of chili pepper may be changed according to family taste.

Scalloped Salmon, Almonds and Noodles

1 cup Thin White Sauce (*p. 387*)
1 can (7 oz.) red sockeye salmon, flaked
1 to 2 tbsp. lemon juice (from ½ lemon)
hot boiled noodles (4 oz. uncooked) (*p. 281*)
⅓ cup slivered almonds toasted
crushed WHEATIES, buttered bread crumbs
    or buttered cracker crumbs

Heat oven to 350° (mod.). Make thin white sauce, increasing salt to 1 tsp. Remove from heat. Sprinkle lemon juice over salmon. Add noodles, toasted almonds and white sauce and toss lightly. Turn into 8 individual shells or buttered baking dishes. Top each with crushed WHEATIES. Bake *10 to 15 min. 8 servings.*

Lasagne

It is said that on Christmas Eve the grandmother in an Italian household measures the width of the children's mouths to know how wide to make the lasagne noodles.

Make Tomato Sauce (*p. 286*). Meanwhile, cook ½ lb. lasagne noodles according to directions on pkg. Drain. Prepare meat balls (*p. 286*). Brown in hot fat, add a small amount of water, cover and simmer *30 min.* Heat oven to 350° (mod.). Place the following ingredients in layers in oblong pan, 13x9½x2" in order listed, beginning and ending with the sauce. Repeat until all ingredients are used up.

sauce
single layer of noodles
mixture of:
    ¾ lb. Ricotta cheese or cottage cheese
    1 tbsp. minced parsley
    1 tsp. oregano
¾ cup grated Parmesan cheese
¾ lb. Mozzarella cheese, grated

Bake *30 min.* Let stand 15 min., cut in squares and serve with meat balls. *6 to 8 servings.*

American Lasagne

Donna Hosler (Mrs. James E. Hosler) brought us this easy version of the popular Italian lasagne.

1 lb. ground beef
2 cloves garlic, minced
1 tbsp. hot fat
1 can (6 oz.) tomato paste
1 can (1 lb. 4 oz.) tomatoes (2½ cups)
1 tsp. salt
¾ tsp. pepper
½ tsp. oregano
hot boiled wide noodles (8 oz. uncooked) (*p. 281*)
8 oz. Swiss cheese, cut up (1½ cups)
1 carton (12 oz.) cottage cheese

Brown beef and garlic in hot fat. Add tomato paste, tomatoes, seasonings. Cover and simmer *20 min.* Heat oven to 350° (mod.). In oblong baking dish, 11½x7½x1½" alternate layers of cooked noodles, Swiss cheese, cottage cheese and meat sauce. Bake *20 to 30 min.* Serve with grated Parmesan cheese. *6 to 8 servings.*

MAIN DISHES *Ideal for buffet serving.*

Deviled Crabmeat

So easy and quick . . . often served by Ruth G. Anderson, former editor of Betty Crocker cook books, at informal Sunday night suppers at "White Pickets," her lovely home.

1 cup milk
1½ cups soft bread crumbs
2 cups flaked cooked crabmeat (two 7-oz. cans)
whites of 5 hard-cooked eggs, finely sliced
yolks of 5 hard-cooked eggs, mashed
1½ tsp. salt
¼ tsp. dry mustard
⅛ tsp. cayenne pepper
⅓ cup butter, melted

Heat oven to 450° (hot). Combine milk and crumbs. Gently stir in crabmeat and egg whites. Blend in rest of ingredients. Pour into buttered oblong baking dish, 10x6x1½". Sprinkle with WHEATIES or buttered bread or cracker crumbs. Bake *15 min.* Serve hot. *6 servings.*

Dried Beef Casserole

Rich, nutritious and easy. Mix ingredients, refrigerate until ready to bake. From Peggy Elvehjem Henninger, formerly of our staff.

1 can (10½ oz.) condensed cream of mushroom soup
1 cup milk
1 cup finely cut Cheddar cheese (about ¼ lb.)
1 cup uncooked elbow macaroni
3 tbsp. finely chopped onion
¼ lb. dried beef, cut in bite-size pieces
2 hard-cooked eggs, sliced

Stir soup to make a creamy consistency. Add rest of ingredients except eggs. Fold in eggs. Turn into buttered 1½-qt. baking dish. Store covered in refrigerator at least 3 to 4 hr. or overnight. *Heat oven to 350° (mod.). Bake 1 hr. uncovered. 4 to 6 servings.*

Chicken-Macaroni en Casserole

hot boiled elbow macaroni (1½ cups or 6 oz. uncooked) *(p. 281)*
2 cups grated Cheddar cheese
1 can (12 oz.) chicken, diced (1½ cups)
1 can (10½ oz.) cream of chicken soup plus enough milk to make 2 cups
1 cup sliced canned mushrooms
¼ cup diced pimiento

Heat oven to 350° (mod.). Mix all ingredients. Pour into buttered 2-qt. baking dish. Bake *60 min. 6 to 8 servings.*

Shrimp Supreme

This rich, savory luncheon dish is often served by a very gracious hostess, Mrs. Richard Folsom Tickle.

1 lb. fresh mushrooms, sliced
2 tbsp. butter
9 Special Deviled Eggs *(below)*
2 lb. fresh green shrimp, cooked and deveined or two cans (4½ oz. each) shrimp
2 cups grated mild Cheddar cheese
2 cups Medium White Sauce *(p. 387)*

Heat oven to 350° (mod.). Sauté mushrooms in butter. Spread on bottom of baking dish, 11½x7½x1½". Top with halves of deviled eggs. Arrange shrimp on top of eggs. Fold 1 cup of the grated cheese into white sauce. Pour this sauce over all and sprinkle with remaining 1 cup grated cheese. Bake *30 min. 6 to 8 servings.*

Special Deviled Eggs: Cut 9 hard-cooked eggs in halves. Slip out yolks; mash with fork. Mix in 3 tbsp. mayonnaise, 1 tbsp. chopped sweet pickle, 2 tsp. vinegar, ½ tsp. dry mustard, dash *each* of Worcestershire sauce and pepper. Refill egg whites.

Baked Tuna Chow Mein Casserole

A favorite of Hazel Smith, formerly of our staff, whose living accounts of her travels abroad are so eagerly read by her many friends.

1 cup chopped celery
¼ cup chopped onion
2 tbsp. chopped green pepper
1 tbsp. butter
1 can (7 oz.) tuna
1 can (10½ oz.) cream of mushroom soup, thinned with ¼ cup milk and ¼ cup water
3 oz. (1⅓ cups) chow mein noodles (save ⅓ cup for topping)
¾ cup (4 oz.) salted cashew nuts
¼ tsp. flavor enhancer (monosodium glutamate)
⅛ tsp. pepper

Heat oven to 350° (mod.). Sauté celery, onion and green pepper in butter. Mix in rest of ingredients; pour into buttered 1½-qt. baking dish. Sprinkle with ⅓ cup chow mein noodles. Bake *30 min. 4 to 6 servings.*

Lasagne See p. 289.

Sandwich Fillings

Use a variety of breads: pumpernickel, rye, whole wheat or oatmeal.

Meat

Leftover beef roast (ground), chopped pickle and celery, prepared mustard or horse-radish, mayonnaise.

Leftover baked ham (ground), chopped pickle, mustard, mayonnaise.

Ground cooked ham or canned luncheon meat, cheese, sweet pickle and mayonnaise.

Liverwurst, slice of tomato, lettuce, mayonnaise.

Fish

Flaked tuna or salmon, sweet pickle, celery and mayonnaise.

Flaked crabmeat, or chopped shrimp, chopped celery, lemon juice and mayonnaise.

Egg

Chopped hard-cooked egg, pickle relish, pimiento, salad dressing.

Chopped hard-cooked egg, ripe olives, mayonnaise.

Chopped hard-cooked egg, chopped ham, minced onion and green pepper, salad dressing.

Fried or scrambled egg on whole wheat bread with catsup.

Cheese

Cream cheese, chopped stuffed olives and nuts.

Sliced Cheddar cheese, thinly sliced fried ham, prepared mustard.

Swiss cheese, ham and pickle.

Cream cheese, Roquefort cheese and chopped nuts.

Swiss cheese and mustard on rye bread.

Cottage cheese, minced green pepper and onion on whole wheat bread.

Unusual

Baked beans, chili sauce, thinly sliced onion.

Sliced radishes on rye or whole wheat.

Peanut butter and chopped crisp bacon.

Elegant Sandwich Loaf See p. 120.

Broiled Turkey and Cheese Sandwiches

Make sandwiches of toasted-on-one-side bread (buttered on untoasted side) and slices of roast turkey. Cover each sandwich with a thin slice of cheese. Place under broiler until cheese is melted. Serve hot with Mushroom Sauce (*p. 387*).

Hot French Toasted Sandwiches

Make chicken, turkey or ham sandwiches. Dip into beaten egg (or mixture of 1 beaten egg and ½ cup milk). Brown on both sides in butter in hot skillet. Or bake on greased baking sheet in 400° oven. Serve hot.

Grilled Cheese Sandwiches

Make cheese sandwiches. Brush lightly with melted butter or spread with soft butter on both sides and bake until golden brown on electric grill or heavy skillet.

Open Grilled Cheese Sandwiches: Toast bread slices on one side. Cover lightly buttered untoasted side with Cheddar cheese. Place under broiler until cheese melts. Sprinkle with paprika, garnish with parsley, pickles and tomato wedges. Serve at once.

Tuna or Chicken Burgers

1 can (7 oz.) tuna, flaked, or 1 cup cut-up
   cooked chicken
1 cup chopped celery
1 small onion, minced
½ cup diced Cheddar cheese
½ cup chopped ripe olives
¼ cup mayonnaise
salt and pepper to taste
6 hamburger buns

Mix filling ingredients. Fill buttered buns with mixture. Place in paper sandwich bags or wrap in aluminum foil. Fold and fasten bags with paper clips. Refrigerate. Just before serving, heat *at 350°* (mod.) *15 to 20 min. 6 servings.*

Club Sandwich

Lightly toast 3 slices bread for each sandwich. Top first buttered slice with cold sliced chicken, top with second slice buttered on both sides. Top second slice with lettuce leaf, sliced tomato and 2 slices crisply fried bacon. Top with buttered third slice toast. Use mayonnaise on chicken layer, if desired. Secure corners with toothpicks or cut in halves or fourths.

Reuben's Sandwich

Full meal in a sandwich. Adapted from the sandwich around which Reuben of New York built his reputation.

1 can (1 lb.) sauerkraut, drained (2 cups)
¼ cup plus 2 tbsp. mayonnaise
½ lb. sliced turkey
½ lb. Swiss cheese, sliced
1 pkg. (4 oz.) corned beef
1 loaf rye bread

Marinate sauerkraut and mayonnaise 30 min. Arrange pieces of turkey, Swiss cheese and corned beef on 6 buttered slices of rye bread. Spread ⅓ cup marinated sauerkraut on each slice of bread. Top with bread slice; cut into halves. Sandwich will be 1½ to 2" high. *6 servings.*

Rachael's Sandwich

The ladies love this version of Reuben's Sandwich (above) with cole slaw instead of sauerkraut.

Follow recipe above—*except* omit sauerkraut and mayonnaise and substitute Almond Cole Slaw.

Almond Cole Slaw

Crisp together 2½ cups shredded cabbage, ½ cup chopped celery, ¼ cup diced green pepper, ¼ cup diced cucumber and 3 tbsp. minced onion. Add ¼ tsp. salt and dash of pepper. Just before serving, add ½ cup toasted slivered almonds and toss lightly with about ½ cup mayonnaise mixed with 2 or 3 tbsp. cream.

Easy Denver Sandwich

¼ cup minced onion
¼ cup minced green pepper
1 tbsp. butter
4 eggs
¼ cup milk
½ cup minced cooked ham
salt and pepper

Sauté onion and green pepper slowly in hot butter until onion is yellow in 8 or 9" skillet. Beat eggs slightly with milk, stir in ham, salt and pepper. Pour into skillet; scramble gently with onion-pepper mixture over low heat just until set. Spoon into hot toasted buns or serve between buttered slices of bread or toast. *Makes 4 sandwiches.*

Barbecued Hamburger Mix

Teen agers clamor for this at their parties.

1 cup chopped onion
2 tbsp. butter
4 lb. ground beef
1 bottle (14 oz.) catsup
1 cup water
½ cup chopped celery
¼ cup lemon juice
2 tbsp. brown sugar
1 tbsp. Worcestershire sauce
1 tbsp. salt
2 tsp. vinegar
1 tsp. flavor enhancer (monosodium glutamate)
½ tsp. dry mustard

Sauté onion in butter. Add ground beef; brown lightly. Drain off excess fat. Add rest of ingredients and simmer covered *30 min. Use to fill 30 to 40 warm hamburger buns.*

Or, cool and freeze in five 1-pt. freezing containers. Seal and label with name and date. Freeze at 0° or lower. Before serving, heat mixture slowly in skillet. *1 pt. fills 6 to 8 hot buttered hamburger buns.*

Saucy Sandwich Rolls

Our good friend Cissy Gregg, charming and talented food editor of the Louisville Courier Journal, says this snack in a sack is fun for a backyard picnic or a cozy supper by the living room fire.

1 lb. wieners, chopped or sliced
1 medium onion, finely chopped
3 tbsp. bacon fat
¼ cup GOLD MEDAL Flour
¾ tsp. salt
dash of pepper
½ tsp. *each* dry mustard, Worcestershire sauce
½ cup *each* catsup and water
1 cup chopped celery
½ cup grated cheese
12 hot dog buns

Brown wieners and onion in hot fat. Remove from heat. Blend in flour, seasonings, catsup, water and celery. Cook about *5 min.*, or until celery is tender, stirring constantly. Add cheese. Heat until cheese melts. Remove from heat. Remove some of soft centers from buns. Fill pockets with mixture. Wrap in heavy waxed paper or aluminum foil, twisting ends tightly. Just before serving, heat in shallow pan *at 350°* (mod.) *10 to 15 min. Makes 12 sandwich rolls.*

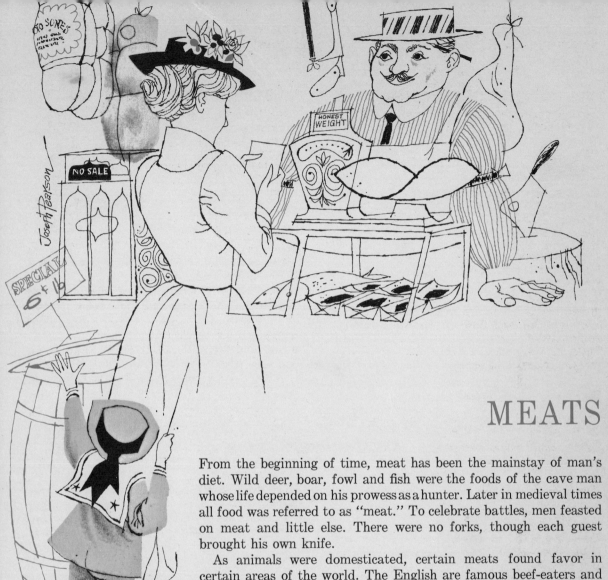

MEATS

From the beginning of time, meat has been the mainstay of man's diet. Wild deer, boar, fowl and fish were the foods of the cave man whose life depended on his prowess as a hunter. Later in medieval times all food was referred to as "meat." To celebrate battles, men feasted on meat and little else. There were no forks, though each guest brought his own knife.

As animals were domesticated, certain meats found favor in certain areas of the world. The English are famous beef-eaters and Americans of English descent soon placed beef at the top of our meat preference list. Our southern neighbors in Argentina raise and enjoy excellent beef. The deeds of their gauchos and our cowboys have built a colorful folklore around beef-raising.

The Italians roast the paschal lamb at Easter, the English love lamb chops, while the Near East prefers shish-kabobs.

Rich, flavorful pork, long a favorite in China, the Pacific isles and in Africa, is second only to beef in our country.

In Italy and France, chefs and homemakers alike, know the art of cooking the delicate, tender veal; and we Americans would do well to learn from them.

With the following chapter as your guide, tender, flavorful meats will be yours for the cooking.

MEAT MAKES THE MEAL

(complete index in back of book)

FROZEN MEAT FACTS

GROUND MEAT AND VARIETY MEATS should be frozen if held over 24 hr. Freeze other meats planned for use three days or more after buying.

Do not freeze canned hams.

NEVER RE-FREEZE ANY MEAT!!

Do not freeze ready-to-serve (bologna, etc.) or cured meats or frankfurters. Salt favors the development of rancidity when meat is frozen.

Freezer storage time for meats is 60 days.

Freeze leftover meats in gravy or sauce for prolonged storage life.

COOKING FROZEN MEAT: Defrosted meats are cooked by the same methods as fresh meats.

Frozen roasts require approximately $\frac{1}{3}$ to $\frac{1}{2}$ again as long for cooking as roast which has been defrosted. The time required for cooking frozen steaks and chops varies according to the surface area and thickness of the meat. Thick frozen steaks and chops must be broiled more slowly than defrosted ones.

DEFROSTING MEAT: Meat may be defrosted in the refrigerator, at room temperature or during cooking. The method of defrosting does not noticeably affect the flavor, tenderness or juiciness of cooked meat cuts. Choice of specific method depends upon the time, the facilities (space in refrigerator, etc.) available.

DEFROSTING TIME is affected by several factors. The lower the defrosting temperature, the longer the time required. Chunky pieces of meat require more time than long, thin cuts of the same weight. Wrapped frozen meats require more time for defrosting than those not wrapped.

FISH AND GAME: Prompt freezing is very important. Cool game quickly. If immediate freezing is not possible, pack in crushed ice. Clean fish; remove feathers (*p. 325*) or skin and clean game. Freeze small fish whole, fillet or steak large fish. Freeze game birds whole; cut up or steak large game. Wrap. To cook: partially or completely defrost in wrapper; cook while still chilled.

SHELL FISH: Do not store cooked peeled shrimp longer than two to three months and cooked unpeeled shrimp longer than four to six months.

WHAT EVERY COOK NEEDS TO KNOW ABOUT MEATS AND FISH

BUY AND STORE WITH CARE

Buying and cooking meat is a great challenge to the homemaker, as meat is one of the most expensive foods and because meat protein is so important for body growth (p. 35). Your choice of beef, pork, lamb, veal, fish or poultry depends on family preferences while your choice of tender or less tender cuts of meat depends on the amount of time available for cooking and the amount of money available for its purchase.

Consider the amount of waste when selecting meat. If a piece has much bone, fat, connective tissue and gristle, it may be more costly than its price indicates.

Knowledge of meat grades and brands (p. 299) is helpful in wise buying, too.

Fall is the time to expect lower prices in meats. Beef is in good supply, and therefore less expensive, Sept. 1 through Jan. 1. Pork is very plentiful Oct. 1 through Jan. 1. Lamb, too, is lower in price during the fall. Veal, however, is almost constant in supply and price.

In deciding the amount of meat to buy for your family, allow ¼ lb. (boneless) to ½ lb. (bone in) per person per meal. Once bought, protect your meat investment by storing it wisely (p. 299).

. . . .

COOK AND SERVE WITH FLAIR

Tender cuts of meat, such as roasts and steaks (pp. 300–301) are cooked by dry heat in an open pan, either over the heat as in pan-broiling, under direct heat as in broiling or in the oven as in roasting. Less tender cuts, from muscular areas like the shoulder or boney areas like the ribs, are cooked by moist heat (pp. 302–303) in a covered pan, usually with liquid added, either on top of the range or in the oven.

Meats roasted at the low temperatures (300–350°) suggested in these recipes are better eating, are more uniformly done and have less shrinkage.

Choose a vegetable to complement the meat (p. 408) and choose an attractive garnish (p. 24) for the meat dish.

NEW ADVENTURES IN MEAT, FISH AND POULTRY

Baked Fish Au Gratin or Golden Fish Puffs (p. 330)—Delicious dinner from frozen fish fillets.

Crown Roast of Pork (p. 309)—Perfect for a big party and so easy to carve.

Liver 'n Bacon Patties (p. 315)—Attractive way to serve your family rich-in-iron liver.

Mixed Grill (p. 312)—Thick lamb chops, chicken livers and sausages with tomatoes and mushrooms.

Oriental Burgers (p. 305)—A tangy sandwich filling of beef, soy sauce and Chinese vegetables.

Roast Cornish Game Hens (p. 318)—Serve one apiece with a necklace of cranberries.

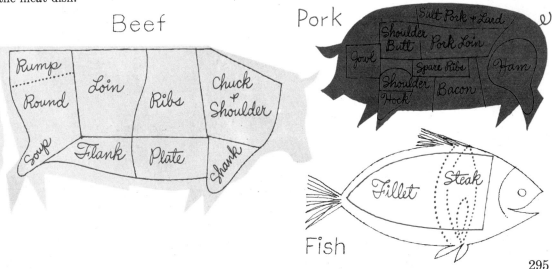

FOUR MAIN DISHES FROM A LEG OF LAMB

Roast Lamb, page 312 *Lamb Curry, page 313* *Broiled Lamb Steak, page 312*
Shish-Kabobs, page 313

SEVERAL MEALS FROM ONE CUT OF MEAT

Larger cuts are often cheaper per pound and are sometimes meat market specials. If you have thought these cuts were too big for your family or there would be too much for leftover meals, consider dividing them so you can make 2, 3 or even 4 different tasting fresh-cooked meat meals. Your meat man will make these cuts for you.

Leg of Lamb

Especially recommended at the time of year when lamb legs run 7 to 9 lb. See picture on opposite page.

Meal 1: Roast Leg of Lamb (*p. 312*). Add Oven-Browned Potatoes (*p. 300*) and serve with parsley-buttered onions.

Meal 2: Broiled Lamb Steaks (*p. 312*). Garnish with pear halves centered with mint jelly.

Meal 3: Shish-Kabobs (*p. 313*). Cut meat from shank and cut into cubes. See recipe. Serve with fluffy rice.

Meal 4: Lamb Curry (*p. 313*). Cut leftover roast into cubes. See recipe.

Beef Chuck

Have a round-bone pot roast cut thick.

Meal 1: Pot Roast (*p. 302*). For one meal.

Meal 2: Old-fashioned Beef Stew (*p. 303*). Cut off a boneless piece to cube for beef stew.

Meal 3: Swiss Steak (*p. 304*). Split other end to make 2 Swiss Steaks.

Pork Butt

The whole fresh pork shoulder butt weighs from 5 to 7 lb. and is nearly boneless. This piece can be divided at home.

Meal 1: Roast Pork (*p. 309*). Use piece with bone.

Meal 2: Pork Steaks. Slice ½" thick. Follow any of the pork chop recipes (*p. 309*).

Meal 3: Oriental Pork Casserole (*p. 279*). Cut remaining meat into cubes.

Pork Loin

In late fall and winter there are good buys in pork. And it's economical to buy a loin rack.

Meal 1: Roast Pork (*p. 309*). A 2 to 3 lb. piece.

Meal 2: Pork Chops (*p. 309*). Slice between ribs after backbone is removed.

Meal 3: Pork Tenderloin (*p. 310*). Strip out pork tenderloin with sharp knife, cut in 2" pieces. Flatten with a cleaver.

Meal 4: Country Backbone. Have bone sawed off, leaving 1" of meat. Cook like spareribs (*p. 310*).

Rib Roast

Expensive but a good value when used as follows:

Meal 1: Roast Beef (*p. 300*). Make Yorkshire Pudding (*p. 300*) for special treat.

Meal 2: Beef Short Ribs Jardiniere (*p. 302*).

Half a Ham

The shank halves of ham usually cost less. Be sure to buy a full shank.

Meal 1: Baked Ham (*p. 311*). Bake the piece with bone in.

Meal 2: Boiled Dinner. Use in place of corned beef in New England Boiled Dinner (*p. 303*).

Meal 3: Ham Slice (*p. 311*). Broil or pan-fry.

Meal 4: Scalloped Ham and Potatoes (*p. 264*).

We are indebted to Beth Bailey McLean and Thora Hegstad Campbell for helpful information and recipes from their book, "The Complete Meat Book".

METHODS OF MEAT COOKERY

DRY HEAT METHODS *(for tender cuts)*		BEEF	PORK	LAMB	VEAL
Roasting	1. Season with salt and pepper. 2. Place fat side up, on rack in roasting pan. 3. Do not add water, do not cover. 4. Roast at 325° (except fresh pork—350°) until done.	Ribs Rump (high quality) Sirloin tip Meat loaf	Loin Leg Spareribs Ham Picnic Ham loaf	Leg Shoulder	Leg Shoulder Loin Meat loaf
Broiling	1. Set oven for broiling. 2. Broil 2 to 3″ from heat until top is brown. 3. Season with salt and pepper. 4. Turn and broil until done. 5. Season and serve at once.	Steaks—rib, loin, T-bone, porter-house, strip Ground	Ham and picnic slices Bacon	Chops—shoulder, rib, loin Ground Kidney Leg steaks	Liver
Pan-Broiling	1. Place meat in heavy skillet. Cook slowly. 2. Do not add fat or water; do not cover. 3. Turn occasionally to brown and cook meat evenly. 4. Pour off fat as it accumulates. 5. Cook until done (do not over-cook); season and serve.	Same as for Broiling	Same as for Broiling	Same as for Broiling	Same as for Broiling
Pan-Frying	1. Brown on both sides in small amount of hot fat. 2. Season with salt and pepper. 3. Do not cover. 4. Cook over medium heat until done, turning occasionally.	Same steaks as for broiling, only thin-ner Liver	Thin chops Tenderloin Smoked ham slice Bacon	Chops—shoulder, rib, loin Ground Liver	Chops Liver Steak or cutlets Ground
MOIST HEAT METHODS *(for less tender cuts)*		BEEF	PORK	LAMB	VEAL
Braising	1. Brown on all sides in fat in heavy pan. 2. Season with salt and pepper. 3. Add small amount of liquid, if necessary. 4. Cover tightly and cook at low temperature until tender.	Pot roasts Short ribs Steak—round or flank Stew meat Liver Oxtails	Shoulder steaks Chops Cutlets Spareribs Liver Heart	Neck slices Shanks Stew meat Riblets Breast Heart	Breast Shoulder Chops Steaks or cutlets Stew meat Liver
Cooking in Liquid	1. Brown on all sides in own fat or other fat. 2. Season with salt and pepper. 3. Add liquid; cover kettle and cook below boiling until tender. 4. Add vegetables just long enough before serving to be cooked.	"Boiling beef" Corned beef Tongue	Fresh or cured —hocks, spareribs, picnic, butt	Shanks	Tongue Heart Sweet-breads

"BUY MEAT WISELY . . . STORE IT CAREFULLY"

says Reba Staggs of the National Live Stock and Meat Board, Chicago, who contributed much information to help us.

"Meat offers greater variety in kinds and cuts and a wider price range than almost any other kind of food. It is important to know the kinds and cuts of meat, for this assures varied and interesting menus. Not only are there many cuts of beef, veal, pork and lamb but also the variety meats and many different kinds of sausages and ready-to-serve meats. Select the grade and cut best fitted to your budget and the way you plan to cook it." All grades of meat have essentially the same nutritive value.

Look for the purple inspection stamp indicating government-inspected meat. It is required for your protection on all meat shipped interstate.

The grade and brand names used on meat and meat products include the grade and brand names of packers and retailers and the grade names of the United States Department of Agriculture.

There is no composite list of the grade or brand names used by individual meat packers and retailers, but each company will provide information concerning its own grade or brand names.

Information on the government grades of meat may be obtained from the Meat Grading Branch, Livestock Division, Agricultural Marketing Service, United States Department of Agriculture, Washington 25, D.C.

Grade and brand names are applied to meat with a roller stamp which leaves its mark the full length of the carcass, or if wholesale cuts are being graded, the full length of the cuts.

The marking fluid used for the meat inspection and grading stamps is harmless.

HOW TO STORE MEAT

1. Fresh Meat: Remove from market wrapping paper. Meat pre-packaged by the meat retailer (self-service) should have the wrapper loosened before placing it in the refrigerator unless the meat is to be used the same day as purchased. Fresh meat which is not pre-packaged should be removed from the market wrapping paper and stored unwrapped or loosely wrapped in waxed paper or aluminum foil. All fresh meat should be stored in the coldest part of the refrigerator or the meat storage compartment. The temperature should be as low as possible without actually freezing the meat.

While it is not generally recommended to freeze meat purchased for immediate consumption, it is usually desirable to freeze meat if it is to be held for more than three days.

    a. Ground Meat: Does not keep as well as whole cuts. Store as fresh meat. Cook within 24 hours. If kept longer, wrap meat and freeze it.

    b. Variety Meats: Store same as ground meat.

2. Cooked Meat: Cover tightly in dish or with foil to prevent drying, store in coldest part of refrigerator. Do not cut, grind or slice until ready to use.

3. Processed Meat: (cured, ready-to-serve, canned). Cured and ready-to-serve meats should be stored in the coldest part of the refrigerator. They should be stored in the original wrapper for a period not to exceed 1 week for ready-to-serve meats (luncheon meats, etc.) or 1 to 2 weeks for cured meats (hams, picnics, bacon). It is not advisable to freeze cured meats and ready-to-serve meats because the salt present in the meat favors the development of rancidity. Also, freezing harms the texture of ready-to-serve meats such as frankfurters. When freezing is absolutely necessary, the meat must be properly wrapped for freezing and the length of storage time must be limited. It should not exceed sixty days.

Canned hams, unless storage recommendations on the can read to the contrary, should be stored in the unopened can in the refrigerator until ready to use. Canned hams should not be frozen. Other canned meats do not require refrigerator storage unless label indicates it.

4. Frozen Meat: Store at a temperature of 0° or lower. It may be placed in the refrigerator under ordinary refrigeration if it is to be used immediately after defrosting. Never re-freeze meat.

HOW TO ROAST BEEF, VEAL, PORK AND LAMB

Roasting meats at low temperatures gives more and juicier servings per pound, does away with spattered ovens and reduces the amount of shrinkage.

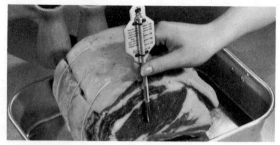

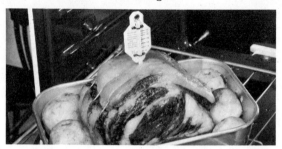

1. Season meat with salt and pepper.

2. Place fat-side-up on rack in open roasting pan. For very lean cuts, such as veal, lay piece of pork or beef fat, strips of bacon or salt pork over top. Do not sear meat.

3. If you have one, insert meat thermometer through outside fat in thickest part of muscle so point does not rest on fat or bone.

4. Roast in preheated slow oven (325°) (325° to 350° for pork). Use this temperature throughout. Do not add water, do not cover, do not baste.

5. Remove when meat thermometer registers desired degree of doneness or follow time in recipe. Allow the longer time for smaller cuts of meat.

Roast Beef

Choose:

Standing Rib

Rolled Rib

Allow ⅓ lb. with bone or ¼ lb. rolled for each serving.

Rump (of prime or high quality) in piece or rolled may also be roasted. Roast *at 325°* (slow mod.). See How to Roast (*above*).

	Min. per Lb.	Meat Thermometer
Rare..................	22 to 26	140°
Medium.............	26 to 30	160°
Well done...........	33 to 35	170°

For rolled roasts, add 10 min. per lb.
For frozen roasts, partial thawing is recommended as it cuts down cooking time.

HOW TO CARVE STANDING RIB ROASTS

Have ribs at left of carver, rib ends toward him. Start at right outside edge. Slice toward ribs in ¼" slices. When knife reaches rib, cut along full length of bone with knife tip.

Fillet of Beef Tenderloin

An excellent roast for company dinner because it cooks in a short time, is easy to carve, and is sure to be tender. Best served crusty brown on the outside and rare inside.

Select a 4 to 6-lb. tenderloin with a little outside fat. Have it trimmed and larded. Place on rack in roasting pan; brush with melted butter or oil. Roast *at 450° to 500°* (hot to very hot) *30 min. for rare; 40 min. for medium; 50 min. for well done.* Extreme tenderness and lack of fat make high temperature preferable. If desired, cut small gashes in tenderloin and insert slices of garlic before roasting. *8 to 12 servings.*

Oven-Browned Potatoes

Boil pared potatoes until almost done; drain, then place in pan with roast the last *30 min.* Turn to brown evenly.

Yorkshire Pudding

In England, Yorkshire Pudding is a "must" with roast beef.

Twenty minutes before beef roast is done, make batter for Popovers (*p. 89*). Heat in oven a square pan, 8x8x2". Remove roast from oven. Spoon off about ½ cup hot drippings. *Increase oven temperature to 425°* (hot). Return roast to oven. Place hot drippings in heated pan. Pour in batter. Bake *20 min.* Remove roast and continue baking pudding *another 15 to 20 min.* Cut pudding in squares and serve immediately. *6 to 9 servings.*

HOW TO BROIL MEAT

Broiling is the favorite method for tender steaks, ground meat patties, lamb chops and smoked ham steaks. Broiling is not recommended for any cut of veal.

1. Slash through outside fat 1″ apart to keep cut from curling.

2. Set regulator at 550° or "broil."

3. Place meat on rack in broiler pan or in smaller shallow pan with rack in it. Place under broiler so top is 2″ from heat (more for thicker cuts).

4. With door closed in gas range, door slightly ajar in electric range, broil until meat is well browned. Season with salt and pepper.

5. Turn and brown other side. Turn only once.

6. Season and serve immediately on hot platter as broiled meats cool quickly.

Broiled Steak

Choose:

Club   T-bone   Porterhouse

Tenderloin (Filet Mignon)   Sirloin

Allow ⅓ to ¾ lb. with bone or ⅓ to ½ lb. boneless for each serving.

Broil in oven. See How to Broil (*above*).

	1″ thick	2″ thick
Rare	5 min. each side	16 min. each side
Medium	6 min. each side	18 min. each side
Well Done	8 min. each side	20 min. each side

Pan-broiling will take about same length of time. Steaks over 1″ thick should be oven-broiled or charcoal-grilled, not pan-broiled.

HOW TO CARVE PORTERHOUSE STEAKS

Have flank end at left of carver. With knife tip, cut around bone. Remove bone. With knife at right angle to platter, slice across full width of steak (1″ slices). Cut across flank end the same way.

How to Pan-Broil

1. Use heavy skillet, rubbing it with suet or greasing it lightly if you wish. Place meat in skillet. Cook slowly.

2. Do not add fat or water; do not cover.

3. Turn occasionally to brown and cook meat evenly. Pour off fat as it accumulates.

4. Cook until done (do not overcook); season and serve.

How to Pan-Fry

Add a little fat, then proceed just as for pan-broiling, using medium heat. Pan-fry rather than pan-broil when meat has very little fat or is floured or breaded.

Minute or Cube Steaks

Minute and cube steaks are inexpensive cuts of beef, ¼ to ½″ thick, scored or cubed by a machine that cuts the fibers and makes the meat more tender.

Dip steaks in flour, shaking off any surplus. Place in sizzling hot skillet in which just enough butter to keep meat from sticking has been melted. Pan-fry on one side *2 to 6 min.*, or until browned as your prefer. Turn, and pan-fry on other side *2 to 6 min.* (The flour keeps juices in the steaks and helps them brown.) Remove to hot platter, sprinkle with salt and pepper; spread with softened butter, if desired. Serve immediately.

301

HOW TO BRAISE MEAT

Braising is sometimes called pot roasting. It is browning meat in a little hot fat, then cooking slowly with small amount of water in a tightly covered pan.

1. Season with salt and pepper, roll in flour. Or roll in Seasoned Flour (*at right*).

2. Brown meat slowly and thoroughly on all sides in a little hot fat.

3. Add small amount of liquid (2 to 3 tbsp.); cover tightly. If liquid cooks away, more may be added.

4. Cook over low heat at a simmering temperature on top of range or in oven at 325° (slow mod.) until meat is tender.

5. Vegetables may be added 30 to 45 min. before meat is done. Continue cooking until meat and vegetables are tender.

6. Meat and vegetables may be removed to hot platter and kept warm while liquid is thickened for gravy, if desired.

Seasoned Flour means 1 tsp. salt, ¼ tsp. pepper, mixed with 1 cup GOLD MEDAL Flour. If desired, ¼ tsp. paprika may be added.

Pot Roast

Choose:

Blade-bone Chuck

Round-bone Chuck

Boned Rump

Sirloin Tip

Allow ⅓ lb. with bone or ¼ lb. boneless for each serving.

Rub roast with ½ cup Seasoned Flour (*above*). Brown in hot fat in heavy kettle *20 to 30 min.* (A low rack or 3 jar lids punched with holes will keep meat from burning during cooking.) Add about 1 cup water and, if desired, other seasonings and ½ cup sliced onion. Cover tightly and simmer.

Weight	Thickness	Total Time
3 lb. (bone-in)	2"	2½ to 3 hr.
5 lb. (bone-in)	3"	3½ to 4 hr.

For large boneless roasts, allow 1 hr. more.

Pressure Cooking Meats

Cuts of meat that require braising or cooking in water may be cooked in a pressure cooker at a good saving of time. Follow cooker directions.

Pot Roast and Vegetables

For special flavor spread browned meat with ½ cup horse-radish.

Select 4 to 5 lb. pot roast. Make Pot Roast (*at left*)—*except* omit onions. About 45 min. before roast is done, add 8 to 10 small onions, 8 to 10 medium carrots, 8 to 10 stalks celery, cut up, 8 to 10 small potatoes or 4 large, quartered, and 1 tsp. salt. Remove meat and vegetables to hot platter. Thicken juice for gravy, if desired. *8 servings.*

Beef Short Ribs Jardiniere

Use 3 lb. short ribs (cut in serving pieces) in place of Pot Roast (*at left*). Cook ribs slowly *1½ hr.* Add 2 large carrots, cut up, 1 green pepper, cut up, and 2 or 3 stalks of celery, cut up; cook *30 min.* longer. Remove meat and vegetables. Thicken liquid for gravy. *6 servings.*

Stuffed Flank Steak

Have flank steak scored. Season with salt; spread with Bread Stuffing (*p. 324*). Roll crosswise and fasten with metal skewers. Brown on all sides in hot fat in heavy skillet. Add 1 cup water. Cover and bake *at 350°* (mod.) *2 hr.* To serve, cut across roll in 1" slices.

HOW TO COOK MEAT IN LIQUID

This method is usually used for cooking a large piece of less tender meat in a large amount of water.

1. Cover meat with hot water.

2. Season with salt and pepper (unless it is smoked or cured meat). Add onion, herbs and spices, as desired.

3. Cover and cook over low heat at simmering temperature until done. See recipe.

4. Vegetables may be added *30 to 45 min.* before meat is done.

Old-fashioned Beef Stew

"My husband worked with this recipe until he had just the right amounts of vegetables and seasonings," says Mrs. Edward Kruger of St. Louis, Missouri. See color picture p. 307.

2-lb. chuck or bottom round (cut in 2″ pieces)
1 tbsp. fat
1 qt. hot water
2 cups diced potatoes (3 medium)
1 cup diced turnips
1 cup diced carrots
½ cup diced parsnips
1 cup diced celery or 1 celery root, diced
1 green pepper, diced
½ cup diced onion (8 small), if desired
1 tbsp. salt
2 beef bouillon cubes

Roll meat in Seasoned Flour *(p. 302)*. Brown thoroughly in hot fat. Cover with the hot water. Simmer *2 hr.*, adding water if necessary. Add remaining ingredients. Cook until vegetables are tender, about *30 min.* If desired, thicken liquid for gravy. The flavor of this stew gets better each time it is reheated. *8 servings.*

Thicken liquid for gravy.

New England Boiled Dinner

3 to 4-lb. corned brisket of beef
8 small onions
8 whole carrots
4 potatoes, halved or quartered
2 turnips, cubed (if desired)
1 green cabbage, cut in wedges

Place meat in heavy kettle. Cover with hot water. Cover tightly and simmer *about 3 hr.* Skim off excess fat and add onions, carrots, potatoes and turnips. Cover and cook *20 min.* Add cabbage and continue cooking *10 to 15 min.* *8 servings.*

Beef Brisket With Horse-radish Sauce

3 lb. beef brisket
2 tbsp. vinegar
2 tbsp. sugar
2 tsp. salt
4 whole cloves
1 bay leaf
1 clove garlic
2 stalks celery, chopped

Place beef in heavy kettle with enough water to cover. Add rest of ingredients. Cover and simmer *3 hr.*, or until tender. Remove meat and slice. Serve with Horse-radish Sauce (below).

Horse-radish Sauce

⅓ cup bottled horse-radish
¼ tsp. dry mustard
1 cup Medium White Sauce *(p. 387)*
paprika

Combine horse-radish, mustard and white sauce in saucepan. Heat thoroughly. Sprinkle with paprika.

Swiss Steak

Pound ½ cup Seasoned Flour (*p. 302*) into both sides of 3 lb. round steak (2″ thick). Brown 2 onions, sliced, in hot fat in heavy skillet. Remove onions and brown meat well on both sides. Top with onions and add 2 cups cooked tomatoes. Cover and cook slowly until tender, *2½ to 3 hr. 8 to 10 servings.*

Country-fried Steak

Brown thoroughly and cook slowly for dark, rich flavor.

Choose 1½ to 2 lb. bottom round, top round, rump, shoulder or sirloin tip. Dredge with flour; brown in hot fat. Sprinkle with salt, pepper and seasoned salt. Add ½ cup water; cover and simmer *30 min.* Top with 1 onion, sliced. Cover and simmer *1 hr. 6 servings.*

Round Steak Royale

Rub 1 lb. round steak (1″ thick) with cut clove of garlic. Cook as for Country-fried Steak (*above*) *2 hr.* topping with ¼ cup sliced onions and 1 can (4 oz.) mushrooms (sautéed in butter) after browning. Remove steak and add ½ cup commercial sour cream; thin to gravy consistency with water. Heat and serve with meat. *4 servings.*

Beef Stroganoff

½ lb. fresh mushrooms, sliced
1 large onion, chopped
¼ cup butter
2 lb. round steak (¼ to ½″ thick)
1 tsp. salt
1 can (10½ oz.) bouillon or consommé, diluted to make 2 cups
1 cup commercial sour cream

Sauté mushrooms and onion in 2 tbsp. butter and remove from pan. Remove fat and bone from steak. Cut into strips 2½″ long and ¾″ wide. Melt additional 2 tbsp. butter in pan. Toss strips of meat in flour, coating thoroughly. Brown meat in butter. Add salt and bouillon-water mixture. Simmer, stirring occasionally, until meat is tender, *about 1¼ hr.* Add mushrooms, onions and sour cream; heat. Serve over noodles or rice. *6 servings.*

Chicken-fried Steak

Cut 1 lb. round steak in 4 pieces. Dip in Seasoned Flour (*p. 302*), then in 1 egg and 2 tbsp. water, beaten together. Dip again in flour. Brown on both sides in hot fat. Cover and cook slowly *20 to 30 min.* To make gravy, remove meat, add ¼ cup Seasoned Flour mixed with 2 cups milk. Stir until gravy comes to a boil; boil 1 min. *4 servings.*

Sauerbraten

A famous German dish; a sweet-sour beef to be served with boiled potatoes and sweet-sour red cabbage.

3½ to 4 lb. chuck roast
2 onions, sliced
2 bay leaves
6 whole cloves

12 peppercorns
12 juniper berries, if desired
2 tsp. salt
1 pt. red wine vinegar

Place roast in an earthenware bowl with onions and seasonings. Pour over a mixture of red wine vinegar and ½ cup water (heated to boiling). Marinate 3 days or more. Turn meat twice a day with 2 wooden spoons; never pierce with a fork. Keep in a cool place. To cook: drain meat and brown thoroughly on all sides in hot fat in heavy skillet. Add marinade, cover pan and simmer slowly *3 to 4 hr.*, or until tender. Serve meat with Gingersnap Gravy (*below*). *6 to 8 servings.*

Gingersnap Gravy: When meat is done remove to platter. Pour off any excess fat. Add 2 tsp. sugar and 8 crumbled gingersnaps and cook *10 min. longer.* Thicken with a flour-water paste (1 tbsp. flour per cup of liquid). Bring to boil; boil 1 min. Season and serve.

Fluffy Meat Loaf

Moist, seasoned just right. Save some for sandwiches.

1 lb. ground beef or veal
½ lb. ground lean pork
3 medium slices soft bread, torn in pieces, and
   1 cup milk or 1 cup dry bread crumbs and
   1¼ cups milk
1 egg, beaten
¼ cup minced onion
1¼ tsp. salt
¼ tsp. *each* pepper, dry mustard, sage,
   celery salt and garlic salt
1 tbsp. Worcestershire sauce

Heat oven to 350° (mod.). Mix all ingredients thoroughly. For better browning, shape into loaf on shallow baking pan. Bake *1½ hr.*, or until done. Serve hot or cold. For Catsup-topped Loaf, spread 3 tbsp. catsup on top before baking. *8 servings.*

Beef Loaf: Use 1½ lb. ground beef for the meat in Fluffy Meat Loaf (*above*). In place of mustard and sage, use 1 tbsp. *each* horse-radish and catsup.

Barbecued Beefies

(Individual Meat Loaves)

Shape mixture for Fluffy Meat Loaf (*above*) into 8 individual loaves (3x2x1"). Place in greased shallow pan with thin slices of onion on each. Pour Texas Barbecue Sauce (*p. 310*) over all. Baste often.

Skillet Meat Loaf

"My guests like this," says Helen Ayres Davis, who combines homemaking with an advertising career.

1½ lb. lean ground beef
1 can (8 oz.) tomato sauce
6 to 10 large stuffed olives, sliced
1 medium onion, chopped fine (½ cup)
⅓ cup rolled oats
1 egg
1 tsp. salt
¼ tsp. pepper

Heat oven to 350° (mod.). Mix beef, ⅓ cup of the tomato sauce, olives, onion, oats, egg and seasonings. Spread in heavy 10" skillet. Cover with remaining ⅔ cup tomato sauce. Bake *1 hr.* Remove excess fat from skillet before serving. Cut in wedges to serve. *6 servings.*

Broiled Hamburgers

Use 1 tsp. salt and ¼ tsp. pepper for each lb. ground beef. For extra juicy hamburgers, add ½ cup water or milk per lb. of meat. Broil 3" from heat, or pan-broil turning once. *1 lb. makes 4 thick or 8 thin patties.*

Swedish Meat Balls

Center of many a smorgasbord.

1 lb. ground beef
½ lb. ground pork
½ cup minced onion
¾ cup fine dry bread crumbs
1 tbsp. minced parsley
1½ tsp. salt
⅛ tsp. pepper
1 tsp. Worcestershire sauce
1 egg
½ cup milk

Mix all ingredients thoroughly. Shape into balls the size of a walnut. Brown in ¼ cup hot fat or vegetable oil. Remove meat balls and make Gravy (*below*). Return meat balls to gravy; cook *15 to 20 min. 6 to 8 servings.*

Meat Ball Gravy: Stir ¼ cup GOLD MEDAL Flour, 1 tsp. paprika, ½ tsp. salt and ⅛ tsp. pepper into hot fat in skillet. Stir in 2 cups boiling water and ¾ cup commercial sour cream.

Oriental Burgers

A Far Eastern sloppy Joe . . . tangy meat and sauce, with Chinese vegetables.

1 medium onion, sliced
1 lb. ground beef
2 tbsp. vegetable oil
1 can (1 lb.) bean sprouts, drained
1 can (5 oz.) water chestnuts, sliced (¾ cup)
⅓ cup soy sauce
⅓ cup water
1 tbsp. dark molasses
2 tbsp. cornstarch
2 tbsp. water

Sauté onion and beef in oil until browned. Add bean sprouts, water chestnuts, soy sauce, ⅓ cup water and molasses. Cook *about 5 min.* Add mixture of 2 tbsp. water and cornstarch. Bring to boil; boil 1 min. Salt to taste. Serve on hamburger buns. *8 servings.*

Veal is delicate in flavor and juicy when properly cooked. It combines well with other flavors. From the young beef, veal is lacking in fat and should not be broiled.

Roast Veal

Choose:

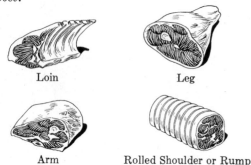

Loin   Leg

Arm   Rolled Shoulder or Rump

Allow ⅓ to ½ lb. bone-in or ¼ to ⅓ lb. boneless for each serving. Roast should be at least 3 lb.

If roast lacks fat covering, cover with bacon or salt pork. Roast in oven *at 325°* (slow mod.). *(See p. 300 for How to Roast.)*

	Weight	Cooking Time	Meat Thermometer
Loin........	5 lb.	3⅓ hr.	180°
Leg.........	3 lb.	2 hr.	180°
Shoulder...	3 lb.	2 hr.	180°
Boned and rolled.....	4 lb.	2⅔ hr.	180°

Veal roasts may also be braised or pot-roasted *(see p. 302)*, and if desired vegetables may be cooked with roast.

Veal Daube

An example of the superb French cuisine of New Orleans.

4 to 5-lb. veal rump or shoulder roast
cut clove of garlic
1 tsp. salt
⅛ tsp. pepper
¼ tsp. allspice
½ tsp. each thyme and sage
2 bay leaves, crushed
¼ cup GOLD MEDAL Flour
1 onion, minced
4 carrots, sliced
2 stalks of celery, diced
1 cup boiling water

Rub roast with cut clove of garlic. Mix seasonings with flour; rub well into meat. Brown in fat in deep heavy kettle. When well browned, remove from kettle. Brown onion, carrots and celery. Return browned roast to kettle and add boiling water. Cover and cook slowly until tender, *2 to 2½ hr.* Thicken liquid for gravy. *8 servings.*

Veal Cutlets, Chops, Steaks

Rib Chop   Loin Chop   Shoulder Blade Chop or Steak   Shoulder or Leg Steak

Allow ⅓ to ½ lb. bone-in or ¼ to ⅓ lb. boneless for each serving.

Dip cutlets, chops or steaks in flour or corn meal, then in beaten egg mixed with a little water, then in fine cracker or dry bread crumbs. Brown on both sides in hot fat. Season with salt and pepper. Add small amount of water (cream or diluted canned cream soup may be used), cover tightly, and cook slowly *45 to 60 min.* on top of range or in oven *at 325°* (slow mod.).

Stuffed Breast of Veal

Make same as Stuffed Shoulder of Lamb *(p. 312)* —*except* use Sausage Stuffing or Apple Stuffing *(p. 324).*

Veal Birds

1-lb. veal steak (¼" thick)
1" cube salt pork, finely chopped
½ cup fine dry bread crumbs
1 egg, slightly beaten
hot water to moisten
1 cup cream (20% butterfat)
¼ tsp. thyme

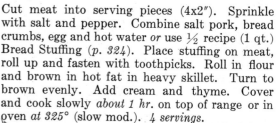

Cut meat into serving pieces (4x2"). Sprinkle with salt and pepper. Combine salt pork, bread crumbs, egg and hot water *or* use ½ recipe (1 qt.) Bread Stuffing *(p. 324)*. Place stuffing on meat, roll up and fasten with toothpicks. Roll in flour and brown in hot fat in heavy skillet. Turn to brown evenly. Add cream and thyme. Cover and cook slowly *about 1 hr.* on top of range or in oven *at 325°* (slow mod.). *4 servings.*

MAKING OLD-FASHIONED BEEF STEW

Recipe, page 303.

Veal à la Madelon

1 clove garlic, minced
2 tbsp. butter
2 lb. boneless veal, cut in bite-size pieces
2 tbsp. flour
1 tsp. salt
¼ tsp. pepper
two 1″ wide strips lemon peel
1 cup boiling water
1 cup whipping cream (35% butterfat)

Sauté garlic in butter in skillet. Remove garlic and brown veal in butter. Sprinkle flour, salt and pepper over meat. Brown again. Add lemon peel and water. Cover. Simmer until tender *about 1 hr.* Remove lemon peel. Stir in cream. Heat through. Serve over hot fluffy rice. *6 servings.*

Veal Supreme

1 lb. veal shoulder, cut in ½″ cubes
½ cup sliced mushrooms
¼ cup finely chopped onion
1 cup tomato juice
½ cup water
pinch of chervil and rosemary
½ bay leaf, if desired
¾ cup commercial sour cream
1 cup diced celery

Roll veal in Seasoned Flour (*p. 302*). Brown in hot fat. Add mushrooms and onion and sauté. Add tomato juice, water and herbs. Simmer until meat is tender, *about 25 min.* Add sour cream and celery. Cover and continue cooking *15 min.* Serve in center of a ring of cooked noodles (use 2 cups uncooked noodles, 4-oz. pkg.). *6 servings.*

NOTE: The noodles may be added with the sour cream and all poured into a greased oblong pan, 10x6x1½″. Garnish with blanched almonds. Bake in oven *at 350° (mod.) 15 to 30 min.*

Veal Paprika

A gourmet dish of distinction . . . sent us by Mrs. W. H. Stutzman, Kirkwood, Missouri.

Roll individual servings of veal steak (2 lb. cut ½″ thick) in Seasoned Flour (*p. 302*). Brown in hot fat in skillet rubbed with garlic. Add 1 cup hot water, cover, simmer *1½ hr.* Arrange meat on hot platter around Poppy Seed Noodles (*p. 288*). Into gravy left in pan, stir 1 cup cream; heat and pour over noodles. Sprinkle with paprika. *6 servings.*

Veal Cordon Bleu

"The different ingredients make a rich, well seasoned dish," says Mrs. Leonard Strauss of St. Louis, Missouri.

1½ lb. veal, cut up for stew
2 tbsp. butter
2 tbsp. flour
1 large tomato, sliced, or 1 cup cooked tomatoes
1 onion, minced
3 fresh mushrooms, sliced, or
  1 can (3 oz.) mushrooms, drained
1 tbsp. tomato paste
1½ cups beef bouillon
1 bay leaf

Brown veal in butter. Remove from pan. Blend in flour. Stir in tomato, onion, mushrooms and tomato paste. Gradually stir in bouillon and bay leaf. Bring to boil; add browned meat. Season to taste with salt and pepper. Simmer until tender, *about 1 hr.*, adding more liquid, if necessary. Serve with rice or noodles. *4 servings.*

Schweizerschnitzel

A member of our staff brought this recipe back from a small German restaurant near Munich.

8 small veal cutlets (boneless)
4 thin slices ham
4 thin slices cheese

Pound cutlets very thin. Place a slice of ham and cheese on 4 cutlets. Top with rest of cutlets. Roll in flour, then in beaten egg and then in dry bread crumbs. Sauté quickly in hot fat to a golden brown on each side. *4 servings.*

Veal Parmesan

Remove white fibers from veal cutlets or serving-size pieces of veal steak . . . and flatten. Sprinkle with salt, pepper and paprika. Coat with grated Parmesan cheese. Sauté in hot fat until lightly browned, *3 min.* on each side. Serve hot with Poppy Seed Noodles (*p. 288*).

Oriental Veal Casserole See p. 279.

The flavor of pork is improved by browning the fat and by slow cooking. All pork should be thoroughly cooked. Pork may be roasted, braised, stewed, but never broiled.

Roast Pork

Choose:

Pork Loin

Loin End   Center Cut

Shoulder—fresh

Butt   Picnic   Fresh Ham

Allow ⅓ to ½ lb. with bone or ¼ to ⅓ lb. boneless for each serving.

Any of the shoulder or leg cuts may also be sold as ham. Roast in oven *at 350°* (mod.). (*See p. 300 for How to Roast.*)

	Minutes per Lb.	Meat Thermometer
Loin...............	35 to 40	185°
Leg...............	25 to 40	185°
Shoulder, picnic.....	35 to 40	185°
Butt...............	45 to 50	185°

The longer time is for small roasts.

Crown Roast of Pork

Have crown made at meat market from two strips of pork loin containing about 20 ribs (6 to 8 lb.). (For easy carving, have backbone removed.) Season with salt and pepper. Place in roasting pan, bone ends up; wrap bone ends in aluminum foil to prevent excessive browning. Roast uncovered in oven *at 325°* (slow) *3 hr.* or until meat thermometer registers 185°. An hour before meat is done, fill center with 2 qt. Apple Stuffing (*p. 324*).

To Serve: Replace foil wraps on bone ends with crab apples or paper frills. Garnish platter with parsley. Slice by running knife close to bone of each rib down to platter. Remove each chop, one at a time. *About 20 servings.*

Braised Pork Chops

Chops from the loin are choicest . . . those from ribs or shoulder, most economical. Use this method for pork steaks (fresh ham), too.

Trim excess fat from chops. Lightly grease hot skillet with fat edge of one chop. Brown chops slowly on both sides in heavy skillet. (*Allow 3 min. on each side.*) For thicker chops, add ¼ cup water; cover tightly. For thin chops, add no liquid—a tight-fitting cover and low heat are all that is needed to keep them moist. Cook slowly on top of range or in oven *at 350°* (mod.) until tender and well done. Season after cooking.

	Thickness	Minutes per Lb.
Rib or loin chops.....	1″	30 to 35 min.
Rib or loin chops.....	½″	20 min.
Shoulder chops.......	½″	20 min.

Stuffed Pork Chops

Have pork chops cut double thick with a pocket on the bone side. Stuff pocket with Bread Stuffing (*p. 324*). Braise as above for 1½ hr.

Pork Chops Supreme

4 lean pork chops, 1″ thick
4 thin onion slices
4 thin lemon slices
¼ cup brown sugar (packed)
¼ cup catsup

Heat oven to 350° (mod.). Season well with salt. Place in 13x9½x2″ pan or large baking dish. Top each pork chop with an onion slice and a lemon slice. Place one tablespoon of brown sugar and one tablespoon of catsup on top. Cover and bake *1 hr.* Uncover and bake *30 min. longer*, basting occasionally. *4 servings.*

For Party Pork Chops: Use 1½ to 2″ thick pork chops. Bake *covered 2 hr., uncovered 30 min.*

HOW TO CARVE ROAST LOIN OF PORK

Turn rib side up. Run knife blade along close to back bone, removing bone. Place on platter with side from which bone was removed toward the carver. Use ribs as a slicing guide. Start at right end of roast, cutting vertical slices.

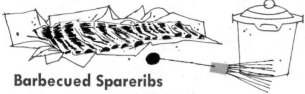

Barbecued Spareribs

Place 3 lb. spare or loin ribs, cut in serving-size pieces, on rack in shallow baking pan. Do not cover. Do not add water. On each piece, place a lemon slice. Sprinkle ½ cup chopped onion over all. Bake in oven *at 450° (hot) about 30 min.* Pour Texas Barbecue Sauce *(below)* over ribs. Continue baking *at 350° (mod.) 1½ to 2 hr.* Baste with sauce every 15 min. If sauce thickens, add a little hot water. To prevent excessive browning, cover last 30 min. of baking. *3 to 4 servings.*

Texas Barbecue Sauce

Mix in saucepan 2 tbsp. brown sugar, 1 tbsp. paprika, 1 tsp. salt, 1 tsp. dry mustard, ¼ tsp. chili powder, ⅛ tsp. cayenne pepper, 2 tbsp. Worcestershire sauce, ¼ cup vinegar, 1 cup tomato juice, ¼ cup catsup, ½ cup water. Simmer *15 min.,* or until slightly thickened.

Roast Spareribs

Allow ¾ to 1 lb. ribs per person. Spareribs require very long, slow cooking because of the large amount of bone. Place spareribs on rack in shallow baking pan. Season with salt, pepper and crushed bay leaf. Roast in oven *at 350° (mod.) about 1½ hr.,* or until tender. Serve.

Baked Stuffed Spareribs

Brown bony side of 2 sets of ribs in roasting pan on top of range. Turn 1 set brown side up; spread with Bread Stuffing or Apple Stuffing *(p. 324).* Cover with other set, brown side next to stuffing. Season with salt. Bake in oven *at 350° (mod.) 1½ to 2 hr.* If necessary, add ¼ cup water.

Spareribs and Sauerkraut

Cut 2 lb. spareribs into 3 or 4-rib pieces. Season with salt and pepper. Brown over medium heat in heavy skillet. Add small amount of water; cover and cook slowly *1 hr.* Empty 1 can (1¾ lb.) sauerkraut into kettle. Top with ribs using 3 tbsp. of the fat and ¼ cup water. Cook slowly *1 hr.*

NOTE: For variety, add ½ tsp. caraway seeds, 3 tbsp. sugar and 3 tbsp. chopped onion to sauerkraut. Or add ¼ cup brown sugar and 2 apples, cut in eighths.

Pork Tenderloin Patties

Brown tenderloin patties in a little hot fat in skillet over medium heat. Add small amount of milk, commercial sour cream, tomato juice or diluted cream of mushroom soup; cover, simmer *20 to 30 min.*

Savory Patties

Brown 1 lb. tenderloin patties in a little hot fat in skillet over medium heat. Pour over patties sauce made of ½ cup commercial sour cream, 2 tbsp. orange juice, 1 tbsp. grated orange rind and ¼ tsp. Worcestershire sauce. Cover and simmer *20 min. 4 servings.*

Pork Cutlets Mornay

Boneless pieces of pork steak. Elegant for a party dish.

Flatten 1 lb. pork cutlets. Season and dip in beaten egg and bread crumbs. Fry in hot fat until golden brown on both sides. Reduce heat, add a small amount of water, cover tightly and braise until tender, *about 30 min.* Place on hot baking pan coated with tomato sauce. Cover with Sauce Mornay *(p. 388).* Sprinkle with ½ cup grated Cheddar cheese and paprika. Place under broiler until hot and bubbly. *6 servings.*

Pork Teriyaki

Of Japanese origin. Also delicious grilled outdoors.

Marinate ¼ to ½″ thick slices of fresh pork (pork butt or pork shoulder) in Teriyaki Sauce *(below)* overnight in refrigerator. Turn occasionally. *Heat oven to 350° (mod.).* Place pork on cake rack with pan under it, lined with foil, to catch drippings. Bake *about 50 min.,* turning and basting frequently until pork is tender.

Teriyaki Sauce

Mix ½ cup soy sauce, ¼ cup honey, ½ tsp. flavor enhancer (monosodium glutamate) and 1 clove garlic, minced, or ½ tsp. ginger.

There are many kinds of cured and smoked ham. *Ready-to-eat means it is safe to eat without further cooking; but cooking will improve texture and flavor. Tenderized refers to a method of curing; it does not mean the ham has been cooked. Canned hams are ready-to-eat, or they may be reheated. Ham will vary greatly in price, the fully cooked or boned hams and the center cuts are costly. Read directions on wrapping carefully before cooking.*

Baked Ham

See color picture pp. 320-321.

Choose:

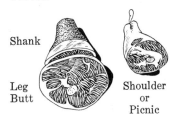

Shank

Leg Butt   Shoulder or Picnic   Boneless Shoulder Butt

Allow ½ to ¾ lb. uncooked with bone, ⅓ lb. boneless, ⅓ lb. cooked with bone, ⅛ to ¼ lb. boneless for each serving.

Follow directions for How to Roast *(p. 300)*, omitting seasoning. Half an hour before ham is done, take from oven and remove rind. Score fat; insert a whole clove in each square, if desired; add glaze and return to oven *at 400°* (mod. hot) for browning, *15 to 20 min.*

	Minutes per Lb.	Meat Thermometer
Whole ham, uncooked	18 to 20	160°
Whole ham, ready-to-eat . . .	10	130°
Half ham, uncooked	22 to 25	160°
Half ham, ready-to-eat	10	130°
Picnic	30 to 35	170°
Boneless Butt	40 to 45	170°

Ham and picnics will carve more easily if allowed to rest out of oven 15 to 20 min. Add this time plus the 10 min. for scoring and glazing.

Glazes for Ham

1. 1 cup brown sugar, 1 tbsp. dry mustard, ½ cup pickle juice or spiced fruit juice may be added.

2. 1 cup brown sugar and ¾ cup crushed pineapple.

3. 1 cup cranberry or currant jelly.

To Precook Ham

Uncooked picnics or shoulder butts should be simmered in water. They will be milder in flavor than when baked the full time. A 6 to 8-lb. picnic will take *3½ hr.*; a boneless 2-lb. shoulder butt, *2 hr.* After cooking in water, add glaze and brown in oven *at 400°* (mod. hot) *15 to 30 min.*

Ham Slice

Cut slashes in edge of a 1″ thick center cut slice of ham. **To Bake:** Sprinkle with 1 tsp. dry mustard and ¼ cup brown sugar. Place in heavy skillet or baking pan. Pour on milk at side of ham slice until it barely reaches top. Bake uncovered in oven *at 350°* (mod.) *1¼ hr.* **To Broil:** Broil *10 min.* 3″ from heat. Turn and broil on second side *10 min.* For ready-to-eat ham, cut time in half.

Pan-Broiled Ham Slice

Rub skillet lightly with ham fat. Place ¼ to ½″ slices of cured ham or Canadian bacon in skillet. Cook slowly until brown; turn and brown other side. For ready-to-eat or cooked ham, browning is all that is necessary.

Ham Loaf Superb

¾ lb. ham
½ lb. veal
¼ lb. pork
2 eggs, beaten
¾ cup soft bread crumbs
¾ cup milk
dash of pepper
2 tsp. prepared mustard
¼ cup brown sugar
⅓ cup pineapple juice or pickled peach juice

Heat oven to 350° (mod.). Grind together ham, veal and pork. Mix in eggs, bread crumbs, milk and pepper. Pat mixture in loaf pan, 9x5x3″. Spread mixture of mustard and brown sugar on top of loaf. Pour juice over loaf. Bake *1½ hr.* Baste loaf several times during baking. Serve with Easy Horse-radish Sauce *(p. 332)*. *5 to 6 servings.*

HOW TO CARVE WHOLE HAM

Place shank end at carver's right. Cut a few slices from near side. Turn ham on cut, flat surface. Holding with fork, remove small wedge 6″ from shank end. Cut thin slices down to bone; run knife along bone to release.

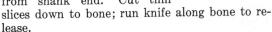

Lamb may be roasted or broiled, depending on the cut. A few of the less tender cuts are braised or made into stew. We are most familiar with lamb chops and leg of lamb, but there are many other cuts and delicious ways to prepare them.

Roast Lamb

See color picture p. 296.

Choose:

French Leg

Sirloin

Rib-crown Roast

Square Cut Shoulder

Cushion Shoulder

Rolled Shoulder

Allow ¼ to ½ lb. bone-in leg roast, ½ to ¾ lb. bone-in shoulder roast, ¼ to ⅓ lb. boneless for each serving.

The "fell," a paper-like covering, may or may not be removed. Those who like a definite lamb flavor prefer to leave the fell on. Season. Roast in oven *at 325° (slow mod.). (See p. 300 for How to Roast.)*

	Weight	Approx. Cook. Time	Meat Therm.
Leg (Medium)......	6 lb.	3 hr.	175°
(Well done).....		3½ hr.	182°
Crown..............	5 lb.	3¾ hr.	182°
Shoulder (bone-in)..	4 lb.	2¼ hr.	182°
Shoulder (cushion) .	4 lb.	2½ hr.	182°
Shoulder (rolled)....	4 lb.	2½ hr.	182°

▶ **ALL YOU HAVE TO DO**

For special seasoning: (1) cut slits in roast with tip of knife, insert slivers of garlic, (2) spread mint or currant jelly over roast, baste occasionally, (3) rub marjoram, thyme or rosemary into surface before roasting.

Stuffed Shoulder of Lamb

Have shoulder of lamb cut "cushion style" with bone removed. Lace string across open side. Fill pocket with Bread Stuffing (*p. 324*) or Apple Stuffing (*p. 324*). Fasten edges with skewers and lace tightly with string. Roast, following time above.

HOW TO CARVE LEG OF LAMB

Leg of lamb is carved just as a whole ham is; see directions on p. 311.

Lamb Chops and Steaks

See color picture p. 296.

Choose:

Sirloin Chop

Rib Chop

Loin Chop

Shoulder Chop

Shoulder Blade Chop

Leg Steak

English Chop

Allow ½ to ¾ lb. chops for each serving; ⅓ to ½ lb. steaks for each serving.

Broil in oven. (*See p. 301 for How to Broil.*)

		Time—each side	
	Thickness	Medium	Well done
Rib or Loin......	1″	6 min.	7 min.
	1½″	9 min.	11 min.
Sirloin..........	1″	6 min.	7 min.
English Chop....	2″	12 min.	15 min.
Shoulder Chops..	1″		8 min.
Leg Steaks.......	1″		8 min.

Pan-broiling requires about same time. (*See p. 301 for How to Pan-Broil.*)

Party Lamb Chops

Heat oven to 325° (slow mod.). Season eight 1″ thick loin or shoulder lamb chops, boned, generously on both sides with salt. Place in roasting pan. On each chop place: 1 onion slice, 1 thin slice processed Swiss cheese and 1 tbsp. commercial sour cream. Bake *uncovered 30 min.; cover and bake 2 to 2½ hr. longer,* or until tender. 8 servings.

Mixed Grill

Place 6 lamb chops, cut 1 rib thick, 6 small pieces calves liver *or* chicken livers, 6 pork sausages *or* slices of bacon on broiler rack. Broil 3″ from heat *5 min.* Season chops and liver with salt and pepper. Turn meat with tongs. Broil *5 min. more.* Add 5 large mushroom caps (rounded side up), brushed with 3 tsp. butter, and 6 tomato slices (½″ thick) seasoned with 2 tsp. salt, ½ tsp. pepper and ½ tsp. basil. Broil *5 min. more. 6 servings.*

Shish-Kabobs

"Popular in Russia," says Marylee Duehring of our staff who demonstrated Betty Crocker convenience foods at the American National Exhibition at Sokolniki Park in Moscow, which she calls, "the city of contradictions." See color picture p. 296.

1½ lb. lamb shoulder or shank, cut into 1" cubes
1 small onion, thinly sliced
1½ tsp. salt
¼ tsp. coarsely ground pepper
½ to 1 tsp. oregano
2 green peppers, cut in 1" pieces
1 large onion, cut in 1" pieces
2 firm tomatoes, cut in 1" pieces

Place lamb cubes in a bowl. Tuck in onion slices. Add seasonings. Refrigerate 1 to 2 hr. Alternate meat cubes, pieces of pepper, onion and tomato on metal skewers. Roll in vegetable oil. Broil 3" from heat, allowing *15 to 20 min.* Turn as meats and vegetables brown. *6 servings.*

Braised Lamb Shanks

Famous German dish.

4 lamb shanks, bones cracked
salt and pepper to taste
¼ tsp. thyme
½ tsp. rosemary
2 cups hot water
1 cup cut-up carrots
1 cup cut-up potatoes
½ cup cut-up celery
1 medium onion, chopped

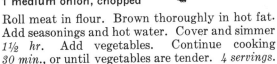

Roll meat in flour. Brown thoroughly in hot fat. Add seasonings and hot water. Cover and simmer 1½ hr. Add vegetables. Continue cooking 30 min., or until vegetables are tender. *4 servings.*

Lamb and Carrot Meat Balls

Delicious gravy thickens as these meat balls simmer.

¾ lb. shoulder of lamb, ground
1½ cups finely grated carrots
1 medium onion, finely chopped
1 egg
2 tsp. salt
⅛ tsp. pepper
2 tbsp. hot fat
¼ cup GOLD MEDAL Flour
1½ cups hot water
½ tsp. basil, if desired

Mix lamb, carrots, onion, egg, salt and pepper. Shape into 12 balls. Sauté in hot fat until brown. Remove from heat. Blend in flour. Stir in water. Add basil. Cover skillet and simmer *30 to 40 min.* *4 to 6 servings.*

Lamb Curry

See color picture p. 296.

3 large apples, pared, cored and sliced
1 onion, sliced
1 clove garlic
2 to 3 tbsp. flour
1 tbsp. curry powder
1 tbsp. lemon juice
2 cups meat stock or bouillon
1 tsp. gravy flavoring
grated rind of ½ lemon
½ cup raisins
3 whole cloves
2 cups cubed leftover cooked lamb

Sauté apples, onion and garlic in butter until golden brown. Remove garlic. Blend in flour and curry powder. Combine lemon juice, stock and gravy flavoring; stir in gradually. Stir in lemon rind, raisins and cloves. Cover, simmer *30 min.* Add lamb. Heat thoroughly. Serve with rice on a hot platter with a side dish of chutney.

Lamb Stew

2 lb. lamb shoulder, cut in 2" cubes
4 cups hot water
3 carrots, diced
1 small turnip, diced
1 onion, sliced
2 cups cubed potatoes
2 tsp. salt
¼ tsp. pepper
1 bay leaf
3 tbsp. minced parsley

Brown meat well in hot fat. Place in deep kettle. Add water. Simmer, covered, *about 2 hr.* Then add remaining ingredients. Continue cooking until vegetables are tender, *about ½ hr.* If desired, thicken broth with ¼ cup flour mixed with ½ cup cold water. Dumplings *(p. 86)* may be cooked on top of stew. *6 servings.*

Bacon is sold in ½ and 1-lb. pkg. (16 to 20 slices per lb.) or in slabs (to be sliced as desired). Bacon squares are economical and are used for seasoning vegetables. Buy only enough bacon for 1 week, as flavor and aroma fade after that. Never freeze bacon.

Pan-Fried Bacon

Place slices in cold skillet. Heat slowly. As bacon heats, separate slices. Do not overcrowd. Turn to cook evenly. Drain on absorbent paper.

Broiled Bacon

Place separated slices on broiling rack 3″ from heat. Turn once to brown evenly.

Baked Bacon

Place separated slices on rack in pan. Bake in oven *at 400°* (mod. hot) *about 10 min.* Do not turn.

Canadian Bacon (*Smoked boneless pork loin*)

Comes sliced 22 to 26 slices per lb., or in a piece (for baking). Allow 2 to 4 oz. for each serving. Pan-fry. Or broil as for bacon (*opposite*).

Baked Canadian Bacon

Canadian bacon in the piece may be roasted like ham. Remove casing. For 2-lb. piece, roast 1½ hr.; for a 4-lb. piece, 2⅓ hr. or 170° on meat thermometer. Use glazes (*p. 311*) as for ham the last 15 min.

Sausage comes in bulk or in casings as links. There are: plain sausage links, country sausage, smoked coarse-ground Polish sausage (smoked with garlic flavor) in large links or coils, thuringer sausage and Swedish sausage. Brown 'n serve sausages are the newest variety. Other sausages, such as bologna, liverwurst and salami are usually served cold or in sandwiches.

Pork Sausage Links

Place in skillet; add small amount of water. Cover and simmer *5 min.* Never prick. Drain. Pan-fry until brown or bake in oven *at 400°* (mod. hot) *20 to 30 min.*

Delicious served with scrambled eggs, applesauce, on top of a casserole of mashed sweet potatoes or corn or with Spanish rice.

Pork Sausage Patties

Form bulk pork sausage into patties or cut from roll. Place in cold skillet; cook over low heat *12 to 15 min.*, or until brown. Pour off fat as it gathers. Or bake as for Pork Sausage Links (*above*).

Country Sausage and Polish Sausage

Simmer, covered, in a little water *10 min.* Drain and brown evenly, *10 min.*

Sausage and Hominy

Cook Country or Polish Sausage (*above*). Remove sausage; add drained hominy and cook *5 min.* Stir to brown evenly. Serve with sausage.

Sausage and Kraut

Place canned sauerkraut in skillet; top with Country or Polish Sausage. Cover. Bake in oven *at 350°* (mod.) *1 hr.*

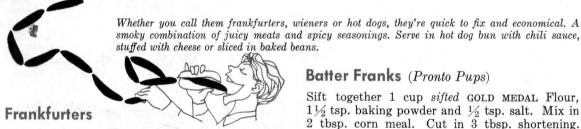

Whether you call them frankfurters, wieners or hot dogs, they're quick to fix and economical. A smoky combination of juicy meats and spicy seasonings. Serve in hot dog bun with chili sauce, stuffed with cheese or sliced in baked beans.

Frankfurters

To Simmer: Drop in boiling water; reduce heat, cook *5 to 8 min.* **To Grill:** Heat slowly in hot fat, turning to brown. **To Broil:** Slice diagonally every inch or so, not cutting through. Rub with butter or vegetable oil; broil 3″ from heat, turning to brown.

Batter Franks (*Pronto Pups*)

Sift together 1 cup *sifted* GOLD MEDAL Flour, 1½ tsp. baking powder and ½ tsp. salt. Mix in 2 tbsp. corn meal. Cut in 3 tbsp. shortening. Add 1 egg and ¾ cup milk; stir until blended. Dip 8 to 12 frankfurters into batter, one at a time. Fry in deep hot fat (365°) until brown, *2 to 3 min.* on each side. Drain on absorbent paper. Insert wooden skewer in end of each frankfurter. Serve with catsup or mustard. *8 to 12 servings.*

Many of these recipes using variety meats were shared with us by Helen Hallbert, Director of the Betty Crocker Kitchens. Any meal in her home becomes a special one because it is planned with loving care and served with a flair.

Pan-Fried Liver *(calf, beef or lamb)*

Allow ¼ lb. for each serving. Pre-cook only when it is to be ground. Avoid overcooking.

Dip ½″ slices in flour, brown in hot fat. Season. Reduce heat. Cook over low heat *8 to 10 min.*, turning once.

Liver and Bacon: Pan-fry 2 slices bacon for each serving of liver. Remove and keep hot while frying liver.

Liver and Onions: Peel and slice sweet onions. Cook in bacon fat until golden. Cover and cook slowly until tender. Pan-fry liver in another skillet. Serve topped with onions.

Braised Liver *(older beef or pork)*

Cut into ½″ slices. Roll in flour. Brown in a little hot bacon fat. Season, reduce heat. Cover and cook until tender, *20 min.*

Braised Liver with Vegetables

Braise liver *(above)—except* brown with the liver chopped onions, carrots and celery. Season. Place in greased baking dish, vegetables on bottom, liver on top. Add ½ cup liquid. Cover. Bake in oven *at 350°* (mod.) or cook on top of range *30 min.*

Broiled Liver *(calf or lamb)*

Slice ⅓ to ½″ thick; brush well with melted butter. Broil *3 min.* Turn once, broil *2 min.*

Oxtail Stew

2 lb. disjointed oxtails
¼ cup fat
1 cup tomato juice
½ cup water
1 cup chopped onion
1 tsp. salt
4 whole allspice
1 bay leaf, crumbled
1 clove garlic, minced
2 tbsp. lemon juice

Roll oxtails in Seasoned Flour *(p. 302)*. Brown thoroughly in hot fat. Add tomato juice, water, onion, salt, allspice, bay leaf and garlic. Cover and simmer *3 hr.* Remove allspice and bay leaf. Add lemon juice. Serve with hot buttered noodles. *4 to 6 servings.*

Liver 'n Bacon Patties

4 slices bacon
1 lb. sliced beef liver
1 small onion
1 egg, slightly beaten
1 tsp. salt
⅛ tsp. pepper
1 to 1½ cups crushed WHEATIES

Place bacon in cold skillet; cook until lightly browned. Remove bacon. Brown liver on both sides. Grind together bacon, liver and onion. Add egg, salt and pepper. Mix well. Shape into 6 patties. Coat with crushed WHEATIES and brown in hot fat. *6 servings.*

Liver Loaf

Brown 1 lb. beef liver in hot fat. Put through food chopper with ½ lb. bulk pork sausage. Add 1½ cups soft bread crumbs, 2 tbsp. minced onion, 1 tsp. Worcestershire sauce, 1 tbsp. lemon juice, 1 tsp. salt, ⅛ tsp. pepper, 1 tsp. celery salt, 2 eggs and ½ cup bouillon. Pat out mixture into loaf pan, 9x5x3″. Top with 2 slices bacon. Bake in oven *at 350°* (mod.) *45 min.*

Heart *(beef, lamb, veal, pork)*

To Prepare: Trim off blood vessels and fat. Wash thoroughly by running water through it. Loosen and trim out small thread-like cords. Wipe with damp cloth.

To Cook: Cover heart with water. Add ½ to 1 tsp. salt. Cover. Simmer until tender: veal and lamb heart, *1 to 1½ hr.*; beef and pork heart, *2 hr.* Grind, chop or slice and use in dishes calling for cooked meat.

Chicken-fried Heart

Slice heart in ¼″ thick pieces. Dip in Seasoned Flour *(p. 302)*. Brown on both sides in hot fat. Add a small amount of hot water. Cover and simmer *20 to 30 min.*

Stuffed Beef Heart

Fill cavity of trimmed and washed heart with Bread Stuffing *(p. 324)*. Fasten with skewers and string. Roll in Seasoned Flour *(p. 302)*. Brown in hot fat. Add ½ cup hot water. Cover. Simmer until tender or bake in oven *at 350°* (mod.) *about 2 hr.*

Tongue *(beef, lamb, veal or pork)*

Always a favorite, hot or cold. Sold fresh, smoked, cured and pickled.

To cook fresh tongue: cover with cold water. Add 1 tbsp. salt, 1 small onion, few peppercorns and 1 bay leaf. Simmer until tender, *1 to 1½ hr. per lb.* Cool slightly; remove connective tissue, bones and skin. Slice and serve hot or cold.

Popular Combinations

Hot tongue is good with buttered chopped spinach or Harvard beets.

Cold tongue is an excellent choice for the cold meat platter, with potato salad or for sandwiches.

Sweetbreads

A very special delicacy. Always precook.

Drop sweetbreads into boiling salted water. Reduce heat and simmer *25 to 35 min.* Drain. Plunge into cold water. Remove membranes. Store covered in refrigerator. Allow ¼ lb. for each serving. To serve, prepare as suggested below.

Pan-Fried Sweetbreads

Dip cooked sweetbreads in flour, then in beaten egg, then in fine cracker crumbs. Fry in hot butter until brown on all sides. Serve hot with tomato sauce, broiled ham or bacon.

Creamed Sweetbreads

Combine 1 lb. cooked sweetbreads, 2 cups Medium White Sauce *(p. 387)* and 1 cup cooked peas, mushrooms, asparagus tips, chicken, ham or veal. Season well and serve in patty shells or on toast.

Baked Sweetbreads and Mushrooms

Elegant company luncheon dish. We serve it frequently to guests.

Divide cooked sweetbreads into serving-size pieces. Roll in Seasoned Flour *(p. 302)* and pan-fry in 3 tbsp. butter until light brown. Place in baking dish. Sauté ½ lb. sliced mushrooms in 3 tbsp. butter . . . then make Thin White Sauce *(p. 387)* in the pan. Pour over sweetbreads. Bake *at 350° (mod.) 30 min.* Serve on rounds of toast or thin ham or Canadian bacon slices; garnish with water cress. *1 lb. sweetbreads makes 5 to 6 servings.*

Spiced Tongue

An inviting summertime supper dish. From Myrna Johnston, Food Editor of Better Homes and Gardens, who serves it at outdoor suppers in her own garden.

Add 1 lemon, sliced, 1 tsp. mixed pickling spices and 2 tsp. salt to the hot water in which a 3-lb. beef tongue is to be simmered. Serve either hot or cold with Easy Horse-radish Sauce *(p. 332)*.

HOW TO CARVE TONGUE

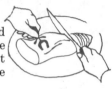

Have tip of trimmed, skinned tongue at right of carver. Slice at an angle from this part straight down so as to produce the largest slices.

Breaded Brains

You'll never know how good they are unless you try them.

Soak 1 lb. brains in salted water 15 min. Drop into boiling water; add 1 tsp. salt; cover and simmer *15 min.* Drain, plunge into cold water; drain again. Remove membrane just before using. Cut cooked brains in 1″ cubes. Mix 1 egg, 2 tbsp. milk and 1 tsp. salt; pour over brains and stir with fork to coat. Roll in ½ cup fine cracker crumbs. Brown slowly in ¼ cup melted butter, turning carefully to avoid breaking. Serve hot with lemon slices or tart pickle relish. *4 servings.*

Broiled Kidney and Bacon

A real delicacy.

Wash lamb kidney. Remove outer membrane. Split through center lengthwise. Remove fat and white tissue. Do not soak. Wrap half a kidney in half a slice of bacon; fasten with toothpick. Broil 3″ from heat *15 min.*, turning once. Serve 2 to a person.

Breaded Kidneys

Wash lamb, veal, beef or pork kidney. Remove outer membrane. Split through center lengthwise. Remove fat and white tissue. Do not soak. Dip kidney in flour, then in slightly beaten egg, then in bread crumbs. Pan-fry *15 min.* in hot fat. Serve with Piquant Brown Sauce *(p. 389)*.

The special flavor, texture and shape of poultry make it adaptable to many interesting dishes. Kathryn B. Niles of the Poultry and Egg National Board in Chicago very kindly gave us this information and pictures.

How to Roast Chicken, Turkey, Duckling or Goose

Have bird completely clean. Rinse with cold water. Pat dry. Rub cavity of bird lightly with salt. Just before roasting, stuff (*p. 324*), if desired, and truss.

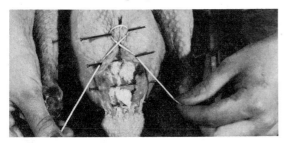

1. Stuff body cavity lightly. *Do not pack.* (Stuffing will expand while cooking.) Fasten opening with skewers . . . then lace shut.

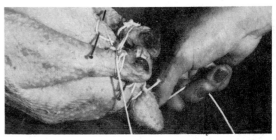

2. Tie leg ends to tail. Bring cord crisscross over back around base of wings. Tie. Insert stuffing in wishbone (neck) cavity.

3. Fasten neck skin to back with skewer. Lift wing tip up and over back for natural brace when turned over.

4. Brush entire bird with cooking fat. Place on rack, breast up. Insert meat thermometer in breast, being sure that tip does not touch bone.

Roast Turkey

Traditional for the holiday feast.

If you want a turkey between 8 and 15 lb., ask for a hen. If you want one between 16 and 25 lb., ask for a tom. Allow ½ to ¾ lb. ready-to-cook weight for each serving.

Prepare turkey for roasting (*above*). If you use a meat thermometer, insert it so the bulb reaches the center of the inside thigh or breast muscle. Place in preheated oven. *Do not cover.* For time and temperature, follow chart (*p. 318*). When light golden brown, place over turkey a piece of aluminum foil about 5″ longer than turkey. Pinch foil at ends, pressing lightly to anchor it. Leave loose at top and sides.

When turkey is about ⅔ done, cut the cord or the band of skin holding the drumstick ends to the tail to release the legs. This permits the heat to reach the inside thigh to assure thorough cooking.

To test for doneness: Press fleshy part of drumstick between fingers, protected with paper or cloth; meat should feel very soft. Move the drumstick up and down, the drumstick should move readily or twist out of the joint. Meat thermometer should register 190° when turkey is done. Remove from pan and keep hot while preparing gravy with drippings in roasting pan.

Half a Turkey

Skewer skin to breast to prevent shrinkage. Roast skin-side-down until ¾ done (see chart). Remove from oven, place stuffing shaped to fill cavity on heavy paper on rack in pan. Place turkey over stuffing and continue roasting until done.

CHART FOR ROASTING POULTRY

*Ready-to-Cook Weight	Oven Temperature	**Total Cooking Time
Turkey		
4 to 6 lb.........	325°	3 to 3¾ hr.
6 to 8 lb.........	325°	3¾ to 4½ hr.
8 to 12 lb.........	325°	4 to 5 hr.
12 to 16 lb.........	325°	5 to 6 hr.
16 to 20 lb.........	325°	6 to 7½ hr.
20 to 24 lb.........	325°	7½ to 9 hr.
Chicken		
4 to 5 lb.........	375°	1½ to 1¾ hr.
over 5 lb.........	375°	1¾ to 2 hr.
Goose		
6 to 8 lb.........	325°	3 to 3½ hr.
10 to 12 lb.........	325°	3¾ to 4¼ hr.
Duckling		
4 to 6 lb.........	325°	1½ to 2 hr.

*****Stuffed weight** of a bird is about the same as weight before it is drawn.

******For **well done,** add 5 to 10 min per lb.

Roast Chicken

Liked by many for holiday dinners. Two may be baked at one time. See color picture pp. 320–321.

A plump young bird, 3 lb. or over, is good for roasting. The capon, weighing from 4 to 7 lb., is especially tender and flavorful with a large amount of white meat. Prepare for roasting (*p. 317*). Follow time chart (*above*).

HOW TO CARVE TURKEY OR CHICKEN

Have leg at right of carver. Cut leg from body, first bending it back with left hand. Sever and lift to plate. Sever thigh from drumstick. Slice meat from leg. Then with fork astride breast, cut down sharply on joint joining wing to body. Cut thin slices of breast where wing was, working up to breast bone.

318

Roast Rock Cornish Game Hens

Roasted—or any other way—Danish pianist-humorist, Victor Borge, loves Rock Cornish game hens, for raising them is his other-than-show-business business.

Thaw four 12 to 15-oz. frozen game hens. Wash and pat dry. *Heat oven to 425°* (hot). Rub cavities of *thawed* hens with salt and pepper. If desired, stuff with 1½ to 2 tbsp. Bread Stuffing (*p. 324*). Place breast-side-up in roasting pan. Brush hens with unsalted fat. Roast *about 1 hr.*, or until fork tender, brushing hens with fat 2 or 3 times during roasting. Serve immediately.

Roast Goose

Prepare for roasting (*p. 317*)—except do not brush with fat. Pour off fat as it accumulates. If very fat, parboil *20 min.* Goose may be roasted in brown paper sack to eliminate fat spattering. Fasten end. When ⅔ done, puncture 6 to 8 holes in top of bag and turn. Excess fat drains into roasting pan.

Roast Duckling

Follow directions for Roast Goose (*above*)—except stuff with an onion, quartered apple and a few celery stalks. Discard stuffing after roasting.

Roasting Turkey in Aluminum Foil

This method shortens roasting time; also prevents spattering of the oven. Turkey is really steam-roasted and will be a light golden brown.

Prepare turkey for roasting (*details on p. 317*). Place bird on aluminum foil; wrap snugly. Seal securely to prevent drippings from escaping into the pan. Place foil-wrapped turkey, breast up, in bottom of a shallow pan. Place in 450° oven (very hot) and roast to within 15 or 20 min. of total roasting time given in the timetable. Remove from oven. Quickly fold foil away from bird to edges of pan. Return to oven and continue roasting until done.

Ready-to-Cook Weight	Oven Temperature	Total Roasting Time
8 to 10 lb.........	450°	2¼ to 2½ hr.
10 to 12 lb.........	450°	2¾ to 3 hr.
14 to 16 lb.........	450°	3 to 3¼ hr.
18 to 20 lb.........	450°	3¼ to 3½ hr.
22 to 24 lb.........	450°	3¼ to 3¾ hr.

Broiled Chicken

Select young chickens, not over 2 lb. in weight. Split in half lengthwise. Break joints to keep flat. Skewer wing and leg to body.

Place chicken on broiler pan (no rack). Brush with melted butter. Broil 5 to 7" from heat, skin-side-down. Broil slowly; regulate heat so chicken begins to brown in 15 min. Turn and brush with butter several times. Broil *35 to 50 min.*, or until tender.

Delmarvelous Broiled Chicken

Prize-winning recipe in a national chicken cooking contest in Salisbury, Maryland.

Make Broiled Chicken (*above*)—*except* rub entire surface of broilers with cut lemon (squeezing to release juice). Coat with melted butter. Sprinkle with mixture of 1 tsp. *each* salt and sugar, ¼ tsp. paprika and ⅛ tsp. pepper for each half.

Broiled Turkey

Split young turkey (about 4 lb.); snap joints to flatten. Brush with vegetable oil, season and place skin-side-down on broiler pan. Broil 7 to 9" from heat, basting often with Tart Turkey Baste (½ cup wine vinegar, ½ cup fresh lemon juice, ½ cup vegetable oil and 2 tsp. salt). Broil slowly *40 to 45 min.*, or until nicely browned. Turn and finish broiling, basting frequently. Allow 1¼ to 1½ hr. cooking time.

Pan-Fried Turkey

Small young turkeys may be fried like chicken or oven-fried (*p. 323*). Brown thoroughly for *15 to 20 min.* Cover and cook slowly until tender—*45 min.* for a 4-lb. bird; *50 to 60 min.* for a 5-lb. bird. If skillet does not have tight-fitting cover, add 1 or 2 tbsp. water. Uncover last 10 min. to recrisp.

Fried Chicken

Crisp on the outside, tender on the inside . . . according to the best Southern traditions.

2½ to 3-lb. frying chicken, cut in pieces
1 cup Seasoned Flour (*p. 302*)

Place a few chicken pieces in paper bag with seasoned flour. Shake well to coat chicken. Remove. Repeat until all chicken is coated. Starting with meaty pieces, place chicken in heavy skillet in hot vegetable oil, ½ to 1" deep. Cover; cook *10 to 15 min.* over medium heat. Remove cover, reduce heat and keep turning chicken until all pieces are uniformly browned, *20 to 25 min.* Drain on absorbent paper.

Maryland Fried Chicken

Dip chicken pieces in flour, then in beaten egg mixed with water, then in fine dry bread crumbs or cracker crumbs. Fry as above. Make Cream Gravy (*p. 390*) from drippings and serve over or with chicken.

Batter Fried Chicken

Cut larger fryer in serving-size pieces. Wash. Partially cook in boiling water, simmering *20 min.* Drain. Sprinkle with a mixture of salt, celery salt and pepper. Dip in Fritter Batter (*p. 87*). Drop into deep fat at 360° (cube of bread browns in 60 sec.). Fry until rich golden brown, *5 to 7 min.* Serve immediately.

Midwest Fried Chicken

Coat cut-up 3 to 4-lb. fryer by shaking in sack containing 1 cup Seasoned Flour (*p. 302*). Starting with meaty pieces, place in heavy skillet in ½" hot fat. Turn to brown evenly, *15 to 20 min.* Add 3 tbsp. water, cover and cook over low heat on top of range or bake *in 325° oven* (slow mod.) *45 to 60 min.*, or until tender. Uncover last 5 to 10 min. to recrisp.

Smothered Chicken

Make Midwest Fried Chicken (*above*)—*except* use only ½ cup Seasoned Flour, sprinkling any remaining flour over chicken. Pour 2 cups hot cream (20% butterfat) over browned chicken. Bake just until tender, then cream will be less likely to separate.

COMPANY'S COMING

Broiled Stuffed Lobster, page 329
Baked Fish with Vegetable Stuffing,
   page 327
Baked Ham, page 311
Roast Chicken, page 318, with
   Currant Glaze, page 325

Barbecued Chicken

Wash and dry cut-up or quartered fryer. Coat by shaking in a bag of Seasoned Flour (*p. 302*). Melt ¼ cup fat (half butter) in baking pan in oven *at 425°* (hot). Place chicken in pan in single layer, skin-side-down. Bake *45 min.* Pour off fat and turn. Spoon hot Barbecue Sauce (*below*) over chicken and bake *at 375°* (quick mod.) *30 to 45 min.*, or until tender. Baste with sauce during baking.

Barbecue Sauce

1 tsp. salt
½ tsp. pepper
1 tbsp. paprika
1 tsp. sugar
1 medium onion, finely chopped
1 cup tomato purée or catsup
¼ cup butter
½ cup hot water
⅓ cup lemon juice
1 tbsp. Worcestershire sauce

Mix all ingredients in saucepan. Heat to boil and remove from heat.

Burmese Chicken Curry

From former staff member Barbara Beck Thomson, whose husband's assignments in the United States Information Service have taken them to Bombay, India, and Rangoon, Burma. The Burmese serve this curry with rice cooked in milk made from grated coconut.

2 to 2½-lb. broiler-fryer chicken
4 small onions, grated
1 clove garlic, minced
2 tbsp. soy sauce
2 tsp. chili powder or cayenne pepper
1 tsp. turmeric
1 tsp. powdered ginger
½ cup vegetable oil
1 cup water

Wash and dry chicken. Remove skin. Remove meat from bones and cut into 1 to 2" pieces. Combine chicken, onions, garlic, soy sauce and seasonings in saucepan. Blend thoroughly. Stir in oil and water. Cover and cook over medium heat until chicken is tender, *30 to 40 min.* Serve over fluffy white rice. Burmese serve about 1½ cups rice and ½ cup chicken curry per serving. *4 to 6 servings.*

Stewed Chicken

For dishes made with cooked chicken.

4 to 5-lb. stewing hen
1 sprig parsley
1 celery stalk with leaves, cut up
1 carrot, sliced
1 slice onion (2 slices if older hen)
2 tsp. salt
½ tsp. pepper

Clean and cut up chicken. Place in kettle with just enough boiling water to cover; add remaining ingredients. Cover. Simmer gently until tender, *2 to 3 hr.* Add more water if necessary. Let cool in stock. Remove meat from bones in pieces as large as possible to use in chicken dishes. *A 5-lb. chicken gives 4 cups of cut-up cooked chicken and 3 to 4 cups of chicken stock.*

Chicken Fricassee

Roll cut-up pieces of a 4½ to 5-lb. stewing chicken in Seasoned Flour (*p. 302*). Brown in thin layer of hot fat in deep heavy kettle. Drain off fat and save. Add 1 cup water and, if desired, chopped onion, lemon juice or herbs such as rosemary or thyme. Cover tightly and cook slowly 2½ to 3½ hr. Add more water if needed. Remove chicken and make gravy using 1½ tbsp. of the saved fat and 1½ tbsp. flour to each cup of liquid. Serve with fluffy rice, cooked noodles or mashed potatoes.

Chicken Fricassee with Dumplings

A fricassee without dumplings is like a wedding without a bride.

Make Chicken Fricassee (*above*)—*except* make Dumplings (*p. 86*) before making the gravy. Arrange dumplings around the pieces of stewed chicken on hot platter. Serve hot . . . with gravy poured over chicken.

Butter-kist Chicken

Even an older chicken will be tender fixed this way.

Melt ¼ cup butter in a heavy skillet. Drop in chicken pieces and cover tightly. Simmer for *2 to 2½ hr.*, turning pieces occasionally and sprinkling them with flavor enhancer (monosodium glutamate) and salt. As necessary, add small amounts of water (about 2 tbsp. at a time) to keep chicken from drying out and browning. When meat is tender, remove cover and brown. Just before serving, remove chicken pieces to serving platter and make Cream Gravy (*p. 390*). Season.

Country Captain

So-tender chicken in a delicious subtly-flavored tomato sauce.

3 to 4-lb. frying chicken, cut up
¾ cup GOLD MEDAL Flour
2 tsp. salt
¼ tsp. cayenne pepper
1 tsp. paprika
½ cup shortening
1 onion, chopped
1 clove garlic, chopped
1 can (20 oz.) tomatoes (2½ cups)
1 cup hot water
1 tsp. salt
1 tsp. curry powder
½ tsp. *each* parsley, thyme
¼ tsp. pepper
3 to 4 cups cooked rice (1 cup uncooked)

Shake chicken in paper bag with flour, salt, pepper and paprika. Brown chicken on all sides in hot shortening. Add onion and garlic and sauté until onion is transparent. Add tomatoes, water and seasonings. Bring to boil. Cover and cook over low heat *1½ hr.*, or until tender. Serve with fluffy white rice. *4 to 6 servings.*

Chicken Breasts Baked in Cream

3 lb. chicken breasts
½ cup chopped onion
1 clove garlic, minced
1 cup cream (20% butterfat)
1 cup chicken broth
2 tsp. salt
⅛ tsp. pepper
1 tbsp. Worcestershire sauce

Heat oven to 300° (slow). Brown chicken breasts in hot fat. Add remaining ingredients. Cover tightly. Bake *about 2 hr.*, or until tender. Just before serving, remove chicken and keep warm while making gravy. *6 to 8 servings.*

To make gravy: Blend mixture of 2 tbsp. flour and ½ cup water into drippings in baking pan. Cook *2 to 3 min.* If too thick, thin with milk.

Chicken and Wild Rice See p. 280.

Oven-fried Chicken

1 cup GOLD MEDAL Flour
2 tsp. salt
¼ tsp. pepper
2 tsp. paprika
½ cup shortening (half butter)
1 cut-up frying chicken

Heat oven to 425° (hot). Mix flour, salt, pepper and paprika in paper bag. Put shortening in oblong pan, 13x9½x2" and set in oven to melt. Shake 3 or 4 pieces of chicken at a time in bag to coat thoroughly. Place chicken, skin-side-down, in single layer in hot shortening. Bake *30 min.* Turn skin-side-up and bake *another 30 min.*, or until chicken is tender. *4 servings.*

Chicken and Biscuits

Chicken fries in the oven and biscuits bake in the same pan.

Make Oven-fried Chicken (*above*)—*except* bake *45 min.*, then push chicken to one end in pan. Place Biscuits (*p. 76*) in single layer on other end. Bake *another 15 min.*, or until biscuits are lightly browned and chicken tender.

Lemon Barbecued Chicken

Make Oven-fried Chicken (*above*)—*except* after baking *45 min.* pour over Lemon Barbecue Sauce (*below*). Continue baking *15 min.*, or until tender.

Lemon Barbecue Sauce

Mash 1 small clove garlic with ½ tsp. salt. Add and mix well ¼ cup vegetable oil, ¼ to ⅓ cup lemon juice (2 lemons), 2 tbsp. finely chopped onion, 1 tsp. black pepper and ½ tsp. thyme.

Turkey or Chicken Cream Pie

Encore . . . leftovers take a bow!

Pastry for 8" Two-crust Pie (*pp. 337-339*)
2 cups cold stuffing
2 cups gravy
2 cups cut-up turkey or chicken
¼ cup cut-up pimiento

Heat oven to 425° (hot). Roll pastry 1" larger than top of 2-qt. baking dish. Put stuffing in baking dish. Heat gravy, meat and pimiento together; pour over stuffing. Cover with pastry. Fold under; flute around inside edge. Cut slits in center. Bake *25 to 30 min.* *6 to 8 servings.*

Bread Stuffing

1 qt. for 4-lb. chicken

⅓ cup butter
¼ cup finely minced onion
4 cups (1 qt.) coarse or fine crumbs or cubes
½ cup chopped celery (stalks and leaves)
1 tsp. salt
¼ tsp. pepper
1 tsp. dried sage, thyme or marjoram
poultry seasoning (to taste)

3 qt. for 12-lb. turkey

1 cup butter
¾ cup finely minced onion
12 cups (3 qt.) coarse or fine crumbs or cubes
1½ cups chopped celery (stalks and leaves)
1 tbsp. salt
1 tsp. pepper
1 tbsp. dried sage, thyme or marjoram
poultry seasoning (to taste)

Melt butter in large heavy skillet. Add onion and cook until yellow, stirring occasionally. Stir in some of bread crumbs. Heat, stirring to prevent excessive browning. Turn into deep bowl. Mix in remaining ingredients lightly. For dry stuffing, add little or no liquid. For moist stuffing, mix in lightly with fork just enough hot water or broth to moisten dry crumbs. Cool and place stuffing in bird when ready to bake.

Giblet Stuffing

Simmer the heart, gizzard and neck from chicken or turkey in seasoned water until tender, *1 to 2 hr.* Add the liver the last 5 to 15 min. Chop the cooked giblets and add to Bread Stuffing (*above*).

Sausage Stuffing

Excellent for pheasant and veal.

Make Bread Stuffing (*above*)—*except* add ⅓ lb. bulk pork sausage, crumbled and browned, for each quart. Omit salt; use sausage fat as part of fat.

Apple Stuffing

Make Bread Stuffing (*above*)—*except* add 1 cup chopped apples for each quart.

Oyster Stuffing

Make Bread Stuffing (*above*)—*except* add 1 cup chopped drained oysters for each quart.

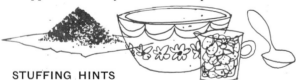

STUFFING HINTS

Mix dressing, ready to stuff, ahead. Chill. Stuff the bird just before roasting to avoid possibility of food poisoning. After the meal, remove stuffing from bird and chill.

A 1-lb. loaf of bread makes 8 cups loosely packed crumbs or cubes (2 qt.).

Plan a cup of stuffing for each pound of ready-to-cook weight.

Pecan Stuffing

Make Bread Stuffing (*above*)—*except* add ⅔ cup coarsely chopped pecans for each quart.

Garden Vegetable Stuffing

Combine 2 cups fine dry bread crumbs, 1 cup finely grated raw carrots, 1 cup finely chopped onion, sautéed in butter, 1 cup chopped raw mushrooms, ½ cup chopped parsley, 1 egg, 1½ tbsp. lemon juice, 1 clove garlic, minced, 2 tsp. salt, ¼ tsp. marjoram and ¼ tsp. pepper. Mix well and pack lightly in cavity of 4 to 5-lb. chicken or 6 to 8-lb. fish.

Mushroom-Wild Rice Stuffing

Sauté ½ lb. sliced mushrooms (or 4-oz. can) in ¼ cup butter *5 min.* Remove mushrooms, add ¼ cup minced onion, 1 tbsp. minced parsley and ½ cup chopped celery; cook until onions are yellow. Add 2 cups cooked wild rice (part brown or white rice may be used), ¾ tsp. salt and dash of pepper. Stuff 4 to 5 lb. chicken.

If the family has divided tastes about texture and seasoning of stuffing, pack some of each one in body cavity.

Bake extra stuffing separately in a pie pan during last 30 to 45 min. of roasting time. Baste occasionally with poultry fat.

2 to 4-day old bread is best for stuffing. Cut off crusts. Pull into ¼ to ½" crumbs or cut in cubes.

Pack stuffing loosely into bird. Packing too tightly makes it heavy and soggy.

Game includes all wild animals and fowl used for food. The main difference between game and domesticated is that wild animals are leaner so need a layer of fat before they are cooked. They may have developed strong muscles from exercising so the meat needs marinating or other tenderizing.

Pheasant and Prairie Chicken

Pheasant is more plentiful. Wells Wilbor, star hunter of General Mills, says, "Add white wine when you cook it as it tends to be dry."

Prepare like chicken (any method). Especially delicious baked in cream—follow recipe for Chicken Breasts Baked in Cream (*p. 323*), using half the amounts of ingredients. If roasted, use Sausage Stuffing (*p. 324*).

Poached Pheasant

The epicurean way . . . as served at dinnertime by Mr. and Mrs. Edward Heum, formerly of Minneapolis, now of San Diego, California.

Poach sections of the breast of pheasant in hot butter in chafing dish at the table. Cook only until it loses its transparency, *5 to 10 min.* The dark meat, legs, etc. can be served later in a main dish.

Quail and Ruffed Grouse

Called bob white and partridge (the most delicate of all game). Mostly breast meat.

Split in halves and pan-broil breast-side-down in lots of butter. Baste often. Or wrap in strips of bacon and bake *at 350°* (mod.) *30 to 35 min.*

Squab and Guinea Hen are domesticated game birds. Prepare as for Broiled Chicken (*p. 319*). Also good fried, braised or roasted. One squab makes 1 generous or 2 small servings. Allow ¾ to 1 lb. guinea hen for each person.

HOW TO REMOVE FEATHERS FROM FOWL

Wet picking is quick and when done properly retains the fine appearance and excellent flavor. Pheasants, grouse and quail have fairly tender skins and should be dipped in water heated to just 130°. Mallard ducks require water heated from 150 to 160°. Dip up and down in hot water until coarse wing and tail feathers can be pulled out easily. Wrap in several thicknesses of cloth and let steam a few minutes. Feathers then can be removed quickly and cleanly. Singe and remove pin-feathers.

Badly shot birds are often skinned but this removes the fat and reduces the fine flavor. Dry picking is very tedious and for most people it is impractical.

Roast Wild Duck

Lewis Child, a crack-shot hunter, says they cook a large Mallard about an hour in a hot oven . . . basting it with wine.

Prepare as for Roast Duck (*p. 318*). Place quartered apples, sliced orange, slices of onion and celery leaves in the cavity (discard after roasting) or fill with the suggested vegetable stuffing below.

To Roast . . . for a brown crispy crust, roast uncovered *at 425°* (hot). Baste several times with hot water at first, then with juices in pan or a wine, until moderately well done . . . tender and juicy (½ to 1 hr. depending on size and age of duck). If preferred, duck can be roasted longer *at 350°*. **To Glaze** . . . brush with a mixture of orange juice and currant jelly the last few minutes and just before serving. Garnish with slices of orange topped with currant jelly.

For Stuffed Wild Duck . . . use a mixture of equal parts of chopped carrots, onion and celery sautéed in butter and serve duck surrounded with the vegetables—the flavor is extended in them.

Venison (*Deer, Moose, Elk*)

Meat from a young animal should "age" for a week, from an older animal for two to three weeks at about 38°. The meat may be cooked like tender cuts of beef. To tenderize meat from an older animal, marinate in buttermilk. Fat should be cut off and replaced with other fat such as salt pork or beef suet. Venison may be served rare, medium or well done. For a special touch baste the roast with red wine. Never overcook venison!

Rabbit and Squirrel

Wild are best in fall and early winter. Domesticated are available anytime. Fur-bearing animals should be eviscerated at once and skinned as soon as possible.

Rabbit and squirrel may be prepared according to any of your favorite recipes for chicken. Remember that the flesh is lean and extra fat should be used in cooking. Roast or fry the tender young animals; older ones are best braised or fricasseed.

FISH *How to chart your fish course.*

FISH FACTS

We are grateful to Rose G. Kerr, home economist with the fisheries branch of the Department of Interior, whose helpful booklets were one of the sources of information for these pages.

Fresh fish have clear, bulging eyes; elastic, firm flesh; reddish pink gills; are free from strong odor. Buy fish stored and displayed on crushed ice . . . just before using. (The fresher the better.)

Frozen fish are available the year 'round (in steaks and fillets). For best results, thaw frozen fish (preferably in refrigerator) just before cooking. Never refreeze. Prepare as fresh fish. Have flavor and texture of fresh-caught fish.

AMOUNT TO BUY

Whole or round fish . . . . .1 lb. per serving
Dressed fish . . . . ½ lb. per serving
Steaks, fillets, sticks . . . . ⅓ lb. per serving

Smoked fish are delicious plain or very simply prepared (boiled, steamed, baked). Most popular are salmon, whitefish, finnan haddie.

Salted cured fish, such as cod and mackerel, require removing excess salt. Soak overnight in cold water. (Or soak for 2 hr. . . . then simmer in fresh water for *30 min.*). Cook as desired.

Fat fish have oil running through all the flesh and are generally best for broiling, baking and planking. Examples:

Mackerel	Barracuda
Pompano	Tuna
Salmon	Shad
Lake Trout	Sturgeon
Rosefish	Whitefish
Herring	Catfish

Lean fish have a drier flesh with the oil stored mainly in the liver and are generally best for boiling and steaming. When baking, add strips of bacon; when broiling, baste with melted fat. Examples:

Bass	Cod
Haddock	Buffalofish
Pike	Perch
Carp	Flounder
Red Snapper	Whiting
Halibut	Croaker

Both fat and lean fish may be pan or deep fat fried.

HOW TO IDENTIFY CUTS OF FISH

Whole or Round
Exactly as caught.

Drawn
Entrails removed.

Dressed
Entrails, head, tail, fins removed.

Pan Dressed
Small sizes of dressed fish (such as crappie).

Fillets
Sides cut lengthwise. Usually boneless.

Butterfly Fillets
Double fillet held together by skin.

Steaks
Cross section slices of large dressed fish.

Sticks
Uniform pieces of fillets.

HOW TO FILLET FRESH FISH

Cut down the back of fish from head to tail on either side of and close to backbone. Cut the flesh free from the rib bones. Skin fish, if desired, beginning at tail end. (Fish with scales are scaled before filleting.)

HOW TO SCALE AND CLEAN FRESH FISH

Hold fish by the tail. Scrape with a blunt knife (or fish scraper) from tail to head in short, firm strokes. Slit underside, remove entrails. Wipe out well.

Because swimming is easy, fish have no tough muscles and need be cooked only briefly. Fish is done when it flakes easily with fork. Serve immediately on preheated platter (fish becomes soggy on standing).

OVEN METHODS

Baked Fish

Suitable for any size or cut.

Heat oven to 350° (mod.). Place fish on aluminum foil in shallow baking pan or in greased shallow pan. Sprinkle with salt, pepper and melted butter. Bake *20 min. for fillets, 30 min. for steaks, 15 min. per lb. for whole fish.* Serve with Egg Sauce (*p. 387*) or Anchovy Velouté Sauce (*p. 388*).

Baked Fish with Stuffing

See color picture pp. 320–321.

For whole fish, fill cavity ⅔ full with Garden Vegetable or Bread Stuffing (*p. 324*) and sew shut.

For fillets, place stuffing between 2 pieces of fish and hold sides secure with toothpicks. Bake as above except longer.

Planked Fish

Elegant for whole fish.

Place fish on hot greased plank (hickory, oak or ash 1½″ thick) or on heatproof glass. Sprinkle with salt, pepper and melted butter. Bake as above. When fish is almost done, arrange a border of hot mashed potatoes around it. Brown under broiler. Garnish. Serve on plank at table.

Broiled Fish

For fillets, small whole fish.

Dip 4 or 6 fish fillets in oil. Sprinkle with salt and paprika. Place skin-side-down on greased broiler pan or baking pan in oven *at 500°* (very hot). Broil 2 to 3″ from heat for *3 min.* Remove and pour over 2 to 4 tbsp. chicken broth (or bouillon cube dissolved in water). Return to *450° oven for 10 min.* Pour 1 tsp. lemon juice and ¼ cup melted butter over fillets just before serving.

Sauces for Fish

Tartar Sauce: Mix 1 cup mayonnaise, 1 tsp. grated onion, 2 tbsp. minced dill pickle, 1 tbsp. minced parsley, 2 tsp. cut-up pimiento.

Cocktail Sauce: See p. 56.

TOP-OF-RANGE METHODS

Pan-Fried Fish

For small game fish; trout, perch, sunfish, crappies.

Sprinkle fish with salt and pepper. Dip in flour or corn meal. Pan-fry in hot skillet with fat ⅛″ deep (part butter gives superb flavor) over medium heat until golden brown. Turn carefully and brown other side, *about 10 min.* in all. Drain on absorbent paper. Serve hot.

Crispy Fried Fish

Cover fish fillets . . . pike, smelt, flounder, etc. with buttermilk. Sprinkle with salt (allow 1 tsp. salt for each lb.). Let stand about ½ hr. Drain. Dip each fillet in flour. Pan-fry. Serve with lemon.

Deep Fat Fried Fish

Perfect for fillets.

Heat fat in deep kettle until a cube of bread browns in 50 seconds (375°). Dip fish in flour, then in slightly beaten egg . . . then in bread or cracker crumbs and drop into hot fat. Fry quickly until golden brown, *3 to 6 min.* Drain on absorbent paper. Serve with lemon slice and Tartar Sauce (*at left below*).

Poached Fish

For steaks and large pieces of fish.

Tie fish in cheesecloth. Lower into boiling water to which 1 sliced onion, carrot, several sprigs of parsley, 2 whole cloves, 1 bay leaf, 2 peppercorns, salt and a little vinegar have been added. Simmer *6 to 10 min. per lb.* depending on thickness. Serve with Egg Sauce (*p. 387*) or Golden Cucumber Sauce (*p. 328*). Or use in salads, creamed dishes or dishes like Pompano en Papillote (*p. 270*).

Steamed Fish

For steaks and large pieces of fish.

Place fish in cheesecloth or cooking parchment on perforated rack or in wire basket directly above boiling water. Cover pot tightly. Cook until done, *10 to 15 min. per lb.* depending on thickness. Remove skin and bones. Season and serve immediately with choice of sauces.

FISH *A "string" of good fish.*

Poached Fish with Golden Cucumber Sauce

A recipe from the collection of Warren Posey, advertising executive of New Orleans, whose hobbies are fishing and gourmet cookery.

To Poach Fish: In large deep skillet, heat to boiling, water about 1½" deep, 1 tsp. salt, 2 peppercorns, 3 lemon slices, 3 sprigs parsley and 1 bay leaf. Place 4 to 6 white fish fillets carefully in boiling mixture and simmer covered *4 to 6 min.*, until fish flakes easily with fork. Remove fish carefully with spatula. Serve immediately with Golden Cucumber Sauce *(below). 4 to 6 servings.*

Golden Cucumber Sauce

¼ cup vegetable oil (such as Wesson)
2 tbsp. flour
2 cups milk
3 egg yolks, slightly beaten
1 medium cucumber, peeled, seeded, diced
   (½" cubes)
1 can (4½ oz.) shrimp, coarsely chopped
1 tsp. salt
½ tsp. Tabasco
½ tsp. nutmeg
⅛ tsp. pepper

Blend oil and flour in saucepan until smooth. Slowly stir in milk, mixing thoroughly. Bring to boil over low heat, stirring constantly. Boil 1 min. Remove from heat. Gradually stir at least half of hot mixture into slightly beaten egg yolks. Then blend into hot mixture in saucepan. Boil 1 min. more, stirring constantly. Blend in remaining ingredients. Serve warm over fillets.

Fillet de Sole Bonne Femme

Originally French, this unusual recipe for preparing sole was brought to us from Scotland by Mrs. M. D. McKenzie of De Land, Florida.

Mix 2 tbsp. melted butter, 2 to 3 tbsp. lemon juice (1 lemon) and ¼ cup finely chopped onion. Pour into an oblong baking dish, 11½x7½x1½". Dip 1 lb. fillet of sole or flounder in this mixture and turn to coat. Bake skin-side-up *at 350°* (mod.) *20 to 30 min.* Place on hot serving platter; pour over a thick fresh mushroom sauce thinned with the juices in which the fish was baked.

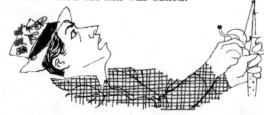

Salmon Loaf

2 cans (16 oz. each) salmon
2 eggs
1½ cups liquid (salmon liquid plus milk)
3 cups coarse cracker crumbs
2 tbsp. lemon juice
2 tsp. chopped onion
¼ tsp. *each* salt and pepper

Heat oven to 350° (mod.). Grease a loaf pan, 9x5x3". Flake salmon and remove bones and skin. Blend in eggs. Stir in remaining ingredients. Spoon lightly into pan. Bake *45 min.* Garnish with lemon wedges. *8 servings.*

Scallop Casserole

1 pt. scallops
½ to ¾ cup cream (20% butterfat)
3 cups soft bread crumbs
½ cup butter, melted
1 tsp. salt
¼ tsp. pepper
1 tbsp. celery seeds

Heat oven to 375° (quick mod.). Grease an oblong baking dish, 11½x7½x1½". Arrange scallops in dish. Pour part of cream over scallops. Combine remaining ingredients and sprinkle over scallops. Pour over remaining cream (it should come ¾ way up on scallops). Sprinkle with paprika. Bake *30 to 40 min. 4 servings.*

Golden Broiled Steaks

Use shad, salmon, gar, cod, buffalofish, etc.

Arrange fish steaks (cut ¾" thick) on greased broiler rack. Spread with part of mixture of grated onion, soft butter, lemon juice, salt, pepper and a little marjoram. Broil *10 min.* (2" under heat); turn and spread with remaining mixture. Broil until golden brown. Serve hot with parsley garnish.

Lutefisk

At holiday time, Scandinavians serve lutefisk with butter, boiled potatoes, lefse, lingonberry sauce, rice pudding and sandbakkels.

Buy a 2-lb. pkg. frozen boneless lutefisk (specially treated cod). You will find directions on the pkg. for cooking in its pliofilm wrapping. Serve lutefisk hot with melted butter or Medium White Sauce *(p. 387).* Pass butter in pitcher or have a little cup of it at each place.

HOW TO BUY SHELLFISH

Crabs, lobster, turtles (move lively), clams, mussels, oysters (tight shells) should be alive. Shrimp are not alive (headless), smell fresh, have green color, close fitting shell. Have soft-shelled crabs cleaned by dealer.

Shucked: Meat removed from shell of clams, oysters and scallops. Must be refrigerated.

Cooked-in-Shell: Such as hard-shelled crabs, lobsters, shrimp. Must be refrigerated.

Cooked, Shell Removed: Such as lobster, crab and shrimp. Must be refrigerated.

Canned: All shellfish are available. Some are smoked.

HOW TO CLEAN SHRIMP

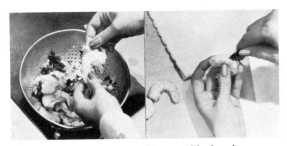

Peel off pink shells.   Remove black vein.

Broiled Lobster

Place live deep sea lobster on back; kill by cutting through head with a sharp knife or plunge into boiling water for 2 to 3 min. With sharp knife, split lobster open from head to tail. Remove black vein, small sac back of head and spongy lungs. Crack claws. Place lobster, top shell-side-up, on broiler rack 4″ from heat. Cut tail crosswise twice (to help prevent curling). Brush with melted butter. Broil *6 to 8 min.*, turn over and brush again with melted butter. Broil *4 to 6 min.*, or until meat and shell are pink (or stuff as below and broil). Serve with melted butter and lemon.

Baked Stuffed Lobster

See color picture pp. 320–321.

Kill and clean lobster as directed above. For each lobster, mix the coral roe and the green liver with 2 tbsp. dry bread crumbs, ¼ tsp. Worcestershire sauce and 1 tsp. chopped parsley and stuff in cavity. Brush meat liberally with melted butter. Bake at *450° (hot) 12 to 15 min.* Serve hot.

Louisiana Boiled Shrimp

Boiled shrimp seasoned to perfection. So tangy in flavor, there is little need for a cocktail sauce.

2 qt. water
3 cups diced celery
1 cup chopped onion
2 lemons, quartered
2 cloves garlic, minced
6 bay leaves
3 tbsp. salt
1 tbsp. whole allspice
2 tsp. cayenne pepper
3 lb. headless frozen or fresh shrimp (with shells still on)

Bring water to boil in large kettle. Add all ingredients except shrimp. Simmer *15 min.* Add shrimp; bring back to boil; simmer *15 min.*, or until shell turns pink and shrimp is tender. Remove from heat. Let shrimp stand 20 min. in shrimp boil; drain. Peel off shells; remove black vein. Serve on platter of cracked ice with favorite cocktail or horse-radish sauce. *3 to 4 main dish servings; 6 to 8 appetizer servings.*

Boiled Crab

Plunge live hard-shelled crab into boiling water well seasoned with lemon, parsley, celery leaves, etc. Bring to boil, then simmer *about 20 min.* (until red). Drain. Let cool at room temperature.

To Serve: break off claws and legs from cooked crab; crack; remove meat. Break off tail or "apron." Force shell apart. Discard spongy material. Remove meat with nut pick; or if Dungeness Crab, tap crab against inside of dish. *6 crabs yield about 1 cup meat for salads, hot dishes, etc.*

▶ ALL YOU HAVE TO DO

To cook soft-shelled crabs: season prepared crabs. Roll in crumbs . . . beaten egg . . . and crumbs. Deep fat fry, broil or pan-fry lightly.

Broiled Lobster Tails

Buy a 6 to 8-oz. South African rock lobster tail for each serving. Thaw frozen tails; cut away thin undershell with kitchen scissors. To keep tails from curling while they broil, bend each backward toward shell to crack. Place on broiler rack, shell-side-up, about 3″ from heat; broil *5 min.* Turn flesh-side-up, brush with melted butter, sprinkle with paprika, broil *8 min. longer.* Serve with melted butter and lemon wedges.

Lobster Thermidor See p. 269.

FISH *One of man's earliest foods.*

Fried Oysters

Select large oysters. Dip in flour; then in 1 egg beaten with 2 tbsp. water; then in fine dry bread or cracker crumbs with salt and pepper added. Fry in hot fat (375°) until golden brown, *2 to 5 min.* Drain on absorbent paper. Serve with lemon or Hot Tartare Sauce (*p. 388*).

Scalloped Oysters

Heat oven to 450° (hot). Mix 1½ cups dry bread or cracker crumbs with ½ cup melted butter. Spread ⅓ of the crumbs in a greased baking dish, 10x6x1½". Arrange over crumbs in 2 layers: 1 pt. oysters, drained, ½ tsp. salt, ¼ tsp. pepper, ¼ cup diced celery, 2 tbsp. minced parsley, ⅔ cup liquid (half oyster liquor, half milk or cream) and the remaining crumbs. Top layer will be crumbs. Bake *about 30 min.* 4 to 6 servings.

Baked Fish au Gratin

2 lb. white fish fillets, fresh or frozen, thawed
8 slices Cheddar cheese
1 tsp. thyme or oregano
¼ cup chopped parsley
2 medium onions, chopped (about 1 cup)
2 tbsp. vegetable oil
2 tbsp. flour
1 tsp. salt
⅛ tsp. pepper
1 cup milk

Heat oven to 400° (mod. hot). Place half of fillets in greased baking dish, 9x9x1¾". Cover with 4 slices of cheese. Top with another layer of fillets and cheese. Sprinkle with thyme and parsley. Sauté onions in oil over medium heat until clear and lightly browned. Blend in flour, salt and pepper. Slowly stir in milk; bring to boil over low heat, stirring constantly. Boil 1 min. Pour over fish. Bake *20 to 30 min.* 6 to 8 servings.

Fillets Almondine

Wonderful for fillets of sole, pike, whitefish.

Bake, broil or pan-fry fish. When fish is done, pour Almond Butter (*below*) over top. Serve immediately.

Almond Butter: Brown ¼ cup butter in small skillet. Add ¼ cup toasted slivered blanched almonds, ¼ tsp. salt and 2 tsp. lemon juice.

French Fried Sea Food

Shrimp, clams, scallops.

Roll the sea food in Seasoned Flour (*p. 302*). Dip into egg, then into dry bread crumbs. Fry in hot fat (375°). Drain on absorbent paper. Serve with catsup or Tartar Sauce (*p. 327*).

Steamed Clams

Scrub clams, discarding any that are open. Add 1" water to kettle with clams. Cover tightly and steam *about 10 min.*, or until shells begin to open. Serve in shells with individual dishes of melted butter and lemon juice. Serve strained broth in bouillon cups. *½ peck serves 4.*

Old-time Fried Clams

Dip clams in Fritter Batter (*p. 87*) and deep fat fry (*p. 327*).

Oysters on Half Shell See p. 56.

Golden Fish Puffs

1 pkg. (16 oz.) frozen pike fillets, thawed
⅛ tsp. salt
1 egg white
¼ cup mayonnaise
¼ tsp. dill seed
¼ tsp. onion juice

Heat oven to 425° (hot). Place fillets in greased baking dish, 9x9x1¾". Season with salt and pepper. Add salt to egg white and whip until stiff but not dry. Fold in mayonnaise, dill and onion juice. Spoon onto fillets. Bake *about 12 min.*, or until fish flakes easily and top is puffed and brown. *4 servings.*

Crispy Browned Hash

1 cup chopped cooked beef chuck
1 cup chopped cooked potatoes
1 onion, minced
1 tbsp. minced parsley
salt and pepper to taste
½ cup milk

Combine all ingredients except milk. Place a little fat in a hot heavy skillet over medium heat. When fat is very hot, spread hash evenly in skillet. The pan should be hot enough to brown the bottom of the hash quickly, *10 to 15 min.* Add milk and mix. Cover and cook slowly until crisp, *about 10 min. 2 to 3 servings.*

Chopped cooked veal, lamb, ham, chicken or turkey may be used in place of beef when making hash.

Meat Croquettes

1 cup Thick White Sauce (*p. 387*)
1 tsp. *each* minced onion and parsley
2 cups coarsely ground or finely chopped cooked meat (beef, pork, ham, veal, lamb or chicken)

Mix all ingredients. Spread out on plate or pie pan. Chill thoroughly. Shape into balls or cylinders. Roll in flour, then dip in mixture of 1 egg, slightly beaten, and 2 tbsp. water, then in fine dry bread crumbs. Fry in deep hot fat (365°) until delicately browned, *1½ to 2 min.* Be careful not to puncture during frying. Drain on absorbent paper in 350° oven until serving time. Serve with hot Mushroom Sauce (*p. 387*) or Tomato Sauce (*p. 389*). *8 croquettes.*

Ham or Chicken Timbales

Delicate individual molds.

4 eggs, slightly beaten
1¼ cups milk
1 tsp. *each* salt and onion juice
⅛ tsp. pepper
¼ tsp. paprika
1½ to 2 cups chopped cooked ham or chicken

Heat oven to 350° (mod.). Mix all ingredients. Spoon into buttered custard cups. Set in pan of water (1″ deep). Bake *about 30 min.*, or until silver knife inserted 1″ from edge comes out clean. Unmold. Serve with hot Béchamel Sauce (*p. 388*). *6 servings.*

Monday Macaroni. See p. 283.

Savory Meat Pie

Glorifies leftover roast. Have mixture hot when topping goes on to insure a thoroughly baked crust.

¼ cup chopped onion
2 tbsp. chopped green pepper
2 cups diced cooked meat (beef, lamb, veal from leftover roast)
2 cups diced cooked vegetables (fresh or leftover—such as carrots, celery, peas, corn, turnips, parsnips
1½ to 2 cups well seasoned gravy thinned with milk or stock
dough for Southern Biscuits (½ recipe p. 76)

Heat oven to 425° (hot). Sauté onion and green pepper in hot fat. Combine with meat, vegetables and gravy in 2-qt. baking dish. Heat in oven *15 min.* Cover with biscuit dough. Cut slits in top for steam to escape. Bake *about 20 min.*, or until golden brown. *6 servings.*

Gilded Pot Roast

A good way to dress up a pot roast the second day.

Sauté 1 onion, finely chopped, and ½ lb. mushrooms, sliced, in 3 tbsp. butter. Stir in 1 cup cream. Simmer *10 min.* Season with salt and pepper. Pour out on large baking pan. Thinly slice leftover pot roast; arrange overlapping slices on mushroom mixture. Spread chopped leftover vegetables over meat. Pour over any meat juices. Cover with 1 cup grated Parmesan cheese. Place under broiler to brown slightly.

Fish Turbot

Arrange alternate layers of flaked cooked pike, trout or bass with Medium White Sauce (*p. 387*) seasoned with onion salt, minced parsley, lemon juice, mace and 1 egg yolk to each cup of sauce. Cover with buttered cracker crumbs and bake *at 400° (mod. hot) about 25 min.*, or until browned on top. Serve hot.

Curried Pork Slices

Arrange slices of cooked pork roast in a baking dish. Top each with a cooked apricot half. Pour Curry Sauce (*p. 387*) over top, sprinkle with a little minced onion, if desired. Top with sautéed mushrooms. Heat *at 350° (mod.) 15 to 20 min.*

Meat or Chicken Shortcakes

Split hot biscuits. Serve plenty of cut-up cooked meat or chicken in well seasoned gravy between and over top.

331

Whole Cranberry Sauce

Boil 2 cups water and 2 cups sugar together *5 min.* Add 4 cups cranberries. Boil, without stirring, until all skins pop, *about 5 min.* Cool. *Makes 4½ cups.*

Molded Cranberry Sauce: Boil Cranberry Sauce (*above*) until thick and cranberries are clear, *15 min.* Pour into mold and chill.

Cranberry-Orange Relish

Put rind and pulp of 1 large orange and 4 cups cranberries through food chopper. Mix in 2 cups sugar and let stand several hours.

Orange-Currant Sauce

For roast duck, lamb, ham or chicken.

Empty ½ cup red currant jelly into bowl and break up with fork. Add grated rind of 1 orange, ⅛ tsp. *each* salt and cayenne pepper and 1 tbsp. prepared mustard dissolved in juice of 2 oranges. Beat well. Serve hot or cold.

Red Cinnamon Apple Rings

Cut cored, pared apples in ½" rings or slices and cook until tender in syrup of 2 cups sugar, 1 cup water, ⅓ cup red cinnamon candies and a few drops red food coloring. Use as a garnish for meat.

Cranberry Ice

"No holiday dinner is complete without it!" says Dr. W. P. Duerre of Lake City, Minnesota. It's a wonderful accompaniment to turkey; also makes a colorful holiday dessert with pistachio ice cream. Serve in avocado halves for holiday appetizer.

1 qt. cranberries (4 cups)
2 cups water
2 cups sugar
¼ cup lemon juice (2 lemons)
1 tsp. grated orange rind or ½ cup orange juice
2 cups cold water (part raspberry juice may be used)

Cook cranberries in water until skins are broken, about *10 min.* Rub through a fine sieve to make smooth pulp. Stir in rest of ingredients. Pour into refrigerator tray. Freeze until firm, 2 to 3 hr., stirring 2 or 3 times. *8 servings.*

Raisin Sauce

A perennial favorite for baked ham.

Melt 2 tbsp. butter over low heat in heavy saucepan. Blend in 2 tbsp. flour. Remove from heat, stir in 2 cups apple cider and ½ cup seedless raisins. Bring to boil, stirring constantly. Boil 1 min. Remove from heat. Serve hot. *Makes 2 cups.*

Currant-Mint Sauce

Good on wild rice.

¼ to ⅓ cup finely chopped mint leaves
2 tbsp. grated orange rind
¼ cup sugar
1 jar (8 or 10 oz.) currant jelly

Combine mint leaves, orange rind and sugar; let stand 1 hr. Mix in jelly with fork. Serve warm. (Jelly will not dissolve.)

NOTE: If fresh mint is not available, use 1 jar mint jelly. Add with currant jelly. Use only 2 tbsp. sugar.

Easy Horse-radish Sauce

Always welcome with ham loaf or tongue.

Fold 3 tbsp. well drained horse-radish and ½ tsp. salt into ½ cup whipping cream, whipped. *Makes 1 cup.*

Old-fashioned Applesauce See p. 219.

Spiced Peaches

Delicious with ham or chicken. Another day use this mixture to spice pears to serve with lamb.

Mix 1 cup vinegar, 1 cup honey, 3 whole cloves and 3 sticks cinnamon in saucepan. Heat to a simmer. Add 6 cups canned peach halves. Cool. Chill several hours or overnight. Drain. Serve fruit with some of the liquid over it.

Pickled Beets

Drain juice from 1 can (16 oz.) sliced beets. Add water to make 1 cup. Add ½ cup vinegar, 1 cup sugar and 1 stick cinnamon; bring to a boil. Pour over beets. Marinate several hours or overnight in refrigerator. Part of the liquid may be poured off when served. *4 servings.*

PIES

Pies, the favorite American dessert, originated in ancient Greece, according to legend. Later the Romans conquered the Greeks, and learned from them the art of making pastry. The Romans filled their pastries with beautiful fruits from near and far.

The flaky tender pastry we know today was developed about 1790 and each country soon perfected its own national specialty: the flans from England, the Napoleons and other puff paste delicacies from France, the fruit-filled strudels from Germany.

Here, during the first lean years in New England, pioneer mothers contrived simple "pyes." They sliced the tops off pumpkins, scooped out fiber and seeds, filled the pumpkins with milk and baked them on the open hearth. The first American pie pans were designed round to cut the corners and shallow so pies would "go a long way."

But soon bounty blessed our land and pies grew large and richly crusted. Settlers in each region of our country created pies according to their old country origin and the ingredients at hand: the fruit and shoo-fly pies of the Pennsylvania Dutch, the apple pies of New England, the sweet potato and nut pies of the French colonists in the Carolinas and Louisiana, and, later, the citrus fruit pies of California and Florida. Today there are pies for every taste and every occasion—delectable fillings encased in flaky pastry.

PIES TO PLEASE

(complete index in back of book)

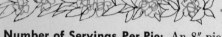 TIMESAVING TIPS

Number of Servings Per Pie: An 8″ pie cuts into 5 or 6 pieces. A 9″ pie cuts into 7 or 8 pieces.

TOPPINGS

Pies often have more appetite appeal if you spoon sweetened whipped cream or whipped ice cream on the top. Add chopped nuts or dates, crushed peanut brittle or grated orange rind. Or sprinkle the top with shaved chocolate, toasted slivered almonds or toasted coconut. Cut Cheddar cheese in fancy shapes to top a favorite apple pie.

NUT BROWN GLAZE

Blend 2 tbsp. soft butter and ¼ cup brown sugar (packed). Stir in 1½ tbsp. cream and ¼ cup pecan halves. Spread over baked pie (warm or cooled). Place under broiler 3″ from source of heat. Broil *3 to 5 min.*, or until glaze bubbles and browns. Serve while glaze is still warm.

SHORT PIE

Heat oven to 450° (hot). Put 1 cup Bisquick and ¼ cup soft butter (½ stick) in 9″ pie pan. Add 3 tbsp. boiling water and stir vigorously with fork until dough forms a ball and cleans the pan. Dough will be puffy and soft. With fingers and heel of hand, pat dough evenly into pie pan. This may seem skimpy but will not be when baked. Flute edge if desired. Bake *8 to 10 min.* Cool and fill with a cooked fruit filling of your choice or fresh fruit in season.

PIE FROM THE PANTRY SHELF

For the Crust: Use Betty Crocker Instant Mixing Pie Crust Mix.

For the Filling: Use pudding mixes for cream pies. For fruit pies, try a prepared canned filling such as cherry, blueberry or apple.

 MEALTIME MAGIC

SUNDAY RELAXING

Pink Bunny (*p. 274*) on Crackers
Crisp Vegetable Relishes
Lemon Mallow Pie (*p. 358*)
Coffee

WEEK-END COMPANY DINNER

Butter-kist Chicken (*p. 322*)
Mashed Potatoes   Green Peas
Cranberry-Grape Salad (*p. 379*)
Biscuits
Old-fashioned Mince Pie (*p. 348*)

Note: You no longer need to sift flour for recipes in this chapter. Measure Gold Medal flour by dipping nested measuring cups into flour and leveling off with spatula.

WHAT EVERY COOK NEEDS TO KNOW ABOUT PIES

BAKE WITH CARE

The cook who is renowned for her pies has learned the trick of making tender flaky pastry, luscious fillings and high meringues.

Pastry, like biscuits, is made of simple ingredients and its success depends largely on the skill of the cook. Follow the step pictures (*pp. 337–339*) remembering to mix and roll the dough *lightly*. Try not to pull the pastry as you fit it into the pan—if you do, it may shrink out of shape in baking. During longer baking periods it is wise to protect the crust with aluminum foil.

Perfect fruit pies are filled with just-tender fruit of lively natural flavor and color in slightly thickened fruit juice. These fruit juices sometimes bubble up through the crust and out of the pan, so save a clean-up job by placing another pan on a shelf below the pie.

Custard pies present a difficult cookery problem since pie crusts require a high temperature for crispness while the custard filling should be baked at a low temperature to prevent weeping and curdling. Slip-Slide Custard Pie (*p. 349*) solves the problem by baking the two separately and then slipping the custard into the shell.

Cream pies are easily made by pouring *hot* cooked filling into the baked shell, immediately topping with a soft meringue and browning.

Four tips to prevent weeping between the meringue and filling (and the formation of those little amber beads on the meringue): 1. gradually beat sugar into the frothy egg whites, 2. continue beating until sugar is dissolved and meringue stands in stiff peaks, 3. seal meringue securely to edge of crust, 4. do not overbake meringue.

. . . .

SERVE WITH FLAIR

It's fun to make pies party-pretty. If you are making a fruit pie, try a lattice top (*p. 340*) or a fancy edge (*p. 340*) or mark a plump apple with tiny leaf on the top crust of an apple pie.

A mound of whipped cream, then a sprinkle of chopped nuts, toasted coconut, chocolate curls (*p. 135*), or grated fruit rind, will dress up chiffon pies.

NEW ADVENTURES IN PIES

Blueberry-Peach Pie (*p. 343*)—A delightful combination of fresh fruit.

Crunchy-Nut Crust (*p. 341*)—Delicious filled with ice cream.

Date-Caramel Pie (*p. 352*)—Oh so good.

Minute Cream Pies (*p. 359*)—Easy to make.

Red Cherry-Banana Pie (*p. 346*)—Colorful and so refreshing.

AMERICA'S FIRST CHOICES IN PIES

Lemon Meringue Pie, page 353   *Apple Pie, page 342*   *Cherry Pie, page 343*

Standard Pastry for One or Two-crust Pie

Made with solid shortening. Flaky and tender. Definite measurements give perfect results!

For 8 or 9″ One-crust Pie
1 cup GOLD MEDAL Flour
½ tsp. salt
⅓ cup lard (or ⅓ cup plus 1 tbsp. hydrogenated shortening)
2 tbsp. water

For 8″ Two-crust Pie
1½ cups GOLD MEDAL Flour
¾ tsp. salt
½ cup lard (or ½ cup plus 2 tbsp. hydrogenated shortening)
3 tbsp. water

For 9″ Two-crust Pie
2 cups GOLD MEDAL Flour
1 tsp. salt
⅔ cup lard (or ⅔ cup plus 2 tbsp. hydrogenated shortening)
¼ cup water

1. Measure flour by dip-level-pour method or by sifting (*see p. 6*). Mix flour and salt in bowl. Cut in shortening with pastry blender until particles are size of peas.

2. Sprinkle with water, 1 tbsp. at a time, mixing with fork, until flour is moistened. Gather dough together with fingers so it cleans bowl. Press into ball. Turn out on lightly floured cloth-covered board.

3. If making two-crust pie, divide dough about in half; round up larger part on board. Prepare rolling pin by covering with stockinet. (Flour rubbed into covered board and stockinet keeps dough from sticking, yet is not taken up by dough.)

4. Flatten with hand, roll out not quite ⅛″ thick. Roll lightly, being careful not to add extra flour as that makes pastry tough. Keep rounding edge of pastry. If it begins to break, pinch broken edges together immediately.

5. Keep pastry circular and roll it about 1″ larger all around than inverted pie pan. Fold pastry in half. Carefully transfer to pie pan.

6. Unfold and ease pastry loosely into pan, being careful not to stretch. (Stretching causes pastry to shrink during baking.) To finish one-crust pie, see step 11.

FOR TWO-CRUST PIE

7. Prepare desired filling and place in pastry-lined pan. Trim off overhanging edges with scissors. Roll second part of dough for top crust large enough to extend 1″ beyond edge of pie pan. Measure by holding pie pan over rolled round of pastry.

8. Fold pastry for top crust in quarters. Make several slits near center to allow steam to escape or top crust will puff up. Moisten edge of bottom pastry with water. Carefully place folded pastry evenly on filling. Unfold. Trim pastry with scissors ½″ from edge of pan.

9. Fold edge of top pastry under edge of lower pastry on rim. Seal thoroughly by pressing with fingertips. Build up a high stand-up rim. Form a fluted edge by firmly placing the right index finger on the inside of rim, left thumb and index finger on outside of pastry at that point. Pinch. Repeat all around edge of pie. Sharpen points by pinching each one firmly.

10. To prevent edge of crust from becoming too brown cover with a 1½″ strip of aluminum foil. Bake pie as directed in each recipe. Remove aluminum foil about 15 min. before end of baking time, so edge will brown slightly.

FOR ONE-CRUST PIE

(These steps follow step 6, *p. 337.*)

For One-crust Pie (*baked with filling*)

For Baked Pie Shell

11. Trim pastry with scissors ½″ from edge of pan. Fold pastry under, even with pan. Flute (see step 9). Hook points as shown under pan rim to help prevent shrinking during baking. (Other finishes, p. 340.) DO NOT PRICK. Fill and bake according to recipe.

12. Trim and flute as in step 11. Prick pie shell. Bake at *475°* (very hot) *8 to 10 min.* Fill with cream or chiffon-type fillings, fruit glacés, meringue pie fillings or other refrigerated fillings. Finish according to recipe.

Oil Pastry

Made with easy-to-measure oil—what could be quicker! More step pictures on p. 337 and opposite.

For 8 or 9" One-crust Pie or Baked Shell

1 cup plus 2 tbsp. GOLD MEDAL Flour
½ tsp. salt
⅓ cup vegetable oil
2 tbsp. cold water

For 8 or 9" Two-crust Pie

1¾ cups GOLD MEDAL Flour
1 tsp. salt
½ cup vegetable oil
3 tbsp. cold water

For One-crust Pie or Baked Shell: Heat oven to 450° (hot). Measure flour by dip-level-pour method or by sifting (*see p. 6*). Mix flour, salt. Add oil; mix with fork until it looks like meal. Sprinkle with water; mix with fork. Gather dough together. *If too dry, add 1 to 2 tbsp. more oil.* Press into ball.

Immediately roll crust between two long strips of waxed paper crossed in center—double layer of paper forms 12" square. Roll in circle to edges of square (12" diameter). Wipe table with damp cloth to keep paper from slipping. Peel off top paper, place crust in pan, paper-side-up. Peel paper; fit pastry loosely into pan. Trim, leaving ½" overhanging edge. Fold under, flute, prick thoroughly. Bake shell *12 to 15 min.*, or until light brown. DO NOT PRICK if crust and filling will be baked together. Bake as recipe directs.

For Two-crust Pie: Heat oven to 425° (hot). Make pastry above; divide almost in half. Use larger half for bottom; roll as above. Fill, trim. Roll top same way. Cut slits; place over filling. Trim ½" beyond rim, fold under. Seal, flute. Bake as recipes in this chapter direct. To prevent overbrowning of edges, cover with 1½" strip aluminum foil. Remove strips 15 min. before end of baking.

1. Stir with fork until mixed. If dry, add 1 to 2 tbsp. more oil.

2. Roll crust between two long strips waxed paper, crossed in the center.

3. Place paper-side-up in pie pan.

Beat until sugar is dissolved.

Pie Meringue

For 8" Pie

2 egg whites
*¼ tsp. cream of tartar
¼ cup sugar
¼ tsp. flavoring

For 9" Pie

3 egg whites
*¼ tsp. cream of tartar
6 tbsp. sugar
½ tsp. flavoring

Heat oven to 400° (mod. hot). Beat egg whites with cream of tartar until frothy. Gradually beat in sugar, a little at a time. Continue beating until stiff and glossy. *Do not underbeat. Beat until sugar is dissolved.* Beat in flavoring. Pile meringue onto *hot* pie filling, being careful to seal the meringue onto edge of crust to prevent shrinking or weeping. Swirl or pull up points for decorative top. Bake *8 to 10 min.*, or until delicately browned. Cool away from drafts.

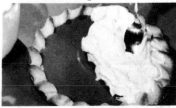

*1 tsp. lemon juice may be substituted for cream of tartar in meringue for Lemon, Lime or Orange Meringue Pies.

Pile onto *hot* filling.

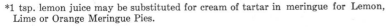

Easy Edges

Fork: Fold edge of pastry under. Use the sharp tines of a fork to press around the edge. To prevent sticking, dip your fork in flour occasionally. For variety, press fork at intervals around edge of pie.

Shell: Fold edges of pastry under and build up rim. Place thumb on edge of pie and press and twist the knuckle of the index finger toward the thumb.

Ruffle: Fold edge of pastry under and build up rim. Place left thumb and index finger ½" apart on outside of pastry rim. With right index finger, pull pastry between fingers. Repeat.

Pastry Cutouts

Cut rolled pastry for top crust into desired shapes, such as pumpkins for Halloween, bells for Christmas. Brush them with water and sprinkle with sugar (colored, if desired). Bake on baking sheet at 475° a few minutes, until golden brown. Cool. Place on filled pie.

Glamour Tops

Lattice Top: Line pan with half of pastry for Two-crust Pie. Trim, leaving 1" overhanging edge. Fill. Roll rest of pastry; cut into ½" strips. (Pastry wheel makes a pretty edge.) Moisten edge of bottom pastry with water. Lay half of pastry strips across filling 1" apart. Weave first cross strip through center. Add another cross strip, first folding back every other strip going the other way. Continue weaving until lattice is complete. Fold lower crust over pastry strips. Press firmly around edge to seal.

Rimless Lattice Top: (Shown in picture on *p. 336*.) Make Lattice Top (*above*) but leave only ½" overhanging. Fold under. When lattice is completely woven, fold pastry strips under folded edge. Press to seal.

Spiral Top: Line pie pan with half of pastry for Two-crust Pie. Fill pie, trim pastry to edge of rim. Roll rest of pastry ⅛" thick; cut into seven ¾" strips 10" long. Use a pastry wheel for a pretty effect. Starting with one strip, twist and lay in spiral on top of pie (adding additional strips as needed by pinching moistened ends together). Finish with twisted strip of pastry on outside of rim. Bake.

For a Shiny Top: Brush top crust with milk before baking.

For a Sugary Top: Using fingers, moisten top crust with water; sprinkle evenly with granulated sugar before baking.

For a Glazed Top: Brush top crust lightly with beaten egg or with egg yolk mixed with a little water before baking.

Graham Cracker Crust

Good with refrigerated pies.

For 9″ Pie

1½ cups graham cracker
   crumbs (18 crackers)
3 tbsp. sugar
⅓ cup butter, melted

For 8″ Pie

1¼ cups
   (15)
2 tbsp.
¼ cup

Heat oven to 350° (mod.). Mix graham cracker crumbs and sugar in bowl. Add butter; mix thoroughly. If desired, save ¼ cup mixture for topping. Press remaining mixture firmly and evenly against bottom and sides of pie pan. Bake *10 min.* Cool; fill with chiffon or cream-type filling.

Ginger, Chocolate or Vanilla Cooky Crusts

Make Graham Cracker Crust (*above*)—*except* use gingersnaps or chocolate or vanilla wafers in place of graham crackers and omit sugar.

Peanut Butter Crust

It's extra-special . . . crunchy!

Make Graham Cracker Crust (*above*)—*except*, in place of butter, use: for 9″ pie, ¼ cup *each* butter and creamy-style peanut butter; for 8″ pie, 3 tbsp. butter and ¼ cup creamy-style peanut butter. Melt together and add to crumb mixture.

Crunchy Nut Crust

Of nuts, sugar and butter. For your fancy parties.

1½ cups finely chopped walnuts or pecans or thinly
   sliced Brazil nuts
3 tbsp. sugar
2 tbsp. soft butter

Heat oven to 450° (hot). Place ingredients in bowl. Stir until nuts are thoroughly coated. Press mixture firmly and evenly against bottom and sides of buttered 9″ pie pan. Bake *6 to 8 min.* Cool. Fill with a chiffon pie filling and chill several hr. before serving. Or, chill empty shell and serve filled with your favorite ice cream.

Butter Crunch Crust

½ cup butter
¼ cup brown sugar (packed)
1 cup GOLD MEDAL Flour
½ cup chopped pecans, walnuts or coconut

Heat oven to 400° (mod. hot). Measure flour by dip-level-pour method or by sifting (*see p. 6*). Mix all ingredients with hands. Spread in oblong pan, 13x9½x2″. Bake *15 min.* Take from oven, stir with spoon. Press 2 cups hot Butter Crunch against bottom and sides of 9″ pie pan. Cool.

Other Ways with Butter Crunch: Serve over ice cream, pudding or warm fruit pie filling.

Coconut Crust

2 tbsp. soft butter
1½ cups shredded coconut (4-oz. can)

Heat oven to 325° (slow mod.). Spread butter evenly in 8″ pie pan. Press coconut with fingertips firmly and evenly against bottom and sides of pie pan. Bake *15 to 20 min.*, or until golden brown. Cool. Fill with favorite ice cream and serve immediately or fill with chiffon pie filling and chill until ready to serve.

Chocolate-Coconut Crust

Easy to make, confection-like pie crust.

2 sq. unsweetened chocolate (2 oz.)
2 tbsp. butter
2 tbsp. hot milk
⅔ cup *sifted* confectioners' sugar
1½ cups shredded coconut, cut up

Melt chocolate and butter in saucepan over low heat. Add milk, sugar and coconut; mix well. Press mixture firmly in an even layer against bottom and sides of greased 8 or 9″ pie pan. Refrigerate 2 hr. Fill with your favorite chiffon or cream filling. Sprinkle with grated unsweetened chocolate, if desired. Chill until serving time.

Apple Pie

From about 1630, Apple Pie was served almost daily in New England . . . when the newly planted orchards were bearing fruit. See color picture on p. 336.

Know your apples! Select tart, firm, juicy apples, such as Jonathans, Winesaps, Greenings, Duchess, Wealthies or Roman Beauties. 1 lb. equals 3 medium apples or 3 cups sliced apples. Peel apples, core and slice ¼" thick. If apples are dry, sprinkle with a little water. For more tartness, add a little lemon juice. Make Pastry for Two-crust Pie of desired size. Line pie pan. (*See pp. 337–338.*)

For 9" Pie	*For 8" Pie*
¾ to 1 cup sugar	½ to ¾ cup sugar
1 tsp. cinnamon or nutmeg	¾ tsp. cinnamon or nutmeg
6 to 7 cups sliced pared apples	4 to 5 cups sliced pared apples
1½ tbsp. butter	1 tbsp. butter

Heat oven to 425° (hot). Mix sugar and cinnamon. Mix lightly through apples. Heap up in pastry-lined pie pan. Dot with butter. Cover with top crust which has slits cut in it. Seal and flute. Cover edge with 1½" strip of aluminum foil to prevent excessive browning. Bake *50 to 60 min.*, or until crust is nicely browned and apples are cooked through (test with fork). Serve warm or cold . . . may be topped with cream, whipped cream or ice cream. Or serve with a slice of cheese.

Green Apple Pie

"When trees in apple orchards with fruit are bending down." Even 16th century English cook books refer to "pyes of greene apples."

Make Apple Pie (*above*)—*except* use about ½ cup more sugar for tart green apples and only ½ tsp. nutmeg or cinnamon. For extra juicy apples, mix 2 tbsp. flour with the sugar to thicken juice.

French Apple Pie

Make Pastry for One-crust Pie. Line pie pan. (*See pp. 337–339.*) Add filling as in recipe for Apple Pie (*above*) using minimum amount of sugar. Sprinkle with

Crumb Topping

For 9" Pie	*For 8" Pie*
½ cup butter	⅓ cup
½ cup brown sugar (packed)	⅓ cup
1 cup GOLD MEDAL Flour	¾ cup

Mix all ingredients until crumbly. Bake *at 400°* (mod. hot) *45 to 55 min.* Serve warm with cream or ice cream.

Dutch Apple Pie

"Perfectly delicious!" says Blythe Parriott Thompson.

Make Apple Pie (*above*)—*except* make extra large slits in top crust. Then, 5 min. before baking time is up, remove pie from oven. Pour ½ cup whipping cream through slits in top crust. Return to oven and finish baking.

Applescotch Pie

Make Pastry for 9" Two-crust Pie. Line pie pan. (*See pp. 337–338.*)

5 cups sliced pared *tart* apples
1 cup brown sugar (packed)
¼ cup water
1 tbsp. lemon juice
¼ cup GOLD MEDAL Flour
2 tbsp. granulated sugar
1 tsp. vanilla
¾ tsp. salt
3 tbsp. butter

Mix apples, brown sugar, water and lemon juice in saucepan. Cover; cook slowly until apples are *just* tender, 7 to 8 min. Blend flour and granulated sugar; add to apples. Cook uncovered, stirring, until syrup thickens (about 2 min.). Remove from heat. Add vanilla, salt and butter. Cool. *Heat oven to 425°* (hot). Pour apples into pastry-lined pie pan. Cover with top crust which has slits cut in it. Seal and flute. Bake *40 to 45 min.*, or until crust is nicely browned.

Cheese-Apple Pie

5 cups thinly sliced pared apples
¾ cup sugar
3 tbsp. flour
⅛ tsp. salt
½ tsp. nutmeg or cinnamon
1 cup grated American processed cheese
3 tbsp. whipping cream

Toss together all ingredients except cream. Pile into pastry-lined pie pan. Pour cream over filling. Finish and bake as for Apple Pie (*above*).

Fresh Berry Pie (*Blueberry, Blackberry, Raspberry, Strawberry, Loganberry or Boysenberry*)

With thick juice bubbling through the crust.

Select ripe, juicy berries—blueberries, blackberries, raspberries, strawberries, loganberries or boysenberries, etc. Berries picked at the height of the season are more flavorful, require less sugar and make the most delicious pies.

Wash berries, drain well. Then pick them over. Remove stems and hulls. Halve large strawberries.

Use the smaller or larger amount of sugar according to your taste and the sweetness of the fruit. Very tart fruit may require even more sugar (up to 1½ cups for 1 qt.).

Make Pastry for Two-crust Pie of desired size. Line pie pan. (*See pp. 337–338.*)

For 9" Pie	*For 8" Pie*
1 to 1½ cups sugar	⅔ to 1 cup sugar
⅓ cup GOLD MEDAL Flour	¼ cup GOLD MEDAL Flour
½ tsp. cinnamon	½ tsp. cinnamon
4 cups fresh berries	3 cups fresh berries
1½ tbsp. butter	1 tbsp. butter

Heat oven to 425° (hot). Mix sugar, flour and cinnamon. Mix lightly through berries. Pour into pastry-lined pie pan. Dot with butter. Cover with top crust which has slits cut in it. Seal and flute. Cover edge with 1½" strip of aluminum foil to prevent excessive browning. Bake *35 to 45 min.*, or until crust is nicely browned and juice begins to bubble through slits in crust. Serve slightly warm, not hot.

Dutch Blueberry Pie

Make Blueberry Pie (*above*)—*except* pour ½ cup whipping cream through slits in crust before baking.

Fresh Cherry Pie

The chosen dessert to top off a mountain trout luncheon at that charming, steeped-in-tradition resort, The Broadmoor, Colorado Springs, Colorado. See color picture on p. 336.

Make Fresh Berry Pie (*above*)—*except* use pitted sour pie cherries in place of berries; increase sugar, add almond flavoring. Use:

For 9" Pie	*For 8" Pie*
1⅓ cups sugar	1 cup
4 drops almond flavoring	3 drops

Grape and Red Raspberry Pie

¾ cup sugar
¼ cup GOLD MEDAL Flour
dash of salt
1½ cups washed red raspberries
1½ cups slightly crushed washed seedless green grapes
1 tsp. lemon juice
1 tbsp. butter

Prepare and bake as for 8" Fresh Berry Pie (*above*).

Pick berries over, remove stems.

Peach or Apricot Pie

Make Fresh Berry Pie (*above*)—*except* use sliced firm peaches or apricots instead of berries. Use minimum amount of sugar and 1 tbsp. less flour.

Blueberry-Peach Pie

Make a 9" Fresh Berry Pie (*above*)—*except* use 2 cups fresh blueberries and 2½ cups pared and sliced fresh peaches in place of berries. Pour blueberries in bottom of pastry-lined pie pan, sprinkle half of sugar-flour mixture over, arrange peach slices on top, sprinkle with rest of sugar-flour mixture. Bake *40 to 50 min.*

Grape Pie

Prize of the harvest season. Sweet, tart, juicy, fragrant with purple grapes, from Mrs. Philip Gearty of Minneapolis.

Make Pastry for Two-crust Pie of desired size. Line pie pan. *(See pp. 337–338.)*

For 9" Pie	*For 8" Pie*
5⅓ cups Concord grapes	4 cups Concord grapes
1⅓ cups sugar	1 cup sugar
¼ cup GOLD MEDAL Flour	3 tbsp. GOLD MEDAL Flour
1¼ tsp. lemon juice	1 tsp. lemon juice
dash of salt	dash of salt
1½ tbsp. butter	1 tbsp. butter

Heat oven to 425° (hot). Remove and save skins from grapes (pinch grape at end opposite stem—fruit pops out). Put pulp into saucepan without water and bring to a rolling boil. While hot, rub through strainer to remove seeds. Mix strained pulp with skins. Mix sugar and flour lightly through grapes. Sprinkle with lemon juice and salt. Pour grapes into pastry-lined pie pan. Dot with butter. Cover with top crust which has slits cut in it. Seal and flute. Cover edge with 1½" strip of aluminum foil to prevent excessive browning. Bake *35 to 45 min.,* or until crust is nicely browned and juice begins to bubble through slits in crust. Serve cool or slightly warm, not hot.

Cranberry-Apple Pie

Make Pastry for 9" Two-crust Pie. Line pie pan. *(See pp. 337–338.)*

3 cups sliced cooking apples (about 3 medium)
2 cups whole fresh or thawed frozen cranberries
1¾ cups sugar
¼ cup GOLD MEDAL Flour
1½ tbsp. butter

Heat oven to 425° (hot). Mix apples and cranberries lightly in mixture of sugar and flour. Pour into pastry-lined pie pan. Dot with butter. Cover with top crust which has slits cut in it. Seal and flute. Bake *40 to 50 min.,* or until crust is nicely browned and juice begins to bubble through slits in crust. Cool.

Early American Pear Pie

Make Pastry for Two-crust Pie of desired size. Line pie pan. *(See pp. 337–338.)*

For 9" Pie	*For 8" Pie*
6 cups sliced pears	4 cups
¾ cup sugar	½ cup
1 tsp. nutmeg or cinnamon	¾ tsp.
2 tbsp. flour	1½ tbsp.
1½ tbsp. butter	1 tbsp.

Heat oven to 425° (hot). Pare and slice firm pears (1 pear makes about 1 cup sliced). Mix sugar, spice and flour. Mix lightly through pears. Pour into pastry-lined pie pan. Dot with butter. Cover with top crust which has slits cut in it. Seal and flute. Bake *35 to 45 min.* Serve cool.

Hawaiian Banana Pie

From Erma Meeks Boyen, Home Service Director of the Hawaiian Electric Company, Honolulu, who terms her state a gourmets' paradise.

Make Pastry for 9" Two-crust Pie. Line pie pan. *(See pp. 337–338.)*

6 cups sliced bananas, ripe but firm
¾ cup pineapple juice
¾ cup sugar
1 tbsp. flour
1½ tsp. cinnamon
1 tbsp. butter

Soak bananas in pineapple juice 20 to 30 min. Drain, saving juice. *Heat oven to 400°* (mod. hot). Place bananas in pastry-lined pie pan. Blend sugar, flour and cinnamon; sprinkle over bananas. Add 3 tbsp. of the pineapple juice; dot with butter and cover with top crust which has slits cut in it. Seal and flute. Bake *30 to 45 min.,* or until crust is browned.

Fresh Rhubarb Pie

Tart, refreshing, springtime delight.

For mild flavor, choose early pink rhubarb. If tender and pink, do not peel. Cut into 1″ pieces (1 lb. makes 2 cups). Amount of sugar depends on tartness of rhubarb. Early rhubarb requires less sugar. Make your pie shallow.

Make Pastry for Two-crust Pie of desired size. Line pie pan. *(See pp. 337–338.)*

For 9″ Pie
1⅓ to 2 cups sugar
⅓ cup GOLD MEDAL Flour
4 cups cut-up rhubarb
1½ tbsp. butter

For 8″ Pie
1 to 1½ cups sugar
¼ cup GOLD MEDAL Flour
3 cups cut-up rhubarb
1 tbsp. butter

Heat oven to 425° (hot). Mix sugar and flour. Mix lightly through rhubarb. Pour into pastry-lined pie pan. Dot with butter. Cover with top crust which has slits cut in it. Sprinkle with sugar. Seal and flute. Cover edge with 1½″ strip of aluminum foil to prevent excessive browning. Bake *40 to 50 min.,* or until crust is nicely browned and juice begins to bubble through slits. Serve slightly warm.

Strawberry or Blueberry-Rhubarb Pie

An inspiration of Mrs. Sherman Child of Minneapolis.

Make Fresh Rhubarb Pie *(above)—except* substitute fresh strawberries or blueberries for half the rhubarb. Use the minimum amount of sugar.

Pineapple-Rhubarb Pie

Make Fresh Rhubarb Pie *(above)—except* substitute about 1 cup drained crushed pineapple for about 1 cup of the rhubarb. Use the minimum amount of sugar.

Pear-Rhubarb Pie

Make Pastry for 9″ Two-crust Pie. Line pie pan. *(See pp. 337–338.)*

1 to 1¼ cups sugar
¼ tsp. salt
⅓ cup flour
2½ cups fresh pears, peeled and diced (about 4)
1½ cups fresh rhubarb (cut in 1″ pieces)
2 tbsp. butter

Heat oven to 425° (hot). Mix sugar, salt and flour. Mix lightly with combined fruits and pour into prepared pie pan. Dot with butter. Cover with top crust; flute edges. Make slits for steam to escape. Cover edge with 1½″ strip of aluminum foil to prevent excessive browning. Bake *40 to 50 min.*

Deep Dish Fruit Pie

Fresh fruit baked with top crust only. Use rhubarb, berries, cherries, peaches or apricots.

Make Pastry for One-crust Pie *(see pp. 337–339).* Roll into 10″ square; make several slits to allow steam to escape during baking. *Heat oven to 425° (hot).* Make Fresh Rhubarb Pie *(above)* or Fresh Berry, Cherry, Peach or Apricot Pie *(p. 343)* —*except* double the amount of filling for 9″ pie. Place in 9″ square pan. Cover with pastry square. Fold edge of crust under; flute just inside edge of pan. Bake *40 to 50 min.,* or until lightly browned. Serve warm with whipped cream or ice cream.

Deep Dish Apple Pie

Lots of apples . . . no bottom crust.

Using oblong pan, 13x9½x2″: Make pastry for 8″ Two-crust Pie *(see pp. 337–338).* Double filling recipe for 9″ Apple Pie *(p. 342). 12 generous servings.*

Using square pan, 9x9x2″: Make pastry for One-crust Pie *(see pp. 337–339).* Double filling recipe for 8″ Apple Pie *(p. 342).* 6 to 8 servings.

Heat oven to 425° (hot). Roll pastry about 1″ larger around than baking pan. Make several slits in crust for steam to escape during baking. Place crust on filling, fold edge over and flute just inside edge of pan. Bake *about 50 min.,* or until lightly browned.

French Strawberry Glacé Pie

An exciting and sparkling combination—flaky pastry, cream cheese and ripe red berries.

Make Baked Pie Shell of desired size (*pp. 338–339*).

1 qt. strawberries	3 tbsp. cornstarch
1 cup water	1 pkg. (3 oz.) cream cheese, softened
1 cup sugar	

Wash, drain and hull strawberries. Simmer 1 cup strawberries and ⅔ cup water about 3 min. Blend sugar, cornstarch and remaining ⅓ cup water; add to boiling mixture. Boil 1 min., stirring constantly. Cool. Spread cream cheese over bottom of cooled baked pie shell. Save out ½ cup choice berries; put remaining 2½ cups berries in baked pie shell. Cover with cooked mixture and garnish with the ½ cup berries. Refrigerate until firm—about 2 hr. Serve with Sweetened Whipped Cream (*p. 232*) or ice cream.

French Raspberry, Blackberry, Blueberry or Cherry Glacé Pie

Make French Strawberry Glacé Pie (*above*)—except in place of strawberries, use fresh raspberries, blackberries, blueberries or pitted sweet cherries.

Streusel Cream Peach Pie

Make Pastry for 9″ One-crust Pie (*pp. 337–339*).

4 cups quartered peeled peaches (8 to 10)
½ cup sugar
½ tsp. nutmeg, if desired
1 egg
2 tbsp. cream
¼ cup brown sugar (packed)
½ cup GOLD MEDAL Flour
¼ cup soft butter

Heat oven to 425° (hot). Arrange peaches in pastry-lined pie pan. Sprinkle sugar and nutmeg over peaches. Beat egg and cream together, then pour over peaches and sugar. Mix brown sugar, flour and butter until crumbly. Sprinkle crumb mixture over fruit in pie pan. Bake *35 to 45 min.*, or until browned. Serve slightly warm. For a special garnish, pass a bowl of whipped ice cream or commercial sour cream.

Red Cherry-Banana Pie

A color and flavor combination that rates rave notices.

Make 9″ Baked Pie Shell (*pp. 338–339*).

1 can (1 lb. 4 oz.) pitted tart red cherries
1 cup sugar
3½ tbsp. cornstarch
1 tbsp. butter
½ tsp. cinnamon
1 tsp. almond flavoring
2 to 3 medium bananas
1 cup whipping cream, whipped stiff

Boil cherries, juice, sugar and cornstarch together 1 min., or until clear and thick, stirring constantly. Add butter and cool. Blend in cinnamon and almond flavoring. Place layers of sliced bananas in pie shell. Pour filling over bananas and chill. Spoon wreath of whipped cream on pie and garnish with banana slices (dipped in lemon, pineapple or grapefruit juice), if desired.

Ice Cream Sundae Pie

A small pastry shell filled with fruit crowns a full-size pastry shell filled with ice cream.

Make Pastry for 8″ Two-crust Pie. (*See pp. 337–338.*)

1 qt. softened ice cream
1½ cups fresh fruit or berries

Roll ⅔ of pastry 1″ larger than inverted 9″ pie pan; ⅓ of pastry ½″ larger than inverted 6″ pan. Ease into pans; flute and prick pastry. Bake *8 to 10 min. at 475°*, or until golden brown. Cool. Spoon ice cream lightly into 9″ pie shell, making hollow in center. Fit smaller shell into hollow and fill with fruit or berries. Serve immediately.

Canned Cherry Pie

Filled to the rim with bright, sparkly fruit and juice.

Canned fruit pies require less fruit than those made with fresh fruit because the fruit has been precooked. To determine amount of sugar needed, look on label to see if fruit was packed in syrup. Use minimum sugar for fruit packed in syrup, maximum sugar for water-packed fruit. The proportion of fruit and juice in the same size can may vary with the brand. Because of this, we measure fruit and juice separately. There are approximately 1¾ cups cherries and 1 cup juice in a 1 lb. 4 oz. can.

Make Pastry for Two-crust Pie of desired size. Line pie pan. (*See pp. 337-338.*)

For 9″ Pie	*For 8″ Pie*
¾ to 1 cup sugar	½ to ⅔ cup sugar
¼ cup GOLD MEDAL Flour	2½ tbsp. GOLD MEDAL Flour
½ tsp. cinnamon	¼ tsp. cinnamon
½ cup fruit juice	⅓ cup fruit juice
3½ cups drained, pitted cherries	2⅓ cups drained, pitted cherries
1 tbsp. butter	1 tbsp. butter

Heat oven to 425° (hot). Mix in saucepan sugar, flour, cinnamon and fruit juice. Cook over medium heat, stirring constantly, until mixture thickens and boils. If desired, brighten color with red food coloring. Pour hot thickened juice over cherries. Mix lightly. Pour into pastry-lined pie pan. Dot with butter. Cover with top crust which has slits cut in it. Seal and flute. Cover edge with 1½″ strip of aluminum foil to prevent excessive browning. Bake *35 to 45 min.*, or until nicely browned and juice begins to bubble through slits in crust. Serve warm.

NOTE: In place of cinnamon, ¼ tsp. almond flavoring may be used in Canned Cherry Pie.

Canned Blueberry or Boysenberry Pie

Make Canned Cherry Pie (*above*)—*except* use drained canned blueberries or boysenberries in place of cherries. Add lemon juice—2 tbsp. for 9″ pie, 1 tbsp. for 8″ pie—before pouring mixture into pastry-lined pie pan.

Canned Apple, Peach or Apricot Pie

Home canned fruit makes this super special.

Make Canned Cherry Pie (*above*)—*except* use canned sliced apples, peaches or apricot halves and juice in place of cherries and juice.

Frozen Fruit Pie

Frozen fruit which retains its shape when thawed (such as cherries, blueberries, peaches and apricots) may be substituted for canned fruit—*except* reduce sugar about ½ cup.

ALL YOU HAVE TO DO

To save pre-cooking fruit and juice before putting into pastry-lined shell: use tapioca instead of flour to thicken the filling. Omit flour. Using 2½ to 3 tbsp. quick-cooking tapioca for 9″ pie, 1½ to 2 tbsp. for 8″ pie, combine sugar, spices, tapioca. Mix through fruit and juice before pouring into pastry-lined pie pan.

Cherry-Pineapple Pie

Make Canned Cherry Pie (*above*)—*except* use 1 cup cut-up canned or fresh pineapple in place of 1 cup of the cherries.

Blushing Peach Pie

Pink peach pie with cinnamon flavor.

Make Pastry for 8″ Two-crust Pie. (*See pp. 337–338.*)

½ cup sugar
2 tbsp. cornstarch
¼ cup peach syrup
3½ cups drained canned peach slices
1 jar (1¾ oz.) cinnamon candies
1 tbsp. butter

Prepare and bake as for Canned Cherry Pie (*above*).

Old-fashioned Mince Pie

One of the earliest pies—meat and fruit minced for a rich, hearty filling. Mrs. Ruth D. Silcox, now of Arlington, Virginia, made One-crust Mince Pies . . . topping the filling with beautiful Pastry Cutouts (p. 340) when she was on our staff.

Make Pastry for Two-crust Pie of desired size. Line pie pan. *(See pp. 337–338.)*

For 9" Pie	*For 8" Pie*
3 cups mincemeat (28 to 30-oz. jar)	2 cups mincemeat (19-oz. jar)
1½ cups chopped apple	1 cup chopped apple

Heat oven to 425° (hot). Mix mincemeat and apple. Pour into pastry-lined pie pan. Cover with top crust which has slits cut in it. Seal and flute. Cover edge with 1½" strip of aluminum foil to prevent excessive browning. Bake *40 to 45 min.*, or until crust is nicely browned. Serve slightly warm.

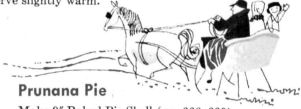

Mince-Ice Cream Pie

Make Pastry for Two-crust Pie of desired size. Line pie pan. *(See pp. 337–338.)*

Heat oven to 425° (hot). Spoon 1½ cups mincemeat (from 28 to 30-oz. jar) into pastry-lined pie pan. Cover with top crust which has slits cut in it. (Top crust forms a slight hollow for ice cream topping.) Bake *30 to 35 min.*, until crust is nicely browned. Just before serving pie, heat rest of mincemeat. Spoon 1 qt. vanilla ice cream onto top crust to fill pie. Serve warm mincemeat over wedges of warm pie.

Twin Fruit Pie

Make 8" Baked Pie Shell *(pp. 338–339).*

about ¼ lb. dried apricots (1 cup cooked)
about ½ lb. dried prunes (1 cup cooked)
1 cup juice (drained from prunes and apricots)
½ cup sugar
2 tsp. lemon juice
2 tbsp. cornstarch

Cook apricots and prunes separately. Drain. Pit prunes. Mix juice, sugar and lemon juice. Bring to boil. Stir in cornstarch, mixed to a paste with small amount of cold water. Cook until thickened. Pour over prunes and apricots. Cool. Pour into cooled baked pie shell.

Prunana Pie

Make 9" Baked Pie Shell *(pp. 338–339).*

2 cups cut-up, drained, sweetened, cooked prunes
  (1 lb. uncooked)
grated rind of 1 lemon (about 1 tbsp.)
1 tbsp. lemon juice
1½ cups sliced bananas (2 large)
½ cup nuts, coarsely chopped, if desired

Mix all ingredients. Chill thoroughly. Just before serving, spoon into cooled baked pie shell. Top with ½ cup whipping cream, whipped with 1 tbsp. confectioners' sugar.

Raisin Pie

Called "Funeral Pie" by the Pennsylvania Dutch because it was always served when relatives and neighbors gathered to pay their "last respects."

Make Pastry for Two-crust Pie of desired size. Line pie pan. *(See pp. 337–338.)*

For 9" Pie	*For 8" Pie*
2 cups seeded raisins	1½ cups
2 cups boiling water	1½ cups
½ cup sugar	⅓ cup
2 tbsp. flour	1½ tbsp.
½ cup chopped nuts	⅓ cup
2 tsp. grated lemon rind	1½ tsp.
3 tbsp. lemon juice	2½ tbsp.

Heat oven to 425° (hot). Cook raisins and water covered until tender (about 5 min.). Stir in mixture of sugar and flour. Cook over low heat, stirring constantly, until boiling. Boil 1 min. Remove from heat. Stir in nuts, lemon rind and juice. Pour hot filling into pastry-lined pan. Cover with top crust which has slits cut in it. Bake *30 to 40 min.*

Custard Pie

Rich, satiny smooth custard baked right in the crust.

Make Pastry for One-crust Pie. Line pie pan. (*See pp. 337–339.*) Build up high fluted edge.

For 9" Pie	For 8" Pie
4 eggs (or 8 egg yolks)	3 eggs (or 6 egg yolks)
⅔ cup sugar	½ cup sugar
½ tsp. salt	¼ tsp. salt
¼ tsp. nutmeg	¼ tsp. nutmeg
*2⅔ cups scalding hot milk	*2 cups scalding hot milk
1 tsp. vanilla, if desired	¾ tsp. vanilla, if desired

*Use part cream for an extra rich pie.

Heat oven to 450° (hot). Beat eggs slightly with rotary beater. Then beat in rest of ingredients. Pour into pastry-lined pie pan. Bake *15 min. then reduce heat to 350° and bake 10 to 15 min. more*, just until a silver knife inserted 1" from side of filling comes out clean. The center may still look a bit soft but will set later. *Caution:* Too long baking makes custard "watery." Serve slightly warm or cold. NOTE: Can be baked at 425° for same time.

Coconut Custard Pie

Make Custard Pie (*above*)—*except* omit nutmeg, stir into custard moist shredded coconut (1 cup for 9" pie, ¾ cup for 8" pie). Sprinkle a little coconut over top. Bake.

Slip-Slide Custard Pie

Certain-sure of a crisp undercrust every time.

Make Custard Pie (*above*)—*except* bake crust and filling separately. Pour filling directly into ungreased pie pan of *same* size as the one in which the crust is baked. Set pan in shallow pan of hot water. Bake custard *30 to 35 min. at 350°*, just until a silver knife inserted 1" from side of filling comes out clean. The center may still look a bit soft but will set later. When lukewarm, slip filling into cooled Baked Pie Shell (*pp. 338–339*) as shown below. Allow to settle a few minutes before serving.

Rhubarb Custard Pie

Something special . . . the tart flavor of rhubarb in a custard filling.

Make Pastry for Two-crust Pie of desired size. Line pie pan. (*See pp. 337–338.*)

For 9" Pie	For 8" Pie
3 eggs	2
3 tbsp. milk	2 tbsp.
2 cups sugar	1½ cups
¼ cup GOLD MEDAL Flour	3 tbsp.
¾ tsp. nutmeg	½ tsp.
4 cups cut-up pink rhubarb	3 cups
1 tbsp. butter	2 tsp.

Heat oven to 400° (mod. hot). Beat eggs slightly; add milk. Mix sugar, flour and nutmeg; stir in. Mix in rhubarb. Pour into pastry-lined pie pan. Dot with butter. Cover with a lattice top (p. 340). Bake *50 to 60 min.*, until nicely browned. Serve slightly warm.

1. Loosen custard around edge of pan with spatula.

2. Shake pan gently to loosen completely.

3. Slip custard into shell, let settle.

AUTUMN PUMPKIN PIE

Recipe, opposite.

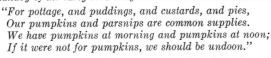

Pumpkin Pie

Pumpkins, or "pompions," were a standby of the early New England settlements. An old verse goes:

> *"For pottage, and puddings, and custards, and pies,*
> *Our pumpkins and parsnips are common supplies.*
> *We have pumpkins at morning and pumpkins at noon;*
> *If it were not for pumpkins, we should be undoon."*

Make Pastry for One-crust Pie. Line pie pan. Build up fluted edge. *(See pp. 337–339.)*

For 9″ Pie	*For 8″ Pie*
1¾ cups mashed cooked or canned pumpkin	1¼ cups cooked or canned pumpkin
½ tsp. salt	¼ tsp. salt
1¾ cups milk	1¼ cups milk
3 eggs	2 eggs
⅔ cup brown sugar (packed)	½ cup brown sugar (packed)
2 tbsp. granulated sugar	1½ tbsp. granulated sugar
1¼ tsp. cinnamon	1 tsp. cinnamon
½ tsp. ginger	¼ tsp. ginger
½ tsp. nutmeg	¼ tsp. nutmeg
¼ tsp. cloves	¼ tsp. cloves

Heat oven to 425° (hot). Beat all ingredients together with rotary beater. Pour into pastry-lined pie pan. (For crispness, have bottom pastry a little thicker than ⅛″.) Bake *45 to 55 min.,* or until a silver knife inserted 1″ from side of filling comes out clean. The center may still look soft but will set later. Serve slightly warm or cold.

Southern Yam or Sweet Potato Pie

Like pumpkin pie, but has a lighter, milder flavor because all granulated sugar was used and cloves omitted.

For 9″ Pie	*For 8″ Pie*
1¾ cups strained mashed cooked yams or sweet potatoes	1¼ cups
1 tsp. salt	¾ tsp.
1½ cups milk	1 cup plus 2 tbsp.
3 eggs	2
1 cup sugar	¾ cup
1 tsp. cinnamon	¾ tsp.
½ tsp. nutmeg	¼ tsp.
½ tsp. ginger	¼ tsp.
1 tbsp. butter, melted	2 tsp.

Mix and bake as for Pumpkin Pie *(above).*

New England Squash Pie

Make Southern Yam or Sweet Potato Pie *(above)—except* use strained mashed cooked Hubbard squash in place of yams or sweet potatoes.

Autumn Pumpkin Pie

The golden pumpkin filling is made with condensed milk. See color picture (p. 350).

Make Pastry for 9″ One-crust Pie *(pp. 337–339).*

1¾ cups mashed cooked or canned pumpkin
1⅓ cups sweetened condensed milk (15 oz.)
1 egg
½ tsp. salt
½ tsp. cinnamon
¼ tsp. *each* nutmeg and ginger
1 cup hot water

Heat oven to 375° (quick mod.). Beat all ingredients together with rotary beater. Pour into pastry-lined pie pan. Bake *50 to 55 min.*

Spicy Pumpkin Pie

Make Pastry for 9″ One-crust Pie *(pp. 337–339).*

2 cups mashed cooked or canned pumpkin
¾ tsp. salt
1⅔ cups evaporated milk (14½ oz.)
2 eggs
¾ cup sugar
1 tbsp. butter, melted
1 to 1¼ tsp. cinnamon
¼ tsp. *each* ginger and nutmeg
⅛ tsp. ground cloves

Mix and bake as for Pumpkin Pie *(above)—except* bake only *40 to 45 min.*

Pecan Pie

Traditional recipe from Tidewater, Virginia. The choice among all desserts served at world renowned Williamsburg Inn in restored colonial Williamsburg.

Make Pastry for One-crust Pie of desired size. Line pie pan. (*See pp. 337–339.*)

For 9" Pie	For 8" Pie
3 eggs	2 eggs
⅔ cup sugar	½ cup sugar
½ tsp. salt	¼ tsp. salt
⅓ cup butter, melted	¼ cup butter, melted
1 cup light or dark corn syrup	¾ cup light or dark corn syrup
1 cup pecan halves	¾ cup pecan halves

Heat oven to 375° (quick mod.). Beat eggs, sugar, salt, butter and corn syrup together with rotary beater. Mix in pecan halves. Pour into pastry-lined pie pan. Bake *40 to 50 min.*, or until set and pastry is nicely browned. Cool. Serve cold or slightly warm.

Spicy Walnut Raisin Pie

Make Pecan Pie (*above*)—*except* omit pecan halves and add:

For 9" Pie	For 8" Pie
½ tsp. cinnamon	¼ tsp.
½ tsp. nutmeg	¼ tsp.
½ tsp. cloves	¼ tsp.
½ cup walnuts, chopped	⅓ cup
½ cup seedless raisins	⅓ cup

Chocolate Brownie Pie

Rich chocolatey version of Pecan Pie developed by Mary R. Jadwin, now Mrs. James Ray Norton of New York City.

Make Pastry for 9" One-crust Pie (*pp. 337–339*).

2 sq. unsweetened chocolate (2 oz.)
2 tbsp. butter
3 eggs
½ cup sugar
¾ cup dark corn syrup
¾ cup pecan halves

Heat oven to 375° (quick mod.). Melt chocolate and butter together over hot water. Beat eggs, sugar, chocolate mixture and syrup together with rotary beater. Mix in pecan halves. Pour into pastry-lined pie pan. Bake *40 to 50 min.*, just until set. Serve slightly warm or cold with ice cream or whipped cream.

Southern Chess Pie

Golden transparent custard, originally from England.

Make Pastry for 9" One-crust Pie (*pp. 337–339*).

4 eggs
1½ cups sugar
½ cup butter
2 tbsp. cream (20% butterfat)
2 tbsp. corn meal
2 tbsp. lemon juice
2 tsp. vanilla
⅛ tsp. salt

Heat oven to 325° (slow mod.). Combine eggs, sugar and butter; beat 5 min. high speed on mixer or with rotary beater. Blend in remaining ingredients. Pour into pastry-lined pie pan. Bake *1 hr.*, or until knife inserted 1" from edge comes out clean.

Date Caramel Pie

Make Pastry for 9" One-crust Pie (*pp. 337–339*).

1 cup light brown sugar (packed)
¼ tsp. salt
1 tbsp. flour
½ tsp. cinnamon
1 egg
1 cup 20% cream or commercial sour cream
1 cup cut-up dates
½ cup coarsely chopped walnuts

Heat oven to 375° (quick mod.). Mix brown sugar, salt, flour and cinnamon. Blend in egg, cream, dates and nuts. Pour into pastry-lined pie pan. Bake *50 to 60 min.*, or until silver knife inserted into side of filling comes out clean. Serve with whipped cream or ice cream.

Lemon Meringue Pie

Robert Taylor's favorite . . . his mother's recipe, featured in our radio cooking school with an interview from this famous star. Its tangy, refreshing flavor makes it our favorite lemon pie, too.

Make Baked Pie Shell of desired size *(pp. 338–339).*

For 9" Pie	*For 8" Pie*
1½ cups sugar	1 cup plus 2 tbsp. sugar
⅓ cup cornstarch	¼ cup cornstarch
1½ cups water	1 cup plus 2 tbsp. water
3 egg yolks, slightly beaten	2 egg yolks, slightly beaten
3 tbsp. butter	2 tbsp. butter
¼ cup lemon juice	3 tbsp. lemon juice
1 tbsp. grated lemon rind	1 tbsp. grated lemon rind

Mix sugar and cornstarch in saucepan. Gradually stir in water. Cook over medium heat, stirring constantly, until mixture thickens and boils. Boil 1 min. Slowly stir at least half the hot mixture into egg yolks. Then blend into hot mixture in saucepan. Boil 1 min. longer, stirring constantly. Remove from heat. Continue stirring until smooth. Blend in butter, lemon juice and rind. Pour into baked pie shell. Cover with Pie Meringue *(p. 339).* Bake. Serve as soon as cool.

Pineapple Meringue Pie

Delicate yellow filling with crushed pineapple.

For 9" Pie	*For 8" Pie*
1 cup sugar	¾ cup
¼ cup cornstarch	3 tbsp.
½ cup water	⅓ cup
1 cup pineapple juice	¾ cup
3 egg yolks, slightly beaten	2
3 tbsp. butter	2 tbsp.
1 tbsp. lemon juice	2 tsp.
1¼ tsp. grated lemon rind	1 tsp.
1¼ cups well drained crushed pineapple	1 cup

Follow method for Lemon Meringue Pie *(above)*— and blend in pineapple at the last.

Quick Orange Meringue Pie

Made from frozen orange juice.

1 cup sugar
¼ cup cornstarch
1⅓ cups frozen concentrate for orange juice (diluted according to directions on can)
2 egg yolks, slightly beaten
2 tbsp. butter

Make an 8" pie following method for Lemon Meringue Pie *(above)*—*except* omit grated rind.

▶ALL YOU HAVE TO DO

To save time: use frozen or canned fruit juices.

To add fresh flavor of lemon or orange: grate just the thin colored rind of fruit (no white).

Lime Meringue Pie

Brought from Florida by Mrs. Myron Hall.

Make Lemon Meringue Pie *(above)*—*except*, in place of lemon, use lime and omit butter. Add a *few* drops of green food coloring for a delicate lime green color.

Grape Meringue Pie

¾ cup sugar
¼ cup cornstarch
1⅓ cups grape juice (6-oz. can frozen grape juice concentrate plus enough water to make 1⅓ cups)
2 egg yolks, slightly beaten
2 tbsp. butter
2 tsp. lemon juice

Make an 8" pie following method for Lemon Meringue Pie *(above)*—*except* omit grated rind.

Vanilla Cream Pie

Velvety smooth filling. Flavor perfect. For richer cream pie, substitute coffee cream for milk. If pie is to be served warm, use 1 tbsp. additional cornstarch. For variety, serve in Peanut Butter Crust (p. 341).

Make Baked Pie Shell (with high fluted edge) of desired size *(pp. 338–339)*.

For 9" Pie	*For 8" Pie*
⅔ cup sugar	½ cup sugar
3 tbsp. cornstarch	2 tbsp. cornstarch
½ tsp. salt	½ tsp. salt
3 cups milk	2 cups milk
3 egg yolks, slightly beaten	2 egg yolks, slightly beaten
1 tbsp. butter	2 tsp. butter
1½ tsp. vanilla	1 tsp. vanilla

Mix sugar, cornstarch and salt in saucepan. Gradually stir in milk. Cook over medium heat, stirring constantly, until mixture thickens and boils. Boil 1 min. Remove from heat. Gradually stir at least half of hot mixture into egg yolks. Then blend into hot mixture in saucepan. Boil 1 min. more, stirring constantly. Remove from heat. Blend in butter and vanilla. Pour immediately into baked pie shell. Finish with Pie Meringue *(p. 339)*. Let cool at room temperature. Or pie may be chilled thoroughly (2 hr.) and topped with Sweetened Whipped Cream *(p. 232)*.

Coconut Cream Pie

Make Vanilla Cream Pie *(above)*—except fold in ¾ cup moist shredded coconut just before filling baked pie shell. Sprinkle whipped cream or meringue topping with ¼ cup shredded coconut (toasted, if desired).

Chocolate Cream Pie

Smooth, rich . . . the kind to rave about.

Make Vanilla Cream Pie *(above)*—except increase sugar and add cut-up unsweetened chocolate with the milk or cocoa with the sugar, cornstarch and salt. Use:

For 9" Pie	*For 8" Pie*
1½ cups sugar	1 cup
3 sq. unsweetened chocolate (3 oz.), cut up or ½ cup cocoa	2 sq. (2 oz.) or ⅓ cup cocoa

Almond Cream Pie

Crunchy toasted almonds; smooth, soft, creamy custard in crispy pastry.

Make Vanilla Cream Pie *(above)*—except, in place of vanilla, use ½ tsp. almond flavoring and add ½ cup toasted slivered blanched almonds to the cooled filling. Sprinkle a few toasted slivered almonds over whipped cream topping.

Banana Cream Pie

Make Vanilla Cream Pie *(above)* or Chocolate Cream Pie *(left)*—except cool filling. Arrange a layer of sliced bananas ½" deep in pastry shell before pouring in cooled filling.

For 9" Pie	*For 8" Pie*
3 large bananas	2 large bananas

If whipped cream topping is used, garnish with a ring of sliced bananas.

Cherry Cream Pie

Make 9" Baked Pie Shell *(pp. 338–339)*.

Make 9" Vanilla Cream Pie filling *(above)*. Pour into cooled pie shell. Chill. Thaw 1 can (1 lb. 4 oz.) frozen red sour cherries. Drain well, reserving juice. Combine ¼ cup sugar and 2 tbsp. cornstarch in saucepan. Stir in cherry juice. Cook over medium heat, stirring constantly, until mixture boils. Boil 1 min. Add cherries. Heat 1 min. more. Cool. Pour over cream filling in pie shell. Top with Pastry Cutouts *(p. 340)*, or garnish with whipped cream.

Butterscotch Cream Pie

Glossy smooth . . . with the true butterscotch flavor. Merriam Paulson of our staff thinks that "there is nothing better!"

Make Baked Pie Shell of desired size (*pp. 338–339*).

For 9″ Pie	*For 8″ Pie*
1 cup brown sugar (packed)	¾ cup brown sugar (packed)
¼ cup cornstarch	3 tbsp. cornstarch
½ tsp. salt	½ tsp. salt
1 cup water	¾ cup water
1⅔ cups milk	1¼ cups milk
⅓ cup butter	¼ cup butter
3 egg yolks, slightly beaten	2 egg yolks, slightly beaten
1½ tsp. vanilla	1 tsp. vanilla

Mix brown sugar, cornstarch and salt in saucepan. Gradually stir in water and milk. Add butter. Cook over medium heat, stirring constantly, until mixture thickens and boils. Boil 1 min. Remove from heat. Gradually stir at least half of hot mixture into egg yolks. Then blend into hot mixture in saucepan. Boil 1 min. more, stirring constantly. Remove from heat. Blend in vanilla. Pour immediately into baked pie shell. If desired, finish with Pie Meringue (*p. 339*). Let cool at room temperature. Or pie may be chilled thoroughly (2 hr.) and topped with Sweetened Whipped Cream (*p. 232*).

Light Butterscotch Pie

Make Butterscotch Cream Pie (*above*)—*except* use all milk instead of milk and water.

Dark Butterscotch Pie

Make Butterscotch Cream Pie (*above*)—*except* increase brown sugar 2 tbsp. or use dark brown sugar.

Birthday Pie

A happy substitute for a birthday cake . . . especially when you make the favorite pie of the one whose birthday it is.

Make cream pie of your choice. Drop Meringue (*p. 339*) on pie by spoonfuls with one for each candle. Bake. Insert candles (in holders) just before serving.

Quick Lemon Pie

Make 9″ Baked Pie Shell (*pp. 338–339*).

1⅓ cups sweetened condensed milk (15 oz.)
½ cup lemon juice
1 tsp. grated lemon rind or ¼ tsp. lemon flavoring
3 eggs, separated
¼ tsp. cream of tartar
6 tbsp. sugar

Heat oven to 325° (slow mod.). Blend milk, lemon juice, rind and egg yolks. Pour into baked pie shell. Top with meringue made by beating egg whites and cream of tartar until frothy. Gradually beat in sugar and continue beating until stiff and glossy. Pile on top of filling. Bake *15 to 20 min.*, or until lightly browned. Cool.

▶ALL YOU HAVE TO DO

For best flavor in chilled pies: remove from refrigerator 20 min. before serving.

Citrus Fruit Chiffon Pie

Gladys Mason, a food artist and a true Californian, makes this delicious pie with fruit from her native state.

Make Baked Pie Shell of desired size (*pp. 338–339*) or Coconut Crust (*p. 341*).

For 9" Pie	For 8" Pie
½ cup sugar	⅓ cup sugar
1 envelope unflavored gelatin (1 tbsp.)	2 tsp. unflavored gelatin
⅔ cup water	½ cup water
⅓ cup lemon, orange or lime juice	¼ cup lemon, orange or lime juice
4 egg yolks, slightly beaten	3 egg yolks, slightly beaten
1 tbsp. grated lemon, orange or lime rind	2 tsp. grated lemon, orange or lime rind
4 egg whites	3 egg whites
½ tsp. cream of tartar	¼ tsp. cream of tartar
½ cup sugar	⅓ cup sugar

Blend sugar, gelatin, water, juice and egg yolks in saucepan. Cook over medium heat, stirring constantly, until it boils. Add rind. (For lime pie, add a few drops green food coloring to intensify the color.) Place pan in cold water; cool until mixture mounds slightly when dropped from a spoon. Fold into a Meringue of egg whites, cream of tartar and sugar (for method, see *p. 339*). Pile into cooled baked pie shell. Chill several hours until set. Garnish with whipped cream.

Pumpkin Chiffon Pie

Make Baked Pie Shell (*pp. 338–339*) or Ginger Cooky Crust (*p. 341*).

For 9" Pie	For 8" Pie
1 envelope unflavored gelatin (1 tbsp.)	2 tsp.
⅔ cup brown sugar (packed)	½ cup
½ tsp. salt	¼ tsp.
½ tsp. cinnamon	¼ tsp.
½ tsp. nutmeg	¼ tsp.
½ tsp. ginger	¼ tsp.
1¼ cups mashed cooked or canned pumpkin	¾ cup
3 egg yolks	2
½ cup milk	⅓ cup
3 egg whites	2
¼ tsp. cream of tartar	¼ tsp.
½ cup sugar	⅓ cup

Blend gelatin, brown sugar, salt, spices, pumpkin, egg yolks and milk in saucepan. Cook over medium heat, stirring constantly, until it boils. Place pan in cold water; cool until mixture mounds slightly when dropped from a spoon. Fold into a Meringue of egg whites, cream of tartar and sugar (for method, see *p. 339*). Pour into cooled crust. Chill until set (2 hr.). Garnish with whipped cream.

Strawberry Chiffon Pie

Make Baked Pie Shell of desired size (*pp. 338–339*).

For 9" Pie	For 8" Pie
⅔ cup sugar	½ cup
1 envelope unflavored gelatin (1 tbsp.)	2 tsp.
1 cup strawberries, thoroughly crushed	⅔ cup
3 egg whites	2
¼ tsp. cream of tartar	¼ tsp.
⅓ cup sugar	¼ cup
½ cup whipping cream, whipped	⅓ cup

Blend sugar, gelatin and strawberries in saucepan. Cook to a full rolling boil, stirring constantly. Place pan in cold water; cool until mixture mounds slightly when dropped from a spoon. Then fold into a Meringue made from egg whites, cream of tartar and sugar (for method, see *p. 339*). Carefully blend in whipped cream. Pile into cooled baked pie shell. Chill several hours until set. Serve cold, garnished with whole strawberries.

Raspberry Chiffon Pie

Make Strawberry Chiffon Pie (*above*)—except use crushed raspberries in place of strawberries.

Frozen Berries in Chiffon Pies

For summertime flavor in the wintertime.

A 10-oz. pkg. frozen strawberries or raspberries, thawed, may be used in place of fresh berries. Use ¼ cup sugar for 9" pie, 3 tbsp. for 8" pie.

Black Bottom Pie

Famous at the Hollywood Brown Derby. Creamy chocolate and rum-flavored layers in a Ginger Cooky Crust.

Make 9" Ginger Cooky Crust (*p. 341*). Cool.

2 tsp. unflavored gelatin	2 egg yolks, slightly beaten
3 tbsp. cold water	1 sq. unsweetened chocolate (1 oz.), melted
½ cup sugar	* 2 tsp. pure rum flavoring
2 tbsp. cornstarch	2 egg whites
½ tsp. salt	¼ tsp. cream of tartar
2 cups milk	⅓ cup sugar

* If imitation rum flavoring is used, add only 1 tsp.

Soften gelatin in water. Mix sugar, cornstarch and salt in saucepan. Stir milk in gradually. Boil 1 min. on medium heat, stirring constantly. Remove from heat. Stir at least half of hot mixture into egg yolks. Blend into hot mixture in saucepan. Boil 1 min. more, stirring constantly. Remove from heat. Take out 1 cup of mixture. Stir softened gelatin into remaining hot mixture. Place pan in cold water. Add the 1 cup reserved custard to chocolate. Blend well, pour into crust. When custard-gelatin is cool and mounds slightly when dropped from a spoon, blend in flavoring. Fold into Meringue of egg whites, cream of tartar and sugar (for method, see *p. 339*). Pile in crust. Chill until firm. Spread with whipped cream. Sprinkle with shaved chocolate.

Eggnog Chiffon Pie

"Perfect for holiday entertaining!" said Mabel Ross, formerly of our staff.

Make 9" Baked Pie Shell (*pp. 338-339*) or Graham Cracker Crust (*p. 341*). Cool.

2 tsp. unflavored gelatin
½ cup sugar
2 tbsp. cornstarch
¼ tsp. salt
1 cup milk
3 egg yolks, slightly beaten
1½ tsp. vanilla
¼ tsp. almond flavoring
1 cup whipping cream, whipped

Blend gelatin, sugar, cornstarch and salt in saucepan. Stir milk in gradually. Cook over medium heat, stirring constantly, until mixture thickens and boils. Boil 1 min. Remove from heat. Stir hot mixture into egg yolks. Return to saucepan and bring *just* to boiling, stirring constantly. Remove from heat. Add flavoring. Place pan in cold water. Cool until mixture mounds slightly when dropped from a spoon. Fold in whipped cream. Pour into crust, sprinkle with nutmeg. Chill.

Nesselrode Chiffon Pie

Make Eggnog Chiffon Pie (*above*) — *except* reduce sugar to ¼ cup, omit flavorings and add ½ tsp. rum flavoring and 1 jar (10 oz.) Nesselrode mixture with whipped cream. Garnish top of pie with candied fruits.

Chocolate Chiffon Pie

Elegant, fluffy, delightful for a party dessert.

Make Baked Pie Shell of desired size (*pp. 338-339*) or Graham Cracker Crust (*p. 341*). Cool.

For 9" Pie	*For 8" Pie*
1 envelope unflavored gelatin (1 tbsp.)	2 tsp.
½ cup sugar	⅓ cup
½ tsp. salt	¼ tsp.
1⅓ cups water	1 cup
2 sq. unsweetened chocolate (2 oz.), cut up	1½ sq. (1½ oz.)
3 egg yolks, slightly beaten	2
1 tsp. vanilla	¾ tsp.
3 egg whites	2
¼ tsp. cream of tartar	¼ tsp.
½ cup sugar	⅓ cup
½ cup whipping cream, whipped stiff	⅓ cup

Blend gelatin, sugar, salt and water in saucepan. Add chocolate. Cook over medium heat, stirring constantly, until chocolate is melted. Remove from heat. Slowly stir all of mixture into egg yolks. Return to saucepan and cook over medium heat, stirring constantly, *just* until it boils. Immediately remove from heat. Place pan in cold water. Cool until mixture mounds slightly when dropped from spoon. Blend in vanilla. Carefully fold in Meringue of egg whites, cream of tartar and sugar (for method, see *p. 339*). Gently fold in whipped cream. Pile into crust. Chill. Top with sweetened whipped cream, sprinkle with shaved dark chocolate.

Lemon Mallow Pie

A creamy-smooth lemon pie.

Make 9″ Baked Pie Shell *(pp. 338–339)* or Crunchy Nut Crust *(p. 341).*

24 large marshmallows
⅓ cup fresh lemon juice
⅓ cup water
grated rind of 1 lemon

5 to 6 drops yellow food coloring, if
  desired
1½ cups whipping cream, stiffly
  whipped

In saucepan heat marshmallows, lemon juice, water and lemon rind, stirring constantly, just until marshmallows are melted. Add food coloring. Chill until mixture mounds slightly when dropped from spoon. Fold in whipped cream. Pile into baked pie shell. Chill until set (2 to 3 hr.). Serve cold. Garnish with whipped cream and sprinkle with lemon rind, if desired.

Pineapple Mallow Pie

Make 9″ Baked Pie Shell *(pp. 338–339).*

24 marshmallows
1 cup crushed pineapple, undrained
1 tbsp. lemon juice
1½ cups whipping cream, whipped

Heat marshmallows, pineapple and lemon juice in saucepan over medium heat. Stir constantly just until marshmallows are melted. Chill until mixture mounds slightly when dropped from spoon. Fold in whipped cream. Pile into baked pie shell. Top with chopped toasted almonds, if desired. Chill until set (2 to 3 hr.).

Chocolate Mallow Pie

Rich, creamy . . . to please your family and your guests.

Make 8″ Baked Pie Shell *(pp. 338–339).*

½ lb. marshmallows (about 32)
¾ cup milk
¼ tsp. salt
1 cup whipping cream, whipped
1 tsp. vanilla
1 sq. unsweetened chocolate (1 oz.), grated
¼ cup chopped nuts

Heat marshmallows, milk and salt in saucepan over medium heat. Stir constantly just until marshmallows are melted. Chill until mixture mounds slightly when dropped from spoon. Fold in whipped cream, vanilla, chocolate and nuts. Pour into baked pie shell. Chill. Top with grated coconut.

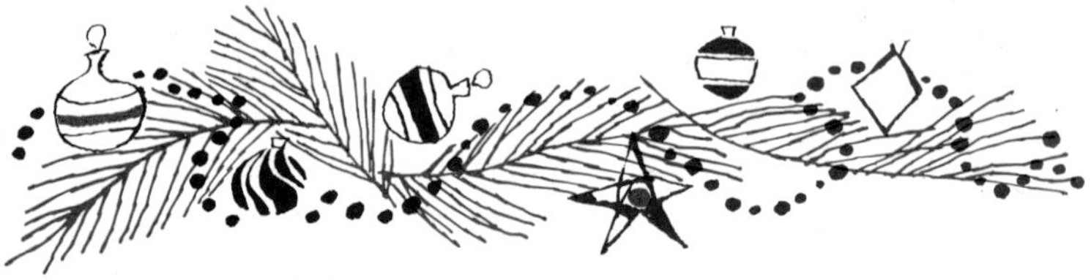

White Christmas Pie

Pure white heavenly concoction created by Ruby Livedalen Peterson (Mrs. Winton R. Peterson), formerly of our staff . . . from an idea brought by Dixie Willson of Mason City, Iowa.

Make Baked Pie Shell (with high fluted edge) of desired size *(pp. 338–339).*

For 9″ Pie	*For 8″ Pie*
½ cup sugar	⅓ cup
¼ cup GOLD MEDAL Flour	3 tbsp.
1 envelope unflavored gelatin (1 tbsp.)	2 tsp.
½ tsp. salt	¼ tsp.
1¾ cups milk	1⅓ cups
¾ tsp. vanilla	½ tsp.
¼ tsp. almond flavoring	¼ tsp.
3 egg whites	2
¼ tsp. cream of tartar	¼ tsp.
½ cup sugar	⅓ cup
½ cup whipping cream, whipped	⅓ cup
1 cup moist shredded coconut	¾ cup

Blend sugar, flour, gelatin and salt thoroughly in saucepan. Gradually stir in milk. Cook over medium heat until mixture boils, stirring constantly. Boil 1 min. Place pan in cold water. Cool until mixture mounds slightly when dropped from spoon. Blend in flavorings. Carefully fold into a Meringue made of egg whites, cream of tartar and sugar (for method, see *p. 339*). Gently fold in whipped cream. Fold in coconut. Pile into cooled baked pie shell. Sprinkle with moist shredded coconut. Chill several hours until set. Serve cold. Delicious topped with crushed strawberries or raspberries.

Baked Alaska Pie

Make shell and fill with fruit and ice cream the night before, top with meringue and brown just before serving.

Make 8" Baked Pie Shell (*pp. 338–339*).

3 cups strawberries   1 pt. firm vanilla ice cream
Meringue for 8" pie (*p. 339*)

Wash, hull, halve, then chill strawberries. Make meringue. *Heat oven to 500°* (very hot). Place 2 cups of the berries in the baked pie shell. Spoon ice cream over the berries. Cover with remaining berries. Spread meringue over pie, being careful to cover all parts. Bake *3 to 5 min.*, until a delicate brown. Serve immediately.

NOTE: Fresh fruit in season . . . such as sliced peaches, Bing cherries, raspberries or blueberries . . . may be used in place of strawberries.

Pink Alaska Pie

A delicious pink-tinted meringue topping strawberry ice cream and peaches.

Make 8" Baked Pie Shell (*pp. 338–339*).

1 qt. strawberry ice cream
Meringue for 8" pie (*p. 339*)
few drops red food coloring
1 pkg. (12 oz.) frozen peaches, thawed

Soften ice cream. Pile into cooled baked pie shell and freeze overnight. *Heat oven to 500°* (very hot). Tint meringue a delicate pink with food coloring. Arrange thawed peaches on ice cream. Spread meringue over pie, covering entire surface and sealing edges. Bake *3 to 5 min.*, or until a delicate brown. Serve immediately.

Strawberry Minute Pie

Easy to make pie with sparkling filling of frozen strawberries and strawberry gelatin.

Make 8" Baked Pie Shell (*pp. 338–339*).

1 pkg. (3 oz.) strawberry-flavored gelatin
1 cup hot water
1 pkg. (16 oz.) *unthawed* frozen strawberries

Dissolve gelatin in hot water. Add strawberries. Break up frozen berries with a fork. As berries thaw, the gelatin thickens. When filling is partially set, pour into the cooled baked pie shell. Chill until completely set. Serve garnished with Sweetened Whipped Cream (*p. 232*).

Raspberry Minute Pie

Make Strawberry Minute Pie (*above*)—*except* use raspberry-flavored gelatin in place of strawberry-flavored gelatin and frozen raspberries in place of frozen strawberries.

Strawberry Minute Cream Pie

A creamy, refreshing fruit and ice cream pie. Easy to make.

Make 9" Graham Cracker Crust (*p. 341*).

1 pkg. (10 or 16 oz.) frozen strawberries
1 pkg. (3 oz.) strawberry-flavored gelatin
1 pt. vanilla ice cream

Place strawberries in large saucepan. Break up with fork and bring to boil. Add gelatin and stir until gelatin is dissolved. Add ice cream to mixture and stir until melted. Place in refrigerator to partially set. (Mixture mounds slightly when dropped from spoon.) Pour into cooled baked crust. Chill until completely set. Garnish before serving.

Raspberry Minute Cream Pie

Make Strawberry Minute Cream Pie (*above*)—*except* use 1 pkg. (10 oz.) frozen raspberries and 1 pkg. (3 oz.) raspberry-flavored gelatin in place of strawberries and strawberry-flavored gelatin.

Ambrosia Minute Cream Pie

Make Strawberry Minute Cream Pie (*above*)—*except* use 1 can (1 lb.) fruit cocktail and 1 pkg. (3 oz.) orange-flavored gelatin in place of strawberries and strawberry-flavored gelatin.

Pineapple Minute Cream Pie

Make Strawberry Minute Cream Pie (*above*)—*except* use 1 can (1 lb. 4½ oz.) crushed pineapple and 1 pkg. (3 oz.) lemon-flavored gelatin in place of strawberries and strawberry-flavored gelatin.

359

Baked Tart Shells *Individual shells to fill as you like. See color picture p. 361.*

Make Standard Pastry for 8″ Two-crust Pie *(pp. 337–338)*. Divide pastry into 8 equal parts. Roll each part into 4″ round or 4″ square.

1. Fit pieces of pastry over backs of muffin cups or custard cups, making pleats so pastry will fit close. (Pastry may be rolled into rounds and fitted into individual pie pans or tart pans.)

2. Prick with fork to prevent puffing during baking. Place the pastry-covered or lined cups or pans on baking sheet. Bake *at 475°* (very hot) *8 to 10 min.*

3. When cool, remove from small cups or pans. Fill with any desired pie filling or special tart filling *(p. 362)*. NOTE: If thinner tart shells are desired, divide pastry into 10 equal parts.

Filled Tart Shells

See color picture p. 361.

Fill Baked Tart Shells *(above)* with fruit *(p. 343)*, cream *(pp. 354–355)* or chiffon filling *(pp. 356–357)*. Top with whipped cream and a sprinkling of nuts.

Simplified Tarts

Do not require tart pans. Make pastry and filling ahead and put together before serving. See color picture p. 361.

Roll pastry ⅛″ thick. Cut with cooky cutter into 3″ rounds. Place on ungreased baking sheet. Prick with fork. Bake *at 475°* (very hot) *8 to 10 min.*, or until delicately browned. Top with softened cream cheese, then with sweetened or glazed fruit; or top with a cream pie filling, then with whipped cream, nuts, etc.

Glacé Fruit Tarts

Your choice of fresh fruit. See color picture p. 361.

Line Baked Tart Shells *(above)* with a thin layer of cream cheese beaten with a little milk, pineapple or orange juice. Fill with fresh or frozen berries, sliced peaches or other fruits. Top with glaze of melted currant or other bright jelly.

In-A-Jiffy Pastry Shells

Make ahead of time and freeze.

Cut rolled pastry into 4 or 5″ circles. Prick with fork; stack with waxed paper between circles. Place in plastic bag or wrap in aluminum foil and freeze. When ready to use, *heat oven to 475°* (very hot). Place frozen circles over inverted custard cups on baking sheet or over inverted muffin cups. Bake *8 to 10 min.*

Sundae Tarts

See color picture p. 361.

Fill cooled Baked Tart Shells *(above)* with ice cream. Top with chocolate or butterscotch sauce, fresh or frozen fruit. Or sprinkle with chopped nuts, shaved chocolate or coconut.

Josephines

Like Napoleons, but daintier and not so rich. Tiny pastry delicacies, put together with cream filling and topped with frosting and nuts.

Make Pastry for 9″ Two-crust Pie *(pp. 337–338)*. Roll ⅛″ thick and cut into 24 oblongs, 3x2″. Place on baking sheet, prick. Bake *at 475°* (very hot) *8 to 10 min.*, or until delicately browned. Just before serving, spread tops of half the oblongs with Easy Creamy Icing *(p. 202)*, then sprinkle with chopped nuts. Put together in pairs with chilled Vanilla Cream filling *(p. 354)* for 8″ pie.

Leftover Pastry Dainties

Roll out trimmings from pie crust. Sprinkle with grated cheese or with mixture of sugar and cinnamon. Cut into fancy shapes. Bake as for tarts. Serve with salads or tea.

THE QUEEN OF HEARTS MADE SOME TARTS

Josephines	*Strawberry Glacé Tart*	*Sundae Tart*
Chocolate Tart	*Blueberry Simplified Tart*	
Lemon Tart	*Blueberry Glacé Tart*	
Cherry Tart	*Nutjammer Squares*	

Nutjammer Squares

Flaky pastry with a secret ingredient—cream cheese; easy filling of nuts and jam. Adapted from the prize-winning recipe submitted by Mrs. Anthony Saccaro of Grand Gorge, New York.

1 cup butter
1 pkg. (8 oz.) cream cheese
2 cups GOLD MEDAL Flour
½ tsp. baking powder
2 cups finely chopped walnuts
1 jar (12 oz.) apricot or peach jam
2 tsp. granulated sugar
⅓ cup confectioners' sugar

Cream butter and cheese. Measure flour by dip-level-pour method or by sifting (*see p. 6*). Mix flour and baking powder; add to creamed mixture. Chill 2 to 3 hr. *Heat oven to 375°* (quick mod.). Mix nuts, jam and granulated sugar. Divide into 4 parts; work with ¼ at a time; refrigerate remaining. Roll very thin (1/16″) on lightly floured cloth-covered board. Cut 2″ squares. Place on baking sheet. Place 1 tsp. nut mixture in center of square and top with another square. Press edges together with fork. Bake *15 to 20 min.* When cooled, sprinkle with confectioners' sugar. *Makes about 5 doz.*

Favorite Coconut Tarts

A delectable use for extra egg yolks.

Make 8 Baked Tart Shells (*p. 360*).

1 cup sugar
2 tbsp. cornstarch
½ tsp. salt
1 cup water
3 egg yolks, slightly beaten
¼ cup butter
1 tsp. vanilla
2 tsp. lemon juice
1 cup moist shredded coconut
¼ cup chopped filberts
¼ cup toasted coconut

Mix sugar, cornstarch and salt in saucepan. Stir water in gradually. Cook over medium heat, stirring constantly, until mixture boils. Boil 1 min. Remove from heat. Stir at least half of hot mixture into egg yolks. Then beat into hot mixture in saucepan. Boil 1 min. longer, stirring constantly. Remove from heat. Continue beating until smooth. Stir in butter, vanilla, lemon juice, 1 cup coconut and filberts. Pour into cooled baked tart shells. Sprinkle ¼ cup coconut over top.

Southern Chess Tarts

Elegant little tarts to serve for teas or fancy occasions.

Make Pastry for 8″ Two-crust Pie (*pp. 337–338*). Divide pastry into 24 equal parts and roll each into circle 3½ to 4″ in diameter. Line 24 tiny tart pans with pastry.

½ cup brown sugar (packed)
¼ cup granulated sugar
½ tbsp. flour
1 egg
1 tbsp. milk
½ tsp. vanilla
¼ cup butter, melted
½ cup pecans or walnuts

Heat oven to 425° (hot). Mix sugars and flour. Beat in thoroughly egg, milk, vanilla and butter. Fold in nuts. Put a scant tablespoon of mixture in each tart. Bake *15 to 20 min.*, or until set.

Banbury Tarts

Specialty of the famous Banbury Cross region near London. A favorite with Charles II.

Make Pastry for One-crust Pie (*pp. 337–339*). Roll into large square, 12x12″. Cut into nine 4″ squares.

½ cup raisins, chopped
½ cup sugar
1½ tbsp. fine cracker crumbs
1 egg yolk
½ tbsp. soft butter
dash of salt
1 tbsp. lemon juice
1 tbsp. grated lemon rind
2 tbsp. chopped walnuts

Mix all ingredients. Spread filling over half of each square. Moisten edges, fold into triangles and press edges together with tines of fork. Prick tops. Bake at 450° (hot) *12 to 15 min.*, or until delicately browned.

SALADS

The story of salads begins with the ancient Egyptians who served oil and vinegar mixed with Oriental spices on raw greens. And though Greeks cultivated lettuce for food, the Romans are credited with popularizing salads. In fact, Augustus Caesar built an altar honoring the healthful qualities of lettuce. The name salad comes from the Latin "sal" because salt was the only dressing the Romans used on greens.

Salads gained mealtime importance during the Golden Age of the European monarchies; sometimes as many as thirty ingredients were used in a single salad. When Spain's Catherine of Aragon went to England as the bride of Henry the Eighth, it was necessary to order her favorite greens from abroad.

From Spain, too, came this proverb, suggesting that four persons are needed to make the dressing for a salad of greens: "a spendthrift for oil, a miser for vinegar, a counselor for salt and a madman to stir it up." Following the French revolution, the general public was introduced to salads by the chefs of the deposed royalty who then opened restaurants.

Today's emphasis on good nutrition and fewer calories has brought renewed attention to salads and to the contrast in texture, color and flavor which they lend to our meals.

SALADS OF ALL SORTS

(complete index in back of book)

TIMELY TIPS

To vary tossed salads: add fringed cucumber slices, green pepper rings, latticed vegetables, cauliflowerets or broccoli buds (see how to cut them on p. 25).

To make cranberry cut-outs: slice canned jellied cranberry sauce, then cut into shapes using cooky cutters. Serve with a pineapple slice as a salad or as a garnish for meats.

For a gourmet touch: use tarragon, wine-flavored or herbed vinegar for French Dressings. Add new touches to favorite salads with herbs and spices (see pp. 51–52).

To take salads on a picnic: carry the dressing in a closed jar and the greens wrapped in a damp cloth. Mix just before eating.

For a pretty edge on melon, grapefruit or apple halves: trace a zigzag line around middle. Then cut deeply with point of sharp knife all around.

To hasten the setting of salads using flavored gelatin: use less hot water and ice cubes (see pkg. directions).

To prevent darkening of sliced apples or bananas: dip in lemon or grapefruit juice or in vegetable oil or sprinkle with a powdered ascorbic acid preparation such as Fruit Freeze. Refrigerate until serving time.

To give your salads fancy finishing touches: celery curls, carrot curls, radish roses, pickle fans and frosted grapes. See easy directions and step pictures on pp. 25–26. More garnishes on p. 24.

MEALTIME MAGIC

BRIDAL LUNCHEON

Bouillon (*p. 399*)
Hot Crabmeat Salad (*p. 382*) on Tomato Slices
Tiny Celery Sticks
Toasted English Muffins
Aloha Chiffon Cake (*p. 237*)

SATURDAY NIGHT

Baked Ham
Hot German Potato Salad (*p. 377*)
Green Beans   Relishes
Muffins (*p. 88*)
Gingerbread Party Dessert (*p. 232*)

WHAT EVERY COOK NEEDS TO KNOW ABOUT SALADS

BUY AND PREPARE WITH CARE

Select salad greens (p. 368) with care. Cabbage and lettuce should be heavy in proportion to size and solid to the touch. For variety, choose lacy-leafed escarole or endive and young green spinach. At home, wash greens thoroughly discarding any wilted or discolored leaves.

Tossed green salad is the simplest and most popular of salads. Tossed greens will be crisper and more attractive if you tear them into bite-size pieces rather than cutting with a knife. Weight-watchers can enjoy tossed greens with lemon juice, salt, pepper and perhaps a sprinkling of an herb (p. 51).

Vegetable salads offer a chance to be adventurous. Try green pepper strips, sliced fresh mushrooms, diagonal-cut raw green beans, sliced zucchini or a handful of freshly-shelled green peas as an addition to or garnish for your next vegetable salad.

Fruit salads are well-liked because the wide variety of fruits leads to an almost endless choice of combinations (p. 369) and because many of them may be made ahead and chilled. A word of caution: try not to serve fruit salad with a meal which already includes a fruit dessert, appetizer or meat accompaniment.

Sea food and chicken salads become a meal in themselves when served with a hot bread and light dessert. When taking these salads on picnics, pack with ice or carry in insulated container to avoid any possibility of food poisoning.

Zesty dressings add the finishing touch to salads. Learn to make French Dressing (p. 370), Mayonnaise (p. 371) and Cooked Salad Dressing (p. 371) well, and you will have the basis for many delightful dressings or salads. For salad and dressing mates, see p. 370.

. . . .

SERVE WITH FLAIR

Colorful salads need little to enhance them beyond the right dressing (p. 370) and perhaps a bit of pimiento, a maraschino cherry or a ripe or green olive.

If cooked vegetables are not as popular at your house as they could be, tempt the family with vegetable salads. They will get more valuable vitamins and minerals from the fresh foods, too.

NEW ADVENTURES IN SALADS

Mexican Green Bean Salad (p. 376)—Unusual but tasty.

Peanut Crunch Slaw (p. 376)—Unique flavors in cabbage salad.

Pineapple Boats (p. 374)—Fruit salad served in pineapple shell.

Crab Louis (p. 381)—West coast favorite—delicate crabmeat with rich Louis dressing.

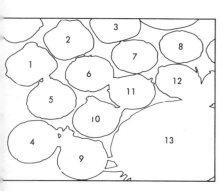

SALAD FOR EVERY DAY

SECRETS OF SALADS

1. *Choose the best salad for your meal.* Light salad with a hearty meal. Tart salad with fish. Hearty or hot salad for main course. Fruit salad as appetizer, dessert or meat accompaniment.

2. *Introduce contrasts in color, texture and form* in your meals with salads. Plan red apple salad with white baked fish; molded salad with a casserole meal; crisp greens with mashed vegetable.

3. *Plan salads with variety.* Serve favorite salads on different greens. Add cauliflowerets, sliced zucchini squash, green pepper strips or cut fresh beans to tossed green salads.

4. *Prepare salad greens with care.* Head lettuce: do not wash—just pull off outer leaves. Refrigerate. Wash as needed to avoid "rusting." Leaf lettuce, endive, spinach, other greens: swish in lukewarm water, washing each leaf separately, drain, wrap in towel, refrigerate.

5. *Match salads and dressings (see p. 370).* Sweet dressings for fruits, tart dressings for greens and vegetables. Use a minimum amount of dressing . . . too much makes a limp salad.

6. *Arrange attractively.* Salads should be simple and casual; not look "fixed." Use a large enough plate or bowl.

1. Break or tear greens. **2.** Add cut-up vegetables. **3.** Toss gently with dressing.

Best Tossed Salad *with Classic French Dressing*

One of the many recipes shared with us by Janette Kelley during the twelve years she was director of our Home Service Department. As a tribute, her many friends have now established a scholarship in her memory.

1 large head lettuce
1 bunch leaf lettuce
½ small bunch endive (about 1 cup)
½ small bag spinach (2 cups)

Use choice part of greens, discard stems and cores. Tear greens into bite-size pieces (do not cut). Have them dry and cold. Before serving, combine as suggested with Classic French Dressing (*opposite*). *6 to 8 servings.*

Classic French Dressing

¼ cup olive oil (or half vegetable oil)
2 tbsp. wine or tarragon vinegar
1½ tsp. salt
1 small clove garlic, put through press or minced
⅛ to ¼ tsp. fresh ground pepper
⅛ to ¼ tsp. flavor enhancer (monosodium glutamate)

Toss salad greens with oil until leaves glisten. Add vinegar combined with rest of ingredients. Toss again. Serve immediately.

A VARIETY OF GREENS MAKES SALADS INTERESTING

Head Lettuce | Boston Lettuce | Chicory | Escarole | Romaine or Cos Lettuce | Beet Greens | Nasturtium Leaves | Bibb Lettuce

Curly Endive | Oak Leaf Lettuce | French Endive | Dandelion Greens | Spinach | Mustard Greens | Cabbage | Water Cress | Bronze Lettuce

FRUIT SALAD FAVORITES

Serve on salad greens with sweet dressing (p. 370).

Cut-up orange sections or mandarin oranges and diced apple or banana slices, garnished with plain or toasted coconut.

Banana slices, rolled in chopped peanuts, and pineapple spears.

Long slices of banana and cubes of jellied cranberry sauce. Or slices of pineapple topped with round slices of jellied cranberry.

Honeydew melon slices with balls of cantaloupe and watermelon.

Cut-up apples, oranges, bananas, grapes, marshmallows and nuts blended with mayonnaise and whipped cream.

Pineapple slices or peach or pear halves topped with cottage or cream cheese.

Fresh or canned pineapple spears, strawberries and halves of blue plums.

Cantaloupe balls, Bing cherries, halved sweet green or Tokay grapes, seeded.

Pineapple chunks, Bing cherries and pecans.

Minted pineapple chunks, green grapes or halved Tokay grapes and cooked diced celery root, garnished with toasted slivered almonds.

Orange and grapefruit sections and avocado slices or slices of unpared red apples, garnished with pomegranate seeds or sliced strawberries.

Apricot, peach or pear half or pineapple slice topped with tiny cream cheese balls rolled in chopped nuts; pistachios are especially attractive.

Prunes or apricots stuffed with cream cheese, cottage cheese or peanut butter.

Sliced fresh pears and halved Tokay grapes, seeded.

Halved sweet green grapes or cherries in hollow of pear or peach halves.

Pear or peach halves with mayonnaise in hollow, topped with grated Cheddar cheese.

Fresh peach slices, small green grapes and peanuts.

Diced fresh pineapple, strawberries and a sprinkling of finely chopped mint.

VEGETABLE SALAD VARIETY

Serve on salad greens with tangy dressing (p. 370).

Cooked green peas, cooked French-style green beans, chopped green pepper, onion and celery, marinated in oil-vinegar dressing overnight and garnished with pimiento.

Grated raw carrots and drained crushed pineapple or diced celery mixed with raisins.

Sliced zucchini, raw cauliflowerets or thinly sliced radishes with tossed greens.

Tomato sections, cucumber slices and cauliflowerets marinated in French dressing, each in its own little lettuce cup.

Cooked baby Lima beans, sliced mushrooms and sliced green onions, seasoned with oregano.

Grated raw carrot, chopped sweet onion, chopped celery, grated rind and sections of 1 orange and lettuce. Or grated raw parsnips, chopped sweet onion, celery and pimiento-stuffed olives tossed with greens.

Small tomatoes stuffed with cottage cheese sprinkled with minced chives, parsley or toasted almonds. Or stuffed with cabbage salad.

Mound of cottage cheese with diced green or red pepper, cucumber and onions.

Asparagus tips on thick tomato slices, sprinkled with grated cheese.

Grated raw carrots and diced celery mixed with raisins or nuts.

Halves of peeled, chilled tomatoes sprinkled with minced parsley, mint or chives. After dressing is added, sprinkle with grated sharp cheese.

Red cherry tomatoes, yellow plum tomatoes with unpared cucumber slices and sliced spring onions.

Overlapping slices of tomato, unpared cucumber slices and onion rings or slices.

French Dressing *(American Version)*

The basis of many delightful variations for simple green salads. For a real zesty flavor, add some grated lemon rind . . . a secret that Harry J. Kleefisch, known to many as "Enrique," learned from a former chef to the King of Italy.

1 cup olive oil, vegetable oil or combination	1 tsp. salt
¼ cup vinegar	½ tsp. dry mustard
¼ cup lemon juice	½ tsp. paprika

Beat all ingredients together with rotary beater or shake well in tightly covered jar. Keep in covered jar in refrigerator. Shake again to mix before using as it separates on standing. *Makes 1½ cups.*

Sweet French Dressing: Add 2 tbsp. *sifted* confectioners' sugar or honey to ½ cup French Dressing.

Piquant Dressing: Add 2 tbsp. sugar, ½ tsp. *each* celery seeds and grated onion to ½ cup French Dressing. Let 1 clove garlic, cut crosswise, stand in dressing 1 hr.

Vinaigrette Dressing: Chop fine: 3 green olives, 1 small dill pickle and 1 hard-cooked egg. Add, with 1½ tsp. minced pimiento, to ½ cup French Dressing. Mix; chill.

Roquefort Dressing: Mash ¼ cup Roquefort cheese with ⅛ tsp. Worcestershire sauce. Blend in ½ cup French Dressing.

Curry Dressing: Add ⅛ tsp. curry powder to ½ cup French Dressing.

Garlic French Dressing: Mix 1 clove garlic, pressed or crushed to fine paste and some freshly ground pepper with ½ cup French Dressing.

Chiffonade Dressing: Add 1 tbsp. chopped ripe olives, 1 tbsp. chopped green pepper, 1 hard-cooked egg (white sieved, yolk mashed) and 1 tbsp. finely cut chives to ½ cup French Dressing.

Lorenzo Dressing: Add 1 tbsp. chili sauce to ½ cup French Dressing.

Poppy Seed Dressing: Add ½ tsp. poppy seeds (or dill, celery, caraway or sesame seeds) to ½ cup French Dressing.

Herb Dressing: Add 2 tsp. minced parsley, ⅛ tsp. thyme and ½ tsp. oregano to ½ cup French Dressing.

SALAD AND DRESSING MATES

For Fruit Salads

Sweet French Dressing (*above*)

Lorenzo Dressing (*above*)

Fruit Salad Mayonnaise (*p. 371*)

1-2-3 Fruit Dressing (*p. 372*)

Lime or Lemonade Dressing (*p. 372*)

Old-fashioned Fruit Dressing (*p. 375*)

Pineapple Fruit Salad Dressing (*p. 372*)

Ruby Red Dressing (*p. 372*)

Poppy Seed Dressing (*above*)

For Meat or Sea Food Salads

Mayonnaise (*p. 371*)

Curry Dressing (*above*)

Tomato-Cucumber Mayonnaise (*p. 371*)

For Salads of Greens or Vegetable Salads

French Dressing (*above*)

Piquant Dressing (*above*)

Vinaigrette Dressing (*above*)

Roquefort Dressing (*above*)

Garlic French Dressing (*above*)

Chiffonade Dressing (*above*)

Herb Dressing (*above*)

Thousand Island Dressing (*p. 371*)

Lorenzo Dressing (*above*)

Russian Dressing (*p. 371*)

Sour Cream Dressing (*p. 372*)

Green Goddess Salad Dressing (*p. 372*)

Tomato Soup Dressing (*p. 372*)

Classic French Dressing (*p. 368*)

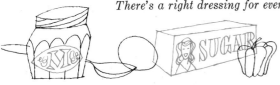

Mayonnaise

The foundation of a myriad of intriguing salad dressings.

1 egg yolk
1 tsp. dry mustard
1 tsp. confectioners' sugar
¼ tsp. salt
dash of cayenne pepper
1 tbsp. lemon juice or vinegar
1 cup vegetable oil
1 more tbsp. lemon juice or vinegar

Beat together with rotary beater egg yolk, mustard, sugar, salt, cayenne and 1 tbsp. lemon juice. Continue beating while adding vegetable oil, at first drop by drop, gradually increasing amount as mixture thickens until all is used. Slowly add the 1 more tbsp. lemon juice. Beat well. Chill before serving. *1½ cups dressing.*

Fruit Salad Mayonnaise

Into ½ cup Mayonnaise (*above*) fold ¼ cup whipping cream, whipped stiff.

Tomato-Cucumber Mayonnaise

Excellent on sea food salads.

To 1 cup Mayonnaise (*above*) add ½ cup *each* drained, diced tomato and cucumber, 1 tsp. minced onion, salt.

Goldenrod Mayonnaise

To 1 cup Mayonnaise (*above*) add finely chopped egg whites from 2 hard-cooked eggs. Top the salad with the sieved egg yolks.

Thousand Island Dressing

Popular on wedges of lettuce.

To ½ cup Mayonnaise (*above*) add 1 tbsp. chili sauce, 1 tbsp. chopped stuffed olives, 1 tsp. minced chives, 1 hard-cooked egg, chopped, ¼ tsp. paprika and additional salt and pepper to taste.

Russian Dressing

With salad greens alone, it makes a perfect dinner salad.

To ½ cup Mayonnaise (*above*) add ¼ cup chili sauce and a few drops of onion juice. An additional teaspoon lemon juice may be added, if desired.

Cooked Mayonnaise

Uses those "extra" egg yolks.

⅓ cup GOLD MEDAL Flour
1 tsp. sugar
1 tsp. salt
1 tsp. dry mustard
¾ cup water
¼ cup mild vinegar or lemon juice
4 egg yolks (or 2 whole eggs)
1 cup vegetable oil

Mix flour, sugar, salt and mustard in saucepan. Gradually add water and vinegar. Cook over low heat, stirring constantly, until mixture boils. Boil 1 min. Remove from heat. Pour into bowl. Beat in egg yolks with rotary beater. Continue beating, adding vegetable oil a little at a time. Chill before serving. When using, modify as desired with whipped cream. *2 cups dressing.*

Cooked Salad Dressing

Also called "boiled" dressing. For potato, cabbage and other hearty salads.

¼ cup sugar
¼ cup GOLD MEDAL Flour
2 tsp. salt
2 tsp. dry mustard
1½ cups milk
½ cup mild vinegar or lemon juice
4 egg yolks, slightly beaten
1 tbsp. butter

Mix sugar, flour, salt and mustard in saucepan. Gradually blend in milk and vinegar. Cook over direct low heat, stirring constantly until mixture thickens and boils. Boil 1 min. Stir at least half of hot mixture into egg yolks. Stir into remaining hot mixture in saucepan. Bring to boil, stirring constantly. Boil 1 min. Remove from heat and stir in butter. Cool. *2 cups dressing.* When using, mix with an equal amount of whipped cream, commercial sour cream or mayonnaise.

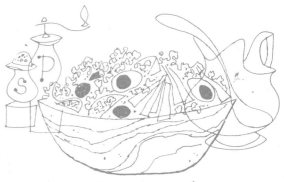

1-2-3 Fruit Dressing

No oil. Tart and refreshing.

1 cup sugar
juice and grated rind of 1 lemon, lime and
   orange
1 egg, well beaten

Combine all ingredients in saucepan. Cook over medium heat, stirring constantly, until boiling. Boil 1 min. Remove from heat. Cool. *About 1½ cups dressing.*

Limeade or Lemonade Dressing

Fresh, zesty . . . so good on fruit.

⅓ cup undiluted frozen concentrate for
   limeade or lemonade
⅓ cup honey
⅓ cup vegetable oil
1 tsp. celery or poppy seeds

Combine all ingredients in small bowl. Beat with rotary beater until smooth. *1 cup dressing.*

Pineapple Fruit Salad Dressing

Use with Fruit Kabobs (p. 56).

1 tbsp. cornstarch
½ cup sugar
2 egg yolks, slightly beaten
⅓ cup water
3 tbsp. pineapple juice
2 tbsp. lemon juice
⅛ tsp. salt

Mix cornstarch and sugar. Add egg yolks and water. Cook over direct heat, bringing mixture to a boil. Boil 1 min., stirring constantly. Remove from heat. Add juices and salt. Cool. Serve in a dish long and deep enough to fit skewer. *1 cup dressing.*

Ruby Red Dressing

*On oranges and citrus things,
It makes a feast that's fit for kings.*

½ cup currant jelly
¼ cup vegetable oil
2 tbsp. lemon juice
dash of salt
few drops onion juice

Beat jelly with fork until smooth. Add rest of ingredients and beat until smooth. *¾ cup dressing.*

Green Goddess Salad Dressing

Most popular at a large San Francisco hotel. Especially delicious on salad greens or sea food. For a milder flavored, thicker dressing, omit vinegar.

1 cup mayonnaise
½ cup commercial sour cream
⅓ cup finely minced parsley
3 tbsp. finely minced chives or green onions
3 tbsp. anchovy paste or finely minced anchovies
3 tbsp. tarragon wine vinegar
1 tbsp. lemon juice
1 clove garlic, crushed or grated
salt and freshly ground pepper to taste

Combine all ingredients. Chill; it mellows and thickens on standing. *2 cups dressing.*

Rancho Roquefort Dressing

Blend 1 cup commercial sour cream, 2 green onions, cut fine, 2 tbsp. mayonnaise, 2 tbsp. lemon juice, ½ cup Roquefort or Bleu cheese, crumbled, and salt and pepper to taste. Let ripen several hours. Serve on lettuce wedges.

Dressing For Lettuce Salad

"Many happy childhood memories are recalled each time I serve this," says Mrs. Burt C. Sloate, Billings, Montana.

Cut or tear into large bowl 4 cups crisp, cold leaf lettuce. Toss with a mixture of ½ cup cream, 3 to 4 tbsp. vinegar, 1 to 1½ tbsp. sugar and ¼ tsp. salt. *6 servings.*

Sour Cream Dressing

Spoon over sliced cucumbers or tender young leaf lettuce. Also delicious on baked potatoes.

Blend 1 cup commercial sour cream, 3 tbsp. minced chives or onion and 2 tbsp. lemon juice (or 1 tbsp. vinegar), 1½ tsp. salt and ⅛ tsp. pepper. *1¼ cups dressing.*

Tomato Soup Dressing

Serve on shredded greens. Contributed by Mrs. E. A. Nierengarten of New Ulm, Minnesota.

1 can (10½ oz.) condensed tomato soup
1 cup *each* vegetable oil and vinegar
1 small onion, grated
1 tbsp. sugar
1 tbsp. Worcestershire sauce
1 tsp. *each* dry mustard, paprika, salt
1 clove garlic, pressed or grated

Combine all ingredients in quart jar. Cover. Shake well. Refrigerate. *3½ cups dressing.*

Caesar's Salad

A connoisseur's salad, made for our staff by a delightful visitor, famous home economist, Essie L. Elliott of California.

In advance: Cover ½ clove garlic with 2 tbsp. vegetable oil; let stand. Also, prepare 2 cups Croutons (*at right below*) except do not butter bread.

Place 3 qt. dry, cold, crisp salad greens in large bowl. Add ⅓ cup *each* vegetable oil, grated Parmesan cheese and crumbled Bleu cheese. Salt and pepper to taste. Break 1 raw egg over greens. Squeeze juice of 2 lemons over egg. Toss well.

Just before serving: Remove garlic from oil; combine oil and croutons and sprinkle over top of salad. *8 servings.*

Palace Court Salad

A luncheon specialty at the Palace Hotel in San Francisco.

Arrange a mound of finely shredded lettuce on salad plate. On top, place a thick large tomato slice. On tomato, place one large cooked artichoke heart (or 3 small). Cover this with pieces of cooked crab, shrimp or chicken. Garnish around edge of lettuce with sieved hard-cooked egg. Serve with Russian Dressing (*p. 371*).

Wilted Greens

Use lettuce, spinach, endive, romaine or a combination of the greens listed on p. 368.

Fry 4 slices bacon, cut up, until crisp. Add ¼ cup vinegar, 2 tbsp. water. Heat. Pour over 1 qt. shredded greens tossed with 2 green onions, chopped, 1 tsp. salt and pepper. Sprinkle 1 hard-cooked egg, chopped, over top.

Onion Chrysanthemum See p. 25.

Chef's Salad

Julienne strips of meat with mixed greens make a hearty main dish salad.

1 head lettuce
½ bunch romaine or endive
½ cup chopped green onion
½ cup sliced celery
1 cup julienne strips of cold cooked meat
    (such as beef, ham, tongue, chicken)
1 cup julienne strips of Swiss cheese
1 can (2 oz.) fillets of anchovy, if desired
½ cup Mayonnaise (*p. 371*)
¼ cup French Dressing (*p. 370*)

Tear greens into bite-size pieces. Toss greens with onion, celery, meat, cheese and anchovies, reserving a few strips of meat and cheese for garnish. Just before serving, toss with dressings. Garnish with strips of meat and cheese, ripe olives and hard-cooked eggs. *4 servings.*

Croutons: Cut buttered bread into cubes, toast in oven.

Julienne: Cut match-like strips of cheese and meat.

Russian Salad

To Chef's Salad (*above*) add some or all: ½ cup *each* diced cooked beets, kidney beans, sauerkraut, ¼ cup *each* diced cucumber and sweet pickles, 1 to 2 tbsp. minced sardines or anchovies, 1 medium potato, diced. Garnish with sieved hard-cooked egg and caviar.

Fresh Spinach Salad

½ lb. washed, dried spinach, torn in
    bite-size pieces (4 cups)
1 small Bermuda onion, sliced
¼ cup diced celery
4 hard-cooked eggs, sliced

Toss all ingredients together lightly. Chill. Before serving, toss lightly with Classic French Dressing (*p. 368*). *8 servings.*

Three-In-One Salad

For beautiful salads, Katharine Eustis lines her lettuce cups with darker green leaves of Bibb lettuce.

tomato salad (small tomato stuffed with cottage
   cheese and chives)
chicken salad sprinkled with slivered,
   salted almonds
grapefruit and orange salad with
   avocado slices
ripe olives, celery, pimiento and water cress
   for garnish

On individual serving plates arrange each salad in separate Lettuce Cup (*below*). Pass double dish of mayonnaise for chicken and tomato salads, sweet fruit dressing for fruit salad.

Lettuce Cups

Slit a lettuce leaf apart and overlap, or overlap two smaller leaves to form cups.

Chicken or Sea Food Salad in Avocado Shells

Serve chicken or sea food salad in peeled avocado halves or on drained round slices of canned pineapple on crisp lettuce. Garnish with sprigs of water cress.

AVOCADO

Run knife down center back of each half . . . cut through center of thin outer rind only. Pull off sections of skin.

Place avocado half on board. Slice as thick as desired. Drench slices with lemon or lime juice to prevent darkening.

Avocado Salad

An avocado is table-ripe when it yields to gentle pressure between the palms of the hands.

Peel and slice 2 avocados. Soak several hours or overnight in refrigerator in about 1 cup French Dressing (*p. 370*), to which 1 clove garlic, crushed, has been added. Drain and serve on greens with more of the dressing. *4 servings.*

Melon Salads

Serve a fruit dressing. For an attractive garnish, roll cream cheese balls in pistachio nuts.

Melon Fruit Cup: Combine watermelon, cantaloupe or honeydew melon balls, cubes or slices. Or use 1 variety combined with other fruits. Serve on greens.

Cantaloupe Ring: See color picture, *p. 366.* Place ¾" thick slice of cantaloupe (rind removed) on bed of salad greens. Fill center with seasonal fruits (melon balls, sweet green grapes, cherries, strips of pears, blackberries). If desired, top with scoop of fruit sherbet.

Melon Boat Salad: See color picture, *p. 366.* Place boat-shaped section of cantaloupe (rind removed) on bed of salad greens. Fill boat with seasonal fruits as in Cantaloupe Ring (*above*).

Melon-Plum-Peach-Grape Salad: Alternate slices of melon, red plums, fresh peaches. Add a few green grapes.

PINEAPPLE BOAT

Cut in two lengthwise. Cut around edge with curved knife, remove fruit. Discard core.

MELON BALLS

Use a ball cutter or a rounded measuring spoon. Cut into melon with circular motion.

Pineapple Boats

Fresh pineapple is plentiful in April, May and June.

Cut the whole pineapple lengthwise into halves or quarters, depending on size. Trim leaves to make a neat appearance. Carefully cut the fruit away from each portion, leaving a wall of fruit about ½" thick on the shell so that it will hold its shape.

Toss pineapple cubes together with other fresh fruits (halved Tokay or sweet green grapes, Bing cherries, orange sections, strawberries, plums, apricot halves, pear sticks) and Sweet French Dressing (*p. 370*). Refill pineapple shell with the fruit salad mixture. Each pineapple boat (half) is an individual serving.

Orange or Grapefruit Salads

Arrange the fruit combinations on salad greens. Garnish gaily with sprigs of water cress or fresh anise. Serve with fruit dressings.

Grapefruit-Orange Salad: Alternate sections of orange and grapefruit.

Apple-Avocado-Orange-Grape Salad: Alternate slices of unpared apple, orange sections and peeled avocado with a sprinkling of halved little green or Tokay grapes.

Grapefruit-Pomegranate Salad: Arrange grapefruit sections in petal fashion. Sprinkle with pomegranate seeds.

Avocado-Grapefruit-Orange Salad: Arrange thin slices of peeled avocado between sections of grapefruit and orange.

Avocado-Grapefruit-Tomato Salad: Place Tomato Flower Cups (*p. 382*) on lettuce leaves. Arrange around each tomato, sections of grapefruit and slices of orange. Insert thin slices of avocado here and there to resemble leaves. Dot with a bit of mayonnaise.

Orange-Bermuda Onion Salad (especially good with wild game): Alternate slices of orange with rings of Bermuda onion. Garnish with sprigs of water cress or chopped fresh mint.

Grapefruit-Avocado-Persimmon Salad: Alternate slices of avocado and persimmon with sections of grapefruit. Garnish.

Grapefruit-Cherry Salad: Put sections of grapefruit together with softened cream cheese. Top with a few large Bing or Royal Anne cherries.

PARING GRAPEFRUIT

Cut thin slice from top . . . then pare 'round and 'round like an apple.

GRAPEFRUIT SECTIONS

Pare, then cut along each dividing membrane. Lift out sections whole.

24-Hour Salad

2 cups drained, pitted, canned white or
    Bing cherries
2 cups drained pineapple bits or chunks
2 oranges, peeled, sectioned and cut up
12 marshmallows, cut in fourths

Toss fruits and marshmallows together. Blend in Old-fashioned Fruit Dressing (*below*). Chill several hours. Serve in large bowl with or without salad greens or in individual Lettuce Cups (*p. 374*). Garnish with orange sections and maraschino cherries. *8 to 10 servings.*

Old-fashioned Fruit Dressing

Beat together with rotary beater 2 eggs, 2 tbsp. sugar, 2 tbsp. vinegar or lemon juice, 2 tbsp. pineapple juice, 1 tbsp. butter and dash of salt. Cook in saucepan over low heat, stirring constantly, just to boiling. Remove from heat. Cool. Fold in ¾ cup whipping cream, whipped.

Frozen Fruit Salad

1 envelope unflavored gelatin (1 tbsp.)
1 cup cold water
⅓ cup mild mayonnaise
1 cup whipping cream, whipped
1 cup drained canned pineapple chunks
1 cup sliced bananas
1 cup cut-up orange
½ cup halved maraschino cherries, dates,
    nuts or a combination
2 tbsp. lemon juice

Soften gelatin in cold water. Dissolve over hot water. Blend into mayonnaise and whipped cream. Fold in remaining ingredients. Pour into refrigerator tray; freeze until firm. *8 servings.*

Waldorf Salad

2 cups diced apple, unpeeled
1 cup diced celery
broken nuts
½ cup mayonnaise (or use 4 to 6 tbsp.
    thinned with cream)

Toss apple, celery and nuts with mayonnaise. Serve in Lettuce Cups (*p. 374*). Top each serving with a maraschino cherry. *4 servings.*

Cabbage Salad (*Cole Slaw*)

2½ cups finely shredded, chopped or grated
  cabbage
1 tsp. salt
Cooked Salad Dressing (*p. 371*) or Mayonnaise
  (*p. 371*) mixed with a little cream

Place cabbage in vegetable crisper or covered dish
in refrigerator 2 or more hours. Then sprinkle
with salt. Moisten with salad dressing or mayonnaise. Toss lightly with fork. Serve immediately.
4 servings.

Delicious Additions

Add 1½ to 2 cups cut-up fruit, vegetables or
nuts (*below*) to Cabbage Salad. Toss lightly again.
6 servings.

Cut-up red apple, celery and nuts.

Drained pineapple, cut-up marshmallows, halved
small green grapes or seeded Tokay grapes.

Grated raw carrots, dill, chopped green pepper.

Raisins, grated carrots, celery or dill seeds.

Cut-up red apple, sliced bananas and salted
peanuts.

Grated turnip, minced onion and pimiento.

Cut-up tomato and cucumber, summer savory.

Minced green pepper, onion and pimiento, sliced
celery, with basil.

Equal parts of cut-up cucumber and minced green
onions, a sprinkling of dill weed.

Old-fashioned Cabbage Slaw

1 tsp. salt
¼ tsp. pepper
½ tsp. dry mustard
½ to 1 tsp. celery seeds
2 tbsp. sugar
¼ cup chopped green pepper
1 tbsp. chopped red pepper or pimiento
½ tsp. grated onion
3 tbsp. vegetable oil
⅓ cup white vinegar
3 cups finely chopped cabbage

Place ingredients in large bowl in order given.
Mix well. Cover and chill thoroughly. Garnish
with water cress and sliced stuffed olives just
before serving, if desired. *4 servings.*

Mexican Green Bean Salad

Marinate 2 cups cooked thinly sliced French
beans or whole cut beans (fresh or frozen) in
2 to 3 tbsp. French Dressing (*p. 370*) with 2 tbsp.
finely chopped onion several hours or overnight.
Add 2 to 3 tbsp. grated Cheddar or Parmesan
cheese. Garnish with thin slices of onion rings. *4
servings.*

Tomatoes Vinaigrette

Serve on luncheon or dinner plate with or without greens.

Arrange 8 or 9 thick tomato slices or smaller whole
tomatoes (with tops cut off) in a square pan,
8x8x2″ or 9x9x1¾″. Spoon over tomatoes a mixture of: 1 cup olive oil, ⅓ cup wine vinegar,
2 tsp. oregano, 1 tsp. salt, 2 cloves garlic (pressed
or minced), ½ tsp. pepper and ½ tsp. dry
mustard. Cover. Chill 2 to 3 hr., basting
occasionally. To serve, sprinkle with minced onion
and parsley and some of dressing. *8 servings.*

Peanut Crunch Slaw

*A prize-winning recipe from Mrs. Hildreth Hatheway,
Santa Barbara, California, famous for her good cooking.*

4 cups shredded cabbage
1 cup finely cut celery
½ cup commercial sour cream
½ cup mayonnaise
1 tsp. salt
¼ cup chopped green onions
¼ cup chopped green pepper
½ cup chopped cucumber
1 tbsp. butter
½ cup salted peanuts, coarsely chopped
2 tbsp. Parmesan cheese

Toss cabbage and celery together. Chill. Mix sour
cream, mayonnaise, salt, onions, green pepper and
cucumber; chill. Just before serving, melt butter
in small skillet; add peanuts and heat until lightly
browned. Immediately stir in cheese. Toss chilled
vegetables with dressing. Sprinkle peanuts on top.
6 to 8 servings.

Potato Salad

A good potato salad is the mark of a good cook.

4 cups cubed cold boiled potatoes
1 tbsp. finely chopped onion
½ tsp. salt
dash of pepper
¼ cup French Dressing (p. 370)
½ cup Cooked Salad Dressing (p. 371) or
  Mayonnaise (p. 371)
2 hard-cooked eggs, cut up

Place potatoes and onion in bowl. Sprinkle with salt and pepper. Mix lightly with French dressing. Chill an hour or two. Toss lightly with salad dressing or mayonnaise. Carefully blend in eggs. Mix in a little minced pimiento and parsley for color. Add extra seasoning and dressing to taste. Serve in bowl or on platter surrounded with salad greens, tomato sections, slices or wedges of hard-cooked eggs, cucumber sticks, etc. Garnish with paprika. *6 servings.*

Special Potato Salad: Add 1 cup chopped celery; 1 cucumber, diced; 1 tsp. celery seeds; 1 cup grated carrots.

Sea Food-Potato Salad: Add 2 cups flaked cooked tuna, salmon, crabmeat, shrimp or lobster and 3 tbsp. chopped crisp pickles.

Meat-and-Potato Salad: Garnish with strips of cooked lean meat such as beef, ham, veal or chicken.

Hot German Potato Salad

Mrs. Joseph Teynor, New Ulm, Minnesota, serves this with baked or boiled ham, baked spareribs or frankfurters.

6 medium potatoes, boiled in jackets
6 slices bacon
¾ cup chopped onion
2 tbsp. flour
1 to 2 tbsp. sugar
1½ tsp. salt
½ tsp. celery seeds
dash of pepper
¾ cup water
⅓ cup vinegar

Peel potatoes and slice thin. Fry bacon slowly in skillet, then drain on paper. Sauté onion in bacon fat until golden brown. Blend in flour, sugar, salt, celery seeds and pepper. Cook over low heat, stirring until smooth and bubbly. Remove from heat. Stir in water and vinegar. Heat to boil, stirring constantly. Boil 1 min. Stir in carefully the potatoes and the crumbled bacon bits. Remove from heat, cover and let stand until ready to serve. *6 to 8 servings.*

Macaroni-Salmon Salad

See color picture p. 380.

2 cups boiled and cooled macaroni
  (1 cup broken uncooked)
1 cup diced cucumber
1 can (8 oz.) salmon, flaked
1 tbsp. grated onion
1 tbsp. minced parsley
¾ cup Mayonnaise (p. 371)
½ tsp. salt
¼ tsp. pepper

Combine ingredients; toss together until blended. Serve on lettuce. Garnish with chopped parsley and paprika, if desired. *4 to 6 servings.*

NOTE: 1½ cups cubed, leftover, cooked meat (chicken, veal, etc.) may be used in place of salmon.

Summer Macaroni Salad

Try this with broiled meat—men love it.

boiled elbow, shell or ring macaroni
  (7 or 8 oz. uncooked)
1 cup cubed Cheddar cheese
1 cup sliced gherkins
½ cup minced onion
½ cup mayonnaise
1 pkg. (10 or 12 oz.) frozen peas (cooked and
  drained)

Drain macaroni and rinse with cold water. Add remaining ingredients. Season with salt and pepper. Chill. Serve in Lettuce Cups (p. 374). *4 to 6 servings.*

Bean Salad

Mrs. Charles Kuoni, Jr. of Glen Ellyn, Illinois, likes to serve this at impromptu luncheons in her suburban home. See color picture p. 380.

2 cups drained cooked kidney beans (1 lb. 4 oz. can)
¼ cup diced celery
3 pickles (dill or sweet), chopped
1 small onion, minced
2 hard-cooked eggs, sliced
½ tsp. salt
⅛ tsp. pepper
about ¼ cup mayonnaise or
  commercial sour cream

Mix all ingredients except mayonnaise. Mix lightly with mayonnaise. Chill thoroughly. Serve on salad greens. Garnish with grated cheese. *6 servings.*

MOLDED SALADS

HOW TO MAKE MOLDED GELATIN SALADS

Choose flavor to make an interesting combination with the fruits or vegetables you add.

1. When gelatin is partially set, add cut-up fruit or vegetables.

2. Pour into individual molds or ring mold. Chill.

3. To unmold, dip in warm water; loosen with spatula; turn upside-down onto plate.

Molded Gelatin Salad

1 pkg. fruit-flavored gelatin (3 oz.)
2 tbsp. lemon juice or vinegar, if desired

1½ to 2½ cups well drained, cut-up fresh or canned fruit, vegetables or sea food

Prepare gelatin according to pkg. directions. If making a vegetable salad, add lemon juice. When partially set (mixture mounds off spoon), add fruit, vegetables or sea food. Pour into 6 or 8 individual molds. Chill until firm. Unmold on individual plates. Garnish with lettuce, endive or water cress. Serve fruit gelatin salads with Fruit Salad Mayonnaise (*p. 371*); serve vegetable or sea food gelatin salads with Mayonnaise (*p. 371*) or Sour Cream Dressing (*p. 372*). *6 to 8 servings.*

NOTE: Double the recipe to fill 9″ ring mold for 12 servings.

Jellied Fruit Medleys

Often served with toasted cheese sandwiches at Sunday night candlelight suppers in the colonial home of Roy and Eleanor Larsen.

Make Molded Gelatin Salad (*above*) using one of the fruit combinations below.

Orange sections, diced apple and banana slices.
Bing cherries and Cling peaches.
Pineapple chunks and sliced strawberries.
Melon balls, Bing cherries and green grapes.

Carrot-Fruit Mold

Make Molded Fruit Gelatin (*above*) using lemon or lime-flavored gelatin, 1½ cups grated raw carrots and 1¼ cups well drained canned crushed pineapple or halved sweet green grapes.

Pacific Lime Mold

Dissolve 1 pkg. (3 oz.) lime-flavored gelatin in 1 cup boiling water. Add juice from 1 can (9 oz.) crushed pineapple; chill until slightly thickened. Beat until frothy. Fold in pineapple, 1 cup creamy cottage cheese, 1 tsp. horse-radish, ½ cup mayonnaise or ½ cup whipping cream, whipped, and ¼ cup chopped nuts. Chill until firm. *6 servings.*

Perfection Salad

Make Molded Gelatin Salad (*above*) using lemon-flavored gelatin, 1 cup finely shredded cabbage, 1 cup finely diced celery, 2 finely chopped pimientos, 6 chopped sweet pickles and 1 tsp. salt.

Creamy Molded Chicken Salad

Bring 1 cup chicken broth to a boil. Add 1 pkg. (3 oz.) lemon-flavored gelatin, stirring until dissolved. Add another ¾ cup chicken broth, ¼ cup mayonnaise, ¼ tsp. salt and dash of pepper. Beat with rotary beater until smooth. Pour into refrigerator tray. Freeze 15 to 20 min., or until firm around edge but soft in center. Turn mixture into bowl and whip until fluffy. Gently fold in 1 cup diced cooked chicken, ½ cup sweet green grapes and ⅓ cup toasted slivered almonds. Pour into 1-qt. mold or 6 individual molds. Chill (not in freezing unit) until firm. Unmold and garnish with pimiento and crisp greens. *6 servings.*

Tangy Tomato Aspic

Colorful, piquant, refreshing.

1 pkg. (3 oz.) lemon-flavored gelatin
1¼ cups hot water
1 can (8 oz.) tomato sauce
1½ tbsp. white vinegar
½ tsp. salt
¾ tsp. onion juice
dash *each* of Tabasco, pepper, ground cloves
    and cayenne pepper

Dissolve gelatin in hot water. Blend in remaining ingredients. Pour into 6 individual molds or 1-qt. ring mold. Chill until firm. Serve on greens with mayonnaise. *6 servings.*

Molded Cheese Salad

1 envelope unflavored gelatin (1 tbsp.)
¼ cup water
1 carton (12 oz.) creamy cottage cheese
1 pkg. (3 oz.) cream cheese
⅓ cup finely chopped celery
2 tbsp. finely chopped chives
¼ tsp. salt
½ cup milk

Soften gelatin in water in custard cup or top of double boiler; place over hot water to dissolve. Meanwhile, beat cottage cheese and cream cheese until fluffy (some small lumps will remain). Blend in celery, chives and salt. Fold in gelatin; stir in milk. (Be sure gelatin is well blended before milk is added to avoid stringiness.) Pour into 6 individual molds or 1-qt. ring mold. Chill until firm. Serve on lettuce with fruit. *6 servings.*

Aspic-Cheese Ribbon Salad

Make Tangy Tomato Aspic (*above*) and pour into a 1¼-qt. ring mold. Chill until *firm.* Top with Molded Cheese Salad (*above*). Chill thoroughly. Unmold ring and fill with a sea food salad or greens. Serve with mayonnaise. *9 to 12 servings.*

Strawberry or Raspberry Salad Glacé

Dissolve 2 pkg. (3 oz. *each*) raspberry or strawberry-flavored gelatin in 2 cups hot water. Add 2 cups cold water. Soften 1 pkg. (8 oz.) cream cheese with cream. Shape into balls, using 1 level tsp. for each. Roll in ½ cup finely chopped nuts. Place some of cheese balls evenly spaced in 9" ring mold. Cover with alternate layers of lightly sugared strawberries or raspberries and cheese balls. Pour cooled gelatin over cheese balls and berries. Chill until set. Unmold. Garnish with large perfect berries. Top with mixture of mayonnaise and whipped cream. *10 to 12 servings.*

Mandarin Duet Salad

Two fruit salads in one—a shimmering, flavorful gelatin ring filled with ambrosia.

Orange Gelatin Ring

2 pkg. (3 oz. each) orange-flavored gelatin
2 cups boiling liquid (water or fruit juice)
1 pt. orange sherbet
1 can (11 oz.) mandarin oranges, drained

Dissolve gelatin in boiling liquid. Immediately add orange sherbet and stir until melted. Add oranges. Pour into 1½-qt. ring mold and chill until firm. Unmold and fill center with Ambrosia Fruit Salad (*below*). *10 to 12 servings.*

Ambrosia Fruit Salad

1 can (11 oz.) mandarin oranges, drained
1 can (13 oz.) pineapple chunks, drained
1 cup flaked coconut
1 cup commercial sour cream or ½ cup
    whipping cream, whipped
1 cup cut-up or miniature marshmallows

Mix all ingredients. Chill several hours or overnight.

Cranberry-Grape Salad

For holiday entertaining. Delicious with tiny hot rolls.

4 cups cranberries
2 cups water
1½ cups sugar
2 envelopes unflavored gelatin (2 tbsp.)
¼ cup cold water
1 cup Tokay grapes (seeded and quartered)
1 cup diced canned pineapple (drained)
½ cup broken walnuts, if desired

Cook cranberries gently in the 2 cups water until skins break. Rub through sieve. Add sugar to pulp. Boil slowly *5 min.* Take off heat. Soften gelatin in cold water. Blend into hot cranberry mixture. Let cool until mixture mounds slightly when dropped from spoon. Add grapes, pineapple and walnuts. Pour into a 9" ring mold or 8 individual molds and chill. When set, unmold and serve on salad greens with mayonnaise or Cooked Salad Dressing (*p. 371*) mixed with whipped cream. *8 to 12 servings.*

MAIN DISH SALADS

Chicken Salad

An all-American favorite.

2 cups cubed cold cooked
  chicken (large chunks)
1 cup diced celery (¼″ pieces)
1 tbsp. lemon juice

salt and pepper to taste
½ cup mayonnaise
2 or 3 hard-cooked eggs, cut up

Toss together chicken, celery, lemon juice and seasonings. Mix in mayonnaise. Carefully fold in eggs. Chill thoroughly. Arrange a mound in each Lettuce Cup (*p. 374*) and garnish with olives or little sweet pickles and parsley. *6 servings.*

Chicken-Fruit Party Salad

Make Chicken Salad (*above*)—*except* omit hard-cooked eggs. Add 1 cup halved sweet green grapes or drained cut-up pineapple. Sprinkle with ½ cup salted almonds.

Chicken and Bacon or Ham Salad

Make Chicken Salad (*above*)—*except* sprinkle with ½ cup finely broken crisp bacon or ½ cup diced ham.

Chicken-Cranberry Salad

Recommended as "something special" by Janet Crawford Taylor (Mrs. Jack Taylor) of Plymouth, Massachusetts, and Ocean Spray Cranberries, Inc.

Make Chicken Salad (*above*)—*except* omit hard-cooked eggs. Sprinkle with 1 cup cubed cranberry jelly.

Mock Chicken Salad

Delicious use for cold roast veal.

Make Chicken Salad (*above*)—*except* use cut-up cooked veal in place of the chicken.

Shrimp Salad

Delicious also with crabmeat, tuna or salmon. Attractive served in Tangy Tomato Aspic ring (p. 379).

1 cup chopped shrimp (or flaked cooked
  crabmeat, tuna or salmon)
1 cup diced celery
1 cup lettuce hearts, cut in small pieces
1 tsp. lemon juice
1 tsp. finely minced onion
salt and paprika to taste

Mix all ingredients lightly. Chill thoroughly. Just before serving, drain and toss together with mayonnaise to moisten. Serve on crisp lettuce. Garnish with tomato sections, wedges of lemon, slices of hard-cooked egg and shiny ripe olives. *4 servings.*

Crab Louis

2 cans (6 oz. each) crabmeat
¾ cup celery, finely chopped
¼ cup pimiento-stuffed green olives, cut in slices
Louis Dressing (*below*)

Just before serving, combine crabmeat, celery, olives and dressing. Serve on salad greens garnished with quartered tomatoes, hard-cooked eggs or ripe olives. *4 to 5 servings.*

Louis Dressing

¾ cup chili sauce
½ cup mayonnaise
1 tsp. freshly minced onion
½ tsp. sugar
¼ tsp. Worcestershire sauce
salt to taste

Toss gently. Refrigerate 30 min. before combining with Crab Louis.

381

Oven Chicken Salad

Bake in individual casseroles or ramekins for easy serving.

2 cups cubed cooked chicken
2 cups thinly sliced celery
1 cup toasted bread cubes
1 cup mayonnaise
½ cup toasted chopped or slivered almonds
2 tbsp. lemon juice
2 tsp. grated onion
½ tsp. salt
½ cup grated cheese
1 cup toasted bread cubes or crushed potato chips

Heat oven to 450° (hot). Combine all ingredients except cheese and 1 cup of bread cubes. Pile lightly into individual baking dishes. Sprinkle with cheese and 1 cup of bread cubes. Bake *10 to 15 min.*, or until bubbly. *6 servings.*

Hot Tuna Salad

Sea food shells may be used for attractive individual servings. See color picture p. 380.

Make Oven Chicken Salad (*above*)—*except* omit chicken and use tuna. Garnish with slice of lemon, twisted.

Hot Crabmeat Salad

Serve this unusual salad in casseroles or spoon onto tomato slices in lettuce cups.

2 cups flaked cooked crabmeat
1 cup chopped celery
⅓ green pepper, chopped
1 large pimiento, chopped
⅓ cup chopped blanched almonds
¼ cup mild vinegar
¼ cup butter
½ cup GOLD MEDAL Flour
1 tsp. dry mustard
⅛ tsp. paprika
1 tsp. salt
1 cup milk
2 egg yolks, slightly beaten

Marinate crabmeat, celery, green pepper, pimiento and almonds in vinegar 2 hr. *Heat oven to 425° (hot).* Melt butter in saucepan. Blend in flour, mustard, paprika and salt. Cook over low heat until mixture is smooth and bubbly. Remove from heat. Stir in milk. Bring to boil; boil 1 min., stirring constantly. Remove from heat. Stir into egg yolks. Combine with the marinated ingredients. Pile lightly into 8 individual baking dishes or an oblong baking dish, 12x8". Bake *12 to 15 min.*, or until bubbly. *8 servings.*

Ham Mousse

A warm weather party dish. Make 3 times the recipe to fill the large fluted mold pictured on p. 380.

Soften 1 envelope unflavored gelatin (1 tbsp.) in ¼ cup cold water and ¼ cup vinegar. Dissolve over boiling water. Stir in 2 cups finely cubed cooked ham, 1 cup finely diced celery, 1 tbsp. sugar, 1 tbsp. pickle relish and 1 tsp. mustard. Fold in ½ cup whipping cream, whipped. Turn into mold and chill until set. Unmold and garnish with water cress. Serve with Easy Horse-radish Sauce (*p. 332*). *4 to 6 servings.*

Salmon Mousse

Make Ham Mousse (*above*)—*except* use 2 cups flaked salmon (1-lb. can) in place of ham and 1¼ tsp. salt. Serve with Tomato-Cucumber Mayonnaise (*p. 371*).

Appetizer Salads

Many hostesses serve salad as the first course for dinner parties.

Tomato Flower Cups on Bibb lettuce. Cut tomatoes almost through into 6 sections so they will open like flowers. Fill with chicken salad. Garnish with sieved hard-cooked eggs. See color picture p. 380.

Artichoke hearts, diced celery, tomato sections and anchovies, Piquant French Dressing (*p. 370*) . . . in Lettuce Cups (*p. 374*). Garnish with strips of green pickles, large green olives.

Grapefruit half with pulp removed, filled with melon balls and topped with Limeade Dressing (*p. 372*).

Avocado half, drenched with lemon juice, seed cavity filled with a little mayonnaise (thinned with lemon juice). Then a spoonful of lemon or cranberry ice. Serve on a bed of water cress.

Antipasto See p. 56.

SAUCES

The art of making sauces flourished in France between the 16th and 18th centuries. Every landed family had a "saucier" whose sole business it was to prepare that part of the menu. Old paintings of banquets in those days show the saucier at work at an elaborately equipped side table. And today, in fine restaurants, the sauce chef ranks second only to the "chef des cuisine."

Diplomats and nobles were proud to give their family names to sauces developed by the chefs in their employ: Soubise, Béchamel, for example. Other well-known sauces bear the name of the cities in which they were first prepared: Béarnaise, Provencale, Bordelaise. "Devote yourself to your sauce," wrote the internationally famous chef, Escoffier. He would not allow any excess in the seasoning of sauces, knowing that heavy seasoning would not correct a badly-made sauce.

We Americans have been reared amidst a tradition of plain, hearty fare. In fact, the only sauce commonly used here is White Sauce, much to the disappointment of the epicure, Brillat Savarin, who said of America, "One hundred religions, and only one sauce." But recently, increased leisure has brought new interest in gourmet cookery. And what simpler way is there to lend subtlety and sophistication to foods than with sauces!

SAUCES TO ENHANCE AND ENRICH

(complete index in back of book)

QUICK SAUCES

When time is short you needn't omit the sauce you've planned to serve—choose a simpler version using a timesaving canned or packaged product.

FOR DESSERTS

Caramel Sauce: Melt ½ lb. vanilla caramels (about 36) in ¼ cup water over hot (not boiling) water. Stir to blend well. *1 cup sauce.*

Quick Custard Sauce: Cook 1 pkg. vanilla pudding mix using 1½ times as much milk as the package directions call for. Increase milk the same amount to make quick lemon, chocolate, butterscotch, coconut cream or strawberry sauce from pudding mix.

Whipped Topping: Place ¼ cup cold water in bowl and add ¼ cup non-fat dry milk slowly. Beat until stiff, *about 10 min.* Add ¼ cup sugar and 1 tbsp. lemon juice. Chill before serving. Use as you would whipped cream. *1¼ cups.*

Speedy Fudge or Caramel Sauce: Follow directions on Betty Crocker Chocolate or Caramel Fudge Frosting Mix packages.

Quick Hard Sauce: Blend ½ cup butter and 1 unbeaten egg white with ½ pkg. (7 oz.) Betty Crocker Creamy White Frosting Mix. Beat on high speed electric mixer 1 minute, or by hand until light and fluffy. Add ½ tsp. rum flavoring, if desired. Chill until hard. *Makes 1½ cups.*

FOR VEGETABLES

Mock Hollandaise Sauce: Blend 1 can (10½-oz.) cream of chicken soup, ¼ cup mayonnaise and 1 tbsp. lemon juice. Cook over low heat, stirring occasionally, until sauce has heated through. Serve over cooked broccoli, carrots or asparagus. *About 1½ cups sauce.*

Sauce Poulette: Sauté 2 tbsp. minced onion in 2 tbsp. butter until yellow. Blend in 1 can (10½-oz.) cream of chicken soup, ⅓ cup milk, 2 tbsp. chopped parsley, 1 tbsp. lemon juice and, if desired, 1 tbsp. cooking sherry. Cook over low heat, stirring occasionally, until heated through. Serve over asparagus, peas or Lima beans.

FOR MEATS AND MAIN DISHES

Mushroom Sauce: Blend 1 can (10½-oz.) cream of mushroom soup, ½ cup milk, ½ tsp. Worcestershire sauce, 2 tbsp. finely chopped pimiento and 1 tbsp. parsley flakes; heat.

Quick Brown Sauce: To 1 can beef gravy, add 1 tsp. gravy flavoring, 1 tbsp. tomato catsup.

Devil Sauce: To 1 can tomato sauce, add 1 beef bouillon cube, 1 tsp. prepared mustard, ¼ cup vinegar.

WHAT EVERY COOK NEEDS TO KNOW ABOUT SAUCES

MAKE WITH CARE

Learning to make White Sauce is your first step in acquiring the art of sauce making. Practice the steps patiently until it is perfectly smooth and just the right consistency: thin enough to flow but thick enough not to saturate food. You'll use White Sauce often—in sauces of many flavors and as the basis for cream soups and main dishes.

Three other sauces may be made with the White Sauce method, simply by varying the liquid: Velouté Sauce (*p. 388*), made with chicken or fish stock; Brown Sauce (*p. 389*), made with beef stock; and Tomato Sauce (*p. 389*), made with tomato juice. Each of these sauces is in turn the basis for many variations.

Gravy is a special variation of White Sauce using the natural meat fats in place of butter and the meat juices, plus water as the liquid.

Choose Pan Gravy or Kettle Gravy (*p. 390*) according to the meat being served. Measure meat fats and juices carefully; it is better to make 1 cup of full-flavored gravy than to make 2 or 3 cups of pale gravy with flavor diluted by water.

Making Hollandaise Sauce (*p. 391*) is another important part of sauce cookery. If you remember to keep the heat low and stir briskly, you can easily make this golden buttery sauce.

Many dessert sauces are simple to make: sugar and fruit juice, cream or water are cooked to a syrup-like consistency. Chocolate, brown sugar, fruits or flavorings are added. Because they are high in sugar, dessert sauces keep well in the refrigerator. Unique is Hard Sauce (*p. 393*), which is not cooked but whipped then chilled until firm.

· ·

SERVE WITH FLAIR

Since sauces themselves are the extra special something complementing meats, vegetables or desserts, little need be said about enhancing the sauces themselves.

Serve hot sauces hot and cold sauces cold, of course. And keep a dainty pitcher or bowl and spoon set handy to serve your sauces in.

NEW ADVENTURES IN SAUCES

Almond Velvet Sauce (*p. 388*)—The French way.

Brown Sauce (*p. 389*)—For meats, rich and dark.

Dill Sauce (*p. 387*)—Gourmet touch for fish.

Old-fashioned Strawberry Sauce (*p. 393*)—Delicious over desserts or pancakes.

Perfection Peach Sauce (*p. 392*)—Serve warm with ice cream or Crème Vanille.

SAUCES TO COMPLEMENT

English Parsley Sauce with Crispy Fried Fish

Hollandaise Sauce on Broccoli   Tomato-Mushroom Sauce over Meat Loaf

White Sauce

The start of creamed dishes and many other sauces. "White Sauce is a good beginning for the small cook," says Virginia Hathaway, Child Psychologist with the Minneapolis Public Schools.

1. Melt butter over low heat in a heavy saucepan. Wooden spoon for stirring is a help.

2. Blend in flour, seasonings. Cook over low heat, stirring until mixture is smooth, bubbly.

3. Remove from heat. Stir in milk. Bring to boil, stirring constantly. Boil 1 min. *Makes 1 cup.*

Thin	*Medium*	*Thick*
Like coffee cream.	Like thick cream.	Like batter.
For creamed vegetables, soup.	For creamed and scalloped dishes.	For croquettes, soufflés.
1 tbsp. butter	2 tbsp. butter	¼ cup butter
*½ to 1 tbsp. flour	2 tbsp. flour	¼ cup flour
¼ tsp. salt	¼ tsp. salt	¼ tsp. salt
⅛ tsp. pepper	⅛ tsp. pepper	⅛ tsp. pepper
1 cup milk	1 cup milk	1 cup milk

*Use smaller amount with starchy vegetables (peas, potatoes), greater with non-starchy (cream of tomato soup).

Cheese Sauce

For vegetable, rice, macaroni and egg dishes.

To 1 cup Medium White Sauce (*above*) add ¼ tsp. dry mustard with the seasonings. Blend in ½ cup nippy Cheddar cheese (cut up or grated). Stir until cheese is melted.

Rich Cheese Sauce

To 2 cups Medium White Sauce (*above*) add 2 cups cut-up or grated nippy Cheddar cheese, 2 tsp. dry mustard, 1 tsp. Worcestershire sauce and 1 tbsp. cooking sherry. Stir until cheese is melted.

Mushroom Sauce

Make 1 cup Medium White Sauce (*above*)—*except* sauté 1 cup sliced mushrooms and 1 tsp. grated onion in the butter 5 min. before adding flour.

Egg Sauce

A pleasant addition to salmon and other fish.

To 1 cup Medium White Sauce (*above*) carefully stir in 2 diced hard-cooked eggs. Season.

Curry Sauce

Combines perfectly with chicken, lamb or shrimp and rice.

Make 1 cup Medium White Sauce (*above*)—*except* sauté ½ tsp. curry powder in the butter before adding flour and other seasoning.

Cucumber Sauce

Refreshing with salmon and other fish.

To 1 cup Medium White Sauce (*above*) add ½ cup cucumber, grated or thinly sliced, and a dash of cayenne pepper. Simmer 10 min.

Dill Sauce

An ideal mate for bland meat or fish.

Make 1 cup Medium White Sauce (*above*)—*except* with the seasonings add 1 tsp. minced fresh dill or ½ tsp. dried dill and a dash of nutmeg. Simmer 2 or 3 min.

Velouté Sauce *(Velvet Sauce)*

As elegant and French as Paris.

2 tbsp. butter
2 tbsp. flour
1 cup chicken or veal or fish stock

salt to taste
dash of white pepper
1/8 tsp. nutmeg

Melt butter over low heat. Stir in flour until well blended. Cook over low heat, stirring until mixture is smooth and bubbly. Remove from heat. Gradually stir in stock. Bring to boil, stirring constantly. Boil 1 min. Blend in seasonings. Serve hot with croquettes, baked or steamed fish or use as a base for special sauces. *Makes 1 cup.*

Béchamel Sauce

Named for Louis de Béchamel, steward to King Louis XIV.

Make Velouté Sauce *(above)—except* blend in 1/2 tsp. salt, 1/8 tsp. pepper, 1/4 tsp. paprika. Then fold in 1/2 cup cream.

Horse-radish Sauce

A nippy touch for canned beef, boiled beef, lamb or ham.

Make Velouté Sauce *(above)—except* stir in 1 tbsp. well drained prepared horse-radish and 1 tsp. prepared mustard.

English Parsley Sauce

Adds color and flavor to new potatoes, green beans or peas. See color picture p. 386.

Make Velouté Sauce *(above)—except* stir hot sauce into 2 egg yolks, well beaten. Boil 1 min. longer, stirring constantly. Add 1/4 cup finely minced parsley.

Almond Velvet Sauce

A typical French touch when used to dress up leftover veal or chicken. Also a delicious accompaniment to sea food.

Make Velouté Sauce *(above)—except* stir in 1/4 cup toasted slivered blanched almonds just before serving.

Sauce Mornay

A rich cheese sauce. Chefs glamorize meats, fish, eggs and vegetables with it.

Make Velouté Sauce *(above)—except* stir in 1 cup cream and 1/8 tsp. cayenne pepper. Heat, stirring constantly. Stir in 1 cup diced sharp Cheddar, Parmesan or Swiss cheese.

Normandy Sauce

For fish mousse, timbales or soufflé.

Make Velouté Sauce *(above)—except* use fish stock. Stir hot sauce into 2 egg yolks. Boil 1 min. longer, stirring constantly. Blend in 1 tbsp. lemon juice and salt, pepper and cayenne pepper to taste.

Anchovy Velouté Sauce

For boiled or baked fish.

Make Velouté Sauce *(above)—except* blend 1 1/2 tsp. anchovy paste into the flour and butter paste. Omit salt and use fish stock instead of veal or chicken stock. Just before serving, add 1 tbsp. minced parsley.

Hot Tartare Sauce

Especially liked by our friend, Helen Clapesattle Shugg of Chicago, Illinois, author of "The Doctors Mayo," when she lunched with us.

Make Velouté Sauce *(above)—except* stir in 1/2 cup mayonnaise, 1 tsp. minced onion, 1 tsp. lemon juice, 1 tbsp. *each* finely chopped sweet pickles, stuffed olives, green pepper and parsley. Heat carefully.

TO GLAMORIZE LEFTOVERS

Allemande Sauce

Make Velouté Sauce *(above)—except* stir hot mixture into slightly beaten egg yolk. Boil 1 min. longer, stirring constantly. Add 1 tsp. lemon juice and 2 tbsp. cream.

Ravigote Sauce

Make Velouté Sauce *(above)—except* stir in 2 tbsp. lemon juice, 1 tbsp. minced onion, 1 tsp. *each* finely minced chervil, tarragon and chives.

Brown Sauce (*Sauce Espagnole*)

Basic dark sauce with a full, rich flavor.

2 tbsp. butter or drippings
½ slice onion
2 tbsp. flour

1 cup beef bouillon (*p. 399*)
salt and pepper to taste

Heat butter in small heavy skillet over low heat until browned. Add onion and sauté until light brown. Remove onion. Stir in flour until well blended. Cook over low heat, stirring constantly, until flour is a deep mahogany brown. Remove from heat. Gradually stir in stock. Bring to boil, stirring constantly. Boil 1 min. Stir in seasonings. Strain, if desired. *Makes 1 cup.*

Bordelaise Sauce

It's fun to experiment with herbs and this is a good beginning. Try it with steaks and chops.

To Brown Sauce (*above*) add ½ tsp. *each* finely minced parsley, thyme, bay leaf and onion.

Provencale Sauce

A real treat for garlic lovers. Use with meat, spaghetti or noodles and vegetables.

To Brown Sauce (*above*) add 1 tomato, chopped, and 1 clove garlic, crushed.

Piquant Brown Sauce

For tongue, beef, veal or fish.

Simmer together 5 min. ½ tbsp. *each* minced onion and chopped capers, 2 tbsp. vinegar, ½ tsp. sugar, dash of paprika and salt. Stir into Brown Sauce (*above*). Then stir in 2 tbsp. thick chili sauce or chopped sweet pickle.

Mushroom Brown Sauce

Adds zest to fish, meat or omelets.

Make Brown Sauce (*above*)—*except* add 1 cup sliced mushrooms to the butter or drippings; brown slowly before adding flour. Stir in a few drops Worcestershire sauce.

Tomato Sauce

A tangy sauce excellent with cheese soufflé and veal cutlet.

2 tbsp. chopped onion
2 tbsp. chopped green pepper
1 tbsp. butter, melted
1 can (8 oz.) tomato sauce
salt and pepper to taste

Sauté onion and green pepper in butter until onion is transparent. Add tomato sauce, salt and pepper and heat over low heat. *Makes 1¼ cups.*

Robert Sauce

Glorifies the humble hamburger.

To Brown Sauce (*above*) add 1 tbsp. vinegar, 1 tbsp. minced onion, 3 tbsp. sliced sour pickles and 2 tsp. prepared mustard.

Brown Devil Sauce

Hot and zippy on steak or meat loaf.

To Brown Sauce (*above*) add 1 tsp. Worcestershire sauce, 1 tsp. vinegar and 1 tbsp. minced parsley.

Mexican Sauce

Edwin Ford of the University of Minnesota tells us he would rather cook than teach. He admits to flipping a mean omelet and tops it with this sauce.

Make Brown Sauce (*above*)—*except* stir in ½ tsp. gravy flavoring, ½ cup tomato catsup, 1 tbsp. *each* minced onion and green pepper sautéed in butter. Season to taste with salt, paprika and celery salt.

Tomato-Mushroom Sauce

Delicious for Spanish omelet, leftover chicken or turkey, cheese soufflé, meat loaf. See color picture p. 386.

1 strip bacon, diced
1 tbsp. flour
1½ tsp. sugar
⅛ tsp. salt
1 cup tomato juice or strained juice from canned tomatoes
*1 can (2 oz.) broken pieces and stems of mushrooms (about ½ cup), drained
1 tbsp. butter
2 tbsp. chopped ripe olives

Sauté bacon. Blend flour, sugar and salt into bacon fat. Cook until smooth and bubbly. Remove from heat. Gradually stir in tomato juice. Bring to boil, stirring constantly. Boil 1 min. Brown mushrooms in butter. Add mushrooms and olives to sauce. *Makes 1⅓ cups.*

* ¼ lb. fresh mushrooms may be used.

Pan Gravy

A rich gravy that makes use of the natural meat fats after cooking roasts, steaks, chops or fried chicken. Most homemakers prefer medium gravy.

For each cup of Thick Gravy

3 tbsp. fat
3 tbsp. flour
1 cup liquid (water, meat stock or bouillon-cube broth)

For each cup of Medium Gravy

2 tbsp. fat
2 tbsp. flour
1 cup liquid

For each cup of Thin Gravy

1 tbsp. fat
1 tbsp. flour
1 cup liquid

1. Remove meat to warm place. Pour off fat; measure amount needed back into pan. *Measure accurately ... too little fat makes gravy lumpy.*

2. Add *level* tablespoons of flour. *Measure flour accurately so gravy is never greasy.* Stir fat and flour together until smooth; then cook over low heat, stirring steadily, until it's all bubbly and brown.

3. Stir in liquid, taking pan off heat to avoid lumps. Always measure liquid—too much weakens flavor. Return pan to heat, stirring and scraping in the rich drippings. Boil 1 min., season and serve.

Creamy Gravy for Chicken, Chops

Use milk for half of liquid in Pan Gravy.

Mushroom Gravy

For beef, veal or chicken.

Brown 1 can (2 oz.) mushrooms, drained, in fat before adding flour in making Pan Gravy. Use mushroom liquor as part of liquid. Blend in ½ tsp. Worcestershire sauce.

Giblet Gravy

Cook gizzard, heart and neck of fowl in 4 cups salted water until tender ... 1 to 2 hr. Add liver last half hr. Remove neck, chop giblets into small pieces, return to cooking water. Use as part or all of liquid in making Pan Gravy.

Kettle Gravy

Made from the liquid in which pot roasts and stews have been simmered.

For each cup of Thick Gravy

1 cup meat broth
¼ cup cold water
3 tbsp. flour

For each cup of Medium Gravy

1 cup meat broth
¼ cup cold water
2 tbsp. flour

For each cup of Thin Gravy

1 cup meat broth
¼ cup cold water
1 tbsp. flour

1. Remove meat to platter. Keep warm. Skim excess fat from meat broth and store for future use in seasoning vegetables. Pour off broth, measure amount needed and return to kettle.

2. Shake water and flour together in covered jar. It is important to *put water in first, flour on top, for a smooth mixture.*

3. Stir flour and water slowly into hot broth. Bring to boil. Boil 1 min. Season and serve.

GRAVY TIPS

The broth will be tastier if you flour meat and brown *slowly* on all sides for about 30 min. before simmering.

For extra richness and flavor, mix paprika with flour when you coat meat for browning.

If there is less than a cup of meat stock (juice) in the pan, add extra liquid to make 1 cup or the amount wanted.

Potato water or water drained from cooked mild vegetables may be used for part or all of the liquid. Or use consommé, sour cream, tomato or vegetable juice as gravy liquid.

Bouillon cubes may be added to increase flavor, or dissolved in water to be used for stock.

For improved flavor in gravy, cook meat with bay leaf, peppercorns, onion, garlic or celery salt.

Hollandaise Sauce

The humblest vegetable, the blandest fish will be company fare when served with this aristocrat of sauces. A favorite of Dr. Reynold A. Jensen, Professor of Child Psychiatry at the University of Minnesota, one of those inspired cooks whose wife, Lil, really likes to have him in the kitchen. See color picture p. 386.

Who said Hollandaise was tricky? It's different, because it's not thickened with flour. But it's easy when made this way—always smooth and creamy. Just follow the two rules: **1.** *Keep heat low.* **2.** *Stir briskly all the time.* And remember, if sauce separates add 1 tsp. water and heat while stirring it in slowly.

2 egg yolks
3 tbsp. lemon juice

½ cup very cold butter (1 stick or ¼ lb.)

In a small saucepan, stir egg yolks and lemon juice with wooden spoon. Add half of butter (½ stick). Stir over very low heat until butter is melted. Add rest of butter. Continue stirring until butter is melted and sauce thickened. Be sure butter melts slowly as this gives eggs time to cook and thicken the sauce without curdling. Serve hot or at room temperature. Any sauce left over will keep in refrigerator. To serve, stir in a little hot water. *Makes 1 cup.*

Cucumber Hollandaise

Party fare over sliced tomatoes, along with roast beef and browned potatoes.

To Hollandaise Sauce (*above*) add 1 cup drained chopped cucumber.

California Hollandaise

Turns asparagus or broccoli into an adventure.

To Hollandaise Sauce (*above*) add 2 tbsp. orange juice and 1 tsp. grated orange rind.

Béarnaise Sauce

A highly flavored Hollandaise.

To Hollandaise Sauce (*above*) add 1 tbsp. minced parsley, ½ tsp. dried tarragon and 1 tbsp. tarragon vinegar.

Mousseline Sauce

Does something wonderful for boiled fish, eggs, artichokes, broccoli, cauliflower or spinach.

To Hollandaise Sauce (*above*) add, when ready to serve, stiffly whipped cream (whip ¼ cup). Serve warm.

Drawn Butter Sauce

To serve with sea food or on vegetables.

Drawn Butter is really melted butter. Put the amount of butter you will need in the smallest skillet or saucepan you have. Melt butter gradually, don't cook it.

Browned Butter Sauce (*Beurre Noisette*)

Heat butter in a tiny skillet or saucepan until it is a delicate brown but not burned.

Black Butter Sauce (*Beurre Noir*)

Let ⅓ cup butter bubble in small saucepan until it is a golden brown. Pour in 1 tbsp. vinegar or lemon juice and let foam up. Add a dash of salt and pepper and serve at once.

Crumb Topping

A buttery, crisp topping for cauliflower, asparagus or other vegetables.

Heat ½ cup dry bread crumbs until golden brown in ¼ cup butter.

Chantilly Sauce

This cool sauce folded into hot peas, asparagus or spinach, makes an interesting combination.

Combine equal quantities of mayonnaise and whipped cream.

FOR ICE CREAM AND FROZEN DESSERTS

Butterscotch Sauce

"It's the best butterscotch sauce in the world!" says Frances Ohm of Los Angeles. "We like to serve it hot over ice cream when we come in from the beach. Sometimes we sprinkle salted almonds over the top."

¾ cup sugar
½ cup light corn syrup
¼ tsp. salt
¼ cup butter
1 cup cream (20% butterfat)
½ tsp. vanilla

Mix in saucepan sugar, syrup, salt, butter and half of cream. Cook over low heat, stirring, to soft ball stage (234°). Stir in remaining cream. Cook to thick, smooth consistency (228°). Remove from heat. Stir in vanilla. Serve hot or cold. *Makes 2 cups.*

Holiday Sauce

Rich and fruity—worthy of the most festive occasion.

1 cup dates, chopped
two jars (4 oz. each) maraschino cherries and juice
1 cup figs, diced
¼ lb. blanched almonds, coarsely chopped and
    toasted, or salted almonds
pinch of salt
½ cup sugar
½ cup water

Combine dates, cherries and figs; let stand several hr. Add almonds and salt. Boil sugar and water 5 min. Add to fruit mixture. Chill. *Makes about 3 cups.*

Kentucky Sauce

A novel blend of flavors.

1 cup granulated sugar
1 cup brown sugar (packed)
½ cup water
1 cup strawberry jam
1 cup orange marmalade
1 cup pecans, cut up
1 lemon (juice and rind, chopped fine)
1 orange (juice and rind, chopped fine)

Cook sugars and water together 5 min. Mix remaining ingredients in thoroughly. Let sauce ripen in a glass jar in refrigerator 2 weeks before using. Will keep indefinitely in refrigerator. *Makes 1 qt.*

Rich Chocolate Sauce

"It's my favorite for faculty parties," says Margaret Kemp Miller, Moorhead, Minnesota.

½ lb. German sweet chocolate
¼ cup water
¼ cup sugar
¼ cup cream (20% butterfat)

Melt chocolate, water and sugar over hot water. Stir until smooth. Take from heat. Blend in cream. Serve hot or cold. *Makes 1 cup.*

Quick Chocolate Sauce

1 pkg. (6 oz.) semi-sweet chocolate pieces
1 can (5½ oz.) evaporated milk
⅛ tsp. salt
* ½ tsp. peppermint flavoring, if desired

Melt chocolate pieces over hot water. Beat in evaporated milk and salt. Blend in flavoring. Serve hot or cold. *Makes about 1½ cups.*

* Be sure to use peppermint flavoring as oil of peppermint is much stronger.

Peppermint Candy Sauce

Karyl Wilson (Mrs. Lawrence W. Wilson), a charming young homemaker friend, often serves this refreshing and colorful ice cream sauce at her parties.

Mix 1½ cups coarsely chopped peppermint stick candy and ½ cup water in small saucepan. Cover. Bring to boil, cook over low heat until candy is melted, about 18 min. Remove from heat. Chill until mixture thickens. Stir in 2 tbsp. coarsely chopped peppermint stick candy. *Makes 1 cup.*

Perfection Peach Sauce

1 pkg. (12 oz.) frozen sliced peaches, thawed
2 tbsp. honey
1 tsp. rum flavoring
1 tsp. lemon juice
2 tbsp. blanched slivered almonds

Drain peaches reserving juice. Cut peach slices into chunks. Purée or rub 3 tbsp. of the chopped peaches through a sieve. Combine peach purée, honey, rum flavoring and drained peach juice in saucepan. Bring to a boil, stirring occasionally. Stir in remaining chopped peaches, lemon juice and almonds. Heat through. Serve warm. *Makes 1 cup.*

FOR STEAMED PUDDINGS, SHORTCAKE, FRESH-FROM-THE-OVEN CAKES

Best Sauce

½ cup *sifted* confectioners' sugar
½ cup soft butter
½ cup whipping cream

Beat sugar and butter until smooth and creamy. Whip cream and heat with the sugar-butter mixture. Boil until foamy. Serve immediately. *Makes 2 cups.*

Almond Cream Sauce

Delicious served over chilled fruits or steamed puddings.

Make Cream Filling (*p. 177*)—except use only 1 tsp. butter; for flavoring use ½ tsp. vanilla and ¼ tsp. almond flavoring. Cool. Fold in ½ cup whipping cream, whipped. *Makes 2 cups.*

Old-fashioned Strawberry Sauce

Serve over ice cream, custard, warm cake, pancakes or waffles.

Wash, drain and hull 2 cups strawberries. Place 1 cup berries in saucepan and cover with ½ cup sugar. Add another layer of berries and ½ cup sugar. Cover and let stand at room temperature overnight. Remove cover. Place over direct heat and bring to boil. Simmer gently 15 min., stirring occasionally. Pour into a bowl or pint jar. Cover and let stand at room temperature 24 hr. Store in refrigerator. *Makes about 2 cups.*

Golden Sauce

¼ cup butter
½ cup brown sugar (packed)
⅛ tsp. salt
2 tbsp. cream
1 tbsp. lemon juice
⅛ tsp. nutmeg

Cream butter, brown sugar and salt. Gradually beat in cream. Blend in lemon juice and nutmeg. Put in serving dish and chill about 1 hr. *Makes 1 cup.*

Old-fashioned Lemon Sauce

Combine in saucepan ½ cup butter, 1 cup sugar, ¼ cup water, 1 egg, well beaten, 3 tbsp. lemon juice (1 lemon) and grated rind of 1 lemon. Cook over medium heat, stirring constantly, just until mixture comes to a boil. *Makes 1⅓ cups.*

Satin Sauce

Beat 1 egg and 1 tbsp. water in saucepan until foamy. Stir in ¾ cup sugar and ¼ tsp. salt. Cook over low heat 1 min., stirring constantly. Remove from heat and stir in 2 tbsp. lemon juice and 1 tsp. vanilla. Serve hot. *Makes 1½ cups.*

Clear Orange Sauce

Mrs. J. King Ross, of Northridge, California, makes this delicious sauce often. "When you live in California," she says, "you find yourself using oranges in some way at almost every meal."

1 cup sugar
¼ tsp. salt
2 tbsp. cornstarch
1 cup orange juice
¼ cup lemon juice
¾ cup boiling water
1 tbsp. butter
1 tsp. *each* grated orange and lemon rind

Mix sugar, salt and cornstarch in saucepan. Stir in orange juice, lemon juice and water. Boil 1 min., stirring constantly. Remove from heat. Stir in butter and rind. Serve hot on Cottage Pudding (*p. 228*) or warm cake. *Makes 2 cups.*

Hard Sauce

Beat ½ cup soft butter in small mixer bowl at high speed until very creamy, fluffy and light in color, 5 min. Gradually beat in 1 cup *sifted* confectioners' sugar. Stir in ½ tsp. vanilla or rum flavoring. Chill about 1 hr. *Makes ¾ cup.*

Creamy Sauce

Rich and smooth; some like it even better than Hard Sauce with steamed puddings.

Beat 1 egg until foamy. Blend in ⅓ cup butter, melted, 1½ cups *sifted* confectioners' sugar and 1 tsp. vanilla. Fold in 1 cup whipping cream, whipped stiff. *Makes 2½ cups.*

FOR FRUITS—FRESH, FROZEN AND CANNED

Raspberry-Currant Sauce

Wonderful on Peach Melba, p. 246.

*1 pkg. (10 oz.) frozen raspberries, thawed
½ cup currant jelly
1 tbsp. cold water
½ tbsp. cornstarch

Blend raspberries and jelly; bring to boil. Stir in a mixture of water and cornstarch. Boil 1 min., stirring constantly. Cool and strain. *Makes 1⅓ cups.*

*Or use 1 cup fresh raspberries. *Makes about ¾ cup.*

Irene's Caramel Sauce

Irene Danielson, who gave us this recipe, uses it on cottage pudding. But we think it makes a special dish of canned peaches or baked apples.

2 egg yolks, beaten
½ cup brown sugar (packed)
½ cup granulated sugar
½ cup water
¼ cup butter
1 tsp. vanilla

Mix all ingredients in saucepan. Cook over medium heat, stirring constantly, until boiling. Boil 1 min. Serve warm or cold. *Makes about 1⅓ cups.*

Easy Caramel Sauce

Mix ¼ to ½ cup brown sugar (packed) and 1 cup commercial sour cream. Spoon over seedless green grapes, sliced peaches or fresh strawberries. *Makes 1 cup.*

Sunshine Sauce

Sometimes called Eggnog Sauce.

2 egg yolks, slightly beaten
¼ cup granulated sugar or ½ cup *sifted* confectioners' sugar
1 tsp. vanilla or 2 tbsp. brandy flavoring
1 cup whipping cream, whipped

Mix egg yolks, sugar and vanilla until blended. Fold sauce into whipped cream. Serve over hot baked pears or peaches. *Makes about 2 cups.*

Coconut Cream Sauce

With baked bananas.

Cut 1 can (4 oz.) moist shredded coconut into shorter shreds or use flaked coconut. Combine with 1 cup cream and let mellow in refrigerator an hour or so. *Makes about 1½ cups.*

Easy Custard Sauce

Make Rich Custard Filling *(below)*—then thin to desired consistency with milk (1½ to 2 cups). *Makes 1 qt.*

Rich Custard Filling

½ cup sugar
⅓ cup GOLD MEDAL Flour
½ tsp. salt
2 cups milk
4 egg yolks (or 2 eggs), beaten
2 tsp. vanilla or other flavoring

Mix sugar, flour and salt in saucepan. Stir in milk. Cook over medium heat, stirring until it boils. Boil 1 min. Remove from heat. Stir a little over half of mixture into egg yolks. Blend into hot mixture in saucepan. Bring *just* to boil. Cool and blend in vanilla.

Mock Devonshire Cream

Mash 1 pkg. (3 oz.) cream cheese. Blend in 2 tbsp. cream and 1 tsp. sugar. Mix until smooth. *Makes about ½ cup.*

Butter Custard Sauce

Delicious over poached fruits.

1 cup sugar
1 cup cream (20% butterfat)
¼ cup butter
1 egg yolk, beaten
1 tsp. vanilla

Combine sugar, cream and butter. Cook over medium heat, stirring constantly, 3 to 4 min. Stir at least half of hot mixture into egg yolk. Return to saucepan. Cook 1 min., stirring constantly. Remove from heat. Blend in vanilla. *Makes about 1½ cups.*

Fresh Mint Sauce

¼ cup finely chopped fresh mint
2 tbsp. sugar
½ cup mint-flavored apple jelly
2 tbsp. water

Combine mint and sugar in small bowl and let stand 1 hr. Melt jelly in saucepan over low heat. Blend in mint-sugar mixture and water. Chill. Serve over chilled fresh, canned or frozen fruit using about 1 tbsp. per serving. Garnish with sprig of fresh mint. *Makes ¾ cup.*

Joseph Pearson

SOUPS

"Soup of the evening, beautiful soup!" wrote Lewis Carroll. In fact, "la soupe" has been the name of the evening meal in parts of rural France for hundreds of years—and the name of our evening meal, supper, is derived from it. Even today these French folk are dipping their spoons into steaming bowls of "pot au feu." This soup, in which the French housewife uses meat bones, vegetable tag ends and herbs, is always cooking slowly at the back of the stove and flavors blend while the soup smiles and chuckles but *never* laughs in a full rollicking boil.

Another present-day word which is a part of the fascinating history of soup is "restaurant." A popular soup of the 16th century was called "restaurant" because it was believed to have "restorative" powers. A chef printed the name over his door to announce that he was serving it, and in time, restaurant came to mean a place where all foods were served.

Nations have become known for distinctive soups: Italy for Minestrone, Russia for Borsch, France for Onion Soup and Bouillabaisse, China for Bird's Nest Soup and the East Indies for Mulligatawny. Here in the United States regional soups are proudly acclaimed: chowders from the East, gumbos from the South, hearty vegetable soups from the Midwest and fish stews from the West coast.

SOUPS TO SAVOR
(complete index in back of book)

 **TIMESAVING TIPS**

SOUP COMBINATIONS

Use a can of each. Dilute with 1½ cups milk or water.

Tomato Soup and Clam Chowder	Cream of Mushroom and Cream of Chicken
Green Pea Soup and Tomato Soup	Clam Chowder and Cream of Celery Soup

HEARTY SOUPS IN A HURRY

Canned soup plus meat or sea food.

Split Pea Soup with ham strips	Vegetable Soup with tiny cooked meat balls
Cream of Mushroom Soup with a can of shrimp	Tomato Soup with a can of minced clams

SOUP TRICKS

Cream of Corn Soup: Combine 1 can (10½ oz.) cream of chicken soup (cream of mushroom or celery), ½ cup mayonnaise, 1½ to 2½ cups milk and 2 cups whole kernel corn. Heat.

Mushroom Soup De Luxe: Stir 1 can clear chicken broth into a can of cream of mushroom soup. Heat gently *5 min.*

Quick Potato Soup, Hot or Cold: For directions for hot Cream of Potato Soup or chilled Vichyssoise, see Betty Crocker Instant Mashed Potatoes pkg.

Hot Buttered Soup: Seasoned butter dropped into soup just before serving.

Hot Soup Cocktail: Tomato soup thinned with bottled clam juice and seasoned with Worcestershire sauce.

Camp-out Soup: Take along lightweight envelopes of dehydrated soups. Mix with water; heat—delicious.

 **MEALTIME MAGIC**

FOR A CHILLY WINTER NIGHT

Chicken and Corn Chowder *(p. 403)*
Grapefruit-Orange Salad *(p. 375)*
Toasted, Buttered Rye Bread
Chocolate Éclairs *(p. 243)*

CHRISTMAS EVE

Oyster Stew *(p. 402)*   Oyster Crackers
Jellied Fruit Medley *(p. 378)*
Christmas Bread Tray
Down East Pudding *(p. 230)* Hard Sauce *(p. 393)*

WHAT EVERY COOK NEEDS TO KNOW ABOUT SOUPS

COOK WITH CARE

Soups, steaming and savory, are a delight to the palate. They may be light or hearty—to tempt or satisfy the appetite.

The popular cream soups (*p. 401*) have a thin White Sauce (*p. 387*) as their basis. Diced, mashed or puréed vegetables are often added to cream soups for color and nutrition. Using consommé as part of the liquid further increases richness and flavor.

Chowders soon left their native New England to become national favorites for lunch or supper. Distant cousins of the cream soups, they are made by stewing meat, sea food or vegetables in milk.

Meat stock is the basis for many of our favorite soups. White stock or Consommé (*p. 399*) is made from chicken or veal bones with meat, brown stock or Bouillon (*p. 399*) of beef. Bones are simmered (never boiled!) with vegetables and seasonings until all the rich meat flavor is extracted. Stock should not be salted until it is served as meats vary in saltiness.

This soup stock is very versatile. It can be served steaming hot from the kettle, with or without additional meat or vegetables. Or, it can be stored for future use in soups and sauces (*p. 389*). Store stock covered in the refrigerator. Remove fat later, when stock is used, as it improves the keeping quality.

. . . .

SERVE WITH A FLAIR

The crispness of crackers is a perfect complement for the smoothness of soup. Hot quick breads and grilled sandwiches go well with soups, too.

Next time you serve a clear soup, garnish each serving with thin slices of lemon, cucumber, radish or avocado. Or sprinkle with minced parsley or chives.

Cream soups are attractive garnished with: slivered salted almonds or cashews, garlic croutons, salted whipped cream, popcorn, crisp ready-to-eat cereal or minced parsley or chives.

NEW ADVENTURES IN SOUPS

Bongo-Bongo (*p. 402*)—An exotic combination of oysters and green peas.

Brunswick Stew (*p. 404*)—This modern version of an old Virginia favorite is a meal in itself.

Corn-Tomato Chowder (*p. 403*)—Hearty, yet inexpensive, sure to please the family.

Gazpacho (*p. 400*)—A chilled vegetable soup of Spanish origin.

Vegetable-Cheese Soup (*p. 402*)—Unique blend of vegetable chunks and rich tangy cheese sauce.

Brunswick Stew, page 404

SOUPS TO SUIT YOUR FANCY

Bongo-Bongo, page 402
Corn-Tomato Chowder, page 403

Gazpacho, page 400
Parisian Onion Soup, page 406

HOW TO MAKE STOCK FOR SOUP

"Stock is to soup what flour is to cake." A savory, richly-flavored stock is essential for good soup. Tips below give general rules for full-flavored soup. This basic stock can be stored several weeks and used as basis for Appetizer Soups (p. 400), Cream Soups (p. 401), other soups in this chapter and sauces, such as Velouté Sauce (p. 388) and Brown Sauce (p. 389).

Bouillon (*Brown Stock*)

1 to 2 lb. marrow bones, cracked
4 lb. shin of beef, cut in small pieces
3 qt. cold water
3 sprigs parsley, minced
¼ tsp. thyme
¼ tsp. marjoram
1 small bay leaf, crumbled
½ cup diced carrots
½ cup chopped onion
½ cup diced celery (with leaves)
10 peppercorns
5 cloves
1 tbsp. salt

Scrape marrow from bones; melt in large kettle over low heat. Add ½ the meat (2 lb.) and brown in marrow fat. Add remaining meat, bones and cold water. Cover and bring slowly to a boil; remove foam. Add remaining ingredients; cover and simmer gently *4 hr.* Remove foam occasionally. Strain and cool quickly. *Makes 2½ qt.*

Consommé (*White Stock*)

5 lb. veal knuckle or chicken with
   bones (or 2½ lb. each)
3 qt. cold water
2 sprigs parsley, minced
¼ tsp. thyme
½ bay leaf, crumbled
⅓ cup diced carrots
⅓ cup chopped onion
½ cup diced celery (with leaves)
6 peppercorns
2 cloves
1 tbsp. salt

Place meat in large kettle (do not brown). Add water and bring slowly to boil; remove foam. Add remaining ingredients. Cover and simmer gently *4 hr.* Remove foam occasionally. Strain and cool quickly. *Makes 2½ qt.*

▶ ALL YOU HAVE TO DO

To skim fat from soup quickly: dip lettuce leaf in soup— lettuce picks up fat! Or, if time permits, pour soup into refrigerator tray, chill, skim off fat when firm.

SOUP TIPS

FOR BEST FLAVOR

Use good bones—A beef shin for brown stock, a veal knuckle or chicken for white stock. Two-thirds meat, one-third bone.

Use a big kettle—A large soup pot with *tight-fitting cover* is essential, whether it be a regular kettle or Dutch oven.

Cook stock slowly and gently—Long, slow simmering over low heat brings out flavors, keeps meat tender, prevents excessive evaporation. The test of a good soup stock: when it cools, it jells.

FOR APPETIZING APPEARANCE

Clarify Stock: Stock must be clarified when used as Bouillon or Consommé in recipes on next page. Clarifying makes soup sparkling-clear.

Egg white and egg shells clarify stock: blend 1 egg white with 1 tbsp. cold water; add to stock with pieces of shell.

Stir until stock boils. Boil *2 min.* Let stand off heat 20 min. Strain through double cheesecloth.

HOW TO STORE STOCK

Store in covered jar in refrigerator. The layer of fat on top helps preserve stock, but must be skimmed off before use in soups and sauces.

A good stock is essential for good appetizer soups. See p. 399 for Bouillon and Consommé recipes.

Spicy Tomato Soup

1½ qt. tomato juice (46-oz. can)
1¼ cups tomato purée (10½-oz. can)
3 tbsp. sugar
5 whole cloves and a dash of ground cloves
1 slice onion
2 cups Bouillon (*p. 399*)
1¼ tsp. salt
1 bay leaf
⅛ tsp. mixed herbs (marjoram, thyme)

Place all ingredients in kettle; bring to boil, stirring occasionally. Simmer *5 min.* Serve with lemon slice. *8 servings.*

Gazpacho

A summer "salad" soup. Cool and thick with chopped vegetables. See color picture p. 398.

¼ cup Consommé (*p. 399*)
¼ cup tomato juice
¼ cup chopped onion
½ cup chopped cucumber, unpeeled
½ cup chopped tomato, unpeeled
½ cup chopped green pepper
1 tbsp. vegetable oil
2 tbsp. wine vinegar
½ tsp. salt

Combine all ingredients. Season to taste with Tabasco and Worcestershire sauce. Chill. Serve as an appetizer. *4 to 6 servings.*

Tomato Bouillon

Heat together equal amounts of beef or chicken bouillon (canned or cubes or use recipe *p. 399*) and tomato juice with 3 or 4 whole cloves. Garnish with lemon slices. (If using bouillon cubes, use 1 cube, ½ cup water and 1 cup tomato juice.)

Madrilene

Heat together equal amounts bouillon (*p. 399*), chicken broth and tomato juice. Garnish with lemon slice.

Consommé Anglaise

Very special . . . wonderful, delicate flavor and interesting texture combination . . . with chicken and toasted almonds.

To each serving of chicken Consommé (*p. 399*), add 1 tbsp. finely chopped cooked chicken and 1 tbsp. chopped toasted blanched almonds.

Consommé Julienne

To each serving of Consommé (*p. 399*), add 1 tbsp. finely chopped shredded vegetables (carrots, beans, leeks, celery, onions). Cook *5 min.*

Consommé Tokyo

To each bowl of Consommé (*p. 399*), add a raw mushroom or carrot slice, a raw spinach or watercress leaf and a cooked shrimp.

Chicken Noodle Soup

To 1 qt. chicken Consommé (*p. 399*), add 1 cup 1 oz.) noodles and cook *10 to 15 min.*

Vichyssoise

Smooth, creamy, rich potato soup. Served chilled.

2 medium onions, sliced
1 tbsp. butter
3 medium potatoes, thinly sliced
½ cup chopped celery
2 cups veal or chicken stock (Consommé, *p. 399*)
½ tsp. salt
1 cup hot milk
1 cup hot cream (20% butterfat)
1 tsp. salt
¼ tsp. nutmeg
⅛ tsp. pepper
3 cups whipping cream (35% butterfat)

Brown onions in butter. Add potatoes, celery, stock and salt; cover and simmer ½ *hr.*, or until vegetables are soft. Press through a fine sieve, forcing through as much of the pulp as possible. To this mixture add milk, cream, 1 tsp. salt, nutmeg and pepper; bring to boil. Chill thoroughly (preferably overnight). When ready to serve, thin with whipping cream. Serve in chilled soup cups. Garnish with chopped chives and paprika. *10 to 12 servings.*

Cream of Vegetable Soup

A basic recipe for creamy-smooth vegetable soup. Variations are pleasing and colorful.

1 tsp. finely chopped onion	⅛ tsp. pepper
2 tbsp. butter	1 cup puréed cooked vegetables
*2 to 3 tbsp. flour	(asparagus, peas, broccoli or others)
1 tsp. salt	4 cups milk (part Consommé *p. 399* or vegetable water may be used)

Sauté onion in butter. Blend in flour, salt and pepper. Cook over low heat, stirring constantly, until smooth and bubbly. Stir in vegetables; bring to boil. Boil 1 min., stirring constantly. Remove from heat. Gradually stir in milk. Heat to serving temperature. *6 servings.*

*Use 2 tbsp. flour for starchy vegetables; 3 tbsp. flour for non-starchy vegetables.

Cream of Celery De Luxe

Make Cream of Vegetable Soup (*above*)—*except* use 1 cup diced cooked celery for vegetables; use 2 cups milk and 2 cups chicken Consommé (*p. 399*) for liquid.

Cream of Spinach De Luxe

Make Cream of Vegetable Soup (*above*)—*except* use 1 pkg. (10 oz.) frozen chopped spinach, thawed, for vegetables. Use 2 cups milk and 2 cups chicken Consommé (*p. 399*) for liquid.

Cream of Chicken Soup

Make Cream of Vegetable Soup (*above*)—*except* use chicken fat instead of butter. Use 3 cups chicken Consommé (*p. 399*) and 1 cup milk or cream for liquid. Blend in ½ cup diced cooked chicken instead of puréed vegetables. Sprinkle each serving with minced chives.

Cream of Mushroom Soup

Make Cream of Vegetable Soup (*above*)—*except* sauté 1 cup (¼ lb. fresh) chopped mushrooms in butter before flour is added. Omit vegetable purée. Use 2 cups chicken Consommé (*p. 399*) for half of liquid. Add paprika and onion salt to taste.

Cream of Corn Soup

Make Cream of Vegetable Soup (*above*)—*except* use 1 can (1 lb.) cream-style corn for puréed vegetables.

Cream of Onion Soup

Ann Burckhardt, of our staff, enjoyed Cream of Onion Soup at a famous resort, then helped us develop this recipe.

2 cups thinly sliced sweet onions
½ cup butter
¼ cup GOLD MEDAL Flour
1½ to 2 tsp. salt
¼ tsp. pepper
4 cups milk

Sauté onions in butter in large saucepan over low heat until tender and transparent (*20 to 30 min.*). Blend in flour and seasonings. Stir over medium heat until mixture is bubbly. Remove from heat. Gradually stir in milk. Bring to boil, stirring constantly. Boil 1 min. *6 servings.*

Cream of Tomato Soup

1 tsp. finely chopped onion
2 tbsp. butter
3 tbsp. flour
2 tsp. sugar
1 tsp. salt
⅛ tsp. pepper
2 cups tomato juice
2 cups *cold* milk

Sauté onion in butter. Stir in flour, sugar, salt and pepper. Cook until smooth and bubbly, stirring constantly. Remove from heat. Gradually stir in tomato juice. Bring to boil, stirring constantly; boil 1 min. Stir *hot* tomato mixture gradually into *cold* milk. Heat rapidly to serving temperature. Serve immediately with chopped fresh mint or dill. *6 servings.*

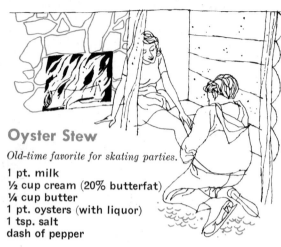

Oyster Stew

Old-time favorite for skating parties.

1 pt. milk
½ cup cream (20% butterfat)
¼ cup butter
1 pt. oysters (with liquor)
1 tsp. salt
dash of pepper

Heat milk and cream to scalding. Just before serving, melt butter in saucepan; add oysters and oyster liquor. Cook gently just until oyster edges curl. Add to scalded milk and cream. Season with salt and pepper; serve immediately with oyster crackers. *4 servings.*

Clam Bisque

Unusually delicious . . . and so easy to make!

1 tsp. grated onion
1 tbsp. butter
1 tbsp. flour
1 tsp. salt
⅛ tsp. pepper
⅛ tsp. celery salt
2 tsp. finely minced parsley
1 cup water or chicken broth (canned)
2 cups milk
1 can (7 oz.) minced clams

Sauté onion in butter; stir in flour, seasonings and parsley. Cook until smooth and bubbly. Remove from heat; stir in water and milk gradually. Bring to boil; boil 1 min. Stir in clams and clam liquor. Heat to serving temperature. Serve sprinkled with minced parsley. *8 servings.*

Oyster Bisque

Make Clam Bisque *(above)—except* use ½ pt. oysters, chopped, and liquor from oysters instead of clams.

Crab, Lobster or Shrimp Bisque

Make Clam Bisque *(above)—except* use 1 can (7 oz.) crabmeat, lobster or shrimp (cut in fine pieces) and liquor from sea food instead of clams.

Vegetable-Cheese Soup

2 cups cubed potatoes
⅔ cup minced onion
½ cup diced celery
½ cup carrots, cut in ½″ slices
½ medium green pepper, diced
2½ cups boiling water
2½ tsp. salt
2 cups Rich Cheese Sauce (*p. 387*)
1 cup tomatoes

Mix vegetables (except tomatoes), water and salt in 3-qt. saucepan. Bring to boil; simmer covered until vegetables are tender, *about 20 min.* Stir in cheese sauce. Add tomatoes. Heat. *6 to 8 servings.*

Bongo-Bongo

An unusual green pea and oyster soup that is similar to the one served in Trader Vic restaurants, which make a specialty of Polynesian food. See color picture p. 398.

1 pkg. frozen green peas, puréed
1 tbsp. butter
1 tbsp. flour
1 tsp. salt
⅛ tsp. pepper
1 cup milk
1 cup fresh oysters, puréed or minced
½ cup whipping cream (35% butterfat)

Prepare peas as directed on pkg. Drain and purée (through sieve or blender). Melt butter in saucepan. Blend in flour, salt and pepper. Cook over low heat, stirring constantly, until smooth and bubbly. Stir in milk, peas and oysters; bring to boil. Boil 1 min., stirring constantly. Remove from heat. Gradually stir in cream and heat just until bubbles form around edge of pan. If desired, top with a dollop of whipped cream and broil until cream browns. *4 to 6 servings.*

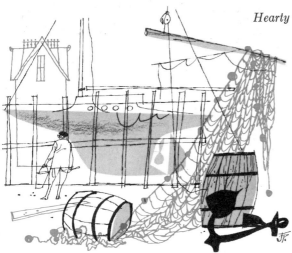

Sea Food Chowder

New England's contribution to the international soup pot.

¼ cup finely cut bacon or salt pork
¼ cup minced onion
1 pt. shucked fresh clams with liquor *or*
   2 cans (7 oz. each) minced or whole clams,
   lobster or other sea food
2 cups finely diced raw potatoes
½ cup water
2 cups milk
1 tsp. salt
⅛ tsp. pepper

Sauté bacon and onion in large kettle. Drain sea food; add liquor, potatoes and water to onion and bacon. Cook until potatoes are tender, *10 min.* Just before serving, add sea food, milk, salt and pepper. Heat to boiling, stirring occasionally. Serve immediately. *6 servings.* NOTE: Butter may be used in place of bacon or salt pork.

Manhattan Clam Chowder

Tomatoes give rosy color.

¼ cup finely cut bacon
¼ cup minced onion
1 pt. shucked fresh clams with liquor *or*
   2 cans (7 oz. each) minced or whole clams
2 cups finely diced raw potatoes
1 cup water
⅓ cup diced celery
1 can (1 lb.) cooked tomatoes
1 tsp. salt
⅛ tsp. pepper
¼ tsp. thyme
2 tsp. minced parsley

Sauté bacon and onion in large kettle. Drain clams; add clam liquor, potatoes, water and celery to onion and bacon. Cook until potatoes are tender, *10 min.* Just before serving, add clams, tomatoes and seasonings. Heat. Serve at once. *6 servings.*

Corn-Tomato Chowder

From Freda De Knight, our vivacious friend, who writes the column, "A Date With A Dish," for Ebony Magazine and is also editor of a cookbook by the same name. See color picture p. 398.

¼ lb. salt pork or bacon
1 small onion, chopped
1 can (1 lb.) whole kernel corn
1 can (1 lb.) tomatoes
2 cups diced raw potatoes
1 tbsp. sugar
*1 tsp. salt
½ tsp. paprika
⅛ tsp. pepper
3 cups boiling water
1 cup evaporated milk

Cut salt pork into small pieces and fry slowly to a golden brown in 3 to 4-qt. saucepan. Add onion and cook slowly without browning *5 min.* Add corn (including liquid), tomatoes and potatoes. Sprinkle with seasonings. Add boiling water and cook slowly until potatoes are tender, *20 to 25 min.* Remove from heat and slowly stir in milk. *6 to 8 servings.*
*When bacon is used, increase salt to 2 tsp.

Chicken and Corn Chowder

A Pennsylvania Dutch recipe obtained for us by Norman E. Dewes.

neck, wings, back and giblets of a hen
1½ qt. boiling water
1 onion, sliced
3 stalks celery (with leaves), chopped fine
1 carrot, diced
1 tbsp. salt
1 can (1 lb.) cream-style corn
2 hard-cooked eggs, chopped fine
Egg Rivvels (*below*)

Place pieces of chicken in large kettle with water, onion, celery, carrot and salt. Cover and simmer until tender, *about 1½ hr.* Slip meat from bones, cut up fine and return to broth. Add corn and simmer *10 min.* Add eggs. Drop Egg Rivvels into soup; simmer *10 min. 6 servings.*

Egg Rivvels: Sift together 1 cup *sifted* GOLD MEDAL Flour and ¼ tsp. salt. Mix 1 egg in with fork, until mixture looks like corn meal. Drop spoonfuls into hot soup.

Ellen's Shrimp Gumbo

From Ellen Connelly, a former member of our staff.

2 onions, sliced
½ green pepper, thinly sliced
2 cloves garlic, minced
¼ cup butter
2 tbsp. flour
1 can (1 lb.) tomatoes
1 can (1 lb.) okra, drained
1 can (6 oz.) tomato paste
3 beef bouillon cubes
4 tsp. Worcestershire sauce
⅛ tsp. ground cloves
½ tsp. chili powder
pinch dried basil
1 bay leaf
1½ tbsp. salt
¼ tsp. pepper
3 cups water
1½ lb. deveined, shelled raw shrimp
3 cups hot cooked rice (1 cup uncooked)
¼ cup minced parsley

In large kettle, sauté onion, green pepper and garlic in butter. Blend in flour; cook over low heat, stirring constantly, until mixture is bubbly and vegetables are tender. Remove from heat; add remaining ingredients except shrimp, rice and parsley. Simmer *45 min.* Just before serving, add shrimp; simmer, covered, *5 min.*, until shrimp are pink and tender. Toss together rice and parsley. Serve gumbo in soup plates over portion of rice and parsley. Or, heap rice in center of individual bowls of gumbo. *8 servings.*

Split Pea Soup

Navy beans, black-eyed peas or other dried peas or beans may be used instead of split peas.

2 cups dried split peas (1 lb.)
3 qt. cold water
1 ham bone or small shank end of ham
1 large onion, minced
3 stalks celery (with tops), chopped fine
1 sprig parsley
salt and pepper

Soak peas in water overnight. (Quick-cooking dried peas and beans do not require overnight soaking.) Add ham, onion, celery and parsley. Heat to boil; cover and simmer *4 to 5 hr.*, until peas are tender and liquid partially cooked down. Season to taste with salt and pepper. For a smoother soup, put through a sieve. Dilute as desired with additional milk or water. Serve hot. *8 servings.*

Brunswick Stew

First made in Brunswick County, Virginia, with rabbit or other game. This flavorful soup is our modernization of the old recipe. See color picture p. 398.

3-lb. stewing hen, cut up
1½ tsp. salt
¼ lb. salt pork, cut in 1″ pieces
4 cups peeled, thickly sliced tomatoes
2 cups fresh cut corn
1 cup coarsely chopped potatoes
1 pkg. (10 oz.) frozen Lima beans
½ cup chopped onion (1 small)
1 tsp. salt
¼ tsp. pepper
dash of cayenne pepper

Place chicken in large heavy kettle or Dutch oven with just enough water to cover. Add 1½ tsp. salt. Cover; simmer gently until tender, *about 2 hr.* Add more water if necessary. Skim excess fat off, if desired. Add pork, vegetables and seasonings. Simmer slowly until soup is thick and well blended, *about 2 hr. 8 to 10 servings.* Flavor improves if refrigerated and reheated.

If Using Canned Vegetables: Substitute in these amounts: 2 cans (1 lb. each) tomatoes, 1 can (1 lb.) whole kernel corn, 1 can (1 lb.) whole new potatoes. Include vegetable liquid, too!

Autumn Soup

A hearty, but inexpensive meat and vegetable soup. Quick and savory.

1 lb. ground beef
1 to 2 tbsp. fat
1 cup chopped onion
4 cups hot water (1 qt.)
1 cup *each* cut-up carrots, celery, potatoes
2 tsp. salt
½ tsp. pepper
1 tsp. meat extract
1 bay leaf, crumbled
pinch basil
6 whole fresh tomatoes, stems removed

Brown beef in hot fat in a heavy kettle. Add onions; cook *5 min.* more. Add water, carrots, celery, potatoes and seasonings. Mix thoroughly. Bring to boil, cover, simmer *20 min.* Add tomatoes; cover and simmer *10 min.* longer. *6 servings.*

Old-fashioned Vegetable Soup

A homemade soup to warm the heart.

1 soup bone with meat
1 to 2 tbsp. fat
4 cups water
1 medium onion, chopped
1 cup sliced carrots (2 or 3 medium)
1 cup cut-up celery and leaves (2 long stalks)
1 can (1 lb.) tomatoes
3 sprigs parsley, cut fine
1 tbsp. salt
½ bay leaf, crumbled
3 peppercorns
¼ tsp. marjoram
¼ tsp. thyme

Cut meat off bone into small chunks. Brown in hot fat in large kettle. Add water and bone and simmer covered 1½ to 2 hr. Remove bone and skim fat from top of soup. Add vegetables, bouquet garni (bay leaf and peppercorns tied in cheesecloth bag), marjoram and thyme; cook an additional 20 to 30 min., until vegetables are tender. Remove bouquet garni before serving. *6 to 8 servings.*

Potato Soup

For a refreshing change sprinkle with grated cheese and pop under the broiler.

1 tbsp. chopped onion
2 tbsp. butter
1 tsp. salt
¼ tsp. celery salt
⅛ tsp. pepper
1 cup mashed potatoes or boiled potatoes, put through a coarse sieve
2 cups hot milk

Sauté onion in butter. Add seasonings and potatoes; stir in milk. Simmer slowly for about 5 min., stirring occasionally. *6 servings.*

Canadian Cheese Soup

1 large potato, finely diced
1 large onion, finely chopped
¼ cup finely diced carrots
¼ cup finely diced celery
1 cup water
2 cups Consommé (*p.399*) or chicken broth (canned)
1 cup grated sharp Cheddar cheese (¼ lb.)
½ cup cream (20% butterfat)
2 tbsp. chopped parsley

In covered saucepan, simmer vegetables in water until tender, 10 to 15 min. Add remaining ingredients except parsley. Heat and serve garnished with parsley. *4 to 6 servings.*

Turkey or Chicken Soup

Last call for the holiday bird.

2 cups cubed cooked turkey or chicken (1″ cubes)
turkey or chicken carcass
1 cup chopped celery (several stalks)
1 carrot, sliced
1 onion, sliced
6 peppercorns
1 bay leaf
4 cloves
salt

Remove meat from carcass of turkey and set aside. Crack bones and place in kettle. Add skin, bouquet garni (peppercorns, bay leaf and cloves in cheesecloth bag). Cover with water. Simmer 2 hr. Cool slightly. Remove bones and bouquet garni by straining. Add meat and vegetables to stock. Chill. Skim off fat. Add salt to taste. Simmer until hot.

Turkey-Potato Soup

A creamy soup . . . smooth and hearty with turkey.

1 tsp. salt
1½ cups water
2 potatoes, thinly sliced
1 medium onion, thinly sliced
1 stalk celery, finely chopped
1 bay leaf
3 cups Thin White Sauce (*p. 387*)
1 tsp. rosemary *or* celery salt
1 cup chopped turkey
½ cup chopped toasted almonds, if desired

Add salt to water in large kettle; bring to boil. Add potatoes, onion, celery and bay leaf. Cook until tender, *about 15 min.* Press through sieve to purée. Add to white sauce. Add seasonings and turkey. Heat through. Serve topped with almonds. *4 to 6 servings.*

NOTE: For thinner soup, add more milk.

French Onion Soup

Dark—made with Bouillon. Full of savory onions. Toasted French bread absorbs flavor ... makes wonderful eating.

6 large, white, sweet onions, thinly sliced
3 tbsp. butter
6 cups Bouillon (*p. 399*) or 6 bouillon cubes dissolved in 6 cups water
1½ tsp. Worcestershire sauce
½ tsp. salt
⅛ tsp. pepper
6 slices French bread or toast
¼ cup grated Parmesan cheese

Brown onions in butter in large deep skillet until tender. Add bouillon and seasonings. Heat thoroughly. Place a slice of toasted bread in each soup bowl and pour soup over it. Sprinkle with cheese. *6 servings.*

Parisian Onion Soup

Light—made with Consommé. A favorite of those who frequent the world-famous Grand Vefour Restaurant, Paris. Monsieur Oliver, the gracious chef-owner, shared this recipe with us. See color picture p. 398.

Make French Onion Soup (*above*)—*except* increase butter to ½ cup. Melt onions in butter by simmering very slowly in covered deep skillet *35 min.* Use chicken consommé (*p. 399*) instead of bouillon. Omit Worcestershire sauce. To serve: place slice of toasted French bread in each bowl, sprinkle with grated Swiss cheese (½ cup in all). Pour soup over; sprinkle with Parmesan cheese (¼ cup in all).

Quick Russian Borsch

This beet soup may be served either hot or cold.

2 small raw beets, finely shredded
1 cup finely shredded cabbage
2 to 4 tbsp. chopped onion
1 can (10½ oz.) bouillon

Add vegetables to bouillon diluted according to directions on can. Bring to boiling and simmer *10 min.* Serve topped with a spoonful of sour cream. *4 servings.*

Potage St. Germaine

Prepare Split Pea Soup (*p. 404*). Garnish each serving with thin slices of bologna sausage. Serve with rye bread.

Italian Minestrone

There's a version for every town in Italy.

1 cup dried kidney beans or white beans
2 cups Bouillon (*p. 399*)
6 cups water
1 large onion, chopped
1 clove garlic, minced
3 large carrots, finely diced
3 stalks celery (with leaves), diced
1 cup diced raw potatoes
2 tbsp. olive oil
1 cup cooked macaroni in ½" pieces (½ cup uncooked)
1 tbsp. salt
¼ tsp. pepper
1 cup cooked tomatoes

Place beans, bouillon and water in large kettle; cook *3 to 4 hr.* Sauté onion, garlic, carrots, celery and potatoes in olive oil. Add vegetables to beans; cover kettle, cook slowly *30 min.*, stirring often. Add macaroni, salt, pepper and tomatoes. Simmer *15 min.* If thinner consistency is desired, add more bouillon. *10 servings.*

Mulligatawny Soup

Curry soup from the East Indies—popular in England.

1 medium onion, sliced
¼ cup butter
1 medium carrot, diced
1 stalk celery, diced
1 green pepper, seeded and diced
1 medium apple, pared, cored and sliced
1 cup cut-up cooked chicken
⅓ cup GOLD MEDAL Flour
1 tsp. curry powder
⅛ tsp. mace
2 whole cloves
1 sprig parsley, minced
2 cups Consommé (*p. 399*)
1 cup cooked tomatoes
salt and pepper to taste

Sauté onion in butter in deep kettle or Dutch oven. Add carrot, celery, green pepper, apple and chicken. Stir in gradually remaining ingredients. Simmer covered ½ *hr.* Serve hot. *6 servings.*

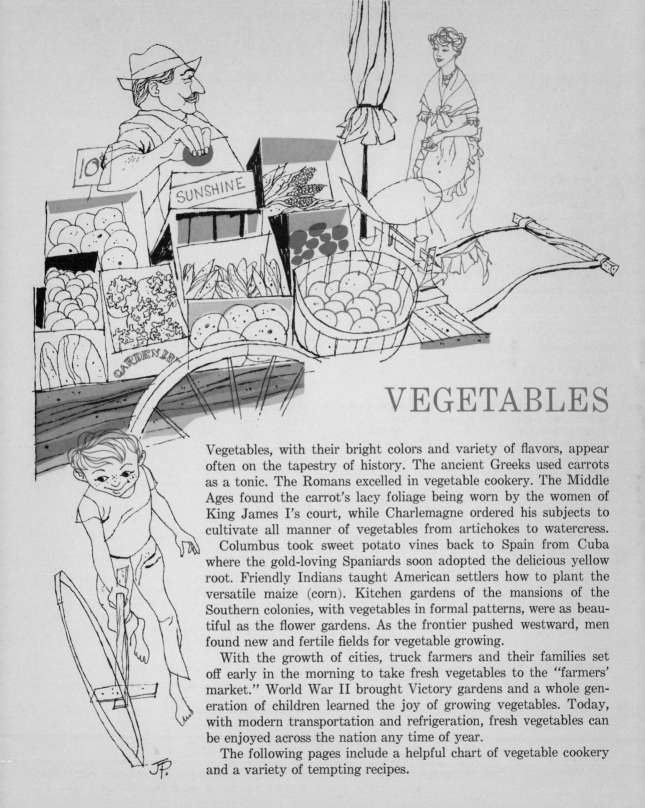

VEGETABLES

Vegetables, with their bright colors and variety of flavors, appear often on the tapestry of history. The ancient Greeks used carrots as a tonic. The Romans excelled in vegetable cookery. The Middle Ages found the carrot's lacy foliage being worn by the women of King James I's court, while Charlemagne ordered his subjects to cultivate all manner of vegetables from artichokes to watercress.

Columbus took sweet potato vines back to Spain from Cuba where the gold-loving Spaniards soon adopted the delicious yellow root. Friendly Indians taught American settlers how to plant the versatile maize (corn). Kitchen gardens of the mansions of the Southern colonies, with vegetables in formal patterns, were as beautiful as the flower gardens. As the frontier pushed westward, men found new and fertile fields for vegetable growing.

With the growth of cities, truck farmers and their families set off early in the morning to take fresh vegetables to the "farmers' market." World War II brought Victory gardens and a whole generation of children learned the joy of growing vegetables. Today, with modern transportation and refrigeration, fresh vegetables can be enjoyed across the nation any time of year.

The following pages include a helpful chart of vegetable cookery and a variety of tempting recipes.

VEGETABLES FOR VARIETY

(complete index in back of book)

VEGETABLES TO COMPLEMENT THE MEAT

Beef: broccoli, cabbage, cauliflower, celery, green beans, tomatoes, beets, mushrooms, eggplant, white turnips, parsnips, kohlrabi.

Pork: cabbage, cauliflower, celery, spinach and other greens, tomatoes, summer squash.

Ham: asparagus, broccoli, Brussels sprouts, celery, green beans, cabbage, cauliflower, spinach and other greens, zucchini.

Fish: tomatoes, peas, green beans, asparagus, cucumbers, celery.

Lamb: artichokes (French), carrots, peas, winter squash, creamed cauliflower, yellow turnips.

Veal: artichokes (French), beets, creamed asparagus, fried eggplant, succotash, winter squash, creamed mushrooms.

Chicken: corn, Lima beans, peas, sweet potatoes.

Turkey: creamed onions, mashed rutabagas, Hubbard squash, sweet potatoes, Brussels sprouts.

QUICK COMPANY SAUCE FOR VEGETABLES

Whip ½ cup whipping cream. Fold in ½ cup mayonnaise and any one of the following:

¼ cup well drained pickle relish (for corn and green beans)

¼ cup prepared horse-radish (for beets and carrots)

¼ cup chopped, well drained cucumber (for broccoli and tomatoes)

¼ cup toasted slivered almonds, salted pecans or cashews (for hot onions and peas)

¼ cup capers (for asparagus and onions)

¼ cup chili sauce (for corn and Lima beans)

2 tbsp. prepared mustard and ¼ tsp. dill (for carrots and cauliflower)

Serve as a topping for hot vegetables, using suggestions above, if desired. *Makes 1¾ cups.*

Be pennywise: use leftover vegetables in soups, main dishes or vegetable combinations (*p. 430*).

VEGETABLE PLATES

A complete meal when you add your favorite beverage and a dessert. See color picture, p. 410.

SATISFYING SANDWICH SUPPER
Buttered Broccoli Spears
Broiled Tomato Halves (*p. 429*)
Broiled Mushroom Caps
Open Grilled Cheese Sandwich (*p. 291*)

POACHED EGG MEDLEY
Buttered Zucchini with Parmesan Cheese
Beets with Orange Sauce (*p. 418*)
Buttered Asparagus
Poached Egg on Toast

DIETER'S DELIGHT
Half Green Pepper, parboiled and stuffed with Succotash
Molded Spinach (*p. 424*) garnished with a slice of hard-cooked egg
Small mound of Cottage Cheese on Bibb Lettuce garnished with apple slices

WHAT EVERY COOK NEEDS TO KNOW ABOUT VEGETABLES

BUY AND COOK WITH CARE

When is a cook an artist? When she chooses the bright greens, golden oranges, snowy whites and warm reds of vegetables to complete her family's meals. And when she retains those colors, as well as the valuable vitamins and minerals, through her skill in vegetable cookery.

Buy vegetables with care. They should be fresh, crisp and firm, have bright color and show no signs of spoilage. When using canned or frozen vegetables, test several brands, choosing the best quality in your price range.

Cook vegetables in a minimum of water just until crisp-tender for best nutrition and color (see vegetable cookery chart, *pp. 411–416*). Since some of the vitamins are dissolved in this vegetable stock, save it for use in soups.

Green vegetables including asparagus, spinach, green beans and peas, should be cooked uncovered the first few minutes so that the chlorophyll will not be affected by heat, then cover.

Red vegetables stay attractive looking if acid is present in cooking. Beets (*p. 418*) contain enough acid to keep their color, but red cabbage (*p. 419*) requires a small amount of vinegar added near the end of the cooking time.

Yellow or orange vegetables including carrots, squash, sweet potatoes and corn, are not as easily changed in color by cooking. Cook them covered in small amount of water for best nutrition in the shortest time.

Many of the white vegetables, turnips and onions together with broccoli, cabbage and Brussels sprouts, are members of the strong-flavored vegetable group (*pp. 415–416*) and must be cooked uncovered in large amount of water to prevent strong odor and flavor.

Though most often and most easily prepared by boiling, some vegetables may be baked or sautéed.

SERVE WITH FLAIR

Vegetables of high quality, carefully cooked, need little more than butter, salt and pepper to make them delicious eating. For variety, pass one of the Glorified Butters (*p. 430*) in a little pitcher. Or add a dash of an herb or spice (*pp. 51–52*).

How versatile are vegetables! They combine beautifully with each other (*p. 430*) and with meats, fish, cheese and eggs. They lend color, texture and precious nutrients to salads, soups and main dishes.

NEW ADVENTURES IN VEGETABLES

De Luxe Creamed Onions (*p. 425*)—Carrots are the surprise ingredient.

Italian Green Peppers (*p. 426*)—Pepper strips with tomato and a dash of oregano.

Skillet Creamed Potatoes (*p. 427*)—Tangy and tasty with sour cream and olives.

Squaw Corn (*p. 423*)—Corn and bacon in scrambled eggs make a quick camp-out supper.

Sweet-Sour Red Cabbage (*p. 419*)—A must for a German-style dinner.

VEGETABLES BRIGHT, VEGETABLES GAY

Poached Egg Medley　　　　*Menus, page 408.*　　　　*Sandwich Supper*
Dieter's Delight

VEGETABLE PREPARATION AND SERVING GUIDE

GENERAL RULE FOR WASHING AND COOKING VEGETABLES

Wash all vegetables thoroughly before cooking. Use lukewarm salty water if vegetables are sandy. Lift vegetables out of water so sand and grit go to bottom. A spray or salad basket helps, too. *Never soak!* Cook with only enough salted water ($\frac{1}{2}$ tsp. salt to 1 cup water, $\frac{1}{4}$ to 1″ deep) to prevent scorching, depending on size and kind of saucepan. Add more water if necessary. Quickly bring water to boil; reduce heat and begin to count cooking time. Cook *only* until "crisp-tender." Cook vegetables in skins whenever possible; some of the nutrients are concentrated next to the skin. Drain off any excess liquid. Store vegetable stock in refrigerator to serve chilled with tomato juice, in gravy, soups, casseroles . . . much of the "goodness" of the vegetable is in the stock. If correctly cooked, the stock will not be excessive.

Fresh Vegetables

For health-giving goodness and palatability.

Vegetables occupy a vital position among the 4 basic foods required for good health. Cook vegetables with special care to retain . . .

Nutritive Value: Health-giving vitamins and minerals.

Texture: The "just done" quality of not being overdone, not underdone, but a satisfying crisp-tender.

Color: Preserving nature's color to satisfy the eye as well as the palate.

Flavor: The true vegetable flavor enhanced with seasonings—not overpowering garnishes and embellishments.

Buttered Vegetables

Most common method of serving.

Use 1 to 3 tbsp. butter, salt and pepper to 2 cups vegetables. Fresh meat drippings are also good. Garnish, if desired (*p. 24*).

Creamed Vegetables

The sauce makes them go further. Use one vegetable or a combination of two or three.

Combine 1 cup hot Medium White Sauce (*p. 387*) with 2 cups hot cooked drained vegetables (use some of stock to make sauce). *4 to 6 servings.*

Sauces for Vegetables

For the gourmet touch.

Sour Cream Dressing (*p. 372*). Hollandaise Sauce (*p. 391*). Mushroom Sauce (*p. 387*). Other Vegetable Sauces (*p. 391*). Tomato Sauce (*p. 389*).

Frozen Vegetables

To use part of the package, saw or cut the frozen block of vegetables.

Amounts: Usually 4 servings per pint package.

How to Cook: Follow directions on package. As a rule, do not thaw before cooking.

Canned Vegetables

Amounts:		
8-oz. can	. . . .	2 servings
16-oz. can	. . . .	3 or 4 servings
1 lb. 4-oz. can	. . . .	4 or 5 servings
1 lb. 13-oz. can	. . . .	6 or 7 servings

How to Cook: Drain off liquid into saucepan. Boil quickly to reduce amount to half. Add vegetables and heat quickly; do not boil. Season.

Scalloped Vegetables

Scallop shells were used originally for baking.

Place Creamed Vegetables (*at left*) in greased baking dish. Sprinkle with Crumb Topping (*p. 391*). Bake *at 350°* (mod.) *20 to 25 min.,* or until it bubbles. *4 to 6 servings.*

Vegetables au Gratin

French for "with crumbs." It usually means the addition of cheese to scalloped vegetables.

Make Scalloped Vegetables (*above*)—*except* use Cheese Sauce (*p. 387*).

411

MILD-FLAVORED VEGETABLES

Follow the general rule on p. 411; leave lid off for first five minutes for green vegetables to allow steam to escape. Then cover pan to finish cooking. This ensures true green color, best flavor and most nutritive value. *Pressure Cooking:* Follow manufacturer's directions for your cooker.

Vegetable	Amount for 4	Preparation	Cooking Time	Popular Ways to Serve
ARTICHOKES French Globe	4 (1 per serving)	Cut off 1" of the top with sharp knife. Trim stems leaving ½" stub. Remove outside lower leaves and thorny leaf tips. Tie leaves to keep in shape. After cooking, cut off stub.	Boil 20 to 45 min., or until leaf pulls away easily.	Place 1 upright per person on a separate plate with main course. Offer Glorified Butter, Hollandaise Sauce or mayonnaise mixed with lemon juice and prepared mustard. See recipes p. 417.
ARTICHOKES Jerusalem	1½ lb.	Pare thin. Leave whole, slice or dice.	Boil 15 to 35 min. Bake at 350° 30 to 60 min.	Buttered, with salt and pepper. Vary with lemon juice and minced parsley. Creamed, French fried or baked.
ASPARAGUS	2 lb.	Break off tough ends as far down as snaps easily. Remove scales if sandy or tough. Leave stalks whole or cut into pieces. Tie whole stalks in bunches with string and cook upright in narrow deep pan or coffeepot. If cut up, cook pieces from lower stems first, add tips the last 5 to 8 min.	Boil whole 10 to 20 min.; 1" pieces 10 to 15 min.; tips 5 to 8 min.	Buttered, with salt and pepper. Vary with dash of lemon juice, mace, garlic powder, minced onion or chives; or sprinkle with slivered almonds or buttered crumbs. May serve with a Cheese, Mushroom or Hollandaise Sauce. See recipes p. 417.
BEANS Green Wax Snap	1½ lb.	Snap off ends. Leave whole, cut French-style into lengthwise strips or crosswise into 1" lengths. If desired, add a clove of garlic or bit of onion while cooking.	Boil whole 15 to 20 min.; cut 15 to 20 min.; French cut 10 min.	Toss with butter, bacon or ham drippings and salt; sprinkle with basil, marjoram, dill weed, savory or thyme. See recipes p. 418.
GREEN LIMAS Butter or Baby Limas (small) Potato or Fordhook (larger)	3 lb. or 1 pt. shelled	Snap pods open; remove beans. Or cut thin strip from inner edge of pod with knife; push beans out.	Boil 20 to 30 min.	Buttered, with salt and pepper. Vary with savory or sage. Or, serve in cream with butter. See recipe p. 418.
BEETS (for Beet Greens, see GREENS)	2 lb. topped	Cut off all but 2" of tops. Save tops. Leave whole with root end. Boil until tender; drain. Run cold water over them and slip off skins and root ends. For quick cooking, pare; then dice, slice, shred or grate coarsely.	Boil in salted water (a little vinegar added to preserve color) to cover. Young whole 30 to 45 min.; sliced 10 to 20 min.; shredded 5 to 10 min.	Buttered, with salt and pepper. Vary with fresh dill, savory, thyme, coriander or caraway. Or with grated orange or lemon rind, lemon juice or vinegar. Pickled, glazed. See recipes p. 418.

Vegetable	Amount for 4	Preparation	Cooking Time	Popular Ways to Serve
CARROTS	1 to 2 lb.	Remove tops; scrub, pare thin or scrape. Leave whole or cut into "coins" (round slices), diagonal slices, strips, cubes or grate coarsely.	Boil large whole 20 to 30 min.; young 15 to 20 min.; sliced 10 to 20 min.; shredded 5 min. Add a pinch of sugar or a bit of orange or lemon peel for extra flavor.	Buttered, with salt, pepper, and minced parsley. Vary with basil, savory, thyme, mint. May also be served with minced chives and lemon juice. Creamed, sautéed, mashed. See recipes p. 420.
CELERY White (bleached) Green (Pascal)	1 bunch	Remove root leaves and coarse strings. Reserve "hearts" to serve raw. Slice outer stalks into 1½ to 2" pieces.	Boil 15 to 20 min. Add bouillon cube for extra flavor.	Buttered, with salt and pepper; creamed; braised. Use in soups, stews, main dishes. See recipes p. 422.
CELERY ROOT (Celeriac)	1½ lb.	Cut away leaves and root fibers. Do not peel.	Boil 40 to 60 min.	Peel, slice and serve with butter, salt and pepper. Creamed; with Hollandaise Sauce.
CELTUCE (Combination of celery and lettuce)	1 bunch	Peel; leave whole. Split lengthwise or cut in small pieces.	See Celery.	Use young leaves in salads or cook as greens. Pale green stalks may be eaten raw or cooked like celery.
CORN Sweet	8 ears	Remove husks, silk, blemishes *just before* cooking. Best when eaten as soon after picking as possible.	Boil 5 to 8 min. in unsalted water to cover. (Salt toughens corn.)	On cob—with butter, salt and pepper. Cut from cob—in cream and butter. See recipes p. 423.
CUCUMBER	2 medium	Leave skins on or pare, if desired. Cut into lengthwise quarters, thick slices or cubes.	Boil 10 to 15 min. To braise, see Celery p. 422.	Buttered, with lemon juice and parsley. Vary with garlic salt, dill weed or chili powder. Creamed.
EGGPLANT	1 medium (about 1½ lb.)	Paring not necessary unless skin is tough. Leave whole or cut in strips or slices 1" thick. Cut when ready to cook as it discolors.	Boil 10 to 15 min. Sauté (fry) 5 to 10 min. in butter or drippings.	Buttered, with salt, pepper, Parmesan cheese, minced chives or parsley. Vary with a few peppercorns, parsley, green onions, crushed garlic or bay leaf. Fried, stuffed, scalloped. See recipes p. 424.
MUSHROOMS	1 lb.	Wash with soft brush. Do not peel. Leave whole or slice parallel with stem.	Sauté (fry) in ¼ cup butter over low heat 8 to 10 min.	Creamed, scalloped, in sauces or soup. Garnish meats. Combine with other freshly cooked vegetables. See recipe p. 265.
OKRA	1 lb.	Cut off stems. Leave small pods whole and cut large pods into ½" slices.	Boil 10 min.	Buttered, with salt and pepper. Vary with dash of vinegar or lemon juice, minced onion or garlic. Use mostly in soups and casseroles. See Creole Celery and Okra p. 422.

413

Vegetable	Amount for 4	Preparation	Cooking Time	Popular Ways to Serve
PARSNIPS	1½ lb.	Pare or scrub with brush. Leave whole or cut in halves, quarters, slices or cubes. Remove core from larger parsnips. A little sugar in water improves flavor.	Boil whole 20 to 40 min.; pieces 8 to 20 min. Bake at 350° 30 to 45 min.	Buttered, with salt and pepper and a sprinkling of minced parsley. Sautéed in butter or drippings; mashed. See recipes p. 425.
PEAS Green	3 lb. unshelled	Shell *just* before cooking. Add 1 tsp. sugar to water, a few pods or leaf of lettuce for additional flavor.	Boil 8 to 15 min.	Buttered, with salt and pepper. Vary with basil, mint, savory, thyme or tarragon. In cream; creamed. Add dash of lemon or lime juice; minced onion.
Black-eyed	½ lb. (1 cup shelled)	Shell as green peas. Cook with ham hock, bacon drippings or salt pork and ½ tsp. sugar.	Boil 30 to 40 min.	Combined with other freshly cooked vegetables. See recipes p. 425.
PEPPERS Green Bell	4	Remove stem, seeds and membrane. Leave whole to stuff and bake.	Parboil whole 5 min., bake at 350° 25 to 30 min. Sauté (fry) 5 min.	Whole—stuffed and baked (p. 264). Cut in slivers or rings. Sauté in butter; season. See recipe p. 426.
POTATOES White	2 lb.	Scrub with brush; remove eyes. Leave skins on whenever possible or pare thin. Leave whole or cut in large pieces or slices. *To Bake:* rub skins with fat for soft skins, prick few holes with fork (for steam to escape).	Boil whole 30 to 35 min.; cut 20 to 25 min. Bake at 375° 1 hr. At 350° bake 1½ hr.	Shake boiled potatoes over low heat to dry; then serve buttered, with salt and pepper. Baked, creamed, fried, scalloped, mashed and others. See recipes pp. 426-427.
New		Scrub lightly or scrape; leave whole.		
PUMPKIN	3 lb. (3 lb. raw equals 3 cups mashed)	Cut in half. Remove seed and stringy interior. Cut in smaller pieces; pare. Bake as for squash or sweet potatoes.	Boil 25 to 30 min. Bake at 400° 1 hr. (varies with size).	Mashed and seasoned with butter, salt and pepper. Unseasoned for pie filling. Use in same ways as squash or sweet potatoes. See recipes pp. 428-429.
SQUASH (Summer) White—Cymling, pattypan or scalloped Yellow—Straight neck or Crookneck Light green—Chayote Dark green—Zucchini (Italian)	2 to 3 lb.	(Soft skins) Remove stem and blossom ends. Remove large seeds (except in zucchini-type), coarse fiber, if any. Leave whole, slice or dice. Paring not necessary.	Boil whole 30 to 60 min.; cut 10 to 15 min. Bake at 350° (whole), 30 to 60 min.	Buttered, with salt and pepper. Vary with marjoram or Parmesan cheese. Baked, mashed, sautéed. See recipes p. 428.

Vegetable	Amount for 4	Preparation	Cooking Time	Popular Ways to Serve
SQUASH (Winter) Banana Hubbard Butternut Acorn Des Moines Table Queen (Danish)	2 to 3 lb.	(Hard skins) Hubbard: pare if desired, remove seeds and fibers, cut into serving pieces. Acorn: do not pare, remove seeds, brush with butter and seasonings before, during and after baking.	Boil 25 to 30 min. Bake at 375° 40 to 60 min. Bake halves of acorn squash cut-side-down, turn after half of baking time. Bake covered for moist top, uncovered for crusty top.	Baked, buttered, glazed, mashed. Spoon brown sugar into hollows the last 15 to 30 min. of baking. Scoop out and mash with cream, nutmeg, candied ginger or with grated orange rind or orange juice. See recipes *p. 428.*
SWEET POTATOES Jersey Sweets Yams	2 lb.	Boil without paring. When tender, drain and slip off skins. To bake whole: scrub, then dry. Rub with a little vegetable oil.	Boil 30 to 35 min. Bake (large) at 350° 50 to 60 min.	Baked with butter, salt and pepper. Mashed, candied, souffléd. See recipes *p. 429.*
TOMATOES	2 lb.	Peel if desired (*see p. 27*). Leave whole or cut in slices or quarters. To cook: cover pan, add no water; add a bay leaf, if desired.	Boil 8 to 10 min. Broil 3 to 5 min.	Buttered, with salt and pepper. Vary with fennel, basil, oregano, sage, tarragon or marjoram. See recipes *p. 429.*
GREENS Mild-flavored: Beet tops, Chicory (outer leaves); Collards, Endive, Dandelion greens (picked before blossoming), Escarole, Lettuce (outer leaves), Romaine (outer leaves), Spinach, Water cress Strong-flavored: Kale, Kohlrabi, Mustard greens, Swiss chard, Turnip greens	1½ to 2 lb.	Follow directions for washing and preparation, p. 411. Save tender young leaves for salads. Remove imperfect leaves and root ends. Cook mild-flavored greens in just the water that clings to leaves. To preserve color, cook uncovered first 5 min. Cook strong-flavored greens with water to cover. Leave cover off pan.	Boil young tender leaves 5 to 15 min., older thicker leaves 20 to 25 min.	Cut with scissors to avoid stringiness. Buttered, with salt, pepper, marjoram, dill weed, mint, rosemary or minced onion. Or serve with lemon or vinegar, hard-cooked egg slices, crumbled crisp bacon, horse-radish, chili sauce, strips of pimiento, slivered toasted almonds or grated Parmesan cheese. Wilted, molded, in soufflés. See recipes *p. 424.*

STRONG-FLAVORED VEGETABLES

Follow general directions on p. 411. If pieces are large or vegetables left whole, cook in large amount of water completely covering the vegetable and without a cover on the pan. This preserves the color and produces a mild flavor. If shredded, or cut in small pieces, cook in small amount of water with cover.

Vegetable	Amount for 4	Preparation	Cooking Time	Popular Ways to Serve
BROCCOLI (Italian Asparagus)	1½ lb.	Remove large leaves and ends of tough stalk parts. If thick, make 3 to 4 gashes through stem so stems will cook as quickly as bud tops. Set upright in pan.	Boil 10 to 15 min.	Buttered, with salt and pepper. Vary with oregano and lemon juice, Hollandaise sauce, grated cheese. Creamed. See recipes *p. 419.*
BRUSSELS SPROUTS (Tom Thumb Cabbage)	1½ lb.	Remove discolored leaves and stem ends. Leave whole.	Boil 8 to 10 min.	Buttered, with salt and pepper. Vary with garlic salt, basil, dill, caraway, savory or cumin. Creamed. See recipe *p. 419.*

Vegetable	Amount for 4	Preparation	Cooking Time	Popular Ways to Serve
CABBAGE White Savoy (yellowish) Red	1 head (1 to 2 lb.)	Remove wilted outside leaves. Shred or cut in wedges. Remove most of core.	Boil 2" wedges 10 to 15 min.; shredded 5 to 8 min.	Buttered, with salt and pepper. Vary with caraway, mint or oregano. Creamed, scalloped. See recipes p. 419.
Chinese or Celery		Remove root ends. Shred or slice thinly.	Boil 4 to 5 min. To braise, see Celery, p. 422.	Buttered, with salt and pepper. Vary with grated cheese, buttered crumbs, Cheese Sauce, Hollandaise Sauce.
CAULIFLOWER	1 large head (3 lb.)	Remove leaves. Leave whole, cutting out center core; or separate into flowerets. Remove any discoloration with knife.	Boil whole 20 to 30 min.; flowerets 8 to 15 min.	Buttered, with salt and pepper. Vary with grated cheese, buttered crumbs, Cheese Sauce, Hollandaise Sauce. See recipes p. 422.
KOHLRABI	4 to 6	Remove leaves (cook as greens). Trim off root and stems. Pare; slice, cube or quarter.	Boil 25 to 40 min. Sauté (fry like potatoes) 10 to 15 min.	Buttered, with salt and pepper. Vary with marjoram. Creamed, sautéed. See recipes p. 428.
ONIONS Small white (for whole-cooked) Yellow or red (domestic—for seasoning) Garlic (for seasoning) Spanish, Bermuda, Italian (sweet—for raw or French fried)	1½ lb.	Peel under running water (prevents tears). Leave whole, slice or quarter, depending on size.	Boil small whole 15 to 25 min.; large whole 30 to 40 min.; sliced 10 min. Bake large whole at 350° 50 to 60 min.	Buttered, with salt and pepper. Vary with thyme or basil. Creamed, scalloped, au gratin, sautéed, baked, stuffed, French fried. See recipes p. 425.
Green onions Pickling onions (very small)	2 bunches		Boil 8 to 10 min.	
Leeks (milder than onions)	2 bunches	Cut off green tops with 2" of white part.	Boil 15 min.	Buttered, with salt and pepper. Vary with thyme, sage or horse-radish butter.
RUTABAGAS Yellow turnip (heavy rutabagas are best)	2 lb.	Pare, slice, dice or cut in strips.	Boil 25 to 40 min. A little sugar in water improves flavor.	Buttered, with salt and pepper. Mashed; in soup. See recipes p. 428.
TURNIPS (for Turnip Greens, see GREENS)	2 lb.	Remove tops (save greens). Pare, slice, dice or cut in strips.	Boil whole 20 to 30 min.; sliced or diced 15 to 20 min.	Buttered, with salt and pepper. Mash, add cream and nutmeg. Vary with minced onion or chives and dash of Worcestershire. See recipes p. 428.

ARTICHOKES *(French or Globe)*

A more sophisticated member of the thistle family, known and used in the Western and Central Mediterranean area thousands of years ago. Served hot as a vegetable or chilled and marinated for appetizer or salad.

Preparation and Serving Guide (pp. 411-412).

Artichoke Hearts Sauté

Serve with any of the Glorified Butters (p. 430) or Hollandaise Sauce (p. 391).

Use cooked fresh, frozen or canned artichoke hearts. Sauté in butter until delicately browned on both sides.

Sour Cream Dip for Artichokes

Serve in individual dishes with cooked artichokes. Delicious as appetizer or first course.

Mix ¾ cup commercial sour cream, ½ cup mayonnaise, 1 tbsp. dehydrated onion soup mix. Chill. *6 servings.*

Graceful Artichoke Eating

Pull off leaf; dip wide end into melted butter mixed with a little lemon juice or Hollandaise Sauce *(p. 391)*; or into mayonnaise mixed with lemon juice and prepared mustard. Scrape soft pulp from base with teeth. Discard the rest. With knife and fork, remove and discard "choke." Dip cut-up "hearts" into sauce.

Jerusalem Artichokes

Neither an artichoke nor does it come from Jerusalem. Cousins in name only, they look like knobby potatoes (a tuberous root of a sunflower plant) with the flavor of an artichoke.

ASPARAGUS

The aristocrat of vegetables; one of the symbols of Springtime. Charles Lamb thought this "vegetable orchid" inspired gentle thoughts . . . exceedingly healthful.

Preparation and Serving Guide (pp. 411-412).

Baked Asparagus

3 tbsp. butter, melted
1 pkg. (10 oz.) frozen asparagus spears (partially cooked) or 12 fresh asparagus spears
2 tbsp. diced onion
2 tbsp. chopped celery
2 tbsp. grated Parmesan cheese
¼ cup bread crumbs
½ tsp. salt
⅛ tsp. *each* pepper and oregano

Heat oven to 375° (quick mod.). Put melted butter in square baking dish, 8x8x2″. Line bottom with asparagus spears. Mix onion, celery, Parmesan cheese, bread crumbs and seasonings. Spread evenly over asparagus. Cover; bake 45 min. *4 servings.*

Asparagus in Cream

1 tbsp. butter
½ cup cream
salt and pepper to taste
2 cups cut-up cooked asparagus, undrained

Add butter, cream, salt and pepper to asparagus just before serving. Reheat, but do not let boil. Serve in custard cups or ramekins. *4 to 6 servings.*

Almond-Cheese Scalloped Asparagus

Good party do-ahead vegetable.

2 pkg. (10 oz. each) frozen cut-up asparagus, thawed
½ cup toasted slivered almonds
½ tsp. salt
dash of pepper
2 cups Rich Cheese Sauce *(p. 387)*
1 cup cracker crumbs

Heat oven to 350° (mod.). Put one half of asparagus in 2-qt. baking dish. Top with half the amounts of remaining ingredients. Cover with rest of asparagus and top with rest of ingredients. Bake *40 to 45 min. 6 to 8 servings.*

Asparagus à la Polonaise

Makes the springtime fresh asparagus even better.

⅓ cup butter
⅓ cup soft bread cubes
2 hard-cooked eggs, chopped
1 tbsp. chopped parsley
salt and pepper to taste
2 lb. fresh asparagus, cooked

Melt butter until foamy. Stir in bread cubes. Cook over low heat until crisp and golden. Remove from heat. Add eggs, parsley and seasonings. Serve over asparagus. *4 servings.*

BEANS *(Green, Wax or Lima)*

The Indians were raising them at the time the Pilgrims arrived. They date back as far as the ancient Romans and their famous feasts. Science has now developed a stringless bean.

Preparation and Serving Guide (pp. 411-412).

German Sweet-Sour Beans

Serve with fried apple rings and pork chops.

2 strips bacon
1 cup minced onion
1 tbsp. flour
½ cup bean liquid
¼ cup water
¼ cup vinegar
2 tbsp. sugar
1 tsp. salt
¼ tsp. pepper
1 pkg. (9 oz.) frozen cut-up green beans, cooked (reserve liquid), or 1 can (1 lb.) green beans, drained

Brown bacon until crisp. Remove bacon. Sauté onion in bacon fat until yellow. Stir in flour. Add liquids and seasonings; bring to boil. Stir in beans. Heat through. Sprinkle with crisp bacon bits. *4 servings.*

Creole Beans

2 tbsp. bacon or ham drippings
⅔ cup celery, diced
2 cups (1-lb. can) stewed tomatoes with green pepper and onions
1 pkg. (9 oz.) frozen cut-up green beans, cooked, or 1 can (1 lb.) green beans, drained
1½ tsp. salt
⅛ tsp. pepper

Sauté celery in bacon drippings. Mix in remaining ingredients. Heat through. *6 servings.*

BEETS

The Greeks served Apollo beet roots on a silver platter. Both beet tops and roots are nutritious.

Preparation and Serving Guide (pp. 411-412).

Harvard Beets

1 tbsp. cornstarch
1 tbsp. plus 1 tsp. sugar
¾ tsp. salt
2 cups cubed or sliced cooked beets
⅔ cup liquid (beet juice and water)
¼ cup vinegar

Mix cornstarch and seasonings. Blend beet liquid and vinegar into cornstarch mixture. Bring to boil; boil 1 min. Add beets; heat. *4 servings.*

To "French" beans, cut in two strips, then cut each strip in two narrow strips.

Green Beans Almondine

Sauté ¼ cup slivered blanched almonds and 2 tbsp. minced onion in 2 tbsp. butter. Toss lightly with 1½ lb. fresh or 1 pkg. (9 oz.) frozen French-style green beans, cooked. *4 servings.*

Green Beans De Luxe

Heat oven to 350° (mod.). Mix 2 pkg. (9 oz. each) frozen French-style green beans, partially cooked, or 2 cans (16 oz. each) green beans, drained, with 1 can (10½ oz.) cream of mushroom soup in 1½-qt. baking dish. Bake *15 min.* Remove from oven and sprinkle with 1 can (3½ oz.) French fried onions. Bake *5 min. more. 6 to 8 servings.*

Succotash

Combine equal amounts hot cooked whole corn with hot cooked green Limas. Add butter, a little cream, season with salt and pepper. Heat.

Beets with Orange Sauce

1 tbsp. butter
¼ cup brown sugar or granulated sugar
1 tsp. cornstarch
¾ cup orange juice
⅛ tsp. *each* salt and pepper
2½ cups diced cooked or canned beets, drained

Melt butter. Mix sugar and cornstarch; blend into butter. Stir in orange juice and cook until thickened, stirring constantly. Add salt, pepper and beets. Cook until beets are heated through. Sprinkle with grated orange rind. *6 servings.*

BROCCOLI

This vegetable is a highly developed form of the cabbage family. A green variety of cauliflower sometimes called Italian asparagus. It was known to the Romans before Pompeii.

Preparation and Serving Guide (pp. 411, 415).

Broccoli Soufflé

Make Spinach Soufflé *(p. 424)—except* use chopped cooked broccoli in place of spinach.

Broccoli Timbales

Make Carrot Timbales *(p. 420)—except* use 1 pkg. (10 oz.) frozen chopped broccoli, cooked and well drained, in place of carrots.

Broccoli-Mushroom-Cheese Scallop

1 to 1½ lb. fresh broccoli or 1 pkg. (10 oz.) frozen broccoli, cooked and cut into 2″ pieces
1 cup Mushroom Sauce *(p. 387)*
¼ cup grated sharp cheese
paprika

Heat oven to 350° (mod.). Spread broccoli in 1-qt. baking dish. Pour mushroom sauce over broccoli. Sprinkle with cheese and paprika. Bake *20 min.,* or until tender and golden brown. *4 servings.*

BRUSSELS SPROUTS

These miniature cabbages receive their name from the Belgian city of Brussels where they were first grown in the 13th century. Sometimes called Tom Thumb Cabbage.

Preparation and Serving Guide (pp. 411, 415).

The Friendly Sprout

Combine cooked Brussels sprouts with cooked onions, peas, beans or celery. Season with butter, cream, salt and pepper.

CABBAGE

One of the best liked and most widely used of all vegetables. It has been said that cabbage, like a good wife, is often taken for granted. It is inexpensive, rich in vitamin C and low in calories.

Preparation and Serving Guide (pp. 411, 416).

Golden Cabbage

Toss together lightly 8 cups shredded cabbage, cooked and drained, 1 egg, slightly beaten, 2 tbsp. butter and 1 tbsp. lemon juice. *6 servings.*

Sweet-Sour Red Cabbage

1 head red cabbage (5 cups shredded)
4 slices bacon, diced
2 tbsp. brown sugar
2 tbsp. flour
½ cup water
⅓ cup vinegar
1 tsp. salt
⅛ tsp. pepper
1 small onion, sliced

Cook cabbage in 2 cups salted water (1 tsp. salt) in covered pan *5 to 8 min.,* or until crisp-tender. Drain. Fry bacon; remove bacon and half of the bacon fat. Add brown sugar and flour to remaining bacon fat; blend. Add water, vinegar, seasonings and onion; cook until thick, *5 min.* Add bacon and cabbage; heat through. Garnish with more diced bacon. *6 servings.*

Philadelphia Cabbage

Cook 3 cups shredded cabbage *(p. 416).* Blend in 1 pkg. (3 oz.) cream cheese (thin with milk or cream), dash of pepper and ¼ tsp. celery seeds. Serve hot. *4 servings.*

Chinese-style Cabbage

1 tbsp. shortening
3 cups finely shredded cabbage
1 cup celery, chopped
1 green pepper, chopped
1 onion, chopped
1 tsp. salt
⅛ tsp. pepper

Heat shortening in skillet. Drop in vegetables; stir well. Cover tightly. Steam *5 min.,* stirring several times. Season with salt and pepper. Serve immediately. *4 servings.*

NOTE: 1 tbsp. soy sauce may be added just before serving.

Cabbage Rolls with Sour Cream Sauce See p. 264.

CARROTS

They may not make your hair curl, but they will help protect your health. One average-sized carrot has only 21 calories yet provides the daily requirement of vitamin A. For variety, cut carrots in circles, strips, chunks and diagonally. Don't forget the Carrot Curls (p. 25).

Preparation and Serving Guide (pp. 411, 413).

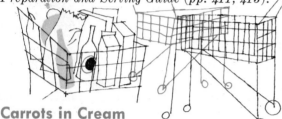

Carrots in Cream

Delicately delicious! Combine with peas, if desired.

Add ½ cup cream, 1 tbsp. butter and salt and pepper to taste to 2 cups hot cooked sliced carrots just before serving. Reheat, but do not let boil. A garnish of parsley adds color. *4 to 6 servings.*

Carrot-Onion-Olive Scallop

An emergency shelf idea . . . but a good one!

Drain liquid from 1 can (1 lb.) diced carrots and 1 can (8 oz.) small whole onions. Use as part of the liquid to make 1 cup Medium White Sauce *(p. 387).* Combine sauce, carrots and onions; heat. Just before serving, add wedges of 3 to 6 ripe olives. *4 to 6 servings.*

Carrot Soufflé

Make Spinach Souffle *(p. 424)—except* use 1 cup sieved cooked carrots in place of spinach.

▶ **ALL YOU HAVE TO DO**

To make cooked carrots look like fresh ones: serve buttered or glazed whole carrots with a sprig of parsley thrust into the end. See color picture p. 421.

Cooked Grated Carrots

Quickly cooked for greatest flavor saving.

4½ cups grated carrots, packed in cup
1 tsp. salt
⅛ tsp. pepper
¼ cup water
3 tbsp. butter or bacon drippings
½ cup finely chopped parsley

Mix first 4 ingredients in saucepan. Cover. Cook until tender, *8 to 10 min.* Drain. Mix in butter and top with parsley. Serve hot. *6 servings.*

Glazed Carrots

Cook 3 to 4 carrots cut crosswise in 1″ pieces. Add 1½ tbsp. butter, ⅓ cup brown sugar (packed) and grated lemon rind and juice to taste. Heat slowly, stirring occasionally, until nicely glazed, *about 15 min. 2 to 3 servings.*

Mint-Glazed Carrots

Simmer 2 cups cooked carrot strips with ¼ cup butter, ¼ cup sugar, 1 tbsp. mint jelly until soft and glazed. *4 servings.*

Carrot Circles and Pineapple

Serve this with chicken, turkey or ham.

½ cup pineapple juice
½ cup carrot stock
1 tbsp. cornstarch
½ tsp. salt
⅛ tsp. pepper
1 tbsp. butter
2 cups cooked sliced carrots
½ cup pineapple chunks, drained

Thicken juices with cornstarch in saucepan; bring just to boil. Add salt, pepper, butter, carrots and pineapple chunks. Heat. *4 servings.*

Carrot Timbales

Sweet carrots baked in a delicate custard and served in individual ramekins—a gourmet's delight.

3 eggs
½ cup milk
½ cup cream (20% butterfat)
2 cups sliced cooked carrots
1 tsp. grated onion
1 tsp. salt
⅛ tsp. pepper

Heat oven to 350° (mod.). Beat egg slightly; add milk, cream, carrots, onion, salt and pepper; mix thoroughly. Bake in ungreased 1-qt. baking dish (set in pan of hot water 1″ deep) *45 min.* or in 8 custard cups or ramekins *20 to 25 min. 6 to 8 servings.*

DRAMATIC VEGETABLE PLATTERS

Cauliflower surrounded by shredded beets in spinach cups and buttered onions.
Stuffed eggplant on a bed of romaine flanked by glazed carrots with parsley garnish.

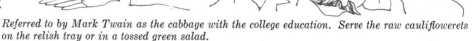

CAULIFLOWER

Referred to by Mark Twain as the cabbage with the college education. Serve the raw cauliflowerets on the relish tray or in a tossed green salad.

Preparation and Serving Guide (pp. 411, 416).

Cauliflower Porcupine

The vegetable becomes a conversation piece.

Tuck toasted, salted, blanched almonds or cashew nuts into whole cooked and seasoned head of cauliflower. Serve with White Sauce or Cheese Sauce (p. 387).

Hungarian Cauliflower

Baked in a sour cream sauce.

Heat oven to 400° (mod. hot). Make 2 cups Medium White Sauce (p. 387)—*except* in place of milk, use 1 cup commercial sour cream and 1 cup water. Stir ¼ tsp. dill weed into sauce. Separate 1 medium head cauliflower into flowerets; arrange in square baking dish, 8x8x2". Pour sauce over cauliflowerets; sprinkle with fine dry bread crumbs. Bake *40 to 45 min.*, or until cauliflower is tender. *4 servings.*

CELERY

Cheese Caulifloweret Scallop

This is a good do-ahead vegetable. The uncooked cauliflower is used. Bake in time to serve.

Heat oven to 400° (mod. hot). Separate 1 medium head cauliflower into sections or flowerets. Arrange in square baking dish, 8x8x2". Pour over 2 cups Medium White Sauce (p. 387) and top with 1 cup grated sharp cheese. Bake *40 to 45 min. 4 servings.*

Variation: Cook cauliflowerets; arrange in baking dish. Cover with White Sauce and sprinkle with cheese. Heat *at 350° 20 min.*, or until cheese melts and sauce is bubbly.

Company Best Cauliflower

Festive. A treat for the family and wonderful for company.

Heat oven to 350° (mod.). Tuck cubes of cheese into whole cooked head of cauliflower. Place in baking dish with about ¼ cup cream. Sprinkle with Crumb Topping (p. 391) and crisp bacon bits. Bake *15 to 20 min.*, or until cheese melts.

A member of the same family as the carrot, fennel, caraway, anise and parsley. The Dutch gardeners near Kalamazoo, Michigan, grew it first in America and sold it on the trains that passed through town. This vegetable appears crispy-crunchy-raw as a relish more often than cooked.

THRIFT TIPS

Serve celery hearts as a relish or salad.

Save small branches and leaves to use in soups, stews, bread stuffings and salads and as garnishes.

Dry leaves in paper bag, then crumble finely. Use as celery seasoning.

Combine a little hot cooked celery with other hot cooked vegetables, such as carrots, string beans, peas or tomatoes to make them go further.

Preparation and Serving Guide (pp. 411, 413).

Creole Celery and Okra

This hearty combination of vegetables would be dandy the night you serve hot dogs or hamburgers.

½ cup chopped onion
½ cup chopped green pepper
2 tbsp. butter
2 to 2½ cups cooked tomatoes
2 cups diced celery
2 cups cut-up fresh or frozen okra
2 tsp. salt
¼ tsp. pepper
½ tsp. basil or oregano

In skillet, sauté onion and green pepper in butter. Stir in remaining ingredients; cook only until celery is crisp-tender, *15 to 20 min. 6 to 8 servings.*

Pan-Braised Celery

Place 3 cups thinly sliced celery and 1 to 2 tbsp. butter in saucepan. Cook, covered, until celery sizzles; reduce heat. Braise *4 to 5 min.* Add a few extra drops of water if necessary. Cook only until crisp-tender. Season with salt and pepper to taste. *3 to 4 servings.*

Pan-Braised Celery Cabbage: Use 3 cups shredded or thinly sliced celery cabbage in place of celery.

CORN

Typically American ... especially the succulent eating of the golden corn on the cob. All America is "corny" in August ... the peak month for corn so serve it often.

Preparation and Serving Guide (pp. 411, 413).

Creamy Skillet Corn

2 cups fresh or 1 pkg. (10 oz.) frozen
    whole kernel corn
2 tbsp. butter
½ cup cream (20% butterfat)
½ tsp. salt
dash of pepper

Combine corn, butter, cream and seasonings in skillet. Cover and simmer *5 to 6 min.*, or until corn is just tender. *4 servings.*

Scalloped Corn

Children love it; for grownups add 2 tbsp. chopped green pepper or pimiento or both.

¼ cup chopped onion
2 tbsp. butter
2 tbsp. flour
1 tsp. salt
½ tsp. paprika
¼ tsp. dry mustard
dash of pepper
¾ cup milk
1 can (1 lb.) whole kernel corn, drained (about
    2 cups fresh)
1 egg, slightly beaten

Heat oven to 350° (mod.). Sauté onion in butter until golden. Blend in flour, seasonings; cook until bubbly. Remove from heat. Gradually add milk. Bring to boil; boil 1 min., stirring constantly. Remove from heat. Add corn and egg. Pour into 1-qt. baking dish. Top with buttered crumbs. Bake *20 to 30 min. 4 servings.*

Corn-Tomato Casserole

1 can (1 lb.) whole kernel corn,
    drained (2 cups)
1 can (1 lb.) tomatoes (2 cups)
1 small green pepper, finely chopped
⅓ cup cracker crumbs
1 tsp. salt
dash of pepper
1 tsp. sugar
2 tbsp. soft butter

Heat oven to 375° (quick mod.). Combine all ingredients in 1½-qt. baking dish. Sprinkle top with additional cracker crumbs and dot with more butter. Bake uncovered *30 min.* Serve in individual dishes. *8 servings.*

Golden Corn Pudding

Bake in a pretty oven-proof dish and serve it for company-best. The delicate custard is so good!

2 cups drained whole kernel corn (canned or
    cooked frozen or fresh)
1 tsp. sugar
1 tsp. salt
¼ tsp. pepper
2 eggs, well beaten
1 cup milk
1 tbsp. butter
2 tbsp. cracker crumbs

Heat oven to 350° (mod.). Mix ingredients thoroughly. Pour into greased 1-qt. baking dish. Set in pan of hot water 1" deep. Bake *60 to 70 min.*, or until silver knife inserted 1" from edge comes out clean. *8 servings.*

Squaw Corn

Quick supper idea for camping trips.

4 slices bacon
1 medium green pepper, chopped
1 small onion, chopped
1 can (1 lb.) cream-style corn (2 cups)
1 tsp. salt
⅛ tsp. pepper
4 eggs, beaten

Fry bacon until crisp. Remove from skillet; drain off most of fat. Sauté green pepper and onion in remaining fat for *5 min.* Stir in corn, salt, pepper and eggs. Stir until eggs are set. Add bacon, broken into small pieces. *4 to 6 servings.*

Succotash See p. 418.

Corn Fritters See p. 87.

Corn Pancakes See p. 93.

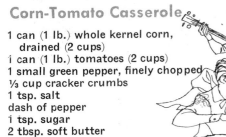

EGGPLANT

This handsome satiny dark purple vegetable brings to the table the flavor of faraway places. It might also be found as the center of a fruit and vegetable centerpiece. Tomato, cheese, onion and parsley are traditional ingredients in the classic eggplant dishes of the East.

Preparation and Serving Guide (pp. 411, 413).

Stuffed Eggplant

A good company vegetable. See color picture p. 421.

1 medium large eggplant
¾ cup sliced mushrooms
2 tbsp. *each* chopped onion and green pepper
1 clove garlic, minced
2 tbsp. butter
2 tbsp. flour
1 tsp. salt
⅛ tsp. pepper
½ cup cream (20% butterfat)
3 tbsp. pimiento

Heat oven to 350° (mod.). Cut large lengthwise slice off eggplant. Remove pulp and cut in cubes. Cook in small amount of boiling salted water, *10 min.* While eggplant is cooking, brown mushrooms, onion, green pepper and garlic in butter. Stir in flour, salt and pepper. Add well drained eggplant, cream and pimiento. Fill shell. Top with 2 tbsp. buttered bread crumbs or 1 tbsp. grated Parmesan cheese or 2 slices crisp bacon, crumbled. Bake *30 min. 4 servings.*

Far East Eggplant

Similar to the way it is prepared in Syria.

¼ cup olive or vegetable oil
1 clove garlic, minced
1 green pepper, chopped
1 onion, chopped
1 medium eggplant, cubed
4 tomatoes, cut-up
2 tsp. salt
¼ tsp. pepper
2 tbsp. grated Parmesan cheese
6 slices crisp crumbled bacon

Cook ingredients except cheese and bacon in skillet until tender. Top with cheese and bacon. Brown under broiler. *4 servings.*

Fried Eggplant

Add a sprinkling of Parmesan cheese at serving time.

Dip strips or slices of eggplant in flour, then in beaten egg, then in cracker crumbs. Sauté in small amount of hot fat *5 to 10 min.,* or until tender and golden brown. Or French fry in hot fat (375°) *2 to 4 min.* on each side. Season with salt and pepper.

GREENS

Greens are principally a salad vegetable, but the outer leaves or tops not tender enough for salads are cooked. There are 15 greens ranging from beet tops to water cress listed on p. 415. Other greens listed on p. 415 may be used in place of spinach in recipes below.

Preparation and Serving Guide (pp. 411, 415).

Spinach Soufflé

1 cup Thick White Sauce *(p. 387)*
1 tsp. grated onion
⅛ tsp. nutmeg
3 eggs, separated
1 cup cooked chopped spinach, drained
¼ tsp. cream of tartar

Heat oven to 350° (mod.). Make white sauce; stir in onion and nutmeg. Stir in 1 egg yolk at a time until blended. Blend in spinach. Beat egg whites and cream of tartar until stiff, but not dry. Fold in spinach mixture. Pour into ungreased 1½-qt. baking dish. Set in pan of hot water 1″ deep. Bake *50 to 60 min.,* or until puffed and golden. Silver knife inserted 1″ from edge will come out clean. Serve immediately. *4 to 6 servings.*

Molded Greens

See color picture p. 410.

Combine hot seasoned chopped* cooked greens with crisp bacon bits or a dash of nutmeg and grated onion. Pack into individual buttered molds (custard cups may be used). Keep warm in very low oven *15 to 20 min.* Unmold and serve with lemon and hard-cooked egg slices.

*Cut the cooked greens with kitchen shears to eliminate stringiness.

Easy Creamed Spinach

Partially thaw and break apart 1 pkg. (9 oz.) frozen chopped spinach. Make 1 cup Thick White Sauce *(p. 387)* in top of double boiler; add spinach, ⅛ tsp. nutmeg. Cover and cook over boiling water *15 min.,* stirring occasionally. *4 servings.*

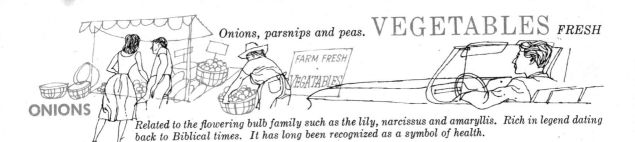

ONIONS

Related to the flowering bulb family such as the lily, narcissus and amaryllis. Rich in legend dating back to Biblical times. It has long been recognized as a symbol of health.

Preparation and Serving Guide (pp. 411, 416).

Fried Onion Rings

Allow one-half onion per serving . . . but there are never enough of these tasty morsels. Best if still crisp inside.

Cut large Spanish or Bermuda onions crosswise into ⅓ to ¼" thick slices. Separate into rings. Dry onion thoroughly, coat generously with flour. Using tongs, dip food into Thin Fritter Batter *(p. 87)*, letting excess drip off. Fry a few at a time in ½ to 1" deep hot fat or oil until golden brown, *about 2 min.* Drain on absorbent paper.

Onion Flavor at Your Fingertips: Keep onion juice and instant minced (dehydrated) onion on the shelf. Use when time is short.

De Luxe Creamed Onions

From Charlotte Johnson of our staff.

2 lb. tiny whole onions
2 tbsp. butter
2 tbsp. flour
¼ tsp. salt
⅛ tsp. pepper
1¼ cups cream (20% butterfat)
1½ cups grated carrots

Peel and cook onions. Melt butter over low heat in heavy saucepan. Blend in flour and seasonings. Cook over low heat, stirring until mixture is smooth and bubbly. Remove from heat. Stir in cream. Bring to boil, stirring constantly. Boil 1 min. Stir in grated carrots and cook *about 3 min.* longer. Pour over drained onions. Serve immediately. *4 servings.*

PARSNIPS

An old-fashioned vegetable making new appearances . . . thin crisp slices of parsnips on a relish tray. If you grow them in your garden, delay harvest until after a sharp frost (flavor improves).

Preparation and Serving Guide (pp. 411, 414).

Candied Parsnips

See Skillet Candied Sweet Potatoes *(p. 429).*

PAR-SNIPS

Intriguing new way to prepare parsnips.

Cut raw parsnips in thin slices. Dip in Seasoned Flour *(p. 302)* or Parmesan cheese or garlic salt. Sauté slowly in butter until golden brown.

PEAS

The most popular of all vegetables. A childhood memory of many is the shelling and eating of the tender young peas direct from the garden. The canned tiny French peas are equally delicious.

Preparation and Serving Guide (pp. 411, 414).

New Peas in Cream

Cook 2 cups peas or 1 pkg. (10 oz.) frozen peas. Drain. Add 1 tsp. sugar, ½ tsp. salt, 2 tbsp. butter, ⅛ tsp. pepper and ½ cup cream (20% butterfat). Heat. *4 servings.*

Peas, French Style

Line bottom and sides of saucepan with washed lettuce leaves. Add peas, sprinkle with salt, pepper, sugar, nutmeg. Add 2 to 4 tbsp. butter. Cover with lettuce leaves. Cook covered over low heat until tender, *20 min.* Discard leaves. Serve.

Favorite Ways with Peas

In cream sauce poured over cooked cauliflower.

In place of Lima beans in succotash.

Mixed with diced cooked yellow turnip.

With new potatoes in cream.

With sautéed fresh mushrooms.

In individual nests of buttered shredded carrots.

With small onions and chopped parsley or celery.

Cooked with a sprig of finely chopped mint or add a tablespoonful of mint jelly after cooking.

PEPPERS *(Sweet Green or Bell)*

The hot spicy varieties are usually referred to as chili peppers. Raw green pepper sticks or rings are good on a relish tray or as a garnish.

Preparation and Serving Guide (pp. 411, 414).

Italian Green Peppers

Attractive and tasty. Genevieve Pagano of our staff serves this with veal or pork.

½ cup sliced onion
2 cloves garlic, minced
2 tbsp. olive or vegetable oil
1 can (1 lb.) stewed tomatoes (2 cups)
2 tsp. sugar

1½ tsp. salt
¼ tsp. pepper
½ tsp. oregano or basil
5 large green peppers, cut in ¾ to 1" strips
1½ qt. boiling water

In large skillet sauté onion and garlic until yellow. Add tomatoes and seasonings. With 2 knives, cut up and blend ingredients. Simmer sauce, uncovered, about *20 min.*, or until slightly thickened. Meanwhile, parboil green pepper strips, uncovered, *about 15 min.* Drain; combine with tomato mixture in skillet. Continue cooking uncovered *about 15 min.*, or until peppers are tender. *4 to 6 servings.*

POTATOES *(White)*

Potatoes are "native" Americans. Potatoes are 75% water—it's what you put on them that's fattening. There are 1500 ways of preparing the potato, from "boiled" to the exquisite "pommes soufflés."

Preparation and Serving Guide (pp. 411, 414).

Mashed Potatoes

Shake drained, cooked potatoes over low heat to dry. Mash with butter, salt, pepper and hot milk (½ cup per 8 potatoes). Whip vigorously until light and fluffy. Sprinkle with paprika, minced parsley or chives.

Mashed Potato Patties

Shape seasoned Mashed Potatoes *(above)* into little patties. Or form into roll; wrap in waxed paper; chill and slice. Dip patties or slices into flour. Fry slowly in hot fat until brown.

Duchess Potatoes

Make Mashed Potatoes *(above)* and stir in beaten eggs (2 eggs for 3 cups potatoes). Spoon into mounds; or with pastry bag and tube form rosettes on a greased baking sheet; or pipe in a border around planked meat or fish. Brush with butter. Brown in 425° (hot) oven.

Potato Puff *(Soufflé)*

Heat oven to 350° (mod.). Add 1 egg yolk and 1 tbsp. butter to 2 cups mashed potatoes. Beat until light and creamy. Beat 1 egg white until stiff and fold into potato mixture. Heap in buttered 1-qt. baking dish. Bake *30 min. 4 servings.*

Baked Potatoes

Bake *(see p. 414)* until they "squeeze soft." Cut crisscross gash on top; squeeze until potato pops up. Pass a bowl of Sour Cream Dressing *(p. 372)*. Shredded cheese, crumbled crisp bacon or freshly ground pepper are delicious atop the sour cream.

Stuffed Baked Potatoes

Sometimes called "Potatoes on the half shell." Do ahead, refrigerate or freeze.

Cut Baked Potatoes *(above)* in halves lengthwise. Scoop out and mash as for Mashed Potatoes *(above)*. Refill potato shells heaping full. Sprinkle with paprika, grated cheese or both. Heat *at 400°* (mod. hot) *20 to 25 min.*, or until golden brown.

French Fried Potatoes

Cut pared potatoes into ⅜″ lengthwise strips. Fill basket ¼ full. Lower slowly into hot fat (375°). If bubbling of fat is excessive, raise and lower basket several times. Use long handled fork to keep potatoes from sticking together. Fry *5 to 7 min.*, or until golden. Drain on absorbent paper. Salt to taste. *4 medium potatoes makes 4 servings.*

Broiler "French Fries"

Wash and pare 4 medium potatoes. Cut lengthwise into strips ¼ to ½″ thick. Dry potatoes with towel. Remove rack from broiler pan. Preheat broiler 5 min. Place potatoes in broiler pan; add ¼ cup vegetable oil and stir to coat potatoes with oil. Place pan about 3″ from heat and broil potatoes *10 to 15 min.*, stirring frequently until golden brown on all sides. Season with salt and serve immediately. *4 servings.*

Oven "French Fries": Make Broiler "French Fries" (*above*)—*except* place potatoes and oil in large shallow pan. Bake *at 425° (hot) 35 to 45 min.* Turn occasionally to brown evenly. Season.

Skillet Creamed Potatoes

6 medium potatoes, boiled
2 cups commercial sour cream
3 tbsp. finely chopped onion
2 tbsp. finely chopped pimiento-stuffed olives
1 tsp. salt
½ tsp. *each* pepper and paprika
1 tbsp. chopped parsley

Dice potatoes. Pour cream into skillet; add potatoes. Heat slowly over medium heat until cream bubbles over potatoes. Add onion and olives. When potatoes are thoroughly heated, add salt and pepper. Serve at once, garnished with paprika and parsley. *6 servings.*

Cottage Fried Potatoes *(Fried Cooked)*

Slice boiled potatoes. Heap slices lightly into skillet with generous amount of hot drippings. Sprinkle with salt, pepper. Brown slowly to crisp. Turn to brown other side.

Lyonnaise Potatoes

Make Cottage Fried Potatoes (*above*)—*except* add onion slices or grated onion to potatoes before frying.

Au Gratin Potatoes See p. 411.

Hashed Browns

"He-man" style. Best if the potatoes are the red variety cooked in their jackets.

4 cups cooled shredded cooked potatoes
2 tbsp. grated onion
1½ tsp. salt
¼ tsp. pepper
2 tbsp. butter
2 tbsp. vegetable oil or drippings

Toss first 4 ingredients together. Heat butter and oil in 9 or 10″ skillet. Add potatoes, leaving a ½″ space around edge. Pack firmly; fry over low heat *10 to 15 min.*, or until bottom crust is a crispy golden brown. Turn potatoes, add 1 tbsp. oil, if necessary, and finish browning, *about 15 min.* Or, finish browning in oven *at 350°* (mod.). To serve, loosen bottom crust with spatula and turn out onto platter. *4 to 6 servings.*

Potatoes Anna *(Raw Fried)*

Turn onto serving plate—golden brown, crisp.

Melt 2 tbsp. butter in heavy skillet. Arrange thinly sliced or grated raw potatoes in 2 or 3 layers. Sprinkle each layer with salt, pepper; dot with butter. Cover; steam *15 min.* Uncover; cook until tender and crispy brown on bottom.

Easy Scalloped Potatoes

Heat oven to 350° (mod.). Arrange 3 to 4 cups thinly sliced or coarsely grated raw potatoes in layers in 1½-qt. baking dish. Sprinkle each layer with minced onion (1 tbsp. in all), salt and pepper; dot with butter. Add 1¼ cups hot milk. Bake uncovered *about 1¼ hr. 4 servings.*

Potato Pancakes

2 cups finely grated raw potato
¼ cup milk
2 eggs, well beaten
2 tbsp. flour
1 tbsp. grated onion
1 tsp. salt
dash of pepper

Mix all ingredients and drop by tablespoonfuls onto well greased griddle or skillet. Bake *about 3 min.* on each side, or until brown. Serve with applesauce as accompaniment to pot roast or braised short ribs. *Makes 12.*

RUTABAGAS, TURNIPS AND KOHLRABIES

Yellow, they are rutabagas; white they are turnips; pale green they are kohlrabies. All cooked and served the same way. Raw rutabagas and turnips are good in salads or on a relish plate.

Preparation and Serving Guide (pp. 411, 416).

Turnip or Rutabaga Puff

Make Potato Puff (*p. 426*)—*except* use mashed turnips or rutabagas in place of potatoes.

Mashed Rutabagas with Potatoes

Combine equal amounts of hot seasoned mashed potatoes and hot seasoned mashed rutabagas or turnips; fold in a small amount of whipped cream.

Green Peas in Rutabaga Nest

Mound up hot buttered shredded rutabagas on platter. Make indentation in center and fill with buttered green peas.

NOTE: Kohlrabies or turnips may be used in place of rutabagas.

Sautéed Turnips or Rutabagas

Cook and slice turnips or rutabagas. Sauté slowly in butter, sprinkling lightly with sugar, *10 min.*, or until nicely glazed.

SQUASH

Varieties of the soft-skinned summer squash are listed on p. 414, hard-skinned winter squash on p. 415. The Indians called squash "askutasquash." Just plain baked "in the shell" with brown sugar and butter spooned into hollows last half of baking is the most popular way to serve.

Preparation and Serving Guide (pp. 411, 414–415).

HOW TO BAKE A MEAL IN AN ACORN SQUASH

1. Place acorn squash halves cut-side-down in pan. Pour in boiling water to ¼″ depth. Bake *at 400°* (mod. hot) *30 min.*

2. Turn squash cut-side-up with fork. Fill centers with partially cooked ground pork sausage. Bake *30 min.*, or until tender. Drain off excess fat. Top with applesauce.

Glazed Squash

Make Skillet Candied Sweet Potatoes (*p. 429*)—*except* use boiled pared Hubbard squash chunks in place of sweet potatoes.

Mashed Squash

Bake Acorn squash until tender. Scoop squash from shell and mash. Season with orange juice and grated orange rind or other additions suggested for Fancy Mashed Sweet Potatoes (*p. 429*).

Squash Continental

8 small squash (zucchini, crookneck or chayote)
¼ cup butter
2 tsp. water
1 clove garlic, crushed
½ tsp. salt
⅛ tsp. pepper

Cut unpared squash in ½″ rounds. Sauté in mixture of butter, water, garlic, salt and pepper. Cook covered *6 to 8 min.* Serve while hot and crisp and holds its shape. Sprinkle with grated Parmesan or Cheddar cheese, if desired. *6 to 8 servings.*

SWEET POTATOES AND YAMS

Yams are more moist and orange-colored . . . also sweeter than the "sweet potatoes." However, prepare the same way. Ham is a natural teammate.

Preparation and Serving Guide (pp. 411, 415).

Fancy Mashed Sweet Potatoes

To cooked mashed sweet potatoes or yams add any of the following: orange juice and grated orange rind, orange marmalade, crushed pineapple or dates. Spoon into baking dish, ramekins or orange shells. Top with cut-up or tiny marshmallows, toasted coconut or chopped peanuts or pecans. Reheat *at 350° (mod.) 15 to 20 min.*, or until heated through.

Meringue-topped Sweet Potatoes

Whip 2 cups cooked sweet potatoes or yams with 1 egg yolk, 2 tbsp. butter and ½ tsp. salt. Pile lightly into buttered 1-qt. baking dish. Top with meringue made from the egg white and 2 tbsp. sugar. Bake *at 350° (mod.) 30 min. 4 servings.*

Sweet Potato Soufflé

Make Spinach Soufflé *(p. 424)—except* substitute 1 cup sieved cooked sweet potatoes or yams and ½ cup chopped pecans for spinach.

Skillet Candied Sweet Potatoes

Mix 1 cup brown sugar, ¼ cup butter, ¼ cup water and ½ tsp. salt in heavy skillet; cook until mixture boils. Add 6 cooked sweet potatoes or yams and cook slowly, turning occasionally, *about 20 min.*, or until potatoes are caramelly. *6 servings.*

Hawaiian Sweet Potato Balls

Attractive platter garnish for turkey or ham.

4 large sweet potatoes or yams, cooked and
  mashed
2 to 3 tbsp. butter
1 tsp. salt
⅛ tsp. pepper
pinch of nutmeg and cinnamon
2 to 3 tbsp. brown sugar (packed)
1 to 1½ cups crushed cereal flakes
8 pineapple slices
8 maraschino cherries

Combine sweet potatoes, butter, seasonings and brown sugar. Drop ⅓ to ½ cup sweet potato mixture onto waxed paper containing crushed cereal flakes and roll into ball. Place ball on pineapple slice in buttered pan. Top with cherry. Heat *at 350° (mod.) 20 min. 8 servings.*

TOMATOES

By cultivation and use it is a vegetable, botanically it is a fruit. The French who popularized its use called it "pomme d'amour" (love apple).

Preparation and Serving Guide (pp. 411, 415).

Stewed Tomatoes

Simmer together *10 min.*: 2½ cups cooked tomatoes, 1 tsp. minced onion, ½ tbsp. sugar, 2 tbsp. butter, ⅛ tsp. pepper and ½ cup soft bread cubes. *4 to 6 servings.*

Broiled Tomatoes

See color picture p. 410.

Dot tomato halves or thick slices of tomato with butter. Sprinkle with salt, pepper, basil, oregano or savory. Broil under low heat *about 3 min.*

Fried Tomato Slices

Dip ¼″ thick tomato slices into Seasoned Flour *(p. 302)*, then into beaten egg, then cracker crumbs. Sauté both sides in butter *about 10 min.*

Stuffed Tomatoes

Heat oven to 350° (mod.). Cut slice from top of 6 unpeeled tomatoes. Scoop out centers and mix pulp with ½ cup crumbled crisp bacon bits (6 slices), ¼ cup chopped celery, 1 small onion, finely chopped, 1 cup soft bread crumbs, ½ tsp. salt, ¼ cup grated cheese. Fill centers. Sprinkle with ¼ cup grated cheese; dot with butter. Bake *about 30 min.* in greased muffin cups or baking dish. *6 servings.*

429

"Waste not, want not," say the old-time New Englanders. It is amazing what can be done with 1 or 2 cups of leftover combined vegetables.

Pennywise Scallop

For odds and ends of cabbage, onion, celery and carrots. Make and freeze; have ready for an emergency.

Combine cooked carrots, celery, cabbage and onions (use some or all) with Medium White Sauce (*p. 387*). Allow 1 cup of white sauce to 2 cups of vegetables. Pour into baking dish; top with Crumb Topping (*p. 391*). Bake *at 375° (quick mod.) 20 to 25 min.*, or until bubbly.

Vegetable Melange

From famous violinist Yehudi Menuhin, who says, "In making this dish, all depends on the seasoning, care and love with which it is done." For a dinner featuring this recipe, see p. 49.

1 lb. summer squash, sliced
1 medium onion, sliced
1 green pepper, cut up
½ eggplant, sliced
4 tomatoes, sliced

Heat oven to 350° (mod.). Sauté each vegetable separately and gently in butter until lightly browned. Season with salt and pepper. Mix lightly and place in buttered 2-qt. baking dish. Top with bread crumbs and grated cheese. Dot with butter. Bake *20 to 25 min.*, or just until vegetables are tender (not mushy). *8 servings.*

NOTE: Mr. Menuhin suggests using organically grown vegetables for his melange, and topping it with crumbs of sea-salt whole meal bread and grated unprocessed cheese.

Tomato-Green Bean Casserole

From Mrs. Ruth M. Kean who, as a former supervisor of home economics teachers in Louisiana, has inspired many to create happier homes.

4 strips bacon
2 cups (1-lb. can) stewed tomatoes with green
    pepper and onions
1 pkg. (9 oz.) frozen green beans, cooked and
    drained, or 1 can (1 lb.) green beans,
    drained (2 cups)
1 tsp. Worcestershire sauce
½ tsp. salt
dash of pepper and cayenne pepper
2 tbsp. mayonnaise
1 cup buttered bread crumbs

Heat oven to 350° (mod.). Fry bacon. Drain off excess fat. Break bacon into pieces. Add tomatoes; simmer a few minutes. Add beans, seasonings and mayonnaise. Place in greased 8" round baking dish. Cover with buttered crumbs. Bake *about 15 min.* (This can be prepared ahead and baked just before serving.)

Flavor-plus Vegetable Combinations

A bit of imagination . . . and Glorified Butters!

Cauliflower and peas
Fresh garden onions (with tops) and carrots
Tiny white onions and peas
Brussels sprouts and celery
Carrot slices with green Limas
Mashed potatoes with mashed rutabagas
Green Limas in acorn squash halves
Stuffed tomatoes in bed of buttered peas
Summer squash, tomatoes and onions
Spinach, parsley and scallions
Peas and mushrooms
Limas, corn and green beans
Squash rings with green peas
Green Limas with sweet red pepper
Carrots and celery, glazed or buttered
Green cabbage and red cabbage
Beets and spinach
Diced carrots in Frenched green bean nests
Cooked grated beets in spinach nests

Glorified Butters for Vegetables

Serve in a small bowl with ladle or in a pitcher. Makes enough for 6 to 8 servings.

To ¼ cup butter heated to golden brown add:

Almond, Cashew or
    Brazil Nut Butter . . . ¼ cup slivered almonds,
        cashews or shaved Brazil
        nuts, ¼ tsp. salt, 2 tsp.
        lemon juice
Caper Butter . . . . 1 tbsp. minced capers
Celery Butter . . . . 1 tsp. celery seeds
Cheese Butter . . . . 2 tbsp. grated Swiss or
        Parmesan cheese
Curry Butter . . . . ¼ tsp. curry powder
Garlic Butter . . . . ¼ tsp. garlic powder
Horse-radish Butter . . . 1 tbsp. horse-radish
Lemon Butter . . . . 2 tbsp. lemon juice, 1 tsp.
        grated rind
Lemon-Chive Butter . . 1 tbsp. minced chives in
        Lemon Butter
Mustard Butter . . . . ¼ tsp. dried mustard, 1 tsp.
        lemon juice, dash of sugar
        and salt
Olive Butter . . . . 2 tbsp. finely chopped
        pitted green or stuffed
        olives
Parsley Butter . . . . few drops lemon juice,
        ¼ cup minced parsley

INDEX

439

445

448

451

452

454

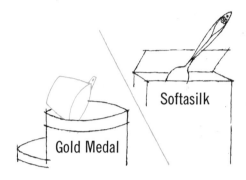

Softasilk

Gold Medal

1 Dip nested measuring cups into flour sack or canister. In using cake flour, spoon flour to overflowing into nested cups.

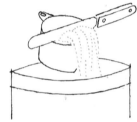

2 Level off with spatula or straight edged knife. (Do not tap cup or pack more flour into cup before leveling off.)

3 Pour flour into mixing bowl with other ingredients. Just stir to blend.

For your information

Dear Homemaker:

As you know, accurate measurements are necessary for good baking results. We have done a great deal of testing in our kitchens and in homes of women throughout the country to determine the best method for measuring flour.

We are happy to tell you that our new, modern "dip-level-pour" method, described on this page, gives consistently uniform measurements and beautiful bakings. Many homemakers prefer this method because of its ease and time-saving convenience. However, you may still follow the traditional sifting method, if you prefer. Use either method without altering the amounts of flour.

Betty Crocker